The Language of Time

The Language of Time

A Reader

Edited by
INDERJEET MANI
JAMES PUSTEJOVSKY
ROBERT GAIZAUSKAS

OXFORD
UNIVERSITY PRESS

OXFORD
UNIVERSITY PRESS

Great Clarendon Street, Oxford OX2 6DP

Oxford University Press is a department of the University of Oxford.
It furthers the University's objective of excellence in research, scholarship,
and education by publishing worldwide in

Oxford New York

Auckland Cape Town Dar es Salaam Hong Kong Karachi
Kuala Lumpur Madrid Melbourne Mexico City Nairobi
New Delhi Shanghai Taipei Toronto

With offices in

Argentina Austria Brazil Chile Czech Republic France Greece
Guatemala Hungary Italy Japan Poland Portugal Singapore
South Korea Switzerland Thailand Turkey Ukraine Vietnam

Oxford is a registered trade mark of Oxford University Press
in the UK and in certain other countries

Published in the United States
by Oxford University Press Inc., New York

© editorial matter and organization Inderjeet Mani, James Pustejovsky, and
Robert Gaizauskas 2005
© the chapters as indicated in their first footnotes

The moral rights of the authors have been asserted

Database right Oxford University Press (maker)

First published 2005

All rights reserved. No part of this publication may be reproduced,
stored in a retrieval system, or transmitted, in any form or by any means,
without the prior permission in writing of Oxford University Press,
or as expressly permitted by law, or under terms agreed with the appropriate
reprographics rights organization. Enquiries concerning reproduction
outside the scope of the above should be sent to the Rights Department,
Oxford University Press, at the address above

You must not circulate this book in any other binding or cover
and you must impose the same condition on any acquirer

A catalogue record for this title is available from the British Library

British Library Cataloguing in Publication Data

Data available

Library of Congress Cataloging in Publication Data

The language of time : a reader / edited by Inderjeet Mani, James Pustejovsky, Robert Gaizauskas.
   p. cm.
   Includes bibliographical references and index.
   ISBN 0-19-926853-3 (alk. paper) – ISBN 0-19-926854-1 (alk. paper) 1. Grammar, Comparative and general–Temporal constructions. 2. Space and time in language. I. Mani, Inderjeet. II. Pustejovsky, J. (James). III. Gaizauskas, Robert.
   P294.5.L36 2005
   425–dc22

2004024155

Typeset by Newgen Imaging Systems (P) Ltd., Chennai, India
Printed in Great Britain on acid-free paper by Biddles Ltd., King's Lynn

ISBN 0-19-926853-3 (hbk)
    0-19-926854-1 (pbk)

10 9 8 7 6 5 4 3 2 1

Contents

Preface	ix
List of Contributors	xi
Acknowledgements	xiii

PART I Tense, Aspect, and Event Structure — 1
Introduction to Part I — 3

1. Verbs and Times — 21
   Z. Vendler

2. The Syntax of Event Structure — 33
   James Pustejovsky

3. The Algebra of Events — 61
   Emmon Bach

4. The Tenses of Verbs — 71
   Hans Reichenbach

5. Tense Logic and the Logic of Earlier and Later — 79
   A. N. Prior

6. Temporal Ontology and Temporal Reference — 93
   Marc Moens and Mark Steedman

7. Deriving Verbal and Compositional Lexical Aspect for NLP Applications — 115
   Bonnie J. Dorr and Mari Broman Olsen

8. A Computational Model of the Semantics of Tense and Aspect — 129
   Rebecca J. Passonneau

PART II Temporal Reasoning — 159
Introduction to Part II — 161

9. A Temporal Logic for Reasoning about Processes and Plans — 173
   Drew McDermott

10. A Logic-based Calculus of Events — 217
    Robert Kowalski and Marek Sergot

11. Extending the Event Calculus with Temporal Granularity and Indeterminacy — 241
    Luca Chittaro and Carlo Combi

12	Towards a General Theory of Action and Time *James F. Allen*	251
13	A Critical Examination of Allen's Theory of Action and Time *Antony Galton*	277
14	Annotating and Reasoning about Time and Events *Jerry Hobbs and James Pustejovsky*	301

PART III Temporal Structure of Discourse ... 317
Introduction to Part III ... 319

15	The Effects of Aspectual Class on the Temporal Structure of Discourse: Semantics or Pragmatics? *David R. Dowty*	333
16	Temporal Interpretation, Discourse Relations, and Commonsense Entailment *Alex Lascarides and Nicholas Asher*	353
17	News Stories as Narratives *Allan Bell*	397
18	Tense as Discourse Anaphor *Bonnie Lynn Webber*	411
19	Tense Interpretation in the Context of Narrative *Fei Song and Robin Cohen*	431
20	An Empirical Approach to Temporal Reference Resolution *Janyce Wiebe, Tom O'Hara, Kenneth McKeever, and Thorsten Öhrström-Sandgren*	443
21	Tense Trees as the 'Fine Structure' of Discourse *Chung Hee Hwang and Lenhart K. Schubert*	461
22	Algorithms for Analysing the Temporal Structure of Discourse *Janet Hitzeman, Marc Moens, and Claire Grover*	475

PART IV Temporal Annotation ... 485
Introduction to Part IV ... 487

23	A Multilingual Approach to Annotating and Extracting Temporal Information *George Wilson, Inderjeet Mani, Beth Sundheim, and Lisa Ferro*	505
24	The Annotation of Temporal Information in Natural Language Sentences *Graham Katz and Fabrizio Arosio*	513

25	Assigning Time-Stamps to Event-Clauses *Elena Filatova and Eduard Hovy*	523
26	From Temporal Expressions to Temporal Information: Semantic Tagging of News Messages *Frank Schilder and Christopher Habel*	533
27	The Specification Language TimeML *James Pustejovsky, Robert Ingria, Roser Saurí, José Castaño,* *Jessica Littman, Rob Gaizauskas, Andrea Setzer,* *Graham Katz, and Inderjeet Mani*	545
28	A Model for Processing Temporal References in Chinese *Wenjie Li, Kam-Fai Wong, and Chunfa Yuan*	559
29	Using Semantic Inferences for Temporal Annotation Comparison *Andrea Setzer, Robert Gaizauskas, and Mark Hepple*	575
Index		585

Preface

The emergence of natural language processing applications that process the wide range of electronic texts now universally available has drawn attention to the need for systems that are *temporally aware*, so that they can extract temporal meaning from documents in various languages. Such capabilities can be useful in question answering, summarization, text mining, and other practical applications.

Perceiving practical needs such as these, various initiatives by the US Government[1] and the European Community[2] have invested in research on related theoretical foundations as well as practical methods. We have also seen a plethora of recent workshops on the subject of temporal information processing for natural language as well as highly relevant workshops on temporal reasoning in general.[3]

Given this level of interest, the time seems ripe for a reference text which collects together fundamental papers to characterize the area. While there is considerable material to draw on, it typically appears scattered across various communities in artificial intelligence, computational linguistics, and formal semantics, with little interaction between them. For progress to be made on temporally aware systems, technical knowledge of the issues addressed in these different disciplines is vital. We believe that an updated and multidisciplinary perspective on the problems of temporal and event interpretation in language can facilitate the wider dissemination of the theoretical and technical solutions offered by this new subfield and provide a consolidated resource for future scientists, engineers, and managers of research.

The book is organized into four parts: Tense, Aspect, and Event Structure; Temporal Reasoning; the Temporal Structure of Discourse; and Temporal Annotation. The first part addresses the core linguistic theories dealing with tense and aspect, as well as computational approaches based on them. The second part turns from linguistic considerations to temporal reasoning from an artificial intelligence perspective. The third part explores how inferences about the temporal structure of discourse can be arrived at based on linguistic and world knowledge. The final part examines the construction of text corpora in which the temporal information has been explicitly annotated, as part of an empirical investigation into how temporal information is conveyed in, or can be extracted from, real text samples.

---

[1] US programs include the *Translingual Information Detection, Extraction, and Summarization* (TIDES) program of the Defense Advanced Research Project Agency, the *Advanced Question and Answering for Intelligence* (AQUAINT) program of the Advanced Research and Development Activity (ARDA), the *Automatic Content Extraction* (ACE) program of the Department of Defense, and the *Information Technology Research* (ITR) program of the National Science Foundation.

[2] European programs include the *Expert Advisory Group on Language Engineering Standards* (EAGLES) and *Semantic Information for Multifunctional Plurilingual Lexica* (SIMPLE).

[3] These workshops include *Spatial and Temporal Granularity* at the conference of the American Association for Artificial Intelligence (AAAI'2000), *Spatial and Temporal Reasoning* at AAAI'2002, *Current Issues in Spatio-Temporal Reasoning* at the European Conference on Artificial Intelligence (ECAI'2000), *Temporal and Spatial Information Processing* at the Conference of the Association for Computational Linguistics (ACL'2001), the *Eighth International Symposium on Temporal Representation and Reasoning* (TIME'2001), *Annotation Standards for Temporal Information in Natural Language* at the International Conference on Language Resources and Evaluation (LREC'2002), the ARDA *Workshop on Time and Event Recognition for Question Answering Systems* (TERQAS'2002), and the ARDA *Workshop on TimeML Annotation Graphical Organizer* (TANGO'2003).

The book contains reprints of classic and contemporary papers. For papers that were previously published at conferences, the authors were invited to add, if desired, a short section with updates on any new developments. In the case of two papers, the updates were substantial enough to constitute new papers (Hobbs and Pustejovsky in Part II and Pustejovsky et al. in Part IV). In addition to the papers, each part is accompanied by an overview of the area that also situates the papers in the section and provides a guide to further reading.

We are grateful to the authors, whose valuable contributions made this collection possible. We would also like to thank our editor John Davey at Oxford University Press as well as our respective institutions for encouragement during this effort. Karen Morgan at OUP and Phyllis Jones at MITRE were helpful in obtaining reprints and permissions. We are also thankful to the US Government's ARDA program (under the direction of John Prange) for funding two summer workshops (TERQAS'2002 and TANGO'2003), which led to the development of the TimeML annotation language and helped synergize some of the interdisciplinary ideas behind this book. Finally, this book would not have been possible without the temporal sacrifices made by our families.
Inderjeet Mani, James Pustejovsky, Robert Gaizauskas

List of Contributors

James Allen, University of Rochester, USA
Fabrizio Arosio, Universita degli Studi di Milano-Bicocca, Italy
Nicholas Asher, University of Texas, USA
Emmon Bach, University of Massachusetts and University of London, UK
Allan Bell, Auckland University of Technology, New Zealand
José Castano, Brandeis University, USA
Luca Chittaro, University of Udine, Italy
Robin Cohen, University of Waterloo, Canada
Carlo Combi, University of Verona, Italy
Bonnie Dorr, University of Maryland, College Park, USA
David Dowty, The Ohio State University, USA
Lisa Ferro, The MITRE Corporation, USA
Elena Filatova, Columbia University, USA
Robert Gaizauskas, University of Sheffield, UK
Anthony Galton, University of Exeter, UK
Claire Grover, University of Edinburgh, UK
C. Habel, University of Hamburg, Germany
M. Hepple, University of Sheffield, UK
Janet Hitzeman, The MITRE Corporation, USA
Jerry Hobbs, University of Southern California (Information Sciences Institute), USA
Eduard Hovy, University of Southern California (Information Sciences Institute), USA
C. H. Hwang, Raytheon Company, USA
Bob Ingria, Deceased
Graham Katz, University of Osnabrück, Germany
Robert Kowalski, Imperial College, UK
Alex Lascarides, University of Edinburgh, UK
Wenjie Li, Hong Kong Polytechnic University, China
Jessica Littman, Brandeis University, USA
Inderjeet Mani, Georgetown University, USA
Drew McDermott, Yale University, USA
K. McKeever, formerly at University of Pittsburgh, USA
Marc Moens, Rhetorical Systems and University of Edinburgh, UK
T. Ohrstrom-Sandgren, formerly at University of Pittsburgh, USA
T. P. O'Hara, University of Maryland, Baltimore County, USA
Mari Olsen, Microsoft Research, USA
Rebecca Passonneau, Columbia University, USA
A. Prior, Deceased
James Pustejovsky, Brandeis University, USA
Hans Reichenbach, Deceased
Roser Sauri, Brandeis University, USA
Frank Schilder, The Thomson Corporation, USA
Lehnart Schubert, University of Rochester, USA
M. Sergot, Imperial College, UK

Andrea Setzer, Sheffield University, UK
Fei Song, University of Guelph, Canada
Mark Steedman, University of Edinburgh, UK
Beth Sundheim, SPAWAR Systems Center, USA
Zeno Vendler, Deceased
Bonnie Webber, University of Edinburgh, UK
Janyce Wiebe, University of Pittsburgh, USA
George Wilson, The MITRE Corporation, USA
Kam-Fai Wong, Chinese University of Hong Kong, China
C. Yuan, Tsinghua University, China

Acknowledgements

The editors and publisher gratefully acknowledge permission granted by copyright holders to include material in this book. Details of the source of each of the following chapters are given in its first footnote.

PART I
Tense, Aspect, and Event Structure

Introduction to Part I

1 INTRODUCTION

The science of computational linguistics requires a variety of tools, both theoretical and practical. In order to process temporal information in natural language, we need core theories from linguistics, computational approaches to interpreting tense, aspect, and discourse structure, as well as temporal reasoning capabilities. The papers in this part cover the core linguistic theories dealing with tense and aspect, as well as computational approaches to interpreting them. To assist the reader in navigating through the various theories, we will first provide some relevant linguistic background, explaining the variety of terminology used in these papers. We then summarize and situate each of the papers in terms of this background.[1]

In order to survive in the world, our ancestors at some point evolved the ability to reason in relative terms like 'near' and 'far' about how far away a source of food was. Likewise, they also evolved the ability to reason about past events and planned or hypothetical events, and thus to reason based on how far away an event was in time. As a result of evolution, by a process which is still largely mysterious, all these kinds of reasoning got built into distinctions found in the languages of the world. In particular, **tense** is a specific mechanism built into language for locating information in time.

Verbs and other expressions in natural languages convey meaning about the temporal properties of events, such as whether events last, change, or complete. **Lexical aspect** or *Aktionsarten* (German for 'kinds of action'), distinguishes between different subclasses of events based on these temporal properties. Languages also provide a variety of resources to distinguish between external versus internal viewpoints on an event. In particular, **grammatical aspect** expresses whether an event is viewed as finished, completed, or ongoing. Finally, the notion of **event structure** is a representation of events as complex objects with specific components. Taken together, aspect and event structure provide what, in computational terms, is called an **event ontology**: a theory of the different subclasses (related by what are sometimes called, in the AI literature, **isa** links), components (related by what are sometimes called **part-of** links), and temporal properties of events. The event ontologies discussed here are motivated by the representational distinctions found in natural language, rather than those motivated by nonlinguistic reasoning tasks. This is appropriate, since the ontologies are used for interpreting natural language.

---

[1] Sections 4 and 5 below make use of logical concepts and notation, as do subsequent parts of this book. The reader who lacks an introductory background in logic may benefit from a text such as Suppes (1999).

2 TENSE

Tense can be defined as 'the grammaticalized expression of location in time' (Comrie 1986: 9). This grammaticalized expression involves marking, via change of form, of particular syntactic elements, e.g. the verb and auxiliaries. For example, in *John ran a marathon*, the past tense morpheme represented as *-ed* (producing the inflected verb form *ran*) is used to indicate that the event occurred at a time earlier than the speech time. In *John will run a marathon*, the modal auxiliary *will* is used to locate the event as occurring at a future time, i.e. later than the speech time. While tense is mainly marked on the verb and auxiliaries associated with the verb group, in some languages, like the North American Indian language Nootka (Comrie 1986), tense is expressed on the noun phrase.

Tense isn't the only mechanism for expressing location in time. In languages such as Mandarin Chinese, which lacks tense morphemes, aspectual markers (see Section 3.2 below) can be used to express location in time, though sometimes even these may be absent (Lin 2003). There are also nongrammaticalized expressions of location in time given by temporal adverbials, e.g. *tomorrow, yesterday, two hours later*, etc. In the case of *tomorrow* or *yesterday*, the temporal location is with respect to the speech time. Temporal locations can also of course be expressed relative to a coordinate system given by a calendar, e.g. 1991 *(AD)*, or a cyclically occurring event, e.g. *morning, spring*, or an arbitrary event, e.g. *the day after he married her*.

The few languages that lack tense altogether are not able to distinguish past from present or future. However, they all have a **realis/irrealis** distinction. In Burmese, for example (Comrie 1986), events that are ongoing or that were observed in the past are expressed by sentence-final realis particles *–te, -tha, -ta*, and *–hta*. In other cases, i.e. for unreal or hypothetical events (including future events, present events, and hypothetical past events), the sentence-final irrealis particles *–me, -ma*, and *–hma* are used.

We now turn to the meanings of individual tenses, as found in English. In English, the **present tense** usually locates events as occurring roughly at the speech time. However, the use of the present does not necessarily mean the event coincides with the speech point. In fact, except for performatives like *I warn you...*, the event doesn't usually coincide with the speech point. The typical use of the English present is the reporting use (as in sports commentaries), and in stative sentences (see below). The present tense can also be used to locate events as occurring in the past, as in *Like, then he tells me....* It can also be used to locate events in the future, as in *I leave next week*, as also to express a habitual use indicating a generalization over a set of times, as in *John loves sushi*.

The **past tense** usually refers to a time prior to speech time. Thus, *John slapped Bill* means that there is a time prior to the speech time when the slapping event occurred. The past tense can also involve **definiteness**, i.e. the speaker has a particular time in mind, as in the example of Partee (1973) *(Oops,) I didn't turn off the stove* (uttered halfway down the turnpike). Note that this reading is stronger than the indefinite reading (there was some unspecified time when the stove wasn't turned off), and weaker than the reading where there is no earlier time when I turned off the stove.

The **future tense** usually refers to a time after the speech time though, like the other tenses, it can also be used to refer to other times, e.g. *He'll be home by now*. Our concept of the future is not symmetric with the past, since the future involves branching. In most Germanic languages, the expression of the future tense always seems to involve the non-tense feature of modality, e.g. *I will/may go tomorrow*. See Comrie (1986) for extensive discussions of tense across languages.

3 ASPECT

3.1 Lexical Aspect

3.1.1 Vendler

VENDLER's classic paper (Chapter 1) groups verbs into various subclasses based on their temporal properties. He notes that verbs which describe **activities** like running, working, etc., express actions that 'consist of successive phases following each other in time.' As a result, it is natural to express events by means of a 'continuous tense', i.e. a verb in the progressive form (*John is running*). Vendler characterizes verbs that describe activities as **processes**. By contrast, **states** do not involve successive phases, as a result, they sound odd in the progressive form, e.g. **John is knowing* (the oddness indicated here with an asterisk). Vendler also observes that 'while running or pushing a cart has no set terminal point, running a mile and drawing a circle do have a "climax".' He points out that a man who stops running did run, while a man who stops running a mile didn't run a mile. He argues that running for half an hour involves running for every subperiod within that half hour, whereas having run a mile in four minutes precludes having run a mile in any subperiod. Thus processes are distinguished from a further class of events that culminate, called **accomplishments**. Processes allow adverbials with 'for' but sound odd with 'in', as in *pushing a cart for/*in half an hour*. Accomplishments have the opposite behavior, e.g. *draw a circle in/*for twenty seconds*. Vendler then goes on to distinguish the class of **achievements**, namely events like reaching a hilltop or winning a race that can be predicated for single moments of time. Since achievements don't extend over time, they can't in general co-occur with 'for' adverbials.

The distinctions Vendler draws and subsequently illustrates with a variety of natural language verb usage examples, are based on solid arguments. His work has stimulated research that has been applied across many languages; see Binnick (2002) for a comprehensive bibliography on lexical aspect. Over the years, a number of refinements have been made to Vendler's scheme, in terms of the lexical and syntactic categories involved, their linguistic tests, and their semantic formalization. These are discussed next.

3.1.2 Refinements

Overall, we can characterize a general class of **eventualities** (also called **situations**), that are either **events** or **states** (also called **statives**), with events being subdivided into **processes** (also called **activities**), **accomplishments**, and **achievements**. We will now describe the linguistic tests for each. It is worth bearing in mind, though, that linguistic tests can vary in reliability. While they provide a well-established form of linguistic argumentation for drawing distinctions between categories, they rely on all-or-nothing judgments of ungrammaticality or awkwardness of sentences; a more graded approach to such judgments may be more realistic. Finally, the tests do have exceptions, but usually such exceptions can be explained (e.g. see the discussion of the *for*-adverbial test for achievements below).

Statives are expressed by verbs like *have, love, believe, know, realize, sit,* and *stand,* etc., but also by adjectives with a copula, as in *is clever, is happy,* and nouns like *killing, accident,* etc. For any state p (like John's being hungry) that holds over a period t, p must also hold for every subinterval of t (Dowty, Chapter 15). This **subinterval property** is a characteristic of states. Statives either denote a situation or entry into the situation (**ingressive** or **inceptive** readings, respectively). Thus, *John sits* is ambiguous: it might denote a state or entry into a state; *John knows* describes a state, whereas *John realizes* describes entry into a state; hence *John is (gradually) realizing what's happening* is acceptable, but **John is knowing what's happening* is odd. Some of the standard linguistic tests for stative readings are as follows:

1. Sentences describing statives (in noninceptive readings) are, as Vendler points out, odd when they occur in the progressive *(*John is knowing Bill)*.
2. Statives are odd in imperatives *(*Know the answer)*.
3. Statives can't be used in pseudo-clefts with *do* *(*What John did was know the answer)*.

Activities (associated with verbs like *walk, run*, etc.) differ from other eventualities in that if an activity *p* (like John's walking) occurs in period *t*, a part of the activity (also an activity) must occur for most subintervals of *t*. Note that here the subinterval property must be constrained so as to allow for gaps. For example, in contrast to Vendler's argument about running, I usually pause while running. Also, only parts of the activity down to a particular **grain size** count as the same activity; clearly, lifting a leg is not running. Thus, X Vs for an hour, where V is an activity, entails X Vs for all/most times in that hour; also X is Ving entails that X has Ved, since the latter sentence is true of a subactivity of V. Some of the standard tests are:

1. Activities take temporal adverbials with *for* (e.g. *John ran for an hour*).
2. Activities do not take temporal adverbial phrases with *in* (e.g. **John ran in an hour*).

Accomplishments (associated with verbs like *build, cook, book*, etc.) are eventualities which can **culminate**. Unlike activities, X Vs for an hour, where V is an accomplishment, does not entail X Vs for all times in that hour; likewise X is Ving does not entail that X has Ved. Thus, John is cooking dinner does not entail John has cooked dinner. Standard tests are:

1. Accomplishments take temporal adverbial phrases with *in* (e.g. *John booked a flight in an hour*).
2. Accomplishment verbs with *stop* indicate that the event did not succeed, e.g. *John stopped building a house* (compare with activities, where they indicate the event succeeded e.g. *John stopped running*).

Achievements (associated with verbs like *win, blink, find, reach*, etc.) are instantaneous (or short-duration) accomplishments, namely events that finish and that occur in a very short time period. The standard tests are:

1. Achievements cannot be modified by temporal *for*-adverbials. Thus, **X Vs for an hour, where V is an achievement verb. For example, **John dies for an hour, *John wins for an hour, *John reached New York for an hour*. In cases where these sentences are acceptable, they tend to have readings which refer to the duration of the result state (e.g. of being dead or a winner) rather than the duration of the achievement event itself.
2. Achievement verbs do not take *stop* (e.g. **John stopped reaching New York*).

Accomplishments and achievements, which are events that can culminate, are sometimes called **telic** eventualities. Achievements are instantaneous, and events in general involve change from the state that held before the event began. Finally, there are also instantaneous activities, called **semelfactives**, like *knock* or *cough*, which are

TABLE 1   Aspectual Features

	Telic	Dynamic	Durative	Example
Stative	−	−	+	*know, have*
Activity	−	+	+	*walk, paint*
Accomplishment	+	+	+	*build, destroy*
Achievement	+	+	−	*notice, win*

instantaneous, atelic, and dynamic. However, they are usually not broken out as a separate class. Based on this, the feature analysis shown in Table 1 can be constructed to capture these distinctions, based on Smith (1991).

So far, these aspectual classes have been defined by linguistic criteria, but not formalized in terms of a semantic theory. Such a formalization is implicit in the work of Dorr and Olsen (Chapter 7), and is carried out explicitly in the paper by Dowty in Part III (Chapter 15).

3.1.3   Aspectual Composition

While these eventuality subclasses characterize individual lexical items, they also can be used to characterize phrases and sentences. In fact, as Dowty points out in his paper in part III, there is a lack of consistency in the literature in terms of what linguistic element the classification applies to. Different approaches have considered different kinds of text units, including lexical items (e.g. *hungry*), verb phrases (e.g. *eating a peach*), sentences, and semantic entities like events. Despite these differences, however, it is clear that expressions of one class can be transformed into one of another class by combining with another expression. This type of transformation is called **aspectual composition**. For example, an activity can be changed into an accomplishment by adding an adverbial phrase expressing temporal or spatial extent, e.g. *I walked* (activity) and *I walked to the station/a mile/home* (accomplishment). Likewise, an accomplishment like *I built my house* can be changed into an activity by combining with a *for*-adverbial, viz., *I built my house for an hour* (activity). A system of rules for carrying out such aspectual composition is called an **aspect calculus**; examples are found in Dowty (1979), see also Dowty (Chapter 15), Jackendoff (1991), de Swart (1998) and Pustejovsky (Chapter 2), among others.

3.2   Grammatical Aspect

While tense allows the speaker to relate the time of an eventuality to a deictic center or some other reference point, grammatical aspect allows the speaker to represent the structure of an eventuality. Here there is a distinction between **perfective aspect**, where an entire eventuality is presented without its internal temporal structure, e.g. *John built a house*, and **imperfective aspect**, where the speaker represents internal phases of the eventuality, e.g. *John is building a house*. Perfective aspect can express termination or completion of an eventuality, while imperfective aspect can express the ongoing nature of an activity. It is important to realize that many of the traditional tenses, e.g. Spanish imperfective, as in *Juan leía cuando entré* (*John was reading when I entered*), may combine both tense and aspect, e.g. past and imperfective. The same is true of the 'complex tenses' in English, such as present progressive, present perfect, etc.

Grammatical aspect is expressed in systematic ways across languages, depending on the lexical aspect of the eventuality. The following account, derived from cross-linguistic arguments by Smith (1991) and work on Chinese by Lin (2003), summarizes some of this systematicity.

In English and French, **perfective aspect** is signaled by verbal tense and aspect morphemes. Termination is expressed in activities, completion is expressed in accomplishments and achievements, and statives can either express termination (e.g. French *passé composé* tense morpheme) or not (English, e.g. *I have lived in Paris*). In Mandarin Chinese, which lacks tense markers but which does have the semantic notion of tense (Lin 2003), the perfective is signaled by morphemes *–le* and *–guo*, usually indicating termination for activities, accomplishments and achievements; completion is indicated by a separate resultative morpheme *–wan*. In Russian, the perfective doesn't apply to statives, but is signaled by prefixes *po-* (short duration) and *pro-* (unexpected interval) in activities.

The **imperfective aspect** is signaled in English by the progressive morpheme *-ing*. It occurs in activities, accomplishments, and achievements. In French, as in Russian, it is signaled by tense morphemes (e.g. the French *imparfait*). In Mandarin, it is signaled by the progressive morpheme *–zai* and resultative morpheme *–zhe*. The particle *-le* can also have an imperfective use with atelic predicates (Lin 2003).

4 EVENT STRUCTURE

As mentioned earlier, from an event ontology standpoint, the component structure of events is of considerable importance, in addition to their various subclasses. In order to represent the internal structure of events, one must first understand how meanings of event-denoting expressions are to be represented. In a logical framework, there are two fundamental ways of representing meaning: (i) the meaning of an accomplishment verb, say *close*, is the predicate *CLOSE*, so that a sentence of the form *X closes Y* is mapped to *CLOSE(X, Y)*; (ii) the meaning of *close* is decomposed into the meaning of primitive elements, e.g. *CAUSE TO BECOME NOT OPEN*, so that a sentence like *X closes Y* can be represented as *CAUSE(X, BECOME(NOT(OPEN(Y))))*.

As Dowty (1979) shows, by decomposing the meaning of any accomplishment verb into a description of a causative event and a result state, we can explain a number of apparent scope ambiguities with adverbs, as well as some data from derivational morphology. For example, *John closed the door again* is ambiguous between an 'external' reading, where John performed the action of closing the door at least once before, and an 'internal' reading, where John merely brought it about that the door is again closed. Postulating a decomposed meaning, the external reading may be explained by *again* having (wide) scope over the entire expression, i.e. *AGAIN(CAUSE(X, BECOME (NOT(OPEN(Y)))))*, whereas in the internal reading, *again* has narrow scope over *closed*, i.e. *CAUSE(X, BECOME(AGAIN(NOT(OPEN(Y)))))*.

Despite Dowty's plausible arguments in favor of his decompositional scheme, decompositional theories are prone to problems, the most crucial of which is the proliferation of primitives. In practical situations, the semantic primitives are often inadequate for the task at hand, and new primitives have to be added. Approaches such as Jackendoff (1990) are hindered by the inability to distinguish differences in meaning among similar words, for example, *run/walk/trot* are all mapped to a *MOVE* primitive. In dealing with this, approaches often end up proliferating 'manner' primitives that help distinguish the different senses. (In addition, some decompositional accounts, such as Schank (1975) are further limited by the lack of a compositional semantics.)

Instead of decomposing meanings in this (somewhat ungainly) way, PUSTEJOVSKY (Chapter 2) suggests a more modular approach. In his approach, rather than the decomposition of event meanings into primitives, the substructure of events, together with meaning-forming rules for 'event composition' give rise to the relationships expressed by decomposed meanings. In particular, he argues that accomplishment events like *close* are made up of two aspectually salient parts, a preparatory process with the meaning $ACT(X, Y)$ & $NOT(CLOSED(Y))$ and a result state with meaning CLOSED (Y). Note that primitives like *CAUSE* and *BECOME* are not explicitly part of the representation. The resulting state overlaps with the event, and can of course extend beyond it. Activities are made up of (an indeterminate number of) subevents each of which corresponds to the activity, e.g. *X pushed Y* would be made up of subevents e each represented as $ACT(X, Y)$ and $MOVE(Y)$. States have no such decomposition, so that *Y is closed* is simply represented as $CLOSED(Y)$. His treatment of achievements is a little less uniform, as it depends on whether it involves an agentive action or not. A non-agentive sentence like *X died* is represented in terms of a preparatory process with the meaning $NOT(DEAD(X))$ and a result state with meaning $DEAD(X)$, while an agentive achievement like *win* is represented just as accomplishments are.

A crucial point about event composition is that it is part and parcel of a compositional semantics. Thus, in *Mary ran to the store, to the store* has a meaning such that it combines with an activity like *ran* to yield a phrase *ran to the store* that is an accomplishment. The latter event has a structure with a preparatory process given by the activity $RAN(X)$ and the result state given by $AT(X, STORE)$. Pustejovsky goes on to apply his account to resultative constructions (like *Mary hammered the metal flat*, where the result state is directly expressed in the construction), and the syntactic behaviors of psychological verbs like *fear* and *frighten*, as well as problems involving the scopes of adverbial modifiers, and the mapping from argument structure to syntactic structure. While the theory has various explanatory advantages, it does not directly relate event structure to temporal structure. For example, the point of culmination of an accomplishment, at which the result is generated, isn't explicitly identified.

The notion of event structure calls out for representational detail. Let us assume that the accomplishment of building a cabin involves a number of subevents as part of its preparatory process, including the accomplishment of hammering in a nail. What sort of precise structure do these events and processes have, given the nesting of subevents? One way of answering this question is by means of an **event algebra**, described by BACH (Chapter 3).

Bach's work draws inspiration from the work of Link (1983) on a lattice-theoretic account of the semantics of mass, count, and plural nouns. In Link's scheme, sets of individuals (as in the case of plurals like *John and Mary*) are individuated by using a join operation that creates super-individuals. Members of the set are linked by an 'individual part-of' relation to the set super-individual. Thus John is an individual part of the plural individual John and Mary, as also of John and the chair, etc. There is a similar structure having to do with the stuff that John (or the chair) is made up of: there is a join operation defined over bits of stuff, with the similar result that the stuff of John is part of the stuff of John and Mary. There is also a mapping between the two structures: the mapping from an individual to the stuff she is made out of can be extended to a mapping from joins of individuals to the joins of the stuff they are made out of.

Bach's goal is to have a similar mapping between telic events and the process stuff they are made out of. His event subclasses are the Vendlerian ones, except that he distinguishes, following Carlson (1977), between two subclasses of achievements, 'happenings' like *recognize* and 'culminations' like *die*. The algebra itself is very concise. (However, please note that there is a misprint in his paper in Section 4, line (2): it should say that the atomic events A_e are a subset of E_e.) Bach shows that the algebra can make precise a variety of intuitions. For example, the process of the event of Sally pounding in a nail is a process-part-of the process of the event of Sally building a cabin. The event of Mary stumbling is an individual part-of the plural event of Mary stumbling and Mary twisting her ankle, and the process of Mary stumbling is a process-part-of the process of Mary stumbling and twisting her ankle. Moreover, events which are distinct, such as John pouring poison into the water (deliberately to kill fish) and John poisoning the populace (which could be unintentional) could be made up of the same processes. The paper then goes on to speculate about other interesting parallels between the domain of nominals and the domain of events.

Further work on event structure applied to event and aspectual semantics is found in the lattice-theoretic work of Hinrichs (1985) and Krifka (1989).

5 FORMAL THEORIES OF TENSE AND ASPECT

5.1 Tense as Anaphor: Reichenbach

We have already seen that times of events can be located with respect to a deictic center, so in a sense they are like pronouns. This anaphoric view of tense derives from the classic work of REICHENBACH, first published in 1947 (Chapter 4). Tensed utterances, according to Reichenbach, introduce references to three 'time points': the speech time S, the event time E, and the **reference time** R. Reference times, for Reichenbach, can coincide with the times of expressions like *Tuesday, the next week, now*, etc., but they aren't necessarily made explicit in text. Now, consider sentence (1). Here the event of leaving is located before the speech time, and also before the time of five o'clock, which coincides with the reference time, which in turn offers a vantage point from which the event of leaving is seen. This would be represented as $E<R<S$. Here $E<R$ means the event time **precedes** the reference time. Likewise, $E=R$ means the event time is **simultaneous** with the reference time.

(1) By five o'clock, John had already left.

Likewise, in (2), the vantage point, which isn't expressed by a temporal adverbial, is some time in the future, so we have E and S before R, with the relation between E and S left unspecified.

(2) John will have caught the train.

Reichenbach used the relations between S, E, and R to represent the meaning of tenses in English and a few other languages. Reichenbach's examples are mainly drawn from English, but in keeping with other well-educated scholars of his time, he also discussed examples in German, French, Latin, and Greek.

Reichenbach's constraint-based analysis of the English tense system is shown in Table 2. Tense (present, past, future) is determined by the relation between R and S. Aspect (simple, anterior, or posterior) is determined by relation between E and R.

TABLE 2 Comparison of Reichenbach and Prior

Relation	Reichenbach's Tense Name	Prior	English Tense Name	Example
E<R<S	Anterior past	PPϕ	Past perfect	*I had slept*
E=R<S	Simple past	Pϕ	Simple past	*I slept*
R<E<S	Posterior past	PFϕ		[*I expected that*]
R<S=E				*I would sleep*
R<S<E				
E<S=R	Anterior present	Pϕ	Present perfect	*I have slept*
S=R=E	Simple present	ϕ	Simple present	*I sleep*
S=R<E	Posterior present	Fϕ	Simple future	*I will sleep*; French: *Je vais dormir*
S<E<R	Anterior future	FPϕ	Future perfect	*I will have slept*
S=E<R				
E<S<R				
S<R=E	Simple Future	Fϕ	Simple future	*I will sleep*; French: *Je dormirai*
S<R<E	Posterior future	FFϕ		*I shall be going to sleep*

Only seven out of thirteen relations are realized in English; there are six different forms, with the simple future being ambiguous. However, as Comrie (1986) points out, the posterior past can be given an unambiguous representation $E>R<S$, and similarly the anterior future can be given an unambiguous representation as $E<R>S$. The progressive forms (not shown) are treated by Reichenbach as having extended intervals in time instead of time points, but are otherwise similar to the simple tenses.

Reichenbach's work has had an enduring influence on subsequent work in formal semantics and computational linguistics. In the Introduction to Part III, we discuss the use of Reichenbachian notions in a formal representation of discourse meaning, namely Discourse Representation Theory (DRT) (Kamp and Reyle 1993). The notion of tense as anaphor is also explicated further in Webber's paper in Part III (Chapter 18).

5.2 Tense as Operator: Prior

When discussing the semantics of the past tense, it was pointed out that *John slapped Bill* means that there is a time prior to the speech time when the slapping event occurred. We might restate this as follows: *John slapped Bill* is true at the speech time if and only if there is some time t before the speech time when *John slaps Bill* is true. This is, in a nutshell, the analysis PRIOR offers of the past tense (Chapter 5).

Prior published most of his work on tense logic in the 1950s and 1960s (Prior 1957, 1967, and 1968). His 1968 paper *Tense Logic and the Logic of Earlier and Later* (Chapter 5 in this volume) has the twin virtues of being self-contained and not requiring the reader to have a technical background in philosophy (this cannot be said of his other papers). The first section of his paper discusses the minimal tense logic K_t developed first by E. J. Lemmon. K_t uses the operators P (for past) and F (for future), defined as below. "Here, ϕ and ψ are propositions in propositional logic."

1. $P\phi$ is true at time t iff there is a t' prior to t such that ϕ is true at time t'.
2. $F\phi$ is true at time t iff there is a t' after t such that ϕ is true at time t'.

Two additional operators H (for 'has always been', defined as *not P not* ϕ) and G ('is always going to be', defined as *not F not* ϕ) are also specified.

The logical system K_t consists of the following four axioms:

(a) $\phi \to H F \phi$: What is, has always been going to be;
(b) $\phi \to G P \phi$: What is, will always have been;
(c) $H(\phi \to \psi) \to (H\phi \to H\psi)$: Whatever always follows from what always has been, always has been;
(d) $G(\phi \to \psi) \to (G\phi \to G\psi)$: Whatever always follows from what always will be, always will be.

The rest of the chapter enhances this logic. First, the minimal propositional tense logic above is related to a minimal calculus defined over instants, that uses the operators *T* and *U*: here *Tap* means 'it is the case at instant *a* that *p*' and *Uab* means 'instant *a* is earlier than instant *b*'. A logic based on the latter calculus forms the first of four logical systems of increasing power developed in the paper. For example, the second logical system relies on allowing the variable *p* in *Tap* to stand for complex expressions like *Tbp* or *Uab*, resulting in expressions like *TaTbp* and *TcUab*.

Unfortunately, the paper by Prior reprinted in Chapter 5 uses a somewhat opaque prefix notation. This notation may be explained as follows, from Prior (1957, chapter 2):

Apq: Either *p* or *q*
Cpq: If *p* then *q*
Epq: Iff *p* then *q*
Kpq: Both *p* and *q*
Np: Not *p*
Σp: For some *p*
Πp: For all *p*

Thus, for example, *CFFpFp* is the same as *FFp* → *Fp* and the rule (*d*) of the System K_t above is the same as *CGC$\phi\psi$CGϕGψ*.

Our illustration of Priorean logic applied to specific English tenses is based in part on de Swart and Verkuyl (1999), and is shown in Table 2. As can be seen, Prior's approach allows free iteration of tense operators to get more complex tenses. However, the free iteration is too powerful: it generates many expressions which can't possibly be natural language (NL) tenses, e.g. *PPPPϕ* **It was the case that it was the case that John had slept*. The progressive isn't distinguished; also, the past perfect has a treatment which is analogous to Reichenbach's. Unlike Reichenbach, however, there is no distinction between present perfect and simple past. Nor is there any operator for present tense. Despite these shortcomings, Prior offers a set of formal logics for representing tense meanings, and it has been extended in various ways, for example, by Kamp (1971) and others. For more on logics for reasoning about time and events, see Part II.

5.3 Imperfective Aspect: Semantics of the Progressive

The **progressive**, which in English expresses imperfective aspect, has attracted the attention of semanticists on account of its peculiar semantic behavior. In the case of activities, the use of the progressive implies culmination: *John was running* implies *John ran*. In the case of telic eventualities, however, this isn't so: *John was running home* doesn't imply *John ran home*. Since the progressive expresses imperfective aspect, this peculiarity or puzzle is referred to as the **imperfective paradox** (Dowty 1979). Note that earlier approaches such as Reichenbach and Prior gave the progressive a similar semantics to the simple tenses.

Dowty addresses this paradox by considering future branches of an event that seem 'normal'. Accordingly, he introduces the concept of an **inertia world**: i.e. a world which is like the current world up to *Now* and is a 'normal' continuation of it thereafter, i.e. a world where nothing 'abnormal' happens. (Such worlds are of course a philosophical abstraction!) He postulates the following meaning for the progressive morpheme (e.g. *-ing*):

> *Progressive V is true in the current world at a time interval I if and only if there is some superinterval I' ⊃ I extending beyond I into the future such that V is true at I' in every corresponding inertia world.*

Consider an event V true at I' in every inertia world. If V is an activity like *John was running*, since it has the subinterval property, V is true at I in every inertia world. Since the inertia world is like the current world up to *Now*, V is true in the current world as well. In contrast, if V is a telic event like *John was running home*, since the subinterval property doesn't hold for it, no such inference can be made about V being true in the current world.

Inertia worlds, while restricted to normalcy, can still result in noncompletion of an event, e.g. *Mary was crossing the street, when a truck hit her* (Vlach 1981). As an alternative, Parsons (1990) proposes a nonmodal theory, where the progressive changes a telic event to be nontelic, i.e. instead of telic V culminating at time t, it merely holds at time t. This approach, Parsons admits, commits to the existence of possibly incomplete objects, e.g. *John was building a house*, on Parson's account, implies that the house exists even if the building event doesn't culminate for some reason (e.g. after some initial activity, the building event might have been aborted due to cost overruns). For more details on the progressive, see Kuhn and Portner (2002), Landman (1992), and White (1994).

5.4 Perfective Aspect: Semantics of the Perfect

The perfect, which is an expression of perfective aspect, poses several semantic puzzles. It has an existential use, locating the event somewhere in the indefinite past. There is also a universal use involving the predicate holding over an entire period, as in *John has lived in Boston*. Whether this period extends up to now or not depends in part on the context.

The present perfect, in particular, also involves **recency**, cf. *Mary has run into trouble*. As Kuhn and Portner (2002) point out, that recency is part of the meaning is supported by the view that the present perfect can always take temporal modifiers that pick out intervals overlapping the present, but never those that pick out intervals entirely preceding the present; viz. *Mary has bought a dress since Saturday*, but **Mary has bought a dress last week*.

The use of the present perfect also involves **felicity conditions**. As Chomsky has noted, *Einstein has visited Princeton* is infelicitous today, but *Princeton has been visited by Einstein* is OK today. As Kuhn and Portner point out, *My mother has changed my diapers many times* is infelicitous when spoken by an adult. For more on the formal semantics of the perfect, see Klein (1994), Kuhn and Portner (2002), and Portner (2003).

6 COMPUTATIONAL APPROACHES

6.1 Introduction

In the above sections, we have introduced some of the theoretical tools that linguistics and logic provide for analyzing temporal information in natural language. These tools supply, at the very least:

(1) a theory, expressed in rules of some form, as to how particular tense features and temporal adverbials contribute to temporally locating events;
(2) an event ontology, namely a description of event subclasses and components, and their temporal properties. In linguistic terms, the ontology falls out of a theory of aspect, including an account of lexical aspect, an aspect calculus, and an account of the semantics of perfective and imperfective aspects, along with a theory of event structure.

The computational approaches in this section demonstrate how some of these tools can be applied in the design of systems to process temporal information in NL. These approaches go well beyond merely applying these tools; they further refine the theories, integrate multiple theories, and test some of the analyses on actual data from an application.

6.2 Computing Aspect: Transition Networks

MOENS AND STEEDMAN (Chapter 6) offer an event ontology with event subclasses that are distinguished similarly to those in Table 1. Telicity is similar to its sense in Table 1, and associated here with a result or consequent state. States are viewed as extending indefinitely in time, while events have beginnings and ends. Event subclasses are also distinguished based on whether they are atomic or extended, analogous to the Durativity feature in Table 1. Thus, there are atomic activities (corresponding to semelfactives) as well as atomic accomplishments (i.e. achievements). In addition to these event subclasses, the event ontology of Moens and Steedman provides a tripartite model of event structure. They represent events that culminate with an event structure consisting of a preparatory process, a culmination, and a result state. Note that the breaking out of the culmination distinguishes it from Pustejovskian version of event structure. Any of these three components can in turn be compound; the preparation for a climb of Everest can include various events, the reaching of the top can be broken down further, and the result state can include further events that are in the same sequence of contingently related events as the culmination. Moens and Steedman motivate this account of event structure by the different readings one gets with *when*-adverbials adjoined to a main clause.

Moens and Steedman go on to develop an aspect calculus, represented as a remarkably compact transition network. Thus, for example, to get an interpretation of *Harry was hiccupping*, the semelfactive (i.e. a point process) *Harry hiccupped* is changed into a process of iteration of the point, and that process of iteration is then in turn changed by the progressive into a progressive state. Temporal adverbials can trigger specific transitions, e.g. *Harry hiccupped for three hours* would be analyzed as a process of iteration of the point event of hiccupping.

Their paper goes on to show how the transition network is able to express a wide variety of aspectual distinctions. It accommodates multiple interpretations for a sentence by allowing for multiple paths through the network. The network can admit ambiguities that seem spurious, for example, *Harry is speaking* could mean a process changed into a progressive state, or a process that is changed into a point and iterated before being changed into the progressive state. The authors show in some detail how particular readings are preferred, and state upfront that the appropriateness of any particular transition is 'conditional on support from (world) knowledge and context'. Their account also doesn't allow transitions out of states, so that a progressive can't be changed into an activity (excluding, for example *He was winning for an hour at the tables when his luck turned*). Their treatment of the progressive is a nonmodal account, and as such it commits to the existence of incomplete objects. Further, some of their assumptions are incorrect, e.g. their claim that the perfect applies only to culminations—what about *John has lived in Boston*? Also, their paper stops short of offering rules for a compositional semantics tied to the specific syntactic structure of sentences. (For an alternative, biologically motivated approach to aspectual composition, see Chang et al. (1998).)

6.3 Computing Aspect: Decomposed Event Ontologies

The work of DORR AND OLSEN (Chapter 7) uses an aspectual classification similar to Table 1. However, they argue, based on Olsen (1994), that while aspectual composition can change a negative feature to positive, the converse doesn't occur. As a result, they get rid of the negative feature values. (This step may be misguided: an accomplishment can change into an activity, as in *Ulrich was winning the race*, and an activity can change into a state, as in a stative treatment of the progressive, as we saw in the Moens and Steedman work.) The result, from a computational point of view, is that features just get added, never deleted, resulting in aspectual composition being a monotonic process. The paper goes on to represent verb meanings in terms of ontological primitives based on the decompositional theory of Jackendoff (1990). Telicity, Dynamicity, and Durativity can then be mapped to the presence of particular primitives in the verb meanings. For example, Jackendoff represents states with one of two primitives; the absence of these is a test for Dynamicity.

Having specified lexical aspect based on the meaning representations of lexical entries (this requires some modification to their pre-existing lexical entries), Dorr and Olsen show how the aspectual class of composed elements can be derived by the same algorithm which determines lexical aspect, namely, by testing for particular elements in the semantic representation. The paper goes on to describe how these aspectual features are exploited to construct translations in Machine Translation applications. For example, their system requires that sentential translations must match in telicity, even if the verb and its translation do not, cf. *marched across the field*, which has the atelic verb *march*, versus the Spanish translation *cruzo el campo marchando* (*crossed the field by marching*), which has the telic *cruzo*. Their lexicon is also available for free use by other researchers (Dorr 2003). This work has also been exploited in natural language generation (Dorr and Gaasterland 2002).

Overall, their approach shows how lexical aspect and aspectual composition can both be derived from a particular decomposed representation for lexical meanings. In other words, the primitives of the event ontology determine aspectual classes of lexical and composed expressions. In their framework, aspectual composition is a side-effect of semantic composition. The downside of their approach is of course that this advantage is won by committing to a decompositional theory that is prone to the problem of proliferation of semantic primitives. Nevertheless, their paper shows how this kind of representation can be made practical in terms of reusable lexical resources.

6.4 Computing Temporal Locations of Actual Events

The final computational paper in this part is that of PASSONNEAU (Chapter 8). Her goal is to process references to eventualities, locating them temporally, as part and parcel of the PUNDIT information extraction system. Passonneau's event ontology distinguishes states, activities, and accomplishments (which she calls 'transition events'). As with Vendler, semelfactives aren't distinguished. Achievements aren't distinguished from accomplishments, since she views them as having short durations rather than being instantaneous; also, whether an achievement is viewed as a point or an interval is considered an issue of granularity. As a result, she doesn't have a Durativity feature. She introduces a feature for Boundedness: states are inherently unbounded, whereas transition events are bounded; activities may be bounded or not depending on sentential context. Like Dorr and Olsen, she uses a decompositional approach to representing aspectual meaning; however, unlike them, she uses the semantic framework of Dowty (1979). Passonneau also independently develops a model of event structure for transition events that is extremely similar to the one proposed by Moens and Steedman.

As in most information extraction research, Passonneau focuses on **actual** events, namely, realis events that are specific, that have occurred earlier or that are occurring at the time of the text. Realis events are characterized as being those not in modal, negated, intentional, or frequency adverbial contexts. Her system works in three steps.

In Step I, each utterance is analyzed in terms of the aspectual class, the tense (past/present) and grammatical aspect (perfect or progressive), the main predicate and its arguments, and (finally) the time over which the event occurs or (in the case of states) holds—the latter is explained below in the account of Step II. Any present tense nonstative event that isn't in the progressive or perfect is treated as nonactual, with all other events, excluding those on a stoplist, being treated as actual.

In Step II, the temporal structure of the eventuality is determined. If it is a state, since it is inherently unbounded, the event producing the state occurs in a subinterval of the state; for example, for the progressive, stative sentence *Metallic particles are clogging the strainer*, the time of the ongoing clogging event is assumed to be an arbitrary moment included within the unbounded interval of the state of being clogged. (Note that unlike Moens and Steedman's approach, there is no notion of iteration here.) In contrast, in the case of a transition event, as in the sentence *The pump failed*, the moment of the event's culmination starts the period of the result state.

In Step III, Reichenbach's tense representation is used to order the event time with respect to the reference time and situation time. In this process, temporal adverbials are interpreted. Thus, given *The compressor failed before the pump seized*, the reference time for each clause is computed as being arbitrary moments included in the failing and seizing events respectively. These reference times are then ordered based on the semantics for *before*.

Passonneau's focus is on the contributions of tense and lexical aspect. Her work is characterized by many interesting details, including the handling of subordinated events. While the theoretical tools she uses (event ontology and tense analysis) are very general, the types of texts her system is used for allow her not to be directly concerned with aspectual composition. Also, checks for realis events in terms of the presence of modal and other contexts aren't discussed in her paper. Her work, nevertheless, demonstrates how these theoretical tools can be used within a practical system to locate events in time. We shall see that such work forms a natural precursor to subsequent work in temporal information extraction, including work discussed in Part IV. We turn now to a system that uses tense and aspect information to locate events in time, but one that is not aimed at the information extraction problem.

Ion Androutsopoulos's work (Androutsopoulos 1996, 2002; Androutsopoulos et al. 1998) addresses problems in natural language interfaces to databases. His NLITDB system allows users to pose temporal questions in natural language to an airport database. NLITDB maps English queries to a temporal extension of the SQL database language, via an intermediate semantic representation. The latter is influenced by the work of Crouch and Pulman (1993), and uses temporal operators, including the Priorean Past operator, along with Reichenbachian indices. (The source code, which relies on Head-Driven Phrase Structure Grammar (HPSG), is freely available.) Although we cannot include a reprint in this volume for reasons of length, we provide a summary of his approach. Readers are referred to his book (Androutsopoulos 2002) for more details.

In NLITDB, verbs in natural language questions are classified into (at least one of the) four aspectual classes based on manual analysis using linguistic tests on question sentences from an application domain test suite. For example, verbs that occur in single-clause questions with nonfuture meanings are treated as states (e.g. *Does any tank contain oil?*). A verb like *land*, which can be used habitually, e.g. *Which flight lands on runway 2?*, or nonhabitually, e.g. *Does flight BA737 land on runway 2 this afternoon?*, will be treated as ambiguous, with a habitual state entry and an accomplishment entry. Activities are distinguished using the imperfective paradox: *Were any flights taxiing?* implies that they taxied, while *Were any flights taxiing to gate 2?* does not imply that they taxied. So, *taxi* will be given an activity verb sense, one that doesn't expect a destination argument, and also an accomplishment verb sense, one that expects a destination argument.

NLITDB has extensive coverage of temporal adverbials. The semantic relation between a question event and the adverbial it combines with is computed by a variety of inference rules. In the case of a state combining with a 'point' adverbial, e.g. *Which flight was queueing for runway 2 at 5:00 pm?*, the state is coerced to an achievement and is viewed as holding *at* the time specified by the adverbial. When an activity combines with a point adverbial, it can mean that the activity holds *at* that time, but an inceptive reading that the activity *starts at* that time is also possible, as in *Which flight queued for runway 2 at 5:00 pm?* An accomplishment may indicate inception or termination; for example, *Which flight taxied to gate 4 at 5:00 pm?* can mean the taxiing starts or ends at 5 pm. In the case of 'interval' adverbials, the event holds for at least part of the adverbial's duration or is included within the duration of the adverbial. The system also has a fairly extensive treatment of *while, before*, and *after* clauses.

7 CONCLUSION

This overview has introduced the theoretical tools for analyzing how natural language expresses the location of events in time (via tense), whether they are ongoing, completed, or terminated (via grammatical aspect), and the ontological distinctions among events that language makes (in terms of aspectual subclasses of events, as well as event structure). We have also explored computational approaches to aspectual composition based on particular event ontologies. Finally, this Introduction has presented information extraction as a means of temporally locating extracted events. It is worth noting that the computational approaches rely heavily on these theoretical tools. In Part III, we will show how the analysis of sentences in a discourse context is used to locate and order events in time, examining formal approaches to discourse analysis. Finally, In Part IV, we will explore current corpus annotation schemes for representing events and their temporal locations, that can in turn give rise to advanced temporal information extraction systems.

REFERENCES

Androutsopoulos, I. (1996). 'A Principled Framework for Constructing Natural Language Interfaces to Temporal Databases'. Ph.D. dissertation, University of Edinburgh.

—— 2002. *Exploring Time, Tense and Aspect in Natural Language Database Interfaces*. Amsterdam: John Benjamins.

—— Ritchie, G. D., and Thanisch, P. (1998). 'Time, tense and aspect in natural language database interfaces', *Natural Language Engineering* 4(3): 229–76. (See <http://www.aueb.gr/users/ion/nlitdb_book/> for freely downloadable software.)

Binnick, R. (2002). 'Project on the Bibliography of Tense, Verbal Aspect, Aktionsart, and Related Areas'. <http://www.scar.utoronto.ca/~binnick/TENSE/Aktions.html>.

Carlson, G. (1977). 'Reference to Kinds in English'. Ph.D. dissertation, University of Massachussetts, Amherst.

Chang, N., Gildea, D., and Narayanan, S. (1998). 'A Dynamic Model of Aspectual Composition', in M. A. Gernsbacher and S. J. Derry (eds.), *Proceedings of the 20th Annual Meeting of the Cognitive Science Society*, Madison, Wisconsin. Mahwah, NJ: Lawrence Erlbaum Associates, 226–31.

Comrie, B. (1986). *Tense*. Cambridge: Cambridge University Press.

Crouch, R. S. and Pulman, S. G. (1993). 'Time and modality in a natural language interface to a planning system', *Artificial Intelligence*, 63: 265–304.

Dorr, B. (2003). 'Lexical Resources' <www.umiacs.umd.edu/~bonnie/LCS_Database_Documentation.html>.

—— and Gaasterland, T. (2002). 'Constraints on the Generation of Tense, Aspect, and Connecting Words from Temporal Expressions'. Technical Report CS-TR-4391, UMIACS-TR-2002-71, LAMP-TR-091, University of Maryland, College Park, MD.

Dowty, D. (1979). *Word Meaning and Montague Grammar*. Boston: D. Reidel.

Hinrichs, E. A. (1985). 'Compositional Semantics for Aktionsarten and NP Reference in English'. Ph.D. dissertation, Ohio State University.

Jackendoff, R. (1990). *Semantic Structures*. Cambridge, MA: MIT Press.

—— (1991). 'Parts and Boundaries', *Cognition* 21: 9–45.

Kamp, H. (1971). 'Formal Properties of "now"', *Theoria* 27: 237–73.

—— and Reyle, U. (1993). *From Discourse to Logic: Introduction to Model-theoretic Semantics of Natural Language, Formal Logic and Discourse Representation Theory*, 2 vols. Dordrecht, Holland: Kluwer.

Klein, W. (1994). *Time in Language*. London: Routledge.

Krifka, M. (1989). 'Nominal Reference, Temporal Constitution, and Quantification in Event Semantics', in R. Bartsch, J. van Benthem, and P. van Emde Boas (eds.), *Semantics and Contextual Expressions*. Dordrecht, Holland: Kluwer, 75–115.

Kuhn, S. and Portner, P. (2002). 'Tense and Time', in D. Gabbay and F. Guenther (eds.), *The Handbook of Philosophical Logic*, vol. 7 (2nd edn.). Dordrecht, Holland: Kluwer.

Landman, F. (1992). 'The Progressive', *Natural Language Semantics* 1: 1–32.
Lin, J-W. (2003). 'Temporal Reference in Mandarin Chinese', *Journal of East Asian Linguistics* 12: 259–311.
Link, G. (1983). 'The Logical Analysis of Plurals and Mass Terms', in R. Bauerle, C. Schwarze, and A. von Stechow (eds.), *Meaning, Use and Interpretation of Language*. Berlin: Walter de Gruyter, 302–23.
Olsen, M. B (1994). 'The Semantics and Pragmatics of Lexical and Grammatical Aspect', Ph.D. dissertation, Northwestern University, Evanston/Chicago, IL.
Parsons, T. (1990). *Events in the Semantics of English*. Cambridge, MA: MIT Press.
Partee, B. (1973). 'Some structural analogies between tense and pronouns in English', *Journal of Philosophy*, 18: 601–10.
Portner, P. (2003). 'The (Temporal) Semantics and (Modal) Pragmatics of the Perfect', *Linguistics and Philosophy* 26: 459–510.
Prior, A. N. (1957). *Time and Modality*. Oxford: Oxford University Press.
——(1967). *Past, Present, and Future*. Oxford: Oxford University Press.
Prior, A. N. (1968). *Papers on Time and Tense*, Oxford: Oxford University Press.
Schank, R. C. (1975). *Conceptual Information Processing*. Amsterdam: North-Holland.
Smith, C. (1991). *The Parameter of Aspect*. Dordrecht, Holland: Kluwer.
Suppes, P. (1999). *Introduction to Logic*. New York: Dover.
Swart, H. de (1998). 'Aspect shift and coercion', *Natural Language and Linguistic Theory* 16: 347–85.
——and Verkuyl, H. (1999). 'Tense and Aspect in Sentence and Discourse'. Ms.
Vlach, F. (1981). 'The Semantics of the Progressive', in P. Tedeschi and A. Zaenen (eds.), *Syntax and Semantics* 14: *Tense and Aspect*, New York: Academic Press, 271–92.
White, M. (1994). 'A Computational Approach to Aspectual Composition', Ph.D. dissertation, University of Pennsylvania.

1

Verbs and Times[1]

Z. VENDLER

1 The fact that verbs have tenses indicates that considerations involving the concept of time are relevant to their use. These considerations are not limited merely to the obvious discrimination between past, present, and future; there is another, a more subtle dependence on that concept: the use of a verb may also suggest the particular way in which that verb presupposes and involves the notion of time.

In a number of recent publications some attention has been paid to these finer aspects, perhaps for the first time systematically. Distinctions have been made among verbs suggesting processes, states, dispositions, occurrences, tasks, achievements, and so on. Obviously these differences cannot be explained in terms of time alone: other factors, like the presence or absence of an object, conditions, intended states of affairs, also enter the picture. Nevertheless one feels that the time element remains crucial; at least it is important enough to warrant separate treatment. Indeed, as I intend to show, if we focus our attention primarily upon the time schemata presupposed by various verbs,[2] we are able to throw light on some of the obscurities which still remain in these matters. These time schemata will appear as important constituents of the concepts that prompt us to use those terms the way we consistently do.

There are a few such schemata of very wide application. Once they have been discovered in some typical examples, they may be used as models of comparison in exploring and clarifying the behavior of any verb whatever.

In indicating these schemata, I do not claim that they represent all possible ways in which verbs can be used correctly with respect to time determination nor that a verb exhibiting a use fairly covered by one schema cannot have divergent uses, which in turn may be described in terms of the other schemata. As a matter of fact, precisely those verbs that call for two or more time schemata will provide the most interesting instances of conceptual divergence in this respect—an ambiguity which, if undetected, might lead to confusion. Thus my intention is not to give rules about how to use certain terms but to suggest a way of describing the use of those terms. I shall present some "*objects of comparison* which are meant to throw light on the facts of our language by way not only of similarities, but also of dissimilarities ... a measuring rod; not as a preconceived idea to which reality *must* correspond."[3]

2 Our first task therefore will be to locate and to describe the most common time schemata implied by the use of English verbs. To do this I need some clear-cut examples

---

Z. Vendler, 'Verbs and Times', ch. 4 of *Linguistics in Philosophy* (Ithaca, NY: Cornell University Press, 1967), 97–121. © 1967 Cornell University Press.

[1] With only minor changes this chapter reproduces an article of the same title which appeared in *The Philosophical Review*, LXVI (1957), 143–160.
[2] I am aware of my duty to explain what exactly I mean by *time schema* in this context. I shall do so in due course.   [3] L. Wittgenstein, *Philosophical Investigations*, I (Oxford: Blackwell, 1953), 130–1.

which, at least in their dominant use, show forth these schemata in pure form. At this stage, I shall try to avoid ambiguous terms and ignore stretched and borderline uses.

I start with the well-known difference between verbs that possess continuous tenses and verbs that do not. The question

What are you doing?

might be answered by

I am running (or writing, working, and so on)

but not by

I am knowing (or loving, recognizing, and so on).[4]

On the other hand, the appropriate question and answer

Do you know ...?
Yes, I do

have no counterparts like

Do you run?
Yes, I do.[5]

This difference suggests that running, writing, and the like are processes going on in time, that is, roughly, that they consist of successive phases following one another in time. Indeed, the man who is running lifts up his right leg one moment, drops it the next, then lifts his other leg, drops it, and so on. But although it can be true of a subject that he knows something at a given moment or for a certain period, knowing and its kin are not processes going on in time. It may be the case that I know geography now, but this does not mean that a process of knowing geography is going on at present consisting of phases succeeding one another in time.

First let us focus our attention on the group of verbs that admit continuous tenses. There is a marked cleavage within the group itself. If it is true that someone is running or pushing a cart now, then even if he stops in the next moment it will be still true that he did run or did push a cart. On the other hand, even if it is true that someone is drawing a circle or is running a mile now, if he stops in the next moment it may not be true that he did draw a circle or did run a mile.[6] In other words, if someone stops running a mile, he did not run a mile; if one stops drawing a circle, he did not draw a circle. But the man who stops running did run, and he who stops pushing the cart did push it. Running a mile and drawing a circle have to be finished, while it does not make sense to talk of finishing running or pushing a cart. Thus we see that while running or pushing a cart has no set terminal point, running a mile and drawing a circle do have a "climax," which has to be reached if the action is to be what it is claimed to be.

Accordingly, the question

For how long did he push the cart?

---

[4] The presence or absence of an object is irrelevant here. *I am pushing a cart* is a correct sentence, while *I am loving you* remains nonsense.

[5] Unless a very different meaning of *running* is involved, which I shall discuss later.

[6] For a clear formulation of this criterion see S. Bromberger's "An Approach to Explanation" in R. J. Butler (ed.), *Analytical Philosophy*, second series, (Oxford: Basil Blackwell, 1965), 72–105. Bromberger correctly points out an error I committed in giving this criterion in the original paper (pp. 74–5).

is a significant one, while

>How long did it take to push the cart?

sounds odd. On the other hand

>How long did it take to draw the circle?

is the appropriate question, and

>For how long did he draw the circle?

is somewhat queer. And, of course, the corresponding answers will be

>He was pushing it for half an hour

and

>It took him twenty seconds to draw the circle

or

>He did it in twenty seconds

and not vice versa. Pushing a cart may go on for a time, but it does not take any definite time; the activity of drawing may also go on for a time, but it takes a certain time to draw a circle.

A very interesting consequence follows. If it is true that someone has been running for half an hour, then it must be true that he has been running for every period within that half hour. But even if it is true that a runner has run a mile in four minutes, it cannot be true that he has run a mile in any period which is a real part of that time, although it remains true that he was running, or that he was engaged in running a mile, during any substretch of those four minutes. Similarly, in case I wrote a letter in an hour, I did not write it, say, in the first quarter of that hour. It appears, then, that running and its kind go on in time in a homogeneous way; any part of the process is of the same nature as the whole. Not so with running a mile or writing a letter; they also go on in time, but they proceed toward a terminus which is logically necessary to their being what they are. Somehow this climax casts its shadow backward, giving a new color to all that went before.

Thus we have arrived at the time schemata of two important species of verb. Let us call the first type, that of *running, pushing a cart*, and so forth, "activity terms," and the second type, that of *running a mile, drawing a circle*, and so forth, "accomplishment terms."[7] The description of these first two categories also illustrates what I mean by exhibiting the "time schemata" of verbs.

When one turns to the other genus, that is, to the verbs lacking continuous tenses, one discovers a specific difference there too. As we said above, verbs like *knowing* and *recognizing* do not indicate processes going on in time, yet they may be predicated of a subject for a given time with truth or falsity. Now some of these verbs can be predicated only for single moments of time (strictly speaking), while others can be predicated for shorter or longer periods of time. One reaches the hilltop, wins the race, spots or recognizes something, and so on at a definite moment. On the other hand, one can know

---

[7] In the absence of a "pure" terminology I am forced to be content with these names (and the other two to be given), which also connote aspects beyond time structure (e.g., that of success). If we do not forget that our point of view is limited to time schemata, however, we shall not be surprised when, for example, *getting exhausted* turns out to be an accomplishment term and *dying* an achievement term in our sense.

or believe something, love or dominate somebody, for a short or long period. The form of pertinent questions and answers proves the point neatly:

> At what time did you reach the top? At noon sharp.
> At what moment did you spot the plane? At 10:53 A.M.

but

> For how long did you love her? For three years.
> How long did you believe in the stork? Till I was seven.

and not the other way around.[8]

Before going any further let us call the first family (that of *reaching the top*) "achievement terms," and the second (that of *loving*) "state terms." Then we can say that achievements occur at a single moment, while states last for a period of time.

3 Our conclusion about achievements is reinforced by a curious feature pointed out by Gilbert Ryle (following Aristotle), namely that "I can say 'I have seen it' as soon as I can say 'I see it.'"[9] As a matter of fact the point can be made stronger still: in cases of pure achievement terms the present tense is almost exclusively used as historic present or as indicating immediate future:

> Now he finds the treasure (or wins the race, and so on)

is not used to report the actual finding or winning, while the seemingly paradoxical

> Now he has found it

or

> At this moment he has won the race

is.

> The fact that we often say things like
>
> It took him three hours to reach the summit
> He found it in five minutes

might tempt a novice to confuse achievements (which belong to the second genus) with accomplishments (which belong to the first). A little reflection is sufficient to expose the fallacy. When I say that it took me an hour to write a letter (which is an accomplishment), I imply that the writing of the letter went on during that hour. This is not the case with achievements. Even if one says that it took him three hours to reach the summit, one does not mean that the "reaching" of the summit went on during those hours.[10] Obviously it took three hours of climbing to reach the top. Put in another way: if I write a letter in an hour, then I can say

> I am writing a letter

at any time during that hour; but if it takes three hours to reach the top, I cannot say

> I am reaching the top

at any moment of that period.

---

[8] Even in *I knew it only for a moment* the use of *for* indicates that a period, though very short, is to be understood.

[9] Gilbert Ryle, *Dilemmas*, (Cambridge: Cambridge University Press, 1954), 102. He quotes Aristotle's *Met.* 1048b. As we shall see later, this particular example is a bit misleading.

[10] For those who like oddities: *It took the battalion twenty minutes to cross the border*; *They are crossing the border*. Such are the borderline cases I mean to ignore at this stage.

As to states, the lack of continuous tenses (e.g., *I am knowing, loving*, and so forth) is enough to distinguish them from activities and accomplishments, and the form of time determination (*How long...? For such and such a period*) should be sufficient to keep them from being confused with achievements.

Still, I think it might be useful to mention, by way of digression, a surprising feature about states which is not strictly connected with considerations of time.

When I say that I could run if my legs were not tied, I do not imply that I *would* run if my legs were not tied. On the other hand, there is a sense of *can* in which

He could know the answer if he had read Kant

does mean that in that case he *would* know the answer. Similarly, in an obvious sense, to say that I could like her if she were not selfish is to say that I would like her if she were not selfish. One feels something strange in

Even if I could like her I would not like her.

It appears, therefore, that in conditionals *could* is often interchangeable with *would* in connection with states. For the same reason, *can* might become redundant in indicative sentences of this kind. Hence the airy feeling about *I can know, I can love, I can like*, and so forth. This also explains why *I can believe it* is very often used instead of *I believe it*. And, to anticipate, the question *Do you see the rabbit?* can be answered equivalently by *Yes, I can see it* or *Yes, I see it*. Later on, in connection with a concrete example, I shall take up this matter again and try to be more specific. For the present, it is enough to mention that while to be able to run is never the same thing as to run or to be able to write a letter is by no means the same as to write it, it seems to be the case that, in some sense, to be able to know is to know, to be able to love is to love, and to be able to see is to see.

One might point out that some achievements also share this feature. Indeed, in some sense, to be able to recognize is to recognize and to be able to spot the plane is to spot the plane. On the other hand, to be able to start or stop running is by no means the same thing as to start or stop running, although to start or to stop running are clearly achievements according to their time schema. Thus here the consideration of the time element is not sufficient; we have to look for another criterion. If we consider that one can start or stop running deliberately or carefully and also that one can be accused of, or held responsible for, having started or stopped running but not of having spotted or recognized something, then we realize that the above-mentioned curious behavior with respect to *can* is proper to verbs denoting achievements that cannot be regarded as voluntary (or involuntary) actions.

Following this lead back to states, we find indeed that one cannot know, believe, or love deliberately or carefully, and none of us can be accused of, or held responsible for, having "done" so either.[11] We may conclude this digression by saying that states and some achievements cannot be qualified as actions at all.[12]

By way of illustration to this section, I add four examples which demonstrate our time schemata from another angle.

For activities: *A was running at time t* means that time instant *t* is on *a* time stretch throughout which *A* was running.

---

[11] They are not "done" or "performed" at all.
[12] In my remarks on *can*, and in taking *deliberately* and *carefully* as criteria for genuine actions, I have made use of my (not very trustworthy) recollection of J. L. Austin's lectures given at Harvard in 1955.

For accomplishments: *A was drawing a circle at t* means that t is on *the* time stretch in which A drew that circle.

For achievements: *A won a race between t_1 and t_2* means that *the* time instant at which A won that race is between t_1 and t_2.

For states: *A loved somebody from t_1 to t_2* means that at *any* instant between t_1 and t_2 A loved that person.

This shows that the concept of activities calls for periods of time that are not unique or definite. Accomplishments, on the other hand, imply the notion of unique and definite time periods. In an analogous way, while achievements involve unique and definite time instants, states involve time instants in an indefinite and nonunique sense.

This division has an air of completeness about it. Perhaps it is more than a mere presumption to think that all verbs can be analyzed in terms of these four schemata.

4 Having thus formed and polished our conceptual tools, in the following sections I shall try to show how they can be used in practice. Here, of course, it would be foolish to claim any completeness: all I can do is to make some remarks on a few verbs or groups of verbs and hope that the reader, if he deems it worth while, will be able to proceed to other verbs in which he is interested.

There is a very large number of verbs that fall completely, or at least in their dominant use, within one of these categories.[13] A little reflection shows that running, walking, swimming, pushing or pulling something, and the like are almost unambiguous cases of activity. Painting a picture, making a chair, building a house, writing or reading a novel, delivering a sermon, giving or attending a class, playing a game of chess, and so forth, as also growing up, recovering from illness, getting ready for something, and so on, are clearly accomplishments. Recognizing, realizing, spotting and identifying something, losing or finding an object, reaching the summit, winning the race, crossing the border, starting, stopping, and resuming something, being born, and even dying fall squarely into the class of achievements. Having, possessing, desiring, or wanting something, liking, disliking, loving, hating, ruling, or dominating somebody or something, and, of course, knowing or believing things are manifestly states.

In connection with the last group, an obvious idea emerges. From the point of view of time schemata, being married, being present or absent, healthy or ill, and so on also behave like states. But then we can take one more step and realize that this is true of all qualities. Indeed, something is hard, hot, or yellow for a time, yet to be yellow, for instance, does not mean that a process of yellowing is going on. Similarly, although hardening is a process (activity or accomplishment), being hard is a state. Now perhaps we understand why desiring, knowing, loving, and so on—the so-called immanent operations of traditional philosophy—can be and have been looked upon as qualities.

Habits (in a broader sense including occupations, dispositions, abilities, and so forth) are also states in our sense. Compare the two questions: *Are you smoking?* and *Do you smoke?* The first one asks about an activity, the second, a state. This difference explains why a chess player can say at all times that he plays chess and why a worker for the General Electric Company can say, while sunbathing on the beach, that he works for General Electric.

It is not only activities that are "habit-forming" in this sense. Writers are people who write books or articles, and writing a book is an accomplishment; dogcatchers are men who catch dogs, and catching a dog is an achievement.

---

[13] For the sake of stylistic simplicity I shall, in what follows, be somewhat casual with respect to the "use versus mention" of verbs.

Now the curious thing is that while cabdrivers—that is, people of whom one can always say that they drive a cab—sometimes are actually driving a cab, rulers—that is, people of whom one can always say that they rule a country—are never actually ruling a country, that is, they are never engaged in a specific activity of ruling a country comparable to the specific activity of driving a cab. A cabdriver might say that he was driving his cab all morning, but the king of Cambodia can hardly say that he was ruling Cambodia all morning. The obvious explanation is that while driving a cab is a fairly uniform thing, as are also smoking, painting, and writing, the actions which a ruler as such is supposed to perform are manifold and quite disparate in nature.[14] Is he "ruling" only while he is addressing the assembly and surveying troops, or also while he is eating lobster at a state dinner? We feel that some of his actions are more appropriate than others to his state as a ruler, but we also feel that none of them in particular can be called "ruling." Of course, a painter also performs diverse actions which are more or less related to his profession (e.g., watching the sunset or buying canvas); nevertheless there is one activity, actually painting, which is "the" activity of a painter.

Adopting Ryle's terminology,[15] I shall call the states of smokers, painters, dogcatchers, and the like *specific* states, and the states of rulers, servants, educators (and grocers, who not only are never actually "grocing" but also do not "groce": the verb *groce* does not happen to exist) *generic* states.

This much it has seemed necessary to say about states, that puzzling category in which the role of verb melts into that of predicate, and actions fade into qualities and relations.

5 As we see, the distinction between the activity sense and the state sense of *to smoke, to paint*, and the like is a general distinction, not peculiar to the concept of smoking or painting alone. Many activities (and some accomplishments and achievements) have a "derived" state sense. There is, however, a group of verbs with conceptual divergences of their own. With respect to many of these verbs, it is hardly possible to establish the category to which they "originally" belong. The group of verbs I have in mind comprises philosophically notorious specimens like *to think, to know, to understand*, on the one hand, and *to see, to hear*, and their kindred on the other.[16] In recent years a number of excellent publications have succeeded in pointing out that the alleged epistemological problems surrounding this family look far less formidable when we become aware of the mistakes of category that are embedded in their very formulation; one can hardly state the problem so long as one refuses to talk incorrect English.

I venture to claim that our categories, based upon time schemata, not only do justice to these recent discoveries but, beyond that, can be employed in exposing and eliminating certain mistakes and oversimplifications which are apt to discredit the whole method. Let us begin with *thinking*. It is clear that it is used in two basic senses. *Thinking* functions differently in

He is thinking about Jones

and in

He thinks that Jones is a rascal.

The first "thinking" is a process, the second a state. The first sentence can be used to describe what one is doing; the second cannot. This becomes obvious when we

---

[14] As pointed out by Gilbert Ryle in *The Concept of Mind* (Chicago: University of Chicago Press, 1949), 44, 118.   [15] *Ibid.*, p. 118.
[16] We shall see that, although knowing remains quite a typical state, at this point it deserves another look.

consider that while

He thinks that Jones is a rascal

might be said truthfully of someone who is sound asleep

He is thinking about Jones

cannot. It shows that thinking about something is a process that goes on in time, an activity one can carry on deliberately or carefully, but this is by no means true of thinking that something is the case. If it is true that he was thinking about Jones for half an hour, then it must be true that he was thinking about Jones during all parts of that period. But even if it is true that he thought that Jones was a rascal for a year, that does not necessarily mean that he was thinking about Jones, the rascal, for any minute of that time.

The last fact shows that *thinking that* is not related to *thinking about* the way *smoking* in its habit sense is related to *smoking* in its activity sense. *Thinking that* is rather like *ruling*, that is, it is based upon actions of various kinds. Consider the behavior of the farmer who thinks that it is going to rain. We may say, then, that *thinking that* is a generic state. On the other hand, the state of a "thinker" is a specific state: he is a man who is very often engaged in thinking about ponderous matters.[17]

It is easy to see that *believing that* is also a generic state. As a matter of fact, *he believes that* can be exchanged for *he thinks that* in most cases. *Believing in*, though different in meaning, belongs to the same category; one can believe in the right cause even while asleep.

Knowing is clearly a state in its dominant uses (*knowing that, knowing how, knowing something* [*somebody*]). Furthermore, since *I am knowing* does not exist in English, knowing seems to be a generic state. For example, the fact that I know that Harvard is in Cambridge is behind a host of my actions that range from addressing letters to boarding buses. Yet none of these actions in particular can be qualified as *knowing*. Doubts might arise, however, from uses like *And then suddenly I knew!* and *Now I know it!* which sound like achievements. Indeed, this insight sense of knowing fits more or less into that category. Yet it would be a mistake to think that this kind of *knowing* is related to the state sense in the way that catching dogs is related to the specific state of dogcatchers. A little reflection shows that they are related rather as getting married (achievement) is to being married (generic state). This is best shown in an example. Suppose someone is trying to solve a problem in mathematics. Suddenly he cries out "Now I know it!" After ten minutes he explains the solution to me. Obviously he still knows it, which means that no flashes of understanding are necessary for him to explain it. Indeed, so long as he knows it (in a state sense), it is logically impossible that he will "know" it (in an achievement sense). *Now I know it!* indicates that he did not know it before.

One is tempted here to say that "knowing" means to start knowing. This is a dangerous temptation; it makes us think that just as to start running begins the activity of running, to start knowing begins the activity of knowing. Of course, the fact that *to start* (*or to stop*) *knowing* does not make sense demonstrates that "knowing" is not the beginning of an activity but the beginning of a state. In general, it is important to distinguish achievements that start activities from achievements that initiate a state.

The same distinctions hold for *understanding*. Its achievement sense, however, is perhaps more common than that of *knowing*; we have just now mentioned "flashes" of

---

[17] I am in doubt about *thinking of something*. Its use is not steady enough. It seems to me, though, that very often it has an achievement sense: *Every time I see that picture I think of you.*

understanding. But these flashes of understanding are also achievements initiating the generic state of understanding.

6 We must keep in mind all these subtleties as we proceed to the arduous task of analyzing the concept of *seeing* from the point of view of temporal structure. In *The Concept of Mind*[18] and also in *Dilemmas*[19] Ryle quite consistently maintains that seeing is not a process nor a state but a kind of achievement or success, in many respects similar to winning a race or finding something. More recently F. N. Sibley has pointed out that in a number of its significant uses, *seeing* functions quite differently from achievement terms, precisely from the point of view of temporal structure.[20] He concludes that since seeing is not, at least not always, an achievement, it may turn out to be an activity after all.

There is no question that seeing can be an achievement in our sense. Uses like *At that moment I saw him*, together with the above-mentioned possibility of saying *I have seen it* as soon as one is able to say *I see it*, show that much. I shall refer to this "spotting" sense of seeing (which is somewhat analogous to the insight sense of *knowing*, or rather *understanding*) as "seeing."

Now, I think, "seeing" is not the only sense of seeing;

How long did you see the killer?
Oh, I am quite tall, I saw him all the time he was in the courtroom. I was watching him.

suggests another possibility.

Do you *still* see the plane?

points in the same direction. Furthermore,

I spotted him crossing the street
I spotted him running

can only be understood in the sense of

I spotted him while he (or I) was crossing the street
I spotted him while he (or I) was running.

On the other hand,

I saw him crossing the street
I saw him running

may also be taken to mean

I saw him cross the street
I saw him run.

Spot refuses this move:
* I spotted him cross the street
* I spotted him run.

Our time schemata explain this difference. Spotting (an achievement) connotes a unique and indivisible time instant. Now running or crossing the street are processes going on in time (the latter also takes time) and as such cannot be broken down into indivisible time instants: their very notion indicates a time stretch. Thus there is a logical difficulty in spotting somebody run or cross the street. One can spot somebody while he is running,

---

[18] Chap. v.   [19] Chap. vii.
[20] "Seeking, Scrutinizing and Seeing," *Mind*, LXIV (1955), 455–78. On p. 472 he is induced to say things like "one must *throughout that length of time* be seeing it."

or on the street, but *while* and *on* here indicate states, and states can be broken down into time instants. Then it is clear that seeing in

I saw him while he was running (or crossing the street)

may mean merely "seeing," but seeing in

I saw him run (or cross the street)

must have a sense that admits a period of time: a process or a state.

But seeing cannot be a process. *What are you doing?* can never, in good English, be answered by *I am seeing....* Thus notwithstanding the fact that one might see something for a long period, it does not mean that he "is seeing" that thing for any period, yet it remains true that he sees it at all moments during that period. In addition, *deliberately* or *carefully* fail to describe or misdescribe seeing, as no one can be accused of or held responsible for having seen something, though one can be accused of or held responsible for having looked at or watched something. Thus seeing is not an action which is "done" or "performed" at all. Finally the curious equivalence of *I see it* and *I can see it* or even *I saw him all the time* and *I could see him all the time* also confirms our claim that seeing is not a process but a state or achievement. Being able to see can hardly be conceived of as a process.

7 At this point, however, a serious difficulty arises. After an eye operation the doctor might say that now the patient can see without suggesting that he sees through the bandage, much as he might say of a patient after an orthopedic operation that he can walk without implying that he is actually walking. Therefore—the objection might go—as the bodily state of being able to walk is not the same thing as walking, the bodily state of being able to see is not the same thing as seeing. Yet they are related the same way: the state of being able to walk is necessary for the activity of walking, and the state of being able to see is necessary for the activity of seeing. Furthermore, as we also suggested, we can say of a man who is sound asleep that he knows geography, or that he thinks that Jones is a rascal, or that he loves Lucy, but no one can say of somebody who is sound asleep that he sees something in any ordinary sense of *seeing*. One might say, however, that he can see, meaning that he is not blind. Thus to be able to see is a state like knowing but seeing is not.

This reasoning confuses two senses of *can*. There are people who can drink a gallon of wine in one draught. Suppose one of them has performed that remarkable feat a minute ago. Then it is quite unlikely that he can do it again now. Should we say then, at this moment, that he can, or rather that he cannot, drink a gallon of wine in one draught? He can and he cannot. Let us refer to the first *can* (in *he can*) as can_2, and to the second (in *he cannot*) as can_1. Of course, he can_2 means that he $could_1$ if his stomach were empty. When his stomach is empty he both can_2 and can_1. Thus can_2 involves can_1 conditionally: he can_1 if certain conditions are fulfilled. Can_1 does not involve any further *can*-s: he can actually. Yet even can_1 *drink a gallon of wine* does not mean that he actually does drink or is drinking that amazing draught.

Now the doctor's *can* in *Now he can see*, spoken while the patient's eyes are still bandaged, is a can_2: if the bandage were removed and if his eyes were open (everything else, like light in the room, and so forth, remaining the same), then he $could_1$ see some things in the room; that is, he *would* see some things in the room. Thus the above-mentioned equivalence holds between *see* and can_1 *see*, that is, the lowest-level *can* that does not involve any further *can*-s conditionally. And this equivalence does not hold for activities: the other patient can_2 walk, though his legs are still tied to the bed; if he were released he could₁ walk, yet it may be he would not be walking.[21]

But my adversary might continue: "You obviously overlook a glaring difference. Walking is a voluntary action, while seeing is a spontaneous one. If you are not blind, if there is some light, and if you open your eyes, then you cannot help seeing something: the spontaneous activity of seeing starts. Digestion, you agree, is a process, yet the equivalence you speak about also holds there, because it also is a spontaneous activity. When I say that I can digest pork, I mean that if I had eaten pork, I could digest pork, that is, I would be digesting pork. If I have not eaten pork, I cannot digest pork. So there is a sense in which *can digest pork* and *is digesting pork* mean the same thing."

This objection is a shrewd one. It is quite true that no one can be running if he is not running, as nothing can be a cat if it is not a cat. But this *can* is a logical modality like *must* in

All cats must be cats.

In this sense, of course, *can be digesting* is the same as *digesting*. But our *can*, if you like, is a physical modality. It is silly to point at a pork chop and say

Now I cannot digest it, but when I have eaten it, I shall be able to digest it for a while, till I have digested it, and then I shall not be able to digest it any more.

But it is by no means foolish to say

Now I cannot see the moon, but when the cloud goes away, I shall be able to see it.

8 We can safely conclude then that seeing has a state sense too. Now, since there is no such process as seeing, yet there is an achievement of "seeing" (the "spotting" sense), the question arises whether "seeing" is related to seeing as catching dogs is related to the state of dogcatchers, or rather as "knowing" (the achievement) is related to knowing (the state). It is quite clear that the latter is the case:

At that moment I saw him (spotted him)

means that I did not see him before that moment. Thus "seeing" is an achievement initiating the generic state of seeing.

As will be recalled, there are scores of activities, accomplishments, and achievements involved in the notion of ruling or knowing that something is the case. Thus the problem remains: what activities, accomplishments, and achievements are connected in this way with the notion of seeing? Did I not know that Harvard is in Cambridge, I could not perform a great number of actions the way I do perform them. In an analogous way, if I do not see my hand, I cannot watch, scan, observe, or scrutinize it; I cannot gaze upon it, keep it in sight, focus my eyes on it, or follow it with my eyes; I cannot see that it is dirty, I cannot notice, or easily find out, tell, or describe what color it has or what it looks like at present; then also I cannot (in a sense) look at it and see it as an instrument or as an animal with five tentacles, and so on.

Of course, none of these actions have to be performed all at the same time, or one after the other, while we see an object. When I am writing, I see the pencil all the time, otherwise I could not write the way I do write. Nevertheless I do not watch, observe,

---

[21] Now it becomes clear that, for instance, *He could₁ know the answer if he had read Kant* means that in that case he would know the answer, but *He could₂ know*...does not mean that in that case he would know the answer.

or scrutinize it; I might not look at it at all; I might even not notice its color. In the same way, when I am walking up and down in my room, absorbed in thoughts, I do not pay any attention to the furniture around me, yet I see it most of the time; otherwise I would bounce against tables and chairs every so often. Think of the way we see our noses or the frame of our spectacles.

Notice that none of the actions I have enumerated is mysterious in the way that seeing is claimed to be mysterious. Any good dictionary can tell us what we mean by *watching, scrutinizing*, and so on, without even mentioning *seeing*.[22] On the other hand the meaning of *seeing* cannot be given, short of a mystery, without realizing its "state" as a state term, that is, without giving the kind of explanation I have tried to give. In much the same way, the meaning of *knowing* remains something ghostly till the kind of explanation is given that, for instance, we find in *The Concept of Mind*; or, for that matter, housekeeping would remain an abstruse activity did we not all know what sort of (by no means abstruse) actions housekeepers are supposed to perform.

9 Before we take leave of *seeing*, I shall mention two borderline senses. If one tells us that he saw *Carmen* last night, he means that he saw all four acts of *Carmen*. Besides, he might say that it took three hours to see *Carmen*. Perhaps one might even answer the question *What are you doing?* by *I am seeing* Carmen *on TV*. Thus there is a queer accomplishment sense of *seeing*. There is another strained usage. A "seer" sees things, and now and then he actually is seeing ghosts or pink rats. Such strained or stretched employment should not worry us. It would be a very serious mistake if one tried to explain the stock uses of *seeing* on the basis of such employment.

Thus there is no one big mystery with regard to seeing, although little puzzles remain as to *observing, watching*, and so forth. One could point out, for example, that while they are activities, they sometimes have—and this is true more of *observing* than of *watching*—an accomplishment sense: it takes some time to observe the passage of Venus across the sun or to watch an ant carrying home a dead fly. There are obvious parallels between the concepts of seeing and hearing and those of watching and listening, and so on. Thus we could continue this kind of investigation, but without any specific problem it would become tedious and idle.

As a conclusion, I think, it is not too much to say that our categories, besides confirming established differences between processes and nonprocesses, may help us in clarifying the often overlooked and embarrassing differences within the class of nonprocesses. We have no reason to fear that seeing, for example, since it is not always an achievement, might turn out to be an activity after all, reviving thereby all the ghosts of epistemology. "What happens when we perceive, and what is it that makes it happen? That is the problem of perception."[23] A sailor on deck looking ahead remarks, "It is pitch dark, I don't see anything." After a while, "Now I see a star." We ask him, "What has happened?" "The cloud's gone." "But what else happened?" "Nothing else." Of course many things happened in the world and in the sailor. But his seeing is not one of them.[24]

---

[22] For example, *The Concise Oxford Dictionary*, 4th ed., defines *watching* (relevant sense): keep eyes fixed on, keep under observation, follow observantly. And *scrutinizing*: look closely at, examine in detail.
[23] Edwin Garrigues Boring, Herbert Sidney Langfeld, and Harry Porter Weld, *Foundations of Psychology* (New York/London: John Wiley & Sons), 216.
[24] I wish to express my gratitude to Professor Israel Scheffler for his helpful comments on the first draft of this chapter.

2

The Syntax of Event Structure*

JAMES PUSTEJOVSKY

I INTRODUCTION

Recent work in linguistic theory has stressed the important role that structured lexical representations can play in natural language, for example, the emergence of argument structure as a distinct level of representation (Grimshaw, 1990; Williams, 1981) and the importance of semantic representations such as f-structure (Bresnan, 1982) and lexical conceptual structure (LCS) (Jackendoff, 1983; Rappaport & Levin, 1988). Similarly, we will explore what advantages there are in positing a separate level indicating the event structures associated with predicates and their arguments.

The conventional view of argument structure is that a verb is given a set of arguments and associated diacritics indicating how they are realized. Some authors, however, have argued that argument structure is a structured representation over which prominence relations are defined (Grimshaw, 1990; Williams, 1981). This structure has profound effects on the behavior of the predicates in the language. Similarly, the conventional view of events (e.g., whether a sentence denotes an activity, a state, etc.) within much of linguistic theory has been that of a single, existentially quantified event variable for sentences in the language (Higginbotham, 1985; Parsons, 1985).[1] Extending this view, we will argue that grammatical phenomena do in fact make reference to the internal structure of events, and that a subeventual analysis for predicates is able to systematically capture these effects. The basic assumptions of the theory are as follows:

(I) A subeventual structure for predicates provides a template for verbal decomposition and lexical semantics. Following Vendler (1967), Dowty (1979), and others, we distinguish three basic event types: states, processes, and transitions, where a predicate in the language by default denotes one particular event type. Unlike previous analyses, however, we assume a more complex subeventual structure of event types, where event types make reference to other embedded types.

(II) By examining the substructure of events, one can describe much of the behavior of adverbial modification in terms of scope assignment within an event structure.

James Pustejovsky, 'The Syntax of Event Structure', *Cognition* 41 (1991): 47–81 © 1991 Elsevier.

*This paper developed out of earlier work on the event semantics of verbs (cf. Pustejovsky, 1989b). I would like to thank Jane Grimshaw, Beth Levin, Jim Higginbotham, Robert Ingria, Noam Chomsky, and Sabine Bergler, for comments on earlier drafts of this paper. Requests for reprints should be sent to James Pustejovsky, Computer Science Department, Ford Hall, Brandeis University, Waltham, MA 02254-9110, U.S.A.

[1] This is assuming that events are represented at all. There are many who still argue that events are not a necessary addition to the ontology of types (see Cresswell, 1985).

(III) The semantic arguments within an event structure expression can be mapped onto argument structure in systematic and predictable ways. The event structure proposed here should be seen as a further refinement of the semantic responsibilities within an LCS (Jackendoff, 1983; Rappaport & Levin, 1988).

We should point out one caveat about the analysis presented below. This paper is not the proper forum for specifying the formal semantics of the event structure proposed here. Rather, what we attempt to show, in broad outline, is the relevance of event structure to lexical semantics and linguistic theory in general. Where appropriate, we will briefly point out the technical details of the analysis, as well as the limitations and shortcomings of the proposal. Details of the formal interpretation of the event semantics presented here can be found in Pustejovsky (1991) and other work in progress.

2 EVENT TYPES

Temporal aspect can be viewed as the behavior of sets of periods involving the concepts of *initial*, *internal*, and *final* temporal subperiods, as they relate to the semantic roles associated with the arguments of predicates.[2] To make this clear, let us examine the meanings of the sentences below:

(1) a. Mary walked.
    b. Mary walked to the store.
    c. Mary walked for 30 minutes.

It is normally assumed that there are at least three aspectual types: *state, process*, and *events*, sometimes distinguishing between *accomplishment* and *achievement* events. The verb *walk* as used in (1a) denotes an activity of indefinite length. That is, the sentence itself does not convey information regarding the temporal extent of the activity. Such a sentence is said to denote a *process* (Dowty, 1979; Kenny, 1963; Mourelatos, 1978; Ryle, 1949; Vendler, 1967; Verkuyl, 1989). Sentence (1b) conveys at least as much information as (1a), with the additional constraint, however, that Mary terminated her activity of walking at the store. Although not making explicit reference to the temporal duration of the activity, (1b) does assert that the process has a logical culmination or duration, such that the activity is over when Mary is at the store. This type of sentence is said to denote an event, or *accomplishment*.

Sentence (1c) also conveys information about a specific activity of walking and its termination. In this sentence, however, there is no explicit mention of a logical culmination to the activity, but rather a durative adverbial is used to impose a temporal specification on the activity's boundedness. Such a sentence denotes a *bounded process*. These examples illustrate the same verb being used for three different aspectual types: process, accomplishment, and bounded process. When the verb *walk* appears alone structurally, it assumes a process interpretation—it is lexically "process-like". The presence of prepositional and adverbial phrases, however, causes the aspectual class of the sentence to change.

Just as the verb *walk* seems to be lexically process-like, there are lexical accomplishments as well. For example, the verbs *build* and *destroy*, in their typical transitive use in (2),

---

[2] Carlson (1981) presents the issues in these terms, and we adopt this statement of the problem.

denote accomplishment events, because there is a logical culmination to the activity performed by Mary:

(2) a. Mary built a house.
    b. Mary destroyed the table.

In (2a) the existence of the house is the culmination of Mary's act, while in (2b) the non-existence of something denotable as a table is the direct culmination of her act. One useful test for whether a sentence denotes an accomplishment is the ability to be modified by temporal adverbials such as *in an hour*, that is, the so-called frame adverbials. Notice in (3) that both "derived" and lexical accomplishments license such modification:

(3) a. Mary walked to the store in an hour.
    b. Mary built a house in a year.

Even though *build* seems lexically to be an accomplishment, observe how it can be used in a context where it appears to denote a process:

(4) Mary built houses for four years.

Sentence (4) means that Mary engaged in the activity of house building for a bounded period of time. The durative adverbial indicates that the sentence has been reinterpreted as a process due to the bare plural in object position (see Bach, 1986; Krifka, 1987).

Another aspectual type mentioned earlier is that of achievement. An achievement is an event that results in a change of some sort, just as an accomplishment does, but where the change is thought of as occurring instantaneously. For example, in sentences (5a), (5b), and (5c) the change is not a gradual one, but something that has a "point-like" quality to it. In fact, modification by *point adverbials* such as *at noon* is a diagnostic that a sentence denotes an achievement (Dowty, 1979):

(5) a. John died at 3 p.m.
    b. John found his wallet at 3 p.m.
    c. Mary arrived at noon.

What are apparently lexical properties of the verb can be affected by factors that could not possibly be lexical. For instance, consider the sentences in (6), where one sees a shift in the meaning of *drink* from an accomplishment as in (6a) to a process as in (6b):

(6) a. Mary drank a beer.
    b. Mary drank beer.

The presence of a bare plural object shifts the interpretation of a logically culminating event to an unbounded process (see Pelletier and Schubert (1989) and Krifka (1987) for details).

Finally, let us consider the behavior of *states*, such as those sentences in (7):

(7) a. Mary is sick.
    b. Mary believes that John loves her.

There is no change occurring in either sentence and no reference to initial or final periods. In fact, it is the homogeneity of states that distinguishes them from the other aspectual types. States are identified by several diagnostics. First, they allow modification by durative adverbials (8a), and secondly, they do not appear as imperatives (8b) (Dowty, 1979):

(8) a. Mary was sick for two months.
  b. *Be sick!

Because of the sometimes elusive nature of aspectual classification, it is useful to consider a few more diagnostics. One well-known test for distinguishing activities from accomplishments, known as the "imperfective paradox" (Bach, 1986; Dowty, 1979), involves the possible entailments from the progressive aspect. To illustrate the nature of this paradox, consider the sentences in (9):

(9) a. John is running. *Entails* John has run.
  b. John is building a house. *Does not entail* John has built a house.

What this difference in entailment indicates is whether an action is homogeneous in nature or has a culmination of some sort. Sentence (9a) is an activity and entails the statement *John has run*. That is, John has already engaged in some running. Sentence (9b), on the other hand, does not allow the entailment *John has built a house* because building is not a homogeneous process, but rather culminates in a changed state, i.e. it is an accomplishment. Thus, if *x is V-ing* entails *x has V-ed*, then either the verb or the predicate is a process. A theory of aspect should be able to account for this behavior, and not just use it to classify propositions into aspectual types.

Finally, there is an important distinction between accomplishments and non-accomplishments based on their interaction with scalar adverbials such as *almost*. Consider the sentences in (10) and the possible interpretations associated with each:

(10) a. John almost swam.
  b. John almost painted a picture.
  c. John almost arrived.
  d. John almost left.

In sentence (10a), what is being expressed is that John almost performed an activity of swimming, but did not even begin it. Sentence (10b), on the other hand, allows for two interpretations. One is similar to (10a), where John almost engaged himself in painting, but then did not. The other interpretation is that John was painting but did not quite complete the picture. The interpretation of (10c), like (10a) is unambiguous, while (10d) permits two readings along the same lines as (10b). Why should there be such a difference? Dowty (1979) claims that an ambiguity arises with *almost* just in case the predicate is an accomplishment. If this ambiguity does not arise, the predicate is not an accomplishment.

Summarizing, we have considered the following categorization of aspectual types for verbs and verb phrases:

(11) a. *Processes:* walk, run
  b. *Accomplishments:* build, destroy
  c. *Achievements:* die, find, arrive
  d. *States:* sick, know, love, resemble

If membership in one of these aspectual classes is viewed as a projection of the lexical properties of the verb, then how is it that the aspectual properties of a sentence may change as the result of other factors, such as adverbials (both durative and frame), the structure of the noun phrase (NP) in an argument position (e.g. definite vs. bare plural), or the presence of a prepositional phrase? In the sections that follow, we will explain these behaviors, which have come to be known as "type-shifting" phenomena (Bach, 1986), in terms of a configurational theory of event structure. We show how the tests normally used as diagnostics for membership in one class or another fall out as the principled consequence of different event structures. Thus, we are able to abandon the feature-based approach to aspect which is generally assumed (e.g., Verkuyl, 1972) in favor of a highly restricted, topological theory of how events are structured.

3 TOWARDS A MODEL OF LEXICAL KNOWLEDGE

In this section, we will outline generally what the basic requirements for a theory of lexical semantics should be. We present a conservative approach to decomposition, where lexical items are minimally decomposed into structured forms (or templates) rather than sets of features. We will provide a generative framework for the *composition* of lexical meanings, thereby defining the well-formedness conditions for semantic expressions in a language.

One can distinguish between two distinct approaches to the study of word meaning: *primitive-based* theories and *relation-based* theories. Those advocating primitives assume that word meaning can be exhaustively defined in terms of a fixed set of primitive elements (e.g., Jackendoff, 1972; Katz, 1972; Lakoff, 1971; Schank, 1975; Wilks, 1975). Inferences are made through the primitives into which a word is decomposed. In contrast to this view, a relation-based theory of word meaning claims that there is no need for the decomposition of word meaning into primitives if words are associated through a network of explicitly defined links (e.g., Brachman, 1979; Carnap, 1956; Collins and Quillian, 1969; Fodor, 1975; Quillian, 1968). Sometimes referred to as *meaning postulates*, these links establish any inference between words as an explicit part of a network of word concepts.[3] What we would like to do is to propose a new way of viewing primitives, looking more at the generative or *compositional* aspects of lexical semantics, rather than the decomposition of words into a specified number of primitives.

Most approaches to lexical semantics making use of primitives can be characterized as using some form of *feature-based* semantics, since the meaning of a word is essentially decomposable into a set of features (e.g., Katz, 1972; Katz and Fodor, 1963; Schank, 1975; Wilks, 1975). Even those theories that rely on some internal structure for word meaning (e.g., Dowty, 1979; Fillmore, 1988) do not provide a complete characterization for all of the well-formed expressions in the language. Jackendoff (1983) comes closest, but falls short of a comprehensive semantics for *all* categories in language. No existing framework, in my view, provides a *method for the decomposition of all lexical categories*.

What, exactly, would a method for lexical decomposition give us? Instead of a taxonomy of the concepts in a language, categorized by sets of features, such a method would tell us the minimal semantic behavior of a lexical item. Furthermore, it should tell us the compositional properties of a word, just as a grammar informs us of the specific syntactic behavior of a certain category. What one is led to, therefore, is a *generative* theory of word meaning, but one very different from the generative semantics of the 1970s (Pustejovsky, 1991). In order to explain why we are suggesting that lexical decomposition proceed in a *generative* fashion rather than the traditional

---

[3] For further discussion on the advantages and disadvantages to both approaches, see Jackendoff (1983).

exhaustive approach, let me take as a classic example the word *closed* as used in (12) (see Lakoff, 1970):

(12) a. The door is **closed**.
 b. The door **closed**.
 c. John **closed** the door.

Lakoff (1970), Jackendoff (1972), and others have suggested that the sense in (12c) must incorporate something like *cause-to-become-not-open* for its meaning. Similarly, a verb such as *give* specifies a transfer from one person to another, e.g. *cause-to-have*. Most decomposition theories of word meaning assume a set of primitives and then operate within this set to capture the meanings of all the words in the language. These approaches can be called *exhaustive* since they assume that with a fixed number of primitives complete definitions of lexical meaning can be given. In the sentences in (12), for example, *closed* is defined in terms of the negation of a primitive, *open*. Any method assuming a fixed number of primitives, however, runs into some well-known problems with being able to capture the full expressiveness of natural language.[4]

These problems are not, however, endemic to all decomposition approaches. We would like to suggest that lexical (and conceptual) decomposition is possible if it is performed *generatively*. Rather than assuming a fixed set of *primitives*, let us assume a fixed number of *generative devices* that can be seen as constructing semantic expressions. Just as a formal language is described in terms of the productions in the grammar rather than its accompanying vocabulary, a semantic language should be defined by the rules generating the structures for expressions rather than the vocabulary of primitives itself.[5]

How might this be done? Consider the sentences in (12) again. A minimal decomposition of the word *closed* is that it introduces an *opposition* of terms: *closed* and *not-closed*. For the verbal forms in (12b) and (12c), both terms in this opposition are predicated of different subevents denoted by the sentences. In (12a), this opposition is left implicit, since the sentence refers to a single state. Any minimal analysis of the semantics of a lexical item can be termed a *generative* operation, since it operates on the predicate(s) already literally provided by the word. This type of analysis draws on Aristotle's *species of opposition* (see Categories, 11b17; Lloyd, 1968), and it will form the basis of one level of representation for a lexical item. Rather than decomposing such a word into primitive terms, evaluate it relative to an opposition.[6]

The essential opposition denoted by a predicate forms part of what we will call the *qualia structure* of that lexical item (Pustejovsky, 1989a, 1991). Briefly, the qualia structure of a word specifies four aspects of its meaning:

- the relation between it and its constituent parts;
- that which distinguishes it within a larger domain;

---

[4] For example, Weinreich (1972) faults Katz and Fodor (1963) for the inability to distinguish between word senses of polysemous elements without requiring an unlimited number of differentiating features.

[5] In my opinion, this approach is also better suited to the way people write systems in computational linguistics. Different people have distinct primitives for their own domains, and rather than committing a designer to a particular vocabulary of primitives, a lexical semantics should provide a method for the decomposition and composition of the meanings of possible lexical items.

[6] Aristotle identifies four species of term opposition:

 (a) Correlation: e.g., "double" vs. "half".
 (b) Contrariety: e.g., "good" vs. "bad".
 (c) Privation: e.g., "blind" vs. "sighted".
 (d) Contradiction: e.g., "sit" vs. "not sit".

See Horn (1989) for discussion of the logic of negation. See Modrak (1987) and Graham (1987) for discussion of Aristotle's theory of explanation and its relation to perception.

- its purpose and function;
- whatever brings it about.

We call these aspects of a word's meaning its *constitutive role*, its *formal role*, its *telic role*, and its *agentive role*, respectively.[7] For example, the telic role of the noun *book* is the predicate *read*, while the agentive role might be *write*.

The minimal semantic distinctions of the qualia structure are given expressive force when combined with a theory of aspectual (or event) types. For example, the predicate in (12a) denotes the *state* of the door being closed. No opposition is expressed by this predicate. In (12b) and (12c), however, the opposition is explicitly part of the meaning of the predicate. Both these predicates denote what we call *transitions*. The intransitive use of *close* in (12b) makes no mention of the causer, yet the transition from *not-closed* to *closed* is still entailed. In (12c), the event that brings about the *closed* state of the door is made more explicit by specifying the actor involved. These differences constitute the *event structure* of a lexical item. Both the opposition of predicates and the specification of causation are part of a verb's semantics, and are structurally associated with slots in the event template for the word. In this case, for example, the *formal* role for the verb *close* is specified as a transition, denoting an opposition. The *constitutive* role specifies the exact content of the event, in terms of what the predicates engaged in opposition actually are (see below). As will be seen in the next section, there are different inferences associated with each event type, as well as different syntactic behaviors (Grimshaw, 1990; Pustejovsky, 1989b).

4 A LEVEL OF EVENT STRUCTURE

As mentioned above, the theory of decomposition being outlined here is based on the central idea that word meaning is highly structured, and not simply a set of semantic features. Let us assume this is the case. We will argue that one level of semantic description involves an event-based interpretation of a word or phrase, that is, the *event structure* mentioned above. Event structure is just one level of the semantic specification for a lexical item, along with subcategorization, argument structure, and qualia structure. Because an event structure is recursively defined in the syntax, "event-type" is also a property of phrases and sentences.[8] There are three primary components to event structure:

- the primitive *event type* of the lexical item;
- the rules of *event composition*;
- the *mapping rules* to lexical structure.

Any verb in natural language can be characterized as belonging to one of three basic event types: *states*, *processes*, or *transitions* (see Bach, 1986; Dowty, 1979; Vendler, 1967).[9] Except where otherwise indicated, the event structure will be interpreted as representing both temporal precedence and exhaustive event inclusion. That is, for an event e, represented as $[e_1\ e_2]$, the intended interpretation is that e is an event containing

---

[7] To a large extent, we follow Moravcsik (1975), who distinguishes the different "aitia" associated with a proposition. For details, see Pustejovsky (1991).
[8] See Tenny (1987) for a proposal on how aspectual distinctions are mapped to the syntax.
[9] Above we distinguished between four aspectual classes. These classes, we argue, collapse to three distinct structural configurations, where transitions subsume both accomplishments and achievements.

two subevents, e_1 and e_2, where the first temporally precedes the second, and there are no other events locally contained in event e.[10] We will distinguish these event types as follows (where E is a variable for any event type):[11]

(13) a. State (S): a single event, which is evaluated relative to no other event
Examples: *be sick, love, know*
Structural representation:

$$\begin{array}{c} S \\ | \\ e \end{array}$$

b. Process (P): a sequence of events identifying the same semantic expression
Examples: *run, push, drag*
Structural representation:

$$\overset{P}{\overbrace{e_1 \ldots e_n}}$$

Following Dowty (1979) and others, we will assume that when P is a process verb, then if the semantic expression P' identified with P is true at an interval I, then P' is true for all subintervals of I larger than a moment:

c. Transition (T): an event identifying a semantic expression, which is evaluated relative to its opposition (Jackendoff, 1972; Lakoff, 1970; von Wright, 1963)[12]
Examples: *give, open, build, destroy*
Structural representation (where E is a variable for any event type):

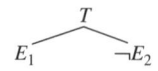

$$\overset{T}{\overbrace{E_1 \qquad \neg E_2}}$$

To illustrate the basic distinction in event types, consider the sentences in (12) from the previous section, repeated below:

(12) a. The door is **closed**.
 b. The door **closed**.
 c. John **closed** the door.

We assume a level of lexical representation similar to that of Dowty (1979), Jackendoff (1983), and Levin and Rappaport (1988), in that verb class distinctions are characterized in terms of an LCS-like structure, which we call LCS'. An LCS is a lexical semantic representation which takes the form of a predicate decomposition. Here we will not assume any fixed set of primitive terms, but rather assume a minimal decomposition of verbs and sentences in terms of the principles of event structure outlined here. This level, using predicates such as $act(x, y)$, $at(x, y)$, and $on(x, y)$, constitutes the LCS'. Thus, the trees represent LCS-like information partitioned according to event structure. Furthermore, we will assume that the LCS representations assumed by Levin and Rappaport (1988) can be constructed by interpreting the event structure together with the LCS', as we will illustrate below. Let us begin with the

---

[10] This does not mean that there is no subeventual structure to these events (see below).
[11] The tree structures are given to illustrate the configurational nature of event structures and their combinations. See Pustejovsky (to appear) for discussion of their formal interpretation; cf. Croft (1990) for an alternative suggestion on how lexical items may structure their internal events.
[12] As mentioned in the previous section, Aristotle's *Categories* (194b) makes the same point.

sentence in (12a) above. The adjectival form *closed* denotes a state where the event structure is that shown in (14b):

(14) a. The door is closed.
   b.
   ES: S
                |
                e
   LCS': |
            [closed(the-door)]
   LCS:
            [closed(the-door)]

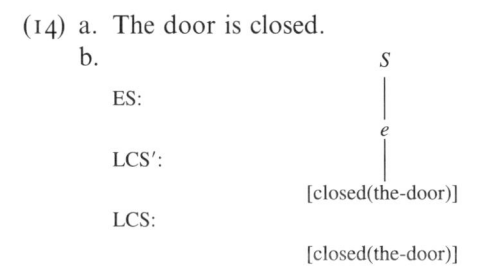

As mentioned in the previous section, a lexical transition, such as *close* in (12b) and (12c), expresses the opposition of a predicate, as illustrated in (15) and (16) below. Here we are assuming that one can interpret the expression of a term opposition as logically equivalent to Dowty's *become* operator (Dowty, 1979, p. 140). Similarly the operator *cause* can be seen as a derivative relation between events, structurally interpreted from an agentive predicate within the initial subevent of an event structure. Furthermore, the conjunction of predicates (&) indicates the simultaneity of the expressions:

(15) a. The door closed.
   b.
                    T
   ES: ╱ ╲
                P   S
   LCS': | |
                       [closed(the-door)]
                [¬closed(the-door)]
   LCS: become([closed(the-door)])

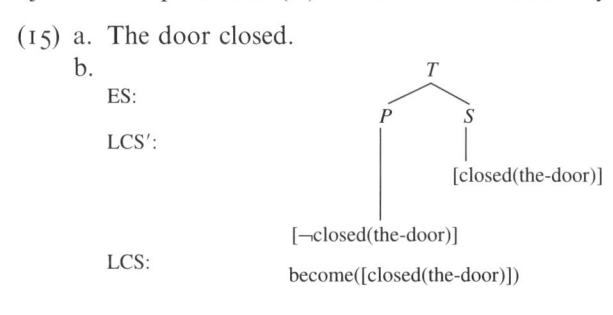

(16) a. John closed the door.
   b.
                    T
   ES: ╱ ╲
                P   S
   LCS': | |
                        [closed(door)]
               [act(j, the-door) & ¬closed(the-door)]
   LCS: cause([act(j, the-door)], become([closed(the-door)]))

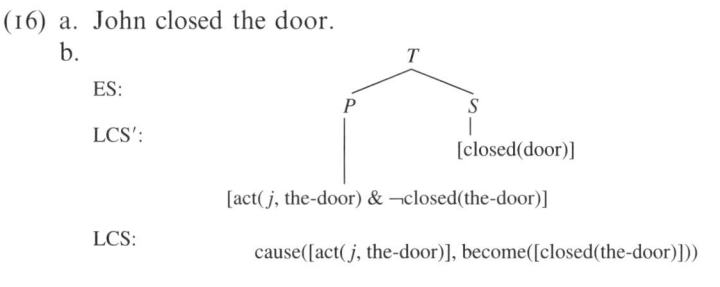

These two structures suggest that *close*, in both the *inchoative* (as in (15)) and *causative* (as in (16)) forms, is a transition from one state to its opposition.[13] Their LCS' representations differ only in the further specification of an action being performed for the causative cases; that is, the expression *and* indicates simultanity of the two expressions within this subevent. But notice that the LCS representations do differ significantly because of the explicit reference to a causal agent. Thus, while the verb *close* is semantically ambiguous at one level (LCS), the logical relatedness of the verb's senses is captured at another (ES and LCS').

---

[13] Hale and Keyser (1986) provide independent motivations for treating the inchoative and causative forms of a verb as essentially identical at some level of representation. In our analysis, they differ only in their LCS, but not in their event structures.

Sentence (17) illustrates how a process verb differs structurally from states and transitions:

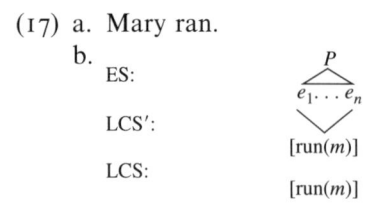

(17) a. Mary ran.
 b. ES:
 $$\overset{P}{\overset{\triangle}{e_1 \ldots e_n}}$$
 LCS':
 [run(m)]
 LCS:
 [run(m)]

The sentence in (18) illustrates how a causative process is represented and subsequently mapped onto an LCS representation:

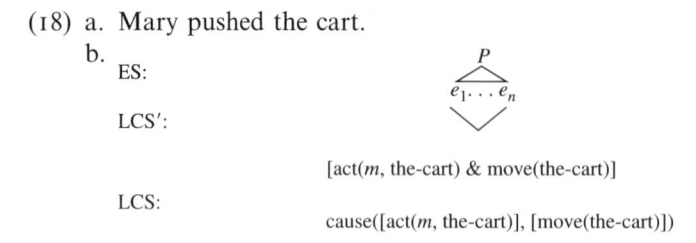

(18) a. Mary pushed the cart.
 b. ES:
 $$\overset{P}{\overset{\triangle}{e_1 \ldots e_n}}$$
 LCS':
 [act(m, the-cart) & move(the-cart)]
 LCS:
 cause([act(m, the-cart)], [move(the-cart)])

The aspectual distinctions made by the above trichotomy do not distinguish between achievements and accomplishments in any structural way, as illustrated above with the inchoative *close* and causative *close*, an achievement and accomplishment, respectively. In fact, we will argue that there is no further distinction necessary in terms of event structure for classifying these two aspectual types. Rather, achievements and accomplishments can be distinguished solely in terms of an agentive/non-agentive distinction. We will characterize the difference as follows. When a verb makes reference both to a predicate opposition and the activity bringing about this change, then the resulting aspectual type is an accomplishment (as in (16)). When the verb makes no explicit reference to the activity being performed, the resulting aspectual type is an achievement (as in (15)). This distinction is illustrated in (19) below:

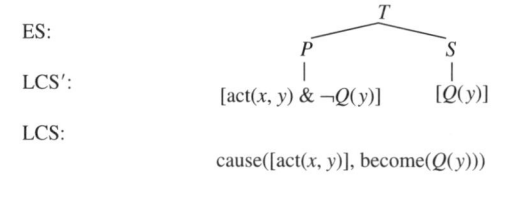

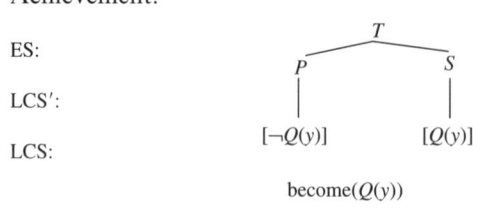

(19) a. Accomplishment:
 ES:
 $$\begin{array}{c} T \\ \diagup \diagdown \\ P \quad\quad S \end{array}$$
 LCS':
 [act(x, y) & ¬Q(y)]   [Q(y)]
 LCS:
 cause([act(x, y)], become(Q(y)))

 b. Achievement:
 ES:
 $$\begin{array}{c} T \\ \diagup \diagdown \\ P \quad\quad S \end{array}$$
 LCS':
 [¬Q(y)]   [Q(y)]
 LCS:
 become(Q(y))

The role of agentivity for distinguishing event types, explored in Dowty (1979), replaces the notion of "event headedness" introduced in Pustejovsky (1989b). As an example of this difference, notice how the transition verbs *build*, *draw*, and *leave* differ in their event structures from *arrive* and *die*, illustrated with *build* and *die*.

(20) a. Mary built a house.

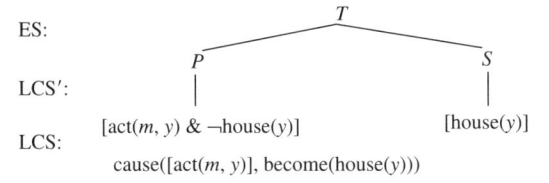

ES:
```
            T
          /   \
         P     S
```
LCS':   [act(m, y) & ¬house(y)]   [house(y)]

LCS: cause([act(m, y)], become(house(y)))

b. Mary died.

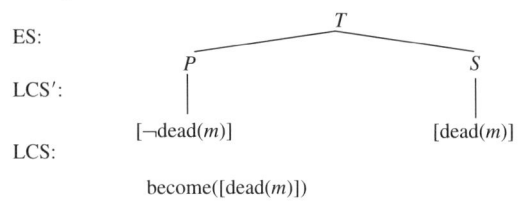

ES:
```
            T
          /   \
         P     S
```
LCS':   [¬dead(m)]   [dead(m)]

LCS: become([dead(m)])

Although this analysis might be intuitive for most cases of achievement verbs, an agentive role does seem implicit in many achievement predicates. For example, the sentences in (21) seem to involve an agent:

(21) a. Mary arrived at the party.
     b. John won the race.

The question, however, is whether the agency is part of the verbal semantics of *arrive* and *win* or is contributed by other means, for example, the animacy of the subject, or pragmatic effects. The position that agency is not intrinsically part of the verb's meaning is not as implausible as it might seem. First, notice the absence of agency in the sentences in (22), with the same verbs as in (21):

(22) a. The package arrived at the office.
     b. Our anniversary has finally arrived.
     c. Mary won the lottery.

The event structure for (22a) is simply the non-agentive transition shown in (22a').

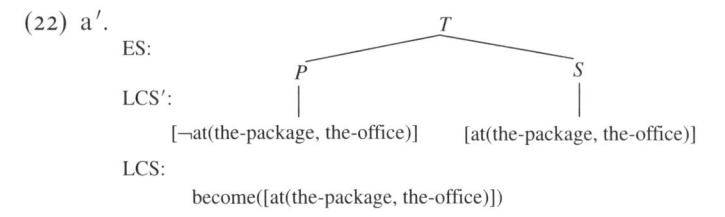

(22) a'.
ES:
```
            T
          /   \
         P     S
```
LCS':   [¬at(the-package, the-office)]   [at(the-package, the-office)]

LCS: become([at(the-package, the-office)])

Rather than being metaphorical uses of an agentive predicate, we argue that the sentences in (22) are typical instances of non-agentive transitions (i.e., achievements). Secondly, notice how intentional adverbials such as *deliberately* cannot felicitously modify predicates such as *win* and *die*.

(23) a. *Mary won the race deliberately. (But cf. Mary lost the race deliberately.)
     b. *Mary deliberately died of cancer.

These data suggest that Dowty's observation concerning agentivity does in fact act to complete the distinctions between the conventional aspectual classes by dividing the class of transitions into two logical subclasses. Configurationally, as event structures, however, the two classes are identical.

5 EVENT COMPOSITION

Having studied the basic event structures associated with verbs, we will now turn to how they interact with other syntactic constituents to form derived event representations, that is, the phenomenon of *event composition*. In particular, we look at two classes of event composition, PP attachment and resultative constructions. There are several types of syntactic constructions that directly affect the event type of a phrase: temporal adverbials, adjunct phrases, complement type (e.g., individuated or not), and aspectual coercion (e.g., the progressive). For reasons of space, we consider only the first two types here (for further discussion see Pustejovsky (to appear)). The basic idea is that the event type for a sentence need not be the event type of the main verb. Category changes may occur because of explicit rules setting out the ways events can compose and be modified.

Briefly, as mentioned in the Introduction, temporal adverbials are sensitive to the type of event being modified (Kenny, 1963; Vendler, 1967). For example, the process verb *run* can be modified by a *durative* adverbial, while the transition *build* cannot:

(24) a. Mary ran *for an hour*.
     b. *Mary built a chair *for an hour*.

Conversely, *build* can be modified by a *frame* adverbial while *run* cannot:

(25) a. *Mary ran *in an hour*.
     b. Mary built a chair *in an hour*.

Within our theory of events, there is one basic principle that accounts for these facts: only when an event contains a logical culmination (e.g., it belongs to the set of transitions) is it modifiable by a frame adverbial. Why should this be? Given our assumptions about the subeventual analysis for verbs, it is possible with our analysis that temporal predicates in the language might make reference to a subevent, or to an assembly of subevents denoted by the verb. Thus, imagine that the frame adverbial *in an hour* requires *two* events to be present for a proper modification, for example, the two subevents of *build*, e_1 and e_2. One can say, then, that this temporal modifier takes as its argument the temporal distance between e_2 and the onset of e_1. The logical form for our sentence (25b) then will be something like (25c):

(25) c. $\exists P, S[\text{build}((P, S)) \wedge \text{agent}(m, (P, S)) \wedge \text{theme}(\text{chair}, (P, S)) \wedge \text{in-an-hour}(P, S)]$

The last conjunct of this expression, *in an hour*, can be interpreted as being:

temporal measure of (time of) S − onset of P = 1 hour

Such an analysis would immediately explain why the other event types (states or processes) are ungrammatical with such adverbials, without the "coerce" reading (cf. (25a)).[14]

---

[14] I would like to thank an anonymous reviewer for pointing out this analysis to me.

A second kind of event composition involves the interaction of a prepositional phrase with the event structure of a verb. These include cases of PP attachment that change the event structure of the verb phrase (VP), as shown in (26) and (27):

(26) a. Mary **ran**.
  b. Mary **ran** to the store.

(27) a. John **pushed** the wagon.
  b. John **pushed** the wagon to Mary.

What the sentence pairs in (26) and (27) have in common is a recognizable shift in their event types. In particular, for each case, a sentence denoting a *process* (in the (a) examples) has been transformed into a *transition* by the presence of a prepositional phrase (PP) denoting a bounded path, a *to*-PP. As Chomsky (1957) notes, these are, in fact, examples of a general phenomenon in language, where the grammar allows a syntactic construction to mirror an already existing lexical representation; that is, in this case, a transition (see also Jackendoff (1983) and Talmy (1985) for similar points). When this structure arises from syntactic composition, we have what we will refer to as *event composition*. Informally, the rule can be stated in the following way. In certain constructions, when the verb denotes a *process* (e.g. *run*, *push*), and there is a phrase present which denotes a function from processes to transitions, then the event type of the entire verb phrase (VP) is construed as a *transition*.[15] Notice that this is the same structure carried by lexically specified transitional verbs such as *build*.

Such a process of composition can be made clearer if we consider a specific example. In (26b) above, the event type of the VP containing the lexical process verb *run* shifts to a transition in composition with the PP. In this example, the notation $\langle P, T \rangle$ is taken to represent a function from processes to transitions:

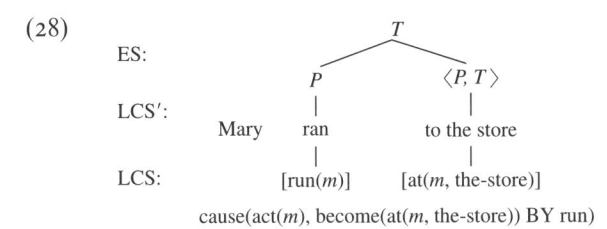

(28)
```
              T
             / \
            P   ⟨P,T⟩
ES:
LCS':       |        |
         Mary  ran   to the store
LCS:            |         |
             [run(m)]  [at(m, the-store)]
         cause(act(m), become(at(m, the-store))) BY run)
```

In this example, the prepositional phrase is able to project its own event structure, the *state* of Mary being at the store. It is easy to verify that the above event structure is a transition, since modification by a frame adverbial is well formed, as illustrated in (29):

(29) Mary ran to the store *in an hour*.

To explain the behavior of this type of event composition, we suggest that the preposition *to* is to be analyzed as denoting a relation between states and processes, such

---

[15] This is a slight simplification for illustration purposes. In Pustejovsky (to appear), prepositions such as "to" are treated as relational event functors, applying first to a state, and then to a process, to give a transition: i.e. $\langle S, \langle P, T \rangle \rangle$. The treatment above, however, is useful as a general description of this case of event type-shifting. It should be pointed out that the event type $\langle P, T \rangle$ has consequences for the mapping to LCS as well. Because the event type of the matrix predicate is actually treated as an argument to $\langle P, T \rangle$, it effectively is subordinated in Levin and Rapoport's (1988) sense, hence creating a "BY manner" expression. For discussion, see Pustejovsky (to appear).

that the resulting event type is a transition. That is, the PP acts like a function from processes to transitions.[16] Importantly, however, as with lexical transitions, this construction sets up a predicate opposition involving the culminating state introduced by the PP. Thus, the LCS derived from this construction looks like that of a lexically specified causative verb.[17]

Similar principles of event composition seem to be operating in the *resultative* construction as well. Resultative constructions are verb phrases, such as those in (30), consisting of a verb with an object, together with an adjunct phrase predicated of the direct object, that specifies the state the object obtains as a result of an action:[18]

(30) a. Mary hammered the metal flat.
　　 b. Mary wiped the table clean.
　　 c. The men drank the pot dry.

Rappaport and Levin (1989) argue that the resultative phrase (e.g. *flat* and *clean*) can only be predicated of the direct object, a restriction they call the *direct object restriction* (*DOR*). We will return to this restriction in Section 7, but for now, let us first examine how this construction is relevant to event composition.

The examples are relevant because the resultative construction involves what appears to be a systematic event-type shifting from processes to transitions. This systematic ambiguity, we argue, is the result of principles of semantic composition, rather than an underlying lexical ambiguity in the verb involved. This follows the general methodology outlined in Pustejovsky (1989a, 1991), where, whenever possible, the logical ambiguity of a word should be generated by general principles operating in the grammar rather than by positing multiple lexical entries. Rappaport and Levin's (1989) analysis assumes a similar position with respect to lexical operations. Although we cannot touch on the richness of the problem (see, for example, the discussion in Rapoport (1990, to appear)), consider the resultative interpretations for the verb *hammer* in (30a) and the verb *wipe* in (30b); they arise from a similar event composition rule to that proposed for PP attachment above. That is, both verbs are underlyingly specified as *processes*, while the adjectival phrases *flat* and *clean* have event interpretations as *states*. Notice, then, how the resultative construction requires no additional word sense for the verb, nor any special semantic machinery in order for the resultative interpretation to be available, beyond the rules of event composition. Briefly, the solution involves analyzing the notion of stage-level predicate (Carlson, 1977) within event semantics as a subset of the states; namely, *those which can be changed by being acted upon*, functions that take processes to transitions, i.e. $\langle P, T \rangle$. Thus, the resultative construction formally reduces to the type of event composition encountered earlier with PP attachment; see (32) below (Ingria and Pustejovsky, 1990) for a discussion of the syntactic consequences of this solution):

(31) a. Mary **hammered** the metal. (*hammer* $\in$ process)
　　 b. Mary **hammered** the metal flat. (*hammer* $\in$ transition)

---

[16] This is similar to the proposals in Hinrichs (1985) and Dowty (1979), where such phrases behave like functions from properties to properties.

[17] For a different approach to such constructions, see Levin and Rapoport (1988), where rules of "lexical subordination" derive such new word senses.

[18] Simpson (1983) and Rappaport and Levin (1989) discuss the connection between resultatives, such as those in (30), and the property of unaccusativity (cf. Perlmutter, 1978). Unaccusatives are intransitive verbs whose subjects behave like direct objects of transitive verbs in many respects (see Levin (1986) and Burzio (1986) for details).

(32)   ES:

```
              T
            /   \
           P    ⟨P, T⟩
           |      |
LCS':   Mary hammer the metal   flat
           |              |
       [hammer(m, the-metal)]  [flat(x)]
LCS:
```

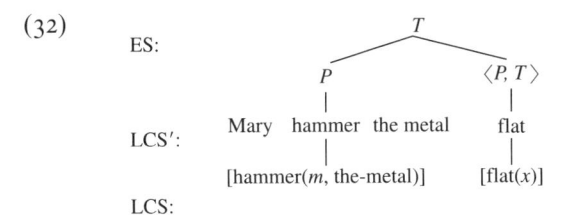

cause(act(m, the-metal), become([flat(the-metal)])) BY hammer

A favorable consequence of this analysis is that it explains why just process verbs participate in this construction, and why the resultative phrase (the adjectival phrase) must be a state. Thus, by proposing that this construction participates in a semantic change at the level of event structure, we can explain the behavior as logically related to that of other subordinating constructions (in Levin and Rapoport's (1988) terms), but where the new sense of the verb arises out of syntactic and semantic composition in the grammar.

To close this section, we will briefly examine the class of psychological predicates such as *fear* and *frighten*, and how event structure contributes to the binding violations associated with the latter set of these verbs. The considerations reviewed briefly here motivate Grimshaw (1990) to analyze such violations in terms of event structure rather than in terms of structural configuration effects.[19]

The normal conditions on anaphoric binding, according to syntactic-based theories of grammar, involve the notions of *precedence*, *c-command*, and a *binding domain*. One class of examples that violates this definition of anaphoric licensing is that involving the *experiencer* verbs (we will not review the literature on this subject here, but will refer the reader to Belletti and Rizzi (1985), Pesetsky (1987), and Grimshaw (1986) for details). The problem can be stated as follows: there are two types of psych predicates—both with an argument structure of (experiencer, theme)—the first where the argument bearing the experiencer role is expressed as the subject (e.g. *fear*) and the second where the argument bearing the theme is expressed as the subject (e.g. *frighten*).[20]

Although these classes seem to have identical argument structures the syntactic behavior of their members is very difficult. For example, the *fear* class behaves as expected by the binding theory, while the *frighten* class allows violations of the c-command requirement on anaphoric binding. Normally, an anaphoric pronoun must be structurally c-commanded by its antecedent, as in (34) or (36). Thus, an anaphor in matrix subject position is ill-formed, because there is no possible antecedent to c-command it as in the *fear* sentences (33a). An exception to this rule comes from the *frighten* class of experiencer verbs, however, as illustrated in (33b, c):

(33) a. *Each other's students fear the teachers.
     b. The pictures of each other frighten the teachers.
     c. ?? Each other's students frighten the teachers.

(34) a. The women fear each other.
     b. The women frightened each other.

---

[19] For discussion of how this phenomenon extends beyond this verb class, see Pustejovsky (1989b) and (to appear).
[20] There are of course two readings for "frighten" type verbs: one which is purely causative (*x* occasions fear in *y*), and the other which is being considered here. As Pesetsky (1987) notes, the backwards binding effect introduced below obtains only in the second interpretation.

(35) a. *Himself fears John.
    b. *Himself annoys John.
(36) a. John fears pictures of himself.
    b. The women frightened each other's students.

Although both classes disallow backward binding when the anaphor is the subject itself (see (35a) and (35b)), when the anaphor occurs embedded within the subject NP, as in (33b, c), binding is permitted with *frighten* verbs. What is it about *frighten* that allows the violation of the normal binding conditions? Following Grimshaw (1986) and Williams (1987),[21] we claim that the argument structure of the verb contributes information that accounts for the binding ability of its arguments. Grimshaw assumes that the argument structures for the members of the two verbs classes is as given in (37), distinguished only by a case-marking diacritic on one argument, Exp_{acc}, indicating it must appear as a direct object:

(37) a. fear (*Exp*(*Th*))
    b. frighten (Exp_{acc}(*Th*))

Grimshaw argues that the notion of *argument command* is as important for licensing anaphoric binding as is c-command. Briefly, this can be defined as in (38):

(38)   Argument command: $(\theta_1(\theta_2 \ldots \theta_n))$: members of outermost lists (recursively) a-command all other arguments.

Equipped with two separate dimensions of evaluation (both c-command and argument command), Grimshaw's theory can predict the subtle grammaticality differences that arise. What is left unexplained, however, is this: if such a minimal structural difference between the two verb classes (see (37)) has such a profound effect on binding possibilities, then there should be strong evidence for this distinction.

We will now demonstrate that the theory of event structure outlined above provides a well-motivated semantic explanation for the structural distinctions between the two experiencer verb types, thereby providing evidence for this distinction. Furthermore, the binding violations that the *frighten* class exhibits are part of a much wider phenomenon. We suggest that the event structure for the *frighten* verbs is that of a transition, while the event structure for *fear* verbs is that of a state. The difference between the two classes of experiencer verbs can be given as follows:

(39) a. Type(*fear*) ∈ state; object is intensional.
    b. Type(*frighten*) ∈ transition; subject is extensional.

Although it has long been noted that verbs such as *fear* are stative and those such as *frighten* are not, there has been little formal use made of this distinction. Furthermore, it is interesting that the *fear* class introduces an intensional object, compared to an extensional subject introduced by *frighten* verbs. This distinction is shown in (40):

(40) a. Mary fears ghosts/big dogs.
    b. Big dogs/*ghosts frighten Mary.

That is, Mary can fear something without there necessarily existing the object of her fears. Something which frightens Mary, however, must exist and be more than an intensional object.

---

[21] Williams' (1987) proposal is somewhat different from Grimshaw's, but we will not review the differences here.

Grimshaw's argument structure distinction between the two classes is supported if one assigns the *fear* class to states and the *frighten* class to transitions, as shown in (41):

(41) a. The movie frightened Mary.
b. Event structure:

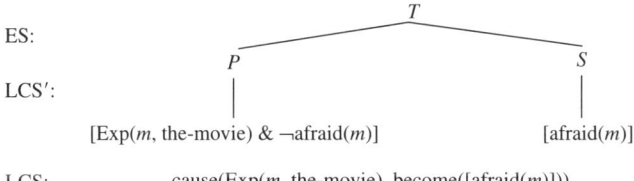

ES:
```
           T
          / \
         P   S
```
LCS':   [Exp(m, the-movie) & ¬afraid(m)]   [afraid(m)]

LCS: cause(Exp(m, the-movie), become([afraid(m)]))

The structure above suggests that the appropriate command relation which exists for verbs such as *frighten* derives from the underlying LCS' relation of *experiencing*, within the initial event. For this example, the experiencer variable *Exp* might be filled by the binary predicate *see(x, y)*. As Grimshaw argues, one possible effect of such "semantic dominance" within a predicate is the licensing of variable binding, for example, anaphora. Thus, the representation provides an explanation for certain syntactic effects which were problematic when analyzed in purely syntactic terms.

6 ADVERBIAL MODIFICATION

In this section we suggest that an event structure provides a natural representation for adverbs as event predicates. We will claim that there are two types of adverbs: *wide-scope* and *narrow-scope*. The ambiguity exhibited by an adverbial, in terms of behaving as a manner- versus speaker-oriented adverb, can be explained in terms of different scope assignments of the same adverb. Such a solution is possible only if we examine the finer structure of the event being modified.

Consider first the examples discussed in Cresswell (1985) and Higginbotham (1989) involving adverbs such as *fatally:*

(42)   Mary fatally slipped

Within a Davidsonian analysis, where adverbs are taken as event predicates, the intended interpretation for this use of the adverb is represented as (43):

(43) $\exists e[slipped(e, m) \wedge fatal(e, m)]$

where one can read this as, "there was a slipping event such that it was fatal to Mary". But there are more complicated examples where the adverb can also be interpreted as a manner adverbial. As McConnell-Ginet (1982) points out, the sentence in (44) has two readings: (a) it was rude of Lisa to depart, and (b) she departed in a rude manner:

(44)   Lisa rudely departed.

The ambiguity arises from there being both a manner and a stative interpretation. McConnell-Ginet's solution involves adding an additional argument to the verb in order to derive the manner reading (45a), while adopting a more traditional Montagovian analysis for the stative interpretation, (45b):

(45) a. *depart(rude, lisa)*
b. *rude(depart(lisa))*

We will not review the details of McConnell-Ginet's proposal here but, as Higginbotham (1989) points out, she has no natural way of accounting for the factivity of the construction under both interpretations.

Higginbotham (1989) proposes an analysis for such constructions in terms of an event semantics which overcomes some of the problems of McConnell-Ginet's solution. In the manner of Davidson (1980) and his own previous work (Higginbotham, 1985), he suggests that quantification over an event variable allows for a first-order treatment of such adverbs. Consider the representations he proposes for (44), illustrated below in (46):

(46) a. $\exists e[depart(e, Lisa) \wedge rude(e, \hat{e}'[depart_0(e')])]$
 b. $\exists e[rude(e, Lisa, \hat{e}'[depart(e', Lisa)]) \wedge depart(e, Lisa)]$

The first expression says that, compared to the set of departing events, Lisa's instance was a rude one. The reading in (46b), on the other hand, says that Lisa was being rude in that she departed (e.g. when she did). For Higginbotham, such modification is another example of θ-*identification*, which results in the conjunction of two attributes predicated of a single individual (or individual variable), and θ-*marking*, which applies the adverb as a function to its argument, the verb. The problem with this analysis is that it assumes a variable adicity for the adverb. That is, *rude* takes two arguments in one case and three in another. Assuming that there is some relationship between the two adverbs, Higginbotham (as well as McConnell-Ginet) must state it independently of the semantics of each lexical item. Following the general methodology outlined above, we show that the ambiguity results from a structural distinction and not from lexical polysemy. In fact, the adverbs in both interpretations are identical, and there is a scope distinction which gives rise to the ambiguity just discussed. To begin with, consider the event structure for a verb such as *depart*, given below:

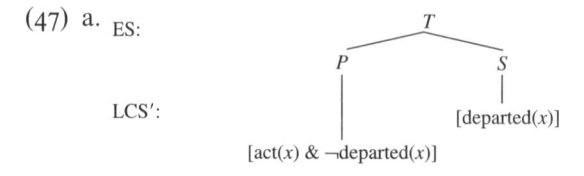

(47) a. ES:

```
                T
              /   \
             P     S
             |     |
                 [departed(x)]
LCS':
        [act(x) & ¬departed(x)]
```

where we minimally distinguish between the action of departing and the resulting state of being departed. This is a transition, annotated by an *act* relation, making it behave like an accomplishment. We will suggest that adverbs such as *rudely*, traditionally termed *manner* adverbials, modify a semantic expression associated with an event structure or an action subevent. Since both the process of leaving and the entire transition are actions, there will be two interpretations possible, resulting from two distinct scopes: over the process (as in (48)); and over the transition (as in (49)). Thus, if one modifies the initial event by characterizing it as *rude*, we arrive at an event predication over the process, that is, a manner interpretation; namely, that the action was performed rudely for those types of actions. The representation for this is given below. In this representation the predicate modifies only the process of *leaving*, and not the state of *having left*:

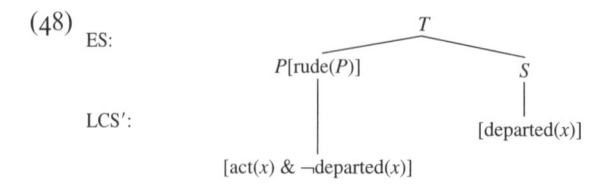

(48) ES:

```
                   T
                 /   \
            P[rude(P)]  S
                |       |
                     [departed(x)]
LCS':
         [act(x) & ¬departed(x)]
```

In this structure the adverbial *rudely* applies to the initial event, and behaves like a *narrow-scope* adverb, relative to the entire event structure. When *rudely* takes scope over the entire event as in (49), it is necessarily interpreted relative to the speaker and situation:

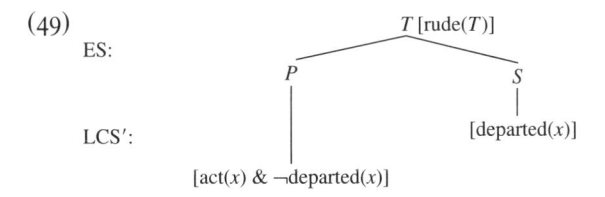

(49) ES:

```
                    T [rude(T)]
                   /          \
                  P            S
                  |            |
LCS':                       [departed(x)]
         [act(x) & ¬departed(x)]
```

Thus, we can represent the ambiguity associated with the adverbial as one of a scope difference of the same lexical item; thus, this provides for a single one-place predicate treatment of the adverbial.

It is interesting to note that adverbs are idiosyncratic in their behavior as event predicates. For example, the adverbial *slowly* in both sentences in (50) refers to the action of walking, while *quickly* in (51) can refer either to the manner of action or to the duration of the entire event:

(50) a. Mary walked to the store slowly.
     b. Mary slowly walked to the store.

(51) a. Mary walked to the store quickly.
     b. Mary quickly walked to the store.

Such information must be associated with the individual adverb, where *quickly* may select for either reading. Notice that if *quickly* selects for a temporal interpretation, it must take wide-scope, since it requires a telic event to measure duration.

One of the diagnostics for aspectual classification discussed in the Introduction was the effect of modification by *almost*. We discovered that accomplishments allow two readings when modified by *almost* while non-accomplishments allow only one. For example, consider the sentences in (52):

(52) a. John almost built a house.
     b. John almost ran.

Both sentences have an interpretation where the act is intended but never carried out, while (52a) carries the additional reading that the action is started but not fully completed. Why is it that *build* allows two interpretations while *run* allows only one?

Following the strategy introduced above, where an event structure allows for richer structural possibilities for adverbs as event predicates, we would expect a sentence to have as many interpretations for an adverbial as there are distinct predicates in the event structure. Since there are two distinct predicates involved in *build*, one within the initial event, and the other in the culminating event, there are two readings for the example in (52a), as illustrated in (53):

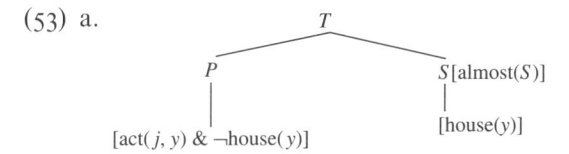

(53) a.
```
                    T
                   / \
                  P    S[almost(S)]
                  |    |
         [act(j, y) & ¬house(y)]  [house(y)]
```

b.
```
        T
       / \
P[almost(P)]  S
     |        |
[act(j,y) & ¬house(y)]  [house(y)]
```

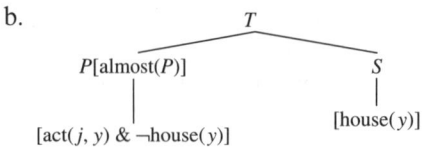

In (53a), by modifying the culmination event, *almost* prevents the assertability of the expression associated with the logical culmination of the event; namely that there exists a house. The other reading, that of intent, is represented as (53b). This is the same reading as that available to (52b), where the *almost* modifies the expression associated with the first event constituent (or the only one as in the case of (52b)):

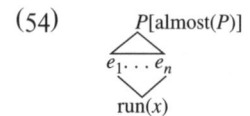

(54)
```
    P[almost(P)]
     /\
   e₁...eₙ
     \/
    run(x)
```

Assuming the proposal above to be correct, then we would assume that the other class of transitions, that is, achievements, should be unambiguous with respect to *almost*, since they involve only one distinct predicate in their event structure. As mentioned in the Introduction, this is in fact the case:

(55) a. John almost died.
 b. Bill almost arrived.
 c. Mary almost won the race.

The only reading available for these sentences is one where something has occurred without the terminus event being achieved (see (56)):[22]

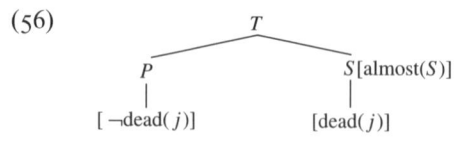

(56)
```
        T
       / \
      P   S[almost(S)]
      |        |
   [¬dead(j)]  [dead(j)]
```

This is the only interpretation available since non-agentive transitions refer to a single predicate and its opposition. Importantly, the privative term is considered a dependent predicate, and does not allow modification by the adverbial.

To close this section, let us return to the topic of temporal adverbials. It is interesting to see what further predictions are made by a subeventual analysis concerning the scope of temporal adverbial modification. With this analysis we would expect that a complex event structure would allow modification by a durative adverbial of one of its *subevents*. This prediction turns out to be correct, in fact, as we see from sentences such as (57):

(57) a. John gave Mary the record for the afternoon.
 b. The company sent John the book for 10 days.
 c. Mary ran into the house for 20 minutes. (See Fillmore, 1988.)

These examples illustrate how the adverbial can modify a subevent of the entire event. In (57a), for example, involving a transition, the interval *the afternoon* modifies only the state referring to Mary having the record, and not the actual act of giving.

---

[22] Higginbotham (1989) proposes a scope analysis for the ambiguities involving "almost". His theory assumes a single event quantification, as proposed in Davidson (1980), and as a result is unable to capture the behavior of achievement verbs and adverbial scope.

This distinction is made explicit using our representation of the lexical semantics for *give*:

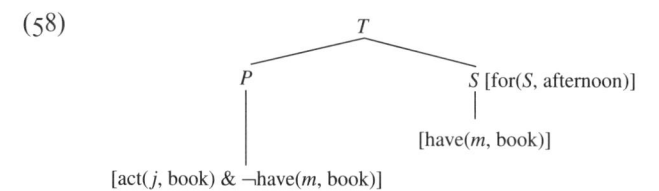

(58)
```
              T
           /     \
          P       S [for(S, afternoon)]
          |       |
          |    [have(m, book)]
  [act(j, book) & ¬have(m, book)]
```

This structure states that the adverbial takes scope over the final event of the giving and not the act itself. In (57b), a similar modification occurs, where the expression *for 10 days* refers to the state of John having the book. Likewise, in (57c), the interval of 20 minutes denotes the time Mary spent inside the house rather than the duration of the act of running itself.

Other examples where the durative adverbial seems to modify the resulting state are given below:

(59) a. John left for a week.
 b. John arrived for the day.
 c. They entered the atmosphere for an hour.

What these examples seem to indicate is that duratives tend to take a narrow scope over any event type that predicates a single property (i.e., state) of an individual. If this is true, then what do we make of the obviously ungrammatical sentence in (60):

(60)   *Mary died for two years.

Why is it not possible to apply the interval to Mary's state of being dead? In fact, it does seem that such cases are marginally permitted, as (61) shows:

(61) ?My terminal died for 2 days last week.

Apparently, the state that is delimited by an interval must be something that is potentially variable relative to the interpretation for the utterance. Thus, sentence (60) predicates *death* of an individual, which to our general mode of interpretation will not vary once predicated. A computer terminal, on the other hand, will allow for this predicate to be applied over and over again. This relates to the *persistence* of a property over an object, and is outside the scope of this discussion. It seems that a stage-level interpretation may be at play here as well (see Carlson, 1977).[23]

7 INTERACTIONS OF EVENT STRUCTURE AND ARGUMENT STRUCTURE

In this section we explore how a level of event structure can contribute to our understanding of the interactions between LCSs and their mappings to argument structure. We suggest that the distinctions provided by event structure are useful in determining how semantic participants in an LCS are realized syntactically. In fact, we argue that an event structure analysis gives further support to Rappaport and Levin's (1989)

---

[23] A reviewer has pointed out that what might be at play here is the "reversibility" of the final event. Thus, sentence (61) is more acceptable because the final event there, that is, the terminal being dead, is reversible, whereas in (60) it is not. The notion of reversibility does seem important here and is worth exploring. This issue is taken up in Pustejovsky (to appear).

argument for deep unaccusativity. Much of our discussion, however, will be merely suggestive and must await further empirical investigations for support. For independent arguments in support of a level of event structure, see Grimshaw (1990) and Grimshaw and Vikner (1990).

We begin by discussing how the different event types translate to different verb classes as defined by their grammatical behavior. It is interesting to note that there is no direct or predictable behavior for the arguments of a verb as determined by its event type alone. For example, the verbs which are specified as transitions appear to form no equivalence class with respect to grammatical behavior. That is, all the verbs in (62) below are lexically transitions, but fall into distinct argument structure verb classes (see Levin, 1989):

(62) a. The bottle broke. (Unaccusative)
    b. Mary broke the bottle. (Causative)
    c. Mary built a table. (Creation)
    d. The movie frightened Mary. (Psychological)

Similarly, those verbs which denote processes are associated with different verb classes, for example, those in (63):

(63) a. Mary slept. (Unergative)
    b. John ran. (Manner of motion)

Using a level of event structure, we will argue that verb classes such as unaccusatives and unergatives correlate with independent principles of mapping from semantics to argument structure.

If we assume that for unaccusative verbs the subject is an underlying object (the "deep unaccusativity" analysis), then the first general behavior we see emerging from the sentences in (62) above is the following:

(A) The semantic participant involved in a predicate opposition is mapped onto the internal argument position of the lexical structure (roughly the d-structure object position).

That is, an event structure like that in (64a) is associated with an argument structure like (64b):

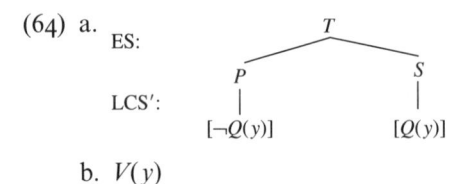

(64) a. ES:
$$\begin{array}{c} T \\ / \backslash \\ P S \end{array}$$
LCS': $ [\neg Q(y)] [Q(y)]$

    b. $V(y)$

As argued in previous sections, all transitions involve a predicate opposition of some sort. Yet, by itself, this property fails to distinguish adequately the verb classes in (62).

Independent of this principle, we argue, following Grimshaw (1990) and Pustejovsky (1989a), that the notions of causer and agent are somehow associated with the initial subevent of an event structure. More explicity, let us propose the following principle:

(B) The agentive participant in the initial subevent of event structure is mapped onto the external argument position of the lexical structure (roughly the d-structure subject).

The result of both principles A and B applying in the structure in (65a) below is the argument structure in (65b) (where an external argument is marked with an asterisk):

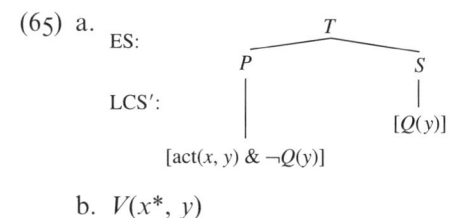

(65) a. ES:
$$\begin{array}{c} \\ P \quad\quad\quad T \\ \quad\quad\quad / \ \backslash \\ \quad\quad\quad P \quad\quad S \end{array}$$

LCS':
$$\quad\quad\quad\quad\quad\quad [Q(y)]$$
$$[act(x, y)\ \&\ \neg Q(y)]$$

b. $V(x^*, y)$

An analysis in terms of event structure allows us to speculate on just what an unaccusative is, in terms of lexical semantic structure. Namely, *an unaccusative is a transition involving a unary predicate opposition, and nothing else.*

Above it was argued that resultative constructions are formed from processes in composition with a phrase denoting a state. Here we show that the apparent counterexamples to this generalization involving unaccusatives, discussed by Rappaport and Levin (1989), are not actually cases of the resultative construction at all, but involve the addition of emphatic (or manner) adjunct phrases. These cases are the following:

(66) a. The river froze solid.
b. The bottle broke open.

These are not true resultatives, for notice that the predication of the adjunct phrase is merely an attribute to the state introduced by the transition/unaccusative verb itself. This becomes clearer when we consider the following data:

(67) a. The river froze in 20 minutes.
b. The river froze solid in 20 minutes.

(68) a. The bottle broke suddenly.
b. The bottle broke open suddenly.

The events in both (67a) and (67b) and (68a) and (68b) are coextensive. That is, it is not the case that the event denoted in (a) is a subpart of that denoted in (b); rather they are the same event, with different information being expressed about it. That is, these are unlike the previous cases where a process shifted to a transition. Thus, in our terms, the examples mentioned in Rappaport and Levin (1989) as resultative constructions are not logically the same as the classic resultative construction. If this is the case, then the generalization that an unaccusative verb is a transition involving a unary predicate opposition strengthens Rappaport and Levin's argument for deep unaccusativity, assuming that only processes enter into resultative constructions.

To conclude this section, we simply state without motivation three final principles involved in mapping from event structure to argument structure. For more detailed discussion, the reader is referred to Pustejovsky (to appear).

(C) If the predicate opposition involves a relation, then both the participants are mapped onto internal argument positions of the argument structure. Otherwise, relational arguments are mapped directly as expressed at event structure; for example, *give* and *put* are examples where the culminating state is a relation, and both arguments are realized as internal arguments.

(D) Any participant in the initial event not expressed by principles (A) or (B) is mapped onto the external argument position.

(E) Each subevent must be associated with at least one argument position at lexical structure.

It is clear from the resultative data and the false reflexive data (e.g. *laugh herself silly*), that certain predicates require the expression of a separate, unsubcategorized argument while others do not, for example, *hammer the metal flat* (see Simpson, 1983). Principle (E) requires that every subevent (in this case, *silly* and *flat*) be associated with at least one argument position. In conjunction with principles (B) and (A), the false reflexive NP serves the function of representing the predicate opposition in the transition, while the external argument represents the causer in the initial event. Therefore, there must be both an internal argument (*herself*) and a unique external argument (*Mary*) to satisfy both conditions. Thus, the reflexive NP acts as a kind of argument epenthesis in the lexical structure:

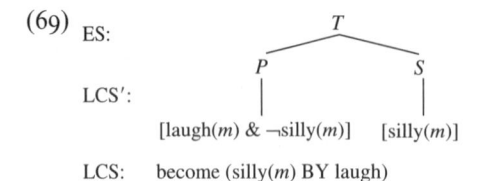

(69) ES:
$$\begin{array}{c} T \\ / \ \backslash \\ P \quad S \end{array}$$

LCS': [laugh(m) & ¬silly(m)]   [silly(m)]

LCS: become (silly(m) BY laugh)

Notice that in the regular resultative cases the principles (A) and (B) are satisfied by the existing argument structure, obviating the need for argument epenthesis.

In this section, we have tried to give some indication of how event structure contributes to the understanding of the mapping between the lexical semantics and syntax, as represented at argument structure. We have glossed over many details and problems which might remain, but the general theme is quite clear: the theory of grammar can be greatly enriched by representations such as those considered here for events. It remains to examine the limitations and further interactions of this system.

8 CONCLUSION

In this paper, we have tried to outline a partial theory of word meaning making use of a rich structural system for the subeventual properties of verbs. We have argued that words lexically specify a specific sequence of subevents organized by a well-defined geometry. Such configurations provide a very restrictive framework for partially defining the lexical semantics of words in the grammar. Metalogical notions such as *cause* and *become* are computed from the aspectual configuration associated with a lexical item and then a sentence.

By looking at the event structure of words in composition, we explained how the lexical specification of a verb's event-type can be overriden as a result of syntactic and semantic compositionality of the verb with other elements in the sentence.

Another advantage of proposing a richer subeventual structure for propositions is that we now have an analysis for the behavior of temporal adverbials, as well as adverbials such as *almost* and *rudely*. It was suggested that the reason accomplishments such as *build* allow two interpretations with such adverbs is due to the number of semantically specified event constituents for its event structure. Achievements, while having a very similar event constituency, have no unique semantic expression associated with the process preceding the culminating state. Finally, we examined briefly how the semantic participants in an event structure are associated with arguments in an argument structure representation. Following Grimshaw (1990), the notion of causer and "external" argument can be linked to a participant in the initial subevent within an event structure.

The purpose of this paper has been to show how verbs decompose into distinct event types with internal structure. Rather than examining the formal semantics of such structures, we have studied the effect that a level of event structure has on the grammar, and how it interacts with other levels of representation. In many ways, the proposal here is preliminary and merely suggestive, but we feel that an appreciation of the internal structure of events for word meaning is an important representational device for lexical semantics.

REFERENCES

Bach, E. (1986). 'The algebra of events', *Linguistics and Philosophy* 9: 5–16.
Belletti, A. and Rizzi, L. (1985). 'Psych verbs and θ-theory'. Manuscript. MIT.
Bennett, M. and Partee, B. (1972). 'Toward the logic of tense and aspect in English'. Distributed by Indiana University Linguistics Club.
Brachman, R. (1979). 'On the epistemological status of semantic networks', in N. Findler (ed.), *Associative Networks: Representation and Use of Knowledge by Computers*. New York: Academic Press.
Bresnan, J. (ed.). (1982). *The Mental Representation of Grammatical Relations*. Cambridge, MA: MIT Press.
Burzio, L. (1986). *Italian Syntax: A Government-binding Approach*. Dordrecht: Reidel.
Carlson, G. (1977). 'Reference to kinds in English'. Ph.D. dissertation, University of Massachusetts.
Carlson, L. (1981). 'Aspect and quantification', in P. Tedeschi and A. Zaenen (eds.), *Syntax and Semantics: Vol. 14, Tense and Aspect*. New York: Academic Press.
Carnap, R. (1956). *Meaning and Necessity*. Chicago: University of Chicago Press.
Chomsky, N. (1957). *Syntactic Structures*. The Hague: Mouton.
Collins, A. and Quillian, M. (1969). 'Retrieval time from semantic memory', *Journal of Verbal Learning and Verbal Behavior* 9: 240–7.
Comrie, B. (1976). *Aspect*. Cambridge: Cambridge University Press.
—— (1985). *Tense*. Cambridge: Cambridge University Press.
Cresswell, M. (1985). *Adverbial Modification*. Dordrecht: Kluwer.
Croft, W. (1990). *Categories and Relations in Syntax: The Clause-level Organization of Information*. Chicago: University of Chicago Press.
Davidson, D. (1980). *Essays on Actions and Events*. Oxford: Clarendon Press.
Dowty, D. R. (1979). *Word Meaning and Montague Grammar*. Dordrecht: Reidel.
Fillmore, C. (1968). 'The case for case', in E. Bach and R. Harms (eds.), *Universals in Linguistic Theory*. New York: Holt, Rinehart, and Winston.
—— (1988). 'The mechanisms of construction grammar'. Manuscript. University of California, Berkeley.
Fodor, J. (1975). *The Language of Thought*. Cambridge, MA: Harvard University Press.
Foley, W. A. and Valin, R. D. van, Jr. (1984). *Functional Syntax and Universal Grammar*. Cambridge: Cambridge University Press.
Graham, R. (1987). *Aristotle's Two Systems*. Oxford: Clarendon Press.
Green, G. (1974). *Semantics and Syntactic Regularity*. Bloomington: Indiana University Press.
Grimshaw, J. (1979). 'Complement selection and the lexicon', *Linguistic Inquiry* 10: 279–326.
—— (1986). 'Nouns, arguments, and adjuncts'. Manuscript, Brandeis University.
—— (1990). *Argument Structure*. Cambridge, MA: MIT Press.

Grimshaw, J. and Vikner, S. (1990). 'Obligatory adjuncts and the structure of events'. Manuscript, Brandeis University.
Gruber, J. (1965). 'Studies in lexical relations'. Ph.D. dissertation, MIT, Cambridge, MA.
Hale, K. and Keyser, J. (1986). 'Some transitivity alternations in English'. Lexicon Project Working Papers 7. Center for Cognitive Science, MIT.
Hale, K. and Laughren, M. (1983). 'The structure of verbal entries'. Walpiri Lexicon Project, MIT, Cambridge.
Higginbotham, J. (1985). 'On semantics', *Linguistic Inquiry 16*: 547–93.
——(1989). 'Elucidations of Meaning', *Linguistics and Philosophy 12*: 465–518.
Hinrichs, E. W. (1985). 'A compositional semantics for Aktionarten and NP reference in English'. Ph.D. dissertation, Ohio State University.
Horn, L. (1989). *A Natural History of Negation*. Chicago: University of Chicago Press.
Ingria, R. and Pustejovsky, J. (1990). 'An active objects approach to syntax, semantics, and parsing', in C. Tenny (ed.), *MIT Working Papers in Parsing*. Cambridge, MA: MIT Press.
Jackendoff, R. (1972). *Semantic Interpretation in Generative Grammar*. Cambridge, MA: MIT Press.
——(1983). *Semantics and Cognition*. Cambridge, MA: MIT Press.
——(1987). 'The status of thematic relations in linguistic theory', *Linguistic Inquiry 18*: 369–412.
——(1990). *Semantic Structures*. Cambridge, MA: MIT Press.
Katz, J. J. (1972). *Semantic Theory*. New York: Harper and Row.
Katz, J. J. and Fodor, J. (1963). 'The structure of a semantic theory', *Language 39*: 170–210.
Kenny, A. (1963). *Actions, Emotions, and Will*. New York: Humanities Press.
Keyser, S. J. and Roeper. T. (1984). 'On the middle and ergative constructions in English', *Linguistic Inquiry 15*: 381–416.
Klein, E. and Sag, I. (1985). 'Type-driven translation', *Linguistics and Philosophy 8*: 163–202.
Krifka, M. (1987). 'Nominal reference and temporal constitution'. Manuscript. Tübingen.
Kunze, J. (1986). 'Phasen, Zeitrelationen und zeitbezogene Inferenzen', in *Probleme der Selektion und Semantik*. Berlin: Akademie-Verlag.
Lakoff, G. (1970). *Irregularity in Syntax*. New York: Holt, Rinehart, and Winston.
——(1971). 'On generative semantics', in D. Steinberg and L. Jakobovits (eds.), *Semantics: An Interdisciplinary Reader*. Cambridge: Cambridge University Press.
Levin, B. (1989). 'Towards a lexical organization of English verbs'. Manuscript, Northwestern University.
——and Rapoport, T. R. (1988). 'Lexical subordination', in *Papers from the 24th Regional Meeting of the Chicago Linguistic Society*, 275–89.
——and Rappaport, M. (1986). 'The formation of adjectival passives', *Linguistic Inquiry 17*: 623–62.
——(1988). 'On the nature of unaccusativity', in J. Carter and R.-M. Dechaine (eds.), *Proceedings of the North East Linguistic Society (NELS 19)*, Cornell University 1988. GLSA Publications.
Levin, L. (1986). 'Operations on lexical forms: Unaccusative rules in Germanic Languages', Ph.D. dissertation, MIT, Cambridge, MA.
Lloyd, G. E. R. (1968). *Aristotle: The Growth and Structure of his Thought*. Cambridge: Cambridge University Press.
McConnell-Ginet, S. (1982). 'Adverbs and logical form: A linguistically realistic theory', *Language 58*: 144–84.
McKeon, R. (1941). *The Basic Works of Aristotle*. New York: Random House.
Modrak, D. (1987). *Aristotle: The Power of Perception*. Cambridge: Cambridge University Press.
Moravcsik, J. M. (1975). 'Aita as generative factor in Aristotle's philosophy', *Dialogue 14*: 622–38.
Mourelatos, A. (1978). 'Events, states, and processes', *Linguistics and Philosophy 2*: 415–34.
Parsons, T. (1985). 'Underlying events in English', in E. LePore and B. McLaughlin (eds.), *Actions and Events*. Oxford: Blackwell.

―― (1990). *Events in the Semantics of English*. Cambridge, MA: MIT Press.
Pelletier, J. and Schubert, L. (1989). 'Mass expressions', in D. Gabbay and F. Guenther (eds.), *Handbook of Philosophical Logic, Vol. 4*. Dordrecht: Reidel, 387–453.
Perlmutter, D. (1978). 'Impersonal passive and the unaccusative hypothesis', *Proceedings of the Annual Meeting of the Berkeley Linguistic Society 4*: 157–87.
Pesetsky, D. (1987). 'Binding problems with experiencer verbs', *Linguistic Inquiry 18*: 126–40.
Pustejovsky, J. (1989a). 'Issues in computational lexical semantics', in *Proceedings of the European Association for Computational Linguistics* (pp. xvii–xxv). Manchester, UK, April 1989.
―― (1989b). 'The geometry of events', in C. Tenny (ed.), *Generative Approaches to Aspect*. Cambridge, MA: MIT Lexicon Project.
―― (1991). 'The generative lexicon'. *Computational Linguistics 17(4): 409–41*.
―― (to appear). *The Generative Lexicon: A Computational Theory of Lexical Semantics*. Cambridge, MA: Bradford Books/MIT Press.
Pustejovsky, J. and Boguraev, B. (1991). 'Lexical knowledge representation and natural language processing'. *IBM Journal of Research and Development 35(4)*.
Quillian, M. R. (1968). 'Semantic memory', in M. Minsky (ed.), *Semantic Information Processing*. Cambridge, MA: MIT Press, 227–70.
Rapoport, T. R. (1990). 'Secondary predication and the lexical representation of verbs'. *Machine Translation 5*: 31–55.
―― (to appear). 'Verbs in depictives and resultatives', in J. Pustejovsky (ed.), *Semantics and the Lexicon*. Dordrecht: Kluwer.
Rappaport, M., Laughren, M. and Levin, B. (to appear). 'Levels of lexical representation', in J. Pustejovsky (ed.), *Semantics and the Lexicon*. Dordrecht: Kluwer.
―― and Levin, B. (1988). 'What to do with theta-roles', in W. Wilkens (ed.), *Thematic Relations*. New York: Academic Press, 7–36.
―― (1989). 'Is there evidence for deep unaccusativity? An analysis of resultative constructions'. Manuscript, Bar Ilan University and Northwestern University.
Reinhart, T. (1976). *The Syntactic Domain of Anaphora*. Ph.D. dissertation, MIT, Cambridge, MA.
Rohrer, C. (1977). 'Die Beschreibung einiger Spanischer Verbalperiphrasen im Rahmen eines Zeitlogischen Systems', in C. Rohrer (ed.), *On the Logical Analysis of Tense and Aspect*. Tübingen: TBL Verlag Gunter Narr.
Rohrer, C. (ed.). (1977). *On the Logical Analysis of Tense and Aspect*. Tübingen: TBL Verlag Gunter Narr.
Ryle, G. (1949). *The Concept of Mind*. London: Barnes and Noble.
Scha, R., and Bruin, J. de (1988). 'The interpretation of relational nouns', in *Proceedings of the 26th Annual Meeting of the Association for Computational Linguistics*. Buffalo, NY, 25–32.
Schank, R. (1975). *Conceptual Information Processing*. Amsterdam: North-Holland.
Simpson, J. (1983). 'Resultatives', in L. Levin and A. Zaenen (eds.), *Papers in Lexical–Functional Grammar*. Bloomington, IN: Indiana University Linguistics Club.
Talmy, L. (1985). 'Lexicalization patterns', in T. Shopen (ed.), *Language Typology and Syntactic Description*. Cambridge: Cambridge University Press.
Tenny, C. (1987). 'Grammaticalizing aspect and affectedness'. Ph.D. dissertation, MIT, Cambridge, MA.
―― (1989). "The aspectual interface hypothesis'. Lexicon Project Working Papers 31, MIT, Cambridge, MA.
Vendler, Z. (1967). *Linguistics and Philosophy*. Ithaca: Cornell University Press.
Verkuyl, H. (1972). *On the Compositional Nature of the Aspects*. Dordrecht: Reidel.
―― (1989). 'Aspectual classes and aspectual distinctions'. *Linguistics and Philosophy 12*: 39–94.

Vlach, F. (1981). 'The semantics of the progressive', in P. Tedeschi and A. Zaenen (eds.), *Syntax and Semantics, Vol. 14, Tense and Aspect*. New York: Academic Press.

Weinreich, U. (1972). *Explorations in Semantic Theory*. The Hague: Mouton.

Wilks, Y. (1975). 'A preferential pattern seeking semantics for natural language inference', *Artificial Intelligence 6*: 53–74.

Williams, E. (1981). 'Argument structure and morphology'. *Linguistic Review 1*: 81–114.

——(1987). 'Binding and linking'. Manuscript, UMASS. Amherst.

Wright, G. H. von (1963). *Norm and Action*. London: Routledge and Kegan Paul.

3

The Algebra of Events

EMMON BACH

1 INTRODUCTION

A number of writers have commented on the close parallels between the mass-count distinction in nominal systems and the aspectual classification of verbal expressions (Allen, 1966; Mourelatos, 1978; L. Carlson, 1981; Hoepelman and Rohrer, 1980) that has been the subject of much attention in recent years in linguistics and philosophy. To take just one class of examples for now, there is a parallel between the two sets of distinctions in their cooccurrence patterns with expressions denoting numbers or amounts, as in Examples (1a)–(4b):

(1) (a) Much mud was in evidence.
    (b) (*)Much dog was in evidence.

(2) (a) John slept a lot last night.
    (b) (*)John found a unicorn a lot last night.

(3) (a) Many dogs were in the yard.
    (b) (*)Many muds were on the floor.

(4) (a) John fell asleep three times during the night.
    (b) (*)John slept three times last night.

(By the use of "(*)" I intend to indicate two things: that we have to do a certain amount of work to impose a special interpretation on the sentence and that the interpretation is shaped by the presence of the number or quantity expression.)

The basic aim of this paper is to try to elucidate this proportion: events: processes:: things: stuff. The account draws heavily on a recent paper by Godehard Link on the count-mass-plural domain (Link, 1983) as well as on the work of a number of writers who have contributed a great deal to our understanding of "verb-classification".[1] In Section 2, I review briefly the classification and in Section 3 Link's analysis for the nominal domain. In Section 4, I set forth our proposals about events and processes and in Section 5 take up a number of problems, some with, some without, solutions.

Emmon Bach, 'The Algebra of Events', *Linguistics and Philosophy* 9 (1986) 5–16. © 1986 Swets & Zeitlinger Publishers.

[1] Besides the writers mentioned in the first paragraph, see for example, the excellent survey in Dowty (1979) and the references cited there. The classic modern works dealing with verb-classification are Kenny (1963), and Vendler (1957). To my knowledge, Verkuyl (1972) was the first extensive work which recognized the importance of these distinctions for linguistic theory.

2 EVENTS, PROCESSES, STATES

Here's a scheme of the kinds of distinctions we want to deal with (based on L. Carlson, 1981, but using our terminology in part):

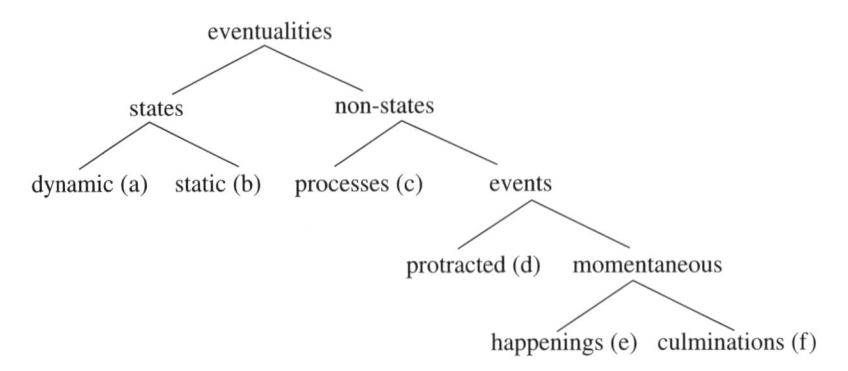

```
                        eventualities
                       /            \
                   states          non-states
                   /    \          /         \
          dynamic (a) static (b) processes (c)  events
                                              /      \
                                       protracted (d)  momentaneous
                                                       /         \
                                                 happenings (e)  culminations (f)
```

Typical examples are:

(a) sit, stand, lie + LOC
(b) be drunk, be in New York, own x, love x, resemble x
(c) walk, push a cart, be mean (Agentive)
(d) build x, walk to Boston
(e) recognize, notice, flash once
(f) die, reach the top

I will take it as given that it is necessary to have at least this much of a classification if we are to deal adequately with the syntax and semantics of English. A great deal of evidence for this point has been given in the last several years, for example in connection with attempts to understand the English progressive and similar constructions in other languages.[2] Most recently, Hans Kamp (1981) and E. Hinrichs (1981) have shown the necessity for these distinctions for interpreting narrative structures.

3 MASS, COUNT, AND PLURAL IN THE NOMINAL SYSTEM

In the work alluded to above, G. Link (1983) argues for the adoption of a somewhat more richly structured model than those made available, for example, in Montague's work.[3] In this section, I will briefly sketch the outlines of Link's system.

The main idea in Link's semantics is to give more structure to the domain of individuals. Along with ordinary individuals like John and Mary as in standard interpretations of the predicate calculus or in Montague's work we are to have plural individuals like those denoted by *the children* or *John and Mary* as well as quantities of "stuff" or matter that corresponds to individuals of both kinds, such as the gold in Terry's ring or the stuff that makes up the plural individual John and Mary.[4]

---

[2] Dowty (1977), Vlach (1981), for example.
[3] It is important to notice that Link's proposals differ crucially from previous attempts to deal with plurals which constructed interpretations for plurals in purely set-theoretic ways, as for example in Bennett's (1974) classic treatment.
[4] Strictly speaking, we will have the corresponding NP denotations, that is, property sets for the individuals mentioned. I ignore this complication throughout the paper.

Moreover, certain relations among these various subdomains and the elements making them up are proposed. I present the essentials in an informal way (for precise details the reader is referred to Link, 1983).

Start with a set A_i of individuals of the more familiar sort, for example, John, Mary, this table, Terry's ring. We extend this domain by means of a join operation to define a superset E as follows:

(i) $A_i \subseteq E_i$
(ii) If $\alpha, \beta \in E_i$ then the *i*-join (individual join: $\alpha \sqcup_i \beta$) of α and $\beta \in E$.

So the *i*-join of John and Mary is in E_i if each of John and Mary is. We establish a partial ordering on the members of E_i ($\leq_i$) by saying that α is "less than or equal to" (or "is an individual part (*i*-part) of") β just in case the *i*-join of α and β is just β itself. Thus the individual John is an *i*-part of the plural individuals John and Mary or Terry's ring and John. The individuals from which we started are atoms in the big structure that we are building.

Among the elements of A_i (and hence E_i) there is a subset which forms a special subsystem of its own. These are the portions of matter or stuff, for example, the gold of which Terry's ring is composed. This subsystem has its own join and partial ordering (*m*-join: $\sqcup_m$; *m*-part: $\leq_m$). Call this set D_i. Finally, we need to specify the relationship between the system of D_i and the rest of the domain. We do this by assuming a mapping h_i from individuals (atomic and plural) to the stuff out of which they are composed. This mapping should satisfy the requirement that the ordering $\leq_i$ among the individuals be preserved in the ordering $\leq_m$ among the quantities of matter making them up (it is a homomorphism). Moreover, $h_i(x) = x$ just in case $x \in D_i$. For example, if John is an *i*-part of the plural individual Terry's ring and John, then the stuff making up John had better be an *m*-part of the stuff making up Terry's ring and John. Note that we have two different part-whole relations. John is an *i*-part of the individual John and Mary, but John's arm is not an individual part of John, both are atoms. On the other hand, the stuff making up John's arm is an *m*-part of the stuff making up John. Note further that the same quantity of stuff can correspond to many different individuals. For example, there may be an individual falling into the extension of the singular count noun *man*, say John, but there is also a plural individual falling under the extension of the plural noun *cells* such that the values for h_i given the two arguments are identical. The two individuals are members of the equivalence class induced by the relation of material identity. Link calls a system of this sort a "Boolean model structure with homogeneous kernel" (*boosk*).

Some consequences of Link's construction that I find interesting and apposite for the present context are these (I haven't given enough details to show that these consequences follow):

(5) Suppose Hengsta is a horse and Hengist is a horse. Then the plural individual Hengsta and Hengist is not a horse, but is in the extension of *horses* (contrast mass terms).

(6) Suppose the plural individual *A* and *B* is in the extension of *horses* and likewise *C* and *D*. Then the plural individual *A, B, C,* and *D* is also in the extension of *horses* (cf. mass terms).

(7) Even if the individual that is the quantity of gold composing Terry's ring is old, Terry's ring need not be.

(8) The two meanings of sentences like *John and Mary lifted the box* (each vs. together) can be nicely represented in Link's semantics by adding the interpretation provided for the plural individual to the interpretation provided, say, in Montague's PTQ.

4 THE ALGEBRA OF EVENTS AND PROCESSES

We now want to try out Link's ideas in the domain of eventualities, that is, to characterize the structure of the model when we extend it to the domain of events and processes, which for the moment I will consider just as new kinds of elements in the (sorted) domain. I will start by considering events to be analogous to the singular and plural individuals and bounded processes ('bits of process') analogous to the portions of matter that make up the 'material extensions' of those individuals.

Our new system will then include the following:

(1) E_e: the set of events with join operations $\sqcup_e$ and partial ordering $\leq_e$ (a complete atomic Boolean algebra);
(2) $A_e \subseteq A_e$: atomic events;
(3) $D_e \subseteq A_e$: bits of process with join $\sqcup_p$ and partial ordering $\leq_p$ (a complete join semilattice);
(4) In addition, we will need two temporal relations on $E_e \times E_e$:
  $\propto$: "strictly precedes" (tr., irr., asymm.),
  $\circ$: "overlaps" (nontr., refl., symm.) (cf. Bach, 1981; Kamp, 1980);
(5) a homomorphism h_e from $\langle E_e, \sqcup_e, \leq_e, \propto, \circ \rangle$ to $\langle D_e, \sqcup_p, \leq_p, \propto, \circ \rangle$ such that
  (i) $h_e(\alpha) = \alpha$ iff $\alpha \in D_e$,
  (ii) $h_e(\alpha \sqcup_e \beta) = h_e(\alpha) \sqcup_p h_e(\beta)$, and
  (iii) $\alpha R \beta \Rightarrow h_e(\alpha) R' h_e(\beta)$ for $R = \leq_e, \propto, \circ$ and $R' = \leq_p, \propto$, respectively.

For purposes of illustration, I will assume that tenseless clauses of English are to be interpreted as denoting sets of eventualities, i.e. members of the domain E_e (for some discussion of the general kind of model structure I assume, see Bach, forthcoming). So here are some examples of the kinds of eventualities that correspond to the above distinctions:

(9) John kiss Mary: atomic event
(10) Mary stumble and Mary twist her ankle: plural event
(11) Mary stumble: atomic event
(12) People discover the hidden cove: plural event
(13) Sally build a cabin: atomic event
(14) Sally pound in a nail: atomic event
(15) Jones poison the populace: atomic event
(16) Jones pour poison into the water main: atomic event

Our homomorphism h (henceforth I will drop subscripts on all symbols where it is clear from context which domain we are considering) will deliver up for us the bounded bits of process corresponding to instances of each of these event types. Just as in the case of the nominal domain it is exceedingly difficult to find English expressions which correspond to these 'pure processes' (cf. our remarks on "(*)" after our first examples). Some intuitions I want to capture with regard to the above examples are these:

Ad (10) and (11): a plural event of type (10) has (necessarily) a singular event of type (11) as an *i*-part, and the processes associated by *h* with the latter is a *p*-part of the process associated with the former.

Ad (13) and (14): an event of type (14) might very well be such that its process is a *p*-part of the process associated with an event of type (13).

Ad (15) and (16): Events of these two types might be materially (processually) equivalent while the events themselves are different. Thus, Jones might very well intentionally pour poison into the water main (in order to rid waterbeds of bedfish) and not intentionally poison the populace (cf. Davidson, 1980, *passim*).

Just as in the nominal domain (Link, 1983), I will assume that our interpretation assigns various predicates to different classes according as they fall under the sort of classification outlined above. (HOW we decide or do this will not be my concern in this paper.) So Dying names an atomic kind of event, Running doesn't, and so on. Familiar properties of these various kinds of eventualities will follow, such as indivisibility and additivity (cf. L. Carlson, 1981; Bach, 1981): no proper *p*-part of a dying is a dying; the fusion of two runnings is a running, but no two dyings are a dying. I will return below to some interesting problems connected with such facts.

5 SOME PARALLELS AND PUZZLES

We have found it quite instructive to think about parallels and differences obtaining between the two domains. In a number of places questions and observations about one of the domains have led us to consider problems in the other domain in a new light.

5.1 Packaging and Grinding

It has frequently been observed that practically any count noun or name[5] can be used as a mass term: *There was dog splattered all over the road; Much missionary was eaten at the festival* (David Lewis's Universal Grinder, cf. Pelletier, 1975). Moreover, the opposite switch occurs as well: *muds* = 'kinds of mud', *ice-creams* = 'portions of ice-cream' (Universal Packager). In each case, we have a change of meaning with no overt marking in the form of the word.

In the verbal domain, we find the same sort of phenomenon. Dowty (1972) observed that practically any process verb can be used 'eventually', given the right context.

One of his examples was the process verb *look for*. One of the characteristics of process verbs is that they don't occur comfortably in the context *NP finished Ving: ? I finishes looking for a unicorn*. Yet in the context of a library with a well-defined search procedure, a sentence like *I finished looking for a book* seems perfectly ordinary.

In English, the way of switching back and forth between count and mass, event and process typically involves no change in the forms involved. The difference is rather induced by the context. In other languages, overt morphological processes or relationships are available or obligatory, for example, in the perfective-imperfective contrasts in Slavic languages. This raises important questions of principle for the analysis of English. Do we want to invoke formation rules with zero-morphology (identity operations in the

---

[5] Link does not deal with the use of names in mass contexts: *They put five pounds of Porky into the stew.*

syntax of words), as in Link's rule for forming the mass-term counterpart to a count noun like *apple*? Or do we want to somehow give meanings for words that are unspecified along this dimension?

It seems to me that there is an asymmetry in these relations between count and non-count meanings that runs in the same direction in the two domains. That is, if we start with a count meaning and derive the non-count meaning (as in Link's rule) there seems to be a regular and predictable meaning. The mass-term *apple* seems to mean the stuff such that there is at least one apple such that that stuff stands in the constitution-relation to the apple (but see below, Section 5.3 for some remaining problems with this account). On the other hand, going in the other direction, the connection seems much less systematic, as already noted. A beer may be a serving of beer or a kind of beer. Similarly, in the verbal domain, when we put a process expression into a count context, we must come up with some kind of corresponding event, but just what it is is relatively free, perhaps the beginning of the process in question, or some bounded portion of it. This asymmetry is predicted by our formal set-up: there is a function (homomorphism) from the count elements to the non-count ones, but it is a many-to-one mapping so that we can't in general expect a unique answer when we ask what count element this portion of non-count stuff might correspond to.

Count elements come as already bounded and discrete items. Therefore we can count them. Non-count elements don't and therefore need some additional specification in order to be used as countable expressions with plurals or numbers. Further, expressions which carve out measures or quantities of stuff—pounds of, portions of, etc.—cannot go with pure count-items in the singular, but demand interpretation of the count-item as mass-term or process counterpart. Moreover, for plurals size and measure are relevant to determining naturalness and usefulness of the particular expressions; *two tons of horses* is odd for practical reasons in a way that *two tons of beans* or *fifty tons of horses* are not (cf. L. Carlson, 1981, on these and many other details). There are interesting puzzles about counting that we will return to below (Section 5.4).

5.2 The Partitive Puzzle

Dowty (1977) and others have discussed the so-called 'imperfective paradox' (I prefer to call it a puzzle). Briefly, the puzzle is this: how can we characterize the meaning of a progressive sentence like (17) on the basis of the meaning of a simple sentence like (18) when (17) can be true of a history without (18) ever being true?

(17) John was crossing the street.

(18) John crossed the street.

(See Vlach, 1981; Dowty, 1979.)

Naturally, we want to use the apparatus we have set up to provide an account of the English progressive, perhaps along the lines of Vlach (1981). Thinking about how to do this has led us to see that there is a perfectly parallel problem in the nominal domain, which we call the 'partitive puzzle'.

Consider Link's account of the following sentence:

(19) There is apple in the salad.

Link's interpretation amounts to this: there are some apples, such that some of the stuff making them up is present in the salad. Note the existential quantification over apples;

the sentence could not be true of a history which never had any apples in it. This seems reasonable enough for this sentence, but consider the following:

(20) This is part of a paper on natural language metaphysics.

(21) We found part of a Roman aqueduct.

It seems as if (20) could be true even though (alas!) the paper in question never reached fulfilment, and (21) true when there no longer is an aqueduct or even if progress on the construction was interrupted forever by hordes of barbarians from the north.

Let us look more closely at Link's account. The denotation of the mass term correspondent m_p of a predicate P is given as this (p. 309):

$$[\![m_p]\!] := \{x \in D | x \leq \sup[h[\![P]\!]]\}.$$

(Here, *sup* stands for *supremum*.) That is, the denotation of *apple* (used as a predicative mass term) is the set of quantities of matter that are *m*-parts of the value of *h* applied to the set of apples in the world. Thus, no apples, no apple. But there could surely be a world in which it was possible to artificially manufacture apple without there being any apples, or for less far-fetched examples, consider again Examples (20) and (21).

Such examples show that we need to allow for a more indirect relation between the denotation of a mass predicative mass term and the corresponding count predicate. Basically, we need to be able to say when certain stuff is of the right kind to qualify as falling under the extension of the mass term, or better we need to *assume* that we can say when this is the case. To actually give criteria is no part of linguistics (cf. Putnam 1975, *passim*).

Further, although we have assumed that the two domains of things and stuff are separate, it seems to me to be reasonable to assume that our knowledge of what qualifies as a quantity of apple or mud or gold is based on our understanding of what is meant by the term phrases *apples, mud*, or *gold*, understood as names for kinds (G. Carlson, 1977) or properties (Chierchia, 1982). Both Carlson and Chierchia argue that such terms are more intensional than the properties of Montague, which are functions from world-time pairs to individuals. We may say that a property or kind determines such a function, which then may be used to get the denotations of the corresponding predicatives *apple, gold*, and *mud*. So to say that there is apple in the salad is to say that there is some stuff in the salad of the right sort as to qualify as apple and the latter involves appealing to our knowledge of the kind of apples or the property of being an apple. It should then fall out of our theory that particular apples are made of apple and so on.

5.3 How Old Is the Gold?

Link provides a nice analysis of the puzzle presented by a sentence like this:

(22) The gold making up Terry's ring is old but the ring itself is new (not old).

Puzzles like this one are among the best evidence for not identifying things with their material counterparts. But there is still a problem.

The interpretation of (22) is this: The x such that x makes up Terry's ring and is gold is old but Terry's ring is not old. No contradiction, since x and Terry's ring are not the same thing, x is just the value of h with Terry's ring as argument. But now consider a sentence like (23):

(23) The snow making up this snowman is quite new but the H_2O making it up is very old (and the H and O even older!).

The interpretation of this sentence comes out like this: The x such that x constitutes the snowman and x is snow is new but the y such that y constitutes the snowman and y is water is very old (not new). This *is* contradictory according to Link's account since x and y must be identical (since h is a function). If we follow Link's sage advice—"our guide in ontological matters has to be language itself" (Link, 1983, pp. 303f.)—then it seems to me that we have to set things up in such a way that we can refer to individuals under a description, somehow. This puzzle is closely connected to the next one.

If we follow Link's advice, then we must acknowledge that two things with contradictory properties cannot be identical. Thus the snow making up the snowman and the H_2O making it up must be different, and neither can be equated with the undifferentiated quantity of matter given by Link's homomorphism. What to do?

The first possibility is to acknowledge that our language allows us to talk about chains of composition, so to speak. The snow in the snowman is itself made up of the water in the snowman (plus air) and so on. What the example shows, then, is that we cannot use the constitution relation directly in an interpretation of a phrase like *the snow making up the snowman*. Our interpretation of such phrases must be such that it does not hold that if x makes up a and y makes up a then $x=y$. We can essentially keep all of Link's apparatus including the homomorphism and the equivalence classes generated by it but merely amend the way in which English words like *make up, constitute* or phrases like *the gold in the ring* are interpreted.

A second way would be to remove altogether the entities in D from the domain of individuals. I explore one way of doing this based on Cresswell's (1973) metaphysics of possible worlds and individuals in Bach, forthcoming. This would amount to saying something like this: *Stoff an sich* (just like the *Ding an sich*) can have no properties, at least as far as our language is concerned.

5.4 How Many Things Are There in the Room?

In both domains many writers have pointed to characteristic properties like additivity, subdivisibility, antiadditivity and antisubdivisibility which play clear roles in giving an account of entailment relations among sentences: Hengist's ear can't be a horse, mud plus mud is mud, a horse plus a horse isn't a horse, and so on. But in both domains there are clear and ordinary examples of count items that don't follow these restrictions. These are words like *thing, event, happen*, and so on. Suppose it is true that something happened, then in the normal case there are smaller subevents that make up the big thing that happened that are also happenings. Similarly for things. In both domains we are at something of a loss to try to answer questions like these:

(24) How many things are there in the room?

(25) How many events took place in the last hour?

Gupta (1980) has stressed the importance of criteria of reidentification and individuation in the logic of common nouns. Our discussion here shows that principles of individuation are crucial for expressions and concepts in the verbal domain as well. We follow Link in *not* requiring that the subdomains D_i and D_e be atomic Boolean algebras. This is as it should be. It is not part of linguistics to decide whether all matter is atomic or all happenings are reducible to little granules of process. Indeed, if contemporary physical theories are to be believed, such ultimate questions are basically incoherent. Events and processes are disjoint, and this seems to be more an artifact of our language or conceptualizations of the world than something about the world itself, so that probably here too our strictly semantic theories should remain silent.

ACKNOWLEDGEMENTS

A large part of the substance of this paper derives from joint work with Barbara Partee, first presented by us at a colloquium at Stanford University, hence the frequent "we". I take full responsibility for errors or infelicities. Grateful acknowledgment is tendered to the Max Planck Institut für Psycholinguistik in Nijmegen, which supported part of the work reported on here.

REFERENCES

Allen, R. L. (1966). *The Verb System of Present-Day English*. The Hague: Mouton.
Bach, Emmon (1981). 'On Time, Tense, and Aspect: An Essay in English Metaphysics', in Peter Cole (ed.), *Radical Pragmatics*. New York: Academic Press, 62–81.
Bach, Emmon (forthcoming). 'The Metaphysics of Natural Language', to appear in *Proceedings of the Seventh International Congress on Logic, Methodology, and Philosophy of Science*.
Bennett, Michael (1974). Some extensions of a Montague fragment of English. Ph.D.
Carlson, Gregory (1977). 'Reference to Kinds in English'. Ph.D. dissertation, University of Massachusetts, Amherst.
Carlson, Lauri (1981). 'Aspect and Quantification', in Philip Tedeschi and Annie Zaenen (eds.), *Syntax and Semantics*, vol. **14**. New York: Academic Press, 31–64.
Chierchia, Gennaro (1982). 'Nominalizations and Montague Grammar: A Semantics Without Types for Natural Language', *Linguistics and Philosophy* **5**, 303–54.
Cresswell, Max J. (1973). *Logics and Languages*. London: Methuen.
Davidson, Donald (1980). *Essays on Actions and Events*. Oxford: Clarendon Press.
Dowty, David R. (1972). 'Studies in the Logic of Verb Aspect and Time Reference in English', unpublished Ph.D. dissertation, The University of Texas, Austin.
——(1977). 'Toward a Semantic Analysis of Verb Aspect and the English "Imperfective" Progressive', *Linguistics and Philosophy* **1**: 45–79.
——(1979). *Word Meaning and Montague Grammar*. Dordrecht: Reidel.
Gupta, Anil (1980). *The Logic of Common Nouns*. New Haven: Yale University.
Hinrichs, Erhard (1981). *Temporale Anaphora im Englischen*, University of Tuebingen, Magisterarbeit.
Hoepelman, J. and Rohrer, C. (1980). 'On the Mass Count Distinction and the French Imparfait and Passe Simple', in C. Rohrer (ed.), *Time, Tense and Aspect*. Tuebingen: Niemeyer, 629–45.
Kamp, Hans (1980). 'Some Remarks on the Logic of Change, Part I', in Christian Rohrer (ed.), *Time, Tense, and Quantifiers*. Tuebingen: Niemeyer, 135–79.
——(1981). 'Événements, représentations discursives et référence temporelle', *Language* **64**: 39–64.
Kenny, Anthony (1963). *Action, Emotion, and Will*. New York: Humanities Press.
Link, Godehard (1983). 'The Logical Analysis of Plurals and Mass Terms', in R. Bäuerle, C. Schwarze, and A. von Stechow (eds.), *Meaning, Use, and Interpretation of Language*. Berlin: Walter de Gruyter, 302–23.
Mourelatos, Alexander P. D. (1978). 'Events, Processes, and States', *Linguistics and Philosophy* **2**: 415–34.
Pelletier, F. J. (1975). 'Non-Singular Reference', in F. J. Pelletier (ed.), *Mass Terms: Some Philosophical Problems*. Dordrecht: Reidel, 1–14.
Putnam, Hilary (1975). *Mind, Language, and Reality*, Philosophical Papers, Vol. 2. Cambridge: Cambridge University Press.
Vendler, Zeno (1957). 'Verbs and Times', *Philosophical Review* **56**: 143–60.
Verkuyl, Henk (1972). *On the Compositional Nature of the Aspects*. Dordrecht: Reidel.
Vlach, Frank (1981). 'The Semantics of the Progressive', *Syntax and Semantics* **14**: 271–92.

4

The Tenses of Verbs

HANS REICHENBACH

A particularly important form of token-reflexive symbol is found in the tenses of verbs. The tenses determine time with reference to the time point of the act of speech, i.e., of the token uttered. A closer analysis reveals that the time indication given by the tenses is of a rather complex structure.

Let us call the time point of the token the *point of speech*. Then the three indications, 'before the point of speech', 'simultaneous with the point of speech', and 'after the point of speech', furnish only three tenses; since the number of verb tenses is obviously greater, we need a more complex interpretation. From a sentence like 'Peter had gone' we see that the time order expressed in the tense does not concern one event, but two events, whose positions are determined with respect to the point of speech. We shall call these time points the *point of the event* and the *point of reference*. In the example the point of the event is the time when Peter went; the point of reference is a time between this point and the point of speech. In an individual sentence like the one given it is not clear which time point is used as the point of reference. This determination is rather given by the context of speech. In a story, for instance, the series of events recounted determines the point of reference which in this case is in the past, seen from the point of speech; some individual events lying outside this point are then referred, not directly to the point of speech, but to this point of reference determined by the story. The following example, taken from W. Somerset Maugham's *Of Human Bondage*, may make these time relations clear:

But Philip ceased to think of her a moment after he had settled down in his carriage. He thought only of the future. He had written to Mrs. Otter, the *massière* to whom Hayward had given him an introduction, and had in his pocket an invitation to tea on the following day.

The series of events recounted here in the simple past determine the point of reference as lying before the point of speech. Some individual events, like the settling down in the carriage, the writing of the letter, and the giving of the introduction, precede the point of reference and are therefore related in the past perfect.

Another illustration for these time relations may be given by a historical narrative, a quotation from Macaulay:

In 1678 the whole face of things had changed ... eighteen years of misgovernment had made the ... majority desirous to obtain security for their liberties at any risk. The fury of their returning loyalty had spent itself in its first outbreak. In a very few months they had hanged and half-hanged, quartered and emboweled, enough to satisfy them. The Roundhead party seemed to be not merely overcome, but too much broken and scattered ever to rally again. Then commenced the reflux of public opinion. The nation began to find out to what a man it had intrusted without conditions all its dearest interests, on what a man it had lavished all its fondest affection.

Hans Reichenbach, 'The Tenses of Verbs', section 51 of *Elements of Symbolic Logic* (New York: The Macmillan Company, 1947), 287–98. © 1947 Maria Reichenbach.

The point of reference is here the year 1678. Events of this year are related in the simple past, such as the commencing of the reflux of public opinion, and the beginning of the discovery concerning the character of the king. The events preceding this time point are given in the past perfect, such as the change in the face of things, the outbreaks of cruelty, the nation's trust in the king.

In some tenses, two of the three points are simultaneous. Thus, in the simple past, the point of the event and the point of reference are simultaneous, and both are before the point of speech; the use of the simple past in the above quotation shows this clearly. This distinguishes the simple past from the present perfect. In the statement 'I have seen Charles' the event is also before the point of speech, but it is referred to a point simultaneous with the point of speech; i.e., the points of speech and reference coincide. This meaning of the present perfect may be illustrated by the following quotation from Keats:

> Much have I traveled in the realms of gold,
> And many goodly states and kingdoms seen;
> Round many western islands have I been
> Which bards in fealty to Apollo hold.

Comparing this with the above quotations we notice that here obviously the past events are seen, not from a reference point situated also in the past, but from a point of reference which coincides with the point of speech. This is the reason that the words of Keats are not of a narrative type but affect us with the immediacy of a direct report to the reader. We see that we need three time points even for the distinction of tenses which, in a superficial consideration, seem to concern only two time points. The difficulties which grammar books have in explaining the meanings of the different tenses originate from the fact that they do not recognize the three-place structure of the time determination given in the tenses.[1]

We thus come to the following tables, in which the initials 'E', 'R', and 'S' stand, respectively, for 'point of the event', 'point of reference', and 'point of speech', and in which the direction of time is represented as the direction of the line from left to right:

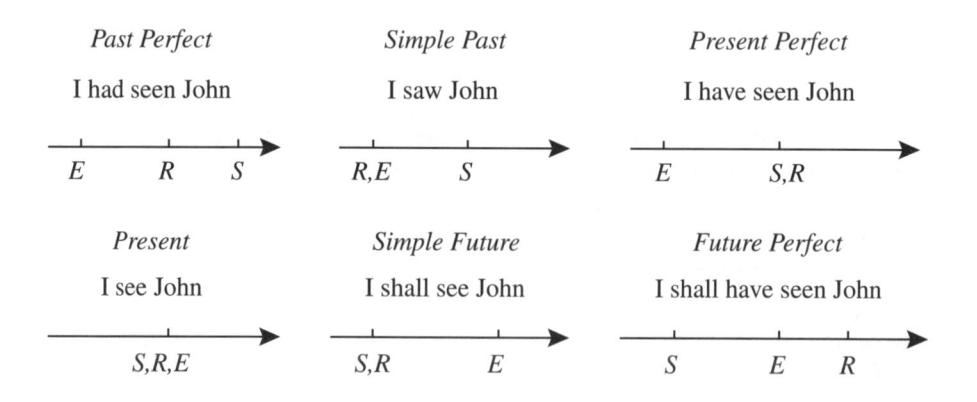

Past Perfect	Simple Past	Present Perfect
I had seen John	I saw John	I have seen John
$E \quad R \quad S \longrightarrow$	$R,E \quad\quad S \longrightarrow$	$E \quad\quad S,R \longrightarrow$

Present	Simple Future	Future Perfect
I see John	I shall see John	I shall have seen John
$S,R,E \longrightarrow$	$S,R \quad\quad E \longrightarrow$	$S \quad E \quad R \longrightarrow$

---

[1] In J. O. H. Jespersen's excellent analysis of grammar (*The Philosophy of Grammar*, H. Holt, New York, 1924) I find the three-point structure indicated for such tenses as the past perfect and the future perfect (p. 256), but not applied to the interpretation of the other tenses. This explains the difficulties which even Jespersen has in distinguishing the present perfect from the simple past (p. 269). He sees correctly the close connection between the present tense and the present perfect, recognizable in such sentences as 'now I have eaten enough'. But he gives a rather-vague definition of the present perfect and calls it 'a retrospective variety of the present'.

In some tenses, an additional indication is given concerning the time extension of the event. The English language uses the present participle to indicate that the event covers a certain stretch of time. We thus arrive at the following tables:

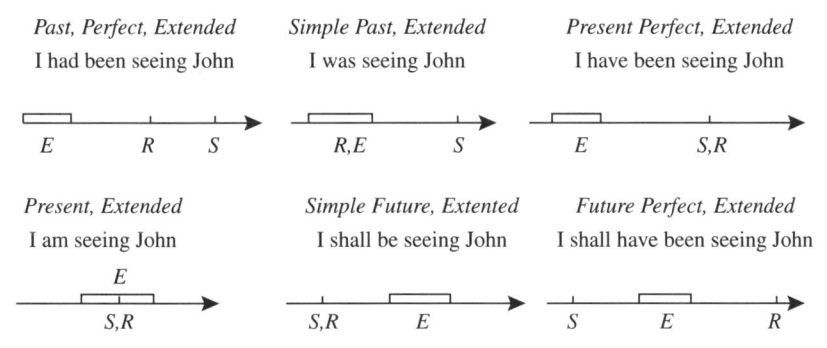

Past, Perfect, Extended *Simple Past, Extended* *Present Perfect, Extended*
I had been seeing John I was seeing John I have been seeing John

E   R   S   R,E   S   E   S,R

Present, Extended *Simple Future, Extended* *Future Perfect, Extended*
I am seeing John I shall be seeing John I shall have been seeing John

E
S,R   S,R   E   S   E   R

The extended tenses are sometimes used to indicate, not duration of the event, but repetition. Thus we say 'women are wearing larger hats this year' and mean that this is true for a great many instances. Whereas English expresses the extended tense by the use of the present participle, other languages have developed special suffixes for this tense. Thus the Turkish language possesses a tense of this kind, called *muzari*, which indicates repetition or duration, with the emphasis on repetition, including past and future cases. This tense is represented by the diagram

Turkish Muzari
görürüm

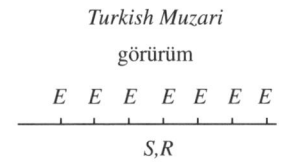

E   E   E   E   E   E
S,R

An example of this tense is the Turkish word 'görürüm', translatable as 'I usually see'. The syllable 'gör' is the root meaning 'see', 'ür' is the suffix expressing the muzari, and the 'üm' is the suffix expressing the first person 'I'.[2] The sentence 'I see' would be in Turkish 'görüyorum'; the only difference from the preceding example is given by the inflection 'üyor' in the middle of the word, expressing the present tense. The Greek language uses the *aorist* to express repetition or customary occurrence in the present tense. The aorist, however, is originally a nonextended past tense, and has assumed the second usage by a shift of meaning; in the sense of the extended tense it is called *gnomic aorist*.[3]

German and French do not possess extended tenses, but express such meanings by special words, such as the equivalents of 'always', 'habitually', and so on. An exception is the French simple past. The French language possesses here two different tenses, the *imparfait* and the *passé défini*. They differ in so far as the *imparfait* is an extended tense, whereas the *passé défini* is not. Thus we have

Imparfait   *Passé défini*
je voyais Jean   je vis Jean

R,E   S   R,E   S

---

[2] Turkish vowels with two dots are pronounced like the German vowels 'ö' and 'ü'.

[3] This shift of meaning is explainable as follows: One typical case of the past is stated, and to the listener is left the inductive inference that under similar conditions the same will be repeated in the future. A similar shift of meaning is given in the English 'Faint heart never won fair lady'. Cf. W. W. Goodwin, *Greek Grammar*, Ginn, Boston, 1930, p. 275.

We find the same distinction in Greek, the Greek imperfect corresponding to the French *imparfait*, and the Greek aorist, in its original meaning as a past tense, corresponding to the French passé défini. Languages which do not have a passé défini sometimes use another tense in this meaning; thus Latin uses the present perfect in this sense (historical perfect).

We may add here the remark that the adjective is of the same logical nature as the present participle of a verb. It indicates an extended tense. If we put the word 'hungry', for instance, in the place of the word 'seeing' in our tables of extended tenses, we obtain the same extended tenses. A slight difference in the usage is that adjectives are preferred if the duration of the event is long; therefore adjectives can often be interpreted as describing permanent properties of things. The transition to the extended tense, and from there to the permanent tense, is seen in the examples 'he produces', 'he is producing', 'he is productive'.

When we wish to express, not repetition or duration, but validity at all times, we use the present tense. Thus we say 'two times two is four'. There the present tense expressed in the copula 'is' indicates that the time argument is used as a free variable; i.e., the sentence has the meaning 'two times two is four at any time'. This usage represents a second temporal function of the present tense.

Actual language does not always keep to the schemas given in our tables. Thus the English language uses sometimes the simple past where our schema would demand the present perfect. The English present perfect is often used in the sense of the corresponding extended tense, with the additional qualification that the duration of the event reaches up to the point of speech. Thus we have here the schema

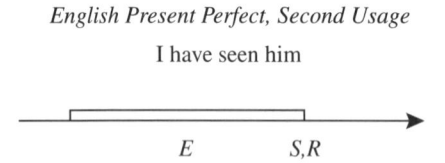

English Present Perfect, Second Usage

I have seen him

$$E \quad\quad S,R$$

In the sense of this schema we say, for instance, 'I have known him for ten years'. If duration of the event is not meant, the English language then uses the simple past instead of the present perfect, as in 'I saw him ten years ago'. German and French would use the present perfect here.

When several sentences are combined to form a compound sentence, the tenses of the various clauses are adjusted to one another by certain rules which the grammarians call the rules for the *sequence of tenses*. We can interpret these rules as the principle that, although the events referred to in the clauses may occupy different time points, the reference point should be the same for all clauses—a principle which, we shall say, demands *the permanence of the reference point*. Thus, the tenses of the sentence, 'I had mailed the letter when John came and told me the news', may be diagramed as follows:

(1) 1st clause: $E_1 - R_1 \quad -S$
    2nd clause: $\quad R_2, E_2 - S$
    3rd clause: $\quad R_3, E_3 - S$

Here the three reference points coincide. It would be incorrect to say, 'I had mailed the letter when John has come'; in such a combination the reference point would have been changed. As another example, consider the compound sentence, 'I have not decided which train I shall take'. That this sentence satisfies the rule of the permanence of the reference point is seen from the following diagram:

(2) 1st clause: E_1—S, R_1
    2nd clause: S, R_2—E_2

Here it would be incorrect to say: 'I did not decide which train I shall take'.

When the reference point is in the past, but the event coincides with the point of speech, a tense R—S, E is required. In this sense, the form 'he would do' is used, which can be regarded as derived from the simple future 'he will do' by a back-shift of the two points R and E. We say, for instance, 'I did not know that you would be here'; this sentence represents the diagram:

(3) 1st clause: R_1, E_1—S
    2nd clause: R_2 —S, E_2

The form 'I did not know that you were here' has a somewhat different meaning; it is used correctly only if the event of the man's being here extends to include the past time for which the 'I did not know' is stated, i.e., if the man was already here when I did not know it. Incidentally, in these sentences the forms 'would be' and 'were' do not have a modal function expressing irreality; i.e., they do not represent a conditional or a subjunctive, since the event referred to is not questioned. The nonmodal function is illustrated by the sentence 'I did not know that he was here', for which the form 'that he were here' appears incorrect.

When a time determination is added, such as is given by words like 'now' or 'yesterday', or by a nonreflexive symbol like 'November 7, 1944', it is referred, not to the event, but to the reference point of the sentence. We say, 'I met him yesterday'; that the word 'yesterday' refers here to the event obtains only because the points of reference and of event coincide. When we say, 'I had met him yesterday', what was yesterday is the reference point, and the meeting may have occurred the day before yesterday. We shall speak, therefore, of the *positional use of the reference point*; the reference point is used here as the carrier of the time position. Such usage, at least, is followed by the English language. Similarly, when time points are compared by means of words like 'when', 'before', or 'after', it is the reference points to which the comparison refers directly, not the events. Thus in the above example (1) the time points stated as identical by the word 'when' are the reference points of the three clauses, whereas the event of the first clause precedes that of the second and the third. Or consider the sentence, 'How unfortunate! Now that John tells me this I have mailed the letter'. The time stated here as identical with the time of John's telling the news is not the mailing of the letter but the reference point of the second clause, which is identical with the point of speech; and we have here the schema:

(4) 1st clause: S, R_1, E_1
    2nd clause: E_2—S, R_2

For this reason it would be incorrect to say, 'Now that John tells me this I mailed the letter'.

If the time relation of the reference points compared is not identity, but time sequence, i.e., if one is said to be before the other, the rule of the permanence of the reference point can thus no longer be maintained. In 'he telephoned before he came' R_1 is said to be before R_2; but, at least, the tenses used have the same structure. It is different with the example, 'he was healthier when I saw him than he is now'. Here we have the structure:

(5) 1st clause: R_1, E_1—S
    2nd clause: R_2, E_2—S
    3rd clause: S, R_3, E_3

In such cases, the rule of the permanence of the reference point is replaced by the more general rule of the *positional use of the reference point*. The first rule, therefore, must be regarded as representing the special case where the time relation between the reference points compared is identity.

Incidentally, the English usage of the simple past where other languages use the present perfect may be a result of the strict adherence to the principle of the positional use of the reference point. When we say, 'this is the man who drove the car', we use the simple past in the second clause because the positional principle would compel us to do so as soon as we add a time determination, as in 'this is the man who drove the car at the time of the accident'. The German uses here the present perfect, and the above sentence would be translated into 'dies ist der Mann, der den Wagen gefahren hat'. Though this appears more satisfactory than the English version, it leads to a disadvantage when a time determination is added. The German is then compelled to refer the time determination, not to the reference point, but to the event, as in 'dies ist der Mann, der den Wagen zur Zeit des Unglücksfalles gefahren hat'. In such cases, a language can satisfy either the principle of the permanence of the reference point or that of the positional use of the reference point, but not both.

The use of the future tenses is sometimes combined with certain deviations from the original meaning of the tenses. In the sentence 'Now I shall go' the simple future has the meaning S, R—E; this follows from the principle of the positional use of the reference point. However, in the sentence 'I shall go tomorrow' the same principle compels us to interpret the future tense in the form S—R, E. The simple future, then, is capable of two interpretations, and since there is no prevalent usage of the one or the other we cannot regard one interpretation as the correct one.[4] Further deviations occur in tense sequences. Consider the sentence: 'I shall take your photograph when you come'. The form 'when you will come' would be more correct; but we prefer to use here the present tense instead of the future. This usage may be interpreted as follows. First, the future tense is used in the first clause in the meaning S—R, E; second, in the second clause the point of speech is neglected. The neglect is possible because the word 'when' refers the reference point of the second clause clearly to a future event. A similar anomaly is found in the sentence, 'We shall hear the record when we have dined', where the present perfect is used instead of the future perfect 'when we shall have dined'.[5]

Turning to the general problem of the time order of the three points, we see from our tables that the possibilities of ordering the three time points are not exhausted. There are on the whole 13 possibilities, but the number of recognized grammatical tenses in English is only 6. If we wish to systematize the possible tenses we can proceed as follows. We choose the point of speech as the starting point; relative to it the point of reference

---

[4] The distinction between the French future forms *je vais voir* and *je verrai* may perhaps be regarded as representing the distinction between the order S, R—E and the order S—R, E.

[5] In some books on grammar we find the remark that the transition from direct to indirect discourse is accompanied by a shift of the tense from the present to the past. This shift, however, must not be regarded as a change in the meaning of the tense; it follows from the change in the point of speech. Thus 'I *am* cold' has a point of speech lying before that of 'I said that I *was* cold'.

can be in the past, at the same time, or in the future. This furnishes three possibilities. Next we consider the point of the event; it can be before, simultaneous with, or after the reference point. We thus arrive at $3 \cdot 3 = 9$ possible forms, which we call *fundamental forms*. Further differences of form result only when the position of the event relative to the point of speech is considered; this position, however, is usually irrelevant. Thus the form $S—E—R$ can be distinguished from the form $S, E—R$; with respect to relations between S and R on the one hand and between R and E on the other hand, however, these two forms do not differ, and we therefore regard them as representing the same fundamental form. Consequently, we need not deal with all the 13 possible forms and may restrict ourselves to the 9 fundamental forms.

For the 9 fundamental forms we suggest the following terminology. The position of R relative to S is indicated by the words 'past', 'present', and 'future'. The position of E relative to R is indicated by the words 'anterior', 'simple', and 'posterior', the word 'simple' being used for the coincidence of R and E. We thus arrive at the following names:

Structure	New Name	Traditional Name
$E—R—S$	Anterior past	Past perfect
$E, R—S$	Simple past	Simple past
$R—E—S$		
$R—S, E$	Posterior past	—
$R—S—E$		
$E—S, R$	Anterior present	Present perfect
S, R, E	Simple present	Present
$S, R—E$	Posterior present	Simple future
$S—E—R$		
$S, E—R$	Anterior future	Future perfect
$E—S—R$		
$S—R, E$	Simple future	Simple future
$S—R—E$	Posterior future	—

We see that more than one structure obtains only for the two *retrogressive* tenses, the posterior past and the anterior future, in which the direction $S—R$ is opposite to the direction $R—E$. If we wish to distinguish among the individual structures we refer to them as the first, second, and third posterior past or anterior future.

The tenses for which a language has no established forms are expressed by transcriptions. We say, for instance, 'I shall be going to see him' and thus express the posterior future $S—R—E$ by speaking, not directly of the event E, but of the act of preparation for it; in this way we can at least express the time order for events which closely succeed the point of reference. Languages which have a future participle have direct forms for the posterior future. Thus the Latin 'abiturus ero' represents this tense, meaning verbally 'I shall be one of those who will leave'. For the posterior past $R—E—S$ the form 'he would do' is used, for instance in 'I did not expect that he would win the race'. We met with this form in an above example where we interpreted it as the structure $R—S, E$; but this structure belongs to the same fundamental form as $R—E—S$ and may therefore be denoted by the same name. Instead of the form 'he would do', which grammar does not officially recognize as a tense,[6] transcriptions are frequently used.

---

[6] It is sometimes classified as a tense of the conditional mood, corresponding to the French conditional. In the examples considered above, however, it is not a conditional but a tense in the indicative mood.

Thus we say, 'I did not expect that he was going to win the race', or, in formal writing, 'the king lavished his favor on the man who was to kill him'. In the last example, the order R—E—S is expressed by the form 'was to kill', which conceives the event E, at the time R, as not yet realized, but as a destination.

Incidentally, the historical origin of many tenses is to be found in similar transcriptions. Thus 'I shall go' meant originally 'I am obliged to go'; the future-tense meaning developed because what I am obliged to do will be done by me at a later time.[7] The French future tense is of the same origin; thus the form 'je donnerai', meaning 'I shall give', is derived from 'je donner ai', which means 'I have to give'. This form of writing was actually used in Old French.[8] The double function of 'have', as expressing possession and a past tense, is derived from the idea that what I possess is acquired in the past; thus 'I have seen' meant originally 'I possess now the results of seeing', and then was interpreted as a reference to a past event.[9] The history of language shows that logical categories were not clearly seen in the beginnings of language but were the results of long developments; we therefore should not be astonished if actual language does not always fit the schema which we try to construct in symbolic logic. A mathematical language can be coordinated to actual language only in the sense of an approximation.

---

[7] In Old English no future tense existed, and the present tense was used both for the expression of the present and the future. The word 'shall' was used only in the meaning of obligation. In Middle English the word 'shall' gradually assumed the function of expressing the future tense. Cf. *The New English Dictionary*, Oxford, Vol. VIII, Pt. 2, S–Sh, 1914, p. 609, col. 3.

[8] This mode of expressing the future tense was preceded by a similar development of the Latin language, originating in vulgar Latin. Thus instead of the form 'dabo', meaning the future tense 'I shall give', the form 'dare habeo' was used, which means 'I have to give'. Cf. Ferdinand Brunot, *Précis de grammaire historique de la langue française*, Masson et Cie., Paris, 1899, p. 434.

[9] This is even more apparent when a two-place function is used. Thus 'I have finished my work' means originally 'I have my work finished', i.e., 'I possess my work as a finished one'. Cf. *The New English Dictionary*, Oxford, 1901, Vol. V, Pt. I, H, p. 127, col. 1–2. The German still uses the original word order, as in 'Ich habe meine Arbeit beendet'.

5

Tense Logic and the Logic of Earlier and Later

A.N. PRIOR

W. V. Quine once wrote a paper entitled 'Three Grades of Modal Involvement'.[1] Tense logic, like modal logic, is something about which some philosophers have misgivings, and like modal logic, it may be presented in a more or a less accommodating manner—it has, in Quine's terminology, its own 'grades of involvement'. I want to present here four such 'grades of tense-logical involvement', by presenting a series of calculi involving the notion of being true (or as Rescher says, 'realized') at an instant, making more and more controversial assumptions at each main stage.

I TENSE LOGICS AND U-CALCULI

We may begin from the juxtaposition of two calculi of E. J. Lemmon's, one a 'minimal' tense logic and one a minimal calculus of the earlier-later relation. Sometimes the tense logic, called K_t, is axiomatized with F (for 'It will be the case that—') and P (for 'It has been the case that—') as primitive symbols, with G (for 'It will always be the case that   ') defined as NFN, and H (for 'It has always been the case that—') as NPN. Here I take G and H as primitive, and define F as NGN and P as NHN, the postulates then becoming

      RG: $\vdash \alpha \to \vdash G\alpha$ RH: $\vdash \alpha \to \vdash H\alpha$
1.1. *CGCpqCGpGq*   1.2. *CHCpqCHpHq*
2.1. *CNGNHpp* (*CFHpp*)   2.2. *CNHNGpp* (*CPGpp*),

these being subjoined to propositional calculus with substitution and detachment. In the associated earlier-later calculus, using *Tap* for 'It is the case at the instant *a* that *p*' and *Uab* for 'The instant *a* is earlier than the instant *b*', we subjoin to propositional calculus and quantification theory these postulates for *T*:

      T1. *CTaCpqCTapTaq*
T2.1. *CTaNpNTap*   T2.2. *CNTapTaNp*

and these for *U*:

UT1. *ETaGpΠbCUabTbp*
UT2. *ETaHpΠbCUbaTbp*.

A. N. Prior, 'Tense Logic and the Logic of Earlier and Later', chapter 11 of *Papers on Time and Tense* (Oxford: Oxford University Press, 1968), 116–34. © 1968 Oxford University Press.

[1] Now printed in his *The Ways of Paradox and other Essays* (New York: Random, 1966), pp. 156–74.

In the T-calculus we may prove the converse of 1, so that 1 and the 2's may be replaced by a pair of equivalences, and in the whole we may prove the formulae *ETaFp ΣbKUabTbp* and *ETaPpΣbKUbaTbp*, relating *U* to *P* and *F*, and giving us the postulates of the U-calculus appropriate to a system with these as primitive. Whether we use the one basis or the other, the tense-logical theses which are provable, preceded by *Ta*, in the minimal U-calculus (e.g. *TaCFHpp*) are precisely those of the minimal tense logic K_t, and the addition of various special conditions on *U* (e.g. *ΠaΣbUab*, giving every instant a *U*-successor) makes possible the proof of new theses of tense logic, preceded by *Ta*.

Here the elementary forms *Tap* and *Uab* of the earlier-later calculus are what Rescher[2] calls 'chronologically definite' propositions, whose truth-value is independent of time; so of course are truth-functions and quantifications of these. If we regard these as propositions *par excellence*, the tensed formulae for which the variables *p, q, r*, etc. may stand may be regarded as *predicates* of the instants 'at' which they are (perhaps loosely) said to be true. Tense logic, we might say, is a logic of pure predicates which are artificially torn away from their subjects and given a spurious independence. Its theses only make sense if we understand them to be implicitly preceded by a *Ta*, as they are explicitly in the U-calculus.

With this conception of the relation between the two calculi, we ought strictly speaking to use different symbols for the *C*'s and *N*'s which occur inside and outside the *Ta*'s; e.g., T1 ought properly to be written as $\mathscr{C}TaCpq\mathscr{C}TapTaq$, T2.1 as $\mathscr{C}TaNp\mathscr{N}Tap$, and UT1 as $\mathscr{E}TaGpΠb\mathscr{C}UabTbp$, with the script letters for proposition-formers and the italics for predicate-formers. Indeed, the four equivalences consisting of T1 and its converse, the T2's, and the UT's, may be replaced by *definitions* of the predicate-formers in terms of the proposition-formers, e.g. the T2's by

$$TaNp = \mathscr{N}Tap,$$

equating 'The instant *a* is (non-*p*)-ish' with 'It is not the case that the instant *a* is *p*-ish'; and UT1 by

$$TaGp = Πb\mathscr{C}UabTbp,$$

equating 'The instant *a* is (*p*-for-evermore)-ish' with 'The instant *a* is earlier than none but *p*-ish instants'. *T* here expresses no more than the attachment of a predicate to its subject, and could be replaced by juxtaposition and bracketing, as in this further transformation of the T2's:

$$(Np)a = \mathscr{N}(pa).$$

The expansion of *pa*, '*a* is *p*-ish', to *Tap*, 'It is true at *a* that *p*', is only a special case of the expansion we sometimes make of '*xφ*'s' to 'It is true *of x* that it *φ*'s'; 'at', we might say, is just this 'of'.

This is what I call the first or lowest grade of tense-logical involvement. Philosophers who are uneasy about tense logic will almost certainly find little in this amount of it to worry about. And there is a nice economy about it; it reduces the minimal tense logic to a by-product of the introduction of four definitions into an ordinary first-order theory, and richer systems to by-products of conditions imposed on a relation in that theory.

It is not *quite* to be taken for granted, however, that the U-calculus is philosophically simpler than a more substantial tense logic would be. For one thing, the U-calculus has two sorts of variables where tensed propositional logic has only one. And if it be replied

---

[2] N. Rescher, 'The Logic of Chronological Propositions', *Mind*, vol. 75, no. 297 (January 1966), pp. 75–96.

that the extra ones are just name-variables, which will have to be introduced sooner or later anyway, the answer to that is that they are names of a very odd kind of entity. Some of us at least would prefer to see 'instants', and the 'time-series' which they are supposed to constitute, as mere logical constructions out of tensed facts. With this motivation, let us try going a little further.

2 ASSIGNMENTS-TO-INSTANTS AS OMNITEMPORAL TENSED PROPOSITIONS

We may begin by ignoring the form *Uab* (we shall of course come back to it), and concentrating on the relations between the form *Tap*, 'It is the case at the instant *a* that *p*', and the simple *p*. If we treat both of these as genuinely propositional, the form *Tap* will be simply a *special case* of the sort of thing for which the variable *p* can stand, and it will make sense to substitute such formulae for the *p*'s and *q*'s both of tense logic and of the U-calculus. *TbTap*, for example, will be as well formed as the simple *Tap*, though there will be a certain vacuity about the initial *Tb*, since we may presume that if it is true at any time, e.g. now, that *p* is true at the instant *a*, this will be equally true at any other time. What this amounts to is that instead of ruling out such forms as *TbTap*, we explicitly lay it down that *TbTap* is equivalent to the plain *Tap*. Again, if forms like *Tap* and *ΠbTbp* are on the same level as the simple *p*, they may occur as arguments of a single truth-function, as in, for example, *KTapq*, *CΠaTapp*.

Allowing ourselves these liberties (which represent the second grade of tense-logical involvement) we may add to T1 and the T2's the following futher postulates for T:

RT: ⊢α → ⊢Taα
T3. *CΠaTapp*
T4. *CΠaTapTbΠaTap*
T5. *CTapTbTap*.

What we now have is equivalent to the System SI of Rescher. In the T-calculus thus enriched, it is easy to prove the converses of T4 and T5; and if we introduce the form *Lα* as an abridgement of *ΠaTaα* in those cases where *a* does not occur free in α, we may prove for this *L* the following:

RL: ⊢α → ⊢Lα
L1. *CLCpqCLpLq* (from T1 by quantification theory and Df. *L*)
L2. *CLpp*   (from T3 by Df. *L*)
L3. *CNLpLNLp*,

the last a little tortuously (using T5). These are Gödel's postulates for the Lewis system S5, which we therefore have for this *L*.

If we now introduce the form *Uab* and draw upon UT1 and UT2, we may prove, for the above *L*, the theses

L4. *CLpGp*
L5. *CLpHp*.

For we obviously have *CΠbTbpΠbCUabTbp* and *CΠbTbpΠbCUbaTbp*, and so *CLpTaGp* and *CLpTaHp* by UT1 and 2; from these we have *CLpΠaTaGp* and *CLpΠaTaHp* by Π2a, and finally L4 and L5 by T3.

We may also, drawing upon UT1 and 2, prove certain results about the prefixing of tense-operators to the form *Tap*. It might be thought that, since *Tap* is 'omnitemporally' true, the forms *FTap, PTap, GTap*, and *HTap* should all be equivalent to the plain *Tap*, but it is not quite as simple as that. The key point is that UT1 and UT2 leave it quite open whether time has or has not a beginning or an end. If there *were* an end of time, *FTap* would be false at the end of time regardless of whether *Tap* itself were true or false, since anything at all beginning with 'It will be the case that—' would be false then. In other words, *CTapFTap* might be false because although *Tap is* true, nothing whatever *will* be true, because there is now no future. And since *Gp* is equivalent to *NFNp*, *GTap* (= *NFTaNp*) would be vacuously *true* at the end of time regardless of the truth or falsity of *Tap*. This means that we have *CFTapTap* and *CTapGTap* but not their converses, and similarly with *P* and *H*. It has already been observed that from T1, the T2's, and UT1 and 2 we have *ETaFpΣbKUabTbp*; hence we have

C (1) *FTap*
K (2) *ΣbKUabTbTap* (1)
K (3) *ΣbKUabTap* (2, Conv. T5)
K (4) *KΣbUabTap* (3)
   (5) *Tap* (4).

And for the other, we clearly have *CTapΠbCUabTap*, and so, by T5, *CTapΠ bCUabTbTap*, i.e. *CTapGTap*. We may prove the converses, as we would expect, if we add the axiom *ΣbUab*, expressing time's forward infinity, and the converses of the corresponding theses in *P* and *H* if we add *ΣbUba*, expressing the infinity of the past.

To prove similar theorems about the form *Uab*, i.e. to prove *CFUabUab*, *CUabGUab*, and their images, it is necessary to add to UT1 and 2 the further postulate (analogous to T5)

UT3. *CUabTcUab*.

The converse of this (like that of T5) is provable.

Finally, if we enrich the U-calculus in the ways suggested, any tense-logical formula which we can prove, preceded by *Ta*, in the U-calculus, we can now prove without this prefix, by passing from *Taϕ* by U.G. to *ΠaTaϕ* and from this to *ϕ* by T3. So we no longer have merely *parallel* tense logics and U-calculi; the tense logics now appear as *parts* of the U-calculi, and this may prepare the way for treating the U-calculi as parts of the tense logics.

3 ALTERNATIVE INTERPRETATION OF THE ENLARGED SYSTEM

The characteristic feature of the present enlargement of the T-calculus, the placing of *Tap* and the plain *p* in the same syntactical category, may well be felt by some to be *the* step which must *not* be taken. Certainly it is essential to what I want to do next. But in itself it does not amount to much, and a person determined to treat tensed propositions as predicates could still do something with the present calculus.

To see what such a person might do with it, we should first observe that even from the point of view of such a person, the calculus of Section 1 has a certain insufficiency about it. It does not suffice to prove, for example, T3 preceded by *Ta*, i.e. *TaCΠaTapp*; but surely even a person who regarded tensed *p*'s as predicates of instants would want to say that it is true of any arbitrary instant *a* that it is '*p*-ish if every instant is *p*-ish'. But the calculus of Section 1 does not even provide for the *formation* of predicates of this sort (i.e. ones like '*p*-ish if every instant is *p*-ish'). In ordinary predicate calculus we may form complex predicates not only by truth-functionally combining simpler ones (as in the predicate 'stands and smokes'), but also by truth-functionally combining predicates and propositions, e.g. we might predicate of John that he 'is coming if and only if Mary is coming'. The predicate-of-instants '—is p-ish if every instant is p-ish', mentioned a few lines higher up, is clearly of this sort; another of the same would be '—is p-ish if the instant b is q-ish'. In defining predicate-formers in terms of proposition-formers we ought therefore to have not only

$$(Cpq)a = \mathscr{C}(pa)(qa)$$

but also

$$(Cp\alpha)a = \mathscr{C}(pa)\alpha$$

and

$$(C\alpha p)a = \mathscr{C}\alpha(pa),$$

where the schematic letter α represents any 'genuine' (i.e. chronologically definite) proposition. Or, doing it with a T-calculus, we could add to the axiom T1 the axiom-schemata

TS1. $\vdash ETaCp\alpha CTap\alpha$
TS2. $\vdash ETaC\alpha pC\alpha Tap$.

We could then obtain, for example, the above-mentioned thesis $TaC\Pi aTap$ by TS2 from $C\Pi aTapTap$, which we have from quantification theory. And if, as is done in some systems of propositional calculus, we defined 'Not p' in terms of a constant false proposition o, the equivalence of $TaNp$ and $NTap$ asserted by our T2's would become simply that case of the schema TS1 in which α is o.

But if someone wanted to replace the *schemata* TS1 and 2 by *axioms* for the key types of α that the system contains, he might well calculate that it would be less cumbersome to do it by running p's and α's together and preventing this confusion from doing any harm by the 'evacuating' postulates T4 and T5 (and UT3). This would mean regarding the theses of the enlarged calculus as all of them preceded by an unexpressed Ta (or ΠaTa) attaching to an arbitrary instant any ostensibly unattached 'predicates' $p, q, r,$ etc. that a thesis might contain, the attachment to it also of 'genuine' propositions being a convenient but empty formality (rather like vacuous quantification).

4 INSTANTS AS PROPOSITIONS

That the last step forward is not a very sensational one, is sufficiently indicated by the fact that we are still left with variables ostensibly representing named or nameable instants as well as ones representing propositions. What I shall call the third grade of tense-logical involvement consists in treating the instant-variables $a, b, c,$ etc. as also representing propositions. We might, for example, equate the instant a with a conjunction of all those propositions which would ordinarily be said to be true at that instant, or we might equate it with some proposition which would ordinarily be said to be true at that instant only, and so could serve as an index of it. When we do this we need of course to find some suitable interpretation for the form Tap, as it scarcely makes sense to speak of one proposition as being true 'at' or 'in' another proposition. We might say, for example, that it is true 'at' or 'in' a that p, if the proposition a at all times implies that p; it can in fact be proved that Tap is logically equivalent to $LCap$. (This follows from the postulates already given, plus two that will shortly be added to them.)

This sounds a highly artificial procedure, but remember that what lies behind it is the belief that 'instants' are artificial entities anyhow, i.e. that all talk which appears to be about them, and about the 'time-series' which they are supposed to constitute, is just disguised talk about what is and has been and will be the case. Certainly this revision of the concept of an instant turns quantification over instants into quantification over a certain sort of propositional variable, and it is important to notice that our third grade of tense-logical involvement commits us to this; but, while I shall not argue the pros and cons here, it seems to me, for reasons that have nothing specially to do with tense logic, that we have to admit such quantifications anyhow.

We take the instant-variables a, b, c, then, as propositional variables, substitutable in theses for the more general propositional variables p, q, r, etc.; though the converse substitution is not possible, since a, b, c, etc. stand only for those propositions which satisfy the postulates RT and T1–T5, together with two that are formulable now that instants are treated as propositions, namely

T6. *Taa*,

i.e. one of the propositions that is true 'at' the instant a is always the instant-proposition a itself; and

T7. *CTapCap*.

Of the theorems which are now provable, the most important are

T8.   *Ma* (=*NLNa*)
T9.   *Σaa*
T10. *CLCapTap*
T11. *CTapLCap*.

T8 may be proved as follows:

1. *CΠbNTbaNTaa*   (U.I)
2. *NΠbNTba*   (1, T6)
3. *CΠbTbNaΠbNTba* (T2, 1, Π1b, Π2b)
4. *NΠbTbNa*   (3, 2)
5. *NLNa*   (4, Df.L);

T9 as follows:

1. *CaΣaa*   (quantification theory)
2. *CTaaTaΣaa* (1, RT, T1)
3. *TaΣaa*   (2, T6)
4. *ΠaTaΣaa* (3, UG)
5. *Σaa*   (4, T3);

T10 thus:

   C (1) *LCap*
   K (2) *ΠbTbCap*   (1, Df.L)
   K (3) *TaCap*   (2, U.I.)
   K (4) *CTaNpTaKNpCap* (3, *CTapCTaqTaKpq*)
   K (5) *CTaNpTaNa*   (4, *CKNpCapNa*, RT, T1)
   K (6) *NTaNa*   (T2.1, T6)
   K (7) *NTaNp*   (5, 6)
      (8) *Tap*   (7, T2.2);

and T11 thus:

1. *CTbTapTbCap* (T7, RT, T1)
2. *CTapTbCap* (1, T5)
3. *CTapΠbTbCap* (2, Π2b).
4. *CTapLCap* (3, Df.*L*).

The addition of T6 and T7 also makes possible certain simplifications of the total system. For example, T3 can now be replaced by the shorter T9 (*Σaa*), since T3 is provable from T9 and T7 as follows:

1. *CΠaTapCap* (T7, Π1a)
2. *CaCΠaTapp* (1, p.c.)
3. *CΣaaCΠaTapp* (2, Σ1a)
4. *CΠaTapp* (3, T9).

We may also drop T4, though the proof of this is a little indirect. From S5 and quantification theory we can prove

$$CΠaLCapLCbΠaLCap,$$

which is what T4 may be transformed into in virtue of the equivalence of *Tap* and *LCap* proved in T10 and T11. And T4 is not itself used in the proof of S5 for *L* or of T10 and T11.

We may also prove *CTabTba* and *CTabCTbcTac*, which with T6 *(Taa)* show that when both its arguments are instant-propositions *T* behaves as an equivalence functor. Indeed we can prove (by T7 and induction on possible contexts of *a* and *b*) the metatheorem that *CTabCf(a)f(b)* holds for any function *f(a)* constructible in the system, so that *Tab* can be used to express a certain sort of identity between instants (*Tab* means that precisely the same propositions are true at *a* as at *b*). We might, indeed, have introduced a propositional identity-function *Ipq* with the usual postulates (*Ipp*, and *CIpqCf(p)f(q)* for all functions of the system), and laid down *CTabIab* instead of T7, thereby equating *T* (with instant-arguments) with this *I* (since T6, *Taa*, is clearly equivalent by identity-theory to *CIabTab*).

When we add the form *Uab* with its axioms UT1 and UT2, we can extend the above metatheorem *CTabf(a)f(b)* to the new functions that we now have, either by introducing *I* and equating *Tab* with *Iab*, or (if we keep the original T7) by adding the further axiom

UT4. *CTabCUcaUcb*.

CTabCUacUbc then becomes provable (making possible the desired extension of the metatheorem). So does UT3, which we can therefore drop as an axiom. We can also, in this extended UT-calculus, prove the theses

T12. *CUabTaFb*,
T13. *CTaFbUab*.

T12 as follows:

C (1) *Uab*
K (2) *Tbb* (T6)
K (3) *ΣcKUacTcb* (1, 2, E.G.)
   (4) *TaFb* (3, UT1).

T13 equates by UT1 to $C\Sigma cKUacTcbUab$, in which quantification theory equates the initial $C\Sigma c$ to ΠcC, and we have $\Pi cCKUacTcbUab$ by UT4.

T12 and T13 mean that we could *define* Uab as $TaFb$, and if we do so we can replace UT1–4 by the last section's L4 ($CLpGp$) and L5 ($CLpHp$) and the tense logic K_t. Proofs of the UT's from these and a system which will shortly be shown equivalent to RT and T1–7, may be found in my *Past, Present, and Future*.[3] Moreover, when further tense-logical postulates are added to K_t, we can prove those conditions on U which make it possible to prove the added tense-logical postulates in the U-calculus; i.e. the traffic between tense logics and U-calculi, given the new T-calculus, is two-way. And since 'at' can no longer mean the predicational 'of', UT1 and UT2 cannot be replaced by definitions, and the movement from them to the tense logic K_t, is less straightforward and natural than the converse one. U-calculi, in short, are now best thought of as by-products of the interaction of the T-calculus and tense logics.

We have still to derive these, however, from tense logic alone. As a step in that direction, but one which in itself commits us to no further 'tense-logical involvements', we shall develop the present T-calculus in a slightly different form.

5 REFORMULATION WITH L PRIMITIVE

In view of T10 and T11, it is possible to develop the calculus sketched in the last section with L instead of T as the one non-tense-logical primitive, defining Tap as $LCap$. This has in fact already been done in *Past, Present, and Future*, using as postulates RL, L1–3, T8 (Ma), T9 (Σaa), and T2.2 ($=CNLCapLCaNp=ALCapLCaNp$). It is from these postulates, with K_t, L4, L5, and the definition of Uab as $TaFb$ ($=LCaFb$), that UT1 and UT2 are there derived; it remains to show their equivalence to those of the last section. The L postulates were proved there and in the preceding section from the T ones; and as to the converse proofs,

(i) given that $Tap=LCap$, it is easy to prove RT, T1 and T4–7 in S5;
(ii) T2.1 follows from modal logic and T8(Ma);
(iii) T3 may be proved from T9 (Σaa) as it was in the T-calculus (since we have the crucial thesis T7 by (i)); and
(iv) of the implications $CLp\Pi aLCap$ and $C\Pi aLCapLp$, jointly equivalent to the definition of L in the T-system as ΠaTa, the first follows from modal logic and the second we prove thus:

1. $C\Pi aLCapp$ (T3)
2. $CL\Pi aLCapLp$ (1, RL, L2)
3. $C\Pi aLLCapLp$ (2)
4. $C\Pi aLCapLp$ (3),

where 3 follows from 2 by the 'Barcan formula' $C\Pi aLf(a)L\Pi af(a)$, known to be provable from S5 and quantification theory, and 4 from 3 by $CLpLLp$, also known to be provable in S5. And if we define Iab as $LEab$, we may prove $CTabIab$ from S5, T2.2 and T8, or (defining Uab as $TaFb$, i.e. $LCaFb$) UT4 from S5, L4, and K_t.

The *consistency* of the whole system may easily be shown by interpreting Lp as p, and the special variables a, b, c, etc. as standing for tautologies. The postulates then all become theses of the propositional calculus.

---

[3] A. N. Prior, *Past, Present, and Future* (Oxford: Oxford University Press, 1967).

This L system is stratified as well as the T system, but on a different principle. The T system divides its postulates into those (T1, T2.1, T2.2) which do not even assume that *Tap* is out of the same syntactical box as the plain *p* (and if *U* is added, UT1 and UT2 do not assume this either); those (RT, T3–5, UT3) which do assume this for *Tap* but not for the plain *a*; and those (T6, T7—and when we add *U*, UT4) which assume it even for *a*. The postulates of the *L* system, on the other hand, divide into those (RL, L1–3 and L4, L5, and K$_t$ when we add them) which do not require the special variables *a*, *b*, *c*, etc. for their formulation, and which thus apply to propositions generally; and those (T8, T9, T2.2) which do require these variables, and give in effect the conditions a proposition must meet to be substitutable for one of the special variables. It must be of such a sort that (i) any such proposition is at some time true (T8), (ii) at any given time some such proposition is true (T9), and (iii) such a proposition permanently implies either the truth or the falsehood of any given proposition (T2.2).

With a little modification of the *L*-system we can do without special variables in favour of a function *Qp* defined as *KMpΠqALCpqLCpNq*; i.e. *Qp* asserts that *p* satisfies T8 and T2.2. We then drop these two postulates, and replace all formulae of the form *Σaf(a)* by *ΣpKQpf(p)*, and all of the form *Πaf(a)* by *ΠpCQpf(p)*, and in theses with free special variables we replace these by ordinary propositional variables and conditions of the form *CQp* at the beginning of the thesis. For example, T2.1, *CLCapNCLaNp* becomes *CQqCLCqpNLCqNp*. But we still need the postulate T9, in the form *ΣpKQpp*. This can be very slightly shortened by dropping from *Qp*, when expanded by its definition, the conjunct *Mp*, which follows from the new conjunct *p*. A still shorter equivalent of *KQpp* which may be used in this axiom is *KpΠqCqLCpq*. The axiom as thus amended asserts that there is something which is now the case, and which is at no time true without everything that is now the case being then true also. (This would fit, for example, a conjunction of all the propositions that are now true; it would also fit a proposition which is true now but not at any other time; cf. our original account of 'instant-propositions' at the beginning of Section 4.) This modification of the L-calculus, however, we can ignore in what follows.

6 THE TENSE-LOGICAL DEFINITION OF L

We would reach a fourth grade of tense-logical involvement if we could give a tense-logical definition of *L*. As to this, it has been shown in *Past, Present, and Future* that (i) if we are prepared to use a richer tense logic than K$_t$, quite simple tense-logical definitions of *L* are possible, e.g. if we assume that time is like a single non-branching line and that the earlier-later relation is transitive, we may define *Lp*, 'It is the case at all times that *p*' as *KKpHpGp*, 'It is and always has been and always will be the case that *p*'; and that (ii) even with the non-committal system K$_t$, if we enlarge our symbolic apparatus a little we can give a tense-logical definition of *L*, provided that we do not allow that there may be several distinct and independent time-series (in which case there would be 'times' which we could not locate from 'now' by any combination of 'will bes' and 'has beens'). But, under (ii), it is possible to improve a little upon the definition given in *Past, Present, and Future*, and upon the proofs there given of the postulates RL and L1–5.

We first define the form $L^n p$ inductively as follows:

$L^0 p = p$
$L^{n+1} p = KHL^n p GL^n p$.[4]

---

[4] For this abridgement of the definition used in *Past, Present, and Future*, I am indebted to Mr. J. R. Lucas.

We then introduce quantifiers binding the n's, and obeying the usual rules, and define Lp as $\Pi n L^n p$. This is equivalent to defining $M^n p$ inductively by

$$M^0 p = p$$
$$M^{n+1} p = APM^n pFM^n p$$

and defining Mp as $\Sigma n M^n p$, i.e. we say that it is true at *some* time that p if and only if either p is itself true now or it is true preceded by *some* combination of 'will be's and 'has been's.

$L^1 p$ it may be observed, is $KHpGp$, and it is easy to show that for this functor, given K_t for H and G, we may prove all but L2 ($CLpp$) of the postulates of the 'Brouwersche' modal system, i.e. RL, L1, L2 and, instead of L3, the weaker $CNpLNLp$, which is equivalent to $CpLMp$ or $CMLpp$ (as L3 itself is equivalent to $CMpLMp$ or $CMLpLp$). Given this result, it is not difficult to show, by induction and the rules for quantifiers, that we have at least the full 'Brouwersche' system for $\Pi n L^n$, i.e. for our defined L. For L2 we have simply

C (1) $\Pi n L^n p$
K (2) $L^0 p$ (1, U.I.)
   (3) p (2, Df.L^0).

For L1, we clearly have $CL^0 CpqCL^0 pL^0 q$ ($=CCpqCpq$) and since we have $CL^1 CpqCL^1 pL^1 q$, we may prove $CL^{n+1} CpqCL^{n+1} pL^{n+1} q$ from any $CL^n CpqCL^n pL^n q$ as follows:

1. $CL^n CpqCL^n pL^n p$ (hyp.)
2. $L^1 CL^n CpqCL^n pL^n q$ (1, RL for L^1)
3. $CL^1 L^n CpqL^1 CL^n pL^n q$ (2, L1 for L^1)
4. $CL^1 L^n CpqCL^1 L^n pL^1 L^n q$ (3, L1 for L^1)
5. $CL^{n+1} CpqCL^{n+1} pL^{n+1} q$ (4, Df.L^{n+1}).

Hence we have $\Pi n CL^n CpqCL^n pL^n q$, from which quantification theory takes us to

$C\Pi n L^n Cpq C\Pi n L^n p\Pi n L^n q$,

i.e. L1 for our defined L. $CMLpp$ is provable similarly.

But in fact we have not only the 'Brouwersche' system but S5 for this L. For Lemmon has shown that not only in S5 but even in the 'Brouwersche' system, supplemented by the usual rules for quantifiers, we may prove the 'Barcan formula' $C\bar{\Pi} n Lf(n) L\Pi nf(n)$. This enables us to prove, for our defined L, the law $CLpLLp$, thus:

1. $C\Pi n L^n pL^{m+k} p$ (U.I.)
2. $CL^{m+k} pL^m L^k p$ (provable by induction)
3. $C\Pi n L^n pL^m L^k p$ (1, 2)
4. $C\Pi n L^n p\Pi k\Pi m L^m L^k p$ (3, $\Pi 2m$, $\Pi 2K$)
5. $C\Pi n L^n p\Pi kLL^k p$ (4, Df.L)
6. $C\Pi^n L^n pL\Pi KL^k p$ (5, Barcan)
7. $CLpLLp$ (6, Df.L).

And it is known that the addition of 7 to the 'Brouwersche' system yields S5. Proofs of L4 and L5 are obvious.

The U-calculus now at last becomes simply a part of tense logic, and the minimal U-calculus is provable from the tense logic K_t, the axioms T8, T9, and T2.2 for the special variables (the M and L which appear in T8 and T2.2 now being seen as tense-logical functors), and quantification theory. From this basis we can in fact prove a little more than the minimal U-calculus; we can also prove a special condition on U, namely

$$\text{UT5.} \quad \Pi a \Pi b (U \cup \check{U} \cup I)_* ab,$$

i.e. every pair of instants is related by the ancestral of the logical sum of U, its converse and identity. This corresponds to the assumption that the time-series (whatever its shape) is unique, i.e. that all instants may be located from 'now' by some combination of 'will be's and 'has been's. This does not yield any new ordinary tense logical formulae (i.e. without such symbols as our $\Pi n L^n$) preceded by Ta; though it does strengthen the conditions on U that may be proved by adding various tense-logical axioms to K_t. And if we add UT5 to RT, T1–7, and UT1–4, we may prove not only K_t, T8, and T9 but the equivalence of Lp ($= \Pi a T a p$) to the tense-logical $\Pi n L^n p$, and so all the postulates used in the present section.

At this stage, however, there is no point in having U and T as primitives in addition to G and H. The latter, it should be noted, we *must* have at all stages but the first, for the formulation of UT1 and 2. At the first stage, these last are definitions, and U is our only primitive constant. At the second, we need U, T, G, and H. At the third, we can get rid of U, and at the fourth of T also, leaving only G and H.

7 RECAPITULATION

The stages of our progress from what could be regarded as a pure earlier-and-later logic to what can be regarded as a pure tense-logic may be tabulated as follows (putting in parentheses those postulates which cease to be independent when a later stage is reached):

        T-Postulates   *UT-Postulates*

System I
  T1.   *CTaCpqCTapTaq*   UT1. *ETaGpΠbCUabTbp*
  T2.1. *CTaNpNTap*   UT2. *ETaHpΠbCUbaTbp*
  T2.2. *CNTapTaNp.*

System II. Add to System I the following:
  T3. *CΠaTapp*   (UT3. *CUabTcUab*)
  (T4. *CΠaTapTbΠaTap*)
  T5. *CTapTbTap.*
  RT: ⊢α → ⊢Taα
    Lp definable as $\Pi a T a p$.

System III. Add to System II the following:
  T6. *Taa*   UT4. *CTabCUcaUcb*
  T7. *CTapCap.*

System equivalent to System IV: Add to System III the following:
                UT5. $(U \cup \check{U} \cup I)_*ab.$

And the stages by which tense-logic so swells as to encompass the earlier-later logic may be tabulated thus (again bracketing those postulates which cease to be independent at a later stage):

System K_t
  RG: $\vdash\alpha \rightarrow \vdash G\alpha$ RH: $\vdash\alpha \rightarrow \vdash H\alpha$
  A1.1. $CGCpqCGpGq$ A1.2. $CHCpqCHpGp$
  A2.1. $CPGpp$ A2.2. $CFHpp$
  P defined as NHN, F as NGN.

System equivalent to System III: Add to K_t the following:

$$\begin{pmatrix} & RL: \vdash\alpha \rightarrow \vdash L\alpha & \\ L1.\ CLCpqCLpLq & & L2.\ CLpp \\ & L3.\ CNLpLNLp & \\ L4.\ CLpGp & & L5.\ CLpHp \end{pmatrix}$$

T8. $NLNa$ T9. Σaa T.2.2. $ALCapLCaNp$
Tap definable as $LCap$, Uab as $LCaFb$.

System IV: Add to the above the following:
  Df.L^n: $L^0 p = p$; $L^{n+1}p = KGL^n p HL^n p$
  Df.L: $Lp = \Pi n L^n p$.

8 THE UNIQUENESS OF THE TIME-SERIES

I want, in conclusion, to look more closely at the beginning and the end of the movement I have sketched.

When the postulates of the tense-logic K_t are no longer regarded as just by-products of definitions in a first-order theory, but substantial assumptions in an independent discipline, it becomes intelligible to question whether they are all true. This possibility I shall not explore here; but there is a converse point, namely that if we do not regard the postulate UT5, in the logic of the earlier-later relation, as a mere by-product of the definition of that relation in tense-logical terms, it becomes intelligible to question *that* postulate, and to wonder whether there are pairs of instants which are *not* connected, even indirectly, by the earlier-later relation. It is certainly intelligible to deny this postulate if we treat instants as genuine objects and the earlier-later relation as undefined; but perhaps we can also do it *without* falling into this 'Platonism' about instants.

Let me lead up to this last possibility by first observing that even if the earlier-later relation is only a logical construction out of tensed facts, we can give a good sense to the assertion that there are an infinity of different *logically possible* time-series. For this could be just a slightly misleading way of saying that not only the futures that have issued from given past states, but the entire course of history, *might* without inconsistency have been different from what it has been and will be, i.e. it *might have been* that we had d and then e and then f instead of a and then b and then c; or *there would be no inconsistency in supposing* that we had d and then e and then f, instead of a and then b and then c. For even if all propositions are tensed, tense logic is not the whole of logic; there is also a logic of such functors as 'There would be no inconsistency in supposing that—'. What we *cannot* say (if 'and then' is tense-logically defined) is that we *do* have a series a, b, c, and also a series d, e, f that is temporally unconnected with it.

Moreover, there is a logic of such functors as 'It appears from a certain point of view that—', and one could therefore give a good sense to talk about an infinity of different 'apparent' time-series. I suspect that the infinity of 'local proper times' which figure in relativistic physics amount simply to what appears from various points of view, or in various 'frames of reference', to be the course of events. And given how the course of events appears from a certain point of view, your relativistic physicist will be able to calculate how it will appear from certain other points of view. He can also indicate what features of the course of events (what temporal orderings of those events) will be common to *all* points of view, and one can work out a 'tense-logic' for that too. (It turns out to be slightly different in the special and the general theories of relativity.) What the relativistic physicists *cannot* calculate from how the course of events appears from certain points of view is how, in all its details, the course of events actually is. It is not clear to me that there is anything surprising or unacceptable in this conclusion, or that we should be driven by it to renounce the use of forms like 'It appears from such-and-such a point of view that p', which assume that there is also a plain p which is or is not the case. Einstein himself[5] once said to Carnap that

> the problem of the Now worried him seriously. He explained that the experience of the Now means something special for men, something different from the past and the future, but that this important difference does not and cannot occur within physics.

If my interpretation of relativistic physics is correct, he had something there.

We can, all the same, develop the logic of 'points of view' on the basis of a syntax which does *not* thus suggest that there is a 'real' (though only partly knowable) course of events which presents these various systematically related appearances. We might describe this alternative syntax in a very general way as follows: instead of using the plain p for a quite impersonal 'It is (really) the case that p', we use it for 'It appears (or is the case) from *this* point of view that p', or 'It is the case with *this* person or particle that p'. That is, the prefix 'It appears from *this* point of view that—' or 'It is the case with *this* person or particle that—' is one which has the same sort of vacuity in this language as 'It is *now* the case that—' has in ordinary tense logic; it does not need to be expressed, but is understood in all that we say. We then describe what appears to be the case from other points of view, or what is the case with other persons or particles, by using quasi-modal operators which take us from 'this' point of view or particle to the other ones, very much as operators like 'It will be the case that—' take us to other 'nows' from 'this' now. They would, I think, be operators corresponding to the 'signal relation' of relativistic physics.[6] Associated with these other points of view or particles are other time-series. These, like 'this' time-series, are just logical constructions out of tensed facts, but they are reached from *our* 'now' not by tenses alone, but by tenses interrupted by the other quasi-modal operators that we use for getting from 'this' point of view or particle to the other ones; it is this that would make UT_5 unprovable.

A language of this sort would have a solipsist ring to it which I find as hard to take as Platonism about instants, but it would have the advantage of making scientifically unanswerable questions not even askable. This is perhaps one of those many cases where the logician's main philosophical function is to show that there is no escape from one or another of a group of not very palatable alternatives.

---

[5] As reported on p. 37 of *The Philosophy of Rudolf Carnap*, ed. Paul A. Schilpp, The Library of Living Philosophers, vol. XI (Chicago, IL: Open Court Publishing Company, 1963).

[6] See R. Carnap, *Introduction to Symbolic Logic and its Applications* (New York: Dover, 1958), chapter G. More accurately, we would need a conjunction corresponding to Carnap's relation C, in terms of which the signal relation is defined.

6

Temporal Ontology and Temporal Reference

MARC MOENS AND MARK STEEDMAN

> "Two weeks later, Bonadea had already been his lover for a fortnight."
> —Robert Musil, *Der Mann ohne Eigenschaften*.

1 INTRODUCTION

It is often assumed that the semantics of temporal expressions is directly related to the linear time concept familiar from high-school physics—that is, to a model based on the number line. However, there are good reasons for suspecting that such a conception is not the one that our linguistic categories are most directly related to. *When*-clauses provide an example of the mismatch between linguistic temporal categories and a semantics based on such an assumption. Consider the following examples, suggested by Ritchie 1979:

(1) When they built the 39th Street bridge...
   a. ...a local architect drew up the plans.
   b. ...they used the best materials.
   c. ...they solved most of their traffic problems.

To map the temporal relations expressed in these examples onto linear time, and to try to express the semantics of *when* in terms of points or intervals (possibly associated with events), would appear to imply either that *when* is multiply ambiguous, allowing these points or intervals to be temporally related in at least three different ways, or that the relation expressed between main and *when*-clauses is one of approximate coincidence. However, neither of these tactics explains the peculiarity of utterances like the following:

(2) # When my car broke down, the sun set.

The unusual character of this statement seems to arise because the *when*-clause predicates something more than mere temporal coincidence, that is, some **contingent** relation such as a *causal* link or an *enablement* relation between the two events. Our knowledge of the world does not easily support such a link for (2), at least if we don't indulge in the fiction that the natural universe is conspiring against the speaker. Nor is the relation predicated between the two events by *when* the one that we normally think of as scientifically causal, for *when* seems to predicate an intransitive relation. Consider:

(3) a. When John left, Sue cried.
   b. When Sue cried, her mother got upset.
   c. When John left, Sue's mother got upset.

From (3a) and (b) it would be unwarranted to conclude the state of affairs that is described in (c). And this causal aspect of the sentence's meaning must stem from the sense-meaning of *when*, because parallel utterances using *while, just after, at approximately the same time as*, and the like, which predicate purely temporal coincidence, are perfectly felicitous.

We shall claim that the different temporal relations conveyed in examples (1) and (2) do not arise from any sense-ambiguity of *when*, or from any "fuzziness" in the relation that it expresses between the times referred to in the clauses it conjoins, but from the fact that the meaning of *when* is not primarily temporal at all. Nor is it simply causal, as Example 3 shows. We will argue instead that *when* has a single sense-meaning, reflecting its role of establishing a temporal focus, which we follow Isard and Longuet-Higgins (1973) in relating to Reichenbach's **reference time**. The apparent diversity of meanings arises from the nature of this referent and the organisation of events and states of affairs in episodic memory under a relation we shall call **contingency**, a term related, but not identical to a notion like causality, rather than mere temporal sequentiality. This contingent, nontemporal relation on the representation of events in episodic memory also determines the ontology of propositions associated with linguistic expressions denoting events and states. It is to these that we turn first.

2 TEMPORAL AND ASPECTUAL CATEGORIES

Propositions conveyed by English sentences uttered in context can, following Vendler, be classified into temporal or aspectual types, partly on the basis of the tenses, aspects, and adverbials with which they can co-occur (cf. Dowty 1979). The term **aspectual type** refers to the relation that a speaker predicates of the particular happening that their utterance describes, relative to other happenings in the domain of the discourse. What the speaker *says* about those relations is of course quite distinct from what those relations objectively *are*. In particular, the speaker's predications about events will typically be coloured by the fact that those events are involved in sequences that are planned, predicted, intended, or otherwise governed by *agencies* of one kind or another. For want of some established term to cover this very general class of dependencies between events, we will use the term **contingency**. Thus an utterance of

(4) Harry reached the top

is usually typical of what we will call a **culmination**—informally, an event which the speaker views as punctual or instantaneous, and as accompanied by a transition to a new state of the world.[1] This new state we will refer to as the **consequent state** of the

---

[1] Readers familiar with Vendler's work will realise that we have changed his terminology. We have done so both for notational convenience and to avoid the considerable confusion that has arisen concerning the precise meaning of the old terms. The new nomenclature is also intended to reflect the fact, also noted by Dowty (1979), that Vendler's "accomplishments," which we will refer to as "culminated processes," are composite events, consisting of a process which is associated with a particular culmination point.

event. It does not necessarily include *all* events that are objectively and in fact consequences. It rather includes only those consequences that the speaker *views* as contingently related to other events that are under discussion, say by causing them or by permitting them to occur. For reasons that are discussed in Section 3.2 below, expressions like these readily combine with the perfect, as in

(5) Harry has reached the top.

The point may perhaps best be made by noting that there is another class of punctual expressions that is *not* normally associated with a consequent state. For example,

(6) John hiccupped

is not usually viewed as leading to any relevant change in the state of the world. It typifies what we call a **point** expression. A point is an event (not necessarily an instantaneous one) that is viewed as an indivisible whole and whose consequences are not at issue in the discourse—which of course does not mean that *de facto* consequences do not exist. Such expressions are evidently not the same as culminations, for they are rather odd in combination with the perfect, as in

(7) #Harry has hiccupped.

The reasons for this will also be discussed below. Sentences like

(8) Harry climbed

typify a third aspectual category, which we will call for obvious reasons a **process**. Most utterances of such sentences describe an event as extended in time but not characterised by any particular conclusion or culmination. As was pointed out by Vendler, expressions like these can be combined with a *for*-adverbial but not with an *in*-adverbial:

(9) Harry climbed for several hours.
    #Harry climbed in several hours.

In contrast,

(10) Harry climbed to the top

typically describes a state of affairs that also extends in time but that *does* have a particular culmination associated with it at which a change of state takes place. We classify most utterances of such sentences as a fourth aspectual type, called a **culminated process**. Culminated processes, in contrast to ordinary processes, combine readily with an *in*-adverbial but not with a *for*-adverbial.

(11) Harry climbed all the way to the top in less than 45 minutes.
    #Harry climbed all the way to the top for less than 45 minutes.

All of the above categories describe what common sense suggests we call **events**—that is, happenings with defined beginnings and ends. We distinguish these "hard-edged" categories from a class of indefinitely extending states of affairs, which, equally commonsensically, we call **states**. Example 12 typically describes one kind of state:

(12) Harry is at the top.

Part of the appeal of Vendler's account, and such descendants as the present proposal, is that it suggests that part of the meaning of any utterance of a sentence is one of

	EVENTS		STATES
	atomic	extended	
+conseq	**CULMINATION** recognize, spot, win the race	**CULMINATED PROCESS** build a house, eat a sandwich	understand, love, know, resemble
−conseq	**POINT** hiccup, tap, wink	**PROCESS** run, swim, walk, play the piano	

FIG. 1

a small number of temporal/aspectual profiles distinguished on a small number of dimensions. In present terms, the event-types can be distinguished on just two dimensions, one concerned with the contrast between punctuality and temporal extension, the other with the association with a consequent state. This subcategorisation can be summarized as in Figure 1.

We have included in Figure 1 examples of verbs which *typically* yield propositions of the relevant types, and we shall assume that such verbs (or, strictly speaking, the associated uninstantiated propositions) are lexically specified as bearing that type. However, it cannot be stressed too often that these aspectual profiles are properties of sentences *used in a context*: sense-meanings of sentences or verbs in isolation are usually compatible with several (or even all possible) Vendlerian profiles, as Dowty and Verkuyl have pointed out—hence the frequent use of words like "typically" and "readily" above. The details of this taxonomy and the criteria according to which utterances can be categorized are less important than the observation that each primitive entity of a given type, such as the culmination event of *Harry's reaching the top*, carries intimations of other associated events and states, such as the process by which the culmination was achieved and the consequent state that followed. What linguistic devices like tenses, aspects, and temporal/aspectual adverbials appear to do is to *transform* entities of one type into these other contingently related entities, or to turn them into composites with those related entities.

For example, we shall argue below that the progressive auxiliary demands that its argument be a process, which it predicates as ongoing. If it is combined with an event type that isn't a process, say with a punctual event as in *Harry was hiccupping*, then it will cause that original event to be reinterpreted as a process, in this case the process of *iteration* or repetition of the basic event. Similarly, we shall argue that a perfect auxiliary demands a culmination, predicating of the time referred to that the associated consequent state holds. The notion of "time referred to" is related to Reichenbach's **reference time** in Section 4.1 below. If the perfect is combined with an event description for which world knowledge provides no obvious culmination, then the ensemble will tend to be anomalous. So, for example, *Harry has reached the top* is fine, but *The clock has ticked*, and *Harry has hummed*, to the extent that they are acceptable at all, seem to demand rather special scenarios in which the tick of the clock and the mere act of humming have a momentousness that they usually lack.

The phenomenon of change in the aspectual type of a proposition under the influence of modifiers like tenses, temporal adverbials, and aspectual auxiliaries is of central importance to the present account. We shall talk of such modifiers as functions which "coerce" their inputs to the appropriate type, by a loose analogy with type-coercion in programming languages (cf. Ait-Kaci 1984). Thus the effect on meaning of the combination of the progressive with an expression denoting an atomic punctual event as in *Sandra was hiccupping* occurs in two stages: first the point proposition is coerced into a process of iteration of that point. Only then can this process be defined as ongoing, and hence as a progressive state. These two stages might be represented as in the following diagram:

(13) (point (*Sandra hiccup*))
↓
(process (iteration (point (*Sandra hiccup*))))
↓
(progressive (process (iteration (point (*Sandra hiccup*)))))

The temporal/aspectual ontology that underlies the phenomenon of aspectual type coercion can be defined in terms of the transition network shown in Figure 2, in which each transition is associated with a change in the content and where, in addition, the felicity of any particular transition for a given proposition is conditional on support from knowledge and context.

Rather than attempting to explain this diagram from first principles, we present below a number of examples of each transition. However, it is worth noting first that many of the permissible transitions between aspectual categories illustrated in Figure 2 appear to be

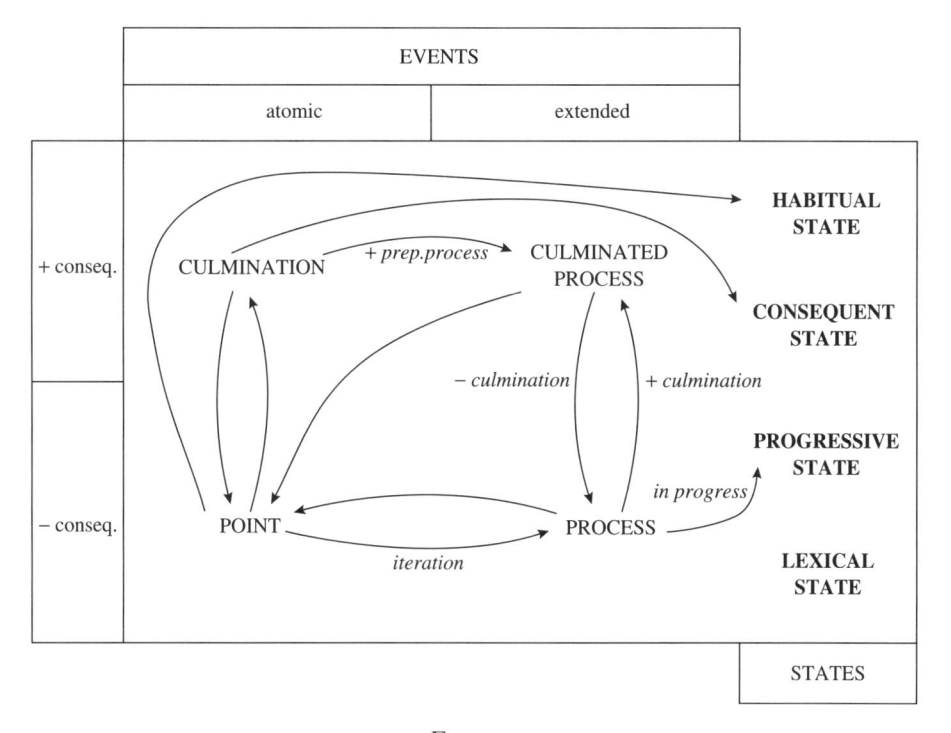

FIG. 2

```
              preparatory process            consequent state
        |////////////////////////\////////////////////////
                                 |
                            culmination
```

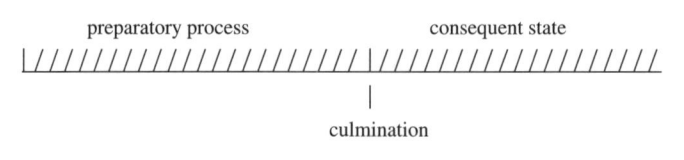

FIG. 3

related to a single elementary contingency-based event structure which we call a **nucleus**. A nucleus is defined as a structure comprising a culmination, an associated preparatory process, and a consequent state.[2] It can be represented pictorially as in Figure 3.

Any or all of these elements may be compound: for example, the preparation leading to the culmination of *reaching the top of Mt. Everest* may consist of a number of discrete steps of climbing, resting, having lunch, or whatever. The consequent state may also be compound; most importantly, it includes the further events, if any, that are in the same sequence of contingently related events as the culmination. Similarly, the culmination itself may be a complex event. For example, we shall see below that the entire culminated process of *climbing Mt. Everest* can be treated as a culmination in its own right. In this case, the associated preparatory process and consequent state will be different ones to those internal to the culminated process itself.

3 ASPECT

3.1 The Progressive

According to the present theory, progressive auxiliaries are functions that require their input to denote a process. Their result is a type of state that we shall call a progressive state, which describes the process as ongoing at the reference time. Thus the following sentence, among other meanings that we shall get to in a moment, can simply predicate of a present reference time that the process in question began at some earlier time and has not yet stopped:

(14) The president is speaking.

If the input to a progressive is atomic then by definition it cannot be described as ongoing. However, as was noted in the introduction, it may be coerced into a process by being iterated, as in

(15) Harry is hiccupping.

There is another route through the network in Figure 2, where the point is coerced into a culmination, i.e., as constituting an atomic event that *does* have consequences associated with it. In this case, the interpretation for (15) parallels the one given for *Harry was reaching the top*, below. However, this particular example is deliberately chosen in order to make that interpretation unlikely.

If a progressive combines with a culminated process, as in:

(16) Roger was running a mile

—then the latter must also first be coerced to become a process. The most obvious way to do this is to strip off the culmination and leave the preparatory process behind.

---

[2] A similar tripartite event structure is proposed in Passonneau (1987).

It is this process that is stated to be ongoing at the past reference time. Another possible coercion is to treat the entire culminated process as a point, and to iterate it. This interpretation appears to be the one that is forced by continuing (16) as in:

(17) Roger was running a mile last week. This week he is up to three.

When a culmination expression like *reach the top* is used with a progressive, it must be coerced to become a process in a slightly more complicated way. The most obvious path through the network in Figure 2 from the culmination node to the process node involves first adding a preparatory process to the culmination to make it a culminated process, then stripping off the culmination point as before. Thus sentences like the following describe this preparatory process as ongoing at the past reference time:

(18) Harry was reaching the top.

Again, an iterated reading is possible in principle, but pragmatically unlikely here.

As a result of the coercions implicit in the last two examples, it is no longer asserted that the culminations in question ever in fact occurred, but only that the associated preparatory processes did. Thus there is no contradiction in continuations that explicitly *deny* the culmination, like:

(19) a. Harry was running a mile, but he gave up after two laps.
b. Harry was reaching the top when he slipped and fell to the bottom.

The fact that, according to the present theory, progressives coerce their input to be a process so that any associated culmination is stripped away and no longer contributes to truth conditions provides a resolution of the **imperfective paradox** (Dowty 1979), without appealing to theory-external constructs like inertia worlds.

3.2 The Perfect

A perfect, as in

(20) Harry has reached the top

is a function that requires its input category to be a culmination. Its result is the corresponding consequent state. The most obvious of these consequences for (20) is that Harry still *be* at the top, although as usual there are other possibilities. Informal evidence that this indeed is the function of the perfect can be obtained by noticing that perfects are infelicitous if the salient consequences are *not* in force. Thus, when I'm on my way to get a cloth to clean up the coffee I accidentally spilled, I can say

(21) I have spilled my coffee.

After cleaning up the mess, however, all the obvious consequences associated with this event seem to be over. In that context, it would be infelicitous to utter (21).

If the input to a perfect is not a culmination, then the perfect will do its best to coerce it to be one, subject to the limitations imposed by contextual knowledge. If the hearer cannot identify *any* relevant consequences, as seems likely for the following example, then coercion may simply fail, in which case a perfect will be infelicitous, as was noted earlier:

(22) #The star has twinkled.

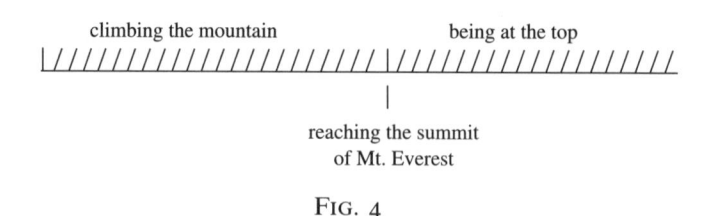

```
            climbing the mountain            being at the top
        |////////////////////////|////////////////////|
                                 |
                          reaching the summit
                             of Mt. Everest
```

FIG. 4

To be able to use a culminated process expression like *climbing Mount Everest* with a perfect auxiliary, it first has to be coerced into a culmination. Requiring such a transition might seem unnecessary since a culminated process already implies the existence of a culmination with consequences to which the perfect could refer. But consider Figure 4 as a possible rendering of the nucleus associated with *climbing Mt. Everest*.

If a perfect could be used to single out the consequences of a nucleus associated with a culminated process expression, then *having climbed Mt. Everest* could be used to refer to the state of having reached the summit or being at the top. However, this does not seem to be the case. A reporter who has managed to establish radio contact with a mountaineer who has just reached the top of Mt. Everest is unlikely to ask

(23) Have you climbed Mt. Everest yet?

The question rather seems to concern consequences of the culminated process as a whole. We capture this fact by making the perfect coerce the culminated process to become a culmination. The transition network allows this to happen if the entire event of climbing Mt. Everest is treated as a single unit by making it a point, so that it can become a culmination in its own right. The perfect then delivers a rather different kind of consequent state.

A process like *work in the garden* can be coerced by a perfect auxiliary in essentially the same way: the process of working, possibly associated with a culmination point, is treated as a single unit. This pointlike entity can then be used as the starting point for the construction of a new nucleus, by treating it as a culmination in its own right, provided that there are associated consequences. As a result, a question like (24) can only be used felicitously if John's working in the garden was (for example) part of a prearranged plan, or a particular task John had to finish before something else could happen:

(24) #Has John worked in the garden?

This account also explains the infelicity of a sentence like (25):

(25) #They have married yesterday.

The sentence could only refer to the consequences of *getting married yesterday* as opposed to getting married some other time. But most of what we think of as consequences of events are *independent* of the specific time at which the event occurred. (In this respect they are different from the preparatory processes, which are argued below to be implicated in certain futurates.) If a certain situation *is* a consequence of an event taking place at a particular time, then a perfect auxiliary may be used to describe that event. Thus a superstitious person believing that disastrous consequences are likely to result from actions performed on an unpropitious date can say:

(26) They have married on Friday the 13th!

But even on Saturday the 14th, such a person still cannot use (25), for it would not provide the essential information about the date, thus flouting Grice's maxim of quantity.

The account given here also explains the well-known contrast between the infelicitous (27a) and its felicitous counterpart, (b):

(27) a. #Einstein has visited Princeton.
b. Princeton has been visited by Einstein.

Whatever causal sequence of events and their consequences associated with the individual (Einstein) we take to be the one we are currently talking about, (a) cannot be used felicitously to refer to a part of that sequence since all such causal sequences seem to be to do with his enduring consciousness and are therefore by definition over. However, (b) *can* be uttered felicitously to refer to that same event because the relevant causal sequence must be one whose event and consequences apply to the institution of Princeton University (whose corporate consciousness endures) and many such consequences are still in train.

The hypothesis we advance that the perfect has only one temporal meaning has a precedent in the work of Inoue 1979. Moens 1987 has extended the present analysis to show that the distinctions McCawley 1971, 1981 and Comrie 1976 draw between different kinds of perfects (such as "perfect of current relevance," "hot news," "result," etc.) are nothing but different consequent states, depending on the nature of the verbal expression and the particular core event it expresses, and the specific kind of episodes in which our general knowledge tells us such core events typically occur.

3.3 Adverbials

For-adverbials can only be used felicitously with process expressions:

(28) John worked in the garden for five hours.

The resulting combination is a culminated-process expression. Evidence for this can be found in the ease with which an expression like (28) can be combined with a perfect, unlike its process counterpart:

(29) # John has worked in the garden.
John has worked in the garden for five hours.

An expression like *playing the sonata* can readily occur with a *for*-adverbial, suggesting that its basic category—by which we mean the type assigned in the lexicon and inherited by the proposition in the absence of any coercion—is that of a process. As a result, (30) carries no implication that Sue *finished* playing the sonata:

(30) Sue played the sonata for a few minutes.

Another route through the network is possible in order to account for examples like (30): Sue's playing the sonata, like any other event, can be viewed as an unstructured point. A transition to turn it into a process then results in an iteration of occurrences at which Sue plays the sonata. This route through the network seems to be ruled out for (30) because it finds no support in our knowledge about sonatas and about how long they typically last. It *does* result, however, in a likely interpretation for a sentence like

(31) Sue played the sonata for about eight hours.

A similar transition path is needed to make sense of examples like the following, in which a culmination is coerced to become a point, and then in turn coerced to become a process by being iterated:

(32) John arrived late at work for several days.

The aspectual network would wrongly predict the existence of a *for*-adverbial paradox, parallel to the imperfective paradox, if *for*-adverbials were permitted to freely coerce culminated processes (and hence culminations) to be (not necessarily completed) processes. The theory might seem to wrongly predict that (a) below would mean roughly the same as (b):

(33) a. #Red Rum won the race for the first few minutes.
     b. Red Rum was winning the race.

However, it is hard to find a context in which (a) means anything at all. The reason for this lies in the way English syntax and morphology control coercion in the aspectual transition network. The transition from culmination to consequent state, for example, demands the presence of a perfect. Similarly, the arc from process to progressive state may be traversed only if a progressive auxiliary is present in the sentence. For other transitions, such as the one resulting in an iterated process or an habitual state, English has no explicit markers and they can be made freely.

The transition from culminated process to process is not one that can be made freely in English, but seems to require the presence of a progressive *-ing*-form. As a result, turning the culmination in (33a) into a process by first adding a preparatory process and then stripping off the culmination point is not allowed. It *is* allowed in (b), but only because the example contains the required progressive *-ing*-form. The only other transition path in the aspectual network that can account for the combination of a culmination with a *for*-adverbial is the one that turns the culmination into a point, and then iterates it to be a process. This interpretation is not felicitous for (33a), either, given our knowledge about what constitutes winning a race. However, as with (32), it *is* acceptable for

(34) Nikki Lauda won the Monaco Grand Prix for several years.

Sometimes, a *for*-adverbial in combination with a culmination seems to describe a time period *following* the culmination rather than an iterated process:

(35) John left the room for a few minutes.

This adverbial is of a different kind, however, expressing intention rather than duration. It is merely by accident that English uses the same device to convey these different meanings. In French or German, for example, the two constructions are clearly distinct, as shown in the following translations of (35) and (32):

(36) Jean a quitté la chambre *pour* quelques minutes.
     Johann verliess *für* einige Minuten das Zimmer.

(37) *Pendant des années* Jean est arrivé en retard au travail.
     Jahrelang erschien Johann zu spät zur Arbeit.

Not all aspectual/temporal adverbials expressing a time span have the same functional type. *In*-adverbials, for example, coerce their input to be a *culminated* process expression, as do related phrases like "it took me two days to...." This means that combination with a culmination expression requires a transition to the culminated process node. According to the aspectual network in Figure 2 this transition is felicitous if the context allows a preparatory process to be associated with the culmination, as in (38):

(38) Laura reached the top in two hours.

The *in*-adverbial then defines the length of this preparatory period.

Since the arcs describe how one must be able to view the world for transitions to be made felicitously, it is obvious that there are expressions that will resist certain changes. For example, it will be hard to find a context in which an *in*-adverbial can be combined with a culmination expression like *Harry accidentally spilled his coffee*, since it is hard to imagine a context in which a preparatory process can be associated with an involuntary act. Indeed, sentences like the following only seem to be made tolerable to the extent that it is possible to conjure up contexts in which the event only *appears* to be accidental:

(39) In fifteen minutes, Harry accidentally spilled his coffee.

A similar problem arises in connection with the following example:

(40) John ran in a few minutes.

The process expression *John ran* has to be changed into a culminated-process expression before combination with the *in*-adverbial is possible. One way in which the network in Figure 2 will permit the change from a process to a culminated process is if the context allows a culmination point to be associated with the process itself. General world knowledge makes this rather hard for a sentence like *John ran*, except in the case where John habitually runs a particular distance, such as a measured mile. If the *in*-adverbial had conveyed a specific duration, such as *in four minutes*, then the analysis would make sense, as Dowty has pointed out. However, the unspecific *in a few minutes* continues to resist this interpretation.

However, another route is also possible for (40): the process of *John running* can be made into an atomic point, and thence into a culmination in its own right. This culmination can then acquire a preparatory process of its own—which we can think of as *preparing to run*—to become the culminated process which the adverbial requires. This time, there is no conflict with the content of the adverbial, so this reading is the most accessible of the two.

Since the transition network includes loops, it will allow us to define indefinitely complex temporal/aspectual categories, like the one evoked by the following sentence:

(41) It took me two days to play the "Minute Waltz" in less than sixty seconds for more than an hour.

The process expression *play the Minute Waltz* is coerced by the *in*-adverbial into a culminated process, including a culmination *of finishing playing the Minute Waltz*. Combination with the *for*-adverbial requires this expression to be turned into a process—the only possible route through the network being that through the point node and iterating. The resulting culminated-process expression describes the iterated process of *playing the Minute Waltz in less than sixty seconds* as lasting for more than an hour. The expression *it took me* ..., finally, is like an *in*-adverbial in that it is looking for a culminated-process expression to combine with. It would find one in the expression *to play the Minute Waltz in less than sixty seconds for more than an hour*, but combination is hampered by the fact that there is a conflict in the length of time the adverbials describe.

In the case of (41), the whole culminated process is instead viewed as a culmination in its own right (via the path through the point node). Knowledge concerning such musical feats then supplies an appropriate preparatory process that we can think of as *practising*. The phrase *it took me two days* then defines the temporal extent of this preparatory process needed to reach the point at which repeatedly playing that piece of music so fast for such a considerable length of time became a newly acquired skill. We assume that the ordering of these successive coercions, like others induced by the perfect and the progressive, are (not necessarily unambiguously) under the control of syntax.

4   TENSE AND TEMPORAL FOCUS

4.1   Tense

The aspects and temporal/aspectual adverbials considered above all act to modify or change the aspectual class of the core proposition, subject to the limits imposed by the network in Figure 2, and by contextual knowledge. However, tenses and certain other varieties of adverbial adjuncts have a rather different character. Tense is widely regarded as an anaphoric category, requiring a previously established temporal referent. The referent for a present tense is usually the time of speech, but the referent for a past tense must be explicitly established. This is done by using a second type of "temporal" adjunct, such as *once upon a time, at five o'clock last Saturday, while I was cleaning my teeth,* or *when I woke up this morning*.

Most accounts of the anaphoric nature of tense have invoked Reichenbach's (1947) trinity of underlying times and his concept of the positional use of the reference time. Under these accounts, temporal adjuncts establish a referent to which the reference time of a main clause and subsequent same-tensed clauses may attach or refer, in much the same way that various species of full noun phrases establish referents for pronouns and definite anaphors.

Reichenbach's account is somewhat inexplicit as far as extended, noninstantaneous events go. In particular, he makes it look as though the reference time is always an instant. However, we believe that the following account is the obvious generalization of his and probably what he intended anyway.

In Reichenbach's system a simple past tense of an atomic event is such that **reference time** (R) and **event time** (E) are identical, while progressives and perfects are such that R and E are *not* identical.[3] The only coherent generalization of his scheme to durative events is to maintain this pattern and assume that R and E are coextensive for an utterance like:

(42) Harry ran a mile.

It follows that R may be an extended period (cf. Steedman 1982). R may also be an extended period for a state such as a progressive, although in this case the corresponding event time is still quite separate, of course.

---

[3] In attributing this view to Reichenbach, we are assuming that there is an oversight or a misprint in his diagram for the past progressive, p. 290: the diagram seems to suggest that R and E are coextensive, whereas what is intended is that the punctual reference time is included in an extended event time, as in his diagram for the present progressive. We also ignore here one of his analyses of the modal future, which we regard as incorrect (cf. Section 5).

What is the nature of this referent, and how is it established? The anaphoric quality of tense has often been specifically compared to *pronominal* anaphora (cf. McCawley 1971; Partee 1973; Isard 1974). However, in one respect, the past tense does not behave like a pronoun: use of a pronoun such as "she" does not change the referent to which a subsequent use of the same pronoun may refer, whereas using a past tense may. In the following example, the temporal reference point for the successive conjoined main clauses seems to move on from the time originally established by the adjunct:

(43) At exactly five o'clock, Harry walked in, sat down, and took off his boots.

Nor is this just a matter of pragmatic inference; other orders of the clauses are not allowed:

(44) #At exactly five o'clock, Harry took off his boots, sat down and walked in.

This fact has caused theorists such as Dowty 1986, Hinrichs 1986, and Partee 1984 to stipulate that the reference time autonomously advances during a narrative. However, such a stipulation (besides creating problems for the theory *vis-à-vis* those narratives where reference time seems *not* to advance) seems to be unnecessary, since the *amount* by which the reference time advances still has to be determined by context. The concept of a nucleus that was invoked above to explain the varieties of aspectual categories offers us exactly what we need to explain both the fact that the reference time advances and by how much. We simply need to assume that a main-clause event such as *Harry walked in* is interpreted as an entire nucleus, complete with consequent state, for by definition the consequent state comprises whatever other events were contingent upon Harry walking in, including whatever he did next. Provided that the context (or the hearer's assumptions about the world) supports the idea that a subsequent main clause identifies this next contingent event, then it will provide the temporal referent for that main clause. If the context does not support this interpretation, then the temporal referent will be unchanged, as in:

(45) At five o'clock, my car started and the rain stopped.

In its ability to refer to temporal entities that have not been explicitly mentioned, but whose existence has merely been *implied* by the presence of an entity that *has* been mentioned, tense appears more like a definite NP (e.g., *the music* in the following example) than like a pronoun, as Webber 1987 points out.

(46) I went to a party last night. The music was wonderful.

4.2 *When*-Clauses

The definite nature of tense together with the notion of the nucleus as the knowledge structure that tensed expressions conjure up explain the apparent ambiguity of *when*-clauses with which this paper began. A *when*-clause behaves rather like one of those phrases that are used to explicitly change topic, such as *and your father* in the following example (cf. Isard 1975):

(47) And your father, how is he?

A *when*-clause does not require a previously established temporal focus, but rather brings into focus a novel temporal referent whose unique identifiability in the hearer's memory is presupposed. Again, the focused temporal referent is associated with an entire nucleus, and again an event main clause can refer to any part of this structure conditional on support from general or discourse specific knowledge. For example, consider again Example 1 with which we began (repeated here):

(48) When they built the 39th Street bridge...
    a. ...a local architect drew up the plans.
    b. ...they used the best materials.
    c. ...they solved most of their traffic problems.

Once the core event of the *when*-clause has been identified in memory, the hearer has two alternative routes to construct a complete nucleus:

(a) to *decompose* the core event into a nucleus and to make a transition to one of the components, such as the preparatory activity of building or to the consequent state of having built the bridge; or
(b) to treat the entire event as a single culmination and *compose* it into a nucleus with whatever preparation and consequences the context provides for the activity of building a bridge, and to make the transition to either one of those.

Either way, once the nucleus is established, the reference time of the main clause has to be situated somewhere within it—the exact location being determined by knowledge of the entities involved and the episode in question. So in Example 48a, the entire culminated process of building the bridge tends to become a culmination (via a path in Figure 2 that passes through the point node), which is associated in a nucleus with preparations for, and consequences of, the entire business, as in Figure 5.

The drawing up of the plans is then, for reasons to do with knowledge of the world, situated in the preparatory phase.

In Example b, in contrast, people tend to see the building of the bridge as decomposed into a quite different preparatory process of building, a quite different culmination of completing the bridge and some consequences that we take to be also subtly distinct from those in the previous case as was argued in Section 3.2. The resulting nucleus is given in Figure 6. The use of the best materials is then, as in (a), situated in the preparatory process—but it is a different one this time. Example c is like (a) in giving rise to the nucleus in Figure 5, but pragmatics seems to demand that the main clause be situated somewhere in the consequent state of building the bridge.

Thus a main clause event can potentially be situated anywhere along this nucleus, subject to support from knowledge about the precise events involved. But Example 2, repeated here, is still strange, because it is so hard to think of *any* relation that is supported in this way:

(49) # When my car broke down, the sun set.

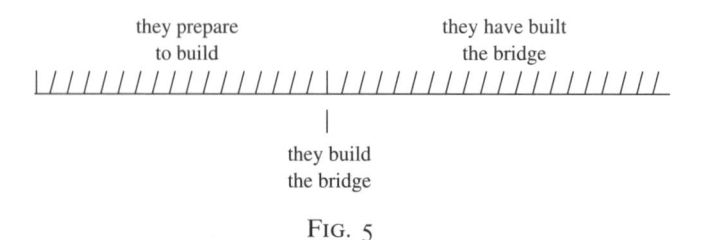

                      they prepare   they have built
                        to build   the bridge
|////////////////////\\\\\\\\\\\\\\\\\\\\\
                                   |
                              they build
                              the bridge

FIG. 5

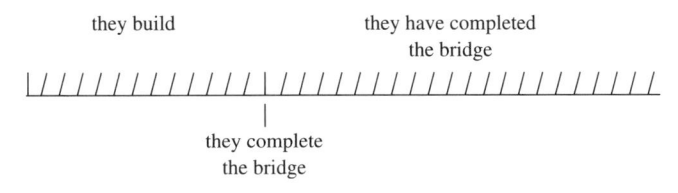

```
          they build                they have completed
                                         the bridge
|////////////////|//////////////////////////|
                 |
            they complete
             the bridge
```

FIG. 6

The *when*-clause defines a nucleus, consisting of whatever process we can think of as leading up to the car's breakdown, the breakdown itself, and its possible or actual consequences. It is not clear where along this nucleus the culmination of *the sun set* could be situated: it is not easy to imagine that it is a functional part of the preparatory process typically associated with a breakdown, and it is similarly hard to imagine that it can be a part of the consequent state, so under most imaginable circumstances, the utterance remains bizarre.

The constraints *when* places on possible interpretations of the relation between subordinate and main clause are therefore quite strong. First, general and specific knowledge about the event described in the *when*-clause has to support the association of a complete nucleus with it. Secondly, world knowledge also has to support the contingency relation between the events in subordinate and main clauses. As a result, many constructed examples sound strange or are considered to be infelicitous, because too much context has to be imported to make sense of them.

In all of the cases discussed so far, the main clause has been an event of some variety. With stative main clauses, as in the following examples, the interpretation strategy is somewhat different. Statives show no sign of being related under what we are calling contingency, presumably because contingency is by definition a relation over events. In particular, they do not enter in a causal or contingent relation with a *when*-clause the way corresponding sentences with events as main clauses do. They therefore merely predicate that the state in question holds at the time of the culmination:

(50) When they built that bridge
 ...I was still a young lad.
 ...my grandfather had been dead for several years.
 ...my aunt was having an affair with the milkman.
 ...my father used to play squash.

However, a stative main clause can be turned into an event expression; in that case, a contingency relation *is* predicated to exist between the two events. Thus the following example seems to involve an inceptive event, which *begins* the state of knowing:

(51) When Pete came in, I knew that something was wrong.

Such changes of type are similar to others discussed above but are not treated in the present paper.

5 REFERRING TO FUTURE EVENTS

Bennett and Partee 1972, speaking of the difference between the present perfect and the simple past, remark that one might expect a similar distinction among future tenses. One could conceive of a construction parallel to the perfect, whose event time would be in the future and whose reference time would be the time of speech, conveying a notion of current relevance; and there could be a construction parallel to the simple past, with both reference and event times in the future. Bennett and Partee suggest that English is *not* as one would expect and follow Reichenbach in saying that these two functions are conflated in a single device, the modal future using *will*. Although it is true that the modal future shares features of both perfect and simple past, it is nevertheless also the case that there are two classes of futurate expressions, with properties parallel to each of the two past expressions.

The candidate for the role parallel to the perfect is the so-called futurate progressive (Smith 1983):

(52) Robert was working on the speech project until he got a job offer from Sussex.

As Dowty 1979, 1986 argues, examples like (52) can be both a past imperfective progressive (answering a question about Robert's past activities) and a past futurate progressive (answering a question about Robert's plans at some past time and meaning something like *Robert was going to work on the speech project, but he didn't*). However, the difference between the two interpretations seems to be a matter of pragmatic world knowledge rather than sense-semantics, corresponding to the two different ways of constructing a nucleus (cf. Section 4). The imperfective progressive decomposes the core event into a nucleus and makes a transition to the preparatory process, indicating that it is in progress at the time of reference. The futurate progressive, through the use of an adverbial signaling an event time posterior to the reference, forces the whole event to be treated as a single unit, which is then composed into a new nucleus. The progressive then indicates that the preparation leading up to the event *as a whole* was in progress at the time of reference (as usual, without asserting that that event or even its onset was ever reached). The futurate progressive thus resembles the perfect in saying something about a (past or present) reference time that is entirely separate from the event time.

The candidate for the role parallel to the simple past among the futurates is to be found in the simple, or nonmodal future, sometimes (confusingly) called the tenseless future:

(53) He leaves on Tuesday.

While the futurate progressive shares with the perfect the property of needing no nonpresent adverbial, the nonmodal future cannot be used in this way. For example, in response to a question about the current state of affairs as specific as *Why are you being so rude to your boss these days?* or as general as *What's new?*, one may respond with an unanchored progressive (54a), much as with a perfect (54b). But one may not reply with an unanchored nonmodal future (54c), although an anchored one (54d) is quite all right.

(54) a. I am leaving.
 b. I have handed in my notice.
 c. *I leave.
 d. I leave next month.

In its requirement for an established nonpresent reference time, the nonmodal future resembles the past tense. The resemblance (which was noted in Leech 1971) is supported by the following further observations. A *when* question concerning the past progressive is ambiguous, reflecting the separation of reference time and event time. By contrast, the nonmodal future does not really seem to occur in the past at all, except of course in reported or indirect speech; it just becomes indistinguishable from the simple past.

It follows that (55) can be answered with (a) or (b). But (56) can only be answered with (a), not with (b).

(55) When were you leaving?
    a. Last week (ambiguous).
    b. Next week.

(56) When did you leave?
    a. Last week (unambiguous).
    b. *Next week.

These similarities suggest the symmetry depicted informally in Figure 7 between the perfect, the simple past, the futurate progressive, and the nonmodal future. The hatching again informally indicates the extent of the consequent state and the preparatory process associated with the perfect and the futurate progressive respectively. That is not to imply that the two are the same sort of entity: they are both states, but of a different kind. The perfect *is* a consequent state; the futurate progressive is a state derived from a preparatory process. This difference is indicated by the presence of a defined upper bound on the latter. The Reichenbach diagram in Figure 7 for the nonmodal future is of course the one that is ascribed (traditionally and by Bennett and Partee) to the modal future, a construction to which we will return in a moment. Before doing so there are some problems remaining to be disposed of.

If the futurate progressive is the true counterpart of the perfect, why is it not subject to the same restriction against nonpresent adverbials?

(57) a. John is leaving (tomorrow).
    b. John has left (*yesterday).

The answer lies in the differences between preparatory processes and consequent states, rather than in the aspects themselves. In both cases the adverbial must associate with the core event of leaving rather than the present reference time. Thus (a) concerns the preparations for *leaving tomorrow* (as opposed to some other time), while (b) concerns the consequences of *leaving yesterday* (as opposed to some other time). As was pointed out in Section 3.2, most of what we think of as consequences of events are *in*dependent of absolute time. This makes it hard to think of consequences associated with John's

PAST

      E
   |////////////|
      | | |
    S,R   E,R   S

   (perfect)   (simple past)

John has left.   John left.

FUTURATE

      E
  |////////////|
     | | |
   S,R   S   E,R

(futurate progressive)   (nonmodal future)

John is leaving (tomorrow).   John leaves tomorrow.

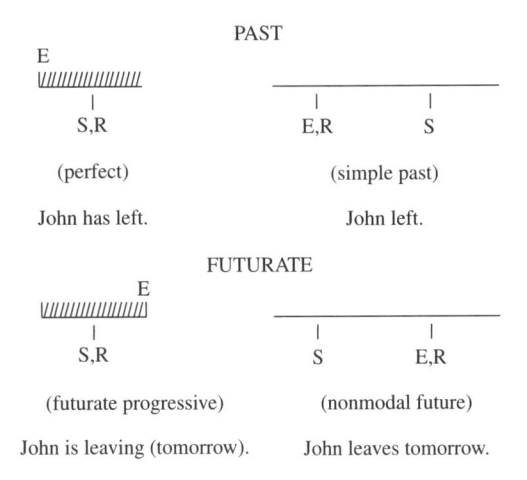

FIG. 7

leaving yesterday as opposed to those associated with John's leaving generally. Preparatory processes do not share this property: the preparatory process associated with John's leaving tomorrow is conceivably very different from that associated with John's leaving next week.

One other difference between the futurate categories and the past categories should be mentioned. If the nonmodal future is the correlate of the simple past, it should be possible to have nonmodal futures of perfects, just as with pasts of perfects. But Vetter 1973 has pointed out that the following is odd:

(58) The Dodgers have finished for the season next Sunday.

Nevertheless, such futurates *do* appear in the context of futurate temporal adjuncts, as in the following example:

(59) Once the Dodgers play the Red Sox next Sunday, they have finished for the season.

The other English futurate expressions also fit into the scheme of Figure 7. The "be going to" construction typified by

(60) I am going to buy a guitar.

clearly belongs with the progressives, being distinguished from them by the nature of the processes that it implicates (see Leech 1971; Palmer 1974; Wekker 1976, and references therein). The "be to" construction typified by

(61) I am to be Queen of the May.

also seems to belong with the progressives, although its modal character has been remarked by Leech and Palmer.

Finally, where does the modal future fit into this scheme? A full analysis of the modals would go beyond the scope of this paper, so the following remarks will be sketchy. The modal future clearly has a reference time not coincident with speech time, like the nonmodal future but unlike the futurate progressive. Nevertheless, Bennett and Partee are quite right that the modal future says something about the present as well as the past. The source of its relevance to the time of speech must therefore have to do with the relation between modals and the time of speech. We make the following tentative suggestion about this relation.

Palmer 1974 pointed out a systematic ambiguity within the epistemic modals as between a futurate and a strictly present meaning, and Steedman 1977 related this to the similar ambiguity of a present-tensed sentence. What needs to be added seems to be the idea that these (suspiciously untensed looking) modals define properties of the time of speech (as is implied by the speech-act theoretic analysis of Boyd and Thorne 1969) and do not of themselves have anything to do with reference time and event time, unlike the true tensed and aspectual auxiliaries. More specifically, *will* says of the time of speech that it leads the speaker to infer a proposition (possibly but not necessarily one concerning the future). *Must* says something very similar but seems to leave the speaker out of it and says that the proposition follows from the state of the world at speech time. *May* says that the proposition is permitted by the state of the world at speech time. These senses are exhibited below.

(62) a. You will be my long-lost brother Willy.
    a'. You will marry a tall dark stranger.

b. You must be my long-lost brother Willy.
b'. You must marry a tall dark stranger.
c. You may (or may not) be my long-lost brother, Willy.
c'. You may (or may not) marry a tall dark stranger.

But, as has often been suggested before, the future epistemic modals have nothing to do with future tense in the strict sense of the word.[4]

6 TOWARD A FORMAL REPRESENTATION

We have argued in this paper that a principled and unified semantics of natural-language categories like tense, aspect, and aspectual/temporal adverbials requires an ontology based on contingency rather than temporality. The notion of **nucleus** plays a crucial role in this ontology. The process of temporal reference involves reference to the appropriate part of a nucleus, where appropriateness is a function of the inherent meaning of the core expression, of the coercive nature of co-occurring linguistic expressions, and of particular and general knowledge about the area of discourse.

The identification of the correct ontology is also a vital preliminary to the construction and management of temporal databases. Effective exchange of information between people and machines is easier if the data-structures that are used to organize the information in the machine correspond in a natural way to the conceptual structures people use to organize the same information. In fact, the penalties for a bad fit between data-structures and human concepts are usually crippling for any attempt to provide natural language interfaces for database systems. Information extracted from natural-language text can only be stored to the extent that it fits the preconceived formats, usually resulting in loss of information. Conversely, such data-structures cannot easily be queried using natural language if there is a bad fit between the conceptual structure implicit in the query and the conceptual structure of the database.

The contingency-based ontology that we are advocating here has a number of implications for the construction and management of such temporal databases. Rather than a homogeneous database of dated points or intervals, we should partition it into distinct sequences of causally or otherwise contingently related sequences of events, which we might call **episodes**, each leading to the satisfaction of a particular goal or intention. This partition will quite incidentally define a partial temporal ordering on the events, but the primary purpose of such sequences is more related to the notion of a plan of action or an explanation of an event's occurrence than to anything to do with time itself. It follows that only events that are contingently related necessarily have well-defined temporal relations in memory.

---

[4] It is an implication of such an analysis that there should be no truly past version of epistemically modal propositions. Where past tenses of the epistemic modals do occur, they must, like the past nonmodal future, always be either counterfactual or indirect or reported speech. This seems to be the case. Mary McCarthy (1974), speaking of David Halberstam's use in *The Best and the Brightest* of "what she could only describe as the Future Past," as in

  i. At a dinner party after the Bay of Pigs Bundy would tell friends...
and
  ii. The power and prestige that the McNamara years would bring...

called it "that awful tense, seeming to endow the author with prophetic powers," signifying "a future already plangent when it has not yet happened." The source of that awful power (which also accrues to the past tenses of the nonmodal future and, as McCarthy also remarks, the modal-like "be to" construction); is of course the shifting of the speech or consciousness time into the past, rather than the reference time.

A first attempt to investigate this kind of system was reported in Steedman 1982, using a program that verified queries against a database structured according to some of the principles outlined above; a more recent extension of this work was reported in Moens 1987. Events are stored as primitives in the database, possibly but not necessarily associated with a time point. Extended events are represented in terms of a pair of punctual events, identifying their starting point as well as the point at which they end (in the case of processes) or culminate (in the case of culminated processes).

Apart from the obvious accessibility relations of temporal precedence and simultaneity, events can also enter into the relation of contingency introduced above. It is significant that the relation used in the implementation is identical to the notion of causality used by Lansky 1986 in an entirely different problem area. She developed a knowledge representation scheme for use in planners in which events are reified and modeled with an explicit representation of their temporal as well as causal relations. In this scheme, a mechanism is provided for structuring events into so-called "locations of activity", the boundaries of which are boundaries of "causal" access. As a result, two events with no causal relation between them cannot belong to the same location of activity—as in the episodes introduced above.

Because we follow Lansky in making the contingency relation intransitive, we avoid certain notorious problems in the treatment of *when*-clauses and perfects, which arise because the search for possible consequences of an event has to be restricted to the *first* event on the chain of contingencies. Thus, when (3) is asserted, repeated here as (63a) and (b), it would be wrong to infer (c):

(63) a. When John left, Sue cried.
 b. When Sue cried, her mother got upset.
 c. When John left, Sue's mother got upset.

The reason is exactly the same as the reason that it would be wrong to infer that Sue's mother got upset *because* John left, and has nothing to do with the purely *temporal* relations of these events. It should also be noted that the notion of contingency used here (in line with Lansky's proposals) is weaker than the notion of causality used in other representation schemes (for example, that of McDermott 1982 or Allen 1984): if Event A stands in a contingent relation to Event B, then an occurrence of A will *not* automatically lead to an occurrence of B: John laying the foundations of the house is a prerequisite for or enables him to build the walls and roof, but does not *cause* it in the more traditional sense of the word and does not automatically or inevitably lead to him building the walls.

The transitions in the network are implemented as inference procedures in the database. Answering a query involving the aspectual auxiliaries and adverbials discussed before consists of finding a matching event description in the database and checking its aspectual type; if the event description is found not to have the required aspectual type, it can be changed by means of the inference procedures, provided such a change is supported by knowledge in the database about the event in question.

7 CONCLUSION

Many of the apparent anomalies and ambiguities that plague current semantic accounts of temporal expressions in natural language stem from the assumption that a linear model of time is the one that our linguistic categories are most directly related to.

A more principled semantics is possible on the assumption that the temporal categories of tense, aspect, aspectual adverbials, and of propositions themselves refer to a mental representation of events that is structured on other than purely temporal principles, and to which the notion of a nucleus, or contingently related sequence of preparatory process, goal event, and consequent state, is central.

ACKNOWLEDGMENTS

We thank Jon Oberlander, Ethel Schuster, and Bonnie Lynn Webber for reading and commenting upon drafts. Parts of the research were supported by: an Edinburgh University Graduate Studentship; an ESPRIT grant (project 393) to CCS, Univ. Edinburgh; a Sloan Foundation grant to the Cognitive Science Program, Univ. Pennsylvania; and NSF grant IRI-10413 A02, ARO grant DAA6-29-84K-0061, and DARPA grant N0014-85-K0018 to CIS, Univ. Pennsylvania. An earlier version of some parts of this paper was presented as Moens and Steedman 1987.

REFERENCES

Ait-Kaci, H. (1984). 'A Lattice Theoretic Approach to Computation Based on a Calculus of Partially Ordered Type Structures'. Ph.D. dissertation, University of Pennsylvania.

Allen, J. F. (1984). 'Towards a General Theory of Action and Time', *Artificial Intelligence* 23: 123–54.

Bennett, M. and Partee, B. (1972). *Toward the Logic of Tense and Aspect in English*. Indiana University Linguistics Club, Bloomington, IN.

Boyd, J. and Thorne, J. (1969). 'The Semantics of Modal Verbs', *Journal of Linguistics* 5: 57–74.

Comrie, B. (1976). *Aspect: An Introduction to the Study of Verbal Aspect and Related Problems*. Cambridge: Cambridge University Press.

Dowty, D. (1979). *Word Meaning and Montague Grammar*. Dordrecht: D. Reidel.

——(1986). 'The Effects of Aspectual Class on the Temporal Structure of Discourse: Semantics or Pragmatics?', *Linguistics and Philosophy* 9: 37–61.

Hinrichs, E. (1986). 'Temporal Anaphora in Discourses of English', *Linguistics and Philosophy* 9: 63–82.

Inoue, K. (1979). 'An Analysis of the English Present Perfect', *Linguistics* 17: 221–2, 561–90.

Isard, S. D. (1974). 'What would you have done if...', *Theoretical Linguistics* 1: 233–55.

——(1975). 'Changing the Context', in E. Keenan (ed.), *Formal Semantics of Natural Language*. Cambridge: Cambridge University Press.

Isard, S. and Longuet-Higgins, C. (1973). 'Modal Tic-tac-toe', in R. J. Bogdan, and I. Niiniluoto (eds.), *Logic, Language and Probability*. Dordrecht: Reidel, 189–95.

Lansky, A. L. (1986). 'A Representation of Parallel Activity Based on Events, Structure, and Causality', in *Workshop on Planning and Reasoning about Action*. Timberline Lodge, Mount Hood, OR, 50–86.

Leech, G. N. (1971). *Meaning and the English Verb*. London: Longman.

McCarthy, M. (1974). 'Sons of the Morning', in *The Seventeenth Degree*. New York, NY: Harcourt Brace Jovanovich.

McCawley, J. D. (1971). 'Tense and Time Reference in English', in C. Fillmore, and T. Langendoen, (eds.), *Studies in Linguistic Semantics*. New York: Holt, Rinehart and Winston, 96–113.

——(1981). 'Notes on the English Present Perfect', *Australian Journal of Linguistics* 1: 81–90.

McDermott, D. (1982). 'A Temporal Logic for Reasoning about Processes and Plans', *Cognitive Science* 6: 101–55.

Moens, M. (1987). 'Tense, Aspect and Temporal Reference'. Ph.D. dissertation. Centre for Cognitive Science, University of Edinburgh, Edinburgh, Scotland.
—— and Steedman, M. (1986). 'Temporal Information and Natural Language Processing'. Research Paper/RP-2. Center for Cognitive Science, University of Edinburgh, Edinburgh, Scotland.
—— (1987). 'Temporal Ontology in Natural Language', in *Proceedings of the 25th Annual Meeting of the Association for Computational Linguistics*. Stanford University, Palo Alto, CA: 1–7.
Palmer, F. (1974). *The English Verb*. London: Longman.
Partee, B. (1973). 'Some Structural Analogies Between Tenses and Pronouns in English', *Journal of Philosophy* 70: 601–9.
—— (1984). 'Nominal and Temporal Anaphora', *Linguistics and Philosophy* 7: 243–86.
Passonneau, R. J. (1987). 'Situations and Intervals', in *Proceedings of the 25th Annual Meeting of the Association for Computational Linguistics*. Stanford University, Palo Alto, CA: 16–24.
Reichenbach, H. (1947). *Elements of Symbolic Logic*. London: Macmillan.
Ritchie, G. D. (1979). 'Temporal Clauses in English', *Theoretical Linguistics* 6: 87–115.
Sag, I. (1973). 'On the State of Progress on Progressives and Statives', in C. Bailey, and R. Shuy, (eds.), *New Ways of Analyzing Variation in English*. Washington, DC: Georgetown University Press, 83–95.
Smith, C. S. (1983). 'States and Dynamics', *Language* 59: 479–502.
Steedman, M. J. (1977). 'Verbs, Time and Modality', *Cognitive Science* 1: 216–34.
—— (1982). 'Reference to Past Time', in R. Jarvella, and W. Klein, (eds.), *Speech, Place and Action*. New York, NY: John Wiley and Sons, 125–57.
Vendler, Z. (1967). 'Verbs and Times', in *Linguistics in Philosophy*. Ithaca, NY: Cornell University Press, chap. 4, 97–121.
Verkuyl, H. J. (1972). *On the Compositional Nature of the Aspects*. Dordrecht: D. Reidel.
Vetter, D. (1973). 'Someone Solves This Problem Tomorrow', *Linguistic Inquiry* 4: 104–8.
Webber, B. L. (1987). 'The Interpretation of Tense in Discourse', in *Proceedings of the 25th Annual Meeting of the Association for Computational Linguistics*. Stanford University, Palo Alto, CA: 147–54.
Wekker, H. (1976). *The Expression of Future Time in Contemporary British English*. Amsterdam:. North Holland.

7

Deriving Verbal and Compositional Lexical Aspect for NLP Applications

BONNIE J. DORR AND MARI BROMAN OLSEN

1 INTRODUCTION

Knowledge of lexical aspect—how verbs denote situations as developing or holding in time—is required for interpreting event sequences in discourse (Dowty, 1986; Moens and Steedman, 1988; Passoneau, 1988), interfacing to temporal databases (Androutsopoulos, 1996), processing temporal modifiers (Antonisse, 1994), describing allowable alternations and their semantic effects (Resnik, 1996; Tenny, 1994), and for selecting tense and lexical items for natural language generation (Dorr and Olsen, 1996; Klavans and Chodorow, 1992; cf. Slobin and Bocaz, 1988). In addition, preliminary pyscholinguistic experiments (Antonisse, 1994) indicate that subjects are sensitive to the presence or absence of aspectual features when processing temporal modifiers. Resnik (1996) showed that the strength of distributionally derived selectional constraints helps predict whether verbs can participate in a class of diathesis alternations, with aspectual properties of verbs clearly influencing the alternations of interest. He also points out that these properties are difficult to obtain directly from corpora.

The ability to determine lexical aspect, on a large scale and in the sentential context, therefore yields an important source of constraints for corpus analysis and psycholinguistic experimentation, as well as for NLP applications such as machine translation (Dorr et al., 1995b) and foreign language tutoring (Dorr et al., 1995a; Sams, 1995; Weinberg et al., 1995). Other researchers have proposed corpus-based approaches to acquiring lexical aspect information with varying data coverage: Klavans and Chodorow (1992) focus on the event-state distinction in verbs and predicates; Light (1996) considers the aspectual properties of verbs and affixes; and Siegel and McKeown (1996) describe an algorithm for classifying sentences according to lexical aspect properties. Conversely, a number of works in the linguistics literature have proposed lexical semantic templates for representing the aspectual properties of verbs (Dowty, 1979; Hovav and Levin, 1995; Levin and Rappaport Hovav, to appear), although these have not been implemented and tested on a large scale.

We show that it is possible to represent the lexical aspect both of verbs alone and in sentential contexts using Lexical Conceptual Structure (LCS) representations of verbs in the classes cataloged by Levin (1993). We show how proper consideration of these universal pieces of verb meaning may be used to refine lexical representations and derive a range of meanings from combinations of LCS representations. A single algorithm may therefore be used to determine lexical aspect classes and features at both verbal and sentential levels. Finally, we illustrate how access to lexical aspect facilitates lexical selection and the interpretation of events in machine translation and foreign language tutoring applications, respectively.

2 LEXICAL ASPECT

Following Olsen (to appear in 1997), we distinguish between lexical and grammatical aspect, roughly the situation and viewpoint aspect of Smith (1991). Lexical aspect refers to the type of situation denoted by the verb, alone or combined with other sentential constituents. Grammatical aspect takes these situation types and presents them as imperfective (*John was winning the race/loving his job*) or perfective (*John had won/loved his job*). Verbs are assigned to lexical aspect classes, as in Table 1 (cf. Brinton, 1988 [p. 57]; Smith, 1991) based on their behavior in a variety of syntactic and semantic frames that focus on their features.[1]

A major source of the difficulty in assigning lexical aspect features to verbs is the ability of verbs to appear in sentences denoting situations of multiple aspectual types. Such cases arise, e.g., in the context of foreign language tutoring (Dorr et al., 1995b; Sams, 1995; Weinberg et al., 1995), where a 'bounded' interpretation for an atelic verb, e.g., *march*, may be introduced by a path PP *to the bridge* or *across the field* or by an NP *the length of the field*:

(1) The soldier marched to the bridge.
    The soldier marched across the field.
    The soldier marched the length of the field.

Some have proposed, in fact, that aspectual classes are gradient categories (Klavans and Chodorow, 1992), or that aspect should be evaluated only at the clausal or sentential level (esp. Verkuyl, 1993; see Klavans and Chodorow (1992) for NLP applications).

Olsen (to appear in 1997) showed that, although sentential and pragmatic context influence aspectual interpretation, input to the context is constrained in large part by verbs' aspectual information. In particular, she showed that the positively marked features did not vary: [+telic] verbs such as *win* were always bounded, for example, in contrast, the negatively marked features could be changed by other sentence constituents or pragmatic context: [−telic] verbs like *march* could therefore be made [+telic]. Similarly, stative verbs appeared with event interpretations, and punctiliar events as durative. Olsen therefore proposed that aspectual interpretation be derived through monotonic composition of marked privative features [+/∅ dynamic], [+/∅ durative] and [+/∅ telic], as shown in Table 2 (Olsen, to appear in 1997, pp. 32–33).

With privative features, other sentential constituents can add to features provided by the verb but not remove them. On this analysis, the activity features of *march* ([+durative, +dynamic]) propagate to the sentences in (1), with [+telic] added by the NP or PP, yielding an accomplishment interpretation. The feature specification of this compositionally derived accomplishment is therefore identical to that of a sentence containing a telic accomplishment verb, such as *produce* in (2).

---

[1] Two additional categories are identified by Olsen (to appear in 1997): Semelfactives (*cough, tap*) and Stage-level states (*be pregnant*). Since they are not assigned templates by either Dowty (1979) or Levin and Rappaport Hovav (to appear), we do not discuss them in this paper.

TABLE 1 Featural identification of aspectual classes

Aspectual Class	Telic	Dynamic	Durative	Examples
State	−	−	+	know, have
Activity	−	+	+	march, paint
Accomplishment	+	+	+	destroy
Achievement	+	+	−	notice, win

TABLE 2 Privative featural identification of aspectual classes

Aspectual Class	Telic	Dynamic	Durative	Examples
State			+	know, have
Activity		+	+	march, paint
Accomplishment	+	+	+	destroy
Achievement	+	+		notice, win

(2) The commander produced the campaign plan.

Dowty (1979) explored the possibility that aspectual features in fact constrained possible units of meaning and ways in which they combine. In this spirit, Levin and Rappaport Hovav (to appear) demonstrate that limiting composition to aspectually described structures is an important part of an account of how verbal meanings are built up, and what semantic and syntactic combinations are possible.

We draw upon these insights in revising our LCS lexicon in order to encode the aspectual features of verbs. In the next section we describe the LCS representation used in a database of 9,000 verbs in 191 major classes. We then describe the relationship of aspectual features to this representation and demonstrate that it is possible to determine aspectual features from LCS structures, with minimal modification. We demonstrate composition of the LCS and corresponding aspectual structures, by using examples from NLP applications that employ the LCS database.

3 LEXICAL CONCEPTUAL STRUCTURES

We adopt the hypothesis explored in Dorr and Olsen (1996) (cf. Tenny, 1994), that lexical aspect features are abstractions over other aspects of verb semantics, such as those reflected in the verb classes in Levin (1993). Specifically we show that a privative model of aspect provides an appropriate diagnostic for revising lexical representations: aspectual interpretations that arise only in the presence of other constituents may be removed from the lexicon and derived compositionally. Our modified LCS lexicon then allows aspect features to be determined algorithmically both from the verbal lexicon and from composed structures built from verbs and other sentence constituents, using uniform processes and representations.

This project on representing aspectual structure builds on previous work, in which verbs were grouped automatically into Levin's semantic classes (Dorr and Jones, 1996;

Dorr, to appear) and assigned LCS templates from a database built as Lisp-like structures (Dorr, 1997). The assignment of aspectual features to the classes in Levin was done by hand inspection of the semantic effect of the alternations described in Part I of Levin (Olsen, 1996), with automatic coindexing to the verb classes (see (Dorr and Olsen, 1996)). Although a number of Levin's verb classes were aspectually uniform, many required subdivisions by aspectual class; most of these divided atelic "manner" verbs from telic "result" verbs, a fundamental linguistic distinction (cf. (Levin and Rappaport Hovav, to appear) and references therein). Examples are discussed below.

Following Grimshaw (1993), Pinker (1989), and others, we distinguish between semantic structure and semantic content. Semantic structure is built up from linguistically relevant and universally accessible elements of verb meaning. Borrowing from Jackendoff (1990), we assume semantic structure to conform to wellformedness conditions based on Event and State *types*, further specialized into *primitives* such as GO, STAY, BE, GO-EXT, and ORIENT. We use Jackendoff's notion of *field*, which carries Loc(ational) semantic primitives into non-spatial domains such as Poss(essional), Temp(oral), Ident(ificational), Circ(umstantial), and Exist(ential). We adopt a new primitive, ACT, to characterize certain *activities* (such as *march*) which are not adequately distinguished from other event types by Jackendoff's GO primitive.[2] Finally, we add a manner component, to distinguish among verbs in a class, such as the motion verbs *run, walk*, and *march*. Consider *march*, one of Levin's *Run Verbs* (51.3.2);[3] we assign it the template in (3)(i), with the corresponding Lisp format shown in (3)(ii):

(3) (i) [$_{Event}$ ACT$_{Loc}$
    ([$_{Thing}$ * 1], [$_{Manner}$ BY MARCH 26])]
  (ii) (act loc
    (* thing 1) (by march 26))

This list structure recursively associates arguments with their logical heads, represented as primitive/field combinations, e.g., ACT$_{Loc}$ becomes (act loc ...) with a (thing 1) argument. Semantic content is represented by a constant in a semantic structure position, indicating the linguistically inert and non-universal aspects of verb meaning (cf. (Grimshaw, 1993; Pinker, 1989; Levin and Rappaport Hovav, to appear)), the manner component by march in this case. The numbers in the lexical entry are codes that map between LCS positions and their corresponding thematic roles (e.g., 1 = *agent*). The * marker indicates a variable position (i.e., a non-constant) that is potentially filled through composition with other constituents.

In (3), (thing 1) is the only argument. However, other arguments may be instantiated compositionally by the end-NLP application, as in (4) below, for the sentence *The soldier marched to the bridge*:

(4) (i) [$_{Event}$ CAUSE
    ([$_{Event}$ ACT$_{Loc}$
      ([$_{Thing}$ SOLDIER],
      [$_{Manner}$ BY MARCH])],

---

[2] Jackendoff (1990) augments the *thematic* tier of Jackendoff (1983) with an *action* tier, which serves to characterize activities using additional machinery. We choose to simplify this characterization by using the ACT primitive rather than introducing yet another level of representation.

[3] The numbers after the verb examples are verb class sections in Levin (1993).

```
        [Path TO_Loc
            ([Thing SOLDIER],
              [Position AT_Loc
                  ([Thing SOLDIER],
                   [Thing BRIDGE])])])]
 (ii) (cause (act loc (soldier) (by march))
        (to loc (soldier)
            (at loc (soldier) (bridge))))
```

In the next sections we outline the aspectual properties of the LCS templates for verbs in the lexicon and illustrate how LCS templates compose at the sentential level, demonstrating how lexical aspect feature determination occurs via the same algorithm at both verbal and sentential levels.

4 DETERMINING ASPECT FEATURES FROM THE LCS STRUCTURES

The components of our LCS templates correlate strongly with aspectual category distinctions. An exhaustive listing of aspectual types and their corresponding LCS representations is given below. The !! notation is used as a wildcard which is filled in by the lexeme associated with the word defined in the lexical entry, thus producing a semantic constant.

(5) (i) **States:**
```
    (be ident/perc/loc
        (thing 2) ... (by !! 26))
```
(ii) **Activities:**
```
    (act loc/perc (thing 1) (by !! 26))
      or (act loc/perc (thing 1)
           (with instr ... (!!-er 20)))
      or (act loc/perc (thing 1)
           (on loc/perc (thing 2))
             (by !! 26))
      or (act loc/perc (thing 1)
           (on loc/perc (thing 2))
           (with instr ... (!!-er 20)))
```
(iii) **Accomplishments:**
```
    (cause/let (thing 1)
      (go loc (thing 2)
        (toward/away_from ...))
          (by !! 26))
      or (cause/let (thing 1)
            (go/be ident
                (thing 2) ... (!!-ed 9)))
      or (cause/let (thing 1)
            (go loc (thing 2) ... (!! 6)))
      or (cause/let (thing 1)
            (go loc (thing 2) ... (!! 4)))
      or (cause/let (thing 1)
            (go exist (thing 2) ... (exist 9))
            (by !! 26))
```

(iv) **Achievements:**
```
(go loc (thing 2) (toward/away_from ...)
   (by !! 26))
or (go loc (thing 2) ... (!! 6))
or (go loc (thing 2) ... (!! 4))
or (go exist (thing 2) ... (exist 9)
   (by !! 26))
or (go ident (thing 2) ... (!!-ed 9))
```

The Lexical Semantic Templates (LSTs) of Levin and Rappaport Hovav (to appear) and the decompositions of Dowty (1979) also capture aspectual distinctions, but are not articulated enough to capture other distinctions among verbs required by a large-scale application.

Since the verb classes (state, activity, etc.) are abstractions over feature combinations, we now discuss each feature in turn.

4.1 Dynamicity

The feature [+dynamic] encodes the distinction between events ([+dynamic]) and states ([Ødynamic]). Arguably "the most salient distinction" in an aspect taxonomy (Dahl, 1985, p. 28), in the LCS dynamicity is encoded at the topmost level. Events are characterized by go, act, stay, cause, or let, whereas States are characterized by go-ext or be, as illustrated in (6).

(6) (i) **Achievements:** *decay, rust, redden* (45.5)
```
(go ident (* thing 2)
   (toward ident (thing 2)
      (at ident (thing 2) (!!-ed 9))))
```
(ii) **Accomplishments:** *dangle, suspend* (9.2)
```
(cause (* thing 1)
   (be ident (* thing 2)
      (at ident (thing 2) (!!-ed 9))))
```
(iii) **States:** *contain, enclose* (47.8)
```
(be loc (* thing 2)
   (in loc (thing 2) (* thing 11))
   (by !! 26))
```
(iv) **Activities:** *amble, run, zigzag* (51.3.2)
```
(act loc (* thing 1) (by !! 26))
```

4.2 Durativity

The [+durative] feature denotes situations that take time (states, activities and accomplishments). Situations that may be punctiliar (achievements) are unspecified for durativity ((Olsen, to appear in 1997) following (Smith, 1991), inter alia). In the LCS, durativity may be identified by the presence of **act, be, go-ext, cause,** and **let** primitives, as in (7); these are lacking in the achievement template, shown in (8).

(7) (i) **States:** *adore, appreciate, trust* (31.2)
```
(be perc
   (* thing 2)
   (at perc (thing 2) (* thing 8)) (by !! 26))
```

(ii) **Activities:** *amble, run, zigzag* (51.3.2)
       (act loc (* thing 1) (by !! 26))
  (iii) **Accomplishments:** *destroy, obliterate* (44)
       (cause (* thing 1)
            (go exist (* thing 2)
               (away_from exist (thing 2)
                  (at exist (thing 2) (exist 9))))
            (by !! 26))

(8) **Achievements:** *crumple, fold, wrinkle* (45.2)
    (go ident
       (* thing 2)
       (toward ident (thing 2)
          (at ident (thing 2) (!!-ed 9))))

4.3 Telicity

Telic verbs denote a situation with an inherent end or goal. Atelic verbs lack an inherent end, though, as (1) shows, they may appear in telic sentences with other sentence constituents. In the LCS, [+telic] verbs contain a Path of a particular type or a constant (!!) in the right-most leaf-node argument. Some examples are shown below:

(9) (i) leave
         (... (thing 2)
            (toward/away_from ...) (by !! 26))
    (ii) enter
         (... (thing 2) ... (!!-ed 9))
   (iii) pocket
         (... (thing 2) ... (!! 6))
    (iv) mine
         (... (thing 2) ... (!! 4))
     (v) create, destroy
         (... (thing 2) ... (exist 9) (by !! 26))

In the first case the special path component, toward or away_from, is the telicity indicator, in the next three, the (uninstantiated) constant in the rightmost leaf-node argument, and, in the last case, the special (instantiated) constant exist.

Telic verbs include:

(10) (i) **Accomplishments:** *mine, quarry* (10.9)
        (cause
           (* thing 1)
           (go loc (* thing 2)
                  ((* away_from 3) loc
                     (thing 2)
                     (at loc (thing 2) (!! 4)))))
    (ii) **Achievements:** *abandon, desert, leave* (51.2)
        (go loc
           (* thing 2)
           (away_from loc
              (thing 2)
              (at loc (thing 2) (* thing 4))))

Examples of atelic verbs are given in (11). The (a)telic representations are especially in keeping with the privative feature characterization (Olsen 1994; to appear in 1997): telic verb classes are homogeneously represented: the LCS has a path of a particular type, i.e., a "reference object" at an end state. Atelic verbs, on the other hand, do not have homogeneous representations.

(11) (i) **Activities:** *appeal, matter* (31.4)
```
(act perc (* thing 1)
      (on perc (* thing 2)) (by !! 26))
```
(ii) **States:** *wear* (41.3.1)
```
(be loc (* !! 2)
      (on loc (!! 2) (* thing 11)))
```

5 MODIFYING THE LEXICON

We have examined the LCS classes with respect to identifying aspectual categories and determined that minor changes to 101 of 191 LCS class structures (213/390 subclasses) are necessary, including substituting act for go in activities and removing Path constituents that need not be stated lexically. For example, the original database entry for class 51.3.2 is:

(12)
```
(go loc (* thing 2)
        ((* toward 5) loc
            (thing 2)
                (at loc (thing 2) (thing 6)))
        (by !! 26))
```

This is modified to yield the following new database entry:

(13) `(act loc (* thing 1) (by march 26))`

The modified entry is created by changing go to act and removing the ((* toward 5) ...) constituent.

Modification of the lexicon to conform to aspectual requirements took 3 person-weeks, requiring 1370 decision tasks at 4 minutes each: three passes through each of the 390 subclasses to compare the LCS structure with the templates for each feature (substantially complete) and one pass to change 200 LCS structures to conform with the templates. (Fewer than ten classes need to be changed for durativity or dynamicity, and approximately 200 of the 390 subclasses for telicity.) With the changes we can automatically assign aspect to some 9,000 verbs in existing classes. Furthermore, since 6,000 of the verbs were classified by automatic means, new verbs would receive aspectual assignments automatically as a result of the classification algorithm.

We are aware of no attempt in the literature to determine aspectual information on a similar scale, in part, we suspect, because of the difficulty of assigning features to verbs since they appear in sentences denoting situations of multiple aspectual types. Based on our experience handcoding small sets of verbs, we estimate generating aspectual features for 9,000 entries would require 3.5 person-months (four minutes per entry), with 1 person-month for proofing and consistency checking, given unclassified verbs, organized, say, alphabetically.

6 ASPECTUAL FEATURE DETERMINATION FOR COMPOSED LCSs

Modifications described above reveal similarities between verbs that carry a lexical aspect feature as part of their lexical entry and sentences that have features as a result of LCS composition. Consequently, the algorithm that we developed for verifying aspectual conformance of the LCS database is also directly applicable to aspectual feature determination in LCSs that have been composed from verbs and other relevant sentence constituents. LCS composition is a fundamental operation in two applications for which the LCS serves as an interlingua: machine translation (Dorr et al., 1993) and foreign language tutoring (Dorr et al., 1995b; Sams, 1993; Weinberg et al., 1995). Aspectual feature determination applies to the composed LCS by first assigning unspecified feature values—atelic [$\emptyset$T], non-durative [$\emptyset$R], and stative [$\emptyset$D]—and then monotonically setting these to positive values according to the presence of certain constituents.

The formal specification of the aspectual feature determination algorithm is shown in Figure 1. The first step initializes all aspectual values to be unspecified. Next the top node is examined for membership in a set of telicity indicators (CAUSE, LET, GO); if there is a match, the LCS is assumed to be [+T]. In this case, the top node is further checked for membership in sets that indicate dynamicity [+D] and durativity [+R]. Then the top node is examined for membership in a set of atelicity indicators (ACT, BE, STAY); if there is a match, the LCS is further examined for inclusion of a telicizing component, i.e., TO, TOWARD, FOR$_{\text{Temp}}$. The LCS is assumed to be [$\emptyset$T] unless one of these telicizing components is present. In either case, the top node is further checked for membership in sets that indicate dynamicity [+D] and durativity [+R]. Finally, the results of telicity, dynamicity, and durativity assignments are returned.

Given an LCS representation L:

1. Initialize: T(L):=[$\emptyset$T], D(L):=[$\emptyset$R], R(L):=[$\emptyset$D]
2. If Top node of L ∈ {CAUSE, LET, GO}
   Then T(L):=[+T]
      If Top node of L ∈ {CAUSE, LET}
         Then D(L):=[+D], R(L):=[+R]
      If Top node of L ∈ {GO}
         Then D(L):=[+D]
3. If Top node of L ∈ {ACT, BE, STAY}
   Then If Internal node of
   L ∈ {TO, TOWARD, FOR$_{\text{Temp}}$}
         Then T(L):=[+T]
      If Top node of L ∈ {BE, STAY}
         Then R(L):=[+R]
      If Top node of L ∈ {ACT}
         Then set D(L):=[+D], R(L):=[+R]
4. Return T(L), D(L), R(L).

FIG. 1 Algorithm for Aspectual Feature Determination.

The advantage of using this same algorithm for determination of both verbal and sentential aspect is that it is possible to use the same mechanism to perform two independent tasks: (1) Determine inherent aspectual features associated with a lexical item; (2) Derive non-inherent aspectual features associated with combinations of lexical items.

Note, for example, that adding the path *to the bridge* to the [∅telic] verb entry in (3) establishes a [+telic] value for the sentence as a whole, an interpretation available by the same algorithm that identifies verbs as telic in the LCS lexicon:

(14) (i) [∅telic]:
    (act loc (* thing 1) (by march 26))
  (ii) [+telic]:
    (cause
      (act loc (soldier) (by march))
      (to loc (soldier)
        (at loc (soldier) (bridge)))))

In our applications, access to both verbal and sentential lexical aspect features facilitates the task of lexical choice in machine translation and interpretation of students' answers in foreign language tutoring. For example, our machine translation system selects appropriate translations based on the matching of telicity values for the output sentence, whether or not the verbs in the language match in telicity. The English atelic manner verb *march* and the telic PP *across the field* from (1) is best translated into Spanish as the telic verb *cruzar* with the manner *marchando* as an adjunct:

(15) (i) E: The soldier marched across the field.
      S: El soldado cruzó el campo marchando.
  (ii) (cause
      (act loc (soldier) (by march))
      (to loc (soldier)
        (across loc (soldier) (field)))))

Similarly, in changing the *Weekend Verbs* (i.e., *December, holiday, summer, weekend,* etc.) template to telic, we make use of the measure phrase (for temp...) which was previously available, though not employed, as a mechanism in our database. Thus, we now have a lexicalized example of 'doing something for a certain time' that has a representation corresponding to the canonical telic frame V *for an hour* phrase, as in *The soldier marched for an hour*:

(16) (act loc (soldier) (by march)
      (for temp (*head*) (hour)))

This same telicizing constituent—which is compositionally derived in the *crawl* construction—is encoded directly in the lexical entry for a verb such as *December*:

(17) (stay loc
    (* thing 2)
    ((* [at] 5) loc (thing 2) (thing 6))
    (for temp (*head*) (december 31)))

This lexical entry is composed with other arguments to produce the LCS for *John Decembered at the new cabin*:

(18) (stay loc (john)
    (at loc (john) (cabin (new)))
    (for temp (*head*) (december)))

This same LCS would serve as the underlying representation for the equivalent Spanish sentence, which uses an atelic verb *estar*[4] in combination with a temporal

---

[4] Since *estar* may be used with both telic *(estar alto)* and atelic *(estar contento)* readings, we analyze it as atelic to permit appropriate composition.

adjunct *durante el mes de Diciembre*: *John estuvo en la cabaña nueva durante el mes de Diciembre* (literally, *John was in the new cabin during the month of December*).

The monotonic composition permitted by the LCS templates is slightly different than that permitted by the privative feature model of aspect (Olsen, 1994; Olsen, to appear in 1997). For example, in the LCS states may be composed into an achievement or accomplishment structure, because states are part of the substructure of these classes (cf. templates in (6)). They may not, however, appear as activities. The privative model in Table 2 allows states to become activities and accomplishments, by adding [+dynamic] and [+telic] features, but they may not become achievements, since removal of the [+durative] feature would be required. The nature of the alternations between states and events is a subject for future research.

7 CONCLUSION

The privative feature model, on which our LCS composition draws, allows us to represent verbal and sentential lexical aspect as monotonic composition of the same type, and to identify the contribution of both verbs and other elements. The lexical aspect of verbs and sentences may be therefore determined from the corresponding LCS representations, as in the examples provided from machine translation and foreign language tutoring applications. We are aware of no attempt in the literature to represent and access aspect on a similar scale, in part, we suspect, because of the difficulty of identifying the aspectual contribution of the verbs and sentences given the multiple aspectual types in which verbs appear.

An important corollary to this investigation is that it is possible to refine the lexicon, because variable meaning may, in many cases, be attributed to lexical aspect variation predictable by composition rules. In addition, factoring out the structural requirements of specific lexical items from the predictable variation that may be described by composition provides information on the aspectual effect of verbal modifiers and complements. We are therefore able to describe not only the lexical aspect at the sentential level, but also the set of aspectual variations available to a given verb type.

REFERENCES

Androutsopoulos, Ioannis. (1996). 'A Principled Framework for Constructing Natural Language Interfaces to Temporal Databases'. Ph.D. dissertation, University of Edinburgh.

Antonisse, Peggy. (1994). 'Processing Temporal and Locative Modifiers in a Licensing Model'. Technical Report 2: 1–38, Working Papers in Linguistics, University of Maryland.

Brinton, Laurel J. (1988). *The Development of English Aspectual Systems: Aspectualizers and Post-Verbal Particles*. Cambridge: Cambridge University Press.

Dahl, Östen. (1985). *Tense and Aspect Systems*. Oxford: Basil Blackwell.

Dorr, Bonnie J. (1997). 'Large-Scale Acquisition of LCS-Based Lexicons for Foreign Language Tutoring', in *Proceedings of the Fifth Conference on Applied Natural Language Processing (ANLP)*, Washington, DC, 139–46.

——(to appear). 'Large-Scale Dictionary Construction for Foreign Language Tutoring and Interlingual Machine Translation', *Machine Translation*, 12(1).

—— Hendler, James, Blanksteen, Scott, and Migdalof, Barrie (1993). 'Use of Lexical Conceptual Structure for Intelligent Tutoring'. Technical Report UMIACS TR 93-108, CS TR 3161, University of Maryland.

Dorr, Bonnie J., Hendler, Jim, Blanksteen, Scott, and Migdalof, Barrie. (1995*a*). 'Use of LCS and Discourse for Intelligent Tutoring: On Beyond Syntax', in Melissa Holland, Jonathan Kaplan, and Michelle Sams, (eds.), *Intelligent Language Tutors: Balancing Theory and Technology*. Hillsdale, NJ: Lawrence Erlbaum Associates, 289–309.

——Lin, Dekang, Lee, Jye-hoon, and Suh, Sungki. (1995*b*). 'Efficient Parsing for Korean and English: A Parameterized Message Passing Approach', *Computational Linguistics* 21(2): 255–63.

——and Jones, Douglas. (1996). 'Role of Word Sense Disambiguation in Lexical Acquisition: Predicting Semantics from Syntactic Cues', in *Proceedings of the International Conference on Computational Linguistics*, Copenhagen, Denmark, 322–33.

——and Olsen, Mari Broman. (1996). 'Multilingual Generation: The Role of Telicity in Lexical Choice and Syntactic Realization', *Machine Translation* 11(1–3): 37–74.

Dowty, David. (1979). *Word Meaning in Montague Grammar*. Dordrecht: Reidel.

——(1986). 'The Effects of Aspectual Class on the Temporal Structure of Discourse: Semantics or Pragmatics?' *Linguistics and Philosophy* 9: 37–61.

Grimshaw, Jane. (1993). 'Semantic Structure and Semantic Content in Lexical Representation'. Unpublished MS., Rutgers University, New Brunswick, NJ.

Hovav, Malka Rappaport and Levin, Beth. (1995). 'The Elasticity of Verb Meaning', in *Processes in Argument Structure,* SfS-Report-06-95, Seminar für Sprachwissenschaft, Eberhard-Karls-Universität Tübingen, Tübingen, 1–13.

Jackendoff, Ray. (1983). *Semantics and Cognition*. Cambridge, MA: MIT Press.

——(1990). *Semantic Structures*. Cambridge, MA: MIT Press.

Klavans, Judith L. and Chodorow, M. (1992). 'Degrees of Stativity: The Lexical Representation of Verb Aspect', in *Proceedings of the 14th International Conference on Computational Linguistics*, Nantes, France, 1126–31

Levin, Beth. (1993). *English Verb Classes and Alternations: A Preliminary Investigation*. Chicago, IL: University of Chicago Press.

——and Rappaport Hovav, Malka (to appear). 'Building Verb Meanings', in M. Butt and W. Gauder (eds.), *The Projection of Arguments: Lexical and Syntactic Constraints*. CSLI.

Light, Marc. (1996). 'Morphological Cues for Lexical Semantics', in *Proceedings of the 34th Annual Meeting of the Association for Computational Linguistics*.

Moens, Marc and Mark Steedman. (1988). 'Temporal Ontology and Temporal Reference', *Computational Linguistics: Special Issue on Tense and Aspect*, 14(2): 15–28.

Olsen, Mari Broman. (1994). 'The Semantics and Pragmatics of Lexical Aspect Features', in *Proceedings of the Formal Linguistic Society of Midamerica V*, University of Illinois, Urbana-Champaign, May, 361–75. In *Studies in the Linguistic Sciences*, 24(2) Fall 1994.

——(1996). 'Telicity and English Verb Classes and Alternations: An Overview'. Umiacs tr 96–15, cs tr 3607, University of Maryland, College Park, MD.

——(to appear in 1997). *The Semantics and Pragmatics of Lexical and Grammatical Aspect*. New York: Garland.

Passoneau, Rebecca. (1988). 'A Computational Model of the Semantics of Tense and Aspect', *Computational Linguistics: Special Issue on Tense and Aspect*, 14(2): 44–60.

Pinker, Steven. (1989). *Learnability and Cognition: The Acquisition of Argument Structure*. Cambridge, MA: MIT Press.

Resnik, Philip. (1996). 'Selectional Constraints: An Information-Theoretic Model and its Computational Realization', *Cognition* 61: 127–59.

Sams, Michelle. (1993). 'An Intelligent Foreign Language Tutor Incorporating Natural Language Processing', in *Proceedings of Conference on Intelligent Computer-Aided Training and Virtual Environment Technology*, NASA: Houston, TX.

——(1995). 'Advanced Technologies for Language Learning: The BRIDGE Project Within the ARI Language Tutor Program', in Melissa Holland, Jonathan Kaplan, and Michelle Sams (eds.), *Intelligent Language Tutors: Theory Shaping Technology*. Hillsdale, NJ: Lawrence Erlbaum Associates, 7–21.

Siegel, Eric V. and McKeown, Kathleen R. (1996). 'Gathering Statistics to Aspectually Classify Sentences with a Genetic Algorithm'. Unpublished MS (cmp-lg/9610002), Columbia University, New York, NY.

Slobin, Dan I. and Bocaz, Aura. (1988). 'Learning to Talk About Movement Through Time and Space: The Development of Narrative Abilities in Spanish and English', *Lenguas Modernas*, 15: 5–24.

Smith, Carlota. (1991). *The Parameter of Aspect*. Dordrecht: Kluwer.

Tenny, Carol. (1994). *Aspectual Roles and the Syntax-Semantics Interface*. Dordrecht: Kluwer.

Verkuyl, Henk. (1993). *A Theory of Aspectuality: The Interaction Between Temporal and Atemporal Structure*. Cambridge and New York: Cambridge University Press.

Weinberg, Amy, Garman, Joseph, Martin, Jeffery, and Merlo, Paola. (1995). 'Principle-Based Parser for Foreign Language Training in German and Arabic', in Melissa Holland, Jonathan Kaplan, and Michelle Sams (eds.), *Intelligent Language Tutors: Theory Shaping Technology*. Hillsdale, NJ: Lawrence Erlbaum Associates, 23–44.

8

A Computational Model of the Semantics of Tense and Aspect

REBECCA J. PASSONNEAU[1]

1 INTRODUCTION

The PUNDIT text-processing system extracts temporal information about real-world situations from short message texts.[2] This involves three complementary analyses. First, PUNDIT determines whether a situation has **actual time** associated with it. A reference to a possible or potential situation, for example, would need a different treatment. Second, it determines the **temporal structure** of the predicated situation, or the manner in which it evolves through time. Finally, it analyzes the **temporal location** of the actual situations with respect to the time of text production or to the times of other situations. These three pieces of information are derived from the lexical head of a predication (verbal, adjectival, or nominal), its grammatical inflections (tense, progressive, perfect), and finally, temporal adverbs such as *before, after,* and *when*. Each of these components of temporal meaning is assigned a context-dependent compositional semantics. A fundamental premise of this approach is that the several sentence elements contributing temporal information can and should be analyzed in tandem (Mourelatos 1981, Dowty 1986) in order to determine the times for which predications are asserted to hold. This is accomplished by means of a model of the semantics of time that incorporates both aspect and a Reichenbachian treatment of tense (Reichenbach 1947).

The temporal analysis component described here was originally designed to handle PUNDIT's first text domain, CASREP messages, which are reports describing equipment failures on navy ships.[3] This domain was a particularly appropriate one for implementing a component to analyze the time information contained explicitly within the individual sentences of a text. CASREPs are diagnostic reports consisting of simple declarative sentences. They present a cumulative description of the current status of a particular piece of equipment rather than narrating a sequence of events. Within one sentence, several different situations may be mentioned, linked together by explicit temporal connectives such as *before* and *after*. It is thus possible to extract a good deal of the important temporal information from these texts without handling intersentential

---

Rebecca J. Passonneau, 'A Computational Model of the Semantics of Tense and Aspect', *Computational Linguistics* 14 (2), 1988, 15–28. © 1988 Association for Computational Linguistics.

[1] Paoli Research Center, Defense systems, UNISYS, formerly Paoli Research Center, SDC—A Burroughs Company.
[2] Prolog UNDerstanding of Integrated Text: it is a modular system, implemented in Quintus Prolog, with distinct syntactic, semantic and pragmatic components (Dahl et al. 1987a, Dahl 1986, Dowding and Hirschman 1987, Palmer et al. 1986).
[3] PUNDIT has now been adapted to four domains.

temporal relations. However, the implementation of the temporal semantic component described here lays the necessary groundwork for eventually computing intersentential relations along lines proposed in Webber 1987.[4] The capacity to process intersentential temporal relations is, of course, essential for adequately handling narrative data.

2 TEMPORAL INFORMATION

The premise of the present work is that accurate computation of the temporal semantics of the verb and its grammatical categories of tense, perfect, and progressive provide a foundation for computing other kinds of temporal information, including the interpretation of temporal adverbials.[5] However, the task of modeling the semantic contribution of the verb and its categories is a complex one because temporal information is distributed across several nonunivocal lexical and grammatical elements. As the extensive linguistic and philosophical literature on tense and aspect demonstrates, the precise temporal contribution of any one surface category of the verb is contingent upon co-occurring verbal categories, as well as upon the inherent meaning of the verb, and even the nature of the verb's arguments (Comrie 1976, Dowty 1979, Mourelatos 1981, Vlach 1981, Vendler 1967). Hence, even a preliminary solution to the computational problems of interpreting temporal information in natural language requires recognizing the relevant semantic interdependencies. This paper proposes a solution to the computational task of extracting temporal information from simple declarative sentences based on separating temporal analysis into distinct tasks, each of which has access to a selected portion of the temporal input. The ultimate goal is to represent temporal information as explicitly as possible at each stage of analysis in order to provide the appropriate information for the next stage. Because the representations are constructed incrementally, it is important that they should be explicit about what has been derived so far, yet sufficiently noncommittal to avoid conflicting with subsequent processing.

The present section of the paper provides the background needed for understanding the information that the algorithm integrating tense and aspect (presented in Section 4) is designed to compute. First, in Section 2.1, I explain what is meant by **actual time** and delimit the scope of the phenomena focused on here. Then in Section 2.2, I describe the components of temporal structure and how they are used to distinguish states, transition events, and two ways of referring to processes. Also in this section I review Dowty's (1979) aspect calculus and introduce how it is used in deriving the representation of temporal structure.

The remaining sections of the paper focus on the implementation. Section 3 describes the input to the temporal component. Section 4 presents the algorithm for computing the situation representations and their temporal location. Part of the computation of temporal location involves determining the reference time of a predication.

---

[4] Webber, in work carried out in part at the Paoli Research Center, proposes a focusing algorithm for computing intersentential temporal relations which is analogous to Sidner's focusing mechanism for definite anaphoric expressions. Future work by Webber and Passonneau will integrate the two dimensions of inter- and intrasentential temporal analysis.

[5] Various types of tenseless predications are processed by PUNDIT's temporal component, including nominalizations, certain clausal modifiers of noun phrases (e.g., *pressure decreasing below 60 psig caused the pump to fail*), and sentence fragments (Linebarger et al. 1988). However, this paper focuses on the simpler case of tensed clauses.

Reference time pertains to the interpretation of relational temporal adverbials, i.e., adverbials that relate the time of a situation to another time (e.g., *The ship was refueled yesterday*, cf. Smith 1981).[6] Temporal connectives, for example, relate the time of a syntactically subordinate predication to a superordinate one. A brief discussion of how the reference time participates in the interpretation of temporal adverbial clauses introduced by connectives such as *before, after*, and *when* is given in Section 5, whose more general topic is the utility of the situation representations for the interpretation of a variety of adverbial types.[7]

2.1 Actual temporal reference

Actual situations are those that are asserted to have already occurred, or to be occurring at the time when a text is produced. This excludes, e.g., situations mentioned in modal, intensional, negated, or frequentative contexts.[8] A predication denotes an actual situation when two criteria are satisfied. First, at least one of the verb's arguments must be interpreted as specific (Dowty 1979, Mourelatos 1981, Vlach 1981). For example, the simple past of *fly* denotes a specific situation in Sentence 1 but not in (2), because the subject of the verb in (2) is a nonspecific indefinite plural.

(1) John flew TWA to Boston.

(2) Tourists flew TWA to Boston.

This paper does not address the interaction of the nature of a verb's arguments with the specificity of references to situations.

The second criterion is that the situation must be asserted to hold in the real world for some specific time. Predications in modal contexts (including the future; cf. Sentence 3) are excluded because their truth evaluation does not involve specific real-world times, but rather, hypothetical or potential times.

(3) The oil pressure should/may/will decrease.

Additionally, frequency adverbials like *always* may force a temporally nonspecific reading, as in (4).

(4) John always flew his own plane to Boston.

PUNDIT's time component does not currently identify modal contexts, frequency adverbials, or nonspecific verb arguments. However, it does identify predications denoting situation types when the form of the verb itself provides this information.

In evaluating actual time, PUNDIT distinguishes between examples like (5) and (6) on the basis of the verb and its grammatical categories. An actual use of the sentence in (5), for example, would report that a particular pump participated in a particular event at a specific time.

---

[6] Reference time also plays a role in intersentential temporal reference (cf. Hinrichs 1988, Moens and Steedman 1988, Nakhimovsky 1988, Webber 1988).

[7] For the sake of brevity, the treatment of temporal adverbs with nominal complements is not described in this paper, but cf. Dahl et al. 1987b.

[8] These are not currently handled in the PUNDIT system. Predications embedded in any one of these contexts do not directly denote specific situations but rather denote types of situations which, e.g., might occur, have not occurred, or tend to occur. Treatment of these contexts awaits the development of a representation which distinguishes between specific situations which hold for some real time and types of situations which hold for some potential time. One such proposal appears in Roberts 1985, which allows for the creation of temporary contexts.

(5) The lube oil pump seized.

(6) The lube oil pump seizes.

(7) The lube oil pump seized whenever the engine jacked over.

Sentences 6 and 7, on the other hand, report on types of recurrent events. In sentence 7, it is the adverb *whenever* that indicates that the main clause refers to a recurrent type of event rather than to a specific event token situated at a particular time. In (6), it is the lexical aspect of the verb *seize* in combination with the present tense that provides that information. A further difference between the two examples is that (7) entails that on at least one past occasion the pump actually seized when the engine jacked over, while (6) does not entail that the lube oil pump ever actually seized. We will see in Section 4.1 that (6) would immediately be determined not to evoke actual time on the basis of the lexical aspect of the verb and its inflectional form. Although PUNDIT does not yet handle frequency adverbials, Section 5 illustrates the procedure by which the main clause of (7) would be processed so that its relation to the subordinate clause event could be identified later.

Lexical aspect is the inherent semantic content of a lexical item pertaining to the temporal structure of the situation it refers to, and thus plays a major role in computing temporal information. The aspectual categories and their relevance to temporal processing are discussed in Section 2.2.

It should be noted that other semantic and pragmatic properties also affect temporal analysis. For example, there are conditions under which the present tense of a verb referring to an event, as in (6), is associated with an actual situation. Under the right conditions, first-person performatives (e.g., *I warn you not to cross me*) accomplish the named event at the moment they are uttered (Austin 1977). Even a sentence like (6) can refer to an actual event if interpreted as a report of a presently unfolding situation, as in a sportscast. Handling tense in these types of discourse would require representing pragmatic features, such as the speaker/addressee relationship, in order to handle the relation of indexicals like tense and person to the speech situation (Jakobson 1957). Section 3 briefly mentions some semantic distinctions pertaining to the verb in addition to lexical aspect, which PUNDIT does handle. Otherwise, however, this paper focuses on temporal analysis of third person descriptions containing verbs whose arguments refer to specific, concrete participants.

2.2 Temporal structure of actual situations

Situations are classified on the basis of their temporal structure into three types: states, processes, and transition events. Each situation type has a distinct temporal structure comprised of one or more intervals. Two features are associated with each interval: kinesis and boundedness. Both terms will be defined more fully below, but briefly, kinesis pertains to the internal structure of an interval, or in informal terms, whether something is happening within the interval. Boundedness pertains to the way in which an interval is located in time with respect to other intervals, e.g., whether it is bounded by another interval.

This approach to the compositional semantics of temporal reference is similar in spirit to interval semantics in the attempt to account for the semantic effects of aspectual class (Dowty 1986, Dowty 1982, Dowty 1979, Taylor 1977). However, interval semantics captures the distinct temporal properties of situations by specifying a truth-conditional relation between a full sentence and a unique interval. The goal of PUNDIT's temporal analysis is not simply to sort references to situations into states, processes, and events, but more specifically to represent the differences between the three situation types *by considering in detail the characteristics of the set of temporal intervals that they hold or occur over* (Allen 1984: 132). Thus, instead of specifying a single set of entailments for each of the three situation types, the temporal semantics outlined here specifies what property of an interval is entailed by what portion of the input sentence, and then compositionally constructs a detailed representation of a state, process, or event from the intervals and their associated features. The critical difference from interval semantics is that while intervals are the fundamental unit from which situation representations are constructed, it is proposed here that intervals have properties that differentiate them from one another.

2.2.1 *Situation types and temporal structure*

The three situation types—states, processes, and transition events—are distinguished from one another entirely on the basis of the grammatically encoded means provided by the language for talking about how and when they occur. People certainly can and do conceptualize finer differences among real-world situations and can even describe these differences, given sufficient time or space. But certain gross distinctions are unavoidably made whenever people mention things happening in the world. Here and in the next section we will examine the temporal distinctions encoded in the form of the verb, often referred to as **aspect**, which are here referred to as temporal structure. Part of the temporal structure, that which Talmy (1985) described as the **pattern of distribution of action through time**, is represented in the time arguments for the three situation types. Another part of the temporal structure, its event time, is the component of temporal structure that gets located in time by tense and the perfect. All the relevant distinctions of temporal structure are represented in terms of intervals and moments of time.

States. Very briefly, a state is a situation that holds over some interval of time, which is both stative and unbounded. A stative interval is one in which, with respect to the relevant predication, there is no change across the interval for which the situation holds. Thus stative intervals are defined here much as stative predications are defined in interval semantics:

An interval I over which some predication ψ holds is stative iff it follows from the truth of ψ over I that ψ is true at all subintervals of I (Dowty 1986: 42).

Sentence 8 is an example of a typical stative predication whose verb phrase is headed by an adjective. During the interval for which the predicate *low* holds over the entity *pressure*, each subinterval is equivalent to any other subinterval with respect to the asserted situation; thus its kinesis is stative.

(8) The pressure is low.

Some of the diagnostic tests for stative predications are that they cannot be modified by rate adverbials (**The pressure was quickly low*), nor referenced with *do it* anaphora (*The pressure was very low. *The temperature also did it/that.*). While inability to occur with the progressive suffix has often been cited as another diagnostic, it is a less reliable one. Dowty 1979 identifies a class of locative stative predications that occur in the progressive (e.g., *The socks are lying under the bed*). Predicates denoting cognition or behavior have often been classified as statives but may occur in the progressive with reference to a cognitive or behavioral process.[9] Although such verbs do not appear in the current domain, they would be treated differently from pure stative verbs.

The intervals associated with states are also inherently unbounded, although a temporal bound could be provided by an appropriate temporal adverbial (e.g., *The pressure was normal until the pump seized*).[10] When an unbounded interval is located with respect to another point in time, it is assumed to extend indefinitely in both directions around that time, as with the punctual adverbial in (9). The moment within the interval that is explicitly located by tense and the punctual adverbial is the situation's event time, depicted as a circle in the middle of the interval, with arrows representing that the interval extends indefinitely into the past and toward the present.

(9) The pressure was low at 0800.

←————————O————————→

Situation type: state
Kinesis: stative
Boundedness: unbounded

This sentence would be true if the pressure were low for only an instant coincident with *0800*, but it is not asserted to hold only for that instant; one thus assumes that it was low not only at the named time, but also prior and subsequent to it. In this sense, the interval is unbounded, as represented graphically above.

Processes. A process is a situation which holds over an active interval of time. Active intervals contrast with stative intervals in that there is change within the interval, a useful distinction for interpreting manner adverbials indicating rate of change, e.g., *slowly* and *rapidly*. Since states denote the absence of change over time, they cannot be modified by rate adverbials; processes can be.

The definition of active intervals is also adapted from the characterization of process predications in interval semantics:

An interval I over which some predication ψ holds is active iff it follows from the truth of ψ at I that ψ is true over all subintervals of I down to a certain limit in size (Dowty 1986: 42).

Active intervals can be unbounded or unspecified for boundedness, depending on whether the verb is progressive. In (10), the active interval associated with the alarm sounding is unbounded and bears the same relationship to the named clock time as does the stative interval in (9) above.

(10) The alarm was sounding at 0800.

←————————O————————→

Situation type: process
Kinesis: active
Boundedness: unbounded

Progressive aspect has often been compared to lexical stativity.[11] Here the commonality among sentences like (9) and (10) is captured by associating the feature of unboundedness both with stative lexical items and with progressive aspect. The temporal structures

---

[9] Cf. discussion of examples like *I am thinking good thoughts*, and *My daughter is being very naughty*, in Smith 1986.

[10] In general, temporal adverbials can modify an existing component of temporal structure or add components of temporal structure.

[11] For comparisons of stativity and the progressive, cf. Vlach 1981, where the two are equated, Smith's counterargument (1986), and the interesting proposal in Mufwene 1984.

of states and unbounded processes are thus identical with respect to boundedness. However, the distinction between the kinesis of (9) and (10) is retained by distinguishing active from stative intervals.

In (11) the interval associated with the alarm sounding is unspecified for boundedness, meaning that the clock time may occur within the interval for which the alarm sounded, or at its onset or termination.

(11) The alarm sounded at 0800.

```
----------------⊖------------------→
```

Situation type: process
Kinesis: active
Boundedness: unspecified

In (10), where the verb is progressive, the clock time is interpreted as falling within the unbounded interval of *sounding,* but in (11), where the verb is not progressive, the clock time can be interpreted as falling at the inception of the process or as roughly locating the entire process.[12] Nonprogressive forms of process verbs exhibit a wide variation in the interpretation of what part of the temporal structure is located by tense. The influencing factors seem to be pragmatic in nature, rather than semantic. The solution taken here is to characterize the event time of such predications as having an unspecified relation to the active interval associated with the denoted process, represented graphically above by the dashed line around the event time.

Transition Events. A transition event is a complex situation consisting of a process which culminates in a new state or process. The new state or process comes into being as a result of the initial process. Since states have no kinesis, they cannot culminate in new situations. The temporal structure of a transition event is thus an active interval followed by—and bounded by—a new active or stative interval.[13]

That there are these three distinct components of transition events can be illustrated by the following sentences in which the time adverbials modify one of the three temporally distinct parts of the predicated event.

(12) It took 5 minutes for the pump to seize.

(13) The pump seized precisely at 14:04:01.

(14) The pump was seized for 2 hours.[14]

The duration *5 minutes* in (12) above applies to the interval of time during which the pump was in the process of *seizing.* The clock time in (13) corresponds to the moment when the pump is said to have made a transition to the new state of *being seized.* Finally, the measure phrase in (14) corresponds to the interval associated with the new state.

Following Dowty 1986, Vendler's (1967) two classes of achievements and accomplishments are collapsed here into the single class of transition events, and for much the

---

[12] Nakhimovsky (1988) makes essentially the same argument, namely that English lacks overt perfective grammatical aspect. In other words, the indeterminacy associated with the simple past of a process verb is evidence for the argument that the **perfective** or **culminated** reading associated with simple past transition event verbs, which are discussed in the next subsection, is a consequence of the interaction between tense and lexical aspect, rather than of the simple past tense itself.

[13] This treatment of transition events closely resembles the **event structure** which Moens and Steedman refer to as a **nucleus.** They define a nucleus as a structure comprising a culmination, an associated preparatory process, and a consequent state (Moens and Steedman 1987).

[14] The durational adverbial in (14) forces a stative reading for a predicate which in isolation would be ambiguous between a passive and the adjectival passive (Levin and Rappaport 1986), in which the past participle is interpreted statively or adjectivally.

same reasons. That is, achievements differ from accomplishments in being *typically of shorter duration* and in not entailing a sequence of subevents, but they nevertheless *do in fact have some duration* (Dowty 1986: 43). Even so-called punctual events (e.g., *They arrived at the station; She recognized her long-lost friend*) can be talked about as if they had duration (Talmy 1985, Jackendoff 1987), apparently depending on the granularity of time involved. It is my belief that handling granularity depends on appropriate interaction with a relatively rich model of the world and of the current discourse, but would not require new units of time; depending on the level of detail required, moments could be exploded into intervals, or intervals collapsed into moments. For these reasons, punctual events are not treated here as a separate class.

With verbs in Vendler's class of achievements, the same participant generally participates in both the initial process and the resulting situation, as in (15):

(15) The engine failed at 0800.

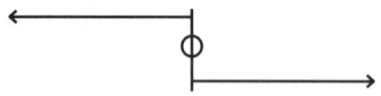

Situation type: transition event
Kinesis: active
Boundedness: bounded

Here, the engine participates in some process (*failing*), which culminates in a new state (e.g., *being inoperative*). In each case, however, there are two temporally distinct intervals, as shown in the diagram above, one bounded by the other.

Causative verbs typically denote accomplishments involving subevents in which the action of one participant results in a change in another participant, as in (16):

(16) The pump sheared the drive shaft.

Here, a process in which the pump participated (*shearing*) is asserted to have caused a change in the drive shaft (*being sheared*). The consequence of the different argument structures of (15) and (16) on the event representation is discussed in the next section.

The boundary between the two intervals associated with a transition event, the transition bound, is defined as a transitional moment between the initial active interval and the ensuing active or stative interval associated with the new situation. An important role played by the transition bound is that it is the temporal component of transition events that locates them with respect to other times. For example, (15) asserts that the moment of transition to the new situation coincides with *0800*. In contrast with examples 9–11, the status of the engine prior to *0800* is asserted to be different from its status at *0800* and afterwards. The components of temporal structure proposed here are intended to provide a basis for deriving what is said about the relative ordering of situations and their durations, rather than to correspond to physical reality. Thus a transition bound is a convenient abstraction for representing how transition events are perceived and talked about. Since a transition event is one which results in a new situation, there is in theory a point in time before which the new situation does not exist and subsequent to which the new situation does exist. This point, however, is a theoretical construct not intended to correspond to an empirically determined time. It corresponds exactly to the kind of boundary between intervals involved in Allen's (1983, 1984) **meets** relation.

2.2.2 Dowty's aspect calculus

The intervals for which situations hold are closely linked with the semantic decompositions of the lexical items used in referring to them. This allows PUNDIT to represent precisely what kinds of situations entities participate in and when. The decompositions include not only *N*-ary relational predicates among the verb's arguments (Passonneau 1986), but also the aspectual operators for processes and events proposed in Dowty 1979. The main clauses for examples 9, 10, 15, and 16 are given below as examples 17–20.

(17) The pressure was low.
Decomposition: low(patient([pressure1]))

(18) The alarm was sounding.
Decomposition: do(sound(actor([alarm1])))

(19) The engine failed.
Decomposition:
become(inoperative(patient([engine1])))

(20) The pump sheared the drive shaft.
Decomposition:
cause(agent([pump1]),become(sheared(patient([shaft1]))))

In (17), the semantic predicate *low* is associated with the predication *be low*, and is predicated over the entity referred to by the subject noun phrase, *the pressure*.[15] The time component recognizes this structure as a stative predication because it contains no aspectual operators.

The decomposition for (18) consists of a basic semantic predicate, **sound**, its single argument, and the aspectual operator **do**, indicating that its argument is in the class of process predicates; the actor role designates the active participant.

The decompositions of transition-event verbs contain the aspectual operator **become**, whose argument is a predicate indicating the type of situation resulting from the event. With inceptive verbs, as in (19), the actor of the initial process is also the patient or theme of the resulting situation, although this dual role is not represented explicitly in the decomposition. If a distinct actor causes the new situation, the verb falls into the class of causatives and the actor of the initial process is conventionally called an **agent**, as in (20). Other decompositional analyses (Dowty 1979, Foley and Van Valin 1984) conventionally represent the initial process of transition-event verbs by associating an activity predicate (e.g., *do*) with the actor or agent of the initial process (e.g., *cause(-do(agent( )), become (inoperative(patient( ))))*). The decompositions in (19) and (20) can be considered abbreviated versions of these more explicit predicate/argument structures.

The **become** operator of transition-event verbs thus provides a crucial piece of information used when deriving representations of transition events. Given a reference to a specific transition event that has already taken place, the temporal component deduces the existence of the new situation that has come into being by looking at the predicate embedded beneath the **become** operator. This is described more fully in Section 4.2.3.

As will be shown in Section 4, PUNDIT represents actual situations as predicates identifying the situation type as a state, process, or event. In order to familiarize the reader with the representation schema without needless repetition of detail, a single example of a situation representation is given below for (17).

---

[15] The atom [*pressure* 1] is an identifier of the entity referred to in the noun phrase and is created by PUNDIT's reference resolution component (Dahl 1986).

(17) The pressure was low.
　　state([low1],
　　　　low(patient([pressure1])),
　　　　period([low1]))

Each situation representation has three arguments: a unique identifier of the situation, its semantic decomposition, and its time argument, in this case, the interval (or *period*) over which the predicate holds. The same pointer (e.g., [low1]) is used to identify both a specific situation and its time argument because the actual time for which a situation holds is what uniquely identifies it. The participants in a situation help distinguish it from other similar situations, but while the same entities can participate in other situations, time never recurs.

Having introduced the distinct situation types and the temporal structures that distinguish them, the next steps are to show how they are computed and how they permit a simple computation of temporal location. This will be done in Section 4. Since the preceding discussions also introduced the representation of lexical aspect and the relevance of the verbal categories, it is now possible to clearly summarize the input which the temporal analysis component receives.

3 INPUT TO THE TEMPORAL COMPONENT

PUNDIT's time component performs its analysis after the sentence has been parsed and recursively after the semantic decomposition of each predicating element in the sentence has been created (Palmer et al. 1986). Although this paper focuses on the temporal analysis of certain kinds of tensed verbs, the basic algorithm described here has been extended to handle other cases as well. Describing the full input to the temporal component provides an opportunity to mention some of them.

The input to the time component for each tensed clause includes not only the surface verb and its tense and aspect markings, but also the decomposition produced by analyzing the verb and its arguments (cf. Section 2.2.2). The input to the time component is thus a list of the following form:

　　[[Tense, Perfect, Progressive],
　　Verb, Decomposition, {Context}]

Each element of the list will be described in turn.

3.1 Verbal categories

The first element in the input list is itself a list indicating the form of the verb, i.e., its grammatical inflection.

[[Tense, Perfect, Progressive],
　　Verb, Decomposition, {Context}]

The tense parameter is either past or present.[16] If the verb is in the progressive or perfect, the corresponding parameter appears while absence of either in the input sentence is reflected in its absence from the list.

---

[16] For sentence fragments such as *erosion of blade tip evident*, the tense parameter is actually *untensed*. The time component assigns present or past tense readings to fragments, depending on the aspectual class of the fragment (Linebarger et al. 1988).

3.2 Three Orders of Verbs

The next two elements in the input to the time component are the surface verb and its decomposition. Lexical aspect is encoded in the decomposition as described in Section 2.2.2 for the cases where it is relevant. However, it is a more fundamental classification pertaining to the verb which helps determine the cases where aspect is relevant.

[[Tense, Perfect, Progressive],
Verb, Decomposition, {Context}]

Since this information is only for treating more complex cases than are described in this paper, the following discussion is intended only to indicate that the model has been extended to cover verbs whose semantic structure contains temporal information of a different order than the inherent temporal structure of an actual situation. After a brief description of three temporal orders of verbs, the discussion will return to explication of the input required for implementing the basic model.

In addition to the aspectual distinction among state, process, and transition-event verbs, there are other distinctions related to temporal semantics. A particularly significant one is among what I call first-, second-, and third-order verbs, by analogy with the distinction among first-, second-, and third-order logics. A first-order verb is one whose arguments are concrete entities, e.g., humans, machines, and other physical objects. A second-order verb takes as its arguments states, processes, and events, but does not in and of itself refer to a situation. Rather, its semantic content is primarily temporal or aspectual (e.g., *occur, follow*). Third-order verbs refer to complex situations (e.g., *result, cause*) whose participants are themselves situations. The aspectual distinctions among verbs referring to states, processes, and transition events are only relevant to first-order verbs.

Second-order verbs can be identified by the impossibility of temporal modification of a situation referred to by the verb, independent of the situation(s) referred to by the verb's argument(s) (Newmeyer 1975), as can be seen by contrasting examples 21 and 22 with (23) and (24).

(21) The failure occurred on Tuesday.

(22) The failure was discovered on Tuesday.

(23) *The failure that happened on Monday occurred on Tuesday.

(24) The failure that happened on Monday was discovered on Tuesday.

Example 22 mentions two distinct situations, a *discovery* and *a failure*. In (21), however, the subject of the sentence, **the failure**, denotes an event, but the verb **occur** does not denote a separate situation. It provides tense and aspect information for interpreting its argument. In other words, the temporal information in (21) is very similar to that contained in (25):

(25) Something failed on Tuesday.

A pragmatic difference between the two sentences is that in (21) it is not necessary to mention what failed whereas in (25), the verb *fail* must have a subject. Other verbs in this class are **follow, precede, continue, happen**, and so on. Because these verbs contribute primarily temporal information, they are conventionally referred to as **aspectual verbs** (Freed 1979, Lamiroy 1987, Newmeyer 1975).

It is easy to see that the analysis of aspectual verbs must be implemented somewhat differently from verbs like *fail*, which directly denote situations. In a sentence like (25), the relevant temporal information is contained in the verb and its tense and aspect marking alone. In contrast, the temporal information in (24) pertaining to the *fail* event is distributed not only in the verb and its tense and aspect markers, but also in its subject. Temporal analysis of sentences like (24) must be performed not only at the main clause level, but also at the level of embedded propositions. In essence, analysis of aspectual verbs is of a different order. Consequently, verbs like *fail* are classified here as first-order verbs while the so-called aspectual verbs are classified as second order.

PUNDIT's temporal component also handles a third class of verbs, classified as third order. A third-order verb denotes a real-world situation, but its arguments are other situations. Consequently, the verb may contribute temporal information about the arguments as well as about the situation it denotes. The verb **result** illustrates this type. Sentence 26 asserts the existence of a **result** situation; the **result** relationship holds between an instigating situation mentioned in the noun phrase *loss of air pressure*, and a resulting situation mentioned in the noun phrase *failure*.

(26) Loss of air pressure resulted in failure.

Additionally, the meaning of **result** includes the temporal information that the instigating situation (the *loss*) precedes the resulting situation (the *failure*). A full temporal analysis of sentences like (26) requires two steps. The first is to analyze the temporal structure of the situation denoted by the verb. The second is to draw the correct temporal inferences about the verb's propositional arguments. Such verbs combine some of the properties of both first- and second-order verbs and thus constitute a third order of analysis. Classifying a verb as a third-order verb drives the search for temporal inferences associated with its arguments.

The classification of these three orders of verbs, summarized in Table 1, is recorded independently of the lexical decompositions used by both the temporal-analysis component and the semantic interpreter. At present, verb-order information is used only by the temporal-analysis component. It essentially selects for the appropriate flow of control through the temporal-processing procedures. Although PUNDIT recognizes the distinction between first-, second-, and third-order verbs, and processes the relevant temporal information in each case, the remainder of the paper will deal only with the analysis of first-order verbs.

TABLE 1   Three orders of verbs

Order	Examples	Definition
First	"fail", "operate"	verbs that denote situations and whose arguments are not propositional
Second	"occur", "follow"	verbs that provide temporal information about their propositional arguments
Third	"result", "cause"	verbs that denote situations but which also provide temporal information about their propositional arguments.

3.3 Lexical aspect

The third element in the input list is the decomposition structure produced by the semantic analysis of the verb and its arguments.

[[Tense, Perfect, Progressive],
Verb, **Decomposition**, {Context}]

The important aspectual features of the decompositions, discussed in Section 2.2.2, can be summarized as follows. If the decomposition of a first-order verb contains a *become* operator, the verb is in the transition-event class; otherwise, if it contains a *do* operator, the verb is in the process class; else, the verb (or other predicate) is stative.

3.4 Discourse context

The final element in the input to the temporal component is a data structure representing the current discourse context.

[[Tense, Perfect, Progressive], Verb, Decomposition, {**Context**}]

The first element of this data structure is a list of unanalyzed syntactic constituents. At this stage of processing, PUNDIT has produced a full syntactic analysis of a surface sentence (or sentence fragment), and a semantic decomposition of some predication within the sentence. After the semantic analysis of a clause, the constituent list contains all those syntactic constituents that do not serve as arguments of the verb, e.g., adverbial modifiers of the verb phrase and sentence adjuncts. After the analysis of the main clause of Sentence 27, for example, the constituent list would contain two unanalyzed constituents; the prepositional phrase introduced by *during*, and the subordinate clause introduced by *when*.

(27) The pump failed during engine start,
when oil pressure dropped below 60 psig.

This list of constituents is processed after the temporal content of a predication is analyzed in the search for temporal adverbials that modify the predication (cf. Section 5 below). The data structure representing the current discourse context contains temporally relevant information, such as the tense and voice of the main clause. The main-clause tense is used for the analysis of situations mentioned in embedded tenseless constituents, while voice is used in analyzing adjectival passives.

The next section describes an algorithm for interpreting the four pieces of information relevant to actual references to states, processes, and events. It demonstrates how the temporal structure and temporal location are generated from the verb's grammatical categories of tense, perfect, and progressive, and from its lexical aspect.

4 ALGORITHM FOR THE TEMPORAL ANALYSIS OF INFLECTED VERBS

The introductory and discussion sections have undoubtedly reinforced the view that semantic processing of temporal information is a complicated problem, even when the scope of the problem is constrained to the simple cases addressed here. Relevant information is distributed within and across distinct constituents, and their contribution to temporal information can depend upon co-occurring elements. Yet these are in no way insurmountable problems. The fundamental design principles behind my approach to temporal processing have been to carefully separate the analysis into distinct subtasks, to pare down to a minimum the information available to each task, and to provide a simple compositional semantics for each kind of temporal input. In this section, I outline the basic algorithm for the temporal analysis of inflected verbs. This algorithm analyzes the four components of the inflected verb described in the preceding section (lexical aspect, progressive, perfect, tense). The output that is generated can then serve as input for further temporal processing. Section 5 illustrates the integration of this basic algorithm into a more global procedure that successively interprets the main and subordinate clauses of complex sentences where the subordinating conjunction is a temporal adverbial.

The basic algorithm for the temporal analysis of inflected verbs has a simple tripartite control structure designed to answer three distinct questions:

1. Does the predication denote a specific situation with **actual time** reference?
2. If so, what is the **temporal structure** of the situation, i.e., how does it evolve through time and how does it get situated in time?
3. Finally, what is the **temporal location** of the situation with respect to the time of text production, and what is the temporal vantage point from which the situation is described?

Figure 1 illustrates the algorithm's global control structure, with the modules corresponding to each question as well as the relevant input for each module. The first

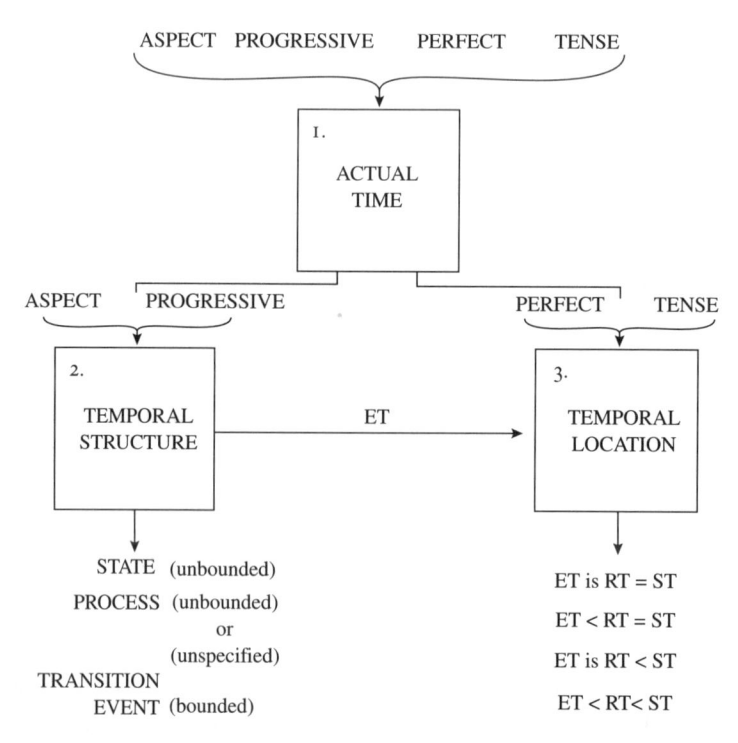

FIG. 1 Algorithm for temporal analysis of inflected verb.

module examines all four temporal parameters described in Sections 3.1 and 3.5 in order to reject certain cases. The second module requires only the two parameters pertaining to the computation of temporal structure. It sends a component of the temporal structure, the event time, to the third module, which locates the event time by analyzing the remaining two temporal parameters, **tense** and **perfect**.

4.1 Module 1: actual time

The first task performed by PUNDIT's temporal component is to identify references to specific situation tokens; that is, instances of situations which have actually occurred. The input is the lexical verb and its grammatical categories. In certain cases, the form of the verb itself can indicate that the predication refers to a type of situation, rather than to a specific token. Thus the screening step described here rejects these cases and otherwise assumes that the predication denotes a specific situation. As pointed out in Section 2.1, the verb itself provides insufficient information in two kinds of cases: those where explicit disconfirming information occurs elsewhere in the sentence (e.g., arguments of the verb, modals, frequency adverbials; cf. examples 2 and 7, repeated below):

(2) Tourists flew TWA to Boston.

(7) The lube oil pump seized whenever the engine jacked over.

and those where pragmatic features of the discourse context affect the interpretation of semantic input (as in a sportscast). While Module 1 currently serves only as a filter, it could be made to generate informative output for subsequent processing of semantically and pragmatically more complex phenomena.

In Section 2.1 it was shown that two classes of inflected verbs generally denote situation types, rather than actual tokens. These are process verbs and transition-event verbs in the simple present tense (i.e., nonprogressive and nonperfect), as exemplified in (28) and (29).

(28) Number 2 air compressor operates at reduced capacity.
(*operate* is a process verb.)

(29) They replace the air compressor every three years.
(*replace* is a transition-event verb.)

For the compound tenses, present tense interacts with the progressive and perfect verbal categories. The progressive alters the aspectual properties of nonstative verbs so that they refer to unbounded situations, and unbounded situations—unlike the other temporal structures—can be located in the actual present (cf. Section 4.2.2). With the perfect forms, the situation being referred to is always located in the past, and tense pertains to the situation's reference time rather than its event time (cf. Section 4.2.3). Thus, as shown in Figure 1, all four elements in the temporal data structure are inspected in order to identify the two cases exemplified in (28) and (29).

Table 2 summarizes the relation between the inflected verb and actual temporal reference.

In the current implementation of PUNDIT, predications that meet the first condition do not receive further temporal analysis.

TABLE 2   Module 1: Actual time

Lexical Aspect	Progressive	Perfect	Tense	Action
Nonstative	no	no	present	reject accept

4.2   Module 2: compute temporal structure

Module 2 computes the first type of specific temporal information associated with reference to an actual situation. It generates an explicit representation of the situation's temporal structure. This structure includes one or more time arguments associated with the semantic predicates in the decomposition, and the situation's event time. Each situation type—state, process, transition event—receives an appropriate situation label, time argument(s), and event time. The temporal structure evoked by an inflected verb can be computed entirely on the basis of the values of the two aspectual elements in its input (Lexical Aspect, Progressive), as shown in Figure 1. The algorithm for Module 2, summarized in Table 3, will be described in the following three sections corresponding to the three situation types.

Though not shown in the figure or in Table 3, Module 2 also receives another input data structure: the semantic decomposition. The decomposition is analyzed during the processing of transition-event situations in order to associate distinct time arguments with distinct semantic predicates in the decomposition. This procedure is explained in the appropriate section below.

4.2.1   States

As shown in Table 3, if the lexical aspect of the predicate is stative (Aspect = stative), then the progressive parameter is irrelevant for computing temporal structure. Lexical stativity is sufficient to identify the situation as a state whose time argument is an unbounded stative interval.

Example 30 gives a simple stative sentence, the relevant input to Module 2, and the final situation representation. Note that (30) illustrates the use of the progressive with a verb in the locative class of statives noted in Dowty 1979, and mentioned in Section 2.2.1.[17]

> (30) Metallic particles are clogging the strainer.
> Lexical Aspect = stative
> Situation Representation:
> state([clog1],
> clog(instrument([material1]),theme ([strainer2])),
> period([clog1]))

As soon as the lexical aspect is recognized to be stative, Module 2 generates the state label and period time argument used in creating the representation depicted above.

---

[17] As noted elsewhere, the aspectual classification of verbs is not completely determinate (Talmy 1985). *Clog* may very well be a verb that can refer either to a process or a state, and it might be possible to decide dynamically the lexical aspect of a specific instance through interaction with a sophisticated model, such as one which incorporates the notion of resource use, as suggested by Nakhimovsky (1988). However, in PUNDIT the aspectual classification of verbs is domain dependent.

TABLE 3 Module 2: temporal structure

Lexical Aspect	Progressive	Label	Time Argument	Event Time (ET)
stative	Yes/No	State	unbounded stative interval	includes ET
process or transition event	Yes	Process	unbounded active interval	includes ET
process	No	Process	unspecified active interval	has ET
transition event	No	Event	transition bound	unifies with ET

A period time argument in the context of a state representation denotes a stative interval. The situation representation in (30) indicates that a specific state, *clog1*, holds over the stative interval, *period([clog1])*; the decomposition in the representation indicates the participants and the relation between them that holds over this interval. By definition, this interval also has an event time associated with it, whose relation to the interval we can determine by its boundedness feature.

Stative intervals are assumed to be unbounded unless an endpoint is provided by further processing (e.g., through adverbial modification, inference). For unbounded intervals, the event time is always an arbitrary moment **included** within the interval. This is represented as a binary predicate of the following form, where the **moment** time argument is the event time:

Event Time = moment([clog1])
such that includes(period([clog1]), moment([clog1]))

This predicate and the state representation given above exemplify the output of Module 2 for state situations. The event time generated here is then passed to Module 3 in order to determine its temporal location. We will return to this same example in the discussion of temporal location in Section 4.3.

4.2.2 Processes

There are three surface forms that denote process situations: nonprogressive process verbs, progressive process verbs, and progressive transition-event verbs. The nonprogressive and progressive cases have distinct temporal structures, due to differences in the relation of the event time to the active interval over which the process holds. Since this is the only difference among the three cases, the similarities in temporal structure will be presented before the event time is discussed.

A nonstative predication that either has a process verb or is in the progressive (i.e., the three combinations of nonprogressive process, progressive process, and progressive transition-event) evokes a process representation. Thus the following three example sentences would each be represented with a process label and a period time argument, representing the active interval over which the process holds. Examples 31 and 32 illustrate the two forms of process verbs that evoke process situations; since they receive the same representation, it is shown only once. Example 33 shows the third type of reference to a process, with a progressive transition-event verb.

(31) The diesel operated.
Lexical Aspect = process
Progressive = no

(32) The diesel was operating.
Lexical Aspect = process
Progressive = yes

(31–32) Situation Representation:
process([operate1],
    do(operate(actor([diesel])))
    period([operate1]))

(33) The pump is failing.
Lexical Aspect = transition event
Progressive = yes
Situation Representation:
process([fail1],
    become(inoperative(patient([fail1]))),
    period([fail1]))

The process representation for (33) contains the full decomposition for the verb *fail* with its aspectual operator **become**. In this context, the **become** operator does not denote a transition to a new situation, but rather, indicates a process of *becoming*, which might or might not culminate in such a transition.

Referring again to Table 3, we note that the active intervals for both (32) and (33) will be unbounded, in contrast to (31), where the active interval is unspecified for boundedness. The consequence of this difference on the representation of the event time is outlined in the following paragraphs.

Unbounded processes. The predicate specifying the relation between the event time of an unbounded process and the period over which the process holds is identical to that for states. That is, the period time argument *includes* an arbitrary moment, which serves as the situation's event time, as shown below.

(32) The diesel was operating.
Event Time = moment([operate1])
such that includes(period([operate1]), moment([operate1]))

(33) The pump is failing.
Event Time = moment([fail1])
such that includes(period([fail1]), moment([fail1]))

The progressive always implies unboundedness, and in this respect resembles lexical statives. Again, it is important to remember that an unbounded interval can acquire endpoints through further processing (e.g., of temporal adverbials, as in *The diesel was operating until the pump failed.*).

Unspecified processes. For nonprogressive process verbs, the period associated with the predication is unspecified for boundedness (cf. discussion of Example 11 in Section 2.2.1). This gives rise to an indeterminate relationship between the event time and the period time argument over which the process holds; i.e., the event time may start, end, or be included within the period. This unspecified relationship is represented by means of a binary *has* predicate, as shown in Example 31.

(31) The diesel operated.
Event Time = moment([operate1])
such that has(period([operate1]), moment
([operate1]))

Both event-time predicates given so far (i.e., *includes*, *has*) indicate a relation between an arbitrary moment and a single interval over which a state or process holds. There is otherwise nothing distinctive about the moment selected to be the event time of a process or state situation. In contrast, as Table 3 indicates, and as discussed in Section 2.2.1, the event time of a transition event is equated with a distinctive component of its temporal structure, viz., the transition bound between a process that initiates the event and the new situation reached at the culmination of the process.

4.2.3 Transition events

Table 3 shows only one component of the temporal structure of a transition event (the relevant line of the table is repeated below).

As noted in Section 2.2.1, a transition event has three temporal components: an initial active interval leading up to a transition, the moment of transition, and the interval associated with the new, resulting situation. In theory, then, one could represent the full temporal structure of a transition-event predication (e.g., *The pump failed*) as three contiguous states of affairs: an initial process (e.g., *failing*) leading up to a transitional moment (e.g., *becoming inoperative*) followed by a new state of affairs (e.g., *inoperative*). At present, PUNDIT explicitly represents only the latter two components of transition-event predications: the moment (transition bound) associated with an event of becoming, and the period associated with the resulting situation. This representation has been found to be adequate for the current applications. Thus transition events are actually assigned two situation representations: an event representation with a moment time argument, represented with the input decomposition, and a resulting state or process situation with a period time argument, for which a new decomposition is derived from the input decomposition. Example 34 illustrates a typical transition-event sentence, the relevant input for computing temporal structure, and the two situation representations.

(34) The pump failed.
Lexical Aspect = transition event
Progressive = no
Situation Representation:
    event([fail1],
        become(inoperative(patient([pump1]))),
        moment([fail1]))
Situation Representation:
    state([fail2],
        inoperative(patient([pump1])),
        period([fail2]))

Lexical Aspect	Progressive	Label	Time Argument	Event Time (ET)
transition event	No	Event	transition bound	*unifies with* ET

from (TABLE 3)

The first situation representation corresponds to the transition event itself. Module 2 generates the event label and moment time argument used in creating the type of event representation shown above for nonprogressive transition event verbs. The moment argument of a transition event is the transition bound implying the onset of a new situation. When Module 2 creates an event with a moment argument, it also creates a representation for the implied situation. In Example 34, the new situation is a state. When creating the representation for the situation resulting from a transition event, it is necessary to determine the appropriate situation label, time argument, and semantic decomposition for the new situation. This is where the semantic decomposition for transition events plays a role, as will be described below.

All transition-event verbs contain a state or process predicate embedded beneath an instance of the aspectual operator **become**. The full decomposition represents the type of situation associated with the moment of transition. The portion embedded beneath **become** is the situation type associated with the new situation. For example, the decomposition passed to the time component for Sentence 34 would be:

become(inoperative(patient([pump1]))).

As shown in (34), this decomposition appears in the representation of the transition event itself. The argument to the **become** operator is then extracted for use in the new situation representation:

inoperative(patient([pump1]))

The extracted decomposition is inspected to determine its aspectual class, completely analogously to the procedure for determining the aspectual class of the input predicate (cf. Section 3). In this case, the embedded predicate decomposition is stative because it contains no aspectual operators. If it contained the *do* operator, the new situation would have been a **process**.[18] In this fashion, the decomposition guides the selection of the situation label and time argument for the situation inferred to result from the transition event.

The final piece of temporal structure derived for a transition event is the temporal relation between the moment associated with the transition event (e.g., moment([fail1])) and the period associated with the resulting situation (e.g., period([fail2])). The event moment is the onset of the period. Following Allen 1983, this is called a **start** relationship. By definition, then, every transition bound starts some period. In the case of Example 34, the moment of failure starts the period for which the pump is in an inoperative state.

start(moment([fail1]), period([fail2]))

The event time of a transitional event is always identified with the transition bound. Thus for examples like (34), the moment time argument serves as the event time of the transition event. This identity relation is not represented as a predicate, but rather, is handled via unification, as indicated in Table 3.

4.3 Module 3: compute temporal location

PUNDIT's temporal component employs a Reichenbachian analysis of tense whereby situations are located in time in terms of three temporal indices: the event time, speech

---

[18] The embedded decomposition never contains the *become* operator; a decomposition with two *become* operators (e.g., *become(become(inoperative(patient([pump1]))))*) would be incoherent.

time, and reference time.[19] It diverges from Reichenbach primarily by distinguishing between the event time and the temporal structure of a situation. While Reichenbach acknowledged that the progressive, for example, pertains to temporal duration, he did not discuss the differences in temporal structure associated with distinct situation types and their interaction with tense. Here, the event time is only a single component of the full temporal structure of a situation. In this section, we will see how this method of defining the event time makes it possible to compute temporal location independently of lexical or grammatical aspect while preserving the distinctive temporal information they contribute to references to actual situations.

The tense and perfect parameters specify the sequencing relations among the event time, reference time, and speech time, with each of the four configurations of tense and perfect specifying a distinct ordering, as shown in Figure 1 and repeated below:

ET is RT = ST   simple present
ET < RT = ST   present perfect
ET is RT < ST   simple past
ET < RT < ST   past perfect

The speech time, or time of text production, is given. It serves as the temporal fulcrum with respect to which the other temporal indices are located. As shown in Table 4, the presence or absence of the perfect indicates whether the event time and reference time are distinct, in which case the event time precedes the reference time, or whether they are identical. Tense is taken to indicate the relation between the reference time and the speech time, following Reichenbach's suggestion: *the position of R[T] relative to S[T] is indicated by the words "past", "present", and "future"* (Reichenbach 1947). Since we are dealing here with actual time, rather than potential or hypothetical time, there is only past or present. That is, the reference time either precedes or coincides with the speech time.

The reference time and the event time are identical to one another for the simple tenses (ET is RT), which has the effect that tense applies to the event time. Thus, for the simple present, the event time and the speech time *coincide*. Note that a distinction is made here between *identity* and *coincidence* of distinct indices. For any speech act or text containing a description of a situation, the speech situation and the described situation are always conceptually and observationally distinct, thus also their respective temporal indices. These indices are therefore represented as distinct times, which, in the present tense, happen to coincide. However, with the simple tenses, there is no reason to create a distinct reference time and a relation saying that it coincides with the event time. Rather, there are two different functions, which, in the case of the simple tenses, are filled by the same temporal index. The function of the reference time is explained more fully below.

TABLE 4 Module 3: temporal location

Parameter	Value	Rules
Perfect	Yes	precedes(ET,RT)
	No	ET is RT
Tense	Past	precedes(RT,ST)
	Present	coincide(RT,ST)

---

[19] Reichenbach's (1947) treatment of tense and other *token reflexive* (indexical) elements is similar to Jakobson's (1957).

Webber (this volume) reviews and expands upon the role reference time plays in intersentential temporal reference. Reference time also plays a role in interpreting relational adverbials like *now*, *yesterday*, *when*, and so on. Adverbs like *now* and *yesterday* relate the reference time of a predication to an implicit time, viz., the speech time. Relational adverbs like *before*, *after*, and *when* relate the time of the predication they modify to an explicitly mentioned time, i.e., the reference time associated with their syntactic complements. In the absence of the perfect, the reference time is identical with the event time, as in (35) and (36).

(35) The pressure is normal now.

(36) The pressure was low yesterday.

In the perfect tenses, the reference time and event time are distinct. The event time of both the present and past perfect predications in (37) and (38) is past, i.e., the moment of *failure* is in the past.

(37) The pump has now failed.[20]

(38) The pump had failed when the gear began to turn.

With the present perfect, it is the reference time that is present, as shown in (37) by the admissibility of the adverb *now*, which also refers to the present. On one reading of (38), the event time, or moment of failure, precedes the reference time, i.e., the time specified by the *when* clause. The perfect tenses can also be used simply to affirm truth or falsehood,[21] thus (38) has another reading in which the perfect does not contribute a distinct reference time, but merely asserts that it is in fact the case that the pump failed when the gear began to turn.

4.3.1 Simple tenses

The distinct relations of event time to temporal structure corresponding to the three categories of boundedness—unbounded, unspecified, and bounded—correlate with distinctive behavior of the present tense. If the temporal structure associated with a predication is an unbounded interval, the simple present locates some time within the interval coincident with the speech time. Examples 39–42 illustrate the simple present in the context of the four types of predications that hold over unbounded intervals.

(39) The pressure is low.
Lexical aspect: stative
Progressive: no

(40) Metal particles are clogging the strainer.
Lexical aspect: stative
Progressive: yes

(41) The pump is operating.
Lexical aspect: process
Progressive: yes

(42) The pump is failing.
Lexical aspect: transition event
Progressive: yes

---

[20] Dowty and others have pointed out that the situation mentioned in a present perfect often persists up to the speech time (1982). However, this is generally not the case with reference to unbounded processes (e.g., *The pump has operated*), and seems to depend on a variety of pragmatic factors for the other situation types.

[21] Cf. McCawley's (1971) discussion of the ambiguities of the perfect, especially the *assertorial* perfect.

In these examples, the predicate is asserted to hold for some interval of unknown duration, which includes the speech time. Since this interval corresponds by definition to actual time, it cannot be known to continue beyond the speech time into the future. However, that it can extend indefinitely into the past is illustrated by (43), where the situations referred to in the first and second conjuncts are assumed to be the same.

(43) The pressure is low and has been low.

Predications involving process or transition-event verbs in the simple present have already been eliminated by Module 1 on the assumption that sentences like (44) and (45) do not refer to actual time.

(44) The pump operates.
Lexical aspect: process
Progressive: no

(45) The pump fails.
Lexical aspect: transition event
Progressive: no

If a predication is not explicitly unbounded, i.e., if it has or may have an endpoint, then the present tense cannot be interpreted as locating the event time in the actual present. An event time located within an unbounded interval corresponds to persistence of the same situation, whereas an event time that may also be an endpoint corresponds to a transition. The way in which examples like (44) and (45) are interpreted can be explained by considering that we cannot announce changes in the world at the exact moment that we perceive them, although in the guise of reportage or sportscasting, we act as though we can.

In contrast to the simple present, the simple past can locate the event time of any temporal structure prior to the speech time. What is distinctive about the past tense in the context of the different temporal structures pertains to the temporal structure surrounding the event time. If the temporal structure is an unbounded interval, then the event time is some moment prior to the speech time within a persisting interval, and the same situation extends unchanged forward towards the present and back into the past. Example 46 illustrates the lack of contradiction in asserting the continuation up to the present of the past, unbounded situation mentioned in the first clause.

(46) The pump was failing and is still failing.

The temporal structure associated with the situation mentioned in the first clause of (47), in the simple past, is an unspecified interval. Here it is unclear whether the two conjuncts refer to the same situation. Since the event time of the first conjunct is represented noncommittally, i.e., it may or may not be an endpoint of the interval, both interpretations are provided for by the representations generated here.

(47) The pump operated and is still operating.

Finally, the simple past of a predication denoting a transition event definitely locates an endpoint. The event time of (48) is the transitional moment between an initial process of *failing* and a resulting state of **being inoperative.**

(48) The pump failed and is still failing.

The first clause of (48) is represented by PUNDIT to assert the following temporal information: there was a moment of transition at which the pump failed, viz., its event time (*moment([fail1])*); this moment started a period in which the pump was inoperative (*start(moment([fail1]), period([fail2])))*; and finally, it preceded the speech time (*precedes(moment([fail1]), Speech Time)*). The second clause cannot refer to the same transition event because a unique transition bound cannot both precede and coincide with the speech time, nor can it both be an endpoint of, and contained within, an interval. Rather, the second clause refers to a distinct situation, either a process that the speaker presumes will eventually result in a new failure, or an iteration of successive failure events. Of these two possibilities for the second clause, PUNDIT currently generates only the former.

4.3.2 Perfect tenses

The perfect tenses have a more complex semantics and pragmatics than the simple tenses. The semantic interpretation given here accounts for the temporal interpretations assigned to the perfect tenses in which the event time and reference time are distinct from one another. There are uses of the perfect that do not have these temporal effects, as pointed out in McCawley 1971, i.e., cases where the event time and reference time would not be distinct. Here we consider only the temporally relevant uses of the perfect, where each perfect tense specifies two temporal relations: in both cases, the event time precedes the reference time; and tense indicates whether the reference time coincides with or precedes the speech time.

The following examples illustrate the present and past perfect with a variety of temporal structures. The only difference between these examples and the simple present tenses examined in the preceding section is the relation between the reference time and event time. The relation between temporal structure, event time, and speech time is the same as for the simple past.

(49) The engine has been operating. (unbounded process)

(50) The engine has operated. (unspecified process)

(51) The pump has failed. (transition event)

(52) The pressure had been low. (state)

(53) The pump had failed. (transition event)

5 INTERPRETING TEMPORAL ADVERBIALS

It is assumed that temporal adverbials can be analyzed in terms of the same components of temporal structure and temporal sequencing constraints that apply to situations. The situation representations developed here provide a foundation for interpreting three distinct types of adverbial modification corresponding to the three features represented in temporal structure, i.e., kinesis, intervals, and moments. Rate adverbs like *slowly* and *rapidly*, which modify the manner in which situations evolve through time, modify active intervals and not stative intervals. For an example like (54), no explicit active interval would be represented, thus one would have to be coerced in order to interpret the adverb.

(54) The pressure was rapidly low.

Examples like (55), on the other hand, provide a motivation for representing the initial active interval of a transition event (cf. Section 4.2.3), since the adverb essentially selects for such an interval.

(55) The engine quickly failed.

Durational adverbials like *for X*, where *X* is a temporal measure phrase, modify any interval, but not their endpoints. Finally, relational adverbs, which specify temporal sequence, modify the reference time of situations.

Adverbials can combine relational and durational elements. *In X*, where *X* is a temporal measure phrase, not only specifies a duration, but also relates the endpoint of this duration to some other time, e.g., the time at which the utterance is produced, as in (56).

(56) The lights will go off in 10 minutes (e.g., *from now*).

Temporal connectives like *before* and *after* can combine with temporal measure phrases to yield complex adverbials specifying both a duration and a relation, as in (57).

(57) The engine seized five minutes before the alarm sounded.

In this section, we will look briefly at the two types of durational phrases compared in Vendler 1967 in order to demonstrate the advantages of the representations developed here for interpreting them. Then we will look briefly at the algorithm for interpreting complex sentences with subordinate adverbial clauses.

5.1 Durational adverbials

Unbounded situations. Predications denoting states and processes have duration, as shown by the interpretation of durational adverbial phrases of the form *for X*, where *X* is a time measure, as in (58) and (59):

(58) The pressure was low for 10 minutes. (state)

(59) The gear was turning for 10 minutes. (unbounded process)

However, as noted in preceding discussions, the past tense in reference to states and unbounded processes does not apply to the whole duration. It applies to the moment within the interval designated as the situation's event time. Since in (58) and (59) the event time is past and the speech time is present, the two temporal indices create an explicit temporal extent within which to locate the durational phrases. The *for* adverbial phrase also evokes an unbounded duration, meaning that the measure phrase does not necessarily encompass the entire duration, as shown by the lack of contradiction in asserting the continuation of the interval up to the present, as in (60) and (61).

(60) The pressure was low for 10 minutes and is still low.

(61) The gear was turning for 10 minutes and is still turning.

The present perfect would allow one to assert something semantically very similar to (60) and (61), but more laconically (e.g., **The pressure has been low for 10 minutes.**). However, a context in which (60) would be more correct than the corresponding perfect is perfectly possible; it would have to be a context where the pressure is now low, was low over some interval of 10 minutes' duration, but where this interval is more than 10 minutes prior to the present, and where the pressure has continued to be low up to the present (e.g., A: *The alarm should go off if the pressure is low for 10 minutes.* B: *Well, the pressure was low for 10 minutes and it's still low, but the alarm still hasn't gone off.*).

The past tense with an unbounded interval evokes a span of time between the past event time and the present speech time within which to situate the measure of time given by a *for* adverbial. However, there is no such span of time associated with the present tense of an unbounded interval, hence the impossibility of a *for* measure phrase in examples (62) and (63).[22]

(62) ? The pressure is low for 10 minutes.

(63) ? The gear is turning for 10 minutes.

Note that the present perfect, like the simple past, does provide a temporal point prior to the present, thereby creating a span of time for the durational phrase to apply to, as in (64) and (65):

(64) The pressure has been low for three hours.

(65) The gear has been turning for five minutes.

The temporal structures generated for examples like (60)–(63) make it possible to correctly interpret the adverbial phrases they contain. The measure phrases in (60) and (61) can be interpreted not simply because the mentioned situations have duration, but more importantly because of the distinctness of the two temporal indices, event time and speech time. In (62) and (63), where event time and speech time coincide, there is no explicit span of time within which to situate the measure phrase. Cases where there is no explicit component of temporal structure in the situation representation to match up with the temporal structure evoked by a temporal adverbial are probably candidates for the kind of coercion discussed in Moens and Steedman 1988.

The durational adverbial phrases in (66)–(68) not only specify a duration, but also an endpoint (Vendler 1967). Since progressive process predications are unbounded, there is no actual endpoint to be mapped to, hence, under one reading, (66) cannot be interpreted as a situation with an actual time; rather, it seems to refer to an activity that was supposed to take place five minutes from some time previously specified in the discourse context (e.g., paraphrasable as *It was to be the case that the gear would turn five minutes from the present*). There is another possible reading, paraphrasable as *It turned out to be the case that the gear turned five minutes after some previously specified time*, as in the context *I applied some lubricant to the gear and it was turning in five minutes*, which, like (62) and (63) above, may be examples requiring coercion.[23] In contrast, examples 67 and 68 can be interpreted as actual situations whose endpoints coincide with the endpoints of the five-minute duration.

(66) The gear was turning in five minutes.

(67) The gear turned in five minutes.

(68) The engine was repaired in five minutes.

The two types of durational adverbials behave differently when modifying the different types of temporal structures in ways that tend to confirm the representations proposed here.

---

[22] Since isolated sentences can generally be given a variety of readings, it is often necessary to add qualifications regarding the intended reading of linguistic examples. Sentences like (60) and (61), for example, can be interpreted as *the pressure is to be low for 10 minutes*. Such interpretations are outside the scope of this paper, for they pertain to hypothetical rather than actual times.

[23] Thanks to Bonnie Webber and Mark Steedman for pointing out the second reading mentioned here.

5.2 Complex sentences

The temporal adverbials encountered in the CASREPs domain consisted predominantly of phrases introduced by temporal connectives, e.g., *when, before,* and *after* (Smith 1981). The general problem in analyzing the strictly temporal information associated with such connectives is to associate some time evoked by the matrix clause with some time evoked by the complement phrase. In general, connectives are represented as associating the reference time of the matrix clause with the reference time of the complement. The procedure involved in analyzing the temporal relations specified by a *before* adverb (or other temporal connective) has the six steps illustrated in (69) below.

(69) The compressor failed before the pump seized.

Step 1: Analyze semantics of the main clause	*The compressor failed*
Step 2: Find reference time of main clause (RT1)	moment([fail1])
Step 3: Recognize temporal adverb	*before*
Step 4: Analyze semantics of subordinate clause	*the pump seized*
Step 5: Find reference time of subord. clause (RT2)	moment([seize1])
Step 6: Look up semantic structure of connective	precede(RT1, RT2)

Result: precedes(moment([fail1]), moment([seize1]))

First, the temporal semantics of the main clause is analyzed. One of the outputs of this analysis is the reference time of the main clause, which in this case would be represented as *moment([fail1])*. Then the time component finds the adverbial phrase *before the pump seized* in the constituent list, which it recognizes as consisting of a temporal connective (*before*) and a complement. The complement clause is sent to the semantic interpreter (Palmer 1985) and is returned to the time component for temporal analysis. The fourth step, the temporal analysis of the subordinate clause, yields the information that the reference time of the subordinate clause is *moment([seize1])*. Finally, the time component looks up the predicate structure representing the semantics of the temporal connective. *Before* is represented as a binary predicate—**precedes**—whose first argument is the reference time of the main clause and whose second argument is the reference time of the complement clause.

Currently, relational adverbs like *before*, *after*, and *when* are represented as predicates relating the reference times of the modified and modifying situations. The procedure for handling temporal connectives assumes a priori that the reference times of the syntactically superordinate and subordinate constituents are the required input. In future work, these and other adverbs will be treated more explicitly as semantic predicates with selectional constraints that guide the search for the appropriate components of temporal structure associated with the referents of the relevant constituents.

6 CONCLUSION

The situation representations presented here model the temporal meaning of inflected verbs by assigning a semantic value to each of four components; the inherent lexical aspect, the tense, and the presence or absence of the perfect and progressive. Two significant advantages to the overall proposal are the simplicity of the algorithm that computes the representations, and the generality of the building blocks used in constructing them. The algorithm accounts for the context dependencies among the four semantic components through a single mechanism, i.e., an appropriate characterization of the event time and its relation to the full temporal structure of a state, process, or transition event. These temporal structures are composed of intervals that may be active or stative, and that may be bounded, unbounded, or unspecified for boundedness.

The situation representations have certain advantages in and of themselves. For example, the linkage between the components of temporal structure and Dowty's aspect calculus, and the incorporation of a Reichenbachian treatment of tense, make it possible to represent very precisely what predicates hold when. Further, the dual possibility of associating the *become* operator either with an unbounded interval or a transition bound between intervals circumvents the so-called imperfective paradox. An additional advantage is the utility of these representations for further processing. The preceding section illustrated how the three building blocks of the representations (i.e., the notion of persistence of some situation through an interval, kinesis of the situation, and boundedness of the interval) make it possible to interpret accurately three corresponding kinds of temporal adverbials, and to identify those cases where coercion is required. Finally, explicit representation of the reference times and event times within distinct types of temporal structures should make it possible to account for the differential contribution of situations to narratives and other types of discourse.

ACKNOWLEDGMENTS

I was fortunate in having the opportunity to consider the problems of temporal analysis in the context of a congenial work environment with stimulating colleagues and a large, relatively comprehensive text processing system. The members of my group provided much useful criticism and commentary, especially Lynette Hirschman, Deborah Dahl, Martha Palmer, and Carl Weir. Bonnie Webber was extremely generous in her encouragement, and offered invaluable suggestions. I also profited from discussions with Mark Steedman, and his careful reading of earlier versions of this paper.

This work was supported by DARPA under contract N00014-85-C-0012, administered by the Office of Naval Research. Approved for public release, distribution unlimited.

REFERENCES

Allen, James F. (1983). 'Maintaining Knowledge about Temporal Intervals', *Communications of the ACM* 26 (11): 832–43.

—— (1984). 'Towards a General Theory of Action and Time', *Artificial Intelligence* 23 (2): 123–60.

Austin, J. L. (1977). *How to Do Things with Words*. Cambridge, MA: Harvard University Press.

Comrie, Bernard (1976). *Aspect: An Introduction to the Study of Verbal Aspect and Related Problems*. Cambridge: Cambridge University Press.

Dahl, Deborah A. (1986). 'Focusing and Reference Resolution in PUNDIT'. Presented at AAAI, Philadelphia, PA.

—— Dowding, John, Hirschman, Lynette, Lang, Francois, Linebarger, Marcia, Palmer, Martha, Passonneau, Rebecca, and Riley, Leslie (1987a). 'Integrating Syntax, Semantics, and Discourse: DARPA Natural Language Understanding Program'. *R&D Status Report*. Unisys Defense Systems, Paoli Research Center. Paoli, PA.

—— Palmer, Martha S., and Passonneau, Rebecca J.(1987b). 'Nominalizations in PUNDIT'. *Proceedings of the 25th Annual Meeting of the ACL*. Stanford, CA, 131–9.

Dowding, John and Hirschman, Lynette (1987). 'A Dynamic Translator for Rule Pruning in Restriction Grammar', *Second International Workshop on Natural-Language Understanding and Logic Programming*. Vancouver, BC, Canada, 79–92.

Dowty, David. (1979). *Word Meaning and Montague Grammar*. Dordrecht: D. Reidel.

——(1982). 'Tenses, Time Adverbials, and Compositional Semantic Theory', *Linguistics and Philosophy* 5: 23–55.

——(1986). 'The Effects of Aspectual Class on the Temporal Structure of Discourse: Semantics or Pragmatics', *Linguistics and Philosophy* 9: 37–61.

Foley, William and Van Valin, R. (1984). *Functional Syntax and Universal Grammar*. Cambridge: Cambridge University Press.

Freed, Alice (1979). *The Semantics of English Aspectual Complementation*. Dordrecht: Reidel.

Hinrichs, E. W. (1988). 'Tense, Quantifiers, and Contexts', *Computational Linguistics* 14: 3–14.

Jackendoff, Ray (1987). 'The Status of Thematic Relations in Linguistic Theory', *Linguistic Inquiry* 18(3): 369–411.

Jakobson, Roman (1957). 'Shifters, Verbal Categories, and the Russian Verb', in *Selected Writings*. The Hague: Mouton.

Lamiroy, Beatrice (1987). 'The Complementation of Aspectual Verbs in French', *Language* 63(2): 278–98.

Levin, Beth and Rappaport, Malka (1986). 'The Formation of Adjectival Passives', *Linguistic Inquiry* 17: 623–62.

Linebarger, Marcia, Dahl, Deborah A., Hirschman, Lynette, and Passonneau, Rebecca J. (1988). 'Sentence Fragments Regular Structures', *Proceedings of the 26th Annual Meeting of the ACL*. Buffalo, NY, 7–16.

McCawley, James (1971). 'Tense and Time Reference in English', in Charles J. Fillmore and D. Terence Langendoen (eds.), *Studies in Linguistic Semantics*. New York: Holt, Rinehart and Winston, 97–114.

Moens, Mark and Steedman, Mark J. (1987). 'Temporal Ontology in Natural Language', *Proceedings of the 25th Annual Meeting of the ACL*. Stanford, CA, 1–7.

——(1988). 'Temporal Ontology in Natural Language', *Computational Linguistics* 14: 15–28.

Mourelatos, Alexander P. D. (1981). 'Events, Processes and States', in P. J. Tedeschi and A. Zaenen (eds.), *Tense and Aspect*. New York: Academic Press, 191–212.

Mufwene, Salikoko S. (1984). 'Stativity and the Progressive'. Indiana University Linguistics Club, Indianapolis, IN.

Nakhimovsky, A. (1988). 'Aspect, Aspectual Class, and the Temporal Structure of Narrative', *Computational Linguistics* 14: 29–43.

Newmeyer, Frederick (1975). *English Aspectual Verbs*. The Hague: Mouton.

Palmer, Martha S. (1985). 'Driving Semantics for a Limited Domain'. Ph.D. dissertation, University of Edinburgh, Edinburgh, Scotland.

——Dahl, Deborah A., Schiffman (Passonneau), Rebecca J., Hirschman, Lynette, Linebarger, Marcia, and Dowding, John (1986). 'Recovering Implicit Information', *Proceedings of the 24th Annual Meeting of the ACL*. Columbia University, New York, NY, 10–19.

Passonneau, Rebecca J. (1986). 'Designing Lexical Entries for a Limited Domain'. Logic-Based Systems Technical Memo No. 42. Paoli Research Center, System Development Corporation. Paoli, PA.

Reichenbach, Hans (1947). *Elements of Symbolic Logic*. New York: The Free Press.

Roberts, Craige (1985). 'Modal Subordination and Anaphora in Discourse'. Paper presented at the 60th LSA. Seattle, WA.

Smith, Carlota S. (1981). 'Semantic and Syntactic Constraints on Temporal Interpretation', in P. J. Tedeschi and A. Zaenen (eds.), *Tense and Aspect*. New York: Academic Press, 213–37.

——(1986). 'A Speaker-based Approach to Aspect'. *Linguistics and Philosophy* 9: 97–115.

Talmy, Leonard (1985). 'Lexicalization Patterns: Semantic Structure in Lexical Forms', in *Language Typology and Syntactic Description: Grammatical Categories and the Lexicon*. Cambridge: Cambridge University Press, 63–163.

Taylor, Barry (1977). 'Tense and Continuity', *Linguistics and Philosophy* 1: 99–220.
Vendler, Zeno (1967). 'Verbs and Times', in *Linguistics in Philosophy*. Ithaca, New York: Cornell University Press, 97–121.
Vlach, Frank (1981). 'The Semantics of the Progressive', in P.J. Tedeschi and A. Zaenen (eds.), *Tense and Aspect*. New York: Academic Press, 271–92.
Webber, Bonnie (1987). 'The Interpretation of Tense in Discourse', *Proceedings of the 25th Annual Meeting of the ACL*. Stanford, CA, 147–54.
——(1988). 'Tense as Discourse Anaphor', *Computational Linguistics* 14: 61–73.

Part II
Temporal Reasoning

Introduction to Part II

I INTRODUCTION

Reasoning about time is an essential competence that all humans possess and a signature of intelligent behavior in any cognitive system. Our ability to represent temporal knowledge of actions and events in the world is essential for modeling causation, constructing complex plans, hypothesizing possible outcomes of actions, and almost any higher-order, cognitive task. It is not surprising, therefore, that temporal reasoning has been a central area of research in artificial intelligence since the 1960s. This overview of Part II will situate some of the work on temporal reasoning, particularly certain aspects that are especially relevant to natural language processing. As we have seen in Part I, natural language expresses temporal information through tense, aspect, temporal adverbials, and other devices. Motivated by linguistic considerations, Part I introduced constraint- and logic-based formalisms for analyzing tense, and event ontologies for representing event classes and structure. These mechanisms were applied in some cases to identification of the temporal location of events mentioned in text. We now turn from linguistic considerations to considerations motivated by artificial intelligence in general.

The problems of temporal reasoning involve in part, as in natural language, locating events in time. Thus, given the narrative,

(1) a. Yesterday, John fell while running.
    b. He broke his leg.

a natural language system may seek to anchor the *falling, running*, and *breaking* events to the particular time (yesterday), as well as order the events relative to each other, e.g. the running precedes the falling, which precedes the breaking. Temporal reasoning is therefore concerned with representing and reasoning about such anchoring and ordering relationships. Temporal reasoning is also concerned with creating the most appropriate formalisms for representing events, states, and their temporal properties. However, the particular form of temporal representation depends on the type of reasoning problem under consideration. In common-sense inference, for example, knowing that the falling occurred before breaking, and that the falling occurred yesterday (facts obtained here from linguistic data), along with common-sense knowledge of the behavior of breakings and fallings, may allow a system to infer that the falling precedes and causes the breaking, and that these events occurred yesterday. In planning, on the other hand, a given outcome is desired (e.g. a robot arriving at a crater), and common-sense knowledge of the behavior of events and states (such as landing, avoiding obstacles, etc.) may allow one to infer what needs to happen when.

Historically, temporal reasoning developed largely out of the planning community in AI, but the ability to perform temporal reasoning in knowledge-intensive environments is critical for many diverse applications. Some of these are listed below:

1. Maintaining temporal consistency in a knowledge base;
2. Temporal question-answering (cf. Androutsopoulos et al. 1998);
3. Scheduling tasks and events; and
4. Causal diagnosis.

There are four features that typically distinguish the structure of time within a model of temporal reasoning:

1. Primitive time unit: the choice of instants (i.e. points) or intervals (i.e. periods) as temporal markers of the flow of time.
2. Branching: whether different time-lines are possible or not.
3. Discreteness: the choice of whether to represent time as a collection of discrete elements, or else as an element between two points.
4. Boundedness: whether time is infinite or finite in each direction.

Each of these issues is addressed in distinct ways in the frameworks represented in this part. Most early approaches to AI, beginning with the frameworks (to be discussed below) of the Situation Calculus (McCarthy and Hayes 1969), the Event Calculus (Kowalski and Sergot, Chapter 10), and also early work in planning (McDermott, Chapter 9), assumes instants to be basic. Other studies, including the papers in this part by Allen and by Hobbs and Pustejovsky, take intervals to be basic.

A flow of time that is a strict partial ordering is said to be linear if any two distinct points are related. A branching model of time can be said to be branching to the future if there is some point that has two unrelated points in its future. Similar remarks hold for the flow of time in the past. When a structure does not branch to the future or the past, it is called a nonbranching (or linear) structure of time. Typically, model-theoretic treatments of tense and aspect in language assume a nonbranching past and possible branching futures. Dowty (1979), for example, invokes the nonlinearity of intensional states inherent in a Montague-style treatment of the progressive, e.g. 'John is crossing the street.' The future branches to many world-time pairs, some of which are inertially closer to achieving the goal state than others. Irrealis contexts also typically require some form of branching future (cf. van Bentham 1983).

Regarding discreteness of time: a dense flow of time exists when, between any two distinct points, there is a third point. A discrete flow supposes that time proceeds in discrete steps, where there is a well-defined next point or period. Finally, the feature of boundedness addresses the issue of the beginning- and end-points in the structure modeling the flow of time. Typical models assume a bounded past and an unbounded future.

The goals of an approach and the specifics of a particular reasoning task will often dictate the choice of one's temporal primitives. For example, from a logical standpoint, instants are attractive since we understand the idea of truth at an instant, but the notion of truth at an interval requires further explication. Dean and McDermott (1987) argue that instants are more efficient for reasoning within temporal database management systems. For reasoning about continuous change, as Galton shows in this part (Chapter 13), we need a notion of durationless events, thus arguing for instants. Galton's paper shows how it is possible to represent intervals in terms of points or have a point-based theory that represents intervals. The differences between point-based and interval-based models have been discussed in considerable detail, for example, in van Bentham (1983) and Shoham (1989).

Each of the temporal reasoning formalisms represented here differs in its expressiveness and efficiency for reasoning about natural language problems. The requirements of a particular reasoning task will largely dictate the topology of time needed, and determine the appropriateness of the data structures and inference rules used. Although early work on natural language was formulated in terms of the basic framework of the Situation Calculus (as with McDermott's paper), most work on the temporal interpretation of text and discourse has assumed some sort of Allen-style interval calculus. The expressiveness inherent in the interval calculus has meshed well with much of the recent work on tense and aspect interpretation in linguistic semantics (e.g. Leith and Cunningham, 2001).

2 TEMPORAL LOGIC

A temporal logic allows one to use the representation and inference mechanisms of logic to reason about time. For this to happen, temporal information needs to be added to the logic. From a logical standpoint, there are two ways to provide for a temporal interpretation of a proposition:

1. Add a modal operator over the propositional expression, so that temporal order is interpreted from the syntactic combination of operators over expressions;
2. Add an additional argument to the predicative expression, one representing time directly as a point or period, or as a time-dependent individual, such as an event.

The latter approach will be discussed below under the Situation Calculus (Section 3). In Part I, we introduced an instance of the first approach, that taken by Prior in the construction of **Minimal Tense Logic**, known as K_t. In such systems, operators play the combined role of verbal tense, temporal adverbials, as well as temporal prepositions and connectives. For K_t, four axioms form the core knowledge about temporal relations (as already stated in the Introduction to Part I):

(2) a. $\phi \rightarrow H\,F\phi$: What is, has always been going to be;
    b. $\phi \rightarrow G\,P\,\phi$: What is, will always have been;
    c. $H(\phi \rightarrow \psi) \rightarrow (H\phi \rightarrow H\psi)$: Whatever always follows from what always has been, always has been;
    d. $G(\phi \rightarrow \psi) \rightarrow (G\phi \rightarrow G\psi)$: Whatever always follows from what always will be, always will be.

F and P are usually referred to as **weak operators**. They can be defined in terms of the other two as follows: $F\phi = \neg G \neg \phi$; $P\phi = \neg H \neg \phi$. K_t becomes a complete inference system when the two rules of temporal inference below are added to the rules of propositional logic:

(3) a. From a proof of ϕ, derive a proof of $H\phi$.
    b. From a proof of ϕ, derive a proof of $G\phi$.

To reason about the truth of expressions in a propositional tense logic, we construct a model, where our interpretation functions (or valuations) make reference to moments of time. Let us define a **temporal frame** as consisting of T, a set of moments in time, and an ordering relation R, the *earlier than* relation. The truth value of an atomic formula ϕ can be determined relative to a frame, according to the following rules:

(4) a. $V_{M,t}(\mathbf{G}\phi) = 1$ iff for every $t_i \in T$ such that tRt_i: $V_{M,t_i}(\phi) = 1$
   b. $V_{M,t}(\mathbf{F}\phi) = 1$ iff for some $t_i \in T$ such that tRt_i: $V_{M,t_i}(\phi) = 1$
   c. $V_{M,t}(\mathbf{H}\phi) = 1$ iff for every $t_i \in T$ such that t_iRt: $V_{M,t_i}(\phi) = 1$
   d. $V_{M,t}(\mathbf{P}\phi) = 1$ iff for some $t_i \in T$ such that t_iRt: $V_{M,t_i}(\phi) = 1$

Examples of the tense logic as applied to natural language sentences are given below:

(5) a. John will have left Boston.
       F(P(leave(j, b)**))**
   b. John was going to leave to Boston.
       P(F(leave(j, b)**))**

Using the model described, we can determine the truth-conditions of the propositional expression for each sentence above. For example, for (5a), we have the following valuation:

(6) a. $V_{M,t}(\mathbf{P}(leave(j,b))) = 1$ iff for some $t_i \in T$ s.t. t_iRt: $V_{M,t_i}((leave(j,b))) = 1$
   b. $V_{M,t}(\mathbf{F}(\mathbf{P}(leave(j,b)))) = 1$ iff for some $t_i \in T$ s.t. tRt_i: $V_{M,t_i}((\mathbf{P}(leave(j,b)))) = 1$

Intuitively, this states that the expression is true if, at some moment of time, t_1, after now (t_0), there is a moment of time, t_2, before t_1, such that 'John leaves Boston' is true. A problem with K_t, as already pointed out in Part I above, is that there is no explicit notion of the present. Notice that in the model above, we just assumed that the base from which we are performing the valuation is conveniently assumed to be the present. This will not be sufficient when we need to model a more dynamic and expansive notion of the present for reasoning tasks.

2.1 Extensions to tense logic

There have been many extensions and modifications to the basic form of the Propositional Tense Logic of System K_t. One major addition was introduced by Kamp (1968), namely the binary temporal operators **S** (since) and **U** (until).

(7) a. $\mathbf{S}\phi\psi$: ψ has been true since a time when ϕ was true.
   b. $\mathbf{U}\phi\psi$: ψ will be true until a time when ϕ is true.

These operators have become standard within computer science in the area of temporal database reasoning systems (as discussed in Manna and Pnueli 1992, and Baudinet et al. 1993), where persistence of database updating functions over relations can be modeled with **S** and **U**, e.g. 'Smith has been manager of Dept. A since Smith was promoted to manager.'

In the 1970s, temporal logic was adopted by computer scientists working in program verification and specification as a standard methodology for program analysis. Pnueli (1977) is one of the first major works in this area, and the growing importance of temporal logic, interval temporal logic, and other extensions to tense logic, is seen in their role in modeling reactive and hybrid systems in computer science (cf. Gabbay et al. 1995 for extensive discussion).

An example of this is **Interval Temporal Logic** (ITL), which is a notation for both propositional and first-order reasoning about periods of time as used in descriptions of hardware and software systems. ITL is able to handle both sequential and parallel composition and offers proof techniques for reasoning about program properties involving safety and liveness. Safety states that something bad will not happen, while liveness properties assert that something good will eventually happen.

3 SITUATION CALCULUS

Perhaps the most widely adopted attempt to model action and change in the early days of AI was the situation calculus (McCarthy 1968; McCarthy and Hayes 1969). This model represents actions and their effects on the world. The world is represented as a set of situations, which model the possible configurations of the world at a particular time. In this sense, there is a strong similarity between possible worlds (Carnap 1947) and situations, although no semantics for the latter was spelled out in the early work. Fluents are time-varying properties of individuals. Actions are functions that map states to states, and hence act as state transformers.

The situation calculus (sc) was used for many different tasks, but was particularly popular in planning paradigms. The major problems with the classic situation calculus are two-fold: (1) concurrent actions cannot be represented; (2) there is no representation for the duration of actions or delayed effects of actions. These problems make the pure SC inadequate for many reasoning tasks, but it has been extended and enriched by numerous researchers and is still a very active area of research (e.g. Reiter 2001).

There are typically two strategies employed for representing the situation calculus within a first-order logical representation (FOL): the use of temporal arguments and the use of metalanguage predicates. The first approach is similar in many respects to Davidson's proposal (1967) for event individuation of predicates; in the case of the Situation Calculus, a state variable is added to every predicate in the language.

The state-based (temporal argument) representation of the Situation Calculus (where temporally-sensitive variables are employed) interprets events as state transform functions. Beginning and end states are characterized as predicates with state variables added. As mentioned above, actions cause state transitions. For example, the state-based representation of sentence (8),

(8)   John gave *Lord of the Rings* to Mary.

is as illustrated in (9).

(9) a. *Have(s1, J, LOTR)*
    b. *Have(s2, M, LOTR)*

The initial state is changed by the application of a state transformer, *give*, modeled as an initiation rule.

(10)   *Have(z, y, Result(give(x, y, z), s))*

The second approach to interpreting the Situation Calculus involves the use of meta-language predicates, which relate the truth value of an expression to a situation. Taking the example in (8) again, this would entail the following representation:

(11) a. *HOLDS(Have(J, LOTR), s1)*
     b. *HOLDS(Have(M, LOTR), s2)*

The *HOLDS* predicate states that a property is true in a specific situation. States are changed by *Initiate* and *Terminate* actions. The way to express the *Initiate* action in this interpretation of SC would be as follows:

(12) *HOLDS(Have(z, y), Result(give(x, y, z), s))*

This interpretation of the Situation Calculus is more expressive than the temporal argument approach, since it effectively creates a second-order representation where predicates can be quantified over. This allows for the treatment of some of the classic problems in aspectual semantics (see Introduction to Part I).

There are some problems with the Situation Calculus that do not disappear under either interpretation outlined above. Chief among these is the fact that situations must be totally ordered, making planning difficult. Frame axioms, rules characterizing the persistence and effects of actions, as we will discuss in Section 6 below, are trivial to express in the Situation Calculus; the number of such rules, however, becomes prohibitively large, as they are proportional to the products of the number of fluents and actions performable over them. In addition, events are not explicitly represented in the model.

3.1 McDermott's Use of the Situation Calculus

McDermott's paper, 'A Temporal Logic for Reasoning about Processes and Plans', (Chapter 9) starts with the general assumptions of the Situation Calculus, but with some important modifications. McDermott frames his contribution as a temporal model with a first-order language, in the spirit of Moore (1980) and Hayes (1979). McDermott assumes the world is defined as discrete situations (states) associated with a date. **Chronicles** are states that are coherently structured into a possible history. McDermott then goes on to define a **fact** as a set of states wherein a particular proposition is true.

He abandons the classical Situation Calculus (cf. McCarthy (1968)) notion of events as fact changers, and defines an **event** as a set of intervals over which a proposition is minimally true (i.e. it happens once). This will be essentially the same intuition that Allen adopts for his definition of event. McDermott's model assumes points as primitive, where intervals can be constructed from a totally ordered convex set of states. This model is continuous (dense time) and has a branching future.

4 EVENT CALCULUS

A somewhat different approach to representing events is taken by Kowalski and Sergot in their paper, 'A Logic-based Calculus of Events' (Chapter 10). This work was originally intended as a model for database update and narrative understanding, but has developed into a richer framework for general issues in temporal reasoning and planning. The main innovation in this model comes in the way that events are represented. Whereas events are viewed as transformers from state to state in the Situation Calculus, they are primitives in the Event Calculus, acting as *updates* on the state of the world. In this sense they are *additive* information operations. More specifically, they are seen as actions that initiate or terminate the properties of individuals (known as fluents, adopted from the Situation Calculus). As in the Situation Calculus, Kowalski and Sergot introduce a *Holds* predicate, which expresses that a property or relationship associated with a specific period of time is true during that period. Hence, for some property, P:

(13) $Holds(P)$

From this, they define the *HoldsAt* relation, which expresses that a relation, u, holds at a specific time instant, t:

(14) $HoldsAt(u, t)$

To illustrate, let us return to the example from the previous section, of John giving *Lord of the Rings* to Mary. Intuitively, the initial and goal conditions can be expressed as below.

(15) a. $HoldsAt(Have(J, LOTR), t_1)$
      b. $HoldsAt(Have(M, LOTR), t_2)$

The *Hold* predicate states that a property is assumed to persist until the occurrence of some event interrupts this property. This is referred to as default persistence. For example, the event of *giving*, e_0, terminates the relation holding at t_1 and then initiates that relation holding at t_2.

(16) a. $terminates(e_0, Have(J, LOTR))$
      b. $initiates(e_0, Have(M, LOTR))$

Time in this model is represented as a partially ordered set of points, and the occurrence of an event is represented by associating it with the time-point at which it occurs. This is accomplished by a metalanguage predicate *happens*, where e is an event instance and t is a time-point:

(17) $happens(e, t)$

Reasoning in the Event Calculus entails deriving the maximal validity intervals (MVIs) over which properties hold, as the result of the actions of events. An MVI is maximal if it cannot be properly contained in any other valid interval.

The paper by Chittaro and Combi (Chapter 11) extends the framework of the Event Calculus to allow for the representation of events with indeterminant temporal anchoring and granularity. They introduce a framework they call the **Temporal Granularity and Indeterminacy Event Calculus** (TGIC) to model these properties. This entails modifying the algorithm for computing maximal validity intervals to allow satisfaction under varying levels of granularity of temporal scale (years, months, days, hours, etc.). This flexibility extends the expressiveness of the Event Calculus to accommodate a more general concept of event. This is illustrated with examples from a clinical domain, showing how varying granularities of events using this procedure can facilitate reasoning.

It should be pointed out that the Event Calculus shares with the Situation Calculus the basic concepts of property initiation and termination, and these similarities are discussed in Kowalski and Sadri (1994). There are some major differences, however, including the following.

1. The Situation Calculus makes use of branching time while the Event Calculus used linear time.
2. The SC has a notion of previous state that is absent from the EC, by virtue of the explicit use of situations.
3. State transitions in the SC are functions but not in the EC.

These are explored in more detail in van Belleghem et al. (1995).

5 ALLEN'S TEMPORAL INTERVAL ALGEBRA

One of the most important works in the area of temporal representation and reasoning is James Allen's article, entitled 'Towards a General Theory of Action and Time' (1984); see Chapter 12. In this system, temporal intervals are considered primitives and constraints (on actions, etc.) are expressed as relations between intervals. There is no branching into the future or the past. In Allen's interval algebra, there are thirteen basic (binary) interval relations, where six are inverses of the other six, excluding equality.

(18) a. before (b), after (bi);
  b. overlap (o), overlappedBy (oi);
  c. start (s), startedBy (si);
  d. finish (f), finishedBy (fi);
  e. during (d), contains (di);
  f. meet (m), metBy (mi);
  g. equality (eq).

These are shown schematically in Figure 1 below. The reasoning system is supported by a transitivity table, which defines the conjunction of any two relations. All thirteen relations can be expressed using *Meet*. For example, for two periods i and j we can define the relation *Before* as follows:

(19) $Before(i, j) =_{df} \exists m[Meets(i, m) \wedge Meets(m, j)]$

5.1 Interpreting intervals

Allen makes a basic distinction between properties, which we have already encountered, and *occurrences*, which are inspired by Davidson's theory of actions and events (Davidson 1967).

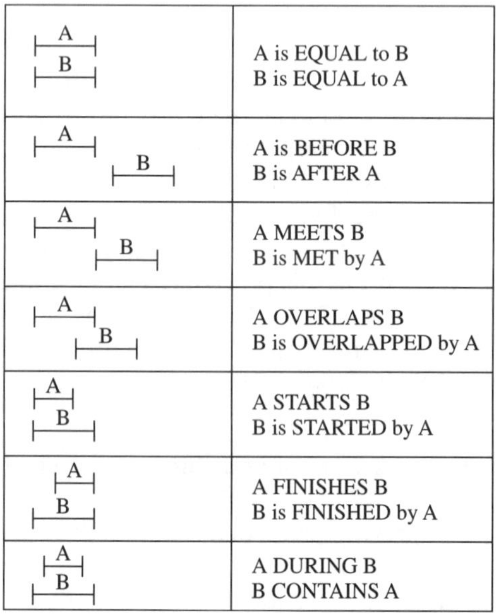

A B	A is EQUAL to B B is EQUAL to A
A B	A is BEFORE B B is AFTER A
A B	A MEETS B B is MET by A
A B	A OVERLAPS B B is OVERLAPPED by A
A B	A STARTS B B is STARTED by A
A B	A FINISHES B B is FINISHED by A
A B	A DURING B B CONTAINS A

FIG. 1

Occurrences are a sort of generalized eventuality category, which divide into two classes: **processes** and **events**.

He then defines metalanguage predicates for each of these three classes.

CLASS	PREDICATE
property	HOLDS
event	OCCUR
process	OCCURRING

HOLDS is used to assert that a property is true during a specified temporal interval.

(20) $HOLDS(p, t)$

is said to be true if and only if the property p holds during the temporal interval t. This predicate is defined in terms of a downward monotonic subinterval property, shown below:

(21) $HOLDS(p, T) \leftrightarrow \forall t [IN(t, T) \rightarrow HOLDS(p, t)]$

This cannot be said of either kind of occurrence, however. For notice that events do not have homogeneous behavior for the properties which live on the interval defining that event. For example, if John dies, then there is a change of state which, as in the situation and event calculi, has to be represented as an opposition of properties. Allen introduces the *OCCUR* relation for events, and defines it as follows (where Allen uses the expression P_t to refer to the necessary and sufficient set of conditions for an event's occurrence in t).

(22) a. $OCCUR(e, t) \wedge IN(t', t) \rightarrow \neg OCCUR(e, t')$
      b. $OCCUR(e, t) \leftrightarrow P_t \wedge \forall t'[IN(t', t) \rightarrow \neg P_{t'}]$

Similarly, because of issues of granularity, even processes are not completely homogeneous in the way that properties are. Imagine the process of playing a piano. Those subintervals when the keys are not being struck are not actual piano playings, hence we need to have a weaker relation interpreting such classes. This is called *OCCURRING* and is defined as follows.

(23) $OCCURING(p, t) \rightarrow \exists t'[IN(t', t) \wedge OCCURRING(p, t')]$

5.2 Discussion of Allen's Theory

The interval algebra as formulated by Allen has enjoyed great favor in natural language processing and AI. In terms of expressiveness, however, Galton (Chapter 13) argues that it is inadequate for representing continuous change. In continuous change, objects occupy locations instantaneously. Galton shows that 'x is at rest at L' and 'x is at L' are indistinguishable in Allen's system, arguing that what one needs is a concept of a property being true at an instant, without requiring that it be true at any interval containing or bounding that instant. Galton attempts to revise Allen's theory based on a combined instant–interval scheme, where instants fall within or limit intervals. A second criticism can be made in terms of computational tractability of interval algebras. Vilain and Kautz (1986) show that consistency and closure computations in the interval algebra are NP-hard. However, they also show that part of the interval algebra can be converted to a point algebra where the computation is tractable (for an application of such an approach, see Pustejovsky et al.'s paper on TimeML in Part IV).

6 TEMPORAL REASONING AND THE FRAME PROBLEM

There are a number of classic problems that relate to temporal reasoning in environments where attributes and individuals change as a result of actions. Chief among these are the following:

1. Frame problem: accounting for those properties of a state that are not changed by performing a particular action.
2. Ramification problem: the explicit effects (direct or indirect) of performing an action.
3. Qualification problem: the conditions under which a particular action is applicable in the first place.

These problems are often collectively grouped under the first term, the **frame problem**. To illustrate what is at play here, consider the *give*-example from above. The action of giving makes explicit only who possesses the book at a certain time. Nothing else about the state of the world is mentioned by this specific action. The frame problem is that of determining what properties (fluents) are not impacted by an action. For example, all things being equal, giving a book to someone will not change the color or weight of the book. All that has basically changed is who has possession of the book. For all other fluent properties in the situation that we are modeling given the occurrence of an action, there must be a logical device to allow them to persist. McCarthy and Hayes (1969) introduced the notion of **inertia** into the Situation Calculus to account for these cases. A frame axiom is a rule associated with a particular action or class of actions that does just this. It keeps the color of the book the same, and so on (Shanahan 1997). Such persistence axioms reflect our knowledge of the way that the world is changed by actions, and how it is updated accordingly. Because the number of frame axioms grows proportionally to the product of possible actions over fluents in a domain, theories of nonmonotonic reasoning have been developed to capture the appropriateness of which properties should change, e.g. McCarthy's theory of circumscription (1986), Reiter's default logic (1980), and Asher and Morreau's non-monotonic reasoning (1991).

The ramification problem examines the related problem of computing those fluents that are impacted by the actions being performed. Rules defining these changes are called **effect axioms**; the computational issues with ramifications involve the appropriate pruning of inferences one can draw from an action. Schubert (1999) has approached the problem as one of finding an adequate explanation of change.

7 CONCLUSION

Given this account of temporal reasoning, we can see that the approaches we have discussed (with the exception of the situation calculus) offer expressive frameworks that can be applied to temporal reasoning in natural language. Both the McDermott and Allen contributions explicitly address problems of temporal inference in natural language. The approaches explore reasoning with states, events, and point and interval representations of time.

Clearly, mapping from natural language representations to such frameworks requires an appropriate representation and annotation of events and the relations between them. As will be seen in Part III, most of the events in discourse have no explicit temporal anchoring and no explicit orderings relative to each other. Therefore, rules must be developed that capture how the text or discourse structures event-orderings. Hobbs and Pustejovsky (Chapter 14) show how an annotation scheme can be linked to a formal theory of time intended for use in representing the temporal content of websites and the properties of web services (the DAML Time Ontology). This linking allows interpretations of documents in terms of the annotation scheme to be mapped to a temporal representation where formal queries can be posed to a temporal reasoning system. The more we can tie in annotation to temporal reasoning, the closer we will come to solving some of the basic understanding problems for reasoning in language. This would be a very important capability in automatic reasoning.

REFERENCES

Abadi, M. and Manna, Z. (1989). 'Temporal Logic', *Programming Journal of Symbolic Computation* 8: 277–95.

Androutsopoulos, I., Ritchie, G. D., and Thanisch, P. (1998). 'Time, tense and aspect in natural language database interfaces', *Natural Language Engineering* 4(3): 229–76.

Asher, N. and Morreau, M. (1991). 'Common Sense Entailment: A Modal Theory of Nonmonotonic Reasoning', in Proceedings to the 12th International Joint Conference on Artificial Intelligence. Sydney, Australia, August 1991, 1–30.

Baudinet, M., Chomicki, J., and Wolper, P. (1993). 'Temporal Deductive Database', in A. Tansel et al. (eds.), *Temporal Databases: Theory, Design and Implementation*. Redwood City, CA: Benjamin-Cummings, 294–320.

Belleghem, K. van, Denecker, M., and De Schreye, D. (1995). 'Combining Situation Calculus and Event Calculus', in Leon Stirling (ed.), *Proceedings of the 1995 International Conference on Logic Programming*. Cambridge, MA: MIT Press, 83–97.

Bentham, J. van (1983). *The Logic of Time*. Dordrecht: Reidel.

Carnap, R. (1947). *Meaning and Necessity: A Study in Semantics and Modal Logic*. Chicago, IL: University of Chicago Press.

Davidson, D. (1967). 'The Logical Form of Action Sentences', in N. Rescher (ed.), *The Logic of Decision and Action*. Pittsburgh: University of Pittsburgh Press, 81–95.

Dean, T. L. and McDermott, D. (1987). 'Temporal data base management', *Artificial Intelligence* 32: 1–55.

Dowty, D. (1979). *Word Meaning and Montague Grammar*. Dordrecht: D. Reidel.

Gabbay, D. M., Hogger, C.J., and Robinson, J. A. (eds.) (1995). *Handbook of Logic in Artificial Intelligence and Logic Programming, Volume 4: Epistemic and Temporal Reasoning*. Oxford: Oxford Science Publications.

Galton, A. P. (1984). *The Logic of Aspect: An Axiomatic Approach*. Oxford: Clarendon Press.

Hanks, H. and McDermott, D. (1986). 'Default reasoning, nonmonotonic logics, and the frame problem', in *Proceedings of the Fifth National Conference on Artificial Intelligence (AAAI-86)*, Philadelphia, PA. Menlo Park, CA: AAAI Press, 328–33.

Hayes, P. (1979). 'Naive Physics Manifesto', in D. Michie (ed.), *Expert Systems in the Microelectronic Age*. Edinburgh University Press.

Hayes, P. (1985). 'Naive Physics I: Ontology for Liquids', in J. Hobbs and R. Moore (eds.), *Formal Theories of the Commonsense World*. Norwood, N.J: Ablex Publications.

Kamp, H. W. (1968). 'Tense Logic and the Theory of Linear Order'. Ph.D. dissertation, UCLA, Los Angeles, California.

Kowalski, R. A. and Sadri, F. (1994). 'The Situation Calculus and Event Calculus compared', in M. Bruynooghe, (ed.), *Logic Programming: Proceedings of the 1994 International Symposium*. Cambridge, MA: MIT Press, 539–53.

Kroger, F. (1987). *Temporal Logic of Programs*. Berlin: Springer-Verlag.

Lamport, L. (1980). '"Sometime" is sometimes "not never": on the temporal logic of programs;' *Proceedings of the 7th ACM SIGPLAN-SIGACT Symposium on Principles of Programming Languages* (POPL). New York: ACM Press, 174–85.

Lamport, L. (1982).'TIMESETS: A New Method for Temporal Reasoning About Programs', in D. Kozen (ed.), *Proceedings of the workshop on Logics of Programs*, Lecture notes in Computer Science, 131. Berlin: Springer-Verlag, 177–96.

Leith, M. and Cunningham, J. (2001). 'Aspect and Interval Tense Logic', *Linguistics and Philosophy* 24: 331–81.

Manna, Z. and Pnueli, A. (1983). 'Verification of Concurrent Programs: A Temporal Proof System', Department of Computer Science, Stanford University, Report No. STAN-CS-83-967.

——(1992). 'Temporal Logic', in Z. Manna and A. Puneli, *The Temporal Logic of Reactive and Concurrent Systems*. Berlin: Springer-Verlag.

McCarthy, J. (1968). 'Situations, Actions and Causal Laws' in M. Minsky (ed.), Semantic Information Processing. Cambridge, MA: MIT Press.

—— (1986). 'Applications of Circumscription to Formalizing Common Sense Knowledge', *Artificial Intelligence* 26(3): 89–116.

——and Hayes, P. (1969). 'Some philosophical problems from the standpoint of artificial intelligence', in B. Meltzer and D. Michie, (eds.), *Machine Intelligence*, vol. 4. Edinburgh: Edinburgh University Press.

Moore, R. C. (1980). 'Reasoning about Knowledge and action', Technical Note 191, SRI International, Menlo Park, CA. October 1980.

Moszkowski, B. (1986). *Executing Temporal Logic Programs*. Cambridge: Cambridge University Press.

Pnueli, A. (1977). 'The Temporal Logic of Programs', *Proceedings of the 18th IEEE Symposium on Foundations of Computer Science*. IEEE Computer Society Press, 46–57.

——(1979). 'The Temporal Semantics of Concurrent Programs', in *Proceedings of the International Symposium on Semantics of Concurrent Computation*. Berlin: Springer-Verlag.

Reiter, R. (1980). 'A logic for default reasoning', *Artificial Intelligence* 13 (1,2): 81–132.

——(2001). *Knowledge in Action : Logical Foundations for Specifying and Implementing Dynamical Systems*. Cambridge, MA: MIT Press.

Richards, B., Bethke, I., Does, J. van der and Oberlander, J. (1989). *Temporal Representation and Inference*. London: Academic Press.

Schubert, L. (1999). 'Explanation Closure, Action Closure, and the Sandewall Test Suite for Reasoning about Change', in H. Levesque and F. Pirri (eds.), *Logical Foundations for Cognitive Agents*. Berlin: Springer-Verlag.

Shanahan, M. P. (1997). *Solving the Frame Problem*. Cambridge, MA: MIT Press.

——(1999*a*). 'The Event Calculus Explained', in M. J. Wooldridge and M. Veloso (eds.), *Artificial Intelligence Today: Recent Trends and Developments*. Springer Lecture Notes in Artificial Intelligence no. 1600. Berlin: Springer-Verlag, 409–30.

——(1999*b*). 'The Ramification Problem in the Event Calculus', in C. S. Mellish (ed.), *Proceedings of the 16th International Joint Conference on Artificial Intelligence (IJCAI)*. Stockholm, Sweden: Morgan Ranfmann, 140–6.

Shoham, Y. (1989). 'Time for action: On the relation between time, knowledge and action', in *Proceedings of the 11th International Joint Conference on Artificial Intelligence (IJCAI)*, Detroit, MI: Morgan Ranfmann, 954–9.

Vilain, M. and Kautz, H. (1986). 'Constraint Propagation Algorithms for Temporal Reasoning', in *Proceedings of the Fifth National Conference on Artificial Intelligence* (AAAI-86), Menlo Park, CA: AAAI Press, 377–82.

9

A Temporal Logic for Reasoning About Processes and Plans*

DREW McDERMOTT

1 INTRODUCTION

A common disclaimer by an AI author is that he has neglected temporal considerations to avoid complication. The implication is nearly made that adding a temporal dimension to the research (on engineering, medical diagnosis, etc.) would be a familiar but tedious exercise that would obscure the new material presented by the author. Actually, of course, no one has ever dealt with time correctly in an AI program, and there is reason to believe that doing it would change everything.

Because time has been neglected, medical diagnosis programs cannot talk about the course of a disease. Story understanding programs have trouble with past events. Problem solvers have had only the crudest models of the future, in spite of the obvious importance of future events.

Many researchers have compensated by modeling the course of external time with the program's own internal time, changing the world model to reflect changing reality. This leads to a confusion between correcting a mistaken belief and updating an outdated belief. Most AI data bases have some sort of operator for removing formulas (e.g., ERASE in PLANNER, Hewitt, 1972). This operator has tended to be used for two quite different purposes: getting rid of tentative or hypothetical assertions that turned out not to be true, and noting that an assertion is *no longer* true. The confusion is natural, since some of the same consequences must follow in either case. For example, if "The car is drivable" follows from "There is gas in the car," then the former statement must be deleted when the latter is, whether you have discovered there to be no gas after all, or the gas has been used up.

But in many cases, the two behave quite differently, and efforts to make them the same have resulted in awkward, inextensible programs. For example, from "x is beating his wife," you are entitled to infer, "x is a bad man." But if x pauses to catch his breath, only the former statement must be deleted from the data base. Clearly, the proper inference is from "If x has beat his wife recently, he is a bad man," and "x is beating his wife," to "For the next year or so, x will have beaten his wife recently," and hence to

---

Drew McDermott, 'A Temporal Logic for Reasoning about Processes and Plans', *Cognitive Science* 6 (1982): 101–55. © 1982 Cognitive Science Society.

*This research was supported by NSF grant MCS 8013710. Thanks to Ernie Davis for technical assistance and ideas; and to Chris Riesbeck and all the members of the Yale Learning Group, who came up with problems for a temporal notation in the field of economics; and to Tony Passera for work on the implementation. I had useful discussions with James Allen, Eugene Charniak, Patrick Hayes, and Robert Moore. The referee is responsible for some improvements in intelligibility. I am responsible for residual confusion and error.

"For the next year or so, x is a bad man." (We must allow for reform.) As far as I know, no AI program has been capable of such inferences.

An even worse flaw than the inability to model present change is the inability to model future possibility. To make this clear, I will sketch an example of where the standard approaches fail.

Say a problem solver is confronted with the classic situation of a heroine, called Nell, having been tied to the tracks while a train approaches. The problem solver, called Dudley, knows that

"If Nell is going to be mashed, I must remove her from the tracks."

(He probably knows a more general rule, but let that pass.) When Dudley deduces that he must do something, he looks for, and eventually executes, a plan for doing it. This will involve finding out where Nell is, and making a navigation plan to get to her location. Assume that he knows where she is, and she is not too far away; then the fact that the plan will be carried out is added to Dudley's world model. Dudley must have some kind of data-base-consistency maintainer (Doyle, 1979) to make sure that the plan is deleted if it is no longer necessary. Unfortunately, as soon as an apparently successful plan is added to the world model, the consistency maintainer will notice that "Nell is going to be mashed" is no longer true. But that removes any justification for the plan, so it goes, too. But that means "Nell is going to be mashed" is no longer contradictory, so it comes back in. And so forth.

Exactly what will happen depends on implementation. The data base manager might loop forever, or it might conclude erroneously that Nell is safe without any action by Dudley. The problem, however, lies deeper than the implementation level. The naive logic we used, a non-monotonic first-order situation calculus (McCarthy, 1968; McDermott and Doyle, 1980), is just inadequate: no implementation can do the right thing here, because the logic doesn't specify the right thing. We need to be able to express, "Nell is going to be mashed *unless* I save her," and *unless* is a non-trivial concept (Goodman, 1947; Lewis, 1973).

In this paper, I will begin an attempt to rectify these problems, by providing a robust temporal logic to serve as a framework for programs that must deal with time. This is in the spirit of Hayes's "naive physics" (Hayes, 1979a), and might be thought of as a "naive theory of time." I will sketch approaches within this framework to what I consider the three most important problems of temporal representation: causality, continuous change, and the logic of problem solving.

One difference between Hayes and me is that I have not been able to turn my eyes away from implementational details as resolutely as Hayes. Consequently, later in the paper I will discuss how these ideas might be embodied in a program. Of course, the use of logic does not constrain us to making the program look like a theorem prover.

So why do I plan to spend any time at all on logic? There are two reasons:

1. We want to be assured that our special-purpose modules are not prone to absurd interactions such as the one I just sketched. One way to guarantee this is to be sure that the modules' actions are sound with respect to an underlying logic. (It is relatively unimportant and in practice unattainable that the programs be logically complete.)
2. Recently it has become clear that a reasoning system must keep track of the justifications for its conclusions, in order to update the data base as assumptions change (Doyle, 1979). For example, a picture of the future based on the assumption

that dinner will be done at 6:00 must be revised if there is a power failure at 5:30. It turns out that constructing and maintaining these justification records, called *data dependencies*, is not trivial. One useful guide is that the data dependencies be equivalent to proofs in the underlying logic.

Many cognitive scientists will not find these reasons reassuring enough. On the one hand, many of them will be intimidated by the use of logical notation. On the other, there is a widespread feeling that psychological experiments have proven that people cannot handle simple syllogisms (see, e.g., Johnson-Laird, 1980), and that, therefore, people cannot possibly operate on logical principles. Together, these considerations cause them to reject papers like this one out of hand.

Let me be a little more reassuring. There is no difference between logical notation and notations like those of Schank (1975) or Charniak (1981), except emphasis. The logical approach aims at expressing the implications used for *inference*, as well as providing an ontological framework (or set of primitives, or vocabulary) for expressing *facts*. But face it—we're all talking about computers performing formal operations on data structures representing beliefs. The only issue is which to nail down first, the organization of the information in memory, or the structure of the inferences.

The experimental results on human processing of syllogisms are much less relevant than they first appear. At best, they show that people have no natural syllogistic machinery accessible to consciousness. This says nothing about logics underlying various kinds of thinking. One might as well investigate frequency-domain analysis in the visual system by asking people to do Fourier transforms in their heads.

In any case, I hope that appreciation of the difficulties raised by time will cause you to stick with me.

2 ONTOLOGY

We shall be doing logic in the style of Robert Moore (1980). The logic of time appears at first glance to be like modal logic, with different instants playing the role of different possible worlds. An expression like "President of the US" seems to denote an intensional object, with a different denotation in different times (worlds). In fact, historically the exploration of this relationship has fueled temporal logic (Prior, 1967; Rescher and Urquhart, 1971).

Moore encountered a similar tradition in his study of knowledge. "Know" had typically been taken as a modal operator. This made it difficult to handle computationally (Moore, 1980). Moore's contribution was to work with a first-order, extensional language that described the *interpretation* of the original modal language. He retained the original modal language as a set of objects manipulated by the first-order semantic language.

We will carry this idea one step further and dispense with the object language altogether, although some of the terminology will hint at vestiges of it. We will talk about a temporal model using a first-order language. The resulting enterprise will look like a hybrid of Moore's work and that of Hayes (1979a).

There are two key ideas to capture in our logic: the "openness" of the future, and the continuity of time. The first idea is that more than one thing can happen starting at a given instant. We model this by having many possible futures. The second idea is that many things do not happen discontinuously. We model this by having a continuum of instances between any two instants. It will be clear eventually why these features are so important.

To capture these ideas, our language will talk of an infinite collection of *states* of the universe. A state is an instantaneous snapshot of the universe. States are partially ordered by a relation "=<." We write (=< s1 s2) to mean that s1 comes before or is identical to s2.

I use "Cambridge Polish" notation for logical formulas. Every term, atomic formula, and combination is of the form (*p* ...), where *p* is a function, predicate, or connective. The rest of the formula after *p* will be the arguments or other subparts. If *p* is a quantifier ("forall" or "exists"), then the subparts are a list of variables and a formula:

(forall (-*vars*-) *fmla*)
(exists (-*vars*-) *fmla*)

For other connectives, the subparts are formulas, as in

(not *fmla*)
(if *fmla1 fmla2*)
(and *fmla1 fmla2* ...)
(or *fmla1 fmla2* ...)
(iff *fmla1 fmla2*)

If *p* is a binary transitive relation, (*p w x y* ... *z*) is an abbreviation for (and (*p w x*) (*p x y*) ... (*p* ... *z*)). I will generally use lower case for logical constants; upper case for sorts (which I will discuss shortly), for Skolem constants, and for domain-dependent predicates and functions; and italics for syntactic variables.

Axiom 1: (iff (and (=< ?s1 ?s2) (=< ?s2 ?s1)) (= ?s1 ?s2))
 (iff (< ?s1 ?s2) (and (=< ?s1 ?s2) (not (= ?s1 ?s2))))

As usual, if (=< s1 s2) and s1 and s2 are distinct, we write (< s1 s2).

Axiom 2: (Density)
 (forall (s1 s2)
  (if (< s1 s2) (exists (s) (< s1 s s2))))

Axiom 3: (Transitivity)
 (forall (s1 s2 s3)
  (if (and (=< s1 s2) (=< s2 s3))
   (=< s1 s3)))

Notice that I assume a sorted logic. Variables beginning with s are states. All this means is that a formula (forall (*x*) *p*), where *x* is a sorted variable, is an abbreviation for

(forall (*x*) (if (is *sort x*) *p*)),

where *sort* is *x*'s sort, or "data type." Sorts will not appear very often, and will be capitalized when they do. They are not very important, and will only save a little typing. We can read (forall (s) ...) as "for all states ...," without having to mention explicitly the condition (is STATE s).

Unbound variables (prefixed with "?") are universally quantified with scope equal to the whole formula (after adding the sort conditions). Anonymous constants of a given sort (used in proofs), so-called "Skolem constants," will be written beginning with the appropriate upper-case letter.

Every state has a time of occurrence, a real number called its *date*. The function d gives the date of a state, as in (=(d S1)D1). Any real number is a valid date: time is infinite and noncircular. Of course, no one in the universe can tell where zero is or what the scale is, so this is harmless. It does mean that two states will have comparable dates, even when they are not related by =<. I will use = < and < for ordinary numerical ordering as well as the partial ordering on states, since the use of sorts will disambiguate. I will not be rigorous about axiomatizing real numbers, but will just assume whatever properties I need as I go. Variables beginning with "r" or "t" are real numbers.

The two orderings are compatible:

Axiom 4: (if (< s1 s2) (<(d s1) (d s2)))

States are arranged into chronicles. A *chronicle* is a complete possible history of the universe, a totally ordered set of states extending infinitely in time.

Axiom 5: (Definition of Chronicle)
 (iff (is CHRONICLE ?x)
   (and ;a set of states
     (forall (y) (if (elt y ?x) (is STATE y)))
     ;totally ordered
     (forall (s1 s2)
       (iff (and (elt s1 ?x) (elt s2 ?x))
         (or (< s1 s2) (> s1 s2) (= s1 s2))))
     ;infinite in time
     (forall (t)
       (exists (s)
         (and (elt s ?x) (=(d s) t))))))

(elt a x) means that a is an element of set x. We won't need any deep set theory, but I will feel free to introduce sets of elements previously introduced, including sets of sets of them. (If variables of some sort begin with a letter "l," then variables bound to sets of objects of that sort begin "ll." So "?ss" is a set of states.)

An immediate consequence of Axiom 5 is that a chronicle is "convex":

(if (is CHRONICLE ?x)
  (forall (s1 s2)
    (if (and (elt s1 ?x) (elt s2 ?x))
      (forall (s)
        (if (< s1 s s2)
          (elt s ?x))))))

Having defined (is CHRONICLE x), we can conceal most uses of it by declaring variables beginning "ch" to be of sort "CHRONICLE."

A chronicle is a way events might go. There may be more than one of them, according to this logic. (See Figure 1.)

Every state is in a chronicle. In fact,

Axiom 6:
 (if (= < ?s1 ?s2)
   (exists (ch) (and (elt ?s1 ch) (elt ?s2 ch))))

whence, by convexity, every state between ?s1 and ?s2 is in ch.

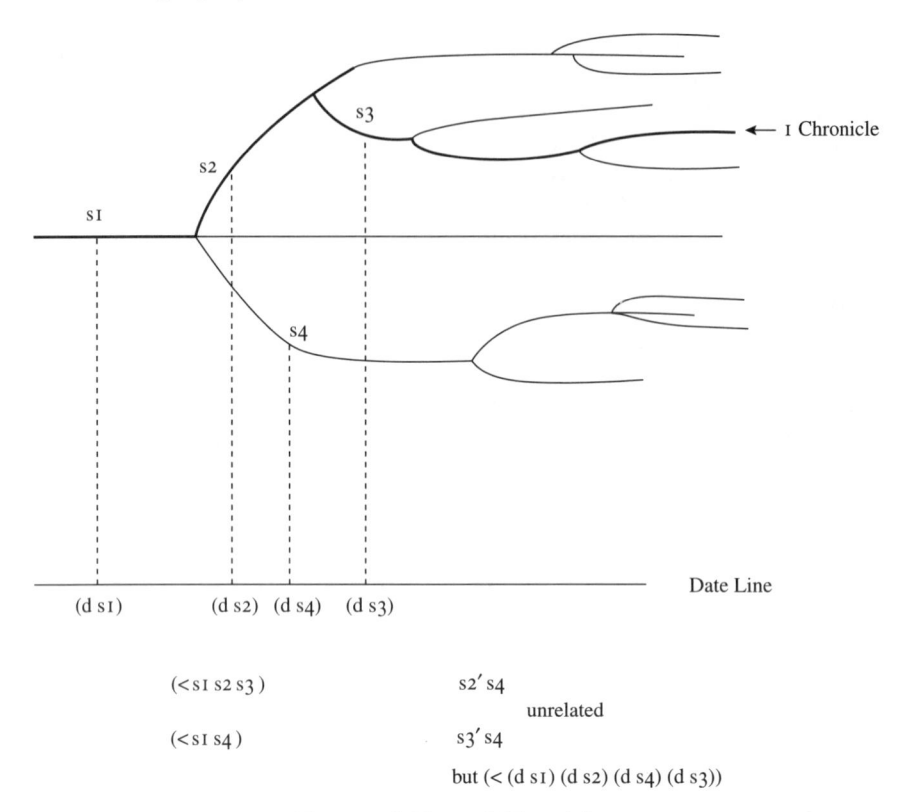

```
       s3
                                  ← 1 Chronicle
   s2

s1

       s4

                                          Date Line
(d s1)    (d s2) (d s4)  (d s3)

         (< s1 s2 s3 )         s2' s4
                                     unrelated
         (< s1 s4 )            s3' s4
                           but (< (d s1) (d s2) (d s4) (d s3))
```

FIG. 1   A Tree of Chronicles.

Chronicles branch only into the future. (See Figure 1.)

Axiom 7:
   (if (and (= < ?s1 ?s) (= < s2 ?s))
      (or (= < ?s1 ?s2) (= < ?s2 ?s1)))

The reason why this is so is that the future is really indeterminate. The past may be unknown, but there is only one past. By contrast, there may be more than one future from a given state. The reason for designing the logic this way is to provide for "free will," in the form of reasoning about actions that *select* one future instead of another. If there were only one future, the most we could do is *discover* it. Of course, both alternatives have unpleasant consequences: the one-future account implies that what we are going to do is unknown but fixed, while the many-futures account implies that the alternative futures to yesterday are as real as this one. For this reason, I do not include any reference to "yesterday" or even "now" in the logic, but simply talk about states in the abstract. The application to the state "now," and the fondness we feel for the "real" chronicle, are matters I defer until the section on implementation.[1]

---

[1] I should point out that the logic I am developing is *not* intended as an analysis of the truth conditions of English or some other natural language. I doubt that this is at all a good way to think about natural language, and even if it is I see no reason why the internal representation should be constrained by the mere presence of words like "now" in natural language.

States and chronicles are important only because they are the stage where facts and events are acted out. *Facts* change in truth value over time. By the usual mathematical inversion, we will take a fact to be a set of states, intuitively those in which it is true. For example, (ON A B) denotes the set of states in which A is on B. ON is a function from pairs of objects to sets of states, that is, facts; it is *not* a predicate.[2] This way of looking at facts is analogous to the logicians' trick of letting propositions denote sets of possible worlds (see e.g., Montague, 1974).

I will let variables beginning with "p" and "q" denote facts. The fact "always" is the set of all states. The fact "never" is the empty set.

We indicate that a fact is true in a state by (elt $s\ p$). As syntactic sugar, we usually write this as (T $s\ p$). ("T" suggests "true-in.") So, we have

Axiom 8:
  (T ?s always)
  (not (T ?s never))

We can think of facts as "propositions" in a Mooresque object language. In particular, we can combine them with connectives. For instance, we can write (T s (& $p\ q$)), where the "&" is *not* part of our own logical notation; instead, it is simply syntactic sugar for set intersection; (& $p\ q$) is just the set of states that are elements of both p and q. Similarly, "V" and " − " in this context denote union and complement (with respect to the set "always"). Then we have things like

(iff (T ?s ?p) (not (T ?s (− ?p))))
(iff (T ?s (& ?p ?q))
   (and (T ?s ?p) (T ?s ?q)))

as trivial set-theory results, after syntactic desugaring.

Events are more difficult to handle than facts. An event is something happening. In the past, the only kind of events handled by AI researchers and most philosophers is what might be called a *fact change*, such as a block being moved from one place to another (McCarthy, 1968; Rescher and Urquhart, 1971). The defining feature of an event on this theory are the changes in facts that the event brings about. This approach suppresses some important features of events. For instance, they take time. A fact change is just a list of two facts; how long it took is not describable. Further, it is meaningless in fact-change formalisms to ask what happens in the middle of a fact change.

Consider the usual emphasis in studies based on McCarthy's situation calculus (McCarthy, 1968; Moore, 1980; Fikes and Nilsson, 1971). In this system, an action like "moving x to y" is reasoned about in terms of a function MOVE that maps a block, a place, and an old situation into a new situation; (MOVE $x\ y\ s$) is the situation resulting from moving x to y in s. The axioms of the calculus talk entirely about the different facts true in s and (MOVE $x\ y\ s$). There is no mention of the infinite number of states occurring during the move.

Some of these problems can be eliminated by simply shifting emphasis, as I will show shortly. But a deeper problem is that many events are simply not fact changes. An example due to Davidson (1967) is "John ran around the track 3 times." The only fact change that occurs is that John is more tired. The amount of fatigue is not terribly

---

[2] It may be considered a predicate in an object language for which this temporal logic is a metalanguage; see below.

different from the amount ensuing on running around 4 times. Besides, surely no one would argue that the *definition* of "run around the track 3 times" is "be here tired." Of course, John might have a memory of having done it, but even "be here tired with a memory of having run around 3 times" is still not a plausible definition, if for no other reason than that John might have lost count. Also, this definition is circular, since John's memory must make reference to the concept to be analyzed, and hence can only mean "I remember [bringing it about that I am tired and have a memory of [bringing it about that I am tired and have a memory of [....]]]"

If you still need to be convinced, consider the (large) class of actions that are done for their own sake, such as visiting Greece, eating a gourmet meal, or having sex. In all these cases, the fact changes are trivial, unappetizing, or only tangentially relevant. One could argue, I suppose, that these things are done only for the memory of having done them. It is true that doing them without remembering them would be a little pointless, but memory fades. Knowing you won't remember much of this trip, meal, or sexual activity 20 years from now is not much of a barrier to doing it now, and does not entail that doing it is logically impossible.

We need a fresh approach. One idea is that events be identified with a certain kind of fact, namely the fact that the event is taking place. Facts occupy time intervals, so we get the ability to talk about what happens during an event. This seems to be adequate for events that consist of some aimless thing happening for a while, such as a rooster crowing in the morning. The rooster-crowing event could just be defined to be the time during which the rooster is crowing. This event happens in a chronicle if any of its states are in that chronicle.

But most events do not fit this mold. Running around a track three times takes time, but cannot be identified with the states during which you are running on the track. The problem is that a given state may be part of a "3 times around" event in one chronicle, and a "2 times around" event in another. But the criterion would have the event happening in both.

We avoid this problem by identifying an event as a set of intervals, intuitively those intervals over which the event happens once, with no time "left over" on either side. An interval is a totally ordered, convex set of states. We can think of each interval as an event token, and the whole set as an event type. So "Fred running around a track 3 times" is the set of all intervals in which exactly that[3] happens.

Now we can indicate that an event happens between states $s1$ and $s2$ by writing (elt [$s1$, $s2$] e). As syntactic sugar for this, I will write (Occ $s1$ $s2$ e). Notice that I let variables beginning with "e" stand for events.

Can we always assume that an event occurs over a closed interval? Let us leave this question unanswered for the time being. In this paper, I will always use the Occ notation, and hence assume that they are closed, but it doesn't seem very important for most events whether they include two extra instants or not. Since we will want to allow for instantaneous events, at least some of them must be closed.[4] The notion of a fact

---

[3] The phrase "exactly that" is intended to rule out "last Tuesday" as a token of this event if Fred ran around the track once on Tuesday (unless it took him 24 hrs). But I do not mean to insist that an event happens over an interval only if it happens over no subinterval. When the event "Fred whistles" happens over an interval, it happens over an infinite number of subintervals. Incidentally, the idea of letting events be sets of intervals was stated by Montague (somewhat differently) in Montague (1960).

[4] Notice, by the way, that if we interpret event intervals consistently (as always closed, always half-open on the right, or whatever), then using them is equivalent to modifying McCarthy's situation calculus by letting actions be *relations* on situations (states) instead of functions.

being true over a period of time is still valuable, even though it wouldn't carry the full load. This is written (subset [s1, s2] p), or, syntactically sugared, as (TT s1 s2 p).

Certain events and facts are closely related. For example, (sunion S), for any set S of sets, is the union of all its elements. The (sunion e) is a fact, true whenever e is "in progress," in the sense that in some possible chronicle e is in the process of occurring. I will use the syntactic sugaring (in-progress e) to mean the same thing as (sunion e), and (Tocc s e) to mean (T s (in-progress e)).

Given a fact, we can work our way back to events in more than one way. For instance, we can take the set of maximal intervals during which the fact is true, or the set of point intervals for all points where the fact is true.

Events can be related to each other in ways similar to those for facts. For instance, if p is a subset of q, then it is as if p implied q: at every state where p is true, so is q. For events, we write (subset e1 e2) as (one-way e1 e2): e1 is one way e2 can happen; every occurrence of e1 is an occurrence of e2. For example, being squashed by a meteor is one way of being squashed.

We used boolean connectives like "&" to combine facts. These are not so useful with events. Instead, we need things like

(seq e1 e2 ... eN)
which stands for
{[s0, sN]: (exists (s1 ... sN-1)
        (and (Occ s0 s1 e1)
            (Occ s1 s2 e2)
            ...
            (Occ sN-1 sN eN)))}

Corresponding to "never," the fact that is never true, there is an event that never happens. This will also be the empty set, so we can call it "never," too, making this the only thing that is both an event and a proposition. There does not seem to be any useful notion of the event that always happens.

More such constructs will be introduced as we go.

Remember that this logic takes an Olympian view of states of the universe. "Now" is not distinguished, so there is no question about representing what has already happened versus what may happen. I will talk about this more in Section 6, below. I should point out, though, that representing tokens of past or expected events as ordered pairs of states, like (s34, s107), is not adequate. A given interval is a token of many different events, which happened to occur at that point. So event tokens must be represented as ordered pairs of events and intervals, or something equivalent.

I want to stress at this point that devising ontologies like this is not an empty philosophical enterprise. On the contrary, I am interested in purely utilitarian ends; I want a way of thinking about time that is useful to a robot. I am not interested in expressing all possible ways of thinking about time, nor am I interested in calculating the truth values of English statements involving time. It may seem that logic and practicality have little to do with each other, that the problem for cognitive science is to build a computational model that reasons about time, and be done with it. Unfortunately, it is not so straightforward. Any program will be based on *some* ontology and assumptions about time. The wrong assumptions will mire us in a swamp of logical conundrums, which much be explicitly faced and conquered. The best way to do this is to make the logical machinery explicit (cf. McDermott, 1978a).

This is what I will be doing in the rest of this paper, examining three major problems that temporal reasoners will face: reasoning about causality and mechanism, reasoning about continuous change, and planning actions. There may be others, but these should suffice. They have been difficult in the past precisely because dangerous assumptions have been made about time, such as that there is a next moment, or that there is only one future. I will try to show that a program based on the logic I propose will have a better chance of avoiding these difficulties.

To illustrate how logical assumptions influence thought, I will try to prove a theorem about a mechanism, and show the power and weakness of what we have assumed so far. The theorem goes like this: Let DEV be a device with two states, DAY and NIGHT. DAY is always followed by NIGHT and NIGHT by DAY. DAY and NIGHT never overlap. Prove that if it is ever DAY or NIGHT, it will always be either DAY or NIGHT.

This may seem simple, but it is just the sort of inference that is beyond the capability of existing reasoning systems. Expressed in our notation, it is

DAY and NIGHT are mutually exclusive (except at boundaries):
  (if (and (Occ ?s1 ?s2 DAY) (Occ ?s3 ?s4 NIGHT))
    (forall (s)
      (if (and (=<?s1 s ?s2) (=<?s3 s ?s4))
        (or (=s ?s2 ?s3)
            (=s ?s1 ?s4)))))

Each takes a nonzero amount of time:
  (if (or (Occ ?s1 ?s2 DAY) (Occ ?s1 ?s2 DAY))
    (<?s1 ?s2))

and each follows the other
  (follows DAY NIGHT)
  (follows NIGHT DAY)

where
  (iff (follows ?e1 ?e2)
    (if (Occ ?s1 ?s2 ?e1)
      (forall (ch) (if (elt ?s2 ch)
        (exists (s3)
          (and (elt s3 ch)
               (Occ ?s2 s3 ?e2)))))))

That is, e2 follows e1 if every occurrence of e1 is followed immediately by an occurrence of e2 in every chronicle containing the occurrence of e1, i.e., in every way events might proceed.

Now to prove
  (if (Occ S1 S2 DAY)
    (forall (s) (if (>s S2) (or (Tocc s DAY)
                                (Tocc s NIGHT)))))

This theorem may seem trivial, but in fact it does not follow from what we have assumed so far. If each succeeding DAY or NIGHT interval is half as long as the previous one, then an infinite number of them could go by in a finite amount of time, after which the state of DEV could be something else. However, this is something we wish to rule out.

```
                P                        –P           P      –P   P  –P
————————————————————————————— ··············· ———————— ····—····
                                                                ↑
                                                                s
                     P violates Axiom 9 at s
```

FIG. 2   How a Well-Behaved Fact Does Not Behave.

We do so with the axiom

Axiom 9:
  (forall (s p)
    (and (exists (s0)
           (or (TTopen s0 s p))
               (TTopen s0 s (– p)))
         (forall (ch)
           (if (elt s ch)
             (exists (s1)
               (and (elt s1 ch)
                    (or (TTopen s s1 p)
                        (TTopen s s1 (– p)))))))))

where
  (iff (TTopen s1 s2 p)
    (and (< s1 s2)
         (forall (s)
           (if (< s1 s s2) (T s p)))))

This axiom, due to Ernie Davis, assures us that, for every fact and an arbitrary state, there is an interval preceding the state during which the fact is always true or always false; and another one following the state, in every chronicle containing it. (See Figure 2.)

The presence of this axiom rules out any super powerful axiom of "comprehension,"[5] which would allow us to infer that any set of states was a fact, such as the set of states during which the temperature in Cleveland is a rational number. This is *not* a fact because, assuming the temperature is smoothly changing, it will change truth value infinitely often in any finite interval.

So we will need special-purpose comprehension axioms for well-behaved facts. I will just assume these along the way as obvious. For example, if p and q are facts, (& p q) is also.[6] When I introduce a function like "in-progress," and announce that its values are from a given domain, like facts, I am implicitly declaring an axiom like

Axiom 10: (In-Progress Comprehension)
   (is FACT (in-progress ?e))

So you can take for granted that (in-progress e) satisfies Axiom 9. This axiom does away with any super powerful comprehension axiom for events, in case you were wondering.

---

[5] An axiom or axiom schema of comprehension states that for every property, there is a set of objects satisfying it. Stating this formally in a way that avoids paradoxes is a major preoccupation of set theorists (Mendelson, 1964).

[6] We could probably recast Axiom 9 as a biconditional and prove these axioms, but set-theoretic parsimony is not really important.

You may now take it on faith that no further assumptions are required to prove that it will always be DAY or NIGHT, or you can bear with me through the following proof. (It is not as arbitrary as it seems; if anyone can find a simpler or clearer proof, I would like to hear about it.)

First, we need a few definitions. Letting sets of events be denoted by variables beginning with "ee," and integers be denoted by variables beginning with "n," we define

Axiom 11:
(iff (chain ?ee 0 ?s1 ?s2) (= ?s1 ?s2))

(iff (chain ?ee (+ ?n 1) ?s1 ?s3)
  (exists (e s2)
    (and (elt e ?ee)
      (Occ s2 ?s3 e)
      (chain ?ee ?n ?s1 ?s2))))

That is, there is an ee chain of length n from s1 to s2, if there is a sequence of abutting events from the set ee that reaches from s1 to s2.

Now reachability is defined thus

Axiom 12:
(iff (reachable ?ee ?ch ?s1 ?s)
  (exists (n s2)
    (and (>= n 0)
      (elt s2 ?ch)
      (chain ?ee n ?s1 s2)
      (= < ?s1 ?s ?s2))))

We read this "?s is ?ee-reachable in ?ch from ?s1."

Some corollaries of these definitions (using Peano arithmetic) are:

(if (reachable ?ee ?ch ?s1 ?s)
  (forall (s')
    (if (< ?s1 s' ?s)
      (reachable ?ee ?ch ?s1 s'))))

(if (reachable ?ee ?ch ?s1 ?s)
  (or (= ?s1 ?s)
    (exists (e s2 s3 n)
      (and (elt e ?ee)
        (elt s3 ?ch)
        (Occ s2 s3 e)
        (= <s2 ?s s3)))))

These state that if ?s is ?ee-reachable from ?s1, then every state between ?s1 and ?s is reachable, and ?s occurs in the middle of some event in ?ee.

Now the proof goes as follows: Assume that S' is a state such that (> S' S2) and (not (Tocc S' DAY)) and (not (Tocc S' NIGHT)). Then by Axiom 6, there is a chronicle CH1 containing S' and S2. Clearly, (not (reachable {DAY, NIGHT} CH1 S2 S')). So, by the properties of real numbers and the first corollary above, there must be a state S, (< S2 S) and (= < S S'), such that every state between S2 and S is {DAY, NIGHT}—reachable in CH1 from S2, and every state from S on is not {DAY, NIGHT}—reachable in CH1 from S2. But, by Axiom 9, there must be an SD3 before S such that either DAY is in progress for all states between SD3 and S, or it is not in progress for all those states.

Temporal Logic for Processes and Plans 185

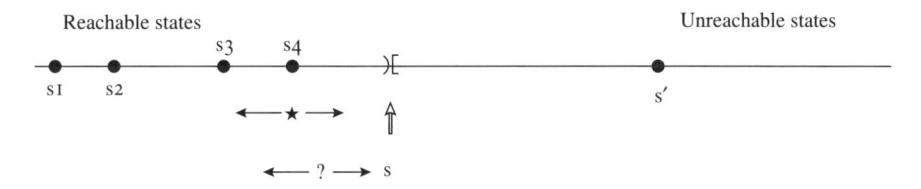

```
       Reachable states                              Unreachable states
                    s3    s4
  •────•────•─────•───────)[───────────────────•──────────────
  s1   s2                                      s'
                 ←──★──→    ⇑
                 ←── ? ──→ s
```

* Either DAY or NIGHT is in progress throughout this interval

FIG. 3   Proof of Eternal DAY or NIGHT.

Similarly, there must be an SN3 before S such that it's NIGHT or it isn't from SN3 to S. Since it can't be neither or both, let S3 be the one for which either it is DAY from S3 to S or NIGHT from S3 to S. Clearly, (< S2 S3) because both DAY and NIGHT occur at least once after S2. Every state from S3 to S is {DAY, NIGHT}—reachable, so, by the second corollary, one of DAY or NIGHT is occurring from S3 to S, and this occurrence ends in some state S4 in CH1. (See Figure 3.)

```
      REACHABLE                )[           NOT REACHABLE
    S1 S2                  S3  S4  S             S'
                         < - * - >
                         < - ? - >
```
*either DAY or NIGHT in progress throughout this interval

S4 must come before S, or else S would be reachable, according to the definition, because S4 would end a chain from S2. But then starting at S4 NIGHT or DAY must occur, so DAY and NIGHT must coexist for more than an instant, which is impossible. So there is no such S, and all instants are reachable—QED.

This may seem quite complicated. But it depended on only one new axiom, Axiom 9. Everything else came from definitions and arithmetic. Of course, this proof is much too complicated to expect a theorem prover to come up with it, but this was never my goal. My intent is similar to Hayes's: to express concepts in a form in which the intuitively plausible inferences are valid. If this is achieved, then we can start worrying about a practical inference program. In fact, I start worrying in Section 6, below. The only thing to point out here is that such a program has no hope of being complete.

I should also assure you that this paper is not crammed full of such long proofs of obvious results. The main purpose of showing you this was to let you get a feel for the generality of the ontological assumptions. They are so general that we have to tame them with Axioms like Axiom 9. But this is all the taming we will want to do.

Also, this result is not entirely academic. It is easily generalizable to a system with a finite number of mutually exclusive states which succeed each other the way DAY and NIGHT do. It gives us the ability to infer infinite loops in simple machines.

Now, as promised, I will examine three major problem areas from the point of view of this logic, before turning to implementation questions.

3   CAUSALITY

Causality is fundamental to a lot of problem solving. A problem solver brings things about by causing other things. What I mean by causality here is that one event (type) always follows another event (type). For example, if x is a loaded gun, pulling its trigger is followed by its firing.

Unfortunately, there must be more to it than that. For example, an exactly analogous case is, If a is approaching from the direction of the sun, the arrival of a's shadow is followed by the arrival of a. But we would not want to say that the arrival of a's shadow causes the arrival of a.

I assume that there is no way to get around this problem, and that there is no way to infer causality merely from correlation. So we will not try to define causality in terms of something more basic. Instead, we will assume whatever causal assertions we need, and infer events from them.

Events can cause two kinds of things: other events, and facts. The two cases are quite different, and the first is simpler.

When an event causes another, there is usually a delay. The scale of the date line attached to the chronicle tree is unknown in the logic, so we cannot use absolute time intervals. Instead, we assume that there are objects called *scales* which occupy some constant amount of time. If "hour" is such a scale, (* 5 hour) is a length of time equal to 5 times the size of hour (see McDermott 1980 for a fuller explanation). We will never be able to evaluate this, but we don't need to; we just need to be able to compare it to other things measured in hours or seconds. We can do the latter because we have as an axiom (=(3,600 second) hour). Note the elision of the * when it is clearly unnecessary.

With this out of the way, we introduce our basic predicate (ecause p e_1 e_2 rf i), which means that e_1 is always followed by e_2, after a delay in the interval i, unless p becomes false before the delay is up. The delay is measured from a point rf through e_1; if $rf=0$, this means from the start of e_1; if $rf=1$, from the end.

Axiom 13:
   (if (ecause ?p ?e1 ?e2 ?rf ?i)
      (if (Occ ?s1 ?s2 ?e1)
         (forall (ch)
            (if (elt ?s2 ch)
               (exists (s3)
                  (and (elt s3 ch)
                     (within-delay s3 ?rf ?i ?s1 ?s2)
                     (or (not (TT ?s2 s3 p))
                        (exists (s4)
                           (and (elt s4 ch)
                              (Occ s3 s4 ?e2))))))))))))

where
   (iff (within-delay ?s ?rf ?i ?s1 ?s2)

      (elt { (d ?s) }
           { − (1 − ?rf)*(d ?s1) }
           { + ?rf*(d ?s2)}
         ?i))

The (within-delay s rf i s_1 s_2) means that state s occurs after s_1 and s_2, with delay i. An rf is a real number that says what point the delay is to be measured from. If it is 0, the delay is to be measured starting at s_1; if 1, from s_2; and so on for any number between 0 and 1. The i is a real interval, like <(3 min), (5 min)>, or [0, (5 hour)]. (An open side of an interval I denote by the usual angle bracket, as in <1, 3] or <1, 3>. A closed interval on the reals, while denoted with square brackets [. . .], is a completely different sort of thing from a state interval.)

As an example of ecause, we can express the idea that if a Republican is elected President, science will progress:

(ecause (POLPARTY ?x REPUBLICAN)
       (elected ?x)
       (INFLUX-MONEY-FOR-DESERVING-RESEARCHERS)
       1 [(1 year), (2 year)]

In these examples, only the parts being illustrated are formalized in a reasonable way.
If the fuse on a powderkeg is lit, the keg will explode if the powder stays dry:

(ecause (& (DRY ?keg) (FUSE-OF ?fuse ?keg))
       (LIT ?fuse)
       (EXPLODE ?keg)
       1 [(30 sec), (2 min)]

If a winch is rotated, an object gets hauled up:

(if (is WINCH ?x)
   (ecause (LOAD-OF ?x ?y)
       (ROTATE ?x)
       (RISE ?y)
       0
       [0, (2 sec)]))

Note that the object might not start rising for a second or two.
We also have the axiom:

Axiom 14:
  (if (ecause ?p ?e1 ?e2 ?rf ?i)
     (forall (s3 s4)
       (if (Occ s3 s4 ?e2)
          (exists (pc ec s1 s2 rfc ic)
             (and (ecause pc ec ?e2 rfc ic)
                (Occ s1 s2 ec)
                (within-delay s3 rfc ic s1 s2))))))

That is, if an event is ever caused, then each of its occurrences is preceded by one of its causes (with the appropriate delay). This might be called the Principle of Paranoia. Its chief virtue is in enabling us to infer that an event must have occurred when it is known to be the only cause of another event that occurred.

The second kind of causality is the causation of a fact by an event. For example, if a boulder falls to the bottom of a mountain, it will *be* at the bottom of the mountain. This is important in problem solving, where the goal is often to bring about some fact by causing one or more events.

One approach might be to say that e causes p if, in all chronicles, p is true for some period of time after e. We could do this, but it would be useless. In this sense, shooting a bullet past someone would be a way of achieving that it was near him.

I must digress here to talk about the speed at which facts change. The real world doesn't change fast most of the time. Many facts remain true for long enough to be depended on. For example, that boulder will probably stay at the bottom of the mountain for years (or centuries). We normally use such facts with confidence, for example, when planning to build a house on the boulder.

On the other hand, we cannot infer with certainty that the boulder will be there. If we could, then there would be no way to plan confidently to remove it. Confidence in the plan would just land us in a contradiction between our belief that the boulder will be gone by next year, and our certainty that it will be there for many years.

This is a classic example of a *non-monotonic* reasoning pattern (McDermott and Doyle, 1980; McDermott, 1981a; and Reiter, 1980). The inference that the boulder will be there is good until you find out that someone is planning to move it. I have resisted introducing non-monotonicity into the logic so far, because it is not that well understood, and what is well understood about it is not all that encouraging. But we are going to need it here.

The problem here is closely related to the *frame problem*. That was the problem that arose in McCarthy's situation calculus (McCarthy, 1968) of not being able to infer anything about a situation resulting from an action in a previous situation, without a large number of axioms of the form "p doesn't change in this transition." A typical axiom would say, "No block's color changes in the transition from s to (MOVE A B s)." The problem is even more acute for us, because almost anything could be happening in an interval. In McCarthy's calculus it was possible to pretend that a situation (MOVE A B So) would persist until the next action, so that the situation after two actions could be denoted by something like (MOVE C A (MOVE A B So)). Now the state of the world changes as the problem solver plans, so there is no term denoting the state of the world when the second action occurs. The frame problem becomes the problem of inferring what's true at the end of an arbitrary interval, given incomplete information about what happened during it.

Part of my expectation in developing a robust logic of time was that we could reason about facts "from the side," inferring that they were true for whole stretches of time. It's no loss that we can't work our way from one state to the "next" any more; that was always a bad idea. But now we find that in general you cannot infer that a fact is true for a period of time.

Let me distinguish this problem from another one that is often held to be solvable with non-monotonic notations. Every AI hacker knows that the example causality axioms I gave earlier are incomplete, and that there is no way to make them complete. For instance, the keg will not explode if the fuse is cut, or if all the oxygen is removed from the keg before the spark reaches it, or the keg is placed in an extremely strong box that can withstand the explosion, or .... But you see the point. It seems pointless to try to list all the ways the rule could fail.

This problem can be solved simply by letting our rules fail now and then. We can't hope to avoid errors, and it normally doesn't matter if a data base is "slightly" inconsistent. When it does matter, we can edit the rules to maintain consistency. So in a sense the theory is "approximately" true, and gets closer to the truth with every edit. Non-monotonic logic could play a role by letting rules "edit themselves" (McDermott and Doyle, 1980), but this hardly seems necessary.

The rule that a boulder stays put for years is not even approximately true in this sense. It would be approximately true only if it were used in a purely passive system. An astronomer observing an uninhabited planet might use the rule this way. He would simply live with errors caused by improbable occurrences like volcanic eruptions that moved boulders. But a problem solver knows full well *both* that it is counting on certain things to be true for a while, *and* that it could make them false any time it wanted to. (Other agents could also make them false, but we neglect this possibility.)

To capture these ideas in the logic, I introduce the notion of *persistence*. A fact p persists from s with a lifetime r, if in all chronicles it remains true until r has gone by or until it *ceases* to be true.

Axiom 15: (Definition of Persist)
  (iff (persist ?s ?p ?r)
      (and (T ?s ?p)
          (forall (s')
             (if (and (within-lifetime s' ?r ?s)
                  (not (T s' ?p)))
           (Occbetween ?s s' (cease ?p))))))

where
  (iff (within-lifetime ?s2 ?r ?s1)
      (and (=< ?s1 ?s2)
          (<(– (d ?s2) (d ?s1)) ?r)))
  (iff (Occbetween ?s0 ?s3 ?e)
      (exists (s1 s2)
          (and (=< ?s0 s1 s2 ?s3)
             (Occ s1 s2 ?e))))

Ceasing does not mean merely that the fact goes from true to false. In fact, ceasing is so rare that it never happens unless we hear about it:

Axiom 16: (Fundamental Property of Ceasing)
  (if (and (persist ?s ?p ?r)
        (within-lifetime ?s' ?r ?s)
        (M (nocease ?s ?p ?s')))
     (not (Occbetween ?s ?s' (cease ?p))))

M is a primitive sentence-forming operator, read "Consistent." Intuitively, if Q cannot be proven false, then (M Q) is true. The (nocease s p s') means that no occurrence of (cease p) occurs between s and s'. To conclude that p actually does not cease, we require only that it be consistent that it not cease; positive information is necessary to override this. The overriding occurs when other rules allow us to infer (not (nocease s p S1)) for some S1 within the lifetime of the persistence; then the M fails, we cannot infer the p does not cease. But if no such rule applies, then we can make the inference.

I hope that this application of non-monotonic logic will not mess everything up. I am depending on a property of the logic of (McDermott, 1981a), namely, that from Axiom 16 and an occurrence of a ceasing within the lifetime of a persistence, we can deduce (not (nocease s p s')). If a weaker logic is used, this should be made explicit in an axiom. However it is done, it is essential that (Occbetween s s' (cease p)) kill off a persistence after s', but leave the persistence "in force" for states between s and s'. Clearly, if (Occbetween s ?s' (cease p)), then (Occbetween s s" (cease p)) for all states s" between s' and the end of the persistence. Then we can infer (not (nocease s p s")) for all those states. We *cannot* infer such a thing for states *before s'*.

What this means is that a plan to remove the boulder five years from now cancels a persistence after that time, but leaves intact the inference that it will be there until then.

By the way, let me make a disclaimer. I try to appeal to non-monotonic deductions as seldom as possible. This is because the logics they are based on (McDermott and Doyle, 1980; McDermott, 1981a; Reiter, 1980; and McCarthy, 1980) are still rather unsatisfactory.

For one thing, even some of the simple deductions in this paper may not be valid in any existing non-monotonic system. For example, the problem with existential quantifiers cited in (McDermott, 1981a) would probably block some of my proofs. (The system of (Reiter, 1980) avoids this problem, but has others.) For another thing, such logics do not distinguish between severities of contradictions; they use the same machinery for "rule edits" of the kind I described and for clipping off a persistent fact. In the usual terminology of such systems, this leads to unexpected "fixed points," or models, in which the wrong assumptions are retracted.

For the time being, we can view these not as problems with this paper, but as problems with non-monotonic logic. In attempting to represent things, it is helpful to be as formal as we can, but if the formal systems cannot keep up with the inferences we want to make, so much the worse for the formal systems. In the long run, I am confident that non-monotonic logics will be developed that capture the inferences we need. Probably the best way to see what inferences those are is to try to get along with the fewest possible non-monotonic inferences, but to feel free to use them when all else fails. If representation designers make it clear what they need, logicians will make it work.

Armed with the idea of persistence, we can make some progress on our original problem. First of all, it seems reasonable that most inferences of facts are actually about persistence of facts. For one thing, many facts have characteristic lifetimes. If x is a boulder, then (AT x *location*) has a lifetime measured in scores of years. If x is a cat, then (AT x *location*) has a lifetime measured in minutes (if the cat is sleeping) or seconds (if the cat is awake).

The senses actually tell you about persistences. I was driven to this by the following problem our logic appears to involve us in. At first blush, we might want an axiom to the effect that if a boulder is at a location loc in state So, then (persist So (AT Boulder Loc) (50 year)). But then we can infer that the boulder will be there in 50 years, when another persistence will start, and so on. We can infer that the boulder will be there for any given time in the future. If this seems harmless, think about the cat instead.

The solution is to scrap such axioms. Instead, we normally start with a persistence and work our way to particular states, not vice versa. This requires that when we see a boulder, our eyes are telling our data base about a persistence, not about an instantaneous fact. Otherwise, as soon as we turned away, we would know nothing about the scene. Once you get used to this idea, it seems perfectly natural.

This brings us back to causation. Clearly, what events must cause directly is persistences, not the truth of facts. So our primitive predicate is (pcause p e q rf i $r1$), which means that event e is always followed by fact q, after a delay in the interval i, unless p becomes false before the delay is up. The delay is measured from a point rf through e; if $rf=0$, this means from the start of e; if $rf=1$, from the end. When q becomes true, it persists for lifetime $r1$. Formally,

```
Axiom 17:
  (if (pcause ?p ?e ?q ?rf ?i ?r1)
    (if (Occ ?s1 ?s2 ?e)
      (forall (ch)
        (if (elt ?s2 ch)
          (exists (s3)
            (and (elt s3 ch)
                 (within-delay s3 ?rf ?i ?s1 ?s2)
                 (or (not T s3 p))
                     (persist s3 ?q ?r1))))))))
```

And we have examples like:

(pcause always)
    (KILL ?x)
    (DEAD ?x)
    1 [0, 0]
    FOREVER)

We pick "FOREVER" to be a very long time, equal to the largest number that can be stored on the machine the universe is being simulated on, or the length of time until the Last Judgement, depending on your religion.

Another example is:

(if (is STOVE ?x)
  (pcause (− (BLACKOUT))
    (TURN-ON ?x)
    (HOT ?x)
    1 [(1 min), (2 min)]
    (24 hour)))

Notice that the persistence time is picked as the time interval over which it is reasonable to infer that the state will remain in existence, assuming you have no intention of changing it. I pick 24 hours here because within that time, either one's spouse will find the burner and turn it off, or the house will burn down. Of course, normally you plan to turn it off sooner. If for some reason you wanted the burner to stay on longer (say you were cooking something that took a really long time), you would just need axioms about putting signs up, or other special tactics. These would say, "If you put a sign up telling someone not to alter a state they won't worry about if they see a sign, then the state will remain as long as the sign is up."[7]

Notice that not all instances of inferring facts "from the side" are direct instances of persistence. Part of the power of the notion comes from the fact that persistent facts have consequences. For example, if everyone in the American embassy is audible (while the embassy is bugged), and Henry is in the embassy for 15 minutes, then he is audible during that period. We don't have to come up with a general lifetime for audibility.

There is no Principle of Paranoia (Axiom 14) for pcause. This is because there are so many ways a fact can come about, including logical consequence, that it does not seem reasonable to look for a cause every time. Also, most true facts are "left-over" persistences. Most boulders in the world have been there longer than any lifetime you would use; the lifetime you can count on is much shorter than the times you observe. By the way, this should make it obvious that the logic does not imply that a persisting fact *stops* being true after its lifetime; we simply lose information after that point.

Since persistences, and not facts, are caused, and since there is usually no persistence that extends back to when a fact became true, there is really no cause for most facts, at least not in the technical senses I have been developing. Of course, many facts of

---

[7] Several people (notably Ernie Davis, James Allen, and Ken Forbus) have suggested that the idea of lifetime should be dropped from persistences. Even though a burner rarely stays on for more than 24 hrs., it *would* if left unattended, and my notation obscures this fact. My main reason for sticking with limited persistences is to take into account the fact that in many cases, we simply lose information about a system for moments too far from our last observation.

interest are the result of observed or inferred events, and *these* will be caused. One interesting case is when an occurrence of (cease p) is inferred using Axiom 15. We can then infer that this ceasing was caused. In fact, we can call this the Special Principle of Paranoia:

> Axiom 18:
> (if (Occ ?s3 ?s4 (cease ?p))
>   (exists (pc ec s1 s2 rfc ic)
>   (and (ecause pc ec (cease ?p) rfc ic)
>   (Occ s1 s2 ec)
>   (within-delay ?s3 rfc ic s1 s2))))

pcause and ecause work hand in hand. Consider the event (PUTON A B) that occurs within minutes after the beginnings of persistences of (CLEARTOP A) and (CLEARTOP B), with lifetimes of several hours. Suppose we have axioms like:

> (pcause (& (CLEARTOP ?x) (CLEARTOP ?y))
>   (PUTON ?x ?y)
>   (ON ?x ?y)
>   1 [0, 0]
>   (10 hour))

and, of course,

> (iff (T ?s (CLEARTOP ?X))
>   (not (exists (y) (T ?s (ON y ?x)))))

We can deduce from the persistence of (CLEARTOP A) and of (CLEARTOP B) that (& (CLEARTOP A) (CLEARTOP B)) will be true for several hours. Hence it will be true during the PUTON. (We will need an axiom about how long PUTONs take.) Hence (ON A B) will persist from the end of the PUTON. Hence (CLEARTOP B), no longer true, must have ceased, and the rule that it doesn't cease is inapplicable. However, it still can be inferred not to have ceased up to the end of the PUTON, so there is no contradiction. I will say more on the subject of reasoning about plans later.

Before going on to other topics, I should pause to review previous work on representing causality. Curiously, Hayes (1979a) argues that there is no isolated body of knowledge about causality. Every branch of "naive physics" has its own way of accounting for things happening. He also says he has found no need for non-monotonicity. I envy him. I think the reason for his good fortune is the "passive" character of his theory. It says how to reason about physical systems; it takes a Buddhist attitude of resignation toward bad things. For example, Hayes's Theory of Liquids (Hayes, 1979b) can be used to infer a flood, in such a way that it is plain contradictory to suppose the flood can be prevented. (This is a bit unfair, since he would presumably make the move of changing the axioms, i.e., the physical setup, as a reflection of the action of the planner. I don't know if this would amount to letting non-monotonicity in by the back door or not.)

The most obvious competitor to the theory I have presented is that of Rieger, who developed a graphical notation for what he calls "Common-Sense Algorithms" (CSA) (Rieger, 1976; Rieger, 1975). This notation included devices for representing concepts like continuous causality, "gated one-shots," thresholds, and much more. There are several problems with this notation, all stemming from Rieger's refusal to state precisely what the links and nodes of his networks *mean*. Apparently, networks representing physical devices and plans are written exactly the same, or are freely mixed. There is a systematic ambiguity about whether a link drawn on a page indicates that *if* something is done, something else will follow; or *that* the thing is actually done and the consequence actually occurs. For example, does the "threshold" link indicate that if the threshold is passed something will happen, or that the threshold is *supposed* to be passed eventually? It seems as if you need to be able to say both. Apparently in the CSA notation you can only say the latter. It seems somehow perverse to make algorithms more basic than physics. In my system, algorithms come in later, in a different form (see Section 5).

Besides this major flaw, there are lots of little places where the CSA notation fails to be precise. For instance, time delays and lifetimes are not mentioned. How is it possible to reason about a plan involving several parallel actions if they are completely unsynchronized?

On the other hand, there is substantial overlap in what he and I have done. His gated causality, and my provision of a gating fact as the first argument to ecause and pcause, are both due to realization of a key fact about causality, that events' behaviors are modified greatly by background facts.

4 FLOW

A system cannot reason about time realistically unless it can reason about continuous change. This has been neglected by all but a handful of people (Hendrix, 1973; Rieger, 1975). The assumption that actions are instantaneous state changes has made it hard to reason about any other kind. If I am filling a bathtub, how do I describe what happens to the water level during (MOVE A B So)?

I will use the term *fluent* for things that change continuously over time. (The term is due to McCarthy (1968), who used it in almost exactly the same sense.) Actually, the notion of fluent is more general than that. It is intended to do the work that is done by "intensional objects" in other systems. The President of the United States is a typical intensional object. Unlike most people, he has lived in the same house for over 150 years. His age sometimes decreases suddenly. These may seem like strange properties, but they are necessary (on some theories) to provide the correct truth value for sentences like "The President lives in the White House" (true), or "In 1955, the President was a movie actor" (false).

In my logic, such objects correspond to fluents. A fluent is a thing whose *value* changes with time. The *value* of a fluent in a given state s is written (V s v). I will use "v" for variables ranging over fluents. So, we can express two different readings for the last example sentence above:

(T 1955 (ACTOR (V 1955 President)))
(T 1955 (ACTOR (V 1981 President)))

In the first, "President" is taken to mean "President at the time of the fact." In the second, it is taken to mean "President at the time of the utterance (1981)." The rules of English make the first reading more likely, under which the sentence comes out false.

Fluents are valuable, not for this sort of playing around, but because physical quantities may be thought of as fluents. For example, "the temperature in Cleveland" is a fluent, which takes on values in temperature space. The changes of the fluent can then be reasoned about. In particular, the fluent's being in a certain region is a fact which might be helpful in causal reasoning. All of the fluents I will look at from now on will have numbers as values. Such fluents I will loosely call "quantities." Most quantities are real-valued and vary continuously as well.

At this point a certain abuse of notation will make life simpler. Strictly speaking, (> v1 v2) is meaningless, because > relates numbers or states, not fluents. What we really need is a function (>* v1 v2), which takes two fluents and returns the fact which is true in all states s for which (V s v1) is greater than (V s v2). Similarly, (>! v1 r) might take a fluent and a real number, and return the fact which is true just when the quantity's value is greater than the number. Clearly, to do this rigorously would be tedious. Instead, I will just assume that all of the red tape can be cleared away, and use (> alpha beta) freely, where alpha and/or beta is a fluent, integer, real number, etc. If either alpha or beta is "polluted" by being a fluent, the result is a fact; if both are numbers, the result is either true or false. Similarly, (+ alpha beta) will produce a new fluent, unless both alpha and beta are numbers, when the result is a number. For safety's sake, I will not do this for anything but simple arithmetic predicates and functions.

By the way, notice that since things like (> (− V1 V2) (* 5 V3)) are facts, they must obey Axiom 9. Ernie Davis has shown that this puts some fairly strong contraints on quantities. A quantity gives rise to a time function in every chronicle; given the time, the fluent delivers a unique value. Axiom 9 constrains this function not to jump around wildly, or ">" will chop it into pieces that disobey the axiom. For instance, we cannot have

$$(V\ s\ V0) = \sin \frac{1}{(d\ s) - t0}$$

in some chronicle, since then (> V0 0) will change truth value infinitely often around $t0$. One way to rule this out is to require that any such function be "finitely piecewise analytic," i.e., that, over any closed interval, the function consist of finitely many fragments that are analytic when extended to the complex plane. ("Analytic" means "infinitely continuously differentiable.") This set of functions is closed under arithmetic operations and differentiation, and always produces well-behaved facts when compared. Restricting ourselves to this set allows for all the discontinuities that quantities exhibit in naive physics, and seems to capture the intuition that normal quantities jump a few times, but basically vary smoothly.

We won't look very hard at requirements like this. We simply let Axiom 9 take its course. But Davis's result is needed to justify the axiom, since otherwise there might not be interesting models satisfying it.

The fundamental event involving fluents is a "vtrans." A (vtrans v r1 r2) denotes the event consisting of all occasions when v changed from r1 to r2.

Axiom 19:
(=(vtrans ?v ?r1 ?r2)
   {[s1, s2]: (and (=(V s1 ?v) ?r1)
                   (=(V s2 ?v) ?r2))})

For example, a winch's rotating corresponds to a vtrans of its phase angle. An increase in inflation is a vtrans of INFLATION from one value to another. A change of Presidents is a vtrans of "President of the US" from one statesman to another.

Knowing that a vtrans occurred tells you nothing about *how* it occurred, unless the quantity involved is *continuous*, when we have an intermediate-value axiom:

Axiom 20:
  (if (continuous ?v)
    (if (Occ ?s1 ?s4 (vtrans ?v ?r1 ?r4))
      (forall (r2 r3)
        (exists (s2 s3)
          (and (=< ?s1 s2 s3 ?s4)
            (if (=< ?r1 r2 r3 ?r4)
              (and (Occ s2 s3 (vtrans ?v r2 r3))
                (forall (s)
                  (if (=< s2 s s3)
                    (=< r2 (V s ?v) r3)))))
            (if (>= ?r1 r2 r3 ?r4)
              (and (Occ s2 s3 (vtrans ?v r2 r3))
                (forall (s)
                  (if (=< s2 s s3)
                    (>= r2 (V s ?v) r3))))))))))))

In English, if *v* changes continuously from *r1* to *r4*, and *r2* and *r3* lie between *r1* and *r4*, then there is a time interval in which *v* changes from *r2* to *r3* without going outside the bounds *r2* and *r3*. That is, it spends a certain period in every subinterval between *r1* and *r4*. (The conclusion of the axiom has two very similar conjuncts, one for the case when *v* is increasing, the other for when it is decreasing.)

Vtranses are normally inferred from "potranses." If (potrans *channel v r*) occurs, that means that "*v* was augmented through the given channel by an amount *r*." A potrans is a potential vtrans.

Potranses are intended to capture the way we reason about things like flows into tanks, and other more general changes. Often we know things like these:

I just poured five gallons of reagent into the vat.
I made 5 thousand dollars consulting today.
Decontrolling oil will tend to increase inflation by 5%.

In all these cases, we are given a fact which all by itself would translate directly into a vtrans: the vat's contents increased by five gallons, my net worth increased by $5,000, inflation increased by 5%. But, as we all know, life is not so simple. If you know about a leak in the vat, the increase is actually 5 gallons MINUS pouring time ∗ rate of leak. The IRS will make sure that my net worth doesn't go up by the amount I made. The Reagan administration hopes that other measures will offset the decontrol of oil.

I adopt a very abstract model of this kind of situation. Many quantities may be thought of as fed by various "channels." These may correspond to physical entities, such as pipes into tanks, but they are never identified with anything physical. They are there almost as a pure technical device to enable us to count potranses. We could not have a potrans of *r* into *v* be an event by itself, since then pouring five gallons into the same vat by two different pipes simultaneously would be just one occurrence of one event.

However, we do assume certain things about channels (which we denote by variables starting with the letter "h"). First, there is the fact (channel-into *h v*), for which we have the axioms:

Axiom 21:
  (iff (exists (s)
         (and (=<?s1 s ?s2)
              (T s (channel-into ?h ?v))))
       (exists (r)
         (Occ ?s1 ?s2 (potrans ?h ?v r))))
  (if (and (Occ ?s1 ?s2 (potrans ?h ?v ?r1))
           (Occ ?s1 ?s2 (potrans ?h ?v ?r2)))
      (=?r1 ?r2))

That is, that one unique amount "flows" through a given channel into a given quantity over any interval. No amount at all flows unless the channel actually "fed" the quantity at some time during the interval.

The fundamental fact about potranses and channels is then:

Axiom 22:
  (if (real-valued ?v)
      (iff (Occ ?s1 ?s2 (vtrans ?v ?r1 ?r2))
           (=(-?r2 ?r1)
              (sumpotrans ?s1 ?s2 ?v
                {h: (exists (s)
                      (and (=<?s1 s ?s2)
                           (T s (channel-into h ?v))))}))))

where
  (=(sumpotrans ?s1 ?s2 ?v {}) 0)
and
  (if (and (=(sumpotrans ?s1 ?s2 ?v ?hh) ?sum)
           (Occ ?s1 ?s2 (potrans ?h ?v ?r)))
      (= (sumpotrans ?s1 ?s2 ?v
                     (union ?hh {?h}))
         (+? sum ?r)))

That is, the change in a real-valued fluent over an interval is the sum of the potential changes in it. (sumpotrans *s1 s2 v set-of-channels*) is the sum of all the potranses through the given channels into *v* from *s1* to *s2*.

Taken together, these two axioms enable us to count the contributions from all channels into a quantity over a given time interval.

Potranses are decomposable:

Axiom 23:
  (iff (Occ ?s1 ?s2 (potrans ?h ?v ?r))
       (forall (s)
         (if (=<?s1 s ?s2)
             (exists (r1 r2)
               (and (Occ ?s1 s (potrans ?h ?v r1))
                    (Occ s ?s2 (potrans ?h ?v r2))
                    (=?r (+r1 r2)))))))

That is, the potrans through a channel over an interval is the sum of the potranses over each subinterval in a partition of it.

If a quantity is continuous, we can decompose potranses into it another way. If a certain amount "flows" into or out of a quantity, then for any smaller amount, the flow began with a subflow of this smaller amount. Formally:

Axiom 24: (An intermediate-value axiom)
(if (continuous ?v)
    (if (Occ ?s1 ?s2 (potrans ?h ?v ?r))
        (forall (r')
            (if (or (=< 0 r' ?r)
                    (>= 0 r' ?r))
                (exists (s)
                    (and (=< ?s1 s ?s2)
                         (Occ ?s1 s (potrans ?h ?v r'))
                         (Occ s ?s2 (potrans ?h ?v
                                     (− ?r r')))))))))

Potranses are not instantaneous:

Axiom 25:
(if (T ?s (channel-into ?h ?v))
    (Occ ?s ?s (potrans ?h ?v 0)))

For example, let's say that we had:

(continuous (WATER-VOL TANK1))

(persist S0 (= {h: (channel-into h (WATER-VOL TANK1))}
              {(INFLOW TANK1), (OVERFLOW TANK1)})
         (6 weeks))

That is, only two channels into TANK1 exist. Notice how casually I sneak new constructs into the fact notation. The $\{x: p\}$ is the set of all x such that p; this is, of course, a fluent. So $(= \{x: p\} \{A, B\})$ is a fact, with an obvious meaning.

The channels have certain special properties. Nothing ever flows in through the overflow, and there is no flow out of it while the level is below some capacity.

(if (Occ ?s1 ?s2
        (potrans (OVERFLOW TANK1) (WATER-VOL TANK1) ?x))
    (=< ?x 0))
(if (TT ?s1 ?s2 (< (WATER-VOL TANK1) (CAP TANK1)))
    (Occ ?s1 ?s2
        (potrans (OVERFLOW TANK1) (WATER-VOL TANK1) 0)))

Notice that the notation allows us to be ambiguous about whether (CAP TANK1) is a fluent or a number. If we decided on the former, we would have to talk about its persistence, so let's pretend it's the latter, and the capacity cannot vary with time. We assume that (> (CAP TANK1) 0).

Nothing ever flows out through the inflow:

(if (Occ ?s1 ?s2
        (potrans (INFLOW TANK1) (WATER-VOL TANK1) ?x))
    (>= ?x 0))

The tank is built so that the capacity is never exceeded:

(=< (V ?s (WATER-VOL TANK1)) (CAP TANK1))

Now, let's say that for some S1 and S3 soon after S0, we have:

(=(V S1 (WATER-VOL TANK1)) 0)

(Occ S1 S3 (potrans (INFLOW TANK1) (WATER-VOL TANK1)
  (+(CAP TANK1) (5 gal))))

Then we can infer that there is a state S2, such that:

(Occ S1 s2 (potrans (INFLOW TANK1) (WATER-VOL TANK1)
  (CAP TANK1)))

(Occ S2 S3 (potrans (INFLOW TANK1) (WATER-VOL TANK1)
  (5 gal)))

(Occ S2 S3 (potrans (OVERFLOW TANK1) (WATER-VOL TANK1)
  (− 5 gal)))

Proof: By Axiom 24, there is a flow of (CAP TANK1) through (INFLOW TANK1), followed by a flow of (5 gal). But during this period, the flow through (OVERFLOW TANK1) must be zero, because it can't be positive, and if it were negative, then by Axiom 22 the volume would never get above (CAP TANK1) during this interval, so it would always be zero, a contradiction. Therefore, at the end of this period, the volume will be (CAP TANK1). This is state S2. Now 5 gal flow into the tank. At least 5 gal must flow out, or the tank capacity would be exceeded at S3. If more than 5 gal flowed out (i.e., less than −5 flowed in), then at the end the tank would be less than full. Then by Axiom 20 there must have been an interval between S2 and S3 during which the volume of water declined from (CAP TANK1) to the final value. But during this interval, either the flow into INFLOW would have had to be negative, or the flow into OUTFLOW would have had to be nonzero, both of which are impossible—QED.

Other examples would be possible, but they would mainly illustrate reasoning about continuous functions. My main goal is the exploration of a logical framework, so I will leave this for somebody else.

Continuous quantities do not in general persist at the same value for very long. For example, the quantity of water in a reservoir will change with rain, evaporation and use. We could try to handle this by indicating that the persistence of time (=WATER-LEVEL k) is (say) one day. But this is almost never right. The level is not likely to stay exactly the same for more than an instant, but it is not likely to double in one day, either, no matter how hard it rains.

We need to introduce the "rate" predicate:

Axiom 26:
  (if (> ?t 0)
    (iff (T ?s (rate ?v ?t ?i))
      (forall (s0 s1)
        (if (and (=< s0 ?s s1)
                 (=(−(d s1) (d s0)) ?t))
          (elt $\frac{?t}{(V\ s1\ ?v) - (V\ s0\ ?v)}$
            ?i)))))

(rate v t i) means that the average rate of change of the quantity v over any interval of length t is within the given interval. The purpose of t is to smooth short-term fluctuations, and to allow us to talk of rates of change of noncontinuous quantities. (t is not allowed to be 0, since then we would have to talk about derivatives, which are hard to define given multiple chronicles, and which don't seem to be necessary for "naive" reasoning about time.)

We also need to delimit rates of potransing:

Axiom 27:
  (if (> ?t 0)
      (iff (T ?s (porate ?h ?v ?t ?i))
          (forall (s0 s1 r)
              (if (and (= < s0 ?s s1)
                       (= (− (d s1) (d s0)) ?t)
                       (Occ s0 s1 (potrans ?h ?v r)))
                  (elt (?r/?t)
                       ?i)))))

Rather than infer persistences of values of numerical quantities, we can infer persistences of their rates of change. I will give an example of such an inference in the next section.

5 PLANNING

With what I have talked about so far, we can reason about causal situations, but only as a spectator. In this section, I will talk about how a program might reason about its own actions. Part of my motivation in defining time the way I did was to support reasoning about interesting actions, like preventing events. The flexibility in my event ontology now carries over to the world of actions: An *action* is in this theory an entity, the doing of which by an agent is an event. Formally, we just need a function (do *agent act*), which is used to name events consisting of an agent performing an action. In this paper, I will completely neglect multiple-agent situations, so the first argument to "do" will be dropped; it will simply map actions into events. Variables denoting actions will begin with "a."

In the first subsection below, I will see how far this takes us. Some actions, like preventing and allowing, just fall out of the ontology. Others, like protecting facts, are still problematical.

In the second subsection, I will explore the notion of "plan." A *plan* is a set of actions, often intended to carry out another action. In one form or another, this idea has been important to several AI researchers, from Sacerdoti (1977) to Schank and Abelson (1977). I will show how the idea gets translated into my temporal-logic framework.

5.1 The logic of action

Many actions are quite straightforward, such as (PUTON x y), which is done whenever the problem solver, or "robot," actually puts x on y. These may correspond to primitive actions the hardware can execute. For each, there will be axioms giving their typical effects as persistences.

But many actions do not fit this mold, such as preventing, allowing, proving, observing, promising, maintaining, and avoiding.

Consider the action "Prevent e," where e is some event. To be concrete, let's have e be the event E1 = "Little Nell mashed by train TR1 in the 5 minutes after state S0." E1 will be prevented if it doesn't happen, assuming it was going to happen if not prevented. (You can't take credit for preventing an unlikely thing.)

This is the sort of thing that past problem solvers have neglected. In the present calculus, it is easy to do. First, we need a notion of event dependence.

Axiom 28:
  (iff (not-occur-if ?e1 ?e2)
    (and (forall (ch)
        (if (hap ch ?e1) (not (hap ch ?e2))))
      (exists (ch) (hap ch ?e2))
      (exists (ch) (not hap ch ?e2))))

where
  (iff (hap ?ch ?e)
    (exists (s1 s2)
      (and (subset [s1, s2] ?ch) (Occ s1 s2 ?e))))

For instance, (not-occur-if E1 E2), where E2 = "I move Little Nell in the 5 minutes after S0."

Now it is easy to define prevention:

Axiom 29:
  (= (prevent ?e) (one-of {a: (not-occur-if (do ?a) ?e)}))

So one way to prevent Little Nell from being mashed is to move her in the next 5 minutes.

In this axiom, I have used "event disjunction," written (one-of {e1 e2 ... }), although this is just syntactic sugar for "sunion." We extend the notation to actions, with the axiom

Axiom 30:
  (= (do (one-of {?a1 ... ?aN}))
    (one-of {(do ?a1) ... (do ?aN)}))

If there are no actions that E is negatively dependent on, then (do (prevent E)) is the empty set, "never." That is, (prevent E) never happens.

Axiom 31:
  (= (do (one-of {})) never)

A finer analysis of impossibility appears below.

As an example, let us take another look at TANK1. Suppose that at S0,

(= (V S0 (WATER-VOL TANK1)) 0),

and (persist S0 (porate (INFLOW TANK1) (WATER-VOL TANK1)
        (1 sec) [R1, R2])
   T0)

where (>R2 R1 0) and (>T0 (/(CAP TANK1) R1)).

A little more terminology: Let (anch s e) stand for {[s, s2]: (Occ s s2 e)}, the set of all occurrences of e starting in s. Let (culm p e) be

{[s1, s2]: (exists (s)
    (and (=<s1 s s2)
      (TT s1 s2 p)
      (Occ s s2 e)))},

the set of all intervals in which p is true and then e happens. Let (holds p) be {[s, s]: (T s p)}, the set of all point intervals at which p is true.

What we want to find is an action to prevent

Eo = (anch S0
    (culm (rate (INFLOW TANK1) (WATER-VOL TANK1)
            (1 sec)<0, infinity>)
    (holds (= (WATER-VOL TANK1) (CAP TANK1)))))

That is, the overflow of the tank that will occur if the water is allowed to run.
We need the action (TURN-OFF (INFLOW TANK1)), defined by this axiom:

Axiom 32:
  (pcause (channel-into ?h ?v)
        (do (TURN-OFF ?h))
        (porate ?h ?v (1 msec) [0, 0])
        1 [0, 0]
        (1 day))

This says that turning off ?h causes the flow through it to become zero. (The fourth argument, 1, says that the effect begins when the action is done; the fifth, [0, 0], says it happens immediately; and the sixth says it persists for one day. See Axiom 17.)

What we want to prove is that if E1 =

  (do (within-time S0 (/(CAP TANK1) R2)
      (TURN-OFF (INFLOW TANK1))))

then
  (not-occur-if E1 E0)

where
  (= (do (within-time ?s ?t ?a))
     {[s1, s2]: (and (Occ s1 s2 (do ?a))
               (= < ?s s2)
               (= <(− (d s2) (d ?s)) ?t))})

The (within-time *s t act*) is the action *act* done within *t* of state *s*.

The proof that turning off the tank in time will prevent the tank from filling requires three steps: (1) showing that Eo is possible; (2) showing that Eo might not happen; and (3) showing that Eo doesn't happen if E1 does.

The first requirement is met by a proof similar to that of Section 4. But to make it go, we have to assume there is a chronicle in which the problem solver refrains from E1. It is tempting to devise an "Axiom of Free Will," which states that any action is avoidable; there is always a chronicle in which you don't do it. But there are counter-examples. If A1 = "snap your fingers within 1 minute of S0," and A2 = "keep from snapping your fingers for 1 minute after S0," then (one-of {A1, A2}) happens in every chronicle containing S0. I will call such an action *unavoidable* in S0. There is no easy way to tell if an action is avoidable or not, so we must just provide axioms to tell in every case, which drive:

Axiom 33:
  (iff (avoidable ?a ?s)
      (exists (ch)
         (and (elt ?s ch) (not (hap ch (do ?a))))))

In the present example, we have (avoidable (TURN-OFF (INFLOW TANK1)) So). E1 is not exactly in this form, but we have the theorem

(if (avoidable ?a ?s)
  (avoidable (within-time ?s ?t ?a) ?s))

If you don't have to do ?a, you don't have to do it within some time. I won't spend any time on the theory of avoidable actions, since it is probably intricate and essentially trivial.

So there is a chronicle in which E1 does not occur. By Axiom 15 and Axiom 16, in this chronicle the water keeps running, so we can infer that the tank will reach capacity during the lifetime of the water's being on.

The third requirement is met by assuming that E1 happens in CH1, and showing that the fact required for "culm" will be cut off. This is pretty obvious.

The second requirement will follow from the third if we can show that the robot is able to turn off this channel. Clearly, we need an axiom to deduce this. For realism, it should be an axiom giving the exact circumstances under which a channel of this sort can be turned off. (You have to be near enough to the tap implementing the channel that you can reach it before (CAP TANK1) / R2.) But this is all tangential, so I won't give details.

To talk about allowing, I first introduce a notion complementary to not-occur-if:

Axiom 34:
  (iff (occur-if-not ?e1 ?e2)
    (and (forall (ch)
          (if (not (hap ch ?e1)) (hap ch ?e2)))
      (exists (ch) (hap ch ?e2))
      (exists (ch) (not (hap ch ?e2)))))

In English, (occur-if-not e1 e2) means that e2 will occur if e1 does not, and e2 may or may not occur.

We need a little bit more. First, the concept of "event negation," written "nev":

Axiom 35:
  (iff (Occ ?s1 ?s2 (nev ?e))
    (and (T ?s1 (possible ?e))
      (T ?s2 (not possible ?e))))

where
  (iff (T ?s (possible ?e))
    (exists (s1 s2 ch)
      (and (elt ?s ch) (elt s2 ch)
        (Occ s1 s2 ?e))))

That is, the negation of an event occurs if that event becomes impossible. For instance, the negation of "Capitalism collapses by the year 1900" occurred in the last half of the nineteenth century.

Now we can define a related operator on actions, "forgo":

Axiom 36:
  (iff (Occ ?s1 ?s2 (do (forgo ?a)))
    (Occ ?s1 ?s2 (nev (do ?a))))

Forgoing an action means doing something that makes doing the action impossible, which may mean just procrastinating until you have lost your chance. It is hard to forgo an action like "Whistling the Star-Spangled Banner" (except perhaps by having your lips removed), but easy to forgo an action like "Move Little Nell within 5 minutes after So." If you don't move her within 5 minutes, you've forgone this action.

Now defining allow is straightforward:

Axiom 37:
  (iff (Occur-if-not (do ?a) ?e)
    (= (allow ?e) (forgo ?a)))
  (if (not (exists (a) (occur-if-not (do ?a) ?e)))
    (= (do (allow ?e)) never))

Related to allowing and preventing are two other actions, forgoing preventing and forgoing allowing. To forgo preventing something is to make it impossible to prevent; this differs from allowing in that the thing might still fail to happen, whereas according to my definition an event that is allowed actually happens.

Forgoing allowing an event is more complex. Let A be an action such that not doing it would entail that the event (E) occurs. To forgo allowing it is to forgo forgoing A. This means doing something that makes it impossible not to do A. This differs from preventing in that E might still occur.

Of course, there is a more mundane notion than either preventing or allowing, in which you actively work to make something happen. I will call this "bring-about." It is described by the axiom:

Axiom 38:
  (= (bring-about ?e)
    (one-of {a: (exists (r i)
        (ecause always (do a) ?e r i))}))

Bringing-about *e* is done by doing an action that (always) causes *e*.

James Allen (personal communication) has raised interesting objections to my analysis of allowing and preventing, which I will repeat here, since they are likely to seem weighty to many people:

Since most things are possible, however improbably, ... every day I allow most of the events that happen in China. If someone was killed there, then since I did 'forgo' the action of boarding a plane, sneaking through customs, and throwing myself in front of the assailant's bullet, I allowed the killing. It gets even worse with prevent. There's probably no way I can ever prevent anything in this world. I have so little control over what happens that whatever I do, there is always some event (however improbable) that is possible and would nullify my efforts.

The first objection, that too many things get allowed, is no trouble for me; one does in fact allow an infinite number of things over any given day, without intending to allow most of them. (Note also that "I allow most of the events... in China" is ambiguous; one certainly does not allow the event consisting of the occurrence of all the events in China over a day.)

The second objection, that too few things get prevented, is more serious. Of course, there is a sense in which one could never *prove* that it is possible to prevent a given event, but this is just another case of excessive caution on the part of formal systems. A dose of non-monotonicity should cure it, one hopes. A deeper problem is that my analysis fails to take probabilities into account. We often plan to prevent something, *knowing* that the plan might not work because of improbable possibilities. But this point applies to all planning, not just prevention. In fact, it applies to a lot of reasoning. As far as I know, there is no theory combining formal logic with probability theory.

In McDermott (1978b), I discussed a classification scheme for actions, used in the NASL problem solver. An important distinction was between "primary" and "secondary" actions. A secondary action was one that was executed correctly when another action was executed in a particular way. For instance, in "Pick up this stick without moving any other stick," the subaction "Don't move any other stick" was a secondary modification of the primary action "Pick up this stick." Another word for a secondary action to which the system was committed was *policy*.

In the present calculus, the distinction does not get made this way. Secondary actions are no weirder than some intuitively primary actions. For instance, (avoid a), where a is an action, is simply an action which is done over any interval in which you don't do a. The key distinction now is between composing actions sequentially or in parallel. Before, I defined (seq e1 ... eN) to be an event consisting of all occurrences of e1, ... eN in order. We can define (seq a1 ... aN) in a similar way. For policies, we must define (par a1 ... aN):

Axiom 39:
  (= (par ?e1 ... ?eN)
     {[s1, s2]: (and (elt [s1, s2] ?e1)
                    (elt [s1, s2] ?e2)
                    ...
                    (elt [s1, s2] ?eN))})

So to do A1 while avoiding doing A2, we do (par A1 (avoid A2)). (Here and from now on, I extend notations defined over events to actions in the obvious way without comment.)

Another secondary action is "protection" (Sussman (1975)). Intuitively, a fact is protected by a problem solver during an interval if it stays true during that interval. However, I think there is more to protection than this, which I do not know how to formalize. There is a distinction between "restorable" and "unrestorable" protections. For instance, if you are protecting the fact, "The fuse (for some keg of dynamite) is not in contact with an open flame," then if the fact becomes false, you have failed. You might try to cut the fuse or run, but it is pointless to move the fuse away from the flame; the damage has been done. In most cases, though, it is worth it to reestablish the protected fact. If I am baby-sitting a child, I try to protect the fact that he is not out of my sight. I do not give up once he is invisible. So the act "Protect p" can often be successful, even if p lapsed a few times. I do not know how to formalize this. Perhaps you could put a time limit on how long the lapses are. So in the baby case, I have failed if he eludes me for more than 5 minutes, while in the dynamite case the maximum allowable lapse is zero. But this seems arbitrary. The only real criteria for success of actions like these are teleological. I am successful with the baby if he's around and in one piece when his parents arrive. I am successful with the dynamite if there's no explosion, and so forth.

I have already mentioned several ways of building new actions out of elementary actions, such as seq, par, forgo, and avoid. Another important class of action-building methods are the traditional programming constructs, like loops and conditionals. A complete study of how these composition methods fit together would start to resemble the study of programming-language semantics (Milne and Strachey 1976). I think we should avoid carrying this resemblance to an extreme. In particular, I think the ability to do simple reasoning about plans would go down the drain if variables and assignment were admitted into the plan language. In most loops that people execute, the outside world keeps all the state information. When a condition is no longer true, it will be false in the world, not in the robot's head.

5.2 The logic of problem solving

So far in this section, I have analyzed actions, without ever introducing the concept of an action that "should be performed." A problem solver may be thought of as a program that takes an action that should be performed, a *task*, and performs it. Hence the notion is of some importance.

I tried once before, in McDermott (1977; and 1978b), to develop the logic of tasks. In that system, NASL, the fundamental predicate was (task *name act*) meaning, *name* denotes an action you should do, to wit, *act*. Unfortunately, the action of a task was usually underspecified. For instance, you might have the tasks:

(task T1 (PUTON A B))
(task T2 (PUTON B C))
(successor T1 T2)

This was where (PUTON B C) was an action that should be performed, but not at an arbitrary time; the "successor" formula constrained it to be after (PUTON A B).

The problem with this approach was that it distorted time relations, in three ways. First, the time dependence between the two actions was not part of their definition. This made it hard to say what "task" meant. If it meant "This action is to be done," then a task assertion didn't describe its action precisely, but only gave a generalization of it. (In the example, (PUTON B C) is a generalization of "Do (PUTON B C) after (PUTON A B).") Second, it wasn't made clear *when* something was a task. As with most previous AI representations, NASL lived only in the present; there was no way to talk about what had been a task or was going to be one. Third, to compensate for this, NASL changed the data base to reflect passing time. When something was no longer a task, it got erased. Unfortunately, when something had been assumed to be a task erroneously, it also got erased. There was no way to distinguish between these two (see Section 1).

In short, three notions of time were confused: the time of an action, the time of a task, and real-world time ("now"). Now that we have a good analysis of time, we can untangle these things.

The correct analysis of task and action seems to be this: A task is an action to which a problem solver is committed. The action must be well enough specified so that the time of commitment is not needed to know what it is the solver is committed to. Therefore, one may have a task like "Visit Greece," satisfiable any time, but usually the action must be more specified than that: "Put block A on block B within 5 minutes after...."

A problem solver's being committed to an action is itself a fact. One may alternately have and not have the task of Visiting Greece. Entirely independently, one may actually visit Greece. There are several ways these might interact:

1. You might have the task and not have done the action yet: In this situation, a rational problem solver will devote resources to accomplishing the action, unless more urgent tasks intrude.
2. You might have the task and have already done the action: In this case, the task has succeeded, and nothing more need be done.
3. You might have done the action and not (now) have the task: This is quite common; an example would be insulting or cheering up someone yesterday without intending to now (or possibly then either).
4. You might have a task for an impossible action: This is quite common too. The action may have been possible when the task began; in this case, the task may

be said to have *failed*. If it was never possible, it is wishful thinking. Philosophers have argued about whether it is ever rational to have such a task. I see no reason why not, in the case of task failure. It seems natural to say that I have a task of meeting that student at 2:30 yesterday as I promised, but I failed to do it.

The last two categories interact in an interesting way. Often when a task fails, there is some other action that was done *instead* of the intended one. For instance, you have a task of hitting the golf ball into the little hole, and you actually hit it into the big pond. Here is a combination of an action with no task and a task with no (possible) action. There should probably be a predicate relating the two: (did-instead act1 act2) would mean that act1 was a task and act2 was done instead (act1 never occurring). (In the example, act1 would be "Hit the ball into the hole on stroke 2 of hole 6 of the golf game played on Tuesday afternoon," and act2 would be "Hit the ball into the pond on stroke 2 of....") Rather than examine this in detail, I will just point out an inadequacy in past representations of task networks. Problem solvers that maintain such networks (Sacerdoti, 1977; McDermott, 1978b) have failed to maintain a complementary *behavior network* that represents what actually happened (or is going to happen). If every task succeeds, the two networks would be isomorphic; where one had "Task a," the other would have "Did a." But if there was failure, there would be a link between the two networks, from "Task a," to "Did b." This would be more useful than simply recording that a task failed or succeeded, and would help the system in explaining its actions.

This is getting ahead of the story, into implementation and away from logic. We need to say more about logic first.

In both NOAH (Sacerdoti, 1977) and NASL (McDermott, 1978b), a key notion is that of one task being a *subtask* of another. This means that the subtask is part of the chosen plan for carrying out the supertask. Every task is either immediately executable or reducible to subtasks, which are executable or reducible, and so on.

A problem solver transforms a task into subtasks by *choosing* a plan for the task, and asserting that every element of the plan is a subtask. This choice mechanism is probably not purely logical. That is, it seems that the solver probably doesn't *infer* a set of subtasks, but must actively choose them, whatever that means.[8]

The requirement that tasks be reduced to subtasks gives rise to a bug. In the current formalism, we can talk of reducing the action A1 to the action (seq B1 B2), but this reduces A to a single subtask. Is there any sense in which B1 and B2 are subtasks of A? It makes sense for B1 to be thought of as a subtask, but just any execution of B2 will cut no ice. We insist that B2 come after B1. To make B2 a subtask would get us right back into the difficulty I raised at the beginning of this section, of tasks being underspecified.

The solution is to take as subtasks B1 and (just-after B1 B2), where just-after is defined as

Axiom 40:
   (=(just-after ?a1 ?a2)
      {[s2, s3]: (and (Occ s2 s3 ?a2)
                     (exists (s1) (Occ s1 s2 ?a1)))})

---

[8] Perhaps I'm wrong on this. But if this relationship really is inferential, it must be an inference of the form: if p is the best plan for a, then every element of p is a subtask of a. Unfortunately, it can happen that there are two equally good plans for a. Since we need to introduce a pure choice here, we may as well accept it in general. Amazingly little has been done on the logic of choices in AI. The work on medical diagnosis (e.g., Shortliffe, 1976), and work on choices by problem solvers (e.g., McDermott, 1978b; Doyle, 1980) are two examples.

The set of actions {B1, (just-after B1 B2)} is such that A is executed in any chronicle in which they are executed; in other words, this set is a plan for A.

Of course, this is not really a solution to the problem, not until we provide rules for reducing tasks of the form (just-after a1 a2). But at least it suggests that what problem solvers do makes some logical sense. That is, in many cases, there is a well-defined plan for a task, each of whose elements must be done in order to carry out the task.

Another example is the classic plan for achieving a conjunction of facts. To analyze this, we need the action (achieve *prop until-prop*), which means "Bring it about that prop is true from the end of the achieve until the until-prop becomes true." This is clearly needed, for the reasons discussed in Section 3; if you were allowed to achieve things for a single instant, the achievement would usually be worthless. So we have:

Axiom 41:
　(iff (Occ ?s1 ?s2 (do (achieve ?p ?q)))
　　　(and (T ?s2 ?p)
　　　　　(forall (s4)
　　　　　　(if (and (< ?s2 s4) (not (T s4 ?p)))
　　　　　　　(exists (s3)
　　　　　　　　(and (< ?s2 s3) (= < s3 s4)
　　　　　　　　　(T s3 ?q)))))))

In English, doing (achieve ?p ?q) amounts to bringing it about that ?p, in such a way that if ?p ever becomes false thereafter, ?q must have become false first.

Historically, tasks of the form "achieve *p*" have been very important. Problem solvers like GPS (Ernst and Newell, 1969) concentrated on these (in the form of "difference reductions"), and this concentration has persisted. An especially interesting case is where *p* is a conjunction of facts (Sussman, 1975; Sacerdoti, 1977). The problem is, of course, that all the facts must be true at once, when the task is complete, and all too often the plan for one conjunct upsets another.

I will introduce the standard plan for achieving conjunctions after some useful definitions. First, we define "to-do" thus

Axiom 42:
　(iff (to-do ?a1 ?a2)
　　　(one-way (do ?a2) (do ?a1)))

That is, *a2* is a way to do *a1* if (do *a2*) is one way that (do *a1*) can happen. Next, we let (plan *aa*) be the action corresponding to the plan consisting of all the actions *aa*.

Axiom 43:
　(iff (Occ ?s1 ?s2 (do (plan ?aa)))
　　　(and (forall (a)
　　　　(if (elt a ?aa)
　　　　　(Occbetween ?s1 ?s2 a)))
　　　(exists (a s)
　　　　(and (elt a ?aa) (Occ ?s1 s a)))
　　　(exists (a s)
　　　　(and (elt a ?aa) (Occ s ?s2 a)))))

That is, a plan is done in any minimal time span in which all of its elements are done. And finally,

Axiom 44:
(iff (T ?s (finished ?a))
    (and (exists (s1 s2)
            (and (Occ s1 s2 (do ?a))
                 (< s2 ?s)))
         (forall (s1 s2)
            (if (= < ?s s2)
                (not (Occ s1 s2 (do ?a)))))))

That is, an action is finished when its last execution is past.

The following theorem then states that one way to achieve a conjunction is to achieve each of its conjuncts, in such a way that each conjunct remains true until the other is achieved.

(if (and (= ?a1 (achieve ?p1 (& ?q (finished ?a2))))
         (= ?a2 (achieve ?p2 (& ?q (finished ?a1)))))
    (to-do (achieve (& ?p1 ?p2) ?q)
           (plan {?a1, ?a2})))

Proof: Assume that the task is to achieve P1 and P2 until Q, and let A1 and A2 be two actions that satisfy the antecedent. Assume that (do (plan {A1, A2})) occurs from So to S2. I will show that (do (achieve (& P1 P2) Q)) also occurs during that interval. According to Axiom 41, we must show that (T S2 (& P1 P2)), and that (& P1 P2) remains true until Q.

To show the first part, without loss of generality assume that A1 finishes before A2 (or no later). (See Figure 4.)

```
                --A1-->              (& P1 P2)           Q              (- P1)
So              S1                   S2                  S3             S4
                ---A2                ->
```

Then A2 is not finished until at least S2, so P1 must be true from S1 to S2. But P2 is true at S2, so (T S2 (& P1 P2)).

To show the second part, let S4 be an arbitrary state after S2 in which (& P1 P2) is false. Then either P1 or P2 is false there. Assume without loss of generality that it is P1. By Axiom 41, there must be a state S3 after S1 in which (& Q (finished A2)) is true, and hence Q is true. This must come after S2, since until then A2 is not finished—QED.

There is one suspicious feature of this plan for conjunction achievement: there is no finite non-circular term for naming either subtask. This rules out certain naive implementations of a problem solver based on this logic. A deeper problem is that there

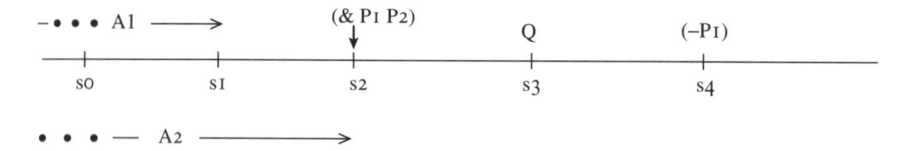

FIG. 4 Conjunction Proof.

may be cases in which there are no actions satisfying the antecedent of my theorem, for instance if ?p1 and ?p2 contradict each other, or they require large amounts of a finite resource, or any of several other cases obtains. It is an open problem how one would go about proving the feasibility or unfeasibility of this plan.

The final problem to be examined in the light of this logic is the "plan decomposition" problem (pointed out by Eugene Charniak, personal communication). When you are writing a plan, say to paint something (Charniak, 1976), you have a choice whether to represent a step as "Dip brush in paint," or "Achieve (paint on brush)." The latter is the purpose of the former, but the former is the most common way of achieving this purpose, so common that it seems wrong not to make it part of the plan. But if the paint in the can is low, the usual step will not work. You will have to tilt the can and grope with the brush, or go buy more paint. On the other hand, it seems wasteful to make "Achieve (paint on brush)" the normal plan step, and rederive the normal sequence every time.

The solution seems to be to store two things: the usual plan, and a proof that it works. The proof in this case would have one fragment that said: "If you dip the brush in the paint, and there is paint deep enough to be dipped into, then you will get paint on the brush. If there is paint on the brush, then stroking the wall with it will get paint on the wall...." The proof is not consulted until the plan fails, that is, until the "dip" step fails to bring about partial immersion of the brush. Then the proof would be consulted to see why this was done. The reason found would mention the bridging fact that "there is paint on the brush." The problem solver could then look for other ways to bring this about.

This sketch requires a lot of work to fill out, but I doubt that problem solvers will be robust and efficient until it is done. One big piece of work is to choose a format for these "proofs" that enables easy access to the relevant fragments. Presumably the proof would be broken into pieces festooned over the plan.

6   SKETCH OF AN IMPLEMENTATION

Up to now, I have avoided discussing data structures and algorithms. If Hayes (1979a) is right, I would be justified in avoiding them for a few more years yet. But I have not been able to keep from thinking about how these ideas would be expressed in a working program, and I think an occasional glimpse in that direction is necessary for even the most dedicated "AI logician." We are engaged in notational engineering, not philosophy.

An implementation must be able to do interesting, useful inferences. What is interesting and useful will vary from application to application. The one I am most interested in is problem solving. A problem solver must exploit the tree of possible chronicles, since it must reason about consequences of different courses of action. It must also be able to reason about the interactions between its actions and inanimate processes, and among its own actions. A typical interaction is the detection that a planned action will cause a persisting fact to cease.

Consider an example from Sacerdoti (1977). Say a problem solver has the tasks of painting the ladder and painting the ceiling. If it works on "paint the ceiling" first, it will notice that the ladder must be climbable, and that it is currently climbable. Therefore, it will persist in being climbable for years. The problem solver concludes that this state will last until the ceiling is painted, which will take a few hours. Now it turns to thinking about painting the ladder. It realizes that this will cause "ladder climbable" to cease, and remain untrue for a day (assuming paint dries this slowly). It then should see that it lacks sufficient information to decide if this is a problem, since it does not know whether it will paint the ladder before painting the ceiling. Since the situation is under its control, it imposes an order that didn't exist before, and decides to paint the ceiling first.

This is similar to Sacerdoti's algorithm, but with some important differences. First, the kind of retrieval that occurs is more generally applicable. If we found out someone was coming to repossess the ladder, exactly the same reasoning would go on, up to the point where we imposed extra order. A different response would be necessary if one of the events was outside our control. But the retrieval problem is the same.

Second, I do not model an action in terms of simple "addlists" and "deletelists," that is, lists of facts that change in truth value as a result of that action. Painting the ladder renders it unclimbable, but only for a while; we could always paint the ceiling tomorrow. In fact, there is no guarantee that we will catch the problem before we have already painted the ladder. Even if we do catch it, there may be some pressing reason why we should paint the ladder first; for instance, we may want to paint the ladder blue, and the ceiling green, and the only way to get green may be to mix our blue with some yellow we have lying around.

In fact, there will in general be many factors on each side of an ordering decision, and I am skeptical that one can casually decide on the basis of one of them how the plan ought to go. Instead, it seems more reasonable to try simulating the plan both ways whenever there is an important uncertainty as to order or outcome (Wilensky, 1980).

For this to work, the implementation must recognize the existence of multiple chronicles. It might seem that we want to keep a description of every relevant chronicle, but, of course, there are an infinite number of chronicles, each with an infinite description; what we really want is a partial description of the typical element of an interesting set of chronicles. For instance, the set of all chronicles in which I fail to prevent Little Nell from being mashed by the oncoming train would be of (somewhat morbid) interest, as would the set of chronicles in which I succeed. A partial description is just a data structure that supports information retrieval, like the action-conflict detection I described before. Let us call this kind of data structure a "time line," without reading too much into the phrase. Every set of chronicles will be represented by a data structure called a *chronset*, which consists of a defining characteristic of the chronicles in the set, plus a time line for accessing the events and facts that occur in those chronicles.

Chronsets are hierarchically organized. When the problem solver detects an important uncertainty in a chronset, it creates two (or more) new chronsets which represent the different outcomes. Almost everything true in the original chronset is true in the new ones; if I am on my way to visit Grandma when I hear Nell's cry for help, then the fact that I will see Grandma tonight is still true in both chronsets. Furthermore, the same chronset can be split more than one way. Before getting involved with Nell at all, I might have been speculating on whether nuclear war would occur by the year 2000, and what that would mean for civilization. The chronsets connected with this possibility have nothing to do with Nell.

Eventually, only one of a pair of alternative chronsets turns out to correspond to reality. This one becomes the new basis for further planning.

So, however time lines are implemented, they will have to be able to inherit properties from "superlines" belonging to higher chronsets. A flexible model of this kind of inheritance is the "data pool" model, developed in Sussman and McDermott (1972) and McDermott (1981b). This allows a distributed data structure to be labeled so that different parts are "visible" in different data pools. Each data pool will correspond to a chronset. So, rather than have different time lines, we can have one big time line, with some parts invisible in some chronsets.

The next question is how time lines are implemented. The idea I am currently pursuing is that they are modeled "spatially," that is, using much the same machinery as in a spatial reasoner like that of McDermott (1980), Davis (1981), and McDermott and Davis (1981).

In our spatial reasoner, every entity is modeled as a "frob"—a frame of reference attached to an object. The frobs are arranged in a graph. If the position of an object is known (fairly precisely) with respect to another object, its position with respect to that object's frame is stored explicitly; otherwise, it is computed when needed. Questions such as, How far is it from A to B? are answered by computation on the coordinates of A and B. Questions such as, What object is near A? are answered by searching through a *discrimination tree* of objects stored with respect to A (McDermott and Davis, 1981, McDermott, 1981c).

Our working hypothesis is that events and facts can be modeled as frobs. The reason this approach may fail is that the frob graphs may just be too complicated; however, it is hard to think of a more promising approach. (But see Allen, 1981.)

In general, a frob's position and other features are "fuzzy," that is, known only to within an interval. Hence we call the aggregation of frobs a *fuzzy map*. The fuzziness is entirely due to uncertainty. The position of the object in the real world is assumed definite. (Objects are not quantum mechanical.) If an event is to be thought of as a frob, there must be a sense in which it is a definite object with uncertain attributes. Of course, this is not what an event is at all. Instead, it is an infinite collection of time intervals. The time during which I sang the Star Spangled Banner is a meaningless quantity, unless you mean the fuzzy interval of all dates from my first singing of it to my last. But this interval will never be reduced to a point by further information.

On the other hand, there does seem to be a notion of temporary uncertainty that gets resolved. I am not sure what time the plumber is coming tomorrow; after she had been here, I am sure. This notion is completely outside the realm of the logic I developed in Sections 1 through 5. Consider a problem solver at state S_0, with a time line including tomorrow, and an event "Plumber comes." It is simply wrong to say that there is uncertainty in what time the plumber is going to come in the day following S_0, because *there are lots of 24-hour periods following S_0*, one per chronicle. Twenty-four hours later, there will be an infinite number of problem solvers, in an infinite number of incomparable states following S_0, each with a slightly different idea of when the plumber came.

So for its own sanity, a problem solver is going to need the notion of the *real* chronicle, the one that is actually going to happen. Actually, for completeness, we will have every chronset contain a unique *realest* chronicle, which must be the real chronicle if the chronset contains it. The uncertainty surrounding the exact time of an event in a given chronset is then the uncertainty about the occurrence of the event in the realest chronicle in the set. And this only makes sense for events that happen at most once in a chronicle: We will call an event or fact being modeled in a time line in this way an *occurrence*.

With these restrictions, it makes sense to apply techniques for mapping time. The existence of chronsets merely forces there to be many competing maps.

Before I discuss time lines in more detail, let me issue a warning about the "real" chronicle and its relatives. I am convinced that no hint of this concept must appear in the logic, because it would lead to some serious paradoxes and a breakdown of the system. (I thank Ernie Davis for discussions leading to this conclusion.) For instance, how do you represent that something is inevitable? In the logic so far, you must say that it will happen in all chronicles. It seems tempting to explore the alternative way of putting this, that the thing will happen in the real chronicle. After all, what can it matter that something happens in an unreal chronicle? But then everything that actually happens was inevitable.

The only conclusion is that the logic we use makes some extreme assumptions about time, which our implementation resolutely ignored. If this bothers you because you think logic ought to encompass everything that goes on in a robot, then this should convince you that it can't. If this bothers you because you want to know who is right, the logic or the implementation, my guess is that the implementation is right, but so what? Neither alternative is very palatable, but neither can be neglected. A system that accepted the idea of many futures would have no grounds for any decision; but neither would a system that accepted the idea of one future. The trick is to resonate between them, betting that there is one real future that matters, relying on a logic that presupposes the opposite.

One other topic falls under the "Implementation" heading. A *data dependency* is a note of the support that an assertion has, expressed as a list of other assertions (Doyle, 1979). In the implementation I am describing, there will be two kinds of dependency: the support for the contention *that* an occurrence will take place in a chronset; and the support for the time *when* it occurs in that chronset. The former is relatively straightforward. A cause will be linked to its effect. A bad occurrence will be linked to the task that prevents it. The only complication is that these links may have to cross chronset boundaries; for example, a task might be there because in another chronset, something bad will happen.

The second kind is more problematic. Times of occurrence are not asserted, but constrained. As constraints accumulate, they become more precisely known, just as in McDermott (1980). How to erase such constraints is still an open problem in the spatial domain, and may also be a problem in the temporal domain.

Consider how this data-dependency system would solve the "Little Nell" problem I started with. Once the system (Dudley) has reasoned out the causal sequence involving the train and Nell, and sees that a bad event is going to happen, it looks for a plan to prevent it. Assuming it finds a candidate, it sets up an alternative chronset in which this plan is successfully executed. (See Figure 5.) It does an analysis of feasibility, and decides that this chronset probably corresponds to reality more closely than the one it started with. However, the data dependency supporting the assertion that "Move Nell"

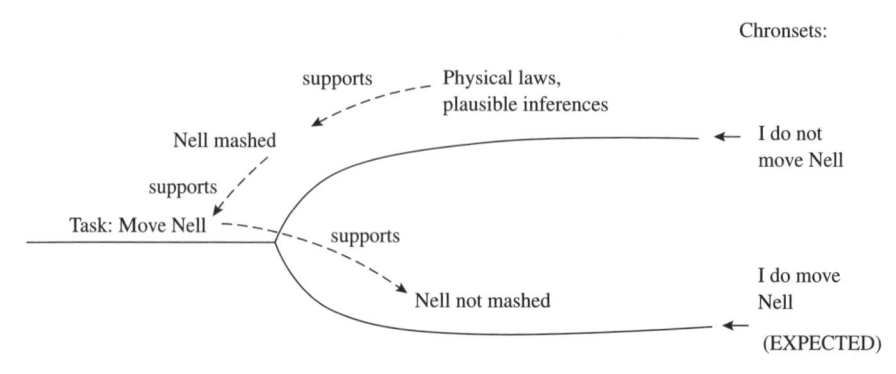

FIG. 5   Tree of Chronsets for the Dudley-Nell Problem.

is a task specifies the occurrence of "Nell is mashed" in the other, original chronset as the justification of the task. It is irrelevant that this chronset is not expected to be realized.

It *is* relevant that in the alternative chronset, she gets mashed. This assertion will be supported by a record of the causal argument (involving the persistence of being tied up, the train schedule, and so on) that led to Dudley's alarm in the first place. If this argument is upset, say by a new assertion that Dick Daring is planning to free Nell in two minutes (thus terminating a crucial persistence), then it is no longer true, even in the alternative chronicle, that Nell is in danger, and the assertion "I have the task of moving Nell" will disappear from Dudley's data base.

As another illustration, let me sketch how this system would handle one straightforward kind of inference—system simulation. This kind of inference is the result of applying ecause and pcause rules to see how a system will behave. That is, starting in some state, we use these rules to predict future states, then start from there to predict more states, and so forth. Each application of a rule creates a new frob, corresponding to the caused effect. This frob will represent a persistence or event. It is also a frame of reference for further simulation; its effects will be frobs fuzzily located in its frame, and so on. Figure 6 shows how each occurrence is located more or less fuzzily, at some offset in the frame of its cause. Each effect then serves as a frame for the next round. Once the structure is built, it can serve to answer queries, like "How soon after F1 will F3 occur?" This requires translating F3's fuzzy coordinates back into frame F0 for comparison. The more steps of translation, the fuzzier the coordinates get.

Just storing the coordinates does not suffice for answering questions such as "What's the first occurrence of... after F1?" This requires other sorts of indexing (McDermott, 1981c).

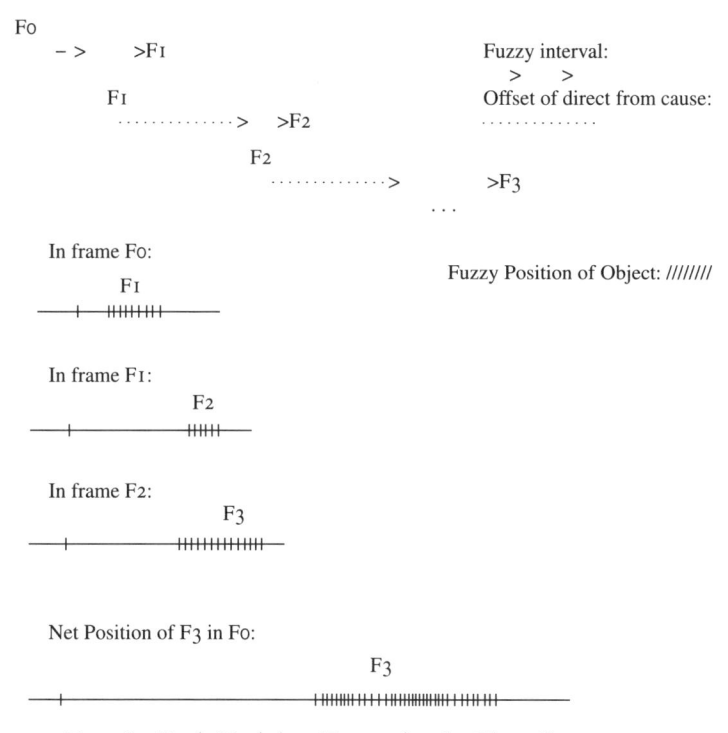

FIG. 6 Each Frob is a Frame for the Next Occurrence.

This sketch is intended only to suggest what one might do. I feel that raw simulation of this sort is actually of little value, except for simple loop-free systems. If a loop is encountered, the unwary simulator will itself go into a loop. Instead, it should be on the lookout for "loopy" patterns, such as a quantity increasing twice, and try to step back and draw more interesting conclusions. I can only point at this problem here, and not hope to solve it.[9]

7 CONCLUSIONS

I set out to develop a temporal logic which captured the openness and continuity of time. To this end, the basic ontology had to include states arranged into a branching set of continua, the "chronicle tree." Doing this enabled us to state facts about causes and effects, continuous change, and plans. In many cases, we could make useful deductions about the course of events. Here is a list of some of the situations considered:

- Causal sequences, including infinite loops
- Continuous change up to some threshold
- Actions taken to prevent the operation of causal systems
- Conflicts among actions done in the wrong order (cf. Sacerdoti, 1977)
- Changes in one's plans forced (or not forced) by changing circumstances

I look at some of these systems more formally than others, for which I emphasized implementational considerations.

I have found that logic and implementation fertilize each other. One often has a vague notion of what one wants a program to do, plus a pile of special cases that don't fit together too well. Sometimes one goes ahead and implements the special cases. I urge consideration of the alternative: temporarily to ignore hard-nosed programming issues, and try to achieve an elegant synthesis of the special cases in the logical domain. If you fail, it is likely that the logical bugs holding you up would have caused the program to exhibit bizarre behavior anyway. If you succeed, the results can often be transferred back to the programming domain. The ontology of the logic will be reflected in the data structures of the program (as chronicles gave rise to chronsets); the commonly encountered proofs will give rise to inference algorithms, and records of them become data dependencies, which help to make the program robust and less opaque. Of course, the program will fail to make inferences the logic allows (and hence, via non-monotonicity, jump to conclusions the logic forbids), but humans have these limitations too.

REFERENCES

Allen, J. (1981). *Maintaining Knowledge about Temporal Intervals* (Technical Report TR86). University of Rochester, Department of Computer Science.

Charniak, E. (1976). *A framed PAINTING: the representation of a common sense knowledge fragment*. Working Paper 28, Fondazione Dalle Molle.

——(1981). 'A common representation for problem-solving and language-comprehension information', *Artificial Intelligence* 16 (3), 225–55.

---

[9] I have implemented a preliminary version of a program for reasoning about simple mechanisms, including some with loops, and will report on it in a later paper.

Davidson, D. (1967). 'The Logical Form of Action Sentences', in N. Rescher (ed.), *The Logic of Decision and Action*. Pittsburgh: Univrsity of Pittsburgh Press, 81–95.

Davis, E. (1981). *Organizing Spatial Knowledge* (Technical Report 193). Yale University, Computer Science Department.

Doyle, J. (1979). *A Truth Maintenance System* (Memo 521). MIT AI Laboratory.

—— (1980). *A Model for Deliberation, Action, and Introspection* (TR 581). MIT AI Laboratory.

Ernst, G. W. and Newell, A. (1969). *GPS: A Case Study in Generality and Problem Solving*. New York: Academic Press.

Fikes, R. and Nilsson, N. J. (1971). 'STRIPS: A new approach to the application of theorem proving to problem solving', *Artificial Intelligence* 2: 189–208.

Goodman, N. (1947). 'The problem of counterfactual conditionals', *Journal of Philosophy* 44: 113–28.

Hayes, P. (1979a). *The Naive Physics Manifesto*. Unpublished.

—— (1979b). *Ontology for Liquids*. Unpublished.

Hendrix, G. (1973). 'Modeling simultaneous actions and continuous processes', *Artificial Intelligence* 4: 145–80.

Hewitt, C. (1972). *Description and Theoretical Analysis (using Schemata) of PLANNER: a Language for Proving Theorems and Manipulating Models in a Robot* (Technical Report 258). MIT, AI Laboratory.

Johnson-Laird, P. N. (1980). 'Mental models in cognitive science', *Cognitive Science* 4 (1): 71–115.

Lewis, D. K. (1973). *Counterfactuals*. Oxford: Basil Blackwell.

McCarthy, J. 'Programs with Common Sense'. In Minsky (ed.), 1968: 403–18.

—— (1980). 'Circumscription: a non-monotonic inference rule', *Artificial Intelligence* 13 (1, 2).

McDermott, D. V. (1977). *Flexibility and Efficiency in a Computer Program for Designing Circuits* (Technical Report 402). MIT, AI Laboratory.

—— (1978a). 'Tarskian semantics or, no notation without denotation!', *Cognitive Science* 2 (3).

—— (1978b). 'Planning and acting', *Cognitive Science* 2 (2), 71–109.

—— (1980). *Spatial Inferences with Ground, Metric Formulas on Simple Objects* (Technical Report 173). Yale University, Computer Science Department.

—— (1981a). 'Non-monotonic logic II: non-monotonic modal theories'. *Journal of ACM*, 1981. (Also Yale CS TR 174.)

—— (1981b). *Contexts and Data Dependencies: a Synthesis*. Submitted to *IEEE Transactions on Pattern Analysis and Machine Intelligence*, 1981.

—— (1981c). *Finding Objects with given Spatial Properties*. (Technical Report 195.) Yale University, Computer Science Department.

—— and Davis, E. (1981). 'Planning and executing routes through uncertain territory'. Submitted to *Artificial Intelligence* 1981.

—— and Doyle, J. (1980). 'Non-monotonic logic I', *Artificial Intelligence* 13 (1, 2) 41–72.

Mendelson, E. (1964). *Introduction to Mathematical Logic*. New York, NY: Van Nostrand.

Milne, R. and Strachey, C. (1976). *A Theory of Programming Language Semantics*. New York, NY: Halsted Press.

Minsky, M. (ed.). (1968). *Semantic Information Processing*. Cambridge, MA: MIT Press.

Montague, R. (1960). 'On the nature of certain philosophical entities', *The Monist* 53: 159–94. (Also in Montague, 1974.)

—— (1974). In R. Thomason, (ed.), *Formal Philosophy*. New Haven, CT: Yale University Press, 148–86.

Moore, R. (1980). *Reasoning about Knowledge and Action* (Technical Report 191). SRI AI Center.

Prior, A. (1967). *Past, Present, and Future*. Oxford: Oxford University Press.

Reiter, R. (1980). 'A logic for default reasoning', *Artificial Intelligence* 13 (1, 2): 81–132.

Rescher, N. (1967). *The Logic of Decision and Action*. Pittsburgh, PA: Pittsburgh University Press.

—— and Urquhart, A. (1971). *Temporal Logic*. New York: Springer-Verlag.

Rieger, C. (1975). 'The commonsense algorithm as a basis for computer models of human memory, inference, belief and contextual language comprehension', *Proceedings of the Theoretical Issues in Natural Language Processing Workshop*. Boston, MA, 180–95.

——(1976). 'An organization of knowledge for problem solving and language comprehension', *Artificial Intelligence* 7: 89–127.

Sacerdoti, E. (1977). *A Structure for Plans and Behavior*. American Elsevier Publishing Company.

Schank, R. C. (1975). *Conceptual Information Processing*. American Elsevier Publishing Company.

——and Abelson, R. P. (1977). *Scripts, Plans, Goals, and Understanding*. Hillsdale, NJ: Lawrence Erlbaum Associates.

Shortliffe, E. H. (1976). *Computer-Based Medical Consultations—MYCIN*. American Elsevier Publishing Company.

Sussman, G. J. (1975). *A Computer Model of Skill Acquisition*. American Elsevier Publishing Company.

——and McDermott, D. V. (1972). 'From planning to conniving—a genetic approach', in *Proceedings of FJCC 41*, 1171. IFIPS.

Wilensky, R. (1980). *Metaplanning*. (Memo UCB/ERL M80/33). Berkeley Department of Computer Science.

10

A Logic-based Calculus of Events

ROBERT KOWALSKI and MAREK SERGOT

1 INTRODUCTION

Formal Logic can be used to represent knowledge of many kinds for many purposes. It can be used to formalize programs, program specifications, databases, legislation, and natural language in general. For many such applications of logic a representation of time is necessary.

Although there have been several attempts to formalize the notion of time in classical first-order logic, it is still widely believed that classical logic is not adequate for the representation of time and that some form of non-classical Temporal Logic is needed. In this paper, we shall outline a treatment of time, based on the notion of event, formalized in the Horn clause subset of classical logic augmented with negation as failure. The resulting formalization is executable as a logic program.

We use the term "event calculus" to relate it to the well-known "situation calculus" (McCarthy and Hayes 1969). The main difference between the two is conceptual: the situation calculus deals with global states whereas the event calculus deals with local events and time periods. Like the event calculus, the situation calculus can be formalized by means of Horn clauses augmented with negation by failure (Kowalski 1979).

The main intended applications investigated in this paper are the updating of databases and narrative understanding. In order to treat both cases uniformly we have taken the view that an update consists of the addition of new knowledge to a knowledge base. The effect of explicit deletion of information in conventional databases is obtained without deletion by adding new knowledge about the end of the period of time for which the information holds.

2 A SIMPLIFIED EXAMPLE

A simple, informal example will illustrate the general idea. Consider the following narrative:

(1) Mary was hired as a lecturer on 10 May 1970.
(2) John left as lecturer on 1 June 1975.
(3) Mary left as professor on 1 October 1980.
(4) Mary was promoted from lecturer to professor on 1 June 1975.

Each sentence in the narrative can be considered as an update which adds new knowledge, starting from an initially empty knowledge base. In the spirit of many natural language processing systems, the meaning of the new knowledge can be formulated in terms of event descriptions. Formulated in event description terms, the sequence of updates becomes:

(1) E1 is an event in which
Mary is hired as lecturer.
E1 has time 10 May 1970.

(2) E2 is an event in which
John leaves as lecturer.
E2 has time 1 June 1975.

(3) E3 is an event in which
Mary leaves as professor.
E3 has time 1 October 1980.

(4) E4 is an event in which
Mary is promoted from lecturer to professor.
E4 has time 1 June 1975.

A typical event causes the start of several (zero or more) periods of time and the end of several others. For example:

An event e of hiring x as y
starts a period of time
for which x has rank y.

This can be formulated as a Horn clause

x has rank y for period after(e)
       if e is an event in which x is hired as y.

Here the term after(e) names the time period as a function of e. The start of after(e) can be defined by a conditionless Horn clause:

The start of after(e) is e.

The end of after(e) is undefined but might be determined by means of additional information later. Similar Horn clauses can be used to express that

an event e of x leaving as y
ends a period of time
for which x has rank y;

an event e of promoting x from y to z
ends a period of time
for which x has rank y and
starts a period of time
for which x has rank z.

By means of these rules it is possible to conclude **after update (1)** that

Mary has rank lecturer for period after(E1)
which starts 10 May 1970.

This can be represented pictorially as shown in Figure 1.

Similarly **after updates (2), (3)**, and **(4)**, it is possible to make the conclusions shown in pictorial terms in Figures 2–4 respectively.

A Logic-based Calculus of Events

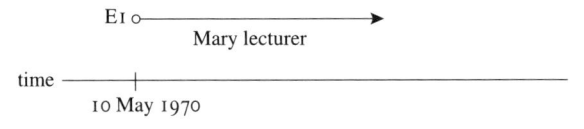

FIG. 1   After update (1).

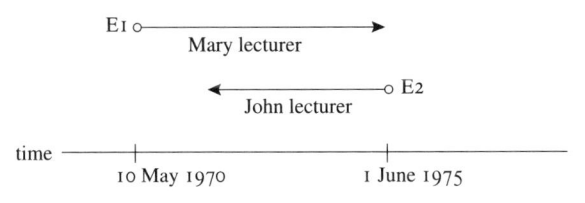

FIG. 2   After update (2).

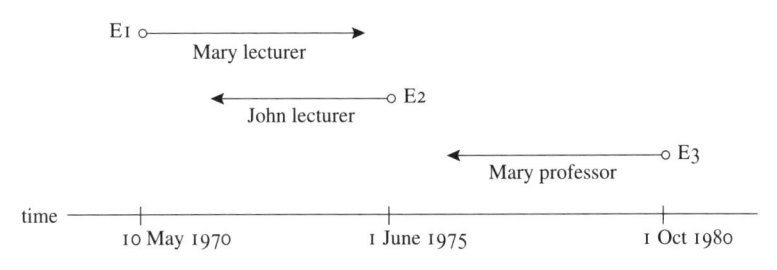

FIG. 3   After update (3).

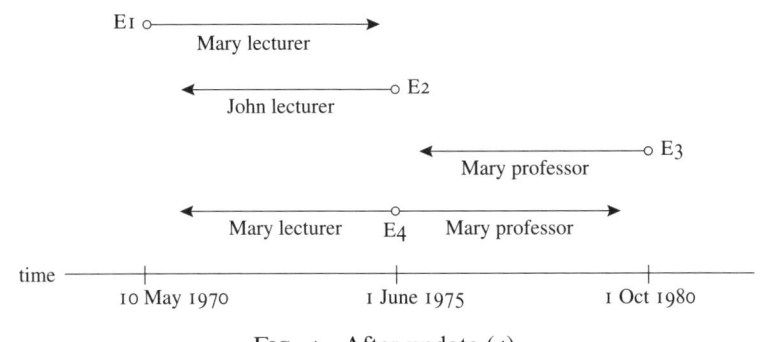

FIG. 4   After update (4).

After update (4) it would be natural to conclude that the event E4 of Mary's promotion ends her previous period after(E1) of lectureship and starts her previously identified, future period before(E3) of professorship. This can be pictured as Figure 5:

The conclusions illustrated in Figure 5 can be justified if we can prove the equalities:

after(E1) = before(E4)
after(E4) = before(E3).

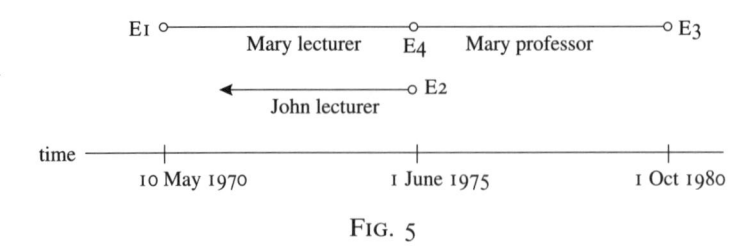

```
 E1 o─────────────────o─────────────────────o E3
         Mary lecturer    E4    Mary professor
              ←──────────────o E2
                John lecturer

time ────┼──────────────────┼──────────────────────┼────
      10 May 1970        1 June 1975           1 Oct 1980
```

FIG. 5

Together with the rules of equality and the fact that E4 ends before(E4) and starts after(E4), these equalities imply that

E4 ends after(E1) and
E4 starts before(E3).

The two equalities can be derived by means of a rule which expresses that

two periods of time are identical
    if   the same individual holds the same rank for both periods,
    and one period starts before the other ends,
    and it cannot be shown that an event has occurred, which affects the individual's rank, after the start of the first period and before the end of the second.

This rule uses default reasoning in the expression "cannot be shown", which can be formalized by negation as failure. Such default reasoning is "non-monotonic" in the sense that conclusions derived with its assistance are automatically withdrawn if contradictory new information is later made available. This might happen in the present example if it were discovered, for instance, that Mary left temporarily in January 1978 and was rehired in October 1979.

Mary's rank at a time instant t can be determined by finding a period of time containing t and determining her rank during that period. This too can be expressed as a Horn clause

x has rank y at time t
    if   x has rank y for period p
    and t in p.

Thus after assimilating our example narrative it should be possible to conclude that

Mary has rank lecturer on 11 May 1970 and
Mary has rank professor on 16 Feb. 1978.

Whether it should also be possible, however, to conclude that

John has rank lecturer on 30 May 1975,

for example, is more problematic. We shall deal with these and related problems later.

The simple example narrative already illustrates several general characteristics of the event calculus approach.

(1) Updates are **additive** in that they **add** but do **not delete** information about events. That a relationship no longer holds is represented by adding information which implies the end of the time period for which the relationship holds rather than by deleting the relationship. This is consistent with our use of classical logic without explicit destructive assignment.

(2) Conventional database systems, in contrast, allow arbitrary additions and deletions of relationships, qualified only by the requirement that integrity constraints be preserved. It might be permissible, for example, to replace the relationship "John has rank lecturer" by the relationship "Mary has rank professor" whether or not this corresponds to any meaningful real world event. The derivation of starts and ends of relationships from event descriptions imposes an extra level of semantic structure on database updates.

(3) Past and future are treated symmetrically. Therefore event descriptions can be assimilated in any order, independently of the order in which the events themselves actually take place. This facilitates dealing with incomplete information, both with new knowledge about the past as well as with hypothetical possibilities for the future. In the example, this is illustrated by the second update which records John's leaving without there being any previous record of his employment.

In a conventional database system the only way to express

"if a person leaves then he must already be employed"

is to formulate an integrity constraint which would reject as inconsistent any update which records an event of leaving without there already being an appropriate record of employment in the database. But such an integrity constraint combines (and confuses) two different kinds of statement: an object-level statement (about the world), that leaving implies a preceding period of employment, with a metalevel statement (about the database) that the database contains a complete record of relevant information about the past. In this paper we ignore problems concerned with the treatment of integrity constraints and preconditions of events.

(4) In the example narrative, a numerical time is associated with every event. In the general case this is not essential; rather it is the relative ordering of events which is important. Knowing the time at which events take place, of course, allows us to define an ordering relation "<" on events in a particularly simple way:

$e < e'$ if   Time(e t) and Time(e' t')
        and t is (chronologically) earlier than t'

In other cases, the event ordering relation can be defined explicitly, without reference to time. Indeed, in many cases it may not be possible to associate explicit times with events at all. For example, the meaning of the sentence

"John went to the theatre
after he came home from work."

can be represented by the event descriptions:

E1 is an event in which
John goes from work to home;
E2 is an event in which
John goes from home to the theatre;

together with a relative ordering of the two events

$E1 < E2$.

In the sequel we shall use the symbol "<" to signify both the ordering relation for events and the chronological (or other) ordering relation on times, and let context disambiguate between the two.

(5) The distinction between events, time periods and time instants makes it possible to deal with concurrent events. In our simple narrative we have such an example. The two events E2 and E4 are distinct even though they take place simultaneously.

(6) Although all the events considered in this paper can be treated as taking place instantaneously, we want to leave open the possibility that events can also have duration. For this reason we do not want time periods to contain wholly the events which start or end them. This is not quite the same as treating time periods as open intervals. Consider for example, an event of moving a block x from place y to place z, which consists in turn of five subevents: grasping, lifting, transporting, lowering, and ungrasping the block. The period for which x is at y ends when x is lifted and the period for which x is at z starts when x is lowered. The relationship between the event and time periods which we previously pictured (Figure 6)

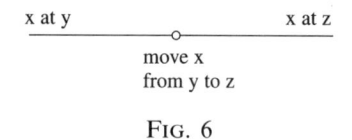

x at y   x at z

move x
from y to z

Fig. 6

can now be pictured (Figure 7).

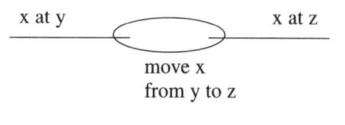

x at y   x at z

move x
from y to z

Fig. 7

To cater for this possibility it suffices to adopt the convention that events occur "after" the periods they end, "before" those they start, and are not wholly contained within them.

(7) Our formalization of events is intended as a formal analysis of the concepts rather than as a program or even as a program specification. Nonetheless, because it can be expressed by means of Horn clauses augmented with negation by failure, it is an executable analysis which in certain circumstances, after appropriate equivalence preserving transformations, runs as a PROLOG program.

(8) The most established alternative treatment of states and actions in classical, first-order logic is the situation calculus (McCarthy and Hayes 1969). Time varying relationships are qualified by a situation parameter, which can be regarded as a global, instantaneous time slice. Events transform one global situation into another.

Because situations are global, it is not possible to deal with simultaneous and partially ordered events. In the usual formalizations, it is difficult also to deal with incomplete information about a situation, and therefore to assimilate new information about the past.

The situation calculus, like the calculus of events, can be formalized by means of Horn clauses augmented with negation as failure (Kowalski 1979) and therefore can be executed as a PROLOG program. However, execution of the situation calculus gives rise to the **frame problem**, the need to reason that a relationship which holds in a situation and is not affected by an event continues to hold in the following situation. This explicit deduction, which is a consequence of the use of global situations, is so computationally inefficient as to be intolerable.

The event calculus was developed, to a large extent, in order to avoid the frame problem. It does so by qualifying relationships with time periods instead of with global situations. Time periods associated with different relationships have different names even if they have the same duration.

(9) There is a vast, related literature (see Bolour et al. 1982) concerned with the formalization of time. Our presentation of the event calculus is similar to those treatments of time which are based on the use of time periods rather than on time instants. Among these, the approach of Allen (1981, 1984) is closest, not only because of its use of time periods, but more importantly because of its emphasis on events and the time periods they start and end. (Since writing this paper, we have discovered the still more closely related work of Lee, Coelho and Cotta (1985), which is also formulated within a logic programming framework.)

We have avoided the use of non-classical logic for two reasons: to obtain greater expressive power, and to exploit the proof procedures which have been developed for classical first-order logic in general and for logic programming in particular. Expressive power is gained by treating time and events explicitly rather than implicitly through the use of natural, but weak modal operators for notions such as "future", "since", and "while". We have potentially sacrificed the greater conciseness of modal logic for the greater expressiveness of an explicit treatment of time and events.

3 THE PROMOTION EXAMPLE IN DETAIL

Before considering the general case, we shall investigate the promotion example in greater detail.

The sequence of updates starting from the initially empty knowledge base can be represented by assertions:

    Hire   (Mary lecturer E1)
    Time   (E1 10.May. 1970)
    Leave   (John lecturer E2)
    Time   (E2 1.June. 1975)
    Leave   (Mary professor E3)
    Time   (E3 1.Oct. 1980)
    Promote (Mary lecturer professor E4)
    Time   (E4 1.June. 1975)

The relationships which start or end as the result of events are defined by general rules:

    Rank (x y after(e))   if Hire(x y e)   P1
    Rank(x y before(e))   if Leave(x y e)   P2
    Rank(x y before(e))   if Promote(x y z e)   P3
    Rank(x z after(e))   if Promote(x y z e)   P4

    Start(after(e) e)   P5
    End(before(e) e)   P6

Notice that we have assumed for the time being that event descriptions are complete. In many cases incomplete event descriptions, such as

    E2 is an event
    in which John leaves,
    E4 is an event
    in which Mary is promoted to professor,

would be more natural. The advantage of complete event descriptions for the present is that they allow us to derive both started and ended relationships from the event descriptions alone. We shall deal with incomplete event descriptions later.

In order to conclude that

End(after(E1) E4)
End(after(E4) E3)
Start(before(E4) E1)
Start(before(E3) E4)

we need additional rules

End(after(e) e')   if after(e) = before(e')   P7
Start(before(e') e) if after(e) = before(e').   P8

To derive that

after(E1) = before(E4)
after(E4) = before(E3)

we use the general rule

after(e) = before(e') if   Rank(x y after(e))   Temp1
                        and Rank(x y before(e'))
                        and e < e'
                        and not after(e) ≪ before(e')

where

p1 ≪ p2

expresses that periods p1 and p2 are **disjoint**, with the end of p1 occurring before the start of p2.

In fact, this rule (and several of the earlier rules) will be generalized later in Section 10 to separate general axioms about events and time from those which are application specific. We shall introduce an axiom which expresses a general property of periods in the event calculus:

any two periods associated with the same relationship
are either identical, or they are disjoint.

(Note that Allen uses the same axiom.) Remembering that periods do not contain their end points, we can formalize the notion of disjoint periods as follows:

p1 ≪ p2 if End(p1 e) and Start(p2 e') and e ≤ e'   Temp2

Pictorially, the definition is illustrated in Figure 8.

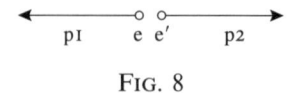

$$\begin{array}{ccc} \longleftarrow & \circ\ \circ & \longrightarrow \\ p1 & e\ e' & p2 \end{array}$$

FIG. 8

Here e ≤ e' means that e occurs before or at the same time as e'.

Note that we allow the case where an event ends and starts the same relationship. For example the event of Mary's taking a sabbatical can be regarded as ending one period of lectureship and starting another.

The negative condition in Temp1 can be interpreted either classically or by means of negation by failure. Interpreting it by negation as failure has the consequence that time periods are assumed to be equal by default, if they cannot be shown to be different.

4 EXECUTION OF THE PROMOTION EXAMPLE

Clauses P1-8 and Temp1–2 are in a form which can be executed as a PROLOG program. Unfortunately, when executed by PROLOG, the program goes into an infinite, non-terminating loop. Suppose for example that we have just the two event descriptions

Hire(Mary lecturer E1)
Promote(Mary lecturer professor E4)
$E1 < E4$

and pose the query

End(after(E1) x) ?   Q1

using P1-8, Temp1-2 and an appropriate definition of $\leq$. The first three conditions of clause Temp1 are solved without difficulty, leaving the query

not after(E1) $\ll$ before(E4) ?   Q2

To show this succeeds we must show that the query

after(E1) $\ll$ before(E4) ?   Q3

fails. There is only one clause we can use, Temp2, and so we must show that the query

End(after(E1) e″) and Start(before(E4) e*) and e″ $\leq$ e* ?   Q4

fails. PROLOG tries to solve the first condition first. But this is just like the original query, and PROLOG goes into a non-terminating loop.

It is possible to eliminate the loop, either by employing a more intelligent problem-solver than PROLOG or by using program transformation techniques. Before presenting a loop-free variant of the "program", however, we have a more serious problem to consider.

5 INCOMPLETENESS AND INCORRECTNESS OF START AND END

Negation by failure is a form of the **closed world assumption**, that the "knowledge base" is complete:

not p is judged to hold if all ways of showing p fail.

If the characterization of p is incomplete then not p may be judged to hold even though it does not. Unfortunately, our characterization of the "Start" and "End" predicates is incomplete. Consequently negation by failure can give incorrect results, allowing us to conclude that two time periods are equal when they are not.

Suppose, for example, that we are given the two event descriptions

Hire(Jack professor J1)
Hire(Jack professor J2)
$J1 < J2$

and nothing more (Figure 9).

```
J1 o————————▶
    Jack professor

            J2 o————————▶
                Jack professor
```

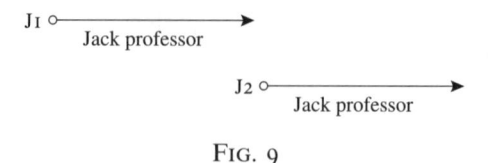

FIG. 9

Clearly some event, as yet unreported, must have occurred somewhere between J1 and J2 to end Jack's first period of professorship. Our existing rules could never find such an end for after(J1). Even if they did not loop, they would only be able to find ends which correspond to named, reported events. The rules we have for "End" are incomplete therefore; by symmetry, so are the ones for "Start".

The rule Temp1, by which we conclude that two periods are equal, relies on the completeness of the program for "$\ll$". The program for "$\ll$", Temp2, relies in turn on the completeness of "Start" and "End". This means that Temp1 may lead us to conclude that two periods are equal, when in fact we should not.

Suppose, for example, we add to the event descriptions above the information that

Leave(Jack professor J3)
J2 < J3.

Pictorially, we have the situation shown in Figure 10.

```
J1 o————————▶
    Jack professor

         J2 o————————▶
             Jack professor

                 ◀————————o J3
                  Jack professor
```

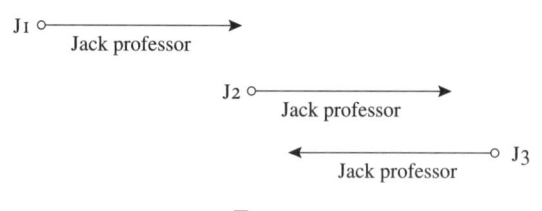

FIG. 10

Even if we eliminated loops, our existing rules could not find an end to after(J1), as argued above. Therefore, we could not show that periods after (J1) and before(J3) are disjoint, and so Temp1 would conclude they are equal. Clearly they are not.

The obvious solution is to complete the definition of the "End" and "Start" predicates. In this example we need rules which allow us to conclude that there exists some end j of after(J1), such that J1 < j ≤ J2 (Figure 11).

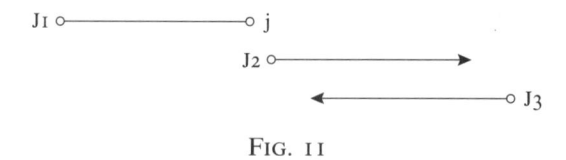

```
J1 o————————o j
      J2 o————————▶
             ◀————————o J3
```

FIG. 11

In fact, as we shall see later, we need similar rules to conclude the existence of ends and starts of time periods in many other cases. In the meanwhile, however, we remark that the problems of incorrectness and looping can both be solved without having first to solve the problem of incompleteness.

If the predicate "$\ll$" is not required for any other purpose, we can solve the problem by finding an alternative program for "$\ll$", which does not rely on the completeness of "Start" and "End". With such a program, the rules we have for "Start" and "End" would still be incomplete but now they would be correct.

A Logic-based Calculus of Events 227

Fortunately, there is such a program. It can be shown that, whenever

Rank(x y after(e))
Rank(x y before(e'))
e < e'

all hold, the condition

after(e) ≪ before(e')

can be replaced by

[Rank(x y' after(e*)) or Rank(x y' before(e*))] and e < e* < e'.

In other words the two time periods are disjoint if (and only if) some other event e* which affects the relationship takes place in between the start of one period and the end of the other.

Notice that the use of the variable y' instead of y implicitly incorporates the "integrity constraint" that no person can hold more than one rank at the same time. We shall deal with such "incompatible" relationships in greater detail later when we deal with the general case.

With this result, we can dispense with the explicit definition of " ≪ ", and write instead

after(e) = before(e') if   Rank(x y after(e))   P9
                            and Rank(x y before(e'))
                            and e < e'
                            and not ([Rank(x y' after(e*)) or
                                         Rank(x y' before(e*))]
                                         and e < e* < e').

This is equivalent to

after(e) = before(e') if   Rank(x y after(e))
                            and Rank(x y before(e'))
                            and e < e'
                            and not[Rank(x y' after(e*)) and e < e* and e* < e']
                            and not[Rank(x y' before(e*)) and e < e* and e* < e'].

This alternative to Temp 1-2 solves both the problem of looping and the problem of incorrectness.

Notice that rule P9 does not cover the case where the events e and e' are too far apart in time for x to have rank y continuously from e to e'. To deal with this case we would need to add another condition to P9, such as

not Too-far-apart(e e')

and define it appropriately.

6   TIME INSTANTS

Using P1-9 PROLOG can be used to determine the time periods for which relationships hold. To determine that a relationship holds at a time instant, however, we need additional rules such as

RankAt(x y t) if   Rank(x y p)   P10
                    and t in p

t in p if   Start(p e1) and End(p e2)   P11
        and Time(e1 t1) and Time(e2 t2)
        and t1 < t and t < t2.

Given the rules P1-11, an appropriate definition of < for time instants, and the description of events E1-E4 in our simple narrative, we can conclude using PROLOG that, for example,

RankAt(Mary lecturer 11.May. 1970)
RankAt(Mary professor 16.Feb.1978).

The rules work for time periods which have a determined start and end. They do not work for periods which have no start or end, or for periods whose starts or ends are implied by other information but are not explicitly determined. These cases can be dealt with in a variety of ways and we shall return to them when we come to consider the general case.

7   A SPECIAL CASE OF THE PROMOTION EXAMPLE

The event calculus approach, the main features of which have been outlined above, may appear more complicated than necessary by comparison with conventional approaches to the treatment of database updates. This is partly because conventional databases deal with a **special case**: events are assimilated in the order in which they take place and the database is assumed to contain a complete record of all relevant past events. It is instructive, therefore, to see what simplifications can be made in the event calculus when we restrict ourselves to the same special case.

One of the most important simplifications is that P1-9 now constitute a complete definition of the troublesome "Start" and "End" predicates. This is because all relationships are first derived in the form

Rank(x y after(e))

before they are (redundantly) re-derived in the form

Rank(x y before(e)).

The existing definitions of "Start" and "End" cover this case. Moreover, as a further simplification, we can avoid the redundancy of deriving the same relationship twice, by restricting attention to the derivation of predicates of the form

Rank(x y after(e))
Start(after(e) e)
End(after(e) e')

which are needed to characterize time periods of the form after(e). Clauses P1-9 can be replaced for these purposes by the clauses

Rank(x y after(e)) if Hire(x y e)   P1
Rank(x z after(e)) if Promote(x y z e)   P4
Start(after(e) e)   P5
End(after(e) e') if   Rank(x y after(e)) and Leave(x y e')   P2'
               and e < e'
               and not [Rank(x y' after(e*)) and e < e* < e']

End(after(e) e') if   Rank(x y after(e)) and Promote(x y z e') P3'
         and e < e'
         and not [Rank(x y' after(e*)) and e < e* < e']

This is a significant simplification over P1-9.

The rules P10 and P11 express that a relationship holds at a particular time instant if it holds after the start of the relationship and before its end. It is appropriate in this special case to assume in addition that a relationship holds after it has started, provided it has not already ended:

   t in p if   Start(p e)   P12
         and Time(e t')
         and t' < t
         and not End(p e')

Here, because the definition of "End" is complete for this special case, the negative condition in P12 does not lead to incorrect results, as it might in the more general case. (These rules are similar to those of Lee, Coelho, and Cotta (1985) who also use negation by failure, but restrict themselves to this special case.)

8   INCOMPLETE EVENT DESCRIPTIONS

For the purpose of simplicity we have assumed that event descriptions are sufficiently complete to derive, directly from the event description alone, the relationships which are started and ended by the event. In many cases, however, **incomplete** event descriptions such as

   E2 is an event in which John leaves,

where there is insufficient information to determine directly what John's rank was when he left, are more natural.

The analysis of natural language by means of semantic networks and semantic cases suggests a way of dealing with such incomplete event descriptions. An event such as

   "John gave the book to Mary",

for example, can be represented as a network (Figure 12)

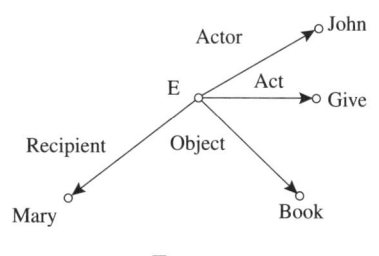

FIG. 12

which can be formalized in turn by using constant symbols to represent nodes and binary predicates to represent arcs:

Actor(E John)
Act(E Give)

Object(E Book)
Recipient(E Mary).

Missing information can be dealt with by representing only the information which is known and ignoring that which is unknown. For example, to represent that Mary was promoted on 1 June 1975:

Act(E4 Promote)
Object(E4 Mary)
Time(E4 1.June.1975).

The advantages of using semantic networks to describe events and of representing such networks in formal logic have been discussed by several authors. The discussion in Kowalski (1979) is especially relevant here.

The clauses P1-4 which presently require complete event descriptions can be modified so that they use the minimum number of conditions needed to establish the conclusion. P1-4 can then be replaced by

Rank(x y after(e)) if	Act(e hire)	P1'
	and Object(e x)	
	and Destination(e y)	
Rank(x y before(e)) if	Act(e leave)	P2'
	and Object(e x)	
	and Source(e y)	
Rank(x y before(e)) if	Act(e promote)	P3'
	and Object(e x)	
	and Source(e y)	
Rank(x y after(e)) if	Act(e promote)	P4'
	and Object(e x)	
	and Destination(e y)	

Thus, for example, P4' does not require the condition

Source(e z)

which identifies the "object's" rank immediately before promotion. The remaining clauses are not affected by this reformulation.

Notice that the new formulation is still symmetric with respect to past and future. However, whereas a complete event description allows us to deduce all possible relationships which are started or ended by an event, an incomplete description might not contain sufficient information to allow such deductions. Nonetheless, it may be possible to complete such an event description by default reasoning.

Suppose, for example, that we are given complete descriptions of the events E1, E2, and E3 as before and then an incomplete description of E4:

Act(E4 promote)
Object(E4 Mary)
Time(E4 1.June.1975).

Pictorially the situation is shown in Figure 13.

The information about E4 is insufficient to allow the derivation of the conclusion

Rank(Mary lecturer before(E4))

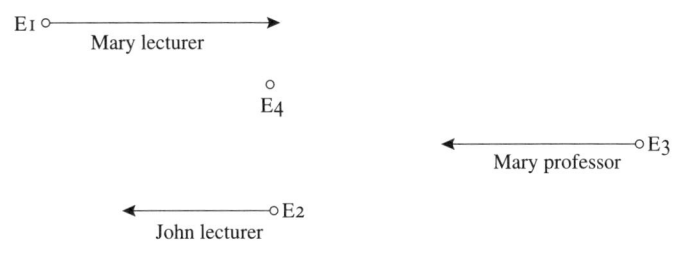

FIG. 13

by means of P3′ and therefore of the further conclusion

End(after(E1) E4).

We can derive these conclusions, however, if we can find a means of completing the event description by deducing

Source(E4 lecturer).

We can do so by adding extra information about promotions: in every event of promotion there must be a "source", even though it may be unknown.

This extra information allows us to deduce that, in event E4, Mary must have been promoted from some rank, and therefore that Mary holds some (unknown) rank throughout the period before(E4). Pictorially we have the situation in Figure 14.

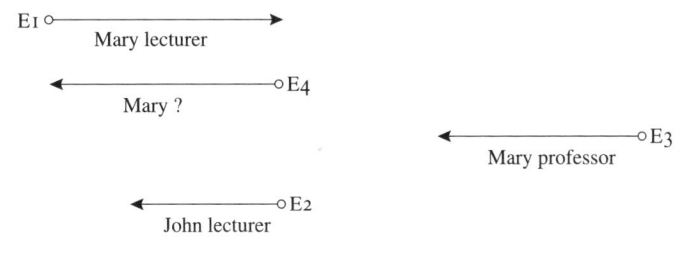

FIG. 14

Mary's ranks during periods after(E1) and before(E4) may be different, or they may be the same.

It is a natural extension of our previous use of default reasoning to assume now that

two ranks are identical
if we cannot show they are different.

This argument justifies adding the extra rule:

Source(e y) if   Act(e promote)
           and Object(e x)
           and Rank(x y after(e′))
           and e′ < e
           and not ([Rank(x y′ after(e*)) or
                   Rank(x y′ before(e*))]
                and e′ < e* < e)

which uses the negative condition to reason by default.

Similarly we can use the additional information that every event of promotion has a "destination" (persons are promoted to **some** rank) to justify the extra rule:

Destination(e y) if   Act(e promote)
          and Object(e x)
          and Rank(x y before(e'))
          and e<e'
          and not ([Rank(x y' after(e*)) or
                     Rank(x y' before(e*))]
          and e<e*<e').

This allows us to deduce

Destination(E4 professor)
Start(before(E3) E4)
End(after(E4) E3).

These conclusions are shown pictorially in Figure 15.

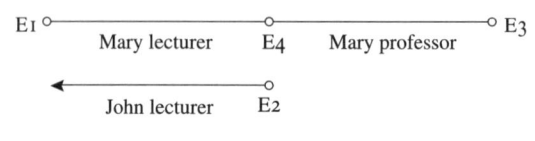

FIG. 15

As usual, conclusions based on default assumptions may be automatically withdrawn after the assimilation of new information.

9   ANOTHER EXAMPLE

Before turning to the general case, it is useful to consider an example in which an event starts and ends more than one relationship. Consider the following narrative:

John exchanged his orange for Mary's apple.
Then Mary exchanged the orange for a pear.

An act of exchanging has two actors and two objects. Suppose we call them the actor, coactor, object and coobject. We can then formalize the narrative by the clauses

Act(E1 exchange)   Act(E2 exchange)
Actor(E1 John)   Actor(E2 Mary)
Object(E1 orange)   Object(E2 orange)
Coactor(E1 Mary)   Coobject(E2 pear)
Coobject(E1 apple)   E1 < E2

Notice that since each exchange event e starts and ends two relationships we need to distinguish the two periods associated with the relationships. We can do so by using terms before(e x) and after(e x), where the second parameter x distinguishes between the two periods. One of the easiest ways of doing this is to use the name of the actor or coactor as the second parameter.

Possesses(x y before(e x)) if   Act(e exchange)   Ex1
                          and Actor(e x)
                          and Object(e y)

Possesses(x y before(e x)) if	Act(e exchange)	Ex2
	and Coactor(e x)	
	and Coobject(e y)	
Possesses(x y after(e x)) if	Act(e exchange)	Ex3
	and Coactor(e x)	
	and Object(e y)	
Possesses(x y after(e x)) if	Act(e exchange)	Ex4
	and Actor(e x)	
	and Coobject(e y)	

In the given example, these clauses allow us to derive

Possesses(John orange before(E1 John))
Possesses(Mary apple before(E1 Mary))
Possesses(John apple after(E1 John))
Possesses(Mary orange after(E1 Mary))
Possesses(Mary orange before(E2 Mary))
Possesses(Mary pear after(E2 Mary))

To derive starts and ends of time periods we need, to begin with, the clauses

Start(after(e x) e)	Ex5
End(before(e x) e).	Ex6

To conclude

after(E1 Mary) = before(E2 Mary)

and therefore that

End(after(E1 Mary) E2)
Start(before(E2 Mary) E1)

we need the clauses

after(e x) = before(e' x) if	Possesses(x y after(e x))	Ex7
	and Possesses(x y before(e' x))	
	and e < e'	
	and not([Possesses(x' y after(e* x')) or	
	Possesses(x' y before(e* x'))]	
	and e < e* < e')	
End(after(e x) e') if after(e x) = before(e' x)		Ex8
Start(before(e' x) e) if after(e x) = before(e' x)		Ex9

Here the negative condition in Ex7 also incorporates the constraint that more than one person cannot "possess" an object at one time.

10 THE GENERAL CASE

We are now in a position to generalize the preceding examples and consider the general case. For this purpose, in order to deal uniformly with events which start or end more than one relationship, it is convenient to name time periods by means of terms

after(e u) and before(e u)

where the second parameter u names the relationship associated with the time period. Moreover, instead of treating time periods as a parameter of time-varying relations, it is convenient to use a general predicate

Holds(p)

which expresses that the relationship associated with p holds for the time period p. Thus we will now write

Holds(before(E2 rank(John lecturer)))

instead of the earlier, simpler notation

Rank(John lecturer before(E2)).

Although in most cases the new notation will be more complicated than necessary, it has the advantage of greater generality. This notation is similar to one we have used elsewhere for the situation calculus. (Kowalski 1979).
Instead of writing rules such as

Holds(before(e rank(x y))) if   Act(e leave)
                            and Object(e x)
                            and Source(e y)
Holds(before(e possesses(x y))) if   Act(e exchange)
                                 and Actor(e x)
                                 and Object(e y)

similar to those we have written before, we can write a single general rule and several specific rules for different applications:

Holds(before(e u)) if Terminates(e u)   G1
Terminates(e rank(x y)) if   Act(e leave)
                         and Object(e x)
                         and Source(e y)
Terminates(e possesses(x y)) if   Act(e exchange)
                              and Actor(e x)
                              and Object(e y).

Similarly

Holds(after(e u)) if Initiates(e u)   G2
Initiates(e rank(x y)) if   Act(e hire)
                        and Object(e x)
                        and Destination(e y)
Initiates(e possesses(x y)) if   Act(e exchange)
                             and Actor(e x)
                             and Coobject(e y).

Notice, however, that to achieve such generality we have had to introduce the new predicates "Initiates" and "Terminates".
The remaining rules are very similar to those we have used for the preceding examples:

Start(after(e u) e)   G3
End(before(e u) e)   G4
Start(before(e' u) e) if after(e u) = before(e' u)   G5

End(after(e u) e')   if after(e u) = before(e' u)   G6

after(e u) = before(e' u) if   Holds(after(e u))   G7
                and Holds(before(e' u))
                and e < e'
                and not Broken(e u e')
Broken(e u e') if   Holds(after(e* u*)) and Exclusive(u u*)   G8
                and e < e* < e'
Broken(e u e') if   Holds(before(e* u*)) and Exclusive(u u*)   G9
                and e < e* < e'

Here "Broken" has been introduced largely as an abbreviation for reuse later on. It is intended that the predicate Exclusive(u u') holds when the relationships u and u' are either identical or incompatible in the sense that not both can hold simultaneously, i.e.

Exclusive(u u)
Exclusive(u u') if Incompatible(u u')

The predicate "Incompatible" needs to be defined by specific rules for particular applications. For example

Incompatible(rank(x y) rank(x y')) if not y = y'
Incompatible(possesses(x y) possesses(x' y)) if not x = x'

y = y.

(Notice that to deal with the case that e and e' are too far apart for u to hold continuously from e to e' we could add extra application-specific rules for the "Broken" predicate.)

To determine that a relationship holds at a time instant we need to modify P10:

HoldsAt(u t) if   Holds(after(e u))
              and t in after(e u)
HoldsAt(u t) if   Holds(before(e u))
              and t in before(e u).

The rule P11

t in p if   Start(p e1) and End(p e2)
        and Time(e1 t1) and Time(e2 t2)
        and t1 < t and t < t2

is adequate as it stands. As before, the rule P12

t in p if   Start(p e)
        and Time(e t')
        and not End(p e')

is appropriate and not incorrect for the special case where events are recorded in the order in which they occur and the database contains a complete record of all relevant past events (and the time between t and t' is not too long for the relationship concerned to hold continuously). However it is incorrect in the general case because our definition of the "End" (as well as "Start") predicate is incomplete. We shall attempt to remedy this defect now.

11 OTHER CASES OF THE START AND END PREDICATES

So far we have rules for the cases

Start(after(e u) e)
End(before(e u) e).

We also have rules which derive end points when time periods are identical (Figure 16):

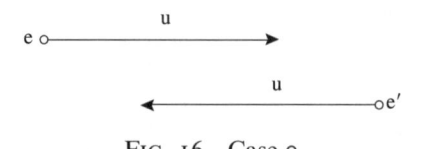

```
        u
e o─────────────▶

        u
◀─────────────o e'
```

FIG. 16   Case 0.

There are other, more difficult, cases which we shall now consider. Pictorially these are shown in Figures 17–19.
In Fig. 17 u and u' are "exclusive" in the sense defined in Section 10.

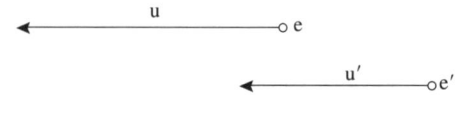

```
        u
◀─────────────o e

           u'
    ◀─────────o e'
```

FIG. 17   Case 1.

In Fig. 18 u and u' are exclusive. (This case is symmetric to case 1.)

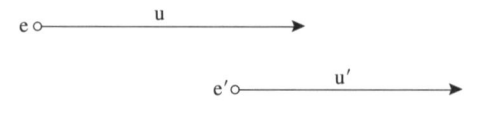

```
        u
e o─────────────▶

           u'
    e'o─────────▶
```

FIG. 18   Case 2.

In Fig. 19 u and u' are "incompatible".

```
        u
e o─────────▶

           u'
    ◀─────────o e'
```

FIG. 19   Case 3.

It can be argued that these four cases exhaust all the situations where time periods interact to imply the existence of end points. In fact, the rules for determining end points in all four cases 0–3 can be systematically derived from a small number of general principles, the most important of which are:

$p1 = p2$ or $p1 \ll p2$ or $p2 \ll p1$ if   p1 instance of u1   Ax1
                        and p2 instance of u2
                        and Exclusive(u1 u2)

not[$p1 = p2$] if   p1 instance of u1   Ax2
                and p2 instance of u2
                and Incompatible(u1 u2)

after(e u)   instance of u if Holds(after(e u))   Ax3

before(e u) instance of u if Holds(before(e u))   Ax4

x < y if Start(p x) and End(p y)   Ax5

p1 ≪ p2 if and only if   Ax6
    there exist e1 and e2 [End(p1 e1) and
        Start(p2 e2) and
        e1 ≤ e2]

Notice that we have previously made use of the "if half" of Ax6 to determine end points in case 0. To determine end points in cases 1–3 we need to use the "only if half". We will not show the derivation of the rules here, but only present the rules themselves.

In **Case 1**, there must exist a start i of before(e' u'), at or after e. Pictorially it is shown in Figure 20.

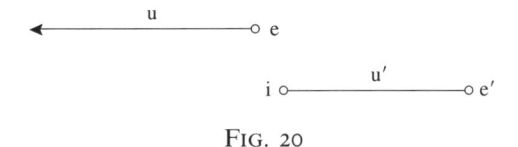

FIG. 20

The new end point can be named as a function of the time period, say init(before(e' u')), and the end point can be derived by the general rule

[Start(before(e' u') init(before(e' u')))
    and
e ≤ init(before(e' u'))]
    if   Holds(before(e u))
    and Holds(before(e' u'))
    and Exclusive(u u')
    and e < e'
    and not Broken(e u' e').

Here we have used the notation

[A and B] if C

as shorthand for the two clauses

A if C
B if C.

Case 2 is similar to case 1:

[End(after(e u) fin(after(e u)))
    and
fin(after(e u)) ≤ e']
    if   Holds(after(e u))
    and Holds(after(e' u'))
    and Exclusive(u u')
    and e < e'
    and not Broken(e u e')

Notice that an attractive consequence of the use of negation as failure is that the **implicit end point** derived by these rules disappears if new information makes it possible to derive the end point explicitly.

Case 3 is similar to cases 1 and 2 but slightly more complicated. In this case there exists an end of after(e u) at or before the start of before(e' u'). These implicit start and end points are shown pictorially in Figure 21.

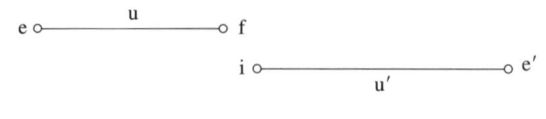

```
          u
e o―――――――――――――o f

          i o―――――――――――――o e'
                u'
```

FIG. 21

[fin(after(e u)) ≤ init(before(e' u'))
    and
Start(before(e' i') init(before(e' u'))))
    and
End(after(e u) fin(after(e u)))]
    if Holds(after(e u))
    and Holds(before(e' u'))
    and Incompatible(u u')
    and e < e'
    and not Broken(e u e')

These clauses complete the definition of the "Start" and "End" predicates.

Notice, however, that our treatment in cases 1 and 2 of both identical and incompatible relationships in the same way suggests the possibility of extending case 3 to include the case where u and u' are identical.

This would mean that in the situation (Figure 22)

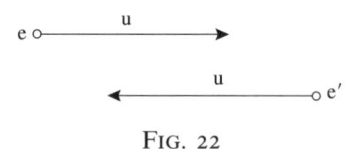

```
            u
e o―――――――――――→

              u
      ←―――――――――――o e'
```

FIG. 22

where we earlier concluded that

after(e u) = before(e' u)

we would need non-Horn clause logic to express that either the equality holds, or the period after(e u) ends before the period before(e' u) starts. Such an expression would have the form

(A or B) if C

where A and B are mutually exclusive. The approach we have taken so far, which rewrites the statement in the form

A if C and not B

and interprets negation as failure, gives disjunction an asymmetric interpretation:

prefer conclusion A to conclusion B
unless it is inconsistent to do so.

12 CONCLUSION

The event calculus attempts to provide a general framework for reasoning about time and events. It is based upon general axioms concerning the notions of events, relationships, and the periods for which they hold. In this paper, we have presented some consequences of these axioms which can be executed as a PROLOG program.

In order to deal with simultaneous and partially ordered events, and to impose semantic structure on knowledge base transitions, events are treated as primitive concepts, and knowledge base states are derived from event descriptions. Event descriptions are symmetric with respect to past and future, implying information about past states as well as about future ones.

In this paper we have concentrated on applications of the event calculus to assimilating both database updates and simple narratives. In particular, we stressed how default reasoning, implemented by negation as failure, deals with the case in which event descriptions are assimilated independently of the order in which they occur. When an update description conflicts with information derived by default reasoning, the update is accepted and the conflicting information previously derived by default is automatically and non-monotonically withdrawn.

In contrast, conventional databases choose to reject updates which are inconsistent with information already in the database. This strategy is appropriate only when updates are reported and assimilated in the order in which they occur, and when the database can be assumed to hold complete information about the past. Making explicit these extra assumptions in the event calculus simplifies the treatment significantly. We have not discussed, however, the processing which is necessary in these circumstances to validate attempted updates and to avoid the violation of database integrity.

These two contrasting approaches to database updates represent extreme ends of a spectrum of possibilities. In general, database systems faced with an attempted update inconsistent with their contents could choose to restore consistency either by rejecting the update or by withdrawing some of the information in the database.

The clauses we presented for assimilating updates and narratives run reasonably efficiently as a PROLOG program. However, they should be regarded not as a program but as a specification. In practice, the clauses would be further transformed and optimized to run more efficiently in specific applications.

A number of extensions can be incorporated straightforwardly into the event calculus. In particular, it is possible to extend the representation of periods to deal with information like

"Mary was a professor when Jim was promoted"

where neither the start nor the end of her period of professorship is known. Important extensions which do need further investigation include the representation of negated facts, and the ability to associate arbitrary sentences, not just conditionless facts, with the periods for which they hold.

Our formalization of the event calculus is deliberately neutral with respect to whether or not events have duration. Fariba Sadri has investigated the treatment of events which have duration, so that we can say, for example, that one event occurs completely, or partially, while another is taking place.

Somewhat more speculatively perhaps, we believe that the assimilation of updates without explicit deletion will contribute to the problem of updating data structures without destructive assignment in logic programming itself. These and other applications remain to be investigated in greater detail.

ACKNOWLEDGEMENTS

We are indebted to Fariba Sadri for her valuable comments, particularly those concerned with completing the definitions of the "Start" and "End" predicates. We also owe thanks to Dov Gabbay for his useful and stimulating discussions about temporal logic and its relationship with classical logic.

This research was supported by the Science and Engineering Research Council.

REFERENCES

Allen, J. F. (1981). 'Maintaining knowledge about temporal intervals', *TR-86*, Computer Science Dept., University of Rochester, January, 1981. Also in *Communications of the (II) (1983): ACM*, 26. 832–43.

——(1984). 'Towards a General Theory of Action and Time', *Artificial Intelligence 23:* 123–54.

Bolour, A., Anderson, T. L., Dekeyser, L. J., and Wong, H. K. T. (1982). 'The role of time in information processing: a survey', *ACM SIGMOD Review 12 (3, April)*.

Kowalski, R. A. (1979). *Logic for Problem Solving*. New York: North-Holland/Elsevier.

Lee, R. M., Coelho, H., and Cotta, J. C. (1985). 'Temporal Inferencing on Administrative Databases', *Information Systems 10 (2):* 197–206.

McCarthy, J. and Hayes, P. J. (1969). 'Some philosophical problems from the standpoint of artificial intelligence', in B. Meltzer and D. Michie (eds.), *Machine Intelligence, 4*. Edinburgh: Edinburgh University Press, 463–502.

11

Extending the Event Calculus with Temporal Granularity and Indeterminacy*

LUCA CHITTARO AND CARLO COMBI

1 INTRODUCTION

In many real-world applications, temporal information is often imprecise about the temporal location of events (*indeterminacy*) and comes at different granularities (Dyreson and Snodgrass 1995). Temporal granularity and indeterminacy are thus emerging as crucial requirements for the advancement of intelligent information systems which have to store, manage, and reason about temporal data. Consider, for example, these events taken from the application—a temporal database for cardiological patients— we are considering in our research (Combi and Chittaro 1999): "between 2 p.m. and 4 p.m. on May 5, 1996, the patient suffered from a myocardial infarction", "he started the therapy with thrombolytics in July 1995", "on October 12, 1996, he had a follow-up visit". The three events happened at the hours, months, and days timelines, respectively. Moreover, the first event cannot be precisely located on its timeline. A temporal reasoning system which has to reason about events and change in this domain must have the capability of representing and reasoning with data at different time scales and with indeterminacy. The two well-known formalisms for reasoning about actions, events and change, i.e., the Situation Calculus (McCarthy and Hayes 1969) and the Event Calculus (EC) (Kowalski and Sergot 1986), do not provide mechanisms for handling temporal indeterminacy and granularity, and very little research has been devoted to the goal of extending them with different granularities. In this paper, we provide an overview of a novel approach (TGIC, Temporal Granularity and Indeterminacy event Calculus) to represent events with imprecise location and to deal with different timelines, using the EC ontology. We then contrast TGIC with the well-known approach to the handling of granularity in EC by Montanari et al. (Montanari et al. 1992). Additional aspects of TGIC are discussed elsewhere: a formalization of the presented concepts is provided in (Chittaro and Combi 1998), while a polynomial algorithm for implementing the reasoning activity of TGIC is described in (Chittaro and Combi 1999). This paper is organized as follows: first, we briefly describe the ontology of EC, and we provide two motivating examples taken from our clinical domain; then we discuss the proposed representation of temporal information in TGIC, and the issues that have to be taken

---

Luca Chittaro and Carlo Combi, 'Extending the Event Calculus with Temporal Granularity and Indeterminacy', in C. Bettini and A. Montanari (eds.), *Spatial and Temporal Granularity: Papers from the AAAI Workshop*. Technical Report WS-00-08. Menlo Park, CA: The AAAI Press, 2000: 53–9. © 2000 American Association for Artificial Intelligence.

* This work has been partially supported by MURST Italian National Project COFIN 2000.

into account by the reasoning activity. Then, we provide a detailed analysis of a previous work extending EC to deal with granularities, and some concluding remarks. The last section summarizes the main further results recently obtained about TGIC.

2 THE ONTOLOGY OF EC

The notions of event, property, timepoint, and time interval are the primitives of the EC ontology: *events* happen at *timepoints* and initiate and/or terminate *time intervals* over which some *property* holds. Properties are assumed to persist until the occurrence of an event interrupts them (default persistence). An event occurrence can be represented by associating the event to the timepoint at which it occurred, e.g. by means of the clause:

```
happens(event, timePoint)
```

EC derives the maximal validity intervals (MVIs) over which properties hold. A MVI is maximal in the sense that it cannot be properly contained in any other validity interval. MVIs for a property p are obtained in response to the query:

```
mholds_for(p, MVI)
```

A property has not to be valid at both endpoints of a MVI: in the following, we thus adopt the convention that time intervals are closed to the left and open to the right.

3 MOTIVATING EXAMPLES

In this section, we present two simple clinical examples concerning patients with cardiological pathologies. In particular, the examples are related to the problem of diagnosing and following up heart failure (ACC/AHA Task Force 1995). We concentrate here on a small fragment of expert knowledge concerning the evaluation of the property hfRisk, i.e., the presence of a heart failure risk which requires special surveillance by clinicians in a considered cardiological patient. Among various factors, this property can be initiated by four different events: (i) smDeltaBP: a measurement of systolic and diastolic blood pressure (BP) on the patient reveals an abnormal difference (too small) between the two values; (ii) saD: sudden appearance of dyspnea is detected; (iii) anginaOnset: the patient starts to experience chest pain; and (iv) amnesiaOnset: the patient starts to experience loss of memory. The smDeltaBP event is acquired from a physiological measurement, saD from a monitoring device, while the other two events are acquired from symptoms reported by the patient. Examples of events terminating the property are a measurement of relevant physiological parameters (blood pressure, heart rate, ECG parameters) with normal values (normPar), or the administration of a specific cardiological drug (cardioDrug). Occurrences of all these events can be given at different calendric granularities (days, hours, minutes, or even seconds with some intensive care devices) and with indeterminacy, depending on what the patient remembers of the symptoms, and what is the accuracy in recording data related to therapies or to physiological measurements.

Case A. An amnesiaOnset happened on October 10, 1998, a smDeltaBP happened at 11:30 on October 10, 1998, and a normPar happened at 10:28 on October 11, 1998. This case is illustrated in Figure 1a. Considering for example the minutes timeline, a temporal reasoning system should provide a single MVI that initiates between 0:00 and 11:30 on October 10 (indeed, after 11.30 we are sure that at least one of the two initiating events—amnesiaOnset and smDeltaBP—actually happened), and terminates at 10:28 on October 11, 1998.

Case B. On the same day (May 3, 1998), an anginaOnset happened at 9, and a normPar happened at 12. Moreover, a saD is reported with an indeterminacy of ten seconds: it happened between 11:59:55 and 12:00:05. This case is illustrated in Figure 1b. Considering for example the hours timeline, a temporal reasoning system should be able to conclude that the property holds necessarily between 9 and 12 hours. Being unknown the relative order of occurrence for saD and normPar, the property could also possibly hold after the saD event if the actual occurrence of saD is after normPar. While the first conclusion is certain, the second one is hypothetical. In this paper, we deal with determining necessary conclusions: this is the perspective adopted in the following sections.

4 REPRESENTING EVENTS AND MAXIMAL VALIDITY INTERVALS (MVIs)

In TGIC, we allow the assignment of an arbitrary interval of time (at the chosen level of granularity) to an event occurrence. This interval specifies the time span over which it is certain that the (imprecise) timepoint is located. More formally, indeterminacy is represented by generalizing the second argument of happens. We use the clause:

happens(event, IOI)

where IOI (*Interval Of Indeterminacy*) is a convex interval over which event happened, and is assumed to be closed to the left and open to the right (according to the adopted time interval convention). For example:

happens(e, [t1, t2])

states that the occurrence time of event e is greater or equal than t1 and lower than t2. TGIC adopts the standard calendric granularities (years, months, days, hours, ...), with the associated mappings among timelines. More generally, it allows one to use any set of granularities where mapping contiguous timepoints from a given granularity to the finest one results in contiguous intervals. Special granularities such as business days or business months (Bettini et al. 1998), which do not meet the general requirement above, are thus not considered. We extend the definition of MVI to accommodate the more general concept of event. A MVI has the form:

⟨Start, End⟩

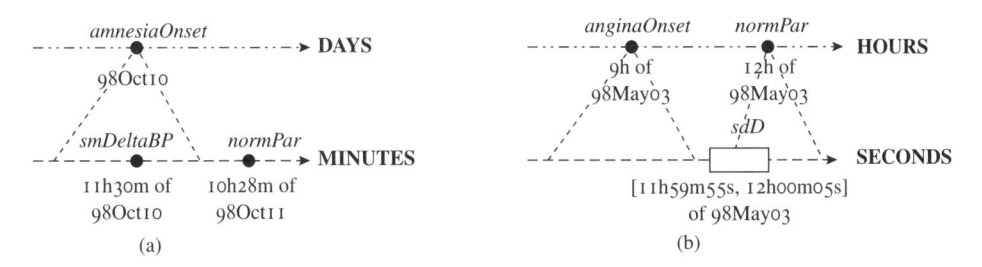

FIG. 1   Case A (a), Case B (b).

where `Start` (`End`) denotes at a given granularity either a specific timepoint, if it is known, or the minimal interval over which the initiation (termination) of the property is necessarily located, in the case of indeterminacy. If `Start` (`End`) is a precise instant, it is trivially the left (right) endpoint of the delimited MVI; if `Start` (`End`) is itself an interval, then the left (right) endpoint of the delimited MVI is the right (left) endpoint of `Start` (`End`). Therefore, a `Start` (`End`) determines (i) the minimal interval over which the initiation (termination) of a property is necessarily located, and (ii) the timepoint at which the property initiates (terminates) is necessarily valid. For example, suppose we have only two events in the database:

`happens(e1, 94Oct10)`

`happens(e2, [12h of 94Dec10, 14h of 94Dec10])`

and `e1` initiates property p, while `e2` terminates p. In this case, we know that the initiation of the property is necessarily located at `94Oct10` and the termination is located over the interval:

`[12h of 94Dec10, 14h of 94Dec10]`
We represent this knowledge, by saying that
⟨`94Oct10, [12hof94Dec10, 14hof94Dec10]`⟩

is a MVI for property p. Therefore, property p is necessarily valid after `94Oct10` and until `12h of 94Dec10`. For conciseness, when an event e initiates (terminates) property p, we refer to the associated IOI as an initiating (terminating) IOI for p.

5 DERIVING MAXIMAL VALIDITY INTERVALS

The relative ordering of a set of events with imprecise occurrence times and/or different granularities can be often only partially known (e.g., in Case B, it is not known whether `saD` happens before, simultaneously, or after `normPar`). Since we are concerned with deriving necessary MVIs, every MVI we derive must be valid in all possible orders consistent with the partial order (Dean and Boddy 1988), resulting from imprecise locations of event occurrences. The approach we propose to derive MVIs is organized in three general steps:

i. the (possibly imprecise) occurrence times of events are mapped to the finest granularity level;
ii. an algorithm which handles partially ordered events is applied only at the finest level to derive necessary MVIs;
iii. the obtained results are mapped at the upper granularity levels required by the user.

5.1 Mapping to the finest granularity

TGIC provides a granularity mapping function to map times between any pair of calendric granularities. This is simply achieved by applying standard mappings among calendric units: for example, hour k is mapped into the interval of minutes $[k * 60, (k+1) * 60]$. These mappings are used both for the first and the third step of MVI derivation.

Temporal Granularity and Indeterminacy

In the case of the first step, the function is used to map the occurrence time of each event to the finest granularity (in our case, the granularity of seconds). For example, the predicate:

happens(smDeltaBP, 11h30m of 98Oct10)

of Case A is mapped into the predicate:

happens(smDeltaBP, [11h30m00s of 98Oct10,
11h31m00s of 98Oct10])

5.2 Handling partially ordered events

We distinguish the three possible kinds of intersection among IOIs the algorithm has to deal with: intersection among initiating IOIs, among terminating IOIs, and among both types of IOIs. Hereinafter, we refer to these three different situations, as I_ALONE, T_ALONE, and I_T_INTERSECT, respectively.

Intersection among initiating IOIs. Let us consider some initiating IOIs for a property p, such that their intersection is non-empty, and there are no intersections with terminating IOIs for p (I_ALONE situation). Let us assume that there are no preceding events, which have already initiated p, so that it is important to derive one single IOI to use as a Start in a MVI. The solution to the problem is given by the interval whose left and right endpoints are the minimum left and right endpoints, respectively, of the given IOIs. Indeed, property p cannot initiate before the minimum left endpoint because there are no other preceding events which initiate it, but it necessarily initiates after or at the minimum left endpoint, and before the minimum right endpoint. The latter delimits the interval of necessary validity for property p, because at least one initiating event happens before it, and there is no lower time that guarantees the same. For example, take the three initiating IOIs (anginaOnset, saD, smDeltaBP) for property hfRisk in Figure 2. In this case, in each of the three intervals [t1,t5], [t2,t3], and [t4,t6], an initiating event happened. The derived Start is thus [t1,t3]: the initiation of hfRisk is necessarily located over [t1,t3].

Intersection among terminating IOIs. Let us consider some terminating IOIs for a property p, such that their intersection is non-empty, and there are no intersections with initiating IOIs for p (T_ALONE situation). Let us assume that p has been initiated by preceding events and no preceding events can terminate it, so that it is important to derive one single IOI to use as an End in a MVI. The solution to the problem is again given by the interval whose left and right endpoints are the minimum left and right endpoints, respectively, of the given IOIs. Indeed, property p cannot terminate before

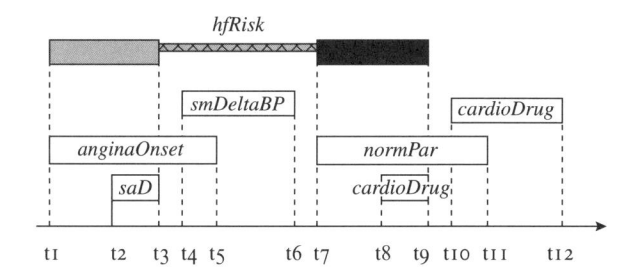

FIG. 2 Examples of I_ALONE and T_ALONE.

the minimum left endpoint because there are no other preceding events which can terminate it, but it necessarily terminates after or at the minimum left endpoint, and before the minimum right endpoint (when the minimum right endpoint is reached, it is certain that at least one terminating event has occurred). The necessity of the validity of property p thus terminates at the minimum left endpoint, because a terminating event can happen after or at that point. For example, considering the three terminating IOIs (normPar and the two cardioDrug) for property hfRisk in Figure 2, the derived End is [t7,t9], and ⟨[t1,t3], [t7,t9]⟩ is a MVI for hfRisk.

Intersection among initiating and terminating IOIs. When an initiating and a terminating IOI for the same property have a non-empty intersection (I_T_INTERSECT situation), it is impossible to establish in what order the corresponding initiating and terminating events happened. As a consequence, it is not possible to conclude anything about the necessary effects of the initiating IOI (a Start could be derived only if we knew that the initiating event happened after the terminating one), while terminating IOIs maintain their capability of being used in an End with respect to previous Starts. For example, if in Figure 3 we considered only the three pairs of intersecting IOIs, nothing could be concluded about the necessary validity of hfRisk: there would be no derivable MVI which is valid in all possible orders of the six indeterminate events. Considering all the (seven) IOIs in the database, the first IOI is a Start for hfRisk, and the first terminating IOI is an End. These two IOIs delimit the only necessary MVI in the database.

If an I_T_INTERSECT occurs when the property does not hold, it is possible (but not necessary) that the property initiates to hold. In these cases, the intersecting IOIs do not allow one to generate a Start, but they have to be considered in relation to a possible subsequent I_ALONE situation. For example, consider the events smDeltaBP and cardioDrug in Figure 4a: since the relative ordering between their occurrences is unknown, they just allow one to conclude that the property hfRisk might have been initiated. Considering also the subsequent event saD, we can conclude that property hfRisk is necessarily valid after t5, because saD has no intersection with terminating IOIs (I_ALONE situation), but to determine the minimal interval for Start, we have to consider also smDeltaBP and cardioDrug. The initiating event for hfRisk can be both smDeltaBP and saD. The IOI of saD will belong completely to Start, while only a part of IOI of smDeltaBP will be included in Start, because when smDeltaBP is the initiating event for the necessary instance of hfRisk, it is impossible for the occurrence of smDeltaBP to be located before the IOI of cardioDrug (the instance of hfRisk initiated by smDeltaBP would be terminated by cardioDrug). Therefore, the Start for hfRisk is given by IOI [t1,t5]: the initiation for the property is necessarily located in that interval. In general, we call Ext the part of Start,

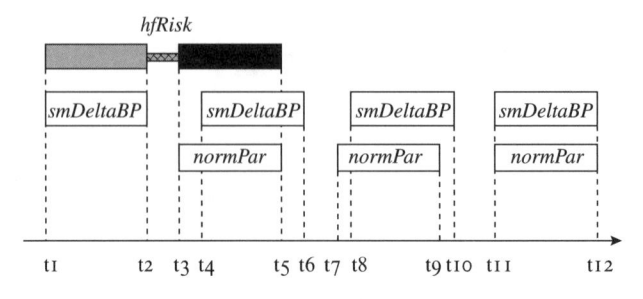

FIG. 3. Three examples of I_T_INTERSECT.

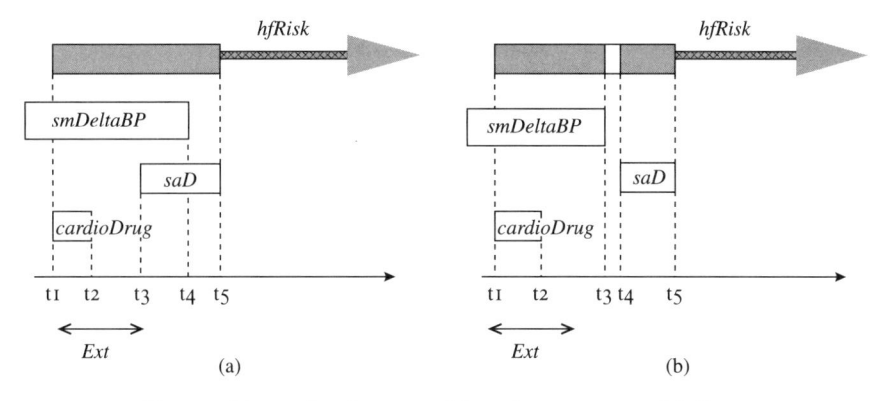

FIG. 4 Example of convex (a) and non-convex (b) Start.

which is produced by considering the I_T_INTERSECT situation preceding the I_ALONE one. The Ext interval in Figure 4a is [t1,t4]. In the general case, a Start needs not to be necessarily convex. This is exemplified in Figure 4b, where, as in the situation of Figure 4a, we can conclude that property hfRisk is necessarily valid after t5, and then we have to similarly consider smDeltaBP and cardioDrug to determine Start. Unlike the case of Figure 4a, smDeltaBP and saD currently do not overlap. Therefore, the Start for hfRisk is given by a nonconvex IOI which comprises [t1,t3] and [t4,t5]: property hfRisk is necessarily valid after t5, and it has been necessarily initiated over the nonconvex interval [[t1,t3], [t4,t5]], which is the union of [t1,t3] (the Ext interval, obtained from I_T_INTERSECT) and [t4,t5] (the interval obtained from I_ALONE).

5.3 Answering queries at multiple granularities

TGIC extends the query predicate mholds_for, to allow one to perform queries at different levels of granularity. The predicate: mholds_for(p,⟨Start, End⟩, granlev) returns the MVIs for property p at the granularity granlev. For example, in Case A (Figure 1a), TGIC derives the MVI: ⟨[00h00m00s of 98Oct10, 11h31m00s of 98Oct10], [10h28m00s of 98Oct11, 10h29m00s of 98Oct11]⟩ for the property hfRisk at the finest level of granularity. The MVI returned by the query mholds_for(hfRisk, MVI, minutes) is ⟨[00h00m of 98Oct10, 11h31m of 98Oct10], 10h28m of 98Oct11⟩. The query: mholds_for (hfRisk, MVI, days) returns the MVI ⟨98Oct10, 98Oct11⟩ as solution. Finally, TGIC provides the predicate:

msg_mholds_for(p, ⟨Start,End⟩)

which tries to automatically choose the most suitable granularity level for Start and End. The most suitable granularity for a Start (End) of an MVI is chosen as follows: starting from the Start (End) derived at the finest level, we move to the coarser levels by using granularity mapping predicates, stopping at the first level where the Start (End) reduces to a time point. For example, for Case A, the query: msg_mholds_ for(hfRisk, MVI) returns the MVI ⟨98Oct10, 10h28m of 98Oct11⟩ as solution. Considering Case B, the latter query returns: ⟨9h of 98May03, 12h of 98May03⟩.

6 RELATED WORK

To the best of our knowledge, the only other approach to deal with temporal granularity in EC has been proposed by Montanari et al. and is described in (Montanari et al. 1992): hereinafter, we refer to this approach as MMCR (the initials of its authors' surnames). MMCR introduces temporal granularity in EC by operating the following extensions.

Multiple timelines. The single EC timeline is extended into a totally ordered set of different timelines $\{T_1,\ldots,T_n\}$, such that each timeline T_i is of finer granularity than the previous timeline T_{i-1}. For example, one could have three timelines corresponding to hours, minutes, and seconds, respectively. In general, the finest timeline is possibly allowed to be continuous, while the other ones must necessarily be discrete.

Granularity mapping predicates. New predicates (*fine_grain_of, coarse_grain_of*) are introduced into the formalism in order to map the occurrence of events from one timeline to the other ones. For example, an event that happened at *2* hrs is mapped at the finer granularity of minutes into the time interval [*120* min, *179* min]; an event that happened at *170* min is mapped at the coarser granularity of hours into the time point *2* hrs.

Reasoning strategy. Derivation of MVIs is extended in order to encompass the presence of events at multiple time scales. In particular, MMCR first maps all the available events at all the different granularity levels, then it exploits the standard EC derivation of MVIs on each of the levels in isolation. The possibility of having contradicting events happening at the same time point as a result of mapping events to coarser time scales is prohibited by means of explicit integrity constraints. Moreover, since the derivation mechanism expects events to happen at time points, the two endpoints of intervals obtained by mapping the occurrence of an event *e* to a finer level of granularity are treated as two endpoints for an interval over which *e* has to occur (temporal indeterminacy).

We have tested MMCR on our clinical domain, and found a number of limitations which can be classified as follows.

Completeness issues. MMCR is often not able to derive the expected MVIs, even for some simple cases. Situations affected by these problems typically involve the presence of intersecting intervals of indeterminacy for different events which have been mapped at finer granularities. MMCR is not able to deal with them properly, as we show below.

Expressiveness issues. MMCR expects one to assign a precise time point on one of the timelines to the occurrence of an event. This is often not possible in real applications where the information available is not so precisely localizable on any available time scale. Events like "between 17:30 and 18:15 the patient had a myocardial infarction", or "between 10:23:05 and 10:23:15, a patient monitoring device detected dyspnea" cannot be handled by MMCR. Moreover, as a result of deriving MVIs in isolation on each timeline, MMCR is not able to return MVIs with starting and ending times given at different granularities.

Efficiency issues. The implementation of MMCR is given in terms of a declarative logic program. Chittaro and Montanari in (Chittaro and Montanari 1996) have shown how a declarative implementation of basic EC is inevitably plagued by a scarce performance, due to a generate-and-test strategy which considers any possible pair of events as a possible candidate for deriving an MVI. This problem is exacerbated in MMCR, because each event has also a counterpart on each of the timelines.

To highlight differences between TGIC and MMCR, let us consider how MMCR would manage the two examples we previously provided. In Case A, MMCR returns three MVIs for property hfRisk: (i) a MVI that initiates at 11:30 on October 10, and terminates at 10:28 on October 11, 1998; (ii) a MVI that initiates between 0:00 and 23:59 on October 10, and terminates at 10:28 on October 11, 1998; and (iii) a MVI that initiates on October 10 and terminates on October 11, 1998. Solution (i) is not satisfying, because the MVI might have possibly started before 11:30, due to the amnesiaOnset event, while solution (ii) is too vague, because it comprises also a large number of time points following 11:30 as possible starting points for the MVI, although the property is certainly valid after 11:30. Instead of producing these two solutions, a temporal reasoning system should provide a single MVI that initiates between 0:00 and 11:30 on October 10, and terminates at 10:28 on October 11, 1998. Solution (iii) is satisfying at the granularity of days.

In Case B, MMCR is unable to handle the saD event, because it is not possible to have temporal indeterminacy unrelated to the mappings among granularity levels. But, even assuming that indeterminacy were handled in general, a second major problem would arise, i.e., the interval of indeterminacy for the initiating event saD has a non-empty intersection with the time of occurrence of the terminating event normPar. As previously discussed, MMCR rules out contradicting events which might possibly happen at the same time point. In this situation, a temporal reasoning system should be able to conclude that the property holds necessarily between 9 and 12 hours.

7 CONCLUSIONS

As we have shown in the previous section, the usefulness of the only other approach dealing with temporal granularity in EC (Montanari et al. 1992), is limited by three serious factors: (i) the possibility of having I_T_INTERSECT situations is prohibited by explicit integrity constraints (that approach is thus often unable to derive the expected MVIs, e.g. in the cases represented by Figures 1b, 3, 4); (ii) the user can associate to an event only a single timepoint on a chosen timeline (indeterminacy is not allowed); and (iii) the implementation is given only in terms of a declarative logic program. Chittaro and Montanari have shown how declarative implementations of EC have significant performance limitations, due to a generate-and-test strategy (Chittaro and Montanari 1996). TGIC overcomes all the above described limitations: it allows and handles I_T_INTERSECT situations; it allows the user to associate any interval of indeterminacy to any event; and an efficient procedural implementation has been provided in Chittaro and Combi (1999).

8 UPDATE

The latest developments of the TGIC project are described in Chittaro and Combi (2002). In particular, besides illustrating different motivating real-world examples, a set-theoretic formalization of TGIC is provided and suitably exemplified. A new procedural implementation for the derivation of necessary MVIs is then formally described and the worst-case data complexity of the proposed improved algorithm is shown to be linear with respect to the number of considered IOIs for a given property. The main idea behind the algorithm, which is formalized in terms of a finite state machine, is that the database of initiating and terminating IOIs is sequentially scanned, by moving a suitable temporal window in chronological order (from the oldest IOIs to the most recent ones): by examining the content of the temporal window, the algorithm is able to determine whether (and when) the considered property starts or ends, deriving the corresponding MVI (if any). We also analyzed the effect of extending TGIC with preconditions, i.e., allowing one to specify that an event initiates and/or terminates at some timepoint the time interval over which some property holds provided that some other properties (i.e., *preconditions*) hold at the considered timepoint. While the proposed TGIC algorithm is able to determine all (and only) the necessary MVIs when no preconditions are used, we have shown the incompleteness and incorrectness issues that arise when preconditions are added. Unfortunately, it is not possible to come up with a polynomial algorithm that is complete and correct when preconditions are used in TGIC: as highlighted by Dean and Boddy (Dean and Boddy 1988), the task of deriving which facts must be true over a given interval from partially ordered events is intractable in the general case (i.e., allowing preconditions), because it requires to explicitly evaluate all possible event orderings. Finally, we extended the comparison of TGIC with related work, considering research projects focusing on extending EC to deal with partially ordered events, on reasoning about temporal constraints, and on modeling and reasoning on time granularities.

REFERENCES

ACC/AHA Task Force. (1995). 'Heart Failure Guidelines', *Journal of American College of Cardiology* 26: 1376–98.

Bettini, C., Wang, X., and Jajodia, S. (1998). 'A general framework for time granularity and its application to temporal reasoning', *Annals of Mathematics and Artificial Intelligence* 22: 29–58.

Chittaro, L. and Combi, C. (1998). 'Temporal Indeterminacy in Deductive Databases: an Approach Based on the Event Calculus', in *Active, Real-time and Temporal Database Systems (ARTDB-97)*, LNCS 1553. Berlin: Springer-Verlag, 212–27.

——(1999). 'Reasoning about Events with Imprecise Location and Multiple Granularities', in *Proceedings of the 10th International Conference on Database and Expert Systems Applications (DEXA-99)*, LNCS 1677. Berlin: Springer-Verlag, 1006–17.

——(2002). 'Temporal Granularity and Indeterminacy in Reasoning about Actions and Change: an Approach Based on the Event Calculus', *Annals of Mathematics and Artificial Intelligence* 1–2: 81–119.

Chittaro, L. and Montanari, A. (1996). 'Efficient temporal reasoning in the Cached Event Calculus', *Computational Intelligence* 12: 359–82.

Combi, C. and Chittaro, L. (1999). 'Abstraction on Clinical Data Sequences: an Object-Oriented Data Model and a Query Language Based on the Event Calculus', *Artificial Intelligence in Medicine* 17: 271–301.

Dean, T. and Boddy, M. (1988). 'Reasoning about Partially Ordered Events', *Artificial Intelligence* 36: 375–99.

Dyreson, C. E. and Snodgrass, R.T. (1995). 'Temporal indeterminacy', in R. T. Snodgrass (ed.), *The TSQL2 Temporal Query Language*. Dordrecht: Kluwer Academic Publishers, 327–46.

Kowalski, R. and Sergot, M. (1986). 'A logic-based calculus of events', *New Generation Computing* 4: 67–95.

McCarthy, J. and Hayes, P. (1969). 'Some philosophical problems from the standpoint of artificial intelligence', in B. Meltzer and D. Michie (eds.), *Machine Intelligence*, 4. Edinburgh: Edinburgh University Press, 463–502.

Montanari, A., Maim, E., Ciapessoni, E., and Ratto, E. (1992). 'Dealing with Time Granularity in the Event Calculus', in *Proceedings of the 1992 International Conference of Fifth Generation Computer Systems (FGCS-92)*. Amsterdam: IOS Press, 702–12.

12

Towards a General Theory of Action and Time

JAMES F. ALLEN

1 INTRODUCTION

The concept of action arises in at least two major subareas of artificial intelligence, namely, natural language processing and problem solving. For the most part, the formalisms that have been suggested in each subarea are independent of each other and difficult to compare, although there is recent work that attempts to merge work from both areas (Charniak 1981). Even considering such work, however, there is presently no computational theory of action that is sufficiently powerful to capture the range of the meanings and distinctions expressible in English. The primary goal of this paper is to suggest a formalism that is considerably more expressive than current theories of action and to explore its use in defining the meanings of English sentences that describe actions and events.

A secondary, but important, requirement on the formalism is that it should be a useful representation for action reasoning (i.e., problem solving). Some effort will be made to describe how the representation could be used by a planning or plan recognition system. This is essential to the natural language research as well, because problem-solving techniques are being used more and more in our models of language comprehension (e.g., see Allen and Perrault 1980). While interest in this approach is growing, progress is inhibited by inadequate representations of actions and plans.

There are at least three major difficulties with nearly all existing models of action in AI. Such models cannot represent:

- actions that involve non-activity (e.g., "I stood on the corner for an hour");
- actions that are not easily decomposable into subactions (e.g., "I spent the day hiding from George");
- actions that occur simultaneously and interact with many others.

The theory outlined below will allow all three of these situations to be represented. Each problem will be examined in detail below when discussing previous work.

1.1 Relevant work

Relevant work on this problem can be divided into three broad categories: representations for natural language systems, problem-solving systems, and work in linguistics and philosophy.

The most common formulation for actions in natural language systems is based on case grammar (Fillmore 1968). Each action is represented by a set of assertions about the semantic roles the noun phrases play with respect to the action denoted by the verb. Such a formalism is useful for interpreting the semantic structure of sentences, but doesn't address the issue of what an action is, or what inferences can be made from the fact that an action occurred. Typically there is only a simple temporal, or causal, ordering on the actions, which is not heavily used. Such representations only work in situations where actions are simply related to each other and no uncertainty exists.

Work in problem solving has used more sophisticated models of action and time. The most influential theory in this work has been the situation calculus (McCarthy and Hayes 1969). The world is represented as a set of situations, each describing the world at a single instant in time. An action is a function from one situation to another, and can be described by a set of prerequisites on the initial situation and a set of effects that will hold in the final situation. While this model has been extremely useful in modeling physical actions by a single agent in an otherwise static world, it cannot easily be extended to account for simultaneous actions and events. For example, the action described by the sentence, "I walked to the store while juggling three balls," seems to be composed of the action of walking to the store and the action of juggling three balls. It is not clear how such a composite action would be defined if we view an action as a function from one instantaneous world description to another. Furthermore, since an action in the situation calculus is equated with change, actions that involve no activity, or restore the world to its original state (e.g., running around a track), cannot be modeled.

The most common implementation inspired by the situation calculus is the *state space model*. The world is described by a data base containing what is presently true, and actions are simulated by adding and deleting facts from the data base. This model suffers from all the above criticisms of the situation calculus and in addition has no model of the past or the future.

None of these formulations can describe the following simple situation. In the blocks world, assume we have two actions, PUSHR, push to the right, and PUSHL, push to the left. Let us also assume that the effect of each of these actions is that the block moves one unit in the appropriate direction. But if two robots perform a PUSHR and a PUSHL simultaneously on the same block, the block doesn't move. Since we cannot express or reason about the simultaneity of actions in any of the above theories, we cannot express this situation. The best we can do will be to have the block oscillate as the robots push alternately.

McDermott (1981) introduces a notion of event that is general enough to address the three problems above. To a first approximation, our two approaches are compatible; however, major differences exist. Some of these differences come about as a result of the difference in intended application, and some as a result of different underlying assumptions in our temporal logics. These issues will be discussed as they become relevant.

Work in linguistics and philosophy has provided many insights for this research, although the theories typically lack a computational viewpoint. The major influences on this paper come from Mourelatos (1978), Jackendoff (1976), and Goldman (1970).

Mourelatos presents a detailed analysis of the different classes of occurrences describable in English, and his terminology will be adopted here. The term *occurrence* is used to describe the class of all events, processes, actions, activities, and accomplishments. This effectively includes all forms of sentence meanings except for assertions of states such as "The building is red" or "I am ten years old". The class of occurrences is further subdivided by Mourelatos, and we will consider this subcategorization later as it becomes relevant.

Goldman presents a detailed theory of human action. At this stage, we need only examine the problem of action individuation, which is demonstrated by the question: if I pull the trigger of a gun, thereby shooting my friend, how many actions have I performed? One view is that only one action is performed, and that it exemplifies two action types (Davidson 1967), pulling the trigger and shooting my friend. Goldman's view is that two distinct—though intimately related—actions are performed. The latter view is adopted here as it provides for a simpler semantics. Thus a physical situation will typically be described as a set of distinct occurrences and actions, and actions may be distinct even if they have the same agent and occur at the same time.

1.2 The proposed theory

The world is described by a set of temporally qualified assertions outlining what is known about the past, present, and future. This includes descriptions of both static and dynamic aspects of the world. The static aspects are captured by *properties* (e.g., Cleo owning a car) that hold over stretches of time. The dynamic aspects are captured by *occurrences* (e.g., Cleo running a race) which describe change of forms or resistance to change over stretches of time. The distinction between properties and occurrences is usually obvious, but situations do arise where it is quite subtle. The most subtle cases arise from situations that can be described from either a static or dynamic perspective. For instance, adopting an example from Jackendoff (1976), we could describe the situation in which a light was on in a house all night by the static description, "the light was on all night", or by the dynamic description, "the light remained on all night". The only difference here appears to be that the latter suggests that it might have been otherwise. In most cases, however, the static/dynamic distinction will be straightforward.

It should be clear that a temporal logic is necessary to support this theory. Time plays a crucial role, and cannot be relegated to a secondary consideration as in most natural language systems or hidden in a search process as in most problem-solving systems. The temporal logic described below is based on temporal intervals, and denies the standard view of mapping time to points on the real number line.

Given a temporal logic, we address how *occurrences* can be defined. In particular, what do we know when we know an occurrence has occurred? In problem-solving systems, actions are described by prerequisites (i.e., what must be true to enable the action), effects (what must be true after the action has occurred), and decomposition (how the action is performed, which is typically a sequence of subactions). While such knowledge is crucial for reasoning about what actions to perform in a given situation, it does not define what we know when we know an action has occurred. To clarify this, consider the simple action of turning on a light.

There are few physical activities that are a necessary part of performing the action of turning on a light. Depending on the context, vastly different patterns of behavior can be classified as the same action. For example, turning on a light usually involves flipping a light switch, but in some circumstances it may involve tightening the light bulb (in the basement) or hitting the wall (in an old house). Although we have knowledge about how the action can be performed, this does *not* define what the action is. The key defining characteristic of turning on the light seems to be that the agent is performing some activity which will cause the light, which was off when the action started, to become on when the action ends. An important side effect of this definition is that we could recognize an observed pattern of activity as "turning on the light" even if we had never seen or thought about that pattern previously.

Thus, we want a level of causal explanation that characterizes the consequences one can draw from a sentence describing an action, or, more generally, an occurrence. Such a description would not replace or subsume the prerequisite/effect/method characterization of actions, although there will be some overlap. For example, the effects of an action should be included, or be derivable from, the causal definition of the action. Some prerequisites would appear in the definition of an action, though others, dealing with an agent's abilities, might not be part of the action definition. Similarly, some parts of a method might be necessary in an action definition, but for the most part, method descriptions do not define what an action is. At a few places in the paper, we shall consider how problem-solving knowledge about actions can be integrated into the proposed framework.

1.3 An outline of the paper

Section 2 introduces an interval-based temporal logic and discusses properties than can hold over intervals. In Section 3, a logic for occurrences is introduced. Occurrences are subdivided into processes and events. Section 4 introduces the notion of action and makes the distinction between definitional knowledge of an action and generational knowledge which is needed for planning actions. Section 5 deals with intentional action and provides a semi-formal notion of plans and of an agent committing to a plan. The paper concludes with an analysis of the meaning of the verb 'to hide', using the formalism developed.

The following conventions will be used throughout. Predicates and constants will be in upper case, and variables will be in lower case. A full range of connectives and quantifiers will be used in their standard interpretation. I use:

    &   conjunction,
    ∨   disjunction,
    ∼   negation,
    ⇒   implication,
    ⇔   equivalence,
    ∀   universal quantifier,
    ∃   existential quantifier,
    ∃!   existence of a unique object.

Any variables that appear with no quantifier are assumed to be universal variables with global scope. I shall often resort to typing variables as in a many-sorted logic. In these cases, the type of the variable will be indicated by its name. Scoping of operators and quantifiers will be indicated by use of parentheses or by indentation of formulas. In general, quantifiers are assumed to be scoped as broadly as possible.

2 A TEMPORAL LOGIC

Before we can characterize events and actions, we need to specify a temporal logic. The logic described here is based on temporal intervals rather than time points. This approach arises from the observation that the only times we can identify are times of occurrences and properties. For any such time, say the time I was opening the door, it appears to be possible to look more closely at the occurrence and decompose it; hence, times can be decomposed into subtimes. In other words, it seems that there is always a more detailed causal explanation if one cares, and is able, to look for it. A good analogy, then, is that times correspond to intervals on the real line. If we accept this, why not allow instantaneous time points as well? First, they do not appear to be necessary. Second, instantaneous time points will present difficulties with the semantics of our logic. If one allows time points, one must consider whether intervals are open or closed. For example, consider the time of running a race, R, and the time following after the race, AR. Let P be the proposition representing the fact that the race is on; P is true over R, and ~P is true over AR. We want AR and R to meet in some sense. Whether both ends of the intervals are open or closed, AR and R must either share a time point or allow time between them. Thus we have a choice between inconsistency or truth gaps, i.e., either there is a time when both P and ~P are true, or there is a time when neither P nor ~P is true. One solution to this problem is to stipulate by convention that intervals are open at the lower end and closed at the upper end, but then every interval has only a single endpoint. The artificiality of this solution reinforces the argument against allowing points. Events that appear to refer to a point in time (e.g., finishing a race) are considered to be implicitly referring to another event's beginning or ending. Thus, time 'points' will be considered to be very small intervals. This will be made more precise below.

The logic is a typed first-order predicate calculus, in which the terms fall into many categories. The following three are needed at present:

- terms of type TIME-INTERVAL denoting time intervals;
- terms of type PROPERTY, denoting propositions that can hold or not hold during a particular time;
- terms corresponding to objects in the domain.

There are a small number of predicates. One of the most important is HOLDS, which asserts that a property holds (i.e., is true) during a time interval. Thus

HOLDS(p, t)

is true if and only if property p holds during t. As a subsequent axiom will state, this is intended to mean that p holds at every subinterval of t as well. Note that if we had introduced HOLDS as a modal operator we would not need to introduce properties into our ontology. We have not followed this route, however, since it seems more complicated in the later development of occurrences.

There is a basic set of mutually exclusive primitive relations that can hold between temporal intervals. Each of these is represented by a predicate in the logic. These relationships are summarized in Fig. 1.

- DURING ($t1$, $t2$): time interval $t1$ is fully contained within $t2$;
- STARTS($t1$, $t2$): time interval $t1$ shares the same beginning as $t2$, but ends before $t2$ ends;
- FINISHES($t1$, $t2$): time interval $t1$ shares the same end as $t2$, but begins after $t2$ begins;
- BEFORE($t1$, $t2$): time interval $t1$ is before interval $t2$, and they do not overlap in any way;
- OVERLAP($t1$, $t2$): interval $t1$ starts before $t2$, and they overlap;
- MEETS($t1$, $t2$): interval $t1$ is before interval $t2$, but there is no interval between them, i.e., $t1$ ends where $t2$ starts;
- EQUAL($t1$, $t2$): $t1$ and $t2$ are the same interval.

Relation	Symbol	Symbol for inverse	Pictoral example
X before Y	<	>	XXX YYY
X equal Y	=	=	XXX YYY
X meets Y	m	mi	XXXYYY XXX
X overlaps Y	o	oi	YYY XXX
X during Y	d	di	YYYYYY XXX
X starts Y	s	si	YYYYY XXX
X finishes Y	f	fi	YYYYY

FIG. 1 The thirteen possible relationships.

Given these predicates, there is a set of axioms that define their behavior. First, given any interval I, there exists an interval related to I by each of the above relationships. Thus, there exists an interval that is before I, that meets I, that is during I, etc. We have axioms asserting that each relationship is mutually exclusive of the others, and we have a large set of axioms describing the transitivity behavior. The full set of transitivity axioms, plus a description of an inference procedure using them, is given in Allen (1981). Two examples of these are:

$$\text{BEFORE}(t1, t2) \text{ \& BEFORE}(t2, t3) \Rightarrow \text{BEFORE}(t1, t3), \quad \text{(T.1)}$$

$$\text{MEETS}(t1, t2) \text{ \& DURING}(t2, t3) \Rightarrow \quad \text{(T.2)}$$
$$(\text{OVERLAPS}(t1, t3) \vee \text{DURING}(t1, t3) \vee \text{MEETS}(t1, t3)).$$

It will be useful to define a predicate that summarizes the relationships in which one interval is wholly contained in another. We define IN as follows:

$$\text{IN}(t1, t2) \Leftrightarrow (\text{DURING}(t1, t2) \vee \text{STARTS}(t1, t2) \vee \text{FINISHES}(t1, t2)). \quad \text{(T.3)}$$

Using this predicate, we can introduce the first crucial property of the HOLDS predicate: If a property p holds over an interval T, it holds over all subintervals of T, i.e.,

$$\text{HOLDS}(p, T) \Leftrightarrow (\forall t.\text{IN}(t, T) \Rightarrow \text{HOLDS}(p, t)). \quad \text{(H.1)}$$

For example, if I owned a car throughout 1982, then I owned a car throughout January of 1982, as well as February, etc.

In fact, it will turn out that we need a slightly stronger axiom in the later development. We shall introduce it here as a second axiom, even though (H.1) can be derived from this axiom plus the properties of the IN relation.

$$\text{HOLDS}(p, T) \Leftrightarrow$$
$$\forall t.\text{IN}(t, T) \Rightarrow (\exists s.\text{IN}(s, t) \wedge \text{HOLDS}(p, s)). \quad \text{(H.2)}$$

The proof that (H.1) can be derived from (H.2) is in Appendix A.

To allow properties to name complex logical expressions, there is a set of functions *and, or, not, all,* and *exists,* that correspond to the logical operators &, ∨, ~, ∀, and ∃ in the following manner.

Conjunction moves through the HOLDS predicate freely:

$$\text{HOLDS}(\text{and}(p, q), t) \Leftrightarrow \text{HOLDS}(p, t) \text{ \& HOLDS}(q, t). \quad \text{(H.3)}$$

Negation is defined by:

$$\text{HOLDS}(\text{not}(p), T) \Leftrightarrow (\forall t.\text{IN}(t, T) \Rightarrow \sim \text{HOLDS}(p, t)) \tag{H.4}$$

Contrast this with $\sim \text{HOLDS}(p, T)$, which by axiom (H.1) is equivalent to

$$\sim (\forall t.\text{IN}(t, T) \Rightarrow \text{HOLDS}(p, t)),$$

which, of course, is equivalent to

$$\exists t.\text{IN}(t, T) \,\&\, \sim \text{HOLDS}(p, t).$$

Thus, the latter asserts that there is at least one subinterval in which p doesn't hold, while the former asserts that p doesn't hold in all subintervals of T.

Using the above definition, we can prove

$$\text{HOLDS}(\text{not}(p), T) \Rightarrow \sim \text{HOLDS}(p, T). \tag{H.5}$$

Also, using (H.4) and (H.2), we can derive

$$\text{HOLDS}(\text{not}(\text{not}(p)), T) \Leftrightarrow \text{HOLDS}(p, T) \tag{H.6}$$

as we would expect from intuition. Mirroring the normal definition of disjunction to define the function 'or', i.e.,

$$\text{HOLDS}(\text{or}(p, q), t) \equiv \text{HOLDS}(\text{not}(\text{and}(\text{not}(p), \text{not}(q))), t),$$

we can derive

$$\text{HOLDS}(\text{or}(p, q), T) \Leftrightarrow \forall t.\text{IN}(t, T) \Rightarrow \tag{H.7}$$
$$(\exists s.\text{IN}(s, t) \wedge (\text{HOLDS}(p, s) \vee \text{HOLDS}(q, s))).$$

Many treatments of temporal logics introduce the notion of branching futures into the model. This is used to analyze the notion of possibility of some event (i.e., there is a branch in which it occurs), and necessity of some event (i.e., it occurs on all branches). The model has also been suggested as a computational framework for reasoning about future actions (e.g., McDermott 1982; Mays 1983).

There is no branching future in the model described here. This is because reasoning about the future is considered to be just one instance of hypothetical reasoning. Other examples include reasoning about the past (i.e., how could the world possibly have arrived at the present state), as well as reasoning independent of time and physical causality (such as mathematics). Since all these forms of reasoning are necessary, it seems arbitrary to put one subclass into the model of time. If there were a good reason to encode such reasoning in a branching time model, then the model should also include a branching past, for the types of mechanisms needed for reasoning about the past and future appear to be identical.

Thus there is a simple single time line (which would correspond to the actual past and actual future in a branching time model). Of course, the reasoner can never totally identify the actual past or future, and reasoning about what actually has occurred or will occur consists of constructing the most plausible hypotheses given what is known about the past, present, and future.

As a final comment, note that this does not mean that the reasoning agent is simply a passive observer of the world. By deciding to do actions, the agent changes his expectations about what the future will actually be. This will be discussed in further detail after we have introduced the notion of events and actions.

3 DEFINING OCCURRENCES

In order to define the role that events and actions play in the logic, let us consider a possible logical form for sentences asserting that an event occurred and see how it fails. The suggestion is that we define a property for each event class such that the property HOLDS over an interval I just in the cases when an instance of the event class occurred over interval I. But this immediately presents problems, for axiom (H.1) would not hold for such properties. In particular, an event such as turning on the light may occur over an interval T, but not occur over any subinterval of T. In other words, T could be the smallest interval over which "turning on the light" occurred. This cannot be captured by a property, for axiom (H.1) would imply the event occurred over subintervals of T as well.

We introduce a new type of object into our ontology, named an *occurrence*. By representing occurrences as objects in the logic, we are following Davidson's suggestion (1967) for representing events. His major argument for this position is that it allows a clean formalism for modeling modifiers and qualifiers of events as predicates acting on the event objects.

Following many others, including Mourelatos (1978), we will divide the class of occurrences into two subclasses, *processes* and *events*. Processes refer to some activity not involving a culmination or anticipated result, such as the process denoted by the sentence, "I am running". Events describe an activity that involves a product or outcome, such as the event denoted by the sentence "I walked to the store". A useful test for distinguishing between events and processes is that one can count the number of times an event occurs, but one cannot count the number of times a process is occurring.

Above, we saw that a property could HOLD over many different time intervals. For example, the property that "my wagon is red" might HOLD in the summer of 1981, but not in 1982, and yet again in 1983. We can view a property as defining a set of time intervals over which it holds. We treat occurrences similarly. For example, the occurrence "I walked from home to school" might OCCUR every weekday morning. We cannot specify a particular instance of an occurrence without specifying the unique time over which it occurred.

Properties, processes, and events may be distinguished by considering the characteristics of the set of temporal intervals that they hold or occur over. As we have already seen, the set of intervals over which a property holds is closed under the IN relation. In other words, if interval I is in the set, all intervals J such that IN(J, I) are also in the set. In contrast, the set of intervals over which an event occurs contains no pair of intervals such that one is IN the other. In other words, an event occurs over the smallest time possible for it to occur. This is the same treatment of events as in McDermott (1982). Processes fall between events and properties. To see this, consider the process "I am walking" over interval I. Unlike events, this process may also be occurring over subintervals of I. Unlike properties, however, it is not the case that the process must be occurring over all subintervals of I. For example, if I am walking over interval I, then I am walking over the first half of I; however, there may be some subintervals of I where I paused for a brief rest.

Let us return to the more formal development of occurrences. We shall start with events, as they are the simplest. The predicate OCCUR takes an event and a time interval and is true only if the event happened over the time interval t, and there is no subinterval of t over which the event happened. Thus for any event e, and times t and t', we have the axiom

$$\text{OCCUR}(e, t) \& \text{IN}(t', t) \Rightarrow \sim\text{OCCUR}(e, t'). \tag{O.1}$$

Related classes of events can be described using functions. For example, consider the set of events consisting of an object changing location. We can define a function CHANGE-POS with three arguments: the object, the source location, and the goal location. Thus,

CHANGE-POS(Ball, x, y)

generates the class of events that consists of a ball moving from x to y. This does not assert that a ball actually did move from x to y. That claim is made by asserting that the event occurred over some time interval. Thus to assert that BALL1 moved from POS1 to POS2 over time T100, we say

OCCUR(CHANGE-POS(BALL1, POS1, POS2), T100).

We can now define necessary conditions for the class of events involving a change of location:

OCCUR(CHANGE-POS(object, source, goal), t) $\Rightarrow \exists t1, t2$.
  MEETS($t1, t$) & MEETS($t, t2$) &
  HOLDS(at(object, source), $t1$) & HOLDS(at(object, goal), $t2$).

Notice that this definition is of the form

$$\text{OCCUR}(e, t) \Rightarrow P_t$$

where e is an event-defining function and P_t is a set of conditions involving t.

If the P_t are necessary and sufficient conditions for an event's occurrence, we can define the event with an assertion of the form

$$\text{OCCUR}(e, t) \Leftrightarrow P_t \& \forall t'.\text{IN}(t', t) \supset \sim P_{t'}.$$

This more complicated form is necessary to ensure the validity of axiom (O.1), which insists that an event occurs only over the smallest interval in which it could have. For example, since the conditions above are sufficient to define a CHANGE-POS event, we could have the assertion

OCCUR(CHANGE-POS(object, source, goal), t) $\Leftrightarrow$
  ($\exists t1, t2$.
    MEETS($t1, t$) & MEETS($t, t2$) &
    HOLDS(at(object, source), $t1$) &
    HOLDS(at(object, goal), $t2$)) &
  ($\forall t'.\text{IN}(t', t) \Rightarrow$
    $\sim$($\exists t3, t4$.
      MEETS($t3, t'$) & MEETS($t', t4$) &
      HOLDS(at(object, source), $t3$) &
      HOLDS(at, (object, goal), $t4$))).

For the sake of readability, we will summarize event definitions by only stating the P_t-conditions and noting whether they are only necessary or are necessary and sufficient.

For example, the above example will be written as:

Necessary and Sufficient Conditions for
OCCUR(CHANGE-POS(object, source, goal), t):

$\exists t1, t2.$
MEETS($t1, t$) & MEETS($t, t2$) &
HOLDS(at(object, source), $t1$) &
HOLDS(at(object, goal), $t2$).

Axiom (O.1) allows us to count events and hence to construct events that are composites of other events. For example, the class of events of repeating an event twice can be defined by:

Necessary and Sufficient Conditions for
OCCUR(TWICE(event), t):

$\exists t1, t2.$
IN($t1, t$) & IN($t2, t$) & $t1 \neq t2$ &
OCCUR(event, $t1$) & OCCUR(event, $t2$).

If we expand this definition out to its full form shown above, we can easily see that it captures repeating exactly twice rather than at least twice.

An event that is a sequence of other events can be defined so that the times of each successive event MEET or are strictly AFTER each other. For example, a two-event sequence with MEET can be defined as follows:

Necessary and Sufficient Conditions for
OCCUR(TWO-MEET-SEQUENCE(event1, event2), t):

$\exists t1, t2.$
STARTS($t1, t$) & FINISHES($t2, t$) & MEETS($t1, t2$) &
OCCURS(event1, $t1$) & OCCURS(event2, $t2$).

Finally, a composite event that will be useful later is the simple composite of two events occurring simultaneously.

Necessary and Sufficient Conditions for
OCCUR(COMPOSITE(event 1, event2), t):

OCCUR(event1, t) & OCCUR(event2, t).

All of the event classes we have considered so far have been fully specified. For example, the CHANGE-POS event class specified both the starting position and ending position of the object. It is possible to deal with less specific events in the same framework as well. For instance, consider the class of events of moving to somewhere (without specifying where from). Thus we can define this new class as follows:

Necessary and Sufficient Conditions for
OCCUR(MOVE-TO(obj, dest), T):

$\exists s.$OCCUR(CHANGE-POS(obj, s, dest), T).

It is here that we see that axiom (O.1) is crucial to allow us to count MOVE-TO events. For example, consider a simple world with three distinguished positions, A, B, and C, and a ball that moves from A to C via B during time T. Now there are three CHANGE-POS events that OCCUR over or within T, CHANGE-POS(Ball1, A, B), CHANGE-POS(Ball1, B, C), and CHANGE-POS(Ball1, A, C). So it would appear that we could have two MOVE-TO (Ball1, C) events that OCCUR over or within T corresponding to the latter two CHANGE-POS events above. If this were the case, we should report that the ball moved to C at least twice during T, an obviously ridiculous conclusion. Axiom (O.1), which is embedded in the definition of MOVE-TO above, guarantees that only the CHANGE-POS from A to C produces a MOVE-TO C event. Thus we have the desired conclusion that the ball moved to C only once during T.

The other major subclass of occurrences is the processes. Processes differ from events in that axiom (O.1) does not hold. If a process occurs over a time interval T, it appears to occur over at least a substantial number of subintervals. For example, if I am walking during interval T, I must be walking during the first half of interval T. I could have stopped walking for a brief period within T, however, and still have been walking during T. Thus, we appear to need some notion of grain of interval size for a given process, where in any subinterval larger than the grain size, the process also occurred. This is too difficult to formalize adequately at present. Thus we will make a weaker claim for processes than we might. In particular, if a process is occurring over an interval T, it must also be occurring over at least one subinterval of T. To formalize this, we introduce a new predicate, OCCURRING, for processes. We then have for all processes p, and time t:

$$\text{OCCURRING}(p, t) \Rightarrow \exists t'.\text{IN}(t', t) \& \text{OCCURRING}(p, t'). \tag{O.2}$$

Related classes of processes will be described using functions in a similar manner as with event classes. For certain classes of processes we can of course define stronger axioms than (O.2). For example, if we let FALLING(object) denote the class of processes involving the object falling, we could have an axiom that it is falling over all subintervals:

$$\text{OCCURRING}(\text{FALLING}(\text{object}), T) \Leftrightarrow (\forall t.\text{IN}(t, T) \Rightarrow \tag{O.3}$$
$$\text{OCCURRING}(\text{FALLING}(\text{object}), t)).$$

Many event classes have closely associated process classes. For example, the event of an object falling from x to y necessarily involves the process of falling. In fact, we could define the falling event as a composite of the CHANGE-POS event introduced above and a falling process. Using a definition of COMPOSITE extended to include processes, we define:

FALL(object, source, goal) =
COMPOSITE(CHANGE-POS(object, source, goal),
FALLING(object)).

Using this definition, we can prove that

OCCUR(FALL(object, source, goal), t) ⇔
OCCUR(CHANGE-POS(object, source, goal), t) &
OCCURRING(FALLING(object), t).

Many events can be decomposed into a fairly 'neutral' event like CHANGE-POS and a process. This appears to formalize the intuition underlying many representations based on verb primitives (e.g., Schank 1975; Jackendoff 1976).

The relation between processes and events becomes more complicated once one considers sentences that describe processes in terms of events. For example, the sentence "John is walking from home to the store" appears to describe a process because it is in the progressive tense, yet does it in terms closer to an event. This sentence may be true even if the event does not occur: John might change his mind on the way and return home. A suggested solution to this problem is that the above sentence really means that John is walking with the intention of going to the store. This does not solve the entire problem, however, for similar sentences can be constructed for inanimate objects, as in "The ball was falling to the ground".

The above solution might be adapted by using a notion of expected outcome to subsume the agent's intention. A solution along these lines, however, is beyond the capabilities of the present formalism. Without further comment, we shall allow such sentences to be expressed by allowing events to be arguments to the OCCURRING predicate. For example, let us assume the sentence "The ball fell onto the table over T" is represented as:

OCCUR(FALL(ball, s, table 1), T).

Then the sentence "The ball was falling to the table over T" would be represented by:

OCCURRING(FALL(ball, s, table 1), T).

Generalizing from this example, we can see that if an event occurred, then it was occurring. In other words, for any event e and time t,

$$\text{OCCUR}(e, t) \Rightarrow \text{OCCURRING}(e, t). \tag{O.4}$$

The converse of this does not hold.

Defining necessary and sufficient conditions for many processes, especially those describing human activity, appears not to be possible. While there may be technical definitions of the differences between walking, strolling, and running, it is unlikely that they would be useful in language comprehension. Such terms appear to be primitive-like processes that may be recognized from the perceptual system. Of course, necessary conditions are likely to be found for these processes, and consequences, such as that they all involve moving, but at different rates, can be described if necessary.

Processes involving physical change, or motion (e.g., falling) may afford precise descriptions. What is necessary to describe these is a workable theory of naive physics (see Hayes 1978). Investigating these issues here will take us too far afield.

An important relationship that we shall need asserts that one event causes another. The nature of causality has been studied extensively in philosophy (e.g., Sosa 1975). Many of the issues considered there, however, will not affect this work. Let us introduce a predicate ECAUSE (event causation), where

ECAUSE($e1$, $t1$, $e2$, $t2$)

is true only if event $e1$'s occurrence at time $t1$ caused event $e2$ to occur at time $t2$. The following facts about causality are important.

If an event occurred that caused another event, then the caused event also occurred.

$$\text{OCCUR}(e, t) \,\&\, \text{ECAUSE}(e, t, e', t') \Rightarrow \text{OCCUR}(e', t'). \tag{O.5}$$

An event cannot cause events prior to its occurrence (though they may be simultaneous).

$$\text{ECAUSE}(e, t, e', t') \Rightarrow \text{IN}(t', t) \vee \text{BEFORE}(t, t') \vee \tag{O.6}$$
$$\text{MEETS}(t, t') \vee \text{OVERLAPS}(t, t') \vee \text{EQUALS}(t, t').$$

Furthermore, the ECAUSE relation is transitive, anti-symmetric, and anti-reflexive.

None of the axioms above can be used to infer a new causal relation from a set of facts involving no causal relations. Thus all inferences about causality come from other already known causal relations, or must be induced from outside the logic. This seems consistent with common treatments in philosophy and artificial intelligence in which causality is irreducible (e.g., Taylor 1966; Norman and Rumelhart 1975; Schank 1975).

4 DEFINING ACTIONS

An important subclass of occurrences are those that involve animate agents performing actions. There are actions that are processes (e.g., "John is running"), and actions that are events (e.g., "John lost his hat"). An action is an occurrence caused in a 'certain' way by the agent. This relation is not simple causality between events, for an agent may be involved in an event without it being an action of that agent. For example, consider two distinct interpretations of the sentence, "Cleo broke the window". The first describes an action of Cleo. The second arises, say, if Cleo is thrown through the window at a wild party. In this case, Cleo is the instrument of the breaking of the window. Thus not all events that are caused by animate agents are actions by that agent.

To avoid this difficulty, we introduce a new form of causality termed agentive causality or ACAUSE. An agent ACAUSES an event only in those cases where the agent caused the event in an appropriate manner for the situation to be called an action of the agent.

Classes of actions can be characterized by the function

ACAUSE(agent, occurrence)

which for any agent and occurrence produces the action of the agent causing the occurrence. As with all other occurrences, such actions may OCCUR or be OCCURRING over a set of time intervals. Particular instances of actions can only be specified by specifying the time of the action.

We can also classify actions in the same manner as all other occurrences by introducing a function for each related class of actions. For example, the class of actions consisting of an agent moving an object from one location to another can be generated by the function

MOVE-ACTION(agent, object, source-location, goal-location)

which can be defined as being equivalent to

ACAUSE(agent, CHANGE-POS(object, source-location, goal-location)).

It is hypothesized that every action can be characterized as an agent ACAUSEing an occurrence. For some actions, such as singing, an occurrence must be introduced that consists of the actual motions involved to produce the activity. Although such an occurrence might never occur independently of the action, introducing it preserves the simplicity of the model.

Again borrowing terminology from Mourelatos (1978), we call the class of actions that consists of ACAUSEing an event to be *performances*, and those that consist of ACAUSEing a process to be *activities*.

We can capture much of the above discussion with the following axioms. If an agent ACAUSEs an occurrence over time t, then the occurrence was OCCURRING over t.

$$\text{OCCURRING}(\text{ACAUSE}(\text{agent}, \text{occurrence}), t) \Rightarrow \qquad (A.1)$$
$$\text{OCCURRING}(\text{occurrence}, t).$$

For every action there is a unique agent and a unique occurrence that the agent ACAUSEs which constitutes the action.

$$\forall \text{action } \exists! \text{ agent}, \text{occurrence action} = \text{ACAUSE}(\text{agent}, \text{occurrence}). \qquad (A.2)$$

For the subclass of performances, we have a stronger version of (A.1) with the OCCUR predicate.

$$\text{OCCUR}(\text{ACAUSE}(\text{agent}, \text{event}), t) \Rightarrow \text{OCCUR}(\text{event}, t). \qquad (A.3)$$

The other important aspects of the ACAUSE relation remain to be considered in the section on intentional action. But first, let us reconsider the individuation of actions.

We have seen simple performances and activities as examples of actions. Using the constructors for composite events we can describe actions that consist of a sequence of actions, or consist of actions being performed simultaneously. Note that a composite action composed of a performance and an activity (e.g., "walking to the store while juggling three balls") is itself a performance. This is easily seen from the observation that we can count the number of occurrences of such composite actions. The only composites that are activities are those that consist entirely of activities.

There are situations which might appear to be simple composite actions, yet, on closer examination, have considerably richer structure. The composite actions we have seen so far consist of actions that can be considered independently of each other; neither is necessary for the success of the other. Thus walking to the store while juggling three balls consists of walking to the store, which could have been done independently, and juggling three balls, which also could have been done independently. Many other composites have subactions that are related in a considerably stronger fashion. Consider the actions performed in the situation described as "Sam hid his coat by standing in front of it".

Taking the position outlined in the introduction, there are at least two distinct actions performed here; namely, "hiding the coat" and "standing in front of the coat". These actions, however, are not independent of each other. They are intimately related, as one was performed by means of performing the other, i.e., the coat was hidden by means of standing in front of it. Note that this is not simply a causal relationship: standing in front of the coat didn't cause John's hiding the coat, it actually constituted the hiding.

A wide range of similar examples exists in the speech act literature (e.g., Searle 1969). For example, I may perform a promise by telling you that I will come to your party, provided I have the appropriate intentions. Again, the act of speaking did not simply cause the promise act, but, in conjunction with the appropriate intentions, it constituted the promise act.

Goldman (1970) terms this relationship between actions as generation. An act A *generates* an act B iff:

(i) A and B are cotemporal (they occur at the same time);
(ii) A is not part of doing B (such as "playing a C note" is part of "playing a C triad" on a piano);
(iii) A occurs in a context C, where the occurrence of A and C jointly imply the occurrence of B.

Goldman distinguishes different types of generation, depending on the nature of the context C. I have not found this a useful division as most examples seem to be combinations of the different types. He identifies three major components of C:

- causal laws: A generates B because the occurrence of A causes the occurrence of B;
- conventional rules: for example, "signaling a left turn on your bike" is generated by "putting your arm out";
- simple (or definitional): A generates B simply by the fact that B is defined as doing A in a certain context; an example of this, namely hiding an object from someone, will be discussed in detail below.

To continue the formal development, let us introduce a predicate GENERATES that takes two actions and a time:

GENERATES(a_1, a_2, t).

This predicate is true only if action a_1 generates action a_2 during time t. GENERATES is transitive, anti-symmetric, and anti-reflexive with respect to its two action arguments.

For example, consider an agent JOHN playing a C triad on the piano. Other actions that JOHN performs simultaneously with this include playing a C note (a part of the first action) and waking up Sue (generated by the first action). We can express this in the formal notation using the following functions. Let:

- PLAY-C-TRIAD(agent, piano) be the action of the agent playing a C triad on the piano;
- PLAY-C(agent, piano) be the action of the agent playing a C note on the piano; and
- WAKE(agent, other) be the action of the agent waking up the other person.

Then the situation above is captured by

OCCUR(PLAY-C-TRIAD(JOHN, P), T_1) &
OCCUR(PLAY-C(JOHN, P), T_1) &
OCCUR(WAKE(JOHN, SUE), T_1)

where

GENERATES(PLAY-C-TRIAD(JOHN, P),
WAKE(JOHN, SUE), T_1)

and ∃-event

PLAY-C-TRIAD(JOHN, P) =
COMPOSITE(PLAY-C(JOHN, P), event).

The notion of generation is crucial for considering how an action was performed, or how to perform an action (i.e., planning). Investigating these issues will take us too far afield, but it is worth briefly considering how planning knowledge and definitional knowledge interact. We have seen two major classes of knowledge about actions. One, the definitional, outlines necessary (and sometimes sufficient) conditions for an action's occurrence. This is crucial for achieving a minimal understanding of what is implied by a sentence describing an action. The second, generational knowledge, outlines how actions can be performed, and is crucial for problem solving. But a sharp distinction in the uses of this knowledge is artificial. Generational knowledge can be used in understanding to infer plausible ways in which an action might have been accomplished, whereas definitional knowledge can be used by a problem solver to identify what actions might be appropriate to solve a certain task that has not been encountered previously.

5 INTENTIONAL ACTION

Before developing the notion of intentional action, let us consider an example that motivates the remainder of the paper, namely, defining the action of hiding an object from someone. We shall not consider the sense of hiding that is equivalent to simply concealing from sight accidentally. The sense here is the sense that arises from an accusation such as "You hid that book from me!" As we shall see, this is an intentional action.

The definition of hiding an object should be independent of any method by which the action was performed, for, depending on the context, the actor could hide the object in many different ways. In other words, the action can be generated in different ways. For instance, the actor could:

- put the object behind a desk;
- stand between the object and the other agent while they are in the same room; or
- call a friend Y and get her or him to do one of the above.

Furthermore, the actor might hide the object by simply not doing something s/he intended to do. For example, assume Sam is planning to go to lunch with Carole after picking Carole up at her office. If, on the way out of his office, Sam decides not to take his coat because he doesn't want Carole to see it, then Sam has hidden the coat from Carole. Of course, it is crucial here that Sam believed that he normally would have taken the coat. Sam couldn't have hidden his coat by forgetting to bring it.

This example brings up a few key points that may not be noticed from the first three examples. First, Sam must have intended that Carole not see the coat. Without this intention (i.e., in the forgetting case), no such action occurs. Second, Sam must have believed that it was likely that Carole would see the coat in the future course of events. Third, Sam must have decided to act in such a way that he then believed that Carole would not see the coat in the future course of events. Finally, for the act to be successful, Sam must have acted in that way. In this case, the action Sam performed was "not bringing the coat", which would normally not be considered an action unless it was intentional.

I claim that these four conditions provide a reasonably accurate definition of what it means to hide something. They certainly cover the four examples presented above. It is also important to note that one does not have to be successful in order to have been hiding something. The definition depends on what the hider believes and intends at the time, not what actually occurs. However, the present definition is rather unsatisfactory, as many extremely difficult concepts, such as belief and intention, were thrown about casually. We shall investigate these issues in the next sections.

5.1 Belief and plans

There is much recent work on models of belief (e.g., Cohen 1978; Moore 1979). I will use a sentential model of belief based on the model of Haas (1982), which is similar to that of Konolidge (1980) and Kaplan (1968). In their work, belief is a predicate taking an agent and a description of a proposition as its arguments and is intended to mean that the agent believes that proposition. In computer models, it means that the agent has a data structure in its memory corresponding to the proposition. To develop this model requires a consistent method of introducing quotation into the predicate calculus so that the usual paradoxes are avoided. I will not develop this fully here as it is not necessary for this paper, but the interested reader should see Perlis (1981) and Haas (1982).

An important thing to notice, though, is that there must be two relevant time indices to each belief; namely, the time over which the belief is held, and the time over which the proposition is believed to hold. For example, I might believe *today* that it rained *last weekend*. This point will be crucial in modeling the action of hiding. To introduce some notation, let

"A believes (during T_b) that p holds (during T_p)"

be expressed as

HOLDS(believes(A, "HOLDS(p, T_p)"), T_b)

and which we shall abbreviate using

BELIEVES(A, p, T_p, T_b).

The quotation of formulas in this development must be viewed only as a notational convenience. A more elaborate system of quotation is required so that variables can be introduced into quoted expressions. In such cases, the variables range over names of terms. I will avoid these issues and simply allow variables within quotation marks. Once we have the capability of describing propositions in the logic, we can specify a wide range of beliefs using quantification over parts of formulas. Proof methods can be developed that allow the simulation of other agents' reasoning. For a rigorous treatment of these issues, see Haas (1982).

Plans are typically characterized in AI as a sequence or partial order of actions (e.g., Fikes and Nilsson (1971); Sacerdoti (1975)). This characterization is adequate when modeling static worlds where the only change is by the agent that constructs the plan. In more general settings, however, plans may involve actions by other agents as well as naturally occurring events. In addition, plans are not made starting from a blank world. There are many external events occurring, and the agent believes that certain other events may occur in the future. This even includes actions that the agent has already decided to do in the future. Thus a more general notion of planning is called for.

Let each *agent* maintain three partial descriptions of the world. Each description is a set of propositions asserting properties and occurrences over time intervals. The first description is called the *expected* world, the second the *planned* world, and the third the *desired* world. The expected world is what the agent believes will happen given that certain known future events will occur and assuming that the agent does nothing. It is a view of the world assuming all agents are as lazy as possible but remain in accordance with the known future events. The expected world obeys a generalized law of momentum. Things in the process of changing continue to change unless prevented, and everything else remains the same unless disturbed.

The desired world contains a description of the properties and occurrences that the agent desires. The planned world is the same as the expected world except that the agent may add or remove actions (by that agent). Thus it is a simulation of what the world would be like if the agent acted differently than what is expected. The goal, of course, is to make the planned world subsume the desired world and then act according to it. A possible algorithm for this would be a generalized GPS model of finding differences between the worlds and introducing actions to reduce the differences. There is not space here to consider the planning algorithm further, but for an initial attempt at building a planner, see Allen and Koomen (1983).

A plan is a set of decisions about performing or not performing actions by the agent. Thus, at any time, there is a plan that specifies the mapping from the expected world to the planned world. A plan can be constructed without the agent intending to actually act in accordance with the plan. Such plans arise from a wide range of activities, from abstract problem solving to the recognition of plans of other agents. It will be important for us here to have a notion of an agent *committing* to a plan. An agent is committed to a plan over a certain time interval if that agent believes he or she will act in accordance with the plan. That is, the planned world becomes the expected world. This then becomes part of the agent's predictions about the future state of the world, and must be considered in any further planning activity done by the agent. For instance, in the hiding example, when Sam decided not to take the coat, he changed an action he had committed to do in order to hide his coat.

Most models of plans in the literature consider a subclass of the set of plans allowed here. In particular, they only allow planning into the immediate future, and with only a few exceptions (e.g., Vere 1981), do not allow occurrences other than actions by the planner. We can express plans which contain occurrences independent of the planner, including actions by other agents, as well as plans not to do some action.

Let us introduce a little notation for use later on. Let the predication

TO-DO(action, time, plan)

be true if the plan specified includes performing the action at the given time, and let

NOT-TO-DO(action, time, plan)

be true if the plan specified includes not performing the action at the given time. This is of course much stronger than asserting ~TO-DO(action, time, plan), which simply asserts that the plan does not contain the indicated action.

The notion of a goal is not part of a plan directly. Rather, goals are part of the desired world and are the usual reason for committing to a plan. Let

IS-GOAL-OF(agent, goal, gtime, t)

be true if the agent's desired world at time t contains the specified goal holding during gtime. Finally, the predicate

COMMITTED(agent, plan, ctime)

is true if the agent is committed over ctime to act in accordance with the specified plan. Being committed to a plan means that the agent believes he or she will perform all actions (by the agent) in the plan.

One can think of a plan as a complex action, and it makes sense to talk of a plan occurring if all its decisions are carried out. This can be expressed by extending the OCCUR predicate to plans according to the following definition:

OCCUR(plan, t) ⇔
   ∀action, t_a.TO-DO(action, t_a, plan) ⇒
     OCCUR(action, t_a) &
   ∀action, t_a.NOT-TO-DO(action, t_a, plan) ⇒
     (∀ t.IN(t, t_a) ⇒
       ~ OCCUR(action, t_a)).

5.2 Intending

There are two senses of intention that are traditionally distinguished in the literature. The first has been termed *prior intention* (e.g. Searle 1980) and arises in sentences such as

"Jim intends to run a mile today".

This intention is prior to the action, and can hold even if the action is never performed (i.e., Jim forgets or changes his mind). We shall model this form of intention simply by asserting that Jim has committed to a plan that has the action as a step. Thus

$$\text{INTEND(agent, ACAUSE(agent, occurrence), atime, itime)} \Leftrightarrow \qquad (\text{I.1})$$
$$(\exists \text{plan COMMITTED(agent, plan, time)} \&$$
$$\text{TO-DO(ACAUSE(agents, occurrence), atime, plan))}.$$

Note that Jim having this intention implies that he believes he will run the mile today. It does not imply that Jim wants to do the action, although in most cases this is a plausible inference. Also plausible is that Jim has some goal that results from this action being performed. The actual nature of this goal is uncertain. For instance, he may want to stay fit (and so he might change his mind and swim instead), or he may want to win a bet that he couldn't run a mile (and so swimming would not be a reasonable alternative). The example does not specify this information.

Many times an intention of an agent is so general that it is expressed in terms of a goal rather than an action. Examples are the actions of "achieving state x", "preventing event E", etc. To express these, we will simply use the IS-GOAL-OF predication introduced earlier.

The last sense of intention is that of intentional action, which arises in sentences such as

"Jack intentionally coughed."

This example is closely related to the notion of prior intention; it appears that Jack coughed as a result of a plan that he was committed to that involved him coughing. This is essentially the treatment suggested in Miller et al. (1960).

But one must be careful with this definition. For instance, if one intentionally does an action A, does one intentionally do all the subparts of A? What about the actions one did to generate A, or the actions that A generates? For instance, if A was the action of Jack intentionally playing a C chord on the piano, did he also

(i) intentionally play a C note (a subpart of A);
(ii) intentionally move his finger (generating (i)); or
(iii) intentionally annoy his neighbors (generated by A)?

One might say no to (i) and (ii), or allow subparts and not generation, or allow all as intentional. Each side has been proposed; which side we should take depends on what is counted to be in a plan. For instance, if a composite action is in a plan, are its subparts in the plan? If so, then (i) is always intentional. If an action is in a plan, the actions that it generates may or may not be in the plan, depending on the knowledge and goals of the actor. Thus, with (iii), it might go either way, depending on why Jack was playing the piano. This last case shows we cannot simply define how intentionality relates to generation. Some actions which are generated could not be denied, however. If Sam intentionally aims and fires a gun at Sue, knowing it is loaded, he intentionally shot her. This appears to be so because there is no other plausible plan that Sam could have had.

Thus, if we assume Sam is a rational being, and does not act at random, we can assume his plan must have been to shoot Sue. Thus, we will only get into difficulty with the plan-based model of intentionality if we make hard and fast rules, such as that all subparts of an action must be in a plan, or all generated actions of an action must be in a plan. If the contents of a plan are left up to plausible reasoning about the motivation of an agent's behavior, the plan model appears to provide a reasonable definition of intentionality.

There are remaining problems with the plan model, however. Davis (1979) gives an example of a person driving a car when a small child runs in front of it. He claims the person intentionally slams on the brakes yet has no time to form a plan to do so. This difficulty may arise from an inadequate model of plan-directed behavior. For the present, however, these examples will not cause us any problems. Searle (1980) presents other difficulties that arise with this simple model, but again, the problems can be ignored at present, as the examples that present them are fairly bizarre.

On the basis of this discussion, and following Goldman (1970), we can say that an agent S intentionally performed an action A at time t iff

(i) S performed A at t;
(ii) A was part of a plan that S was committed to at time t; and
(iii) S performed A because of S's knowledge of (ii).

Introducing a new predicate, we can easily capture the first two conditions above, but it is not clear how to formalize condition (iii). For computational models in which an agent only acts because of an existing plan, however, this should not present any difficulties. Thus we can capture the first two conditions with:

$$\text{INTENTIONAL(ACAUSE(agent, occurrence), time)} \Rightarrow \qquad (I.2)$$
$$\text{OCCURS(ACAUSE(agent, occurrence), time)} \,\&$$
$$\text{INTEND(agent, ACAUSE(agent, occurrence), time, time)}.$$

Finally, let us return to questions about the nature of the ACAUSE relation. The examples in which we have used it have all been intentional actions, so the question arises as to whether it is possible to have an ACAUSE relation to an unintentional action? For instance, if John broke the window unintentionally, did John perform an action? That, he certainly did, but the action he performed might not be breaking the window, it may have been hitting the baseball (which broke the window). If we claim that, even in this case, John performed the action of breaking the window, then we can make the example more complicated. What if John hit the baseball, which landed on the roof of a house, and a few minutes later rolled off and broke the window? Obviously, in this example, the delay and causal chain of events soon gets complicated enough that we would say John did not break the window. So where do actions stop and mere events caused by actions begin?

There seems no easy answer to this question, although a fruitful approach could be to consider the issue of responsibility. If an agent acts in a way that causes some effect which, while unintentional, should have been foreseen, we tend to term that as an action. We do not have the time to pursue this here, so make the simplifying assumption that all actions are intentional, i.e.,

$$\text{OCCUR(ACAUSE(agent, occurrence), } t) \Rightarrow \qquad (I.3)$$
$$\text{INTENTIONAL(agent, ACAUSE(agent, occurrence), } t).$$

In the unintentional case of "John broke the window", we analyze that as John did something intentionally that caused the window to break. This may seem to complicate the analysis of such sentences, but it can be handled in a relatively clean manner. The meaning of a sentence such as "John broke the window" could be

$\exists e, t1, t2$.OCCUR(ACAUSE(John, e), $t1$) &
  OCCUR(BREAK-EVENT(Window), $t2$) &
  ((e = BREAK-EVENT(Window)) $\vee$
   ECAUSE($e, t1$, BREAK-EVENT (Window), $t2$)).

The disjunction captures the ambiguity as to whether the breaking of the window was intentional or not. If e = BREAK-EVENT(Window), then the event that John ACAUSEd was the breaking of the window. If e caused BREAK-EVENT(Window), then the event John ACAUSEd was something else which ECAUSEd the breaking of the window. Finally, if John intentionally broke the window by hitting the baseball, then he performed two actions (intentionally) which are related by the GENERATEs relation.

6 HOW TO HIDE REVISITED

With these tools, we can attempt a more precise definition of hiding. We first define the function

  HIDE(agent, observer, object)

to generate the class of hiding actions. Let us also introduce an event function

  SEE(agent, object),

which generates events of an agent seeing an object, and a property SEEN(agent, object) defined by

  HOLDS(SEEN(agent, object), t) $\Leftrightarrow$
    $\exists t1$.BEFORE($t1, t$) &
    OCCUR(SEE(agent, object), $t1$).

So the necessary and sufficient conditions for Sam to hide the coat from Carole over interval T_h are as follows. He must have initially believed (during T_b) that Carole would have seen the coat during T_h:

$\exists t$.IN(t, T_h) & STARTS($T_b 1, T_h$) & $\quad\quad\quad\quad\quad\quad$ (1)
  BELIEVES(Sam, SEEN(CAROLE, COAT), $t, T_b 1$).

He must have had an intention (during T_h) that Carole not see the coat:

$\quad\quad$IS-GOAL-OF(Sam, not(SEEN(CAROLE, COAT)), T_h, T_h). $\quad\quad\quad\quad$ (2)

Restating conditions (1) and (2) in terms of Sam's plan during $T_b 1$, we see that in his expected world Carole will see the coat, while in the desired world, she will not.

The next conditions describe Sam as he formulates a new plan which achieves his goal of Carole not seeing the coat. To describe this we introduce two new event classes, first the event of an agent committing to a plan, and second the event of an agent changing his or her mind about something. Let

  COMMIT(agent, plan)

denote the class of events defined by

Necessary and Sufficient Conditions for
OCCUR(COMMIT(agent, plan), time):

$\exists t1, t2$.MEETS($t1$, time) &
  MEETS(time, $t2$) &
  $\sim$COMMITTED(agent, plan, $t1$) &
  COMMITTED(agent, plan, $t2$).

Furthermore, let us define the event class

CHANGE-MIND(agent, property, ptime)

by

Necessary and Sufficient Conditions for
OCCUR(CHANGE-MIND(agent, property, ptime), time):

$\exists t1, t2$.MEETS($t1$, time) &
  MEETS(time, $t2$) &
  BELIEVES(agent, property, ptime, $t1$) &
  BELIEVES(agent, not(property), ptime, $t2$).

Using these events, we can state that Sam is adopting a plan with the goal that Carole not see the coat and that he believes it will work:

$\exists$plan, T_b2.MEETS(T_b1, T_b2) & (3)
  OCCUR(COMMIT(Sam, plan), T_b2) &
  ECAUSE(COMMIT(Sam, plan), T_b2,
    CHANGE-MIND(Sam, SEEN(CAROLE, COAT), T_h), T_b2).

These three conditions capture Sam's intention to hide the coat, and if Sam acts in accordance with the plan hypothesized in condition (3), the hide action is performed.

We can put these conditions all together into one definition as follows:

Necessary and Sufficient Conditions for
OCCUR(HIDE(agent, observer, object), T_h):

$\exists t, T_b1, T_b2$, plan.
  STARTS(T_b1, T_h) &
  MEETS(T_b1, T_b2) &
  IN(t, T_h) &
  BELIEVE(agent, SEEN(observer, object), t, T_b1) &
  IS-GOAL-OF(agent, not(SEEN(observer, object)), T_h, T_h) &
  OCCUR(COMMIT(Sam, plan), T_b2) &
  ECAUSE(COMMITS(Sam, plan), T_b2,
    CHANGE-MIND(Sam, SEEN(CAROLE, COAT), T_h), T_b2) &
  OCCUR(plan, T_h).

The condition that the agent changed his mind can be derived from the above conditions and the definition of ECAUSE.

One can see that much of what it means to hide is captured by the above. In particular, the following can be extracted directly from the definition:

- if you hide something, you intended it not to be seen (and thus can be held responsible for the consequences of this);
- you cannot hide something if you believed it was not possible that it could be seen, or if it were certain that it would be seen anyway;
- one cannot hide something simply by changing one's mind about whether it will be seen.

In addition, there are many other possibilities related to the temporal order of events. For instance, you can't hide something by performing an action after the hiding is supposed to be done.

7 CONCLUSION

In the introduction, three problems in representing actions were discussed. These problems have been addressed throughout the paper, but sometimes only implicitly. Let us reconsider each problem. The first problem concerned actions that involve non-activity, such as standing still. These can be modeled with no difficulty. An action class can be defined so that the agent remains in one position over the time of the action's occurrence. Note that such a non-activity must be intentional if it is to qualify as an action in this framework. Otherwise, such non-activity can only be modeled as an event. A more complicated form of non-activity involves not doing an action that was previously expected. These actions can be defined in terms of the beliefs and intentions of the agent. In particular, the agent must have been intending to do the action and later changed his or her mind.

The second problem concerned actions that cannot be defined by decomposition into subactions. The example of "hiding a book from Sue" is a prime example from this class. Any particular instance of hiding a book can be decomposed into a particular set of subactions, but there is no decomposition, or set of decompositions, that defines the class of hiding actions. Rather, hiding can only be defined in terms of the agent's beliefs and intentions. The speech acts also fall into this class. Each occurrence of a speech act is partially decomposable into the act of uttering something, but otherwise depends crucially on the speaker's intentions.

The third problem concerned actions that occur simultaneously and possibly interact. Simultaneous actions can be described directly since the temporal aspects of a plan are separated from the causal aspects. This enables us to describe situations where actions may interact with each other. Building a system that can reason about such interactions while problem solving, however, remains a difficult problem.

This framework is currently being used to study general problem-solving behavior, as well as the problem-solving behavior that arises in task-oriented dialogues. A simple problem solver has been built using this framework and is described by Allen and Koomen (1983). The model is also being used both for plan recognition and plan generation in a system under development at Rochester that comprehends and participates in task-oriented dialogues. The action models are being used to describe a useful set of conversational actions which include the traditional notion of speech acts.

APPENDIX A PROOF THAT (H.2) ENTAILS (H.1)

$$\text{HOLDS}(p, T) \Leftrightarrow (\forall t.\text{IN}(t, T) \Rightarrow \exists s.\text{IN}(s, t) \land \text{HOLDS}(p, s)). \tag{H.2}$$

$$\text{HOLDS}(p, T) \Leftrightarrow (\forall t.\text{IN}(t, T) \Rightarrow \text{HOLDS}(p, T)). \tag{H.1}$$

We assume (H.2) as the definition, and prove (H.1) one direction at a time. The only assumptions we need about the IN relation is that it is transitive, and for every interval I, there exists an interval J such that $\text{IN}(J, I)$.

Proof of $\text{HOLDS}(p, T) \Rightarrow (\forall t.\text{IN}(t, T) \Rightarrow \text{HOLDS}(p, T))$:

(1)	$\text{HOLDS}(p, T)$	hypothesis;
(2)	$\forall t.\text{IN}(t, T) \Rightarrow (\exists s.\text{IN}(s, t) \& \text{HOLDS}(p, s))$	by defn. (H.2), (1);
(3)	$\text{IN}(T1, T)$	assumption;
(4)	$\quad \text{IN}(T2, T1)$	assumption;
(5)	$\quad \text{IN}(T2, T)$	transitivity of IN using (3), (4);
(6)	$\quad \exists s.\text{IN}(s, T2) \& \text{HOLDS}(p, s)$	MP (2), (5);
(7)	$\forall t'.\text{IN}(t', T1) \Rightarrow$	discharging assumption (4);
	$\quad (\exists s.\text{IN}(s, t') \& \text{HOLDS}(p, s))$	
(8)	$\text{HOLDS}(p, T1)$	by defn. (H.2), (7);
(9)	$\forall t.\text{IN}(t, T) \Rightarrow \text{HOLDS}(p, T)$	discharging assumption (3).

Proof of $(\forall t.\text{IN}(t, T) \Rightarrow \text{HOLDS}(p, t)) \Rightarrow \text{HOLDS}(p, T)$:

(1)	$\forall t.\text{IN}(t, T) \Rightarrow \text{HOLDS}(p, t)$	hypothesis;
(2)	$\quad \text{IN}(T1, T)$	assumption;
(3)	$\quad \text{HOLDS}(p, T1)$	MP (1), (2);
(4)	$\quad \forall t'.\text{IN}(t', T1) \supset \exists s'.\text{IN}(s', t') \& \text{HOLDS}(p, s')$	by defn. (H.2), (3);
(5)	$\quad \exists s''.\text{IN}(s'', T1)$	axiom
(6)	$\quad\quad \text{IN}(T2, T1)$	existential elim., (5);
(7)	$\quad\quad \exists s', \text{IN}(s', T2) \& \text{HOLDS}(p, s')$	MP (4), (6);
(8)	$\quad\quad\quad \text{IN}(T3, T2) \& \text{HOLDS}(p, T3)$	existential elim., (7);
(9)	$\quad\quad\quad \text{HOLDS}(p, T3)$	conj. elim., (8);
(10)	$\quad\quad\quad \text{IN}(T3, T1)$	transitivity of IN, (6), (8);
(11)	$\quad\quad\quad \text{IN}(T3, T1) \& \text{HOLDS}(p, T1)$	conj. into. (9), (10);
(12)	$\quad\quad\quad \exists s'.\text{IN}(s', T1) \& \text{HOLDS}(p, s')$	existential intro., (11);
(13)	$\quad \exists s'.\text{IN}(s', T1) \& \text{HOLDS}(p, s')$	existential intro., [12];
(14)	$\forall t.\text{IN}(t, T) \supset \exists s'.\text{IN}(s', t) \& \text{HOLDS}(p, s')$	discharging assumption (2);
(15)	$\text{HOLDS}(p, T)$	by defn. (H.2), (14).

ACKNOWLEDGMENTS

The author wishes to thank Henry Kautz for his detailed criticism of the penultimate version of this paper that forced the clarification of several murky areas. I would also like to thank Jerry Feldman, Alan Frisch, Andy Haas, Margery Lucas, Dan Russell, and Stuart Goldkind for many enlightening comments and improvements on previous versions of this paper, and Drew McDermott and Pat Hayes for discussions on general issues in representing action and time.

REFERENCES

Allen, J. F. (1981). 'Maintaining knowledge about temporal intervals', TR 86, Computer Science Dept., University of Rochester, January 1981; also in *Communications of the ACM* **26** (1983), 832–43.

Allen, J. F. and Koomen, J. A. (1983). 'Planning using a temporal world model', *Proceedings of the 8th International Joint Conference on Artificial Intelligence* (IJCAI), Karlsruhe, West Germany, 741–7.

Allen, J. F. and Perrault, C. R. (1980). 'Analyzing intention in utterances', *Artificial Intelligence* **15**: 143–78.

Charniak, E. (1981). 'A common representation for problem-solving and language-comprehension information', *Artificial Intelligence* **16**: 225–55.

Cohen, P. R. (1978). 'On knowing what to say: Planning speech acts', TR 118, Computer Science Dept., University of Toronto.

Davidson, D. (1967). 'The logical form of action sentences', in N. Rescher (ed.), *The Logic of Decision and Action*. Pittsburgh, PA: University Pittsburgh Press.

Davis, L. K. (1979). *Theory of Action*. Englewood Cliffs, NJ: Prentice-Hall.

Fikes, R. E. and Nilsson, N. J. (1971). 'STRIPS: A new approach to the application of theorem proving to problem solving', *Artificial Intelligence* **2**: 189–205.

Fillmore, C. J. (1968). 'The case for case', in E. Bach and R. J. Harms (eds.), *Universals in Linguistic Theory*. New York: Holt, Rinehart and Winston, 1–90.

Goldman, A. (1970). *A Theory of Human Action*. Princeton, NJ: Princeton University Press.

Haas, A. (1982). 'Planning mental actions', TR 106 and Ph.D. dissertation, Computer Science Dept., University of Rochester, Rochester, NY.

Hayes, P. J. (1978). 'Naive physics I: Ontology for liquids'. Working Paper 63, Institut pour les Etudes Semantiques et Cognitives, Geneva.

Jackendoff, R. (1976). 'Toward an explanatory semantic representation', *Linguistic Inquiry* **7**(1): 89–150.

Kaplan, D. (1968). 'Quantifying in', *Synthese* **19**: 178–214.

Konolidge, K. (1980). 'A first-order formalization of knowledge and action for a multiagent planning system', TN 232, AI Center, SRI International, Menlo Park, CA.

Mays, E. (1983). 'A modal temporal logic for reasoning about change', *Proceedings of the 21st Meeting of the Association for Computational Linguistics*. Cambridge, CA: MIT.

McCarthy, J. and Hayes, P. J. (1969). 'Some philosophical problems from the standpoint of artificial intelligence', in B. Meltzer and D. Michie (eds.), *Machine Intelligence* **4**. Edinburgh University Press, Edinburgh, 463–502.

McDermott, D. (1981). 'A temporal logic for reasoning about processes and plans', RR 196, Computer Science Dept., Yale University, New Haven, CT; also in *Cognitive Science* **6**(2) (1982): 101–55.

Miller, G. A., Galanter, E. and Pribram, K. H. (1960). *Plans and the Structure of Behavior*. New York: Holt, Rinehart and Winston.

Moore, R. C. (1979). 'Reasoning about knowledge and action', Ph.D. dissertation, MIT, Cambridge, MA.

Mourelatos, A. P. D. (1978). 'Events, processes, and states', *Linguistics and Philosophy* **2**: 415–34.

Norman, D. A. and Rumelhart, D. E. (1975). *Explorations in Cognition*. San Francisco, CA: Freeman.

Perlis, D. (1981). 'Language, computation, and reality', TR 95 and Ph.D. dissertation, Computer Science Dept., University of Rochester, Rochester, NY.

Sacerdoti, E. D. (1975). 'The nonlinear nature of plans', *Proceedings of the 4th International Joint Conference on Artificial Intelligence* (IJCAI). Tbilisi, USSR, 206–14.

Schank, R. C. (1975). *Conceptual Information Processing*. New York: North-Holland.

Searle, J. R. (1969). *Speech Acts: An Essay in the Philosophy of Language*. London: Cambridge University Press.

Searle, J. R. (1980). 'The intentionality of intention and action', *Cognitive Science* **4**(1): 47–70.
Sosa, E. (ed.) (1975). *Causation and Conditionals*. Oxford: Oxford University Press.
Taylor, R. (1966). *Action and Purpose*. Englewood Cliffs, NJ: Prentice-Hall.
Vere, S. (1981). 'Planning in time: Windows and durations for activities and goals', Jet Propulsion Laboratory, California Institute of Technology.

13

A Critical Examination of Allen's Theory of Action and Time

ANTONY GALTON

1 INTRODUCTION

It has been recognized for some years now that in many areas of artificial intelligence there is a pressing need for efficient ways of representing everyday reasoning about time. Amongst the work that has been most influential in this area is that of Allen (1981, 1983, 1984) and McDermott (1982). McDermott identifies an adequate treatment of *continuous change* as one of the key requirements for a system to be able to reason about time realistically, and Allen, while not dealing explicitly with continuous change, mentions examples which involve it (e.g. a ball falling onto a table, a block on a rotating table). Examples of AI applications involving continuous change are Bundy's work on mechanics problem solving (1978), Hayes' "naive" ontology for liquids (1985), and Kuipers' qualitative reasoning method for predicting the behaviour of mechanisms characterized by parameters varying continuously in time (1984). More generally, a system cannot hope to interact intelligently with the physical world in real time unless it can reason effectively about continuous change. So it is clear that AI cannot afford to ignore this aspect of temporal reasoning.

In this paper I shall show that Allen's interval-based theory of time is not adequate, as it stands, for reasoning correctly about continuous change. I identify the source of this inadequacy in Allen's determination to base his theory on time intervals rather than on time instants, either banishing the latter entirely or, latterly, relegating them to a subsidiary status within the theory. A consequence of this neglect of instants is that the resulting classification of properties and events and how they are instantiated in time is too crude to encompass continuous phenomena. I argue that in order to overcome this limitation one must be prepared to treat instants and intervals on an equal footing, as well as diversifying the range of predicates assigning temporal locations to properties and occurrences.

In the light of this discussion, I propose some revisions of Allen's theory which overcome the problems encountered with continuous change while adhering closely to the spirit of the original.

2 ALLEN'S LOGIC OF INTERVALS

2.1 Properties and their negations

Allen (1984) sets up his logic of intervals as a framework on which to hang assertions about the instantiation in time of properties and occurrences. For the moment we need only consider properties. In Allen's notation, the formula HOLDS(p, T) says that the property p holds during the interval T. More precisely, what it says is that p holds *throughout* that interval, and to secure this interpretation Allen introduces an axiom

$$\text{HOLDS}(p, T) \Leftrightarrow (\forall t)[\text{IN}(t, T) \Rightarrow \text{HOLDS}(p, t)]. \tag{H.1}$$

In Allen's notation, "IN(X, Y)" means that the interval X is a proper subinterval of Y. Allen immediately follows this axiom with a more complicated one, namely

$$\text{HOLDS}(p, T) \Leftrightarrow \\ (\forall t)[\text{IN}(t, T) \Rightarrow (\exists s)[\text{IN}(s, T) \,\&\, \text{HOLDS}(p, s)]]. \tag{H.2}$$

And he goes on to define, amongst other things, the negation of a property, characterized by the axiom

$$\text{HOLDS}(\text{not}(p), T) \Leftrightarrow (\forall t)[\text{IN}(t, T) \Rightarrow \neg\text{HOLDS}(p, t)]. \tag{H.4}$$

I shall refer to the operator "not" in (H.4) as *property-negation*, to be kept distinct from ordinary sentence-negation, symbolized by "¬." Allen notes that HOLDS(not(p), T) implies ¬ HOLDS(p, T), but not conversely, and that HOLDS(not(not(p)), T) is equivalent to HOLDS(p, T).

2.2 Some problems with property-negation

In this section I shall show that Allen's axioms (H.2) and (H.4) lead to difficulties if we try to apply them in the context of reasoning about continuous change. In particular, I show that (i) Allen's property-negation does not correctly capture what we ordinarily understand by the negation of a property, and that (ii) the kinds of property that are admissible as substituends for p in (H.2) is a restricted subclass of the whole range of properties we need to consider.

In what follows, I shall use "X" as the name of a physical body, "P" as the name of a possible position for X (i.e. a region of space commensurate with X), and "X is at P" to represent the proposition that the body X exactly occupies the position P.

Case 1. Assume that property-negation does exactly capture our intuitive notion of the negation of a property. In that case, if we let "p" stand for "X is at P," then "not(p)" must stand for "X is not at P."

Now suppose X is in continuous motion throughout the interval T. This means that there is no subinterval of T throughout which X is at P; for if there were, then X would be at rest throughout that subinterval, and hence not continuously moving throughout T. Using the abbreviations introduced above, we can write what has just been said as

$$\neg(\exists t) [\text{IN}(t, T) \,\&\, \text{HOLDS}(p, t)],$$

which is equivalent to

$$(\forall t)[\text{IN}(t, T) \Rightarrow \neg \text{HOLDS}(p, t)],$$

and hence, by (H.4), to

HOLDS(not (p), T).

By our assumption, this means that "X is not at P" is true throughout T. Since P can be any possible position for X, it follows that X is never at any position at all at any time during T. Allen's block-manipulating robot will encounter problems lifting that block off the rotating table: according to the robot's own temporal logic, since the block is in continuous motion, it will never be in exactly the right position for the robot to get hold of it! Plainly, we must reject our assumption, and conclude instead that Allen's property-negation does not always tally with our ordinary idea of the negation of a property.

Case 2. Assume now that "X is not at P" is a legitimate substituend for p in axiom (H.2). As before, we shall suppose that X is in continuous motion throughout the interval T, only now we add the further stipulation that the path traced by X during T does not cross itself, so that X does not occupy any position more than once in the course of its motion.

I claim that, given any subinterval t of T, there is a subinterval s of t such that "X is not at P" is true throughout s. For this claim to be false, either (a) "X is not at P" is false throughout t, i.e. X is at P throughout t, which contradicts our assumption that X is continuously moving throughout T, or (b) X returns to P during every subinterval of t, which contradicts our stipulation that X's path is non-self-intersecting.

Representing "X is not at P" by p, we can write what has just been proved as

$(\forall t)[\text{IN}\ (t, T) \Rightarrow (\exists s)\ [\text{IN}\ (s, t)\ \&\ \text{HOLDS}\ (p, s)]]$.

By our assumption, (H.2) holds for this reading of p, allowing us to infer

HOLDS(p, T),

i.e. "X is not at P" is true throughout T. This is the same conclusion as we reached in Case 1; as before, we must reject it, and conclude that there are properties, such as X's not being at P, which cannot be substituted for p in (H.2).

2.3 Another formulation of the arguments

I hope it will not appear to weaken my conviction as to the force of these arguments if I present them in a different form. In doing so, I shall prepare the ground for the subsequent revision of Allen's theory which will circumvent the problems that the arguments reveal.

First, note that Allen recognizes the possibility of one interval following another without any intervening gap. If S and T are two such mutually contiguous intervals, Allen says that *S meets T*, and writes this in predicate form as MEETS(S, T). MEETS is one of thirteen ways in which two intervals can be temporally related, which Allen systematically enumerates and names.

Next, although Allen himself does not take this step, we can posit a function JOIN such that whenever S meets T, JOIN(S, T) is the interval obtained by joining S to T, i.e. the interval which begins when S begins and ends when T ends. If intervals were sets, this would be the set-theoretic union of S and T (but it is important to bear in mind that for Allen, intervals are not sets).

The join of two intervals has the property that if t is a subinterval of JOIN(S, T), then either t is a subinterval of S, or t is a subinterval of T, or t = JOIN($t1$, $t2$), where t_1 and t_2 are contiguous subintervals of S and T respectively. This, I take it, is intuitively clear. It has as a consequence that if a property p holds throughout some subinterval of JOIN(S, T) then in particular p holds throughout some subinterval of either S or T: in symbols,

$$(\exists t)[\text{IN}(t, \text{JOIN}(S, T)) \,\&\, \text{HOLDS}(p, t)] \Rightarrow$$
$$(\exists t)[(\text{IN}(t, S) \vee \text{IN}(t, T)) \,\&\, \text{HOLDS}(p, t)]. \tag{1}$$

We will now show that if the property p either is of the form not(q) for some property q, or satisfies (H.2), then

$$\text{HOLDS}(p, S) \,\&\, \text{HOLDS}(p, T) \,\&\, \text{MEETS}(S, T) \Rightarrow$$
$$\text{HOLDS}(p, \text{JOIN}(S, T)). \tag{2}$$

(In the terminology of Shoham (1986), this means that p is a *concatenable* proposition type.) To prove this for the case that p is not(q), assume that

$$\text{MEETS}(S, T) \,\&\, \neg\text{HOLDS}(\text{not}(q), \text{JOIN}(S, T)). \tag{3}$$

From (H.4), the second conjunct of this is equivalent to

$$\neg (\forall t)[\text{IN}(t, \text{JOIN}(S, T)) \Rightarrow \neg\text{HOLDS}(q, t)],$$

which straightforwardly entails

$$(\exists t)[\text{IN}(t, \text{JOIN}(S, T)) \,\&\, \text{HOLDS}(q, t)],$$

whence, using (1), we can infer

$$(\exists t)\,[(\text{IN}(t, S) \vee \text{IN}(t, T)) \,\&\, \text{HOLDS}(q, t)],$$

This can be rewritten as

$$(\exists t)\,[\text{IN}(t, S) \,\&\, \text{HOLDS}(q, t)] \vee (\exists t)\,[\text{IN}(t, T) \,\&\, \text{HOLDS}(q, T)],$$

which by (H.4) is equivalent to

$$\neg\text{HOLDS}(\text{not}(q), S) \vee \neg\text{HOLDS}(\text{not}(q), T). \tag{4}$$

The implication of (4) by (3) is obviously equivalent to (2).

For the second case, suppose p satisfies (H.2) and suppose HOLDS(p, S) and HOLDS(p, T), where S meets T. Let t be any subinterval of JOIN(S, T); then t must share a common subinterval with at least one of S and T, which means that t has a subinterval throughout which p holds, so we have

$$(\forall t)[\text{IN}(t, \text{JOIN}(S, T)) \Rightarrow (\exists s)[\text{IN}(s, T) \,\&\, \text{HOLDS}(p, s)]].$$

Since p satisfies (H.2), this implies HOLDS(p, JOIN(S, T)), and (2) is proved.

Now suppose X moves from O to P during an interval S, and without stopping at P moves on from P to Q during an interval T. Since X does not stop at P, S must meet T. Assuming that X only passes through P once during JOIN(S, T), we have that "X is not at P" is true throughout S and also throughout T. If we let p stand for "X is not at P," then our postulated motion (which, it must be conceded, is a possible one) implies the truth of the antecedent of (2). If we then allow either that "X is not at P" can be written in the form, not(q), for some property q, or that "X is not at P" is a legitimate substituend for p in (H.2), then by (2) our postulated motion implies that "X is not at P" is true throughout JOIN(S, T); in other words, contrary to our supposition, that X is never at P at all during JOIN(S, T). Hence, just as before, we must conclude that "X is not at P" cannot be expressed in the form not(q), nor can it legitimately be substituted for p in (H.2).

2.4 The Way Out: Instantaneous Property-ascriptions

We showed in the previous two sections that we cannot allow "X is not at P" to be represented in the form "not(p)" in Allen's theory; nor, however else we represent it, can we allow it as a substituend for p in (H.2). On either of these assumptions, continuous motion could not occur, at least not if we allow, as we surely must, that when a moving body passes through a position, then it is *at* that position. So if a body X passes through P without stopping there, then although Allen's "not(X is at P)" must be true throughout some interval in which this happens, "X is not at P" will not be true throughout any such interval.

What *is* true, of course, is that there is an interval throughout which X is never *at rest* at P. It is an entirely consistent interpretation of "not(X is at P)" to read it as "X is not at rest at P." This reading, however, would be just as appropriate as an interpretation of "not(X is at rest at P)." We now have a curious state of affairs on our hands: two apparently distinct properties, namely "X is at rest at P" and "X is at P," turn out to have the same property-negation.

The consequence of this is that in Allen's system these properties are not really distinct after all; that is, Allen's system cannot distinguish between a body's being in a certain position, and its being at rest there. To see this, note that if not(p) and not(q) are the same property, and p and q both satisfy (H.2), then

$$\begin{aligned} \text{HOLDS}(p, T) &\Leftrightarrow \text{HOLDS}(\text{not}(\text{not}(p)), T) \\ &\Leftrightarrow \text{HOLDS}(\text{not}(\text{not}(q)), T) \\ &\Leftrightarrow \text{HOLDS}(q, T), \end{aligned}$$

so p and q must hold throughout exactly the same intervals, and hence are equivalent from the point of view of Allen's logic.

It is indeed true that in the context "...throughout T," the two properties "X is at P" and "X is at rest at P" (which, I take it, do both satisfy (H.2)) are equivalent,[1] for there is nothing more to X's being at rest at P throughout T than its merely being at P throughout T. In a wider context, on the other hand, these properties are not equivalent, since it is perfectly possible for a moving body to be in a position without being at rest there.

Allen's system cannot encompass the idea of a property's being true *instantaneously*, i.e. being true at an instant without being true throughout any interval either containing or bounded by that instant. Yet just this is required if we are to be able to talk about continuous motion, for such motion does involve an object's occupying positions instantaneously in this sense. Some properties, such as "X is at P," then, can be true at isolated instants (others, such as "X is at rest," "X is in motion," "X is not at P" cannot). This being so, we cannot follow Allen in seeking to reduce all ascriptions of properties to times to the form "P holds throughout T." That way, no property

---

[1] Or nearly so! As an exception, consider a gramophone record on a rotating turntable. For objects lacking radial symmetry, the statement in the text holds good. It should be borne in mind throughout this discussion that by "position" I mean a region of space which an object exactly fits, with no room left over; so it is no exception that I can be in my room for an hour without ever being at rest there.

ever gets to be assigned to an instant at all, and we can never talk about continuous change.

Notice, incidentally, that my arguments do not in any way depend on assuming the existence of *space* points. If they did so, then Allen could evade the consequences of the arguments by rejecting space points as well as time points (instants). But the only spatial entities required for my argument are extended regions, namely positions that extended bodies can occupy.

3   REINSTATING INSTANTS

3.1   Allen's argument reconsidered

In order to rescue Allen's theory from the difficulties revealed in the previous discussion, we must first look closely at Allen's attitude to time instants. His attitude has, it appears, changed somewhat over the years. Allen (1984) argues for abolishing instants altogether; Allen and Hayes (1985) show how instants can be constructed as certain special sets of intervals (each instant is identified with the set of intervals that either contain or are bounded by it). This later reinstatement of instants does not help to overcome our difficulty, though, because nothing is said about whether, and if so how, properties can be said to hold at instants.

Allen's original argument for excluding instants from his temporal ontology can be summed up as follows. Suppose we have two intervals S and T such that

$$\text{MEETS}(S, T) \ \& \ \text{HOLDS}(p, S) \ \& \ \text{HOLDS}(\text{not}(p), T),$$

i.e. S and T are contiguous intervals such that some proposition p is true throughout S and false throughout T. Then if we allow the existence of an instant I at the point where S and T meet, one of the following cases must occur:

(a) I is part of both S and T.
(b) I is part of S but not T.
(c) I is part of T but not S.
(d) I is part of neither S nor T.

In case (a), p would have to be both true and false at I, which is absurd; in case (d), p would be neither true nor false at I, which is, according to Allen, equally unacceptable; while as for the remaining cases, since there is nothing to choose between them, any decision either way must be artificial. So, Allen concluded, we ought to banish instants altogether.

The trouble with this argument is that it presupposes that the only way a theory of time can embrace both instants and intervals is by assuming that intervals are made up out of instants, that instants are as it were the atoms out of which intervals are made. Sometimes this idea takes the form of assuming that intervals are sets of instants, though really this is a different notion, since the relationship that a set bears to its members is not that of a whole to its parts. But on either way of treating instants, we run into the kinds of difficulty that Allen was hoping to dispel by the abolition of instants, the difficulty of choosing between the alternatives (a)–(d) above; it is just because this choice seems to have no relevance to real questions about time that there is something attractive about the idea of abolishing instants altogether.

Suppose now that we reject as meaningless the question whether or not a given instant is part of, or a member of a given interval, while retaining the idea of there being an instant at the point where the two intervals meet. We are still left with two important relationships between instants and intervals. First, the instant where *S* meets *T* can be said to fall *within* the join of these two intervals, and second, this same instant can be said to *limit* both *S* and *T*, the former at its end, the latter at its beginning.

I shall write WITHIN(*I, T*) to mean that the instant *I* falls within the interval *T*, and LIMITS(*I, T*) to mean that *I* limits *T*. A coherent theory of instants and intervals can now be built up using these two notions, together with the various relations between intervals catalogued by Allen (as mentioned above, there are thirteen of them: apart from EQUAL, which is its own converse, they are BEFORE, MEETS, OVERLAPS, DURING, STARTS, and FINISHES, and their converses—IN being defined as the disjunction of DURING, STARTS, and FINISHES).

Both WITHIN and LIMITS can be defined for the "nests" introduced in Allen and Hayes (1985), as follows:

$$\text{WITHIN}(\text{BEGIN}(S), T) \Leftrightarrow S(\text{d f oi}) \, T,$$
$$\text{WITHIN}(\text{END}(S), T) \Leftrightarrow S(\text{d s o}) \, T,$$
$$\text{LIMITS}(\text{BEGIN}(S), T) \Leftrightarrow (= \text{s si mi}) \, T,$$
$$\text{LIMITS}(\text{END}(S), T) \Leftrightarrow S(= \text{f fi m}) \, T;$$

but one does not have to accept the nest construction in order to develop the logic of WITHIN and LIMITS. Such a logic can be developed without prejudice to whether instants and intervals are accorded equal status or one is regarded as conceptually prior to the other.

Amongst the required rules of the logic are:

$$(\forall t)(\exists i)[\text{WITHIN}(i, t)], \tag{I.1}$$

$$\text{WITHIN}(I, S) \,\&\, \text{IN}(S, T) \Rightarrow \text{WITHIN}(I, T), \tag{I.2}$$

$$\text{WITHIN}(I, S) \,\&\, \text{WITHIN}(I, T) \Rightarrow (\exists t)[\text{IN}(t, S) \,\&\, \text{IN}(t, T)], \tag{I.3}$$

$$\text{WITHIN}(I, S) \,\&\, \text{LIMITS}(I, T) \Rightarrow (\exists t)[\text{IN}(t, S) \,\&\, \text{IN}(t, T)]. \tag{I.4}$$

Note the convention I adopt for notating instants and intervals: instants are $I, J, \ldots$, and intervals are $S, T, \ldots$, with corresponding lower-case letters for bound variables of each type.

The theory of instants and intervals implied by rules such as these need not be of the set-theoretic or part-whole kind, but rather something weaker, in which the problems which trouble Allen do not arise. Essentially, it is the theory expounded at some length, and with considerable confusion, by Aristotle in the *Physics*. It is all we need for our purpose of revising Allen's theory to embrace an account of continuous change.

3.2 Why Allen's theory needs instants

We may see what Allen has tried to do as an attempt to reduce all ascriptions of states of affairs to times to a basic schema of the form "such-and-such a property holds throughout such-and-such an interval." And we have seen that this attempt encounters difficulties when we try to use it to analyze continuous change, for the essence of such change is that the changing object passes through a continuous range of states, each of which obtains for an isolated instant.

In order to circumvent this difficulty, while remaining within Allen's interval-based system, we should have to find a way of analyzing propositions of the form "such-and-such a property holds at such-and-such an instant" solely in terms of propositions of the form "such-and-such a property holds throughout such-and-such an interval." In this section I shall show that this cannot be done.

Assume that the instant I is given as the meeting point of two contiguous intervals S and T: I shall denote this state of affairs by $I = S*T$. Assume further that some property p holds at I but not at any other time in the interval JOIN(S, T). On this assumption, although p holds at I there is no interval U containing I such that p holds throughout U. It would not, therefore, seem possible to analyze "p holds at I" in terms of "p holds throughout U."

Now consider the negation of p, by which I mean not the property not(p) defined by Allen's axiom (H.4), but rather that property which holds at all and only those times at which p does not hold. For the time being I shall denote this property "neg(p)." Now neg(p) holds throughout S and throughout T (since p itself does not hold at all during these intervals), but it does not hold throughout JOIN(S, T) (since p holds at I); and this combination of holding and not holding on the part of neg(p) uniquely characterizes the situation we have assumed with regard to p. That is, we can define "p holds at the isolated instant $S*T$" to mean the same as "neg(p) holds throughout S and throughout T but not throughout JOIN(S, T)."

There are two problems with this definition. The first problem is that it does not give us a general characterization of holding at an instant: it applies to the case where a property holds at an isolated instant, but not where a property holds at an instant which falls within or limits an interval throughout which it holds. The second problem is that the definition implicitly assumes that we can explain the relationship between p and neg(p) without presupposing a prior understanding of the locution "p holds at instant I."

The first problem is perhaps not too serious. To overcome it, we need only be prepared to accept a disjunctive definition such as:

p holds at I iff *either* neg(p) holds throughout S and throughout T but not throughout JOIN(S, T), where $I = S*T$, or p holds throughout T, where I falls within or limits T.

Note that this definition will only apply to those properties which can hold at isolated instants. Not all properties are of this kind: for example "X is in motion" and "X is not at p" are not. For these latter properties we can define "p holds at I" much more simply by:

p holds at I iff p holds throughout some interval within which I falls.

It is the second problem which really puts paid to any attempt to incorporate talk of properties holding at instants into Allen's theory of intervals. As we have seen, it is no good defining neg(p) as Allen defines not(p), that is by:

neg(p) holds throughout T iff it is not the case that p holds throughout any subinterval of T,

for on this definition, if S meets T, it cannot happen that neg(p) holds throughout S and throughout T but not throughout JOIN(S, T). What we want, of course, is a definition which, once "p holds at I" is defined, will yield the equivalence:

neg(p) holds at I iff p does not hold at I.

But we cannot use this equivalence itself as the definition without circularity.

3.3 States of position and states of motion

In view of these difficulties, I propose to abandon the analysis attempted in the last section and start afresh. The problems encountered in our examination of Allen's system can all be traced to the assumption, implicit throughout Allen's work though never explicitly stated, that all properties should receive a uniform treatment with respect to the logic of their temporal incidence. Our starting point will therefore be to distinguish sharply between two kinds of properties, having different temporal logics; I shall call these properties *states of position* and *states of motion*.

- States of position can hold at isolated instants; and if a state of position holds throughout an interval, then it must hold at the limits of that interval. Examples: a body's being in a particular position, or moving at a particular speed or in a particular direction. More generally, any state which consists of some continuously variable quantity's assuming a particular value is a state of position.
- States of motion cannot hold at isolated instants: if a state of motion holds at an instant then it must hold throughout some interval within which that instant falls. Examples: a body's being at rest or in motion, and more generally any state of affairs which consists of some continuously variable quantity's either remaining fixed or undergoing a change of value.

Note, incidentally, that while a body's being at rest is regarded as a state of motion, its having zero velocity is a state of position. I here take the Aristotelian view that rest is to be defined as a body's remaining in the same place over a period of time, so that a state of rest can only be said to obtain at an instant in the derivative sense of its obtaining throughout an interval within which that instant falls; whereas having zero velocity (a concept unknown to Aristotle) is defined at an instant, in the manner of the differential calculus, in terms of the limit of overall velocities in a diminishing sequence of intervals converging on that instant. If a body is at rest then it has zero velocity, but not conversely. That a body can have zero velocity without being at rest is clear from the often-discussed examples of a ball thrown vertically upward, which acquires zero velocity for an instant at the topmost point of its trajectory, and the bob of a pendulum, which acquires zero velocity for an instant at the end points of each swing.

My terminology "states of position" and "states of motion" is suggested by the paradigmatic cases, but does not imply that everything which satisfies the criteria for one or other of these kinds of state will be such as would naturally be described in these terms. In particular, it will turn out that any given state of position's *not* holding constitutes a state of motion, and vice versa.

Shoham (1986) presents a series of definitions characterizing classes of propositions, with the intention of replacing Allen's trichotomy states/events/processes by a more flexible scheme. For example, Shoham calls a proposition type *downward-hereditary* if whenever it holds in some interval it holds in all subintervals of that interval, and *concatenable* if whenever it holds in two contiguous intervals it holds in their join.

To see how my distinction between states of position and states of motion fits into Shoham's classificatory scheme, we must first agree on how Shoham's locution "holds in" is to be understood. If we take it to mean the same as my "holds throughout" (at least as regards properties—events, processes, etc. are not in question here since they fall outside the range of my present classification), then in Shoham's terminology all states turn out to be both upward- and downward-hereditary, and all states of position and some states of motion are concatenable.[2] If, on the other hand, we understand Shoham's "holds in" so that "p holds in T" is equivalent to "it is not the case that the negation of p holds throughout T" (what I represent by "p holds within T" below), then all states come out as both upward-hereditary and concatenable, but none as downward-hereditary.

It thus appears that in order for Shoham's classification to have any relevance for my distinction between states of position and states of motion, it is necessary to read his "holds in," as applied to states, to mean the same as my "holds throughout"; and in that case my distinction between states of position and states of motion is seen to bear some relation, though not a very tight one, to Shoham's distinction between concatenable and noncatenable proposition types.

4 A REVISED THEORY

Because of the way states of position and states of motion have been defined, it will be necessary to treat them separately in some of the logical development that follows. To begin with, though, a fair amount can be said with sufficient generality to cover both kinds of state.

4.1 Results for general properties

Whereas Allen recognizes only one way of ascribing properties to times, namely to assert that a property holds throughout an interval, we shall find it necessary to introduce three different ways. We want to be able to say not only that a property holds *throughout* an interval, but also that it holds *during* an interval (i.e. at some time during an interval, not necessarily through all of it), and that it holds *at* an instant. I shall represent these three types of statement by the forms HOLDS-ON(p, T), HOLDS-IN(p, T), and HOLDS-AT(p, I) respectively. For the initial, general treatment, I shall take the last of these locutions as primitive, defining the others in terms of it; later I shall show how we can reverse the order of definition if we are determined not to accord instants conceptual priority over intervals.

To begin with, then, we shall define what it is for a property to hold during an interval to be that there is at least one instant within the interval at which the property holds, i.e.

$$\text{HOLDS-IN}(p, T) \Leftrightarrow (\exists i)[\text{WITHIN}(i, T) \,\&\, \text{HOLDS-AT}(p, i)] \qquad (\text{D.1})$$

and similarly, for a property to hold throughout an interval is for it to hold at every instant within that interval:

$$\text{HOLDS-ON}(p, T) \Leftrightarrow (\forall i)[\text{WITHIN}(i, T) \Rightarrow \text{HOLDS-AT}(p, i)]. \qquad (\text{D.2})$$

Here we do not attempt to define WITHIN explicitly, taking it rather as a primitive predicate of the theory, satisfying the rules (I.1)–(I.3) above as axioms (similar remarks apply to LIMITS which we use below). Given these definitions for HOLDS-IN and HOLDS-ON, and making use of our postulates relating instants to intervals, we can easily prove the following theorems:[3]

$$\text{HOLDS-IN}(p, S) \,\&\, \text{IN}(S, T) \Rightarrow \text{HOLDS-IN}(p, T). \qquad (\text{T.1})$$

---

[2] The qualification "some" is needed here because while, e.g. "X is in motion" is concatenable, "X is not at p" is not. "X is at rest" is concatenable so long as all motion is continuous; but if "jumps" can occur, then X can be at rest at P throughout S and at rest at Q throughout T, where P is different from Q and S meets T; and in this case X is *not* at rest throughout JOIN(S, T).

[3] The proofs of these and all subsequent theorems are collected together in the appendix to this paper.

This says that if a property holds within some interval S, then it holds within any interval of which S is a subinterval (e.g. if I was in London last Tuesday then I was in London last week, last fortnight, etc.).

$$\text{HOLDS-ON}(p, T) \,\&\, \text{IN}(S, T) \Rightarrow \text{HOLDS-ON}(p, S). \tag{T.2}$$

This says that if a property holds throughout T then it holds throughout every subinterval of T (e.g. if I was in London all last week, then I was in London all last Monday, all last Tuesday, etc.).

$$\text{HOLDS-ON}(p, T) \Rightarrow \text{HOLDS-IN}(p, T). \tag{T.3}$$

This says that if a property holds throughout an interval, then a fortiori it holds within that interval (e.g. if I was in London all last week then, of course, I was in London last week).

$$\text{HOLDS-ON}(p, T) \Rightarrow (\forall t)[\text{IN}(t, T) \Rightarrow \text{HOLDS-IN}(p, t)]. \tag{T.4}$$

This says that if a property holds throughout an interval T, then it holds within every subinterval of T (e.g. if I was in London all last week, then I was in London last Monday, last Tuesday, etc.).

$$(\exists t)[\text{IN}(t, T) \,\&\, \text{HOLDS-ON}(p, t)] \Rightarrow \text{HOLDS-IN}(p, T). \tag{T.5}$$

This says that if a property holds throughout some subinterval of T then it holds within T (e.g. if I was in London all last Tuesday then I was in London last week).

$$\text{HOLDS-AT}(p, I) \Rightarrow (\forall t)[\text{WITHIN}(I, t) \Rightarrow \text{HOLDS-IN}(p, t)]. \tag{T.6}$$

This says that if a property holds at an instant then it holds within any interval containing that instant (e.g. if I was in London at midday last Tuesday, then I was in London last Tuesday, last week, etc.).

$$(\exists t)[\text{WITHIN}(I, t) \,\&\, \text{HOLDS-ON}(p, t)] \Rightarrow \text{HOLDS-AT}(p, I). \tag{T.7}$$

This says that if a property holds throughout some interval containing an instant I then it holds at I (e.g. if I was in London all last week then I was in London at midday last Tuesday).

We now introduce negation: I shall stop using "neg," replacing it with the more natural "not"; but my definition of "not(p)" will differ from Allen's. In fact, we define:

$$\text{HOLDS-AT}(\text{not}(p), I) \Leftrightarrow \neg\text{HOLDS-AT}(p, I). \tag{D.3}$$

Armed with this definition, the following further theorems are elementary:

$$\text{HOLDS-IN}(\text{not}(p), T) \Leftrightarrow \neg\text{HOLDS-ON}(p, T). \tag{T.8}$$

$$\text{HOLDS-ON}(\text{not}(p), T) \Leftrightarrow \neg\text{HOLDS-IN}(p, T). \tag{T.9}$$

$$\text{HOLDS-AT}(\text{not}(\text{not}(p)), I) \Leftrightarrow \text{HOLDS-AT}(p, I). \tag{T.10}$$

The theorems (T.1)–(T.10) all hold for any property, regardless of whether it is a state of position or a state of motion. In order to find results which distinguish the two kinds of state, we must introduce formal criteria by which they can be recognized. These criteria must encapsulate our informal requirements that a state of position should hold at the limits of any interval throughout which it holds, whereas a state of motion must hold throughout some interval containing any instant at which it holds.

Suppose a state of position p holds throughout an interval T, and let I limit T. Then any interval containing I must share a common subinterval with T and hence p must hold within any such interval. In order to secure the result that p holds at I, it therefore suffices to stipulate that p satisfies the converse of theorem (T.6), namely:

$$(\forall t)[\text{WITHIN}(I, t) \Rightarrow \text{HOLDS-IN}(p, t)] \Rightarrow \text{HOLDS-AT}(p, I). \quad \text{(SP)}$$

We shall stipulate that a property p is a state of position just so long as it satisfies the condition (SP).

Now let p be a state of motion, and suppose p holds at an instant I. We require there to be an interval containing I throughout which p holds. This will follow so long as we stipulate that p satisfies the converse of theorem (T.7), namely:

$$\text{HOLDS-AT}(p, I) \Rightarrow (\exists t)[\text{WITHIN}(I, t) \& \text{HOLDS-ON}(p, t)]. \quad \text{(SM)}$$

This will be our criterion for p to be a state of motion.

4.2 Theorems for states of position

In this section we derive some further theorems which hold so long as p is a state of position.

First, we have the converse of (T.4):

$$(\forall t)[\text{IN}(t, T) \Rightarrow \text{HOLDS-IN}(p, T)] \Rightarrow \text{HOLDS-ON}(p, T). \quad \text{(T.11P)}$$

This says that if p holds in every subinterval of T, then it holds throughout T. For example, if X is at P throughout T_1 and throughout T_2, where $T = \text{JOIN}(T_1, T_2)$, then clearly X is at P in every subinterval of T (since any such subinterval overlaps at least one of T_1 and T_2); so since "X is at P" is a state of position, (T.11P) tells us that X is at P throughout T. The corresponding inference for a state of motion is false: if "X is not at P" holds throughout T_1 and throughout T_2, it does not follow that "X is not at P" holds throughout T, since X might instantaneously pass through P at the instant $T_1^*T_2$ where the two intervals meet.

Next, we can derive a formal expression of the other part of our informal characterization of states of position, namely that such a state must hold at the limits of any interval throughout which it holds:

$$\text{HOLDS-ON}(p, T) \& \text{LIMITS}(I, T) \Rightarrow \text{HOLDS-AT}(p, I) \quad \text{(T.12P)}$$

and we can also derive a result which shows that the negation of a state of position satisfies the criterion for states of motion:

$$\text{HOLDS-AT}(\text{not}(p), I) \Rightarrow (\exists t)[\text{WITHIN}(I, t) \& \text{HOLDS-ON}(\text{not}(p), t)]. \quad \text{(T.13P)}$$

So far we have derived everything on the basis of taking HOLDS-AT to be our primitive locution relating properties to times, defining HOLDS-IN and HOLDS-ON in terms of them. If we want to follow Allen in regarding intervals as conceptually prior to instants, then we had better find a way of reversing this order of definition, so that HOLDS-AT is defined in terms of one or both of the other two relations. To do this, we must find an equivalence between HOLDS-AT(p, I) and some formula not involving HOLDS-AT at all.

If p is a state of position, a suitable equivalence is obtained by conjoining (SP) and (T.6), as follows:

$$\text{HOLDS-AT}(p, I) \Leftrightarrow (\forall t)[\text{WITHIN}(I, t) \Rightarrow \text{HOLDS-IN}(p, t)]. \quad \text{(T.14P)}$$

Further, by conjoining (T.4) and (T.11P), we obtain:

$$\text{HOLDS-ON}(p, T) \Leftrightarrow (\forall t)[\text{IN}(t, T) \Rightarrow \text{HOLDS-IN}(p, t)]. \qquad (\text{T.15P})$$

These two results taken together mean that for states of position we can take HOLDS-IN to be our primitive relation instead of HOLDS-AT. This accords well with the way we locate states of affairs in time in our everyday speech: we often say things like "John was ill last week," meaning by this not that John was ill all last week but that he was ill at some time during last week.

4.3 Theorems for states of motion

In this section we derive a series of theorems for states of motion which runs parallel to the theorems derived for states of position. This parallelism illustrates a fairly thoroughgoing duality between the two kinds of property.

First, we have the converse of (T.5):

$$\text{HOLDS-IN}(p, T) \Rightarrow (\exists t)[\text{IN}(t, T) \,\&\, \text{HOLDS-ON}(p, T)], \qquad (\text{T.11M})$$

which says that a state of motion can only hold in an interval by virtue of holding throughout one of its subintervals (e.g. if I was driving this morning then there must have been a period during the morning throughout which I was driving—whereas I could have been driving at 60 m.p.h. this morning without there being any interval throughout which I was driving at 60 m.p.h., say if I merely passed through that speed instantaneously in the course of accelerating up to 70 m.p.h. and then again when slowing down).

Corresponding to (T.12P), involving limits, we have

$$\text{HOLDS-AT}(p, I) \,\&\, \text{LIMITS}(I, T) \Rightarrow \text{HOLDS-IN}(p, T), \qquad (\text{T.12M})$$

which says that p holds in an interval whenever it holds at one of its limits (e.g. if I was driving at 10.30 a.m. then I must have been driving for at least a short while leading up to that moment, and hence in any interval which ends at 10.30 a.m., and I must have continued driving for at least a short while after, and hence in any interval beginning at 10.30 a.m.).

The duality between the two kinds of state is further exemplified by the next result:

$$\begin{aligned}(\forall t)[\text{WITHIN}(I, t) \Rightarrow \text{HOLDS-IN}(\text{not}(p), t)] \Rightarrow \\ \text{HOLDS-AT}(\text{not}(p), I),\end{aligned} \qquad (\text{T.13M})$$

which shows that the negation of a state of motion is a state of position.

As with states of position, we can find an equivalence which enables us to define HOLDS-AT in terms of one of the other relations, but in this case the other relation is not HOLDS-IN but HOLDS-ON:

$$\text{HOLDS-AT}(p, I) \Leftrightarrow (\exists t)[\text{WITHIN}(I, t) \,\&\, \text{HOLDS-ON}(p, t)]. \qquad (\text{T.14M})$$

This equivalence is obtained by conjoining (SM) and (T.7). By conjoining (T.5) and (T.11M) we obtain an equivalence which allows us to reduce HOLDS-IN to HOLDS-ON for states of motion:

$$\text{HOLDS-IN}(p, t) \Leftrightarrow (\exists t)[\text{IN}(t, T) \,\&\, \text{HOLDS-ON}(p, t)]. \qquad (\text{T.15M})$$

This means that for states of motion we can take HOLDS-ON to be primitive.

For states of motion we also have the following chain of equivalences:

$$\text{HOLDS-ON}(\text{not}(p), T) \Leftrightarrow \neg \text{HOLDS-IN}(p, T)$$
$$\Leftrightarrow \neg (\exists t)[\text{IN}(t, T) \,\&\, \text{HOLDS-ON}(p, t)]$$
$$\Leftrightarrow (\forall t)[\text{IN}(t, T) \Rightarrow \text{HOLDS-ON}(p, t)],$$

which gives us Allen's axiom (H.4) characterizing not(p). In fact, if we take my logic as described here and restrict it by confining the interpretation of p to states of motion and paraphrasing all occurrences of HOLDS-AT and HOLDS-IN in terms of HOLDS-ON, as indicated by (T.14M) and (T.15M), then we will obtain a system similar to Allen's. This in a way vindicates my claim that the revisions proposed here adhere closely to the spirit of Allen's theory; but as we have seen, his theory is too restrictive to encompass a description of the phenomena associated with continuous change.

4.4 The problem of "intermingling"

I now wish to return to Allen's axiom (H.2). It will be convenient to divide this equivalence into two separate implications as follows:

$$(\forall t)[\text{IN}(t, T) \Rightarrow (\exists s)[\text{IN}(s, t) \,\&\, \text{HOLDS-ON}(p, s)]]$$
$$\Rightarrow \text{HOLDS-ON}(p, T). \tag{H.2.1}$$

$$\text{HOLDS-ON}(p, T) \Rightarrow$$
$$(\forall t)[\text{IN}(t, T) \Rightarrow (\exists s)[\text{IN}(s, t) \,\&\, \text{HOLDS-ON}(p, s)]]. \tag{H.2.2}$$

It is easy to see that in our modified system (H.2.1) is satisfied by states of position, while (H.2.2) is satisfied by states of motion. For the first result, we need only use (T.5) to eliminate HOLDS-IN from (T.11P), while for the second, we use (T.11M) to eliminate HOLDS-IN from (T.4).

In introducing (H.2), all Allen says by way of justification is that it will turn out to be needed; but it is not clear from Allen's paper precisely what role, in an intuitive sense, this axiom plays in his system. For enlightenment on this, we must turn to the work of Hamblin (1969, 1971), who introduced a logic of intervals which, once differences in notation have been taken into account, can be seen to be identical to Allen's system. In particular, Hamblin's Axiom 9 corresponds to Allen's (H.1), while Hamblin's Axiom 10 corresponds to the half of Allen's (H.2) which we have labelled (H.2.1); Hamblin does not need an extra axiom to correspond to (H.2.2), since this follows from (H.1).

For Hamblin, the purpose of introducing his Axiom 10 is to exclude "the possibility of indefinitely intermingled periods of redness and non-redness, or of high pitch and low pitch, or of whatever else it is that we take the elementary predicates to represent." (1971: 132). McDermott (1982) also has a rule, his Axiom 9, with this purpose: specifically, McDermott wishes to exclude from his class of facts any state of affairs which can change truth value infinitely often in any finite interval. Prior (1967: 108) referred to such a situation as a "fuzz." Allen himself says nothing about this particular issue, but whether or not he had something like this in mind when he introduced axiom (H.2), it is an interesting exercise to see how our present modification of his system fares with regard to intermingling.

In this context, it is necessary to distinguish between two kinds of intermingling: there is intermingling throughout an interval, such as would occur if p held at instants corresponding to rational numbers but not at instants corresponding to irrational numbers; and there is intermingling in the neighbourhood of an instant, as for example if p held throughout each interval of the form

$$\left[1+\frac{1}{3^n}, 1+\frac{2}{3^n}\right]$$

and at no other times.[4]

Intermingling throughout an interval is ruled out by our axioms. For such intermingling to occur throughout an interval T, it would have to be the case that both p and not(p) hold during every subinterval of T, for some property p. One of p and not(p) must be a state of position; we may suppose without loss of generality that p is. This means, by (T.11P), that p must hold throughout T, so there is no intermingling.

Intermingling in the neighbourhood of a point, however, is not ruled out. If we wish to rule it out, we must do so explicitly. Two new axioms are required, one to rule out intermingling immediately *before* an instant, and another to rule out intermingling immediately *after* an instant.

If intermingling of p and not(p) occurs immediately after an instant I, then for any interval T limited by I at the beginning it is the case that both p and not(p) hold within any initial subinterval of T. So whenever such intermingling occurs, we have, for some interval T:

$(\forall t)[\text{STARTS}(t, T) \Rightarrow (\text{HOLDS-IN}(p, t) \,\&\, \text{HOLDS-IN}(\text{not}(p), t))]$.

To rule out intermingling after an instant, it will suffice to posit the negation of this formula, namely

$(\exists t)[\text{STARTS}(t, T) \,\&\, (\neg \text{HOLDS-IN}(p, t) \lor \neg \text{HOLDS-IN}(\text{not}(p), t))]$

as an axiom. This may be transformed, using (T.8) and (T.9), to the more perspicuous form:

$(\exists t)[\text{STARTS}(t, T) \,\&\, (\text{HOLDS-ON}(p, t) \lor \text{HOLDS-ON}(\text{not}(p), t))]$.

To exclude intermingling immediately before an instant, we may introduce the analogous axiom:

$(\exists t)[\text{FINISHES}(t, T) \,\&\, (\text{HOLDS-ON}(p, t) \lor \text{HOLDS-ON}(\text{not}(p), t))]$.

Together, these two axioms achieve the same effect as McDermott's Axiom 9, which "assures us that, for every fact and an arbitrary state, there is an interval preceding the state during which the fact is always true or always false; and another one following the state, in every chronicle containing it" [1982: 113].

5 PROCESSES AND EVENTS

In addition to properties, Allen goes on to talk about *occurrences*, which he subdivides into *processes* and *events*; in this section I shall show how these items can be accommodated into our modification of Allen's system.

---

[4] I am here identifying instants with real numbers for the sake of giving clear illustrations of the phenomena under consideration; but the possibility of such phenomena depends only on the infinite divisibility of time and not on any specific correlation of instants with numbers.

5.1 Events

Whereas properties *hold* at times, events *occur*; so Allen introduces a predicate OCCUR, with the intended meaning that the sentence OCCUR(e, T) is true so long as T is the unique interval over which the event e happens. An immediate objection to this is that it requires that all events take time; there can be no instantaneous events in Allen's system. But in reality, instantaneous events do occur, paradigmatic examples being the event of something's starting to move, and the event of its coming to rest (cf. Anscombe 1964: 17f).

Suppose, for example, that S and T are two contiguous intervals, such that some body X is in motion throughout S and at rest throughout T, so that we have:

MEETS(S, T) & HOLDS-ON(moving(X), S) & HOLDS-ON(not(moving(X)), T).

Then clearly X comes to rest in the interval JOIN (S, T), but there is no subinterval U of JOIN(S, T) such that this event takes up the whole of U. If we denote the event by e, we cannot represent its occurrence by means of a sentence of the form OCCUR(e, U).

I propose that just as we used three different predicates HOLDS-AT, HOLDS-ON, and HOLDS-IN where Allen uses only the single predicate HOLDS, we should similarly replace Allen's OCCUR by three predicates OCCURS-AT, OCCURS-ON, and OCCURS-IN. The first of these is for locating an instantaneous (i.e. *punctual*) event at the instant at which it occurs, the second for locating an event which takes time (a *durative* event) on the interval over which it occurs (so my OCCURS-ON corresponds to Allen's OCCUR), and the third is for locating any event, whether punctual or durative, in an interval within which it occurs. So in the example just given, we can say both OCCURS-AT(e, $S*T$) (where $S*T$ is the instant at which S meets T), and OCCURS-IN(e, JOIN(S, T)), but we cannot report this occurrence at all using OCCURS-ON.

As an example of a durative event, consider the motion of a body X from one place P_1 to another place P_2, such as is given by the following formula:

HOLDS-ON(at (X, P_1), S) & MEETS(S, T) & ¬HOLDS-IN(at(X, P_1), T) & ¬HOLDS-IN(at (X, P_2), T) & MEETS(T, U) & HOLDS-ON(at(X, P_2), U).

Given this sequence of states, if we use e to represent the event of X's moving from P_1 to P_2, then we can say both OCCURS-ON(e, T) and OCCURS-IN(e, JOIN(S, T, U)), but we cannot report the occurrence of this event using OCCURS-AT.[5]

Some obvious axioms for occurrence are

$$\text{OCCURS-ON}(e, S) \text{ \& IN}(S, T) \Rightarrow \text{OCCURS-IN}(e, T), \qquad (\text{O.1})$$

$$\text{OCCURS-ON}(e, T) \text{ \& IN}(S, T) \Rightarrow \neg\text{OCCURS-ON}(e, S), \qquad (\text{O.2})$$

$$\text{OCCURS-AT}(e, I) \text{ \& WITHIN}(I, T) \Rightarrow \text{OCCURS-IN}(e, T), \qquad (\text{O.3})$$

$$\text{OCCURS-IN}(e, S) \text{ \& IN}(S, T) \Rightarrow \text{OCCURS-IN}(e, T). \qquad (\text{O.4})$$

Note that my (O.2) is the same as Allen's (O.1), if we identify my OCCURS-ON with his OCCURS. If e is durative, we have

$$\text{OCCURS-IN}(e, T) \Rightarrow (\exists t)[\text{IN}(t, T) \text{ \& OCCURS-ON}(e, t)], \qquad (\text{O.5D})$$

---

[5] Note that I here use JOIN(S, T, U) as an abbreviation for JOIN(S, JOIN(T, U)), or , equivalently, JOIN(JOIN (S, T), U).

whereas if e is punctual we have rather

$$\text{OCCURS-IN}(e, T) \Rightarrow (\exists i)[\text{WITHIN}(i, T) \,\&\, \text{OCCURS-AT}(e, i)]. \qquad \text{(O.5P)}$$

Taken together, (O.1) and (O.5D) give rise to the equivalence

$$\text{OCCURS-IN}(e, T) \Leftrightarrow (\exists t)[\text{IN}(t, T) \,\&\, \text{OCCURS-ON}(e, t)] \qquad \text{(T.16D)}$$

which is valid for durative events, while (O.3) and (O.5P) give

$$\text{OCCURS-IN}(e, T) \Leftrightarrow (\exists i)[\text{WITHIN}(i, T) \,\&\, \text{OCCURS-AT}(e, i)] \qquad \text{(T.16P)}$$

valid for punctual events. Note also that (O.4) can be derived as a theorem, the derivation proceeding separately for durative events (using (O.5D) and (O.1)) and for punctual events (using (O.5P) and (O.3)).

All this suggests that we could begin with OCCURS-ON and OCCURS-AT, and define OCCURS-IN in terms of them. In fact, since the treatment of OCCURS-IN has to differ according as the event it is applied to is punctual or durative, there would be something to be said for splitting it into two new predicates, OCCURS-IN for durative events and OCCURS-WITHIN for punctual ones. This move would have the advantage of clearly separating out the cases where our existing OCCURS-IN requires separate treatment for the two kinds of event; but it has the disadvantage that those formulae like (O.4) which at present hold for both duratives and punctuals would now each have to be replaced by two distinct formulae, one for duratives and one for punctuals.

5.2 Processes

Allen gives as examples of processes the occurrences denoted by the sentences "I am running" and "I am walking." To show that these sentences refer to items of a category distinct from both properties and events, Allen argues:

Processes fall between events and properties. To see this, consider the process "I am walking" over interval I. Unlike events, this process may also be occurring over subintervals of I. Unlike properties, however, it is not the case that the process must be occurring over all subintervals of I. For example, if I am walking over interval I, then I am walking over the first half of I; however, there may be some subintervals of I where I paused for a brief rest. (Allen 1984:132)

Arguments like this occur over and over again in the literature; I must confess that I have never really understood them. Suppose that I am walking throughout S and throughout U, with a "brief rest" taking up the interval T, where S meets T and T meets U. Now whether this brief rest counts as a time of my walking or of my not walking depends on just how the term "walking" is meant to be understood here. There are broader and narrower senses: in a narrow sense, I am not walking during T, and in this narrow sense it is not the case that I am walking throughout JOIN(S, T, U) either; in a broader sense, though, I *am* walking during T, and it is only in this broader sense that I am walking throughout JOIN(S, T, U). In whatever sense "walking" is taken, if I am walking throughout JOIN(S, T, U) then in *that* sense I am walking throughout T. Thus (T.2) holds, and "I am walking" reports a property. For further discussion of narrower and broader senses see Galton (1984: 85, 129ff). and also Section 5.3 below.

Note that my distinction between broad and narrow senses has been recognized in passing by Allen and Kautz (1985), but they prefer to treat the distinction as one between broader and narrower senses of the temporal term rather than the property:

The question "What are you working on now?" at a conference refers to a much larger time than the instant the question is asked.

If it didn't, one would have to answer "nothing" every time one had an idle moment. Thus, "now" appears to be ambiguous, and can refer to one of a hierarchy of times based on containment. (Allen and Kautz 1985: 253)

The trouble with this way of looking at things is that it limits recognition of broad and narrow senses to sentences whose temporal term is "now." It would surely be impracticable to extend this idea so that all temporal terms become similarly ambiguous; and in any case, as we have seen, by locating the distinction between broad and narrower senses in the process rather than the time we are enabled to simplify our ontology by subsuming processes under properties.

5.3 Analysis of progressive sentences

Having excluded a separate category of processes from our system, we are left with the task of explaining how to analyze sentences which report events with the verb in the progressive aspect, like Allen's example, "The ball was falling to the table." Allen's method here is to treat the event given by "The ball fell to the table" as if it were a process; formally, instead of putting

$$\text{OCCUR}(\text{FALL}(\text{ball}, s, \text{table}), T)$$

(where s denotes an unspecified initial position from which the ball fell), which says that the ball fell to the table over the interval T, he puts

$$\text{OCCURRING}(\text{FALL}(\text{ball}, s, \text{table}), T)$$

in order to say that the ball was falling to the table over that interval (without necessarily getting there). Here OCCURRING is the predicate used for processes just as HOLDS and OCCUR are used for properties and events respectively. The use of OCCURRING with an argument that would normally denote an event forces us to reinterpret that argument as denoting a process, namely the process whose occurring constitutes the occurrence of the event.

If we wanted to do something analogous to this in my system, taking account of the assimilation of processes to properties, we could adopt the convention that if any HOLDS predicate is applied to an expression denoting a durative event, then the event-expression must be understood as denoting instead the property which consists of that event being in progress. To say that the ball is in the process of falling to the table at instant I we should have

$$\text{HOLDS-AT}(\text{FALL}(\text{ball}, s, \text{table}), I),$$

and to say that the ball was in the process of falling to the table throughout an interval T,

$$\text{HOLDS-ON}(\text{FALL}(\text{ball}, s, \text{table}), T).$$

Care must be taken to distinguish the latter formula from

$$\text{OCCURS-ON}(\text{FALL}(\text{ball}, s, \text{table}), T),$$

which says that the entire event of the ball's falling to the table took up exactly the interval T. Of these two formulae, the latter implies the former, but not conversely. A similar relationship holds between

$$\text{HOLDS-IN}(\text{FALL}(\text{ball}, s, \text{table}), T),$$

which says that the ball was falling to the table at some time during the interval T, and

OCCURS-IN(FALL(ball, s, table), T),

which says that the ball fell to the table at some time during T.

An alternative approach, which I favour, is to make the conversion from event to property explicit by means of a *progressive operator* PROG which when applied to a durative event converts it into the property which consists of that event's being in progress. So the properties expressed by "the ball is falling to the table" and "John is walking to the station" would be expressed in the form "PROG(e)", where e represents the event "The ball falls to the table," in the one case, and "John walks to the station" in the other.

In this approach, instead of writing

HOLDS-AT(FALL(ball, s, table), I),

which is now ill-formed, we must write

HOLDS-AT(PROG(FALL(ball, s, table)), I);

and similarly for the formulae involving HOLDS-ON and HOLDS-IN.

The formalization of PROG presents some problems, especially in view of the need to take into account the broad and narrow sense discussed earlier. Here I cannot do more than present a few preliminaries. To begin with, we must stipulate that all properties of the form PROG(e) are states of motion rather than states of position; this is to rule out the possibility of an event's being in progress at an isolated instant. Second, we must rule that PROG cannot take a punctual event as its argument, since an event which takes no time cannot be in progress.

To formalize the broad/narrow dichotomy, we need to split PROG into two separate operators, say b-PROG and n-PROG for the broad and narrow senses respectively (if we wish to capture a series of degrees of broadness, we will need more than two; but two will be enough to be getting on with, representing the extremes of the scale). A fully formal characterization of these operators is difficult; at present I can only indicate some of the most basic requirements.

For the broad sense, note that if an event e occurs over an interval T, then in the broad sense it is in progress throughout T, so we have:

OCCURS-ON(e, T) ⇒ HOLDS-ON(b-PROG(e), T).

On the other hand, there need only be certain subintervals of T during which e is in progress in the narrow sense:

OCCURS-ON(e, T) ⇒ HOLDS-IN(n-PROG(e), T);

to be specific, e must be narrowly speaking in progress throughout some initial subinterval of T (otherwise we can chop off an initial subinterval which contributes nothing to the occurrence of e, yielding a proper subinterval of T over which e occurs, contravening (O.2)), and again throughout some final subinterval:

OCCURS-ON(e, T) ⇒ ($\exists t$)[STARTS(t, T) & HOLDS-ON(n-PROG(e), t)],
OCCURS-ON(e, T) ⇒ ($\exists t$)[FINISHES(t, T) & HOLDS-ON(n-PROG(e), t)].

Finally, to say that the broad sense is indeed broader than the narrow, we must have

HOLDS-AT(n-PROG(e), I) ⇒ HOLDS-AT(b-PROG(e), I).

Beyond this, it is hard to make any general assertions about the formalization of the progressive operators. Too much seems to depend on the exact nature of the events to which they are applied.

For example, if we consider the event *e* of my driving from Exeter to London, then for n-PROG(*e*) to be true I must be in a car, at the wheel, in the process of actually driving; whereas for b-PROG(*e*) to be true I need only be somewhere between Exeter and London, having driven from Exeter to that point, and if I am not actually driving then I must at least have the intention of carrying on driving as far as London (cf. Galton 1984: chapter 7).

6 CONCLUSION

In this paper I have proposed a series of revisions to Allen's theory of time and action. These revisions seemed to me to be necessary in order to accommodate the possibility of representing facts concerned with continuous change, for which Allen's system is as it stands unsuitable.

The principal revision is to diversify the temporal ontology by introducing instants as well as intervals. These new instants are not related to intervals either as parts to wholes or as members to sets, but in a simpler way that reflects in a modern context Aristotle's theory of time. To some extent, this move is already foreshadowed by the "nest" construction of Allen and Hayes (1985), but in the present paper the instants are integrated more thoroughly into the system by the introduction of a distinction between two kinds of property, called states of position and states of motion, which differ with respect to the logic of their temporal incidence, and in particular in the different ways in which they may be said to hold at instants.

As a consequence of these revisions, it was further found necessary to diversify the range of predicates for asserting temporal locations: both HOLDS and OCCUR are split into three new predicates HOLDS-ON, HOLDS-IN, HOLDS-AT and OCCURS-IN, OCCURS-ON, OCCURS-AT. The last of these predicates makes it possible to talk about instantaneous events, which cannot be done in Allen's system. In addition, I argued that it was unnecessary to introduce a category of processes separate from properties and events.

As far as I can see, there is nothing that can be done in Allen's system that cannot be done in the revised version, and the latter has the advantage over the former of making it possible to reason about continuous change and instantaneous events, both of which, I believe, ought to be accountable for in any general theory of temporal phenomena, and in particular in any such theory that is to be adequate for artificial intelligence applications such as natural language systems and planning systems operating in real time.

Finally, I should like to stress that despite the apparent severity of my revisions, the system I have advocated remains very close in spirit to Allen's.

APPENDIX A PROOFS OF THE THEOREMS

$$\text{HOLDS-IN}(p, S) \,\&\, \text{IN}(S, T) \Rightarrow \text{HOLDS-IN}(p, T). \tag{T.1}$$

Proof. Suppose that (a) HOLDS-IN(p, S) and (b) IN(S, T). Then by (a) and (D.1) there is an instant I such that (c) WITHIN(I, S) and (d) HOLDS-AT(p, I). By (I.2), (b) and (c) we have WITHIN(I, T), which by (D.1) and (d) gives us HOLDS-IN(p, T). □

$$\text{HOLDS-ON}(p, T) \,\&\, \text{IN}(S, T) \Rightarrow \text{HOLDS-ON}(p, S). \tag{T.2}$$

Proof. Suppose that (a) HOLDS-ON(p, T) and (b) IN(S, T). Let I be any instant in S, so we have (c) WITHIN(I, S). By (b), (c) and (I.2), we have (d) WITHIN(I, T). By (a), (d) and (D.2), HOLDS-AT(p, I). This holds for every I in S, so by (D.2), HOLDS-ON(p, S). □

$$\text{HOLDS-ON}(p, T) \Rightarrow \text{HOLDS-IN}(p, T) \tag{T.3}$$

Proof. Suppose that (a) HOLDS-ON(p, T). By (I.1), there is an instant I such that (b) WITHIN(I, T), and by (a), (b), and (D.2) we have (c) HOLDS-AT(p, I). Finally, from (b), (c) and (D.1) we deduce HOLDS-IN(p, t). □

$$\text{HOLDS-ON}(p, T) \Rightarrow (\forall t)[\text{IN}(t, T) \Rightarrow \text{HOLDS-IN}(p, t)]. \tag{T.4}$$

Proof. Suppose that (a) HOLDS-ON(p, T), and let S be any interval. Suppose (b) IN(S, T). Then by (a), (b) and (T.2) we have (c) HOLDS-ON(p, S). From (c) and (T.3) we now have (d) HOLDS-IN(p, S). The inference from (b) to (d) holds for any interval S, so we have $(\forall t)[\text{IN}(t, T) \Rightarrow \text{HOLDS-IN}(p, t)]$. □

$$(\exists t)[\text{IN}(t, T) \ \& \ \text{HOLDS-ON}(p, t)] \Rightarrow \text{HOLDS-IN}(p, T)]. \tag{T.5}$$

Proof. Suppose (a) IN(t, T) and (b) HOLDS-ON(p, t). By (b) and (T.3), we have (c) HOLDS-IN(p, t), and by (a), (c), and (T.1), HOLDS-IN(p, T). □

$$\text{HOLDS-AT}(p, I) \Rightarrow (\forall t)[\text{WITHIN}(I, t) \Rightarrow \text{HOLDS-IN}(p, t)]. \tag{T.6}$$

Proof. Suppose (a) HOLDS-AT(p, I), and let T be any interval. Suppose (b) WITHIN(I, T). By (a), (b), and (D.1), we have (c) HOLDS-IN(p, T). The inference from (b) to (c) holds for any interval T, so we have $(\forall t)[\text{WITHIN}(I, t) \Rightarrow \text{HOLDS-IN}(p, t)]$. □

$$(\exists t)[\text{WITHIN}(I, t) \ \& \ \text{HOLDS-ON}(p, t)] \Rightarrow \text{HOLDS-AT}(p, I). \tag{T.7}$$

Proof. Suppose that (a) WITHIN(I, T) and (b) HOLDS-ON(p, T). Then by (a), (b) and (D.2), HOLDS-AT(p, I). □

$$\text{HOLDS-IN}(\text{not}(p), T) \Leftrightarrow \neg\text{HOLDS-ON}(p, T) \tag{T.8}$$

Proof. By (D.1), the left-hand side of (T.8) is equivalent to

$$(\exists i)[\text{WITHIN}(i, T) \ \& \ \text{HOLDS-AT}(\text{not}(p), i)].$$

By (D.3), this is equivalent to

$$(\exists i)[\text{WITHIN}(i, T) \ \& \ \neg\text{HOLDS-AT}(p, i)],$$

i.e. to

$$\neg(\forall i)[\text{WITHIN}(i, T) \Rightarrow \text{HOLDS-AT}(p, i)],$$

which by (D.2) is equivalent to the right-hand side of (T.8). □

$$\text{HOLDS-ON}(\text{not}(p), T) \Leftrightarrow \neg\text{HOLDS-IN}(p, T) \tag{T.9}$$

Proof. This is proved by an argument exactly analogous to that used in proving (T.8). □

$$\text{HOLDS-AT}(\text{not}(\text{not}(p)), I) \Leftrightarrow \text{HOLDS-AT}(p, I) \tag{T.10}$$

Proof. By (D.3), the left-hand side of (T.10) is equivalent to $\neg\text{HOLDS-AT}(\text{not}(p), I)$. By (D.3) again, this is equivalent to $\neg\neg\text{HOLDS-AT}(p, I)$, i.e. to HOLDS-AT($p$, I). □

$$(\forall t)[\text{IN}(t, T) \Rightarrow \text{HOLDS-ON}(p, t)] \Rightarrow \text{HOLDS-ON}(p, T) \tag{T.11P}$$

Proof. Suppose (a) $(\forall t)[\text{IN}(t, T) \Rightarrow \text{HOLDS-IN}(p, t)]$, and let I be any instant. Suppose (b) WITHIN(I, T). Let S be any interval, and suppose (c) WITHIN(I, S). By (b), (c) and (I.3), there is an interval U such that (d) IN(U, T) and (e) IN(U, S). By (a) and (d), we have (f) HOLDS-IN(p, U). By (e), (f), and (T.1), we have (g) HOLDS-IN(p, S). The inference from (c) to (g) holds for any interval S, so by (SP) we have (h) HOLDS-AT(p, I). Finally, the inference from (b) to (h) holds for any instant I, so by (D.2) we have HOLDS-ON(p, T). □

$$\text{HOLDS-ON}(p, T) \,\&\, \text{LIMITS}(I, T) \Rightarrow \text{HOLDS-AT}(p, I) \qquad \text{(T.12P)}$$

Proof. Suppose (a) HOLDS-ON(p, T) and (b) LIMITS(I, T), and let S be any interval. Suppose (c) WITHIN(I, S). Then from (b), (c) and (I.4), there is an interval U such that (d) IN(U, S) and (e) IN(U, T). From (a), (e) and (T.4), we infer (f) HOLDS-IN(p, U). But from (d), (f) and (T.1) we have (g) HOLDS-IN(p, S). The inference from (c) to (g) holds for any interval S, so by (SP) we have HOLDS-AT(p, I). □

$$\text{HOLDS-AT}(\text{not}(p), I) \Rightarrow$$
$$(\exists t)[\text{WITHIN}(I, t) \,\&\, \text{HOLDS-ON}(\text{not}(p), t)]. \qquad \text{(T.13P)}$$

Proof. Suppose (a) HOLDS-AT(not(p), I). Then by (a) and (D.3) we have (b) ¬HOLDS-AT(p, I). From (b) and (SP), we infer that there must be an interval T such that (c) WITHIN(I, T) and (d) ¬HOLDS-IN(p, T). From (d) and (T.9) we have (e) HOLDS-ON(not(p), T); the conjunction of (c) and (e) gives us the required result. □

$$\text{HOLDS-IN}(p, T) \Rightarrow (\exists t)[\text{IN}(t, T) \,\&\, \text{HOLDS-ON}(p, T)], \qquad \text{(T.11M)}$$

Proof. Suppose that (a) HOLDS-IN(p, T). By (a) and (D.1), there is an instant I such that (b) WITHIN(I, T) and (c) HOLDS-AT(p, I). From (c) and (SM), there is an interval S such that (d) WITHIN(I, S) and (e) HOLDS-ON(p, S). By (b), (d) and (I.3), there is an interval U such that (f) IN(U, T) and (g) IN(U, S). By (e), (g) and (T.2), we have (h) HOLDS-ON(p, U). The conjunction of (f) and (h) gives us the required result. □

$$\text{HOLDS-AT}(p, I) \,\&\, \text{LIMITS}(I, T) \Rightarrow \text{HOLDS-IN}(p, T), \qquad \text{(T.12M)}$$

Proof. Suppose that (a) HOLDS-AT(p, I) and (b) LIMITS(I, T). By (a) and (SM) there is an interval S such that (c) WITHIN(I, S) and (d) HOLDS-ON(p, S). By (b), (c) and (I.4) there is an interval U such that (e) IN(U, S) and (f) IN(U, T). By (d), (e) and (T.4) we have (g) HOLDS-IN(p, U). Finally, from (f), (g) and (T.1) we have HOLDS-IN(p, T). □

$$(\forall t)[\text{WITHIN}(I, t) \Rightarrow \text{HOLDS-IN}(\text{not}(p), t)] \Rightarrow$$
$$\text{HOLDS-AT}(\text{not}(p), I) \qquad \text{(T.13M)}$$

Proof. Suppose (a) $(\forall t)$[WITHIN(I, t)⇒HOLDS-IN(not(p), t)], and let T be any interval. Suppose (b) WITHIN(I, T). Then by (a) and (b) we have HOLDS-IN(not(p), T), which by (T.8) is equivalent to (c) ¬HOLDS-ON(p, T). The inference from (b) to (c) is general, so we have $(\forall t)$[WITHIN(I, t)⇒¬HOLDS-ON(p, t)], which is straightforwardly equivalent to (d) ¬$(\exists t)$[WITHIN(I, t) & HOLDS-ON(p, T)]. By (d) and (SM) we have ¬HOLDS-AT(p, I), which by (D.3) is equivalent to HOLDS-AT(not(p), I), as required. □

REFERENCES

Allen, J.F. (1981). 'An interval-based representation of temporal knowledge', in *Proceedings of the International Joint Conference on Artificial Intelligence* (IJCAI). Vancouver, BC, 221–6.
—— (1983). 'Maintaining knowledge about temporal intervals', *Communications of the ACM* **26**: 832–43.
—— (1984). 'Towards a general theory of action and time', *Artificial Intelligence* **23**: 123–54.

—— and Hayes, P.J. (1985). 'A common-sense theory of time', in *Proceedings of the International Joint Conference on Artificial Intelligence* (IJCAI). Los Angeles, CA, 528–31.

—— and Kautz, H.A. (1985). 'A model of naive temporal reasoning', in J.R. Hobbs and R.C. Moore (eds.), *Formal Theories of the Commonsense World*. Norwood, NJ: Ablex, 251–68.

—— and Koomen, J.A. (1983). 'Planning using a temporal world model', in *Proceedings of the International Joint Conference on Artificial Intelligence* (IJCAI). Karlsruhe, FRG, 741–7.

Anscombe, G.E.M. (1964). 'Before and after', *Philosophical Review* **73**: 3–24.

Bundy, A. (1978). 'Will it reach the top? Prediction in the mechanics world', *Artificial Intelligence* **10**: 129–46.

Galton, A.P. (1984). *The Logic of Aspect*. Oxford: Clarendon Press.

Hamblin, C.L. (1969). 'Starting and stopping', *The Monist* **53**: 410–25.

Hamblin, C.L. (1971). 'Instants and intervals', *Studium Generale* **24**: 127–34.

Hayes, P.J. (1985). 'Naive Physics I: Ontology for liquids', in J.R. Hobbs and R.C. Moore (eds.), *Formal Theories of the Commonsense World*. Norwood, NJ: Ablex, 71–108.

Kuipers, B. (1984). 'Commonsense reasoning about causality: Deriving behavior from structure', *Artificial Intelligence* **24**: 169–203.

McDermott, D. (1982). 'A temporal logic for reasoning about processes and plans', *Cognitive Science* **6**: 101–55.

Prior, A.N. (1967). *Past, Present and Future*. Oxford: Clarendon Press.

Shoham, Y. (1986). 'Reified temporal logics: Semantical and ontological considerations', in *Proceedings of The European Conference on Artificial Intelligence* (ECAI). Brighton, UK, 390–7.

14

Annotating and Reasoning about Time and Events

JERRY HOBBS AND JAMES PUSTEJOVSKY

I INTRODUCTION

The Semantic Web will necessarily require specification of temporal information. For example, someone who does a web search trying to find a place to buy a book needed before next Tuesday may or may not be able to use an online bookstore that promises delivery within five business days. Someone doing a genealogical search may want to specify that the birthdate of a person is between 15 and 45 years before a known marriage date. In response to this need, in connection with the DARPA-sponsored DAML program, we have been developing an ontology of temporal concepts, OWL-Time (originally DAML-Time), that covers the basic topological temporal relations on instants and intervals, measures of duration, and the clock and calendar (Hobbs, 2002). This will enable the statement of and reasoning about the temporal aspects of the contents and capabilities of web resources and of the needs of users.

But most of the information on the Web is in natural language, and there is no chance that it will ever be marked up for semantic retrieval if that has to be done by hand. Natural language programs will have to process the contents of web pages to produce annotations. Remarkable progress has been made in the last decade in the use of statistical techniques for analyzing text. However, these techniques for the most part depend on having large amounts of annotated data, and annotations require an annotation scheme. It is for this reason that the ARDA-funded AQUAINT program has sponsored the development of a mark-up language TimeML for temporal information in texts.

These annotations are most relevant to the Semantic Web enterprise if the annotation scheme meshes well with temporal ontologies used in the Semantic Web. The aim of this paper is to define just such a mapping. In Section 2 of this paper we present TimeML. In Section 3 we present the relevant parts of OWL-Time. In Section 4 we discuss how TimeML is interpreted within OWL-Time in order to provide a temporal grounding for texts that will facilitate reasoning over events, their orderings, and their relative granularity.

Reasoning about time is one of the most important aspects of common-sense reasoning. Linking a formal theory for time with an annotation scheme aimed at extracting rich temporal information from natural language text is significant for at least two reasons. It will allow us to use the multitude of temporal facts expressed in text as the ground propositions in a system for reasoning about temporal relations. It will also constitute a forcing function for developing the coverage of a temporal reasoning system, as we encounter phenomena not normally covered by such systems, such as complex descriptions of temporal aggregates.

2 TIMEML

2.1 The need for temporal annotation

The AQUAINT program is a multiproject effort to improve the performance of question answering systems over free text, such as that encountered on the Web. An important component to this effort is the access of information from text through content rather than keywords. Named entity recognition has moved the fields of information retrieval and information exploitation closer to access by content, by allowing some identification of names, locations, and products in texts. Beyond these metadata tags (ontological types), however, there is only a limited ability at marking up text for real content. One of the major problems that has not been solved is the recognition of events and their temporal anchorings. In this paper, we report on an AQUAINT project to create a specification language for event and temporal expressions in text.

Events in articles are naturally anchored in time within the narrative of a text. For this reason, temporally grounded events are the very foundation from which we reason about how the world changes. Without a robust ability to identify and extract events and their temporal anchoring from a text, the real "aboutness" of the article can be missed. Moreover, since entities and their properties change over time, a database of assertions about entities will be incomplete or incorrect if it does not capture how these properties are temporally updated. To this end, event recognition drives basic inferences from text.

For example, currently questions such as those shown below are not supported by question answering systems.

1. a. Is Gates currently CEO of Microsoft?
   b. When did Iraq finally pull out of Kuwait during the war in the 1990s?
   c. Did the Enron merger with Dynegy take place?

What characterizes these questions as beyond the scope of current systems is the following: they refer, respectively, to the temporal aspects of the properties of the entities being questioned, the relative ordering of events in the world, and events that are mentioned in news articles, but which have never occurred.

There has recently been a renewed interest in temporal and event-based reasoning in language and text, particularly as applied to information extraction and reasoning tasks (cf. Mani and Wilson, 2000, *ACL Workshop on Spatial and Temporal Reasoning*, 2001, Gaizauskas and Setzer, 2002). Several papers from the workshop point to promising directions for time representation and identification (cf. Filatova and Hovy, 2001, Schilder and Habel, 2001, Setzer, 2001). Many issues relating to temporal and event identification remain unresolved, however, and it is these issues that TimeML was designed to address. Specifically, four basic problems in event-temporal identification are addressed:

(a) Time stamping of events (identifying an event and anchoring it in time);
(b) Ordering events with respect to one another (lexical versus discourse properties of ordering);
(c) Reasoning with contextually underspecified temporal expressions (temporal functions such as *last week* and *two weeks before*);
(d) Reasoning about the persistence of events (how long does an event or the outcome of an event last).

The specification language, TimeML, is designed to address these issues, in addition to handling basic tense and aspect features.

2.2 Links

For the full specification of Time ML, see Chapter 27. Here we will focus on the LINK Tag.

The set of LINK tags encode the various relations that exist between the temporal elements of a document. There are three types of link tags.

- TLINK:

  A TLINK or Temporal Link represents the temporal relationship holding between events or between an event and a time, and establishes a link between the involved entities making explicit if they are: simultaneous, identical, before, after, immediately before, immediately after, including, during, beginning, and ending.

- SLINK:

  An SLINK or Subordination Link is used for contexts introducing relations between two events, or an event and a signal. SLINKs are of one of the following sorts: Modal, Factive, Counter-factive, Evidential, and Negative evidential.

- ALINK:

  An ALINK or Aspectual Link represents the relationship between an aspectual event and its argument event. Examples of the aspectual relations to be encoded are: initiation, culmination, termination, continuation.

Below, we present the specification for each link relation.

(1) **TLINK**:

```
attributes ::= [lid] [origin] (eventInstanceID | timeID)
               [signalID]
               (relatedtoEventInstance | relatedtoTime) relType
lid ::= ID
{lid ::= LinkID
LinkID ::= l<integer>}
origin ::= CDATA
eventInstanceID ::= ei<integer>
timeID ::= t<integer>
signalID ::= s<integer>
relatedToEventInstance ::= ei<integer>
relatedToTime ::= t<integer>
relType ::= 'BEFORE' | 'AFTER' | 'INCLUDES' | 'IS_INCLUDED'
            | 'DURING' | 'SIMULTANEOUS' | 'IAFTER' | 'IBEFORE' |
            'IDENTITY' | 'BEGINS' | 'ENDS' | 'BEGUN_BY' |
            'ENDED_BY'
```

To illustrate the function of this link, let us return to the sentence above, now adding the annotation of the TLINK, which orders the two events mentioned in the sentence.

> John left 2 days before the attack.

```
<TLINK eventInstanceID="ei1" signalID="s1"
relatedToEventInstance="ei2" relType="BEFORE"/>
```

(2) **SLINK**:

```
attributes ::= [lid] [origin] [eventInstanceID]
               subordinatedEventInstance [signalID]
               relType
lid ::= ID
{lid ::= LinkID
LinkID ::= l<integer>}
origin ::= CDATA
eventInstanceID ::= ei<integer>
subordinatedEventInstance ::= ei<integer>
signalID ::= s<integer>
relType ::= 'MODAL' | 'EVIDENTIAL' | 'NEG_EVIDENTIAL'
            | 'FACTIVE' | 'COUNTER_FACTIVE'
```

A modally subordinating predicate such as *want* is typed as introducing a SLINK, as shown below.

> Bill wants to teach on Monday.

```
Bill
<EVENT eid="e1" class="I_STATE">
wants
</EVENT>
<MAKEINSTANCE eiid="ei1" eventID="e1" tense="PRESENT"
 aspect="NONE"/>
<SIGNAL sid="s1">
to
</SIGNAL>
<EVENT eid="e2" class="OCCURRENCE">
teach
</EVENT>
<MAKEINSTANCE eiid="ei2" eventID="e2" tense="NONE"
 aspect="NONE"/>
<SIGNAL sid="s2">
on
</SIGNAL>
<TIMEX3 tid="t1" type="DATE" temporalFunction="true"
 value="XXXX-WXX-1">
Monday
</TIMEX3>
<TLINK eventInstanceID="ei2" relatedToTime="t1"
 relType="IS_INCLUDED"/>
<SLINK eventInstanceID="ei1" signalID="s1"
subordinatedEventInstance="ei2" relType="MODAL"/>
```

(3) **ALINK**:

```
attributes :: = [lid] [origin] eventInstanceID [signalID]
    relatedToEventInstance relType
lid :: = ID
{lid :: = LinkID
LinkID :: = l<integer>}
origin :: = CDATA
eventInstanceID :: = ei<integer>
signalID :: = s<integer>
relatedToEventInstance :: = ei<integer>
relType :: = 'INITIATES' | 'CULMINATES' | 'TERMINATES' | 'CONTINUES'
```

To illustrate the behavior of ALINKs, notice how the aspectual predicate *begin* is treated as a separate event, independent of the logically modified event; the "phase" is introduced as the relation within the ALINK.

The boat began to sink.

```
The boat
<EVENT eid = "e1" class = "ASPECTUAL">
began
</EVENT>
<MAKEINSTANCE eiid = "ei1" eventID = "e1" tense = "PAST"
 aspect = "NONE"/>
<SIGNAL sid = "s1">
to
</SIGNAL>
<EVENT eid = "e2" class = "OCCURRENCE">
sink
</EVENT>
<MAKEINSTANCE eiid = "ei2" eventID = "e2" tense = "NONE"
 aspect = "NONE"/>
<ALINK eventInstanceID = "ei1" signalID = "s1"
 relatedToEventInstance = "ei2"
relType = "INITIATES"/>
```

We should point out that the ALINK captures aspectual phase information associated with an event, and is logically (temporally) distinct from the BEGIN relType in the TLINK above. For example, in a sentence *The boat began to sink when the torpedo hit it*, the torpedo hitting the boat is TLINKed to the sinking event through the relType BEGIN, while the beginning of the sinking is ALINKed through the phase relType INITIATE.

In order to provide an interpretation of the TimeML specification of event and temporal expressions described above, we will adopt the OWL-Time ontology for time as a model.

3 OWL-TIME

OWL-Time is an ontology of temporal concepts, for describing the temporal content of web pages and the temporal properties of web services. Its development is being informed by temporal ontologies developed at a number of sites and is intended to capture the essential features of all of them and make them and their associated resources easily available to a large group of web developers and users. In this paper we specify the ontology in predicate calculus; This should be adequate for most applications[*]. A complete specification, due to George Ferguson, in KIF and in an encoding of logic in RDF/DAML developed by McDermott et al. (2001). A complete specification in OWL awaits further development of OWL-Rules. A resource with all the time zone information for the world in OWL-Time can be found at <http://www.isi.edu/pan/timezonehomepage.html>.

3.1 Topological temporal relations

3.1.1 Instants and intervals

There are two subclasses of *TemporalEntity*: *Instant* and *Interval*.

$Instant(t) \supset TemporalEntity(t)$[1]
$Interval(T) \supset TemporalEntity(T)$

The predicates *begins* and *ends* are relations between instants and temporal entities.

$begins(t, T) \supset Instant(t) \land TemporalEntity(T)$
$ends(t, T) \supset Instant(t) \land TemporalEntity(T)$

For convenience, we can say that the beginning and end of an Instant is itself. The converses of these rules are also true.

$Instant(t) \supset begins(t, t)$
$Instant(t) \supset ends(t, t)$

The predicate *inside* is a relation between an Instant and an interval.

$inside(t, T) \supset Instant(t) \land Interval(T)$

This concept of *inside* is not intended to include beginnings and ends of intervals.
The predicate *timeBetween* is a relation among a temporal entity and two instants.

$timeBetween(T, t_1, t_2)$
$\supset TemporalEntity(T) \land Instant(t_1) \land Instant(t_2)$

The two instants are the beginning and end points of the temporal entity.

$(\forall t_1, t_2)[t_1 \neq t_2$
$\supset (\forall T)[timeBetween(T, t_1, t_2)$
$\equiv begins(t_1, T) \land ends(t_2, T)]]$

The ontology is silent about whether the interval from t to t, if it exists, is identical to the instant t.
 The ontology is silent about whether intervals *consist of* instants.
 The ontology is silent about whether intervals are uniquely determined by their starts and ends.
 The core ontology is silent about whether intervals are uniquely determined by their beginnings and ends.

---

[*] On the daml.org website there is an OWL specification of those parts of OWL-Time that are easily expressible in OWL. This can be found at <http://www.isi.edu/pan/damltime/time-entry.owl>.
[1] A note on notation: Conjunction ($\land$) takes precedence over implication ($\supset$) and equivalence ($\equiv$). Formulas are assumed to be universally quantified on the variables appearing in the antecedent of the highest-level implication.

We can define a proper interval as one whose start and end are not identical.

$(\forall\ T)[ProperInterval(T)$
$\equiv Interval(T)$
$\quad \wedge (\forall\ t_1,\ t_2)[begins(t_1,\ T) \wedge ends(t_2,\ T) \supset t_1 \neq t_2]]$

The ontology is silent about whether there are any intervals that are not proper intervals.

3.1.2 Before

There is a *before* relation on temporal entities, which gives directionality to time. If temporal entity T_1 is before temporal entity T_2, then the end of T_1 is before the start of T_2. Thus, *before* can be considered to be basic to instants and derived for intervals.

$(\forall\ T_1,\ T_2)[before(T_1,\ T_2)$
$\equiv (\exists\ t_1,\ t_2)[ends(t_1,\ T_1) \wedge begins(t_2,\ T_2) \wedge before(t_1,\ t_2)]]$

The *before* relation is antireflexive, antisymmetric, and transitive.

$before(T_1,\ T_2) \supset T_1 \neq T_2$
$before(T_1,\ T_2) \supset \neg before(T_2,\ T_1)$
$before(T_1,\ T_2) \wedge before(T_2,\ T_3) \supset before(T_1,\ T_3)$

The end of an interval is not before the beginning of the interval.

$Interval(T) \wedge begins(t_1,\ T) \wedge ends(t_2,\ T) \supset \neg before(t_2,\ t_1)$

The beginning of a proper interval is before the end of the interval.

$ProperInterval(T) \wedge begins(t_1,\ T) \wedge ends(t_2,\ T)$
$\quad \supset before(t_1,\ t_2)$

If one instant is before another, there is a time between them.

$Instant(t_1) \wedge Instant(t_2) \wedge before(t_1,\ t_2)$
$\quad \supset (\exists T)timeBetween(T,\ t_1,\ t_2)$

The ontology is silent about whether there is a time from *t* to *t*.

If an instant is inside a proper interval, then the beginning of the interval is before the instant, which is before the end of the interval. This is the principal property of *inside*.

$inside(t,\ T) \wedge begins(t_1,\ T) \wedge ends(t_2,\ T) \wedge ProperInterval(T)$
$\quad \supset before(t_1,\ t) \wedge before(t,\ t_2)$

The relation *after* is defined in terms of *before*.

$after(T_1,\ T_2) \equiv before(T_2,\ T_1)$

The ontology is silent about whether time is linearly ordered. Thus it supports theories of time, such as the branching futures theory, which conflate time and possibility or knowledge.

3.1.3 Interval relations

The relations between intervals defined in Allen's temporal interval calculus (Allen and Kautz, 1985) can be defined in a straightforward fashion in terms of before and identity on the beginning and end points. We illustrate this with the relations *intMeets* and *intFinishes*.

$(\forall T_1, T_2)[intMeets(T_1, T_2)$
$\equiv [ProperInterval(T_1) \wedge ProperInterval(T_2)$
$\wedge (\exists t)[ends(t, T_1) \wedge begins(t, T_2)]]]$

$(\forall T_1, T_2)[intFinishes(T_1, T_2)$
$\equiv [ProperInterval(T_1) \wedge ProperInterval(T_2)$
$\wedge (\exists t_1)[begins(t_1, T_1)$
$\wedge (\forall t_3)[begins(t_3, T_2) \supset before(t_3, t_1)]$
$\wedge (\forall t_4)[ends(t_4, T_2) \equiv ends(t_4, T_1)]]]]$

These definitions are a bit more complicated than one might at first think necessary, in order to handle unbounded intervals.

3.1.4 Linking Time and Events

The time ontology links to other things in the world through four predicates—*atTime*, *during*, and *timeSpan*. We assume that another ontology provides for the description of events—either a general ontology of event structure abstractly conceived, or specific, domain-dependent ontologies for specific domains.

The term "eventuality" will be used to cover events, states, processes, propositions, states of affairs, and anything else that can be located with respect to time. The possible natures of eventualities would be spelled out in the event ontologies.

The predicate *atTime* relates an eventuality to an Instant, and is intended to say that the eventuality holds, obtains, or is taking place at that time.

$atTime(e, t) \supset Instant(t)$

The predicate *during* relates an eventuality to an interval, and is intended to say that the eventuality holds, obtains, or is taking place during that interval.

$during(e, T) \supset Interval(T)$

If an eventuality obtains during an interval, it obtains at every Instant inside the interval and during every subinterval.

$during(e, T) \wedge inside(t, T) \supset atTime(e, t)$
$during(e, T) \wedge intDuring(T_1, T) \supset during(e, T_1)$

Note that this means that an intermittent activity, like writing a book, does not hold "during" the interval from the beginning to the end of the activity. Rather the "convex hull" of the activity holds "during" the interval.

Whether a particular process is viewed as Instantaneous or as occuring over an interval is a granularity decision that may vary according to the context of use, and is assumed to be provided by the event ontology.

The predicate *timeSpan* relates eventualities to Instants or intervals (or temporal sequences of Instants and intervals). For contiguous states and processes, it tells the entire instant or interval for which the state or process obtains or takes place.

$timeSpan(T, e) \supset TemporalEntity(T) \vee tseq(T)$
$timeSpan(T, e) \wedge Interval(T) \supset during(e, T)$
$timeSpan(t, e) \wedge Instant(t) \supset atTime(e, t)$

$timeSpan(T, e) \wedge Interval(T) \wedge \neg inside(t, T)$
  $\wedge \neg begins(t, T) \wedge \neg ends(t, T)$
  $\supset \neg atTime(e, t)$
$timeSpan(t,e) \wedge Instant(t) \wedge t_1 \neq t \supset \neg atTime(e, t_1)$

Whether the eventuality obtains at the start and end points of its time span is a matter for the event ontology to specify. The silence here on this issue is the reason *timeSpan* is not defined in terms of necessary and sufficient conditions.

In an extension of the time ontology, we also allow temporal predicates to apply directly to events, should the user wish. Thus, *begins(t, e)* says that the instant *t* begins the interval that is the time span of eventuality *e*. (See <http://www.isi.edu/pan/damltime/time-entry-documentation.txt>.)

3.2 Measuring durations

3.2.1 Temporal units

This development assumes ordinary arithmetic is available.

We can consider temporal units to constitute a set of entities—call it Temporal Units—and have a function *duration* mapping Intervals × TemporalUnits into the Reals.

$duration([5:14, 5:17], *Minute*) = 3$

The arithmetic relations among the various units can be stated in axioms like

$duration(T, *Second*)$
  $= 60*duration(T, *Minute*)$

The relation between days and months (and, to a lesser extent, years) is specified as part of the ontology of clock and calendar below. On their own, however, month and year are legitimate temporal units.

3.2.2 Concatenation and Hath

The multiplicative relations above don't tell the whole story of the relations among temporal units. Temporal units are *composed of* smaller temporal units. A larger temporal unit is a concatenation of smaller temporal units. We first defined a general relation of concatenation between an interval and a set of smaller intervals. Then a predicate *Hath* is defined that specifies the number of smaller unit intervals that concatenate to a larger interval.

Concatenation: A proper interval *x* is a concatenation of a set *S* of proper intervals if and only if *S* covers all of *x*, and all members of *S* are subintervals of *x* and are mutually disjoint. From this definition we can prove as theorems that there are elements in *S* that start and finish *x*; and except for the first and last elements of *S*, every element of *S* has elements that precede and follow it.

Hath: The basic predicate for expressing the composition of larger intervals out of smaller temporal intervals of unit length is *Hath*, from statements like "30 days hath September" and "60 minutes hath an hour." Its structure is

$Hath(N, u, x)$

meaning "*N* proper intervals of duration one unit *u* hath the proper interval *x*." That is, if *Hath(N, u, x)* holds, then *x* is the concatenation of *N* unit intervals where the unit is u. For example, if x is some month of September then *Hath*(30, *Day*, x) would be true.

Hath is defined as follows:

Hath(N, u, x)
≡ (∃ S)[card(S) = N
∧ (∀ z)[member(z, S) ⊃ duration(z, u) = 1]
∧ concatenation(x, S)]

That is, x is the concatenation of a set S of N proper intervals of duration one unit u.

We are now in a position to state the relations between successive temporal units, by means of axioms like the following:

duration(T, *Minute*) = 1 ⊃ Hath(60, *Second*, T)

The relations between months and days are dealt with after the calendar has been characterized.

3.3 Clock and calendar

3.3.1 Clock and calendar units

We take a day as a calendar interval to begin at and include midnight and go until but not include the next midnight. By contrast, a day as a duration is any interval that is 24 hours in length. The day as a duration was dealt with in the previous section. This section deals with the day as a calendar interval.

Including the beginning but not the end of a calendar interval in the interval may strike some as arbitrary. But we get a cleaner treatment if, for example, all times of the form 12:xx a.m., including 12:00 a.m. are part of the same hour and day, and all times of the form 10:15:xx, including 10:15:00, are part of the same minute.

For stating general properties about clock intervals, we use

clockInt(y, n, u, x).

This expression says that y is the nth clock interval of type u in x. Here u is a member of the set of clock units, that is, one of *Second*, *Minute*, or *Hour*. For example, the proposition

clockInt(10:03, 3, *Minute*, [10:00,11:00])

holds.

In addition, there is a calendar unit function with similar structure:

calInt(y, n, u, x)

This says that y is the nth calendar interval of type u in x. Here u is one of the calendar units *Day*, *Week*, *Month*, and *Year*. For example, the proposition

calInt(12Mar2002, 12, *Day*, Mar2002)

holds.

Each of the calendar intervals is that unit long; a calendar year is a year long.

calInt(y, n, u, x) ⊃ duration(y, u) = 1

The distinction between clock and calendar intervals is because they differ in how they number their unit intervals. The first minute of an hour is labeled with 0; for example, the first minute of the hour [10:00,11:00] is 10:00. The first day of a month is labeled with 1; the first day of March is March 1. We number minutes for the number just completed; we number days for the day we are working on. Thus, if the larger unit has N smaller units, the argument n in *clockInt* runs from 0 to $N-1$, whereas in *calInt n* runs from 1 to N. To state properties true of both clock and calendar intervals, we can use the predicate *calInt* and relate the two notions with the axiom

calInt(y, n, u, x) ≡ *clockInt*(y, n − 1, u, x).

OWL-Time includes a treatment of weeks and days of the week as well.

3.3.2 Months and years

The months have special names in English, as in

calInt(m, 9, *Month*, y) ∧ *calInt*(y, n, *Year*, e)
≡ *September*(y, x)

That is, the ninth month m in a year y is a September. The number of days in a month have to be spelled out for individual months, by axioms of the following form:

September(m, y)
⊃ (∃ S)*Hath*(30, *Day*, m)

The definition of a leap year is as follows, where $CE(z)$ is the Common Era in time zone z:

(∀ z)[*leapYear*(y)
≡ (∃ n, x)[*CalInt*(y, n, *Year*, CE(z))
∧ [*divides*(400, n)
∨ [*divides*(4, n) ∧ ¬*divides*(100, n)]]]]

Now the number of days in February can be specified.

February(m, y) ∧ *leapYear*(y) ⊃ (∃ S)*Hath*(29, *Day*, m)
February(m, y) ∧ ¬*leapYear*(y) ⊃ (∃ S)*Hath*(28, *Day*, m)

Months can now be defined as a duration, namely, the duration from the nth day of one month to the nth day of the next month, with special provisions for months with unequal numbers of days.

To say that July 4 is a holiday in the United States one can write

(∀ d, m, y)[*calInt*(d, 4, *Day*m) ∧ *July*(m, y) ⊃ *holiday*(d, USA)]

3.4 Time and duration stamps

Standard notation for times list the year, month, day, hour, minute, and second. It is useful to define a predication for this.

timeOf (t, y, m, d, h, n, s, z)

For example, an instant t has the time

5:14:35pm PDT, October 4, 2002

if the following property holds for t:

timeOf (t, 2002, 10, 4, 17, 14, 35, *PDT*)

We can similarly define a predicate that specifies the duration of an interval in standard units.

durationOf (T, y, m, d, h, n, s)

It is straightforward to translate predications of *timeOf* and *durationOf* into ISO 8601 format for dates, times, and durations.

4 INTERPRETING TIMEML IN OWL-TIME

The intended interpretation of the TimeML specifications can now be provided in terms of the OWL-Time ontology. This allows one to move back and forth between the two representations as required for linguistic analysis and reasoning.

There are some aspects of TimeML that relate not to a theory of time but a theory of the structure of events. Among these are aspect, such as "perfective". We do not deal with these here.

The information in the SIGNAL tag is of importance in the automatic recovery of temporal relations, and therefore it is important that signals be annotated. But by the time annotation is complete, that information will have been incorporated into LINK tags, so it is not necessary to interpret signals with respect to the OWL-Time ontology.

The SLINK is about grammatical subordination, or predicate-argument stucture, and the modal or cognitive relation between the dominating and subordinated events. Thus, it is not concerned with the ontology of time as such, although it is important in linking the subordinated possible event into the temporal structure of the whole text.

The TimeML attribute "functionInDocument" refers to a concept in a theory of documents and relates it to times. Essentially, it states an *atTime* relation between a document event, such as publication, and the time referred to by a temporal expression. It is required for the interpretation of deictic expressions such as "now" and "last week". The treatment of deictic time will be addressed in a future release of OWL-Time.

The "tense" attribute of MAKEINSTANCE tags is expressed in terms of a *before* or equality relation, once the deictic anchor ("now") is known.

The "value" in a TIMEX3 tag is a date, time, or duration in the ISO 8601 standard format, as extended by TIDES2. As pointed out above, there is a straightforward mapping between *timeOf* predications and date and time formats, and between *durationOf* predications and duration formats. The "XX" notation in the ISO standard corresponds to existentially quantified variables in the logic.

The "relType" values of the TLINK tag correspond roughly to the interval relations in Allen's interval calculus and can be defined either in terms of these or in a similar manner. For example, an IAFTER relation can be defined as the interval during which one event occurs meeting the interval during which the other occurs. IDENTITY is not a temporal relation but is expressed as equality involving reified events.

The "relType" values of the ALINK tag can be defined similarly. An event that INITIATES another, for example, occurs at the start of the interval during which the other occurs. The ALINK tag conveys something more than just temporal information. As mentioned above, the beginning of a sinking of a boat is not the same event as the event of a torpedo hitting the boat, even if they are simultaneous. This distinction, however, is not part of a theory of time but a theory of the structure of events. Similarly, the distinction between TERMINATES and CULMINATES is not a temporal one but something that would have to come from event theory.

The logical representation of the temporal information in the sentence

John left 2 days before the attack.

can now be read off the TimeML tags in the markup. Recall that the ordering between the events is encoded in a TLINK as:

```
<TLINK eventInstanceID=ei1 signalID=s1 relatedToTime=t1
relType=BEGINS/>
```

Assume e_1 is John's leaving and e_2 is the attack. If the TLINK relType is interpreted as BEGINS, and the type attribute of t_1 is *duration*, then the OWL-Time representation of the temporal information from TimeML is as shown below.

$atTime(e_1, t_1) \wedge atTime(e_2, T_2)$
$\wedge \, before(t_1, t_2) \wedge timeBetween(T, t_1, t_2)$
$\wedge \, duration(T, *Day*) = 2$

Another important component for reasoning about events and their temporal properties within web-based content is an analysis of explicit and implicit causation as expressed in the text. Event causation involves more than proximate temporal precedence of events. However, for a significant number of cases in text, the axioms associated with temporal ordering together with information linked to specific lexical items will be sufficient for deriving causal-like inferences between events.

In TimeML, three distinct cases of event causation in texts are distinguished:

(a) E_1 *cause* E_2:
The rain (E_1) caused flooding (E_2).

(b) *X cause* E_1:
John (X) started a fire (E_1).

(c) E_1 *Discourse_marker* E_2:
John pushed Mary (E_1) and she fell over (E_2)

For a case such as (a) above, the causal predicate *cause* is analyzed as denoting a separate event, which is identified as identical to the initial event in the logical subject position. A TLINK establishes the precedence relation between this event and the flooding event in object position. The TimeML for (a) is illustrated below.

```
The
<EVENT eid="e1" class="OCCURRENCE">
rain
</EVENT>
<MAKEINSTANCE eiid="ei1" eventID="e1" tense="NONE"
  aspect="NONE"/>
<EVENT eid="e2" class="OCCURRENCE">
caused
</EVENT>
<MAKEINSTANCE eiid="ei2" eventID="e2" tense="PAST"
  aspect="NONE"/>
```

the
```
<EVENT eid="e3" class="OCCURRENCE">
flooding
</EVENT>
<MAKEINSTANCE eiid="ei3" eventID="e3" tense="NONE"
  aspect="NONE"/>
<TLINK eventInstanceID="ei1"
  relatedToEventInstance="ei2" relType="IDENTITY"/>
<TLINK eventInstanceID="ei2"
  relatedToEventInstance="ei3" relType="BEFORE"/>
```

The OWL-Time interpretation of (a) will merely express the temporal precedence relation, while leaving a more explicit encoding of causation to other domain interpretations.

rain(e_1) ∧ flooding(e_2)
atTime(e_1, t_1) ∧ atTime(e_2, t_2)
∧ before(t_1, t_2)

For case (b) above, there is no explicit event in subject position, hence the causal predicate alone will be temporally ordered relative to the object event, thereby obviating an "event metonymy" interpretation of the sentence (Pustejovsky, 1993).

Both solutions are adopted for verbs such as the following, in their causative senses: *cause, stem from, lead to, breed, engender, hatch, induce, occasion, produce, bring about, secure*.

For case (c) above, the annotation can optionally identify the discourse marker *and* as a signal for a TLINK introducing the relType BEFORE and a potential interpretation of causation. Such discourse causation relations can then be modeled in terms of discourse rhetorical interpretations, such as Hobbs (1982).

5 RELEVANCE TO SEMANTIC WEB

Significant efforts have been launched to annotate the temporal information in large textual corpora, resulting in the development of the mark-up language TimeML. Significant efforts have also taken place in the Semantic Web community for developing an ontology of time for expressing the temporal content of websites and the temporal properties of web services, resulting in OWL-Time. There is much to be gained by linking these two efforts, and that is what we have begun to do in this paper.

ACKNOWLEDGEMENTS

The authors would like to thank the other members of the TERQAS and TANGO Working Groups on TimeML for their contribution to the specification language presented here: Robert Ingria, Robert Gaizauskas, Graham Katz, Jose Castano, Andrea Setzer, Roser Sauri, Inderjeet Mani, Antonio Sanfilippo, Beth Sundheim, Jess Littman, Bob Kippen, Andrew See, and Andy Latto. This work was performed in support of the Northeast Regional Research Center (NRRC) which is sponsored by the Advanced Research and Development Activity in Information Technology (ARDA), a U.S. Government entity which sponsors and promotes research of import to the Intelligence Community which includes but is not limited to the CIA, DIA, NSA, NIMA, and NRO. It was also funded in part by the Defense Advanced Research Projects Agency as part of the DAML program under Air Force Research Laboratory contract F30602-00-C-0168. We would also like to thank the researchers who have contributed to the development of OWL-Time, including Feng Pan, George Ferguson, James Allen, Richard Fikes, Pat Hayes, Drew McDermott, Ian Niles, Adam Pease, Austin Tate, Mabry Tyson, and Richard Waldinger.

REFERENCES

Allen, J. F. (1984). 'Towards a general theory of action and time', *Artificial Intelligence* 23: 123–54.
—— and Ferguson, G. (1997). 'Actions and events in interval temporal logic', in Oliveiro Stock (ed.), *Spatial and Temporal Reasoning*. Dordrecht: Kluwer Academic Publishers, 205–45.
—— and Hayes, P. J. (1989). 'Moments and points in an interval-based temporal logic', *Computational Intelligence* 5: 225–38.
—— and Kautz, Henry A. (1985). 'A Model of Naive Temporal Reasoning', in Jerry R. Hobbs and Robert C. Moore (eds.), *Formal Theories of the Commonsense World*. Norwood, NJ: Ablex Publishing Corp., 251–68.
Ferro, Lisa, Mani, Inderjeet, Sundheim, Beth, and Wilson, George (2001). 'TIDES Temporal Annotation Guidelines. Version 1.0.2'. MITRE Technical Report, MTR 01W0000041.
Filatova, Elena and Hovy, Eduard (2001). 'Assigning Time-Stamps To Event-Clauses', in *Proceedings of the ACL-2001 Workshop on Temporal and Spatial Information Processing*, ACL-2001, Toulouse, France, 6–11 July, 88–95.
Gaizauskas, Robert and Setzer, Andrea (eds.) (2002). *Annotation Standards for Temporal Information in Natural Language*, LREC 2002.
Hobbs, Jerry (1982). 'Towards an Understanding of Coherence in Discourse', in W. Lehnert and M. Ringle (eds.), *Strategies for Natural Language Processing*. Hillsdale, NJ: Lawrence Erlbaum Associates.
—— (2002). <http://www.cs.rochester.edu/~ferguson/daml/daml-time-nov2002.txt>.
Ingria, Robert and Pustejovsky, James (2002). 'TimeML Specification 1.0', available at <http://timem/.org>.
McDermott, Drew, Borden, Jonathan, Burstein, Mark, Smith, Doug, and Waldinger, Richard (2001). 'A Proposal for Encoding Logic in RDF/DAML', available at <http://www.cs.yale.edu/homes/dvm/daml/>.
Mani, Inderjeet and Wilson, George (2000). 'Robust Temporal Processing of News', in *Proceedings of the ACL'2000 Conference*, 3–6 October 2000, Hong Kong, 69–76.
Pustejovsky, J. (1993). 'Type Coercion and Lexical Selection', in J. Pustejovsky (ed.), *Semantics and the Lexicon*. Dordrecht: Kluwer Academic Publishers, 73–94.
Pustejovsky, James, Gaizauskas, Robert, Sauri, Roser, Setzer, Andrea, and Ingria, Robert (2002). 'Annotation Guideline to TimeML 1.0', available at <http://timem.org.>.
Schilder, Frank and Habel, Christopher (2001). 'From Temporal Expressions To Temporal Information: Semantic Tagging Of News Messages' in *Proceedings of the ACL-2001 Workshop on Temporal and Spatial Information Processing*, ACL-2001, Toulouse, France, 6–11 July, 65–72.
Setzer, Andrea (2001). 'Temporal Information in Newswire Articles: an Annotation Scheme and Corpus Study', Ph.D. dissertation, University of Sheffield.

PART III
Temporal Structure of Discourse

Introduction to Part III

1 INTRODUCTION

Sentences are rarely interpreted in isolation. The context in which a sentence is uttered, including the situation of the speakers involved, is important. In general, the previous **discourse history** plays a crucial role in resolving anaphoric references, including those of pronouns, definite and indefinite noun phrases, and temporal adverbials like *later, that day, then, in June*, etc. An utterance may answer a follow-up question in a dialog, so that the utterance only makes sense in the context of the prior discourse history. Likewise, an utterance may elaborate or express a contrast with a previously established point in an expository text; that previous context is important for understanding the utterance.

In Part I, we discussed the anaphoric view of tense, as expressed in Reichenbach's account. The approaches discussed there modeled tense and aspect without taking into account the prior discourse history. Clearly, when we interpret sentences in succession, we are able to fit them into a temporal structure, allowing us to infer which events occurred roughly when, and in what order they might have occurred, even though the text may not specify those details. Further, we have clear intuitions as to how various states fit into a discourse. This discourse structure can often be inferred without specific information about the exact durations of events and states. How can an agent achieve such an amazing inferential feat? How do tense and aspect information help our understanding of this temporal structure? What other kinds of knowledge are involved in our inferences about this structure?

The papers in this section address these questions. They explore various models of discourse that show how the prior discourse history constrains the interpretation of temporal information in utterances. They clarify the role of different knowledge sources in constructing to a temporal structure for events in an entire discourse.

In order to put these papers in perspective, we will first introduce an account of how the meaning of a sentence can be related in a systematic way to a discourse history. This account is based on the influential work of Kamp (1984), which introduces **Discourse Representation Theory** (DRT). We then follow the representation of tense and aspect in DRT, as elaborated by Kamp and Reyle (1993). Unfortunately, no single source provides a short, self-contained description of DRT and its application to temporal discourse; we have therefore provided such an introduction, which in turn requires a certain level of technical detail in its presentation.

This introduction is followed by a discussion of the relative influence of semantics versus pragmatics in interpreting the temporal order of events in a discourse context. Two different theories are examined here. We then summarize research in discourse analysis that analyzes the temporal orderings found in newspaper texts. Next, we turn to several computational approaches that make inferences about the temporal structure of discourse. We begin with an anaphoric theory of tense, followed by an implementation of such a theory that explores the notion of coherent tense sequences. We then discuss an anaphoric approach to resolving temporal adverbials. Next, we explore the role of compositional semantics. Finally, we examine a system where different knowledge sources are integrated together. Taken together, this section illustrates some of the challenging problems facing computational approaches aimed at discovering temporal relations in discourse, including the need to factor in background knowledge of the world.

2   DISCOURSE REPRESENTATION THEORY

The argument made by DRT is that a semantic theory should provide an interpretation for sentences in the context of a discourse (viewed as a sequence of sentences), rather than sentences in isolation. (This idea is common to DRT as well as several related theories grouped under the rubric of 'Dynamic Semantics'.) In DRT, as each sentence in a discourse gets processed, it contributes its semantic information to a Discourse Representation Structure (DRS), which provides a cumulative semantic representation for the discourse. A DRS can have a hierarchical structure, with sub-DRSs introduced under certain conditions. In processing each sentence, once a syntactic tree is constructed for the sentence, a DRS is constructed for the tree using semantic rules, and this DRS is merged with an existing DRS for the discourse.

DRT is motivated by certain linguistic phenomena which illustrate the interaction between reference and quantification (two very fundamental concerns in the formal semantics of NL). These phenomena are the famous (or infamous) 'donkey sentences' first discussed by Geach (1962):

(1) Pedro owns a donkey.
(2) If Pedro owns a donkey, he beats it.
    $\forall x[[donkey(x) \& owns(Pedro, x)] \rightarrow [beats(Pedro, x)]]$
(3) Every farmer who owns a donkey beats it.
    $\forall x \, \forall y[[donkey(x) \& farmer(y) \& owns(y, x)] \rightarrow [beats(y, x)]]$

The meaning of (1) is that there is a donkey and Pedro owns it, i.e. 'donkey' is existentially quantified. When sentence (1) is embedded in the antecedent of a conditional like 'if', however, the donkey emerges as universally quantified, as in the formula expressing the meaning of (2). Here 'if' seems to have the meaning of *whenever* or *always*. Note that the semantics of (3), shown in its logical formula, seems similar to that of a variant of (2), namely *If a farmer owns a donkey, he beats it*.

In a nutshell, Kamp's approach is to have referring expressions introduce free variables (called **discourse referents**, or **reference markers**), so that the 'x' in 'donkey(x)' in (2) is initially free. Both *every* (as in (3)) and *if* (as in (2)) will capture these variables by means of a universal quantifier. Thus, even though they occur in different syntactic positions, *every* and *if*, in sentences of the form 'Every P ... Vs' and 'If P ..., V ...' are both given a common semantic template $\forall x[[P(x)] \rightarrow [V(x)]]$. Any free variables that aren't quantified are eventually existentially quantified.

Consider (3). The DRS for it is shown in (4).

(4)

x1, x2		x3
farmer (x1)	==>	x3 = x2
donkey (x2)		beats (x1, x3)
owns (x1, x2)		

The DRS in (4) has two subordinate DRSs, linked by a special operator $\Longrightarrow$ that corresponds to the above semantic template. Each subordinate DRS has a set of discourse referents, shown in the first row, together with a set of terms (called DRS-conditions) that are conjoined together. The idea here that a subordinate DRS inherits discourse referents from a superordinate DRS (in this case empty, because (3) is discourse initial), with a DRS to the right-hand side of the $\Longrightarrow$ operator inheriting from the DRS to the left-hand side. Referents in the left-hand side DRS that aren't existentially closed are not accessible outside the containing DRS, so x1 and x2 can't be pronominalized in subsequent sentences. The DRS in (4) is semantically equivalent to the formula in (3).

3 TENSE AND ASPECT IN DRT

3.1 Basic framework

An extensive treatment of tense and aspect within the DRT framework is found in the work of Kamp and Reyle (1993) (hereafter K&R). In their approach, tensed sentences, following Reichenbach, introduce a discourse referent e for the eventuality described by the sentence (we didn't introduce this earlier in order not to complicate the presentation). They also introduce a referent n for the speech time, and another referent t for the time (explicitly mentioned or not) to which the event is anchored, called the **location time**. The representation also includes a relation $time(e, t)$ between e and t. The *time* relation can be specialized to express various temporal relations, e.g. if t is considered an interval, the event might occur during t, before t, etc. Consider the following discourse.

(5) A man entered the White Hart on Sunday.

Here the condition $t < n$ is added to the DRS, since it's in the past tense. In addition, since the lexical aspect is nonstative, the condition $e \subseteq t$ is also introduced, to express the *time* relation, that the event occurs during the location time t. The additional condition Sunday($t1$) is also added, since 'on' makes the reference time coincide with the location time t. The resulting DRS is shown in (6).

(6)
$e, t, n, x, y, t1$
$t<n, e \subseteq t$
enter (e, x, y), man(x)
$y =$ the WhiteHart
Sunday $(t1), t1=t$

If the sentence used a stative verb, as in *A man was ill on Sunday*, the only change (apart from 'being ill' being substituted for 'entering the White Hart') would be to have the condition $e \bigcirc t$ instead of $e \subseteq t$, since statives are assumed to overlap with the location time (however, note that when used in the present tense, statives are assumed to include the location time, i.e. $t \subseteq e$).

3.2 Temporal relations for successive sentences

K&R argue that in *successive past tense sentences which lack temporal adverbials, events advance the narrative forward, while states do not*. This argument, which has been traditional in the formal semantics literature (Partee 1984; Hinrichs 1986), accords with some of our intuitions about the way narratives progress, e.g. (7) below.

(7) A man entered the White Hart. He was wearing a black jacket. Bill served him a beer.

The question therefore arises as to how to define 'advancing the narrative forward'.

At this point, it is worth distinguishing between narrative progression and Reichenbach's reference time (reference point). K&R (p. 594) point out, in some past perfect flashbacks like (8) below, Reichenbach's reference time remains constant (10 a.m. in this instance), but we still have a sense that the narrative progresses, since the location time of each event is displaced forward in narrative order.

(8) Fred arrived at 10. He had got up at 5; he had taken a long shower, had got dressed and had eaten a leisurely breakfast. He had left the house at 6:30.

They therefore introduce a concept (called '**reference point**' (or **Rpt**) to indicate the point in time that the narrative has progressed to. This reference point, which is expressed by the current value of the location time, is distinguished from the Reichenbachian reference time used in the past perfect, which they call the '**temporal perspective point**'. At the start of the discourse (7), Rpt is empty. At the end of the first sentence of the discourse, since it is a nonstative sentence, the Rpt is reset to $e1$. At the end of the second sentence, there is no change to the Rpt, since the second sentence is stative. At the end of the third sentence, since it is nonstative, the Rpt is reset, advancing it to $e3$ (thus, $e1 < e3$, since the second Rpt advances the previous value). This is shown in (9), where dotted lines are used, for clearer exposition, to separate the sentences.

(9)
```
Rpt ← { }
e1, t1, x, y
enter (e1, x, y), man (x), y = the WhiteHart
t1<n, e1⊆t1
Rpt ← e1
- - - - - - - - - - - - - - - - - - - - - - - - - - - - - -
e2, t2, x1, y1
PROG(wear(e2, x1, y1)), black-jacket(y1), x1 = x
t2<n, e2 o t2, e1⊆e2
- - - - - - - - - - - - - - - - - - - - - - - - - - - - - -
e3, t3, x2, y2, z
serve(e3, x2, y2, z), beer(z), x2 = Bill, y2 = x
t3<n, e3⊆t3
Rpt ← e3
e1<e3
```

In summary, then, the timeline constructed by this analysis of (7) has the entering entirely before the serving, with the state of wearing including the entering. One awkward aspect of this analysis is that the Rpt conditions (which represent processing state, rather than semantic conditions from sentence meaning) are always removed from the DRS once set (p. 525). Nevertheless, the simple narrative principle used in DRT allows for narrative moves to be managed using just a register mechanism (Rpt).

3.3 Assessment of DRT

Overall, DRT is a semantic theory with a strongly computational flavor, where the DRS-construction rules are specified at a sufficient level of detail to allow for automatic construction of DRSs. DRT has therefore been quite widely used in computational approaches. Further, tense and aspect information is given an extensive account in the theory, making it highly applicable for temporal informal information processing of natural language. In particular, the temporal ordering of events is based on an anaphoric view of tense. Of course, until systems can accurately and completely parse sentences in the large, DRT isn't readily available for use on unrestricted text.

The analysis shown earlier in (6) is actually a simplified version of the full DRT analysis. In the full scheme (K&R, pp. 616–25), 'Sunday' in the context of (5) results in a quantificational DRS condition stating that the time $t1$ is the past Sunday nearest to n; or, more generally, 'the nearest Sunday, in the "right" direction, to some given [anchor] time $t0$' (K&R, p. 620). This extension is achieved at the expense of complicating the rules for DRS construction. This tendency to force the interpretation of many different kinds of context-dependencies into semantics is also observed in their Rpt mechanism, which, as we show next, ends up with incorrect predictions. We believe that for improved modularity, some of these context-dependencies are best treated in a separate pragmatics module. In Part IV, we will examine annotation schemes for such context-dependent or **'relative' times**, along with computational mechanisms for resolving them. Finally, as we will discuss next, other kinds of pragmatic information also play a role in inferring the temporal structure of narrative discourse. These other kinds of information need to be integrated with a semantic account like DRT.

4 SEMANTIC VERSUS PRAGMATIC INFLUENCES ON TEMPORAL STRUCTURE

Inferences about the temporal structure of discourse appear to depend not just on semantic information from tense and aspect, but also on pragmatic principles governing language use, as well as background world knowledge. We would therefore suspect that DRT in itself will be insufficient.

4.1 Temporal relations and pragmatics

DOWTY (Chapter 15) assumes a compositional semantic theory of aspect where the aspectual classes of lexical items give rise to the aspectual classes assigned to sentences. He first provides definitions for the *Aktionsarten* we discussed earlier in Part I. In his semantic analysis, a sentence is *stative* if it has the **subinterval property**, i.e. if its truth at an interval implies that it is true at all subintervals. *Activity* sentences have a restricted subinterval property: truth at an interval implies truth at all subintervals down to a certain size limit. *Accomplishment* and *achievement* sentences have the property that if they are true at an interval, they are false at any subintervals of the interval. A sentence in the progressive of the form *PROG p* is true at an interval I if there is a superinterval I′ properly containing I such that *p* is true at I′. Dowty shows that this approach accounts for our intuitions that progressive sentences are stative. However, committing to such a view would also mean treating gapped events in the progressive as states.

Dowty posits a pragmatic principle for interpreting the temporal relations of successive sentences in a discourse. This principle, called the **Temporal Discourse Interpretation Principle** (TDIP), uses the Reichenbachian notion of reference time, and states that *the reference time for each sentence is a time consistent with the temporal adverbials in the sentence, if any, or else a time which immediately follows the reference time of the previous sentence.* The notion of 'immediately follows' is intentionally vague, as it depends on context. He goes on to show that the TDIP can account for our intuitions about the past perfect.

Dowty shows that the TDIP partially explains our intuitions about event ordering, in cases where the reference time isn't made explicit. However, he demonstrates that other pragmatic principles also play a role that can sometimes conflict with the TDIP. These include (a) the **perspective** of the narrator or protagonist from whose point of view the events may be described; (b) **expectations** about (violable) discourse conventions such as Grice's Maxim of Manner (Grice 1975), which is a convention that discourses should be exactly as informative as required; and (c) **background knowledge**, e.g. that the state of the man's wearing a black jacket in (7) extends backward in time to overlap with his entering, and that states are assumed to hold for their typical duration unless there's evidence to the contrary, so that the man was still wearing his jacket at the time of the serving of beer.

In summary, Dowty provides a semantic theory of aspect, but argues that event ordering depends on pragmatic principles as well as semantic information from tense and aspect. His approach is therefore opposed to that of DRT, where, as we have seen, rules governing the ordering of events in a discourse (including the Rpt movement rule) are invoked in the course of building a sentence's semantic representation. If we agree with Dowty that pragmatic inferences are important in event ordering, and if such inferences can only be made once the sentence's meaning has been grasped, then it seems that event ordering should not be part of the DRS-construction process for a sentence, but instead, be guided by a later, pragmatics module.

Note, however, that Dowty's theory, unlike DRT, is not a computational one. Further, the TDIP doesn't appear to make the right predictions in cases of successive past tense events where the second is a subevent of the first, as in (12) below, discussed in Section 5.2. However, since the integration of different knowledge sources is not his focus, Dowty cannot be faulted for that. Nevertheless, such integration is crucial in computational approaches.

4.2 Pragmatics and default reasoning

If pragmatics is so clearly involved in inferring temporal relations, how should pragmatics be represented and processed in a computer system? The work of LASCARIDES AND ASHER (Chapter 16) attempts to provide a formal account of the pragmatic influences in event ordering in discourse. Lascarides and Asher (L&A) state that what's needed is a theory that combines common-sense knowledge and pragmatic principles in a formal logic, so that the correct interpretations may be arrived at by means of proofs in this logic. Such a logical scheme, they argue, requires a notion of **defeasible reasoning**—in other words, reasoning is based on default knowledge that can be overridden.

L&A take a non-anaphoric view of tense, dispensing with Reichenbachian notions. In their scheme, tense orders the events just with respect to the speech time. The temporal ordering derived is entirely based on discourse relations that link together DRSs; the extended DRT formalism, called **SDRT**, is discussed separately in Asher (1993).

The approach thus views the temporal ordering as being based on pragmatics rather than semantics. To see their argument, consider sentences like the following:

(10) Max fell. John pushed him.
(11) Max switched off the light. The room was pitch dark.

In (10), the narrative moves backward, contrary to what we may expect from DRT and the TDIP. In (11), the state of being dark begins after the event (in accordance with the TDIP, but not DRT). In addressing phenomena like these, L&A assume that the default ordering of events is in narrative order (i.e. a **Narration** discourse relation), but that this default can be overridden by specific discourse relations (logical ones, based on Hobbs (1985)), such as **Explanation** in (10) and **Result** in (11). In particular, in a case like (10), *normally* the event of the first clause is before the event of the second; however, it is also known that if the second clause describes a pushing event and the first a falling event, *normally* the second clause is before the first. The resolution of this conflict in favor of the more specific inference is licensed by a defeasible inference procedure called the Penguin Principle.

Overall, L&A view the problem of constructing the temporal structure of discourse as the business of a pragmatics module, and argue that a logical framework based on default reasoning is an appropriate mechanism for such a module. However, despite their precise formalization of their account, their approach has not proved that attractive from a computational viewpoint. Each example sentence they discuss seems to require large amounts of **common-sense knowledge** to make the requisite pragmatic inferences to support temporal ordering (i.e. to check if the default ordering needs to be overridden). Thus, for (11), it assumes knowledge that if the room is dark and the light was just switched off, the switching off caused the room to become dark. How is knowledge of this sort to be acquired? While common-sense knowledge bases like CYC (Lenat 1995) have been developed, they have not yet reached the point where they are general enough to allow application and reuse of domain knowledge across different tasks. Until such knowledge acquisition problems are addressed in a satisfactory manner, such a theory has to be put on hold in terms of practical use in computational linguistics.

4.3 Empirical structure of temporal narratives

So far we have been looking at short discourses, mostly examples suggested based on introspection in support of linguistic arguments. What sort of temporal discourse structure do naturally occurring discourses have, as a whole? Labov (1972) notes that personal narratives can be segmented into the following components: an Abstract (a summary of the central action); Orientation (scene setting—who, when, where, and initial situation); Action (the main part—what happened); Evaluation (the significance); Resolution (what finally happened); and Coda (wrap up and return from the time of the narrative to the present). The order of the components is as above (though Evaluation may be mixed into the other elements), and among these components, Action and Evaluation are the only obligatory ones.

BELL (Chapter 17) takes up the Labovian analysis and attempts to extend it to news stories, noting that they are quite different in structure from personal narratives (he arrives instead at a structure based on van Dijk (1988)). In terms of movement of reference times, Bell points out that the narrative convention is not usually followed in the case of news stories; the temporal structure of news is dictated by **perceived news value** rather than chronology. Thus, the latest news is often presented first, with the possibility of multiple backward and forward movements through different timeframes. In addition, news often expresses **multiple viewpoints**, with **commentaries, eyewitness recapitulations**, etc., offered at different speech times. All this makes for a very complicated time structure for news. Interestingly, much of the recent computational work, including that discussed in Part IV, is based on news corpora.

Obviously, future work needs to characterize the temporal structures of entire texts more precisely, in order to be able to derive empirically grounded models of temporal narratives. Work on corpus annotation, described in Part IV, is a first step towards that goal.

5 COMPUTATIONAL APPROACHES

5.1 Introduction

We began the section by mentioning the role the previous discourse history plays in resolving anaphoric references. The first three computational papers we discuss view the problem of interpreting the information from tense and temporal adverbials in terms of anaphoric reference. All use a model of discourse, but differ in the complexity and explicitness of the mechanisms proposed. We then turn to a critique of the kinds of uses Reichenbach's system has been put to, and discuss an implemented system that ties the temporal relationships rather closely to the logical form semantics. Finally, we illustrate how some of the knowledge sources that influence temporal ordering can be integrated together.

5.2 Temporal anaphora

WEBBER (Chapter 18) develops a theory of **anaphoric reference.** She first develops an account of noun phrase anaphora, relating it to the approach of Grosz and Sidner to modeling shifts in what linguists have called 'global focus' based on a **focus-stack** mechanism which allows for subdialogs to be represented and earlier dialog segments to be resumed (see, for example, Grosz and Sidner (1986)). She then shows how tensed clauses can be treated as anaphors just like noun phrases are. Crucial to her account is the notion of a **Discourse Model** which the hearer constructs in interpreting a text, consisting of the entities mentioned in the text along with their relationships (including relationships of ordering, elaboration, etc.). (This work, from 1988, pre-dates SDRT.) Her analysis is Reichenbachian, with an account of event structure similar to the one in Moens and Steedman in Chapter 6. She introduces the concept of a **Temporal Focus** (TF), which captures the idea that at any point in the discourse, there is one entity (usually an event) in the Discourse Model 'that is most attended to and hence most likely to stand in an anaphoric relation with the [reference time] RT of the next clause'.

Given this framework, Webber specifies a number of rules governing the temporal relationships among successive clause pairs in a discourse. In her account, the relation between RT of the second clause's event and the event structure of the first clause's event contributes to the maintenance or movement of the TF across events. The RT can match the initial phase of the event (as in 12), the result phase, or may coincide with it.

(12) John bought Mary some flowers. He picked out three red roses.

Here, of course, Kamp and Reyle's approach and Dowty's TDIP would both make the wrong prediction. (Please note, however, that there is a misprint in Webber's Figure 3: β_{prep} should instead be labeled (b) and β_{conseq} (c).)

In (13), her account predicts correctly that Eb < Ec < Ea < Ed. Here the TF moves to Ea, Eb, and Ec after sentence a, b, and c, respectively, but then returns to Ea after sentence d.

(13) a. John went into the florist shop. b. He had promised Mary some flowers. c. She said she wouldn't forgive him if he forgot. d. So he picked out three red roses.

The way Webber's scheme is described, the tense of the first clause seems not to matter that much. Thus her account has the consequence that past perfect sequences move successively backwards, ruling out extended flashbacks as in (8) above. She also doesn't take aspect into account. Nevertheless, her approach is notable for its intuitively satisfying appeal to event structure in temporal ordering, and it makes a seminal contribution in relating the notion of tense and temporal relations in narrative to a substantial theory of anaphora and discourse modeling.

SONG AND COHEN (Chapter 19) extend Webber's work in an implemented system. Like Webber, they adopt a Reichenbachian tense representation, modified along the lines of Comrie (1986), as explained in Part I, along with a focus-stack mechanism. However, they also represent aspect, based on Passonneau's scheme (see Part I). They carry out an analysis of tense shifts, arriving at the conclusion that only certain kinds of shifts are **coherent.** This leads them to suggest various heuristics to resolve ambiguities in temporal ordering. When the tense moves from simple present to simple past, the event time moves backward, and from simple present to simple future, it moves forward. When the tense of two successive sentences is the same, they argue that the event time moves forward, except for statives and unbounded processes, which keep the same time. (This argument, as we have been pointing out, is in general untenable.) When the tense moves from present perfect to simple past, or present prospective (*John is going to run*) to simple future, the event time of the second sentence is before or simultaneous with the event time of the first sentence.

These heuristics are built into an algorithm for tense interpretation. They report on an evaluation, involving simple stories with indirect speech and nonactual situations excluded from consideration. However, their algorithm incorrectly rules out, among others, present tense to past perfect transitions. These days, of course, large corpora can be used to automatically discover which tense sequences actually occur, providing ample opportunity to test such claims. In addition, as we shall see in Part IV, annotated corpora can be used to find out which temporal relations co-occur with particular tense sequences. Overall, the Song and Cohen tense- and aspect-based approach, while ignoring discourse relations and pragmatic knowledge, is nevertheless interesting as an implemented system for event ordering in narratives. Further work using it is found in Mani and Wilson (2000).

So far, we have been discussing an anaphoric theory of tense. Temporal anaphora can of course also involve temporal adverbials. WIEBE et al. (Chapter 20) develop an empirical investigation of reference resolution in temporal adverbials in corpora of Spanish meeting scheduling dialogs. In their dialogs, there are numerous time expressions, including relative times. Their algorithm resolves the values of these time expressions by using a linear list of all temporal adverbials mentioned earlier. The algorithm distinguishes various types of anaphoric relation, including whether the reference is more specific than the candidate antecedent, e.g. the translated dialog (14), or less specific, e.g. (15).

(14) Speaker 1: How is Tuesday, January 30th?
Speaker 2: How about 2?

(15) Speaker 1: How about Monday at 2?
Speaker 2: OK, Monday sounds good.

For each relation the algorithm considers just the most recent reference for which the relation can be established. It turns out that in their data, out of 215 anaphoric references, the most recent time is the correct antecedent in 95 per cent of the cases; going back one additional time covers the remaining cases. Their algorithm, which is heavily tuned to the particular genre of dialogs, achieves an overall accuracy of over 80 per cent.

Wiebe et al.'s work, when it first appeared, represented a paradigm shift in temporal information extraction, as it is constituted the first empirically driven body of work in this area. They adopt the standard methodology of a corpus-based approach, developing a scheme for coding time values corresponding to the adverbials, and obtaining a moderate-to-high level of **inter-annotator agreement** on the coding. The algorithm is evaluated on a blind test-set. Such methodologies are discussed in Part IV, including the paper by Wilson et al. (Chapter 23) which further explores the assignment of values to temporal expressions.

5.3 Logical form and clausal subordination

So far, we have not addressed specific issues that arise when dealing with sentences that are complex, involving multiple clauses with **subordination** relations. Consider (16).

(16) He will think Mary has left.

HWANG AND SCHUBERT (H&S) (Chapter 21) point out that simply analyzing each tense in (16) on Reichenbachian lines and making a list of the constraints might lead to the conclusion that (16) means that at some future time t (i.e. ahead of the speech time), John will think that Mary's leaving occurred at some time t' before the speech time. However, this is incorrect. This sentence means that at some future time t, he will think that Mary's leaving occurred at some time t' before t. Note that Reichenbach's scheme doesn't specify how to combine together information from the various morphemes involved in the future or present perfect. H&S argue that instead of simply listing Reichenbachian constraints, it is important to consider the compositional semantics of the complex sentence. Thus, they treat 'John would have left' as involving a composition of present, past, future, and perfect operators in the logical form meaning of the sentence. H&S take the logical form of a sentence and convert it automatically into a temporal structure called a **tense tree**, in the course of which temporal relations are postulated between Reichenbach-like temporal indices; the same structure is elaborated to provide a tree for an entire discourse. Here *Aktionsarten* and discourse relations are necessarily involved. However, by virtue of its being driven by the logical form, the tense tree derives the correct interpretation for sentences with embedded clauses like (16).

H&S assign a major role to world knowledge and plausible inference in resolving possible ambiguities in temporal ordering. In practice, this reliance on world knowledge means that their approach is therefore domain-specific. Their main contributions are to show how compositional semantics is crucial in dealing with subordination relations, and how such a semantics can be used in a systematic way to represent the temporal structure of discourse. Their paper was published prior to Kamp and Reyle's book, and as such doesn't offer a comparison to the latter. Their paper also emphasizes being able to deal with various forms of subordination; in particular, since Mary's leaving in (16) is a thought rather than a realis event. The representation of various kinds of subordination relations on events is discussed in the paper on TimeML by Pustejovsky et al. in Part IV (Chapter 27).

5.4 Integrating different knowledge sources

HITZEMAN ET AL. (Chapter 22) examine the interaction of various knowledge sources for event ordering, within the context of an implemented NLP system. They argue that reasoning using background knowledge, as in the Lascarides and Asher approach discussed above, is too computationally expensive. They then enumerate a number of constraints on temporal ordering based on tense and aspect that might be considered as a default when temporal adverbials or explicit cues to a rhetorical relation (like *because*) are absent. They point out, for example, that given a sentence describing a past tense activity followed by one describing a past tense event (accomplishment or achievement), the event can only occur just after the activity; it can't precede, overlap, or be identical to (or presumably be a phase of) it.

Their computational approach is based on assigning weights to different ordering possibilities based on the knowledge sources involved. Temporal adverbials and discourse cues are first tried; if neither are present, then the above default rules based on tense and aspect are used. If the ordering is still ambiguous at the end of this, semantic rules are used based on modeling the discourse in terms of **threads.** The idea here, based on the notion of **temporal centering**, is that there is one 'thread' that the discourse is currently following. Thus, in (13) above, each utterance is associated with exactly one of two threads: (i) going into the florist's shop and (ii) interacting with Mary. Hitzeman et al. prefer an utterance to continue a current thread which has the same tense or is semantically related to it, so that in (13) above, utterance d would continue the thread (i) above based on tense.

The Hitzeman et al. approach shows how different knowledge sources can be related to each other in a computational system for temporal ordering. In place of world knowledge, however, semantic distance between utterances is used, presumably based on lexical relationships. Whether such semantic similarity is effective is a matter for evaluation, which is not discussed in this paper. For example, it isn't clear what would rule out (13c) as continuing thread (i). Recent work by Mani, Schiffman, and Zhang (2003) and Mani and Schiffman (2004) has examined the interaction between such knowledge sources in a corpus-based setting involving machine-learned rules for temporal ordering.

6 CONCLUSION

When we began this section, we observed that humans are able to infer a temporal structure for events in a discourse, even though a lot of information might be implicit.

Our introspection suggests that the cues used by the particular language to express tense and aspect information are clearly involved, as are particular temporal adverbials which locate information, sometimes rather vaguely, in time. We saw our theories suggest that world knowledge plays a role in these inferences, as do pragmatic conventions. We saw also that this ordering need not be a simple timeline, because of partial ordering, the presence of irrealis and subordinated events, and the complex temporal structure of particular genres, such as news texts.

How then do humans actually carry out inferences about temporal ordering? Clearly, psycholinguistic experiments are needed to understand this better. Some preliminary work is reported in Mani and Schiffman (2004), who describe an experiment where subjects were asked to order events in successive clauses, with the clauses being either both past tense, or the first being past tense and the second past perfect. They found that subjects only agree 60 per cent of the time. Subjects have a hard time making fine-grained decisions about Allen-like temporal relations, for example, deciding whether an event is BEFORE or EQUAL to another (e.g. (17)), or whether it is BEFORE or MEETS the other (18).

(17) Shapiro said he *tried on* the gloves and *realized* they would never fit Simpson's larger hands.

(18) They *had contested* the 1992 elections separately and *won* just six seats to 70 for MPRP.

It may be that such fine-grained distinctions are not part of our commonsense representations. Nevertheless, we humans are able to answer fairly complex questions about temporal ordering, even in the face of fairly vague information provided by temporal adverbials. This suggests that underspecified representations of temporal ordering, where certain kinds of ambiguities are collapsed, may be especially relevant to computational approaches, as well as the ability to provide different views of an ordering based on granularity and focus.

Despite the diversity in the approaches we have seen so far, there are clear assumptions one can make about the modules involved in a computational approach to ordering events in discourse. Any such approach must rely on a level of preprocessing of each utterance, including the ability to deal with clause structure and subordination relations. A computational system also needs an event ontology, one which distinguishes at least between events and states, and possibly a representation of event components, e.g. a tripartite model of event structure, as discussed in the overview of Part I (3.2), though putting this to practical use may be difficult. A semantic representation of the events and their temporal properties needs to be built for each sentence; such a representation needs to have resolved temporal adverbials, based on matching antecedents in the prior discourse. A system will need various ordering rules that are sensitive to tense and aspect information in the semantic representation, as well as the logical form of the representation. These rules will, crucially, rely on discourse-level information, and may access discourse-level models of various kinds that address the coherence of a particular ordering (the models discussed above reference structures such as DRSs, temporal foci, tense trees, temporal centers, discourse threads, etc.). Further, these rules may require reasoning based on rhetorical structure (for parsing discourse into rhetorical structures, see Marcu (1997)), as well as formal reasoning based on background knowledge.

Computational systems are not always aimed at simply mimicking human behavior. Machines may be able to reason about consistency and closure in a way that humans may not be able to keep track of, thus using temporal reasoning to answer questions that a human couldn't. In addition, a computational agent may use a variety of patterns that are based on statistical regularities in its environment, that may or may not correspond to the categories arrived at by introspective analysis. For this reason, we believe that it is imperative to study these phenomena on a much larger scale than has been done so far, taking advantage of large corpora to allow machines to learn rules that best explain the distinctions in temporal ordering that humans are able to make reliably. That also means that inter-annotator reliability is important to establish in any coding of linguistic judgments about ordering. Provided the data is annotated with a rich set of features, particular learning methods can use the data to automatically discover the contributions of different knowledge sources. Part IV discusses such methods. Nevertheless, it must be borne in mind that the background knowledge that humans have seems ubiquitous in many of our judgments about temporal ordering, and thus in addition to reasoning about time, formal reasoning about the world is required. The ability to marry corpus-based approaches to discourse-based phenomena, on one hand, with formal reasoning, on the other, thus is an important direction for future research in this area.

REFERENCES

Asher, N. (1993). *Reference to Abstract Objects in Discourse*. Studies in Linguistics and Philosophy, 50. Dordrecht: Kluwer.

Comrie, B. (1986). *Tense*. Cambridge: Cambridge University Press.

Dijk, T. A. van (1988). *News as Discourse*. Hillsdale, NJ: Lawrence Erlbaum Associates.

Geach, P. (1962). *Reference and Generality*. Ithaca, NY: Cornell University Press.

Grice, H. P. (1975). 'Logic and Conversation', in O. P. Cole and J. L. Morgan (eds.), *Speech Acts: Syntax and Semantics*, vol. 3. New York: Academic Press, 41–58.

Grosz, B. and Sidner, C. (1986). 'Attention, Intention, and the Structure of Discourse', *Computational Linguistics* 12(3): 175–204.

Hinrichs, E. (1986). 'Temporal Anaphora in Discourses of English', *Linguistics and Philosophy* 9(1): 63–82.

Hobbs, J. (1985). 'On the Coherence and Structure of Discourse'. Report No. CSLI- 85-37. Stanford, CA: Center for the Study of Language and Information, Stanford University.

Kamp, H. (1984). 'A Theory of Truth and Semantic Representation', in J. A. G. Groenendijk, T. M. V. Janssen, and M. B. J. Stockhof (eds.), *Truth, Interpretation, and Information*. Dordrecht: Foris, 277–322.

Kamp, H. and Reyle, U. (1993). *From Discourse to Logic: Introduction to Model-Theoretic Semantics of Natural Language, Formal Logic and Discourse Representation Theory*, Part 2. Studies in Linguistics and Philosophy, 42. Dordrecht: Kluwer.

Labov, W. (1972). 'The Transformation of Experience in Narrative Syntax'. in W. Labov (ed.), *Language in the Inner City*. Philadelphia: University of Pennsylvania Press.

Lenat, D. B. (1995). 'CYC: A Large-Scale Investment in Knowledge Infrastructure,' *Communications of the Association for Computing Machinery (CACM)* 38(11): 32–8.

Mani, I. and Schiffman, B. (2004). 'Temporally Anchoring and Ordering Events in News', in J. Pustejovsky and R. Gaizauskas (eds.), *Time and Event Recognition in Natural Language*. Amsterdam: John Benjamins (to appear).

——and Zhang, J. (2003). 'Inferring Temporal Ordering of Events in News'. Short Paper. In *Proceedings of the Human Language Technology Conference of the North American Chapter of the Association for Computational Linguistics* (HLT-NAACL'03). Edmonton, Canada. Association for Computational Linguistics, 55-7.

Mani, I., Schiffman, B. and Wilson, G. (2000). 'Robust Temporal Processing of News'. In *Proceedings of the 38th Annual Meeting of the Association for Computational Linguistics (ACL'2000)*. Montreal, Canada: Association for Computational Linguistics, 69–76.

Marcu, D. (1997). 'The Rhetorical Parsing of Natural Language Texts', in *Proceedings of the 35th Annual Meeting of the Association for Computational Linguistics*, ACL'96. Madrid: Association for Computational Linguistics, 96–103.

Partee, B. H. (1984). 'Nominal and Temporal Anaphora', *Linguistics and Philosophy* 7: 243–86.

15

The Effects of Aspectual Class on the Temporal Structure of Discourse: Semantics or Pragmatics?

DAVID R. DOWTY

I INTRODUCTION

The temporal relationship between the events and states that are described in successive sentences in a narrative discourse is often indicated explicitly through definite time adverbials, as in (1), temporal subordinate clauses, or certain tense combinations (e.g. a past perfect sentence within a narrative in the simple past).

(1) John arrived at 8 p.m. He left again at 10.

But in cases where such indicators are absent, it has been observed by Jespersen, and in more detail in a series of recent articles by Helen Dry (1978, ms.), that the aspectual classes of the predicates in the discourse, i.e. their *Aktionsarten*, seem to determine these temporal relationships. (By *aspectual class* I refer to the taxonomy of predicates originating with Aristotle and known in the Anglo-Saxon tradition through the work of Ryle, Kenny and Vendler; I will refer to these classes by Vendler's names *States*, *Activities*, *Accomplishments*, and *Achievements*, and I assume that the reader is acquainted with the syntactic and semantic tests usually employed to distinguish these categories (cf. Vendler, 1967; Dowty, 1979).

If a sentence in a narrative contains an accomplishment or achievement predicate but no definite time adverb, that sentence is understood to describe an event occurring later than the time of the previous sentence's event (or in the literary analyst's terms, narrative time "moves forward" in the second sentence). For example, (2) indicates this phenomenon with an accomplishment, *walk over to him*,

(2) John entered the president's office. The president walked over to him.

and (3) illustrates it with an achievement, *wake up*:

(3) John entered the president's office. The president woke up.

If on the other hand the second sentence of the sequence has a stative predicate, as in the second sentence in (4), or an activity predicate as in the second one in (5), the state or process it describes is most usually understood to overlap with that of the previous sentence: narrative time does not "move" in the second sentence.

(4) John entered the president's office. The president sat behind a huge desk.

(5) John entered the president's office. The clock on the wall ticked loudly.

This lack of temporal advancement is, in fact, almost inescapable when the second sentence is in a progressive tense, no matter whether the verb is an activity as in (6), or an accomplishment or achievement, as in (7).

(6) John entered the president's office. The president was looking out the window.

(7) John entered the president's office. The president was writing a letter.

Some lexical stative verbs (e.g. *stand, sit, realize*), however, seem to be systematically ambiguous between a "stative" and an "inceptive" interpretation; in the latter interpretation these are achievement predicates, and time accordingly "moves" in this interpretation (cf. (8)):

(8) John entered the president's office. The president realized why he had come.

Other stative predicates can be given an inceptive interpretation with the aid of an adverbial like *suddenly* or *in a moment*, and here also time moves:

(9) John sat in his chair going over the day's perplexing events again in his mind. Suddenly, he was asleep.

Activity sentences likewise lend themselves to inceptive interpretations in non-progressive tenses. Progressives, on the other hand, resist the inceptive interpretation in almost all cases.

2 THE ANALYSIS OF KAMP AND HINRICHS

Hans Kamp (1979a, 1980) has recently proposed a theory of the interpretation of narrative discourse that proceeds in two steps: first, discourse rules map a sequence of sentences comprising a discourse into a *discourse representation structure*. Secondly, the discourse representation is given a truth-conditional interpretation relative to a model (whereas the individual sentences are not truth-conditionally interpreted directly).

One task of the discourse-representation construction is the specification of the temporal relationships between adjacent sentences. Kamp proposes that for French, at least, these relationships in discourse structure are a function of the tenses of the sentence. If the sentence is in the passé simple, its event follows and does not overlap with the event of the previous sentence. But if this sentence is in the imparfait, its event overlaps temporally with that of the previous sentence.

Hinrichs (1981) has applied Kamp's ideas to the analysis of English discourses. In accord with the observations I have cited above about the role of aspectual class, Hinrichs subcategorizes sentences syntactically by their aspectual class—statives, activities, etc.—in order that these classes can be referred to by the discourse representation construction rules.

Note however one problem that will arise if this method is adopted. It has been observed (Verkuyl, 1972; Dowty 1972, 1979 and elsewhere) that the aspectual properties of English sentences are not determined simply by their lexical main verbs (as Kenny and Vendler seem to have assumed). Rather, a large variety of syntactic constituents of the sentence play a role in this determination. For example, a prepositional phrase or NP expressing extent can convert an activity into an accomplishment:

(10) a. John walked. (*activity*)
 b. John walked to the station. (*accomplishment*)
 c. John walked a mile. (*accomplishment*)

The presence of an indefinite plural NP or mass NP can render a sentence that would otherwise be an accomplishment into an activity:

(11) a. John noticed the rare seashell on the beach. (*achievement*)
 b. John noticed rare seashells on the beach. (*activity*)
 c. Tourists noticed the rare seashell/rare seashells on the beach. (*activity*)

Since adverbials like *for an hour* are only compatible with states and activities, while adverbials like *in an hour* are only compatible with accomplishments and achievements, the choice between these two kinds of adverbial can in effect disambiguate a verb that is lexically ambiguous between activity and accomplishment interpretations. So as Fillmore (1971) observed, (12a) has the accomplishment interpretation of *read a book* (i.e. read the whole book), (12b) on the other hand has only the activity interpretation (i.e. read from the book):

(12) a. John read a book in two hours.
 b. John read a book for two hours.

One could still try to treat aspectual class as a syntactic property of sentences in spite of these complications; in fact Verkuyl (1972) employs this syntactic approach. To carry out this method, Verkuyl finds it necessary to subcategorize a large variety of syntactic categories for aspectual class—not only verbs, but their complements, verb phrase nodes, NP nodes, and sentence nodes; in addition, elaborate co-occurrence restrictions among these subcategories are needed as well. But, as I have argued elsewhere (Dowty 1972, 1979), this syntactic method misses the point: it is surely the *semantic* properties of verbs, of the prepositional phrase in (10b), of the definite versus indefinite plural NPs in (11), and of the adverbials in (12), etc., that are responsible for the ultimate aspectual properties of the sentences in which they appear, and a syntactically based classification of the aspectual interaction of all of these kinds of constituents would simply recapitulate work that has to be done in the lexical and compositional semantics anyway.

If I am correct in supposing that the aspectual character of full sentences is determinable only in the semantics (and I will indicate in a moment how I think this should be carried out), then this situation poses a dilemma for Kamp's and Hinrichs' approach to the temporal relationships in discourse as I understand it. For if the compositional model-theoretic interpretation of the sentences in a discourse is determined only after a discourse representation has been constructed (as Kamp proposes), and if it is only in the model-theoretic interpretation that the aspectual class of a sentence is fully apparent (as I am arguing), then how can aspectual class have an effect on how the temporal relationships between sentences are represented in the discourse representation? A second problem I see for the application of Kamp's method to English is that in certain cases, the intended aspectual class of a sentence is determined in part by the hearer's real world knowledge; i.e. this knowledge is needed to disambiguate sentences that are potentially ambiguous in aspectual class. These cases will be discussed later on. But in these cases as well, the decision how to order the states and events described by successive sentences in a discourse will depend on the prior decision as to just what aspectual classes the individual sentences fall into. If so, then here again it seems that the temporal relationships among sentences in a discourse depends on the prior determination of the semantics of the individual sentences, contrary to Kamp's proposal as I understand it.

But rather than attempt to argue that Kamp's proposal about discourse representation cannot be amended to account for these apparent problems, I will simply present here an alternative account of the temporal semantics of discourse, one in which discourse semantics depends on sentence semantics and pragmatic principles, and try to show that it gives a simple and natural account of discourse ordering, one that makes use of certain principles that are independently motivated.

In particular, my claim is that the temporal relationships between sentences of a discourse are determined by three things: (1) the semantic analysis of aspectual class using the interval semantics that was proposed by Barry Taylor (1977) and extended in Dowty (1979); (2) a single principle for the interpretation of successive sentences in a discourse, a principle which in itself does not make reference to the aspectual classes of the sentences involved; and (3) a large dose of Gricean conversational implicature and "common-sense" reasoning based on the hearer's knowledge of real world information.

I should add that I will draw heavily on data and observations made in several papers by Helen Dry (1978, 1983), whose analysis rests in part on ideas of Carlota Smith (1978, 1983). Both Dry and Smith speak of aspectual distinctions in terms of "sentences which make reference to the natural beginning points and endpoints of a situation" versus sentences which do not make reference to such points. I should point out that what I say in this paper need not be construed as disagreeing with Dry's and Smith's claims. Rather, my contribution will lie in making precise just what these so-called "natural endpoints of a situation" are in model-theoretic terms (i.e. in terms of moments and intervals of familiar tense-logical models), and also making precise just how the compositional semantics of sentences and discourse is determined, both of which remain unformalized in Dry's and Smith's work.

3 TAYLOR/DOWTY SEMANTICS FOR ASPECTUAL CLASSES

The semantics of aspectual classes used by Taylor and by myself rests on an essential innovation in tense logic first put forward by Bennett and Partee (1972). This is the idea that the recursive semantic clauses are to be stated in terms of the (primitive) notion of truth of a sentence with respect to an interval of time (rather than with respect to a moment of time, as in earlier treatments). In particular, the truth of a sentence with respect to a given interval I is independent of the truth of that same sentence with respect to subintervals of I, or moments within I, or with respect to superintervals of I. Thus to cite an example illustrating the utility of this idea, if it is true that John ran a mile in five minutes, say between 1:00 p.m. and 1:05 p.m., we want to allow it to be false that he ran a mile in any subinterval of this time, say between 1:00 p.m. and 1:03 p.m. Conversely, if a sentence is true of two consecutive intervals, it may yet be false of the interval which is the union of these two intervals. So if John ran a mile between 1:00 and 1:05 p.m. and then, without pausing, ran a mile again between 1:05 p.m. and 1:10 p.m., it need not follow that the sentence "John ran a mile" is true of the interval from 1:00 p.m. to 1:10 p.m. However, sentences with different predicates will obey exactly the conditions which fail with respect to predicates like "run a mile", and it is just in conditions like these that predicates of one aspectual class differ from those of another in the

Dowty/Taylor semantics. The defining criteria of three aspectual classes of predicates are given in (13):[1]

(13) a A sentence φ is stative iff it follows from the truth of φ at an interval I that φ is true at all subintervals of I. (e.g. if John was asleep from 1:00 until 2:00 p.m. then he was asleep at all subintervals of this interval: *be asleep* is a stative).
   b A sentence φ is an activity (or *energeia*) iff it follows from the truth of φ at an interval I that φ is true of all subintervals of I down to a certain limit in size (e.g. if John walked from 1:00 until 2:00 p.m. then most subintervals of this time are times at which John walked; *walk* is an activity.)
   c A sentence φ is an accomplishment/achievement (or *kinesis*) iff it follows from the truth of φ at an interval I that φ is false at all subintervals of I. (E.g. if John built a house in exactly the interval from September 1 until June 1, then it is false that he built a house in any subinterval of this interval: *build a house* is an accomplishment/achievement.)

Note that these criteria make no distinction between two of Vendler's classes, accomplishments versus achievements. This is deliberate. It is often suggested that accomplishments differ from achievements in that achievements are "punctual" in some sense, whereas accomplishments have duration: dying, an achievement, happens all at once, while building a house, an accomplishment, takes time. However, many events usually classed as achievements do in fact have some duration. A physicist may object that reaching the finish line, no matter how defined, has duration, and a physician may likewise view dying as a process with multiple stages happening in sequence.[2] It has also been observed that the test of occurring in the progressive, supposedly a test for distinguishing achievements from accomplishments, also gives inexact results, as it is often possible to put an achievement sentence in the progressive tense (*John was dying when the doctor arrived*). Rather, I think the distinction as Vendler and others must have intuitively understood it is something like the following: achievements are those kinesis predicates which are not only typically of shorter duration than accomplishments, but also those for which we do not normally understand as entailing a sequence of subevents, given our usual everyday criteria for identifying the events named by the predicate. Dying, or reaching the finish line, take place, according to everyday criteria, when one state—being alive or being not yet at the finish line—is recognized as being replaced by another: being dead, or being at the finish line, respectively. Recognizing an accomplishment, such as building a house or running a mile, can normally and usually involve recognizing distinct subevents which may be necessary but not individually sufficient for the accomplishment itself—building the foundation for a house, raising the walls, adding the roof, for example. Thus achievements are "punctual" only in a sense akin to that in which events in a narrative are punctual in Kamp's theories: they are not interrupted by other events in the narrative. (This sense of punctual is a bit stronger than Kamp's actually, for an accomplishment may also be punctual in his sense simply in that it is not interrupted or overlapped by other events mentioned in the narrative in which it occurs: yet because of our knowledge of how events such as house-building normally transpire, we may infer the existence of temporally included subevents for

---

[1] Theses criteria are adapted, with some changes, from Taylor (1977, pp. 206–9, 215) and Dowty (1979). In particular, Taylor gives more complicated versions of (13b) and (13c), so he should not be held responsible for any inadequacies of my formulations here, which are however adequate for purposes of this paper.
[2] See also Kamp (1979*a*) for a sophisticated formulation of the notion of becoming, according to which it does not transpire at a moment.

accomplishments, whether mentioned in the narrative or not. But we do not do so, I suggest, in the case of achievements.)

The criteria in (13) actually give us tests for stative, activity or accomplishment/achievement *sentences*, not predicates. But the criteria for the predicates themselves are straightforwardly derivable from these: if a predicate when combined with enough definite NPs to form an atomic sentence (but without the addition of indefinite plurals, progressives, or aspectual adverbs) meets a certain one of these tests, then the lexical predicate itself is to be classed accordingly. This brings up the point of just what aspectual classes should be classifications of: are these classes of verbs, or verb phrases, or sentences (or possibly events or situations)? This is a question which has generated much confusion in the past. The claim which is thoroughly implicit in the treatments in Dowty (1979) (but which, unfortunately, may not have been made explicit enough), is that we must classify not only lexical predicates but also verb phrases and sentences by these tests. The aspectual class of a verb is of course a property of its lexical meaning (and must be described by meaning postulates or similar means). The aspectual class a phrase or sentence belongs to will thus be determined in a mechanical and completely explicit way by the lexical aspectual class of its main verb and the compositional semantic rules that have applied in combining the NPs, adverbials, tenses and other constituents involved in the whole sentence. This resulting class will often not be the same as that of the lexical verb. To cite a case which will be of importance later on, consider the progressive tense. The semantics for the progressive proposed by Taylor and myself is approximately (14):

(14) [PROG φ](i.e. the progressive form of φ) is true at I iff there is an interval I' properly containing I such that φ is true at I'.

(I have argued elsewhere (Dowty 1979) that (14) is not quite adequate for the English progressive; rather the progressive should be given a kind of modal interpretation involving some but not all possible histories containing I. However, this difference is irrelevant for topics I will discuss in this paper, and I ignore it here for simplicity.)

It now follows as a theorem from (13) and (14) that any sentence with a progressive tense, no matter what the aspectual class of its lexical verb, is a stative sentence. To see this, suppose that a sentence of the form PROG φ is true of interval I_1. Hence φ is true of some superinterval I' of I_1. Now consider some arbitrarily chosen subinterval of I_1. This subinterval of I_1 will also necessarily be a subinterval of I', hence PROG φ will be true of this subinterval as well. Because this conclusion holds of any subinterval of I_1 whatsoever, PROG φ has the criterial property of statives, property (13a). (It has been independently suggested that progressives ought to be considered statives, but as far as I know, no analysis has been given in which this is a consequence of the definitions of the progressive and stativity.)

It can similarly be shown that the negation of any atomic sentence will be a stative sentence, and given an appropriate semantics for modals, any atomic sentence plus a modal will be stative.

Thus to summarize this discussion, let us consider the question what aspectual class is to be found in example (15).

(15) John was walking to the station.

The answer is, three classes: The lexical verb *walk* is an activity. The verb phrase *walk to the station* is an accomplishment, given the semantics for directional adverbials like *to the station* proposed in Dowty (1979), and the sentence as a whole is a stative because of its progressive tense.

It will of course be the aspectual class of the sentence as a whole (rather than any of its subconstituents) which is relevant to the temporal effect on discourse interpretation.

While this analysis of aspect seems to serve us fairly well, taking the notion of the truth of a sentence with respect to an interval of time as primitive (or, in possible world semantics, truth with respect to an index consisting of a possible world and an interval of time), it has been proposed by Kamp (1979a) that we should instead take events as primitive, with orderings of precedence and overlap defined upon these, and then derive the definitions of interval and moment from events. It has also been proposed in situation semantics that we eschew the notion of possible world in favor of situations and situation types (Barwise and Perry, 1983; Cooper, 1986). I am not at all unsympathetic to either of these two proposals, but I would merely point out here that if either or both of these proposals were adopted, it would still be possible, as far as I can tell, to reconstruct the definitions of aspectual classes in (13) in these new frameworks; indeed, I conjecture it will be necessary to do so to properly capture the semantics of verbs, aspectual adverbs, and the progressive tense. For example, if we took events as primitives, then we should require that any "event" satisfying a stative sentence must have temporally located within it another located situation type satisfying this same sentence, and so on. I will also assume, without discussion, that the principles for discourse interpretation I will present shortly will also carry over to these new frameworks.

4 THE TEMPORAL DISCOURSE INTERPRETATION PRINCIPLE (TDIP)

I am now ready to introduce the primary principle for interpreting successive sentences in a discourse temporally, the *temporal discourse interpretation principle* (TDIP), (16):

(16) Given a sequence of sentences $S_1, S_2, \ldots, S_n$ to be interpreted as a narrative discourse, the reference time of each sentence S_i (for i such that $1 < i \leq n$) is interpreted to be:
 a. a time consistent with the definite time adverbials in S_i, if there are any;
 b. otherwise, a time which immediately follows the reference time of the previous sentence S_{i-1}.

Several features of (16) require comment. The term "reference time" here is an allusion to Reichenbach (1947), i.e. in a simple past tense sentence, this is the time at which the event or state mentioned by the sentence occurred (or obtains, respectively), not the time at which the sentence is heard or read by the hearer, which I will rather refer to as the speech time. The semantic theory for the interpretation of tense I have in mind here (though it is not the only one consistent with my approach to discourse time reference) is one I have proposed in various forms in earlier papers (Dowty, 1982, ms.): a theory in which both reference time and speech time are contextual parameters of the utterance. Treating reference time as a contextual parameter enables one to account for examples like Partee's "I didn't turn off the stove" (Partee, 1973) and similar examples. (See also Nerbonne 1986 for a more elaborate development of this idea.) Specifically, I have in mind that the recursive clauses for sentences are stated relative to a pair of times $\langle i, j \rangle$ in which the first time i is a reference time, the second time j is the speech time.

The semantic clauses for the tenses past, present and future require that a certain relation obtains between reference and speech time—that the former is earlier than, the same as, or later than the latter, respectively. The semantic clauses for the perfect, progressive, and for aspectual adverbials, on the other hand, do not mention the speech time j but relate to the reference time i to another reference time i' which bears some specified relation to i. For example, we have already seen in (14) how the progressive asserts that the reference time i is properly contained within the interval i' at which the atomic nonprogressive sentence is true. Definite time adverbials locate the reference time i at a particular time or date. For those who have not seen this two-dimensional approach to the semantics of tense before and find it puzzling, there is no need to go into greater detail for our present purposes: I believe the intuitive, quasi-Reichenbachian notion of "reference time" is all that is required to understand how the TDIP will work.

Secondly, the clause (16a) is necessary for the TDIP to be compatible with successive sentences in which the second has a definite adverbial such as one mentioning a clock time or calendar date. (17) is such an example, and the TDIP instructs us in this case to choose a reference time that can be satisfied by the adverbial "at 2 p.m.".

(17) John arrived at 10 a.m. He departed again at 2 p.m.

(16a) is probably to be subsumed under a more general principle for interpreting indexical expressions, namely "choose values for indexical expressions that allow the sentence to be true wherever possible" (cf. the parallel case of the value of the indexical *I* in *I am John Smith*).

5 THE TDIP AND ACCOMPLISHMENTS/ACHIEVEMENTS

Consider now how clause (16b) will come into play with successive accomplishment/achievement sentences having no time adverbial, such as (18), the same as an earlier example.

(18) John entered the president's office. The president walked over to him.

The TDIP in this case tells us to put the reference time of the second sentence, the time of the president's walking over to John, immediately after that of the first sentence. (As I will explain in a moment, the non-overlap between the two is correctly predicted.) The phrase "immediately after" in (16b) is of course vague, but deliberately so. The reason is that the closeness of the reference time of S_i to that of S_{i-1} at any point in a discourse is only determined by the hearer's understanding of the nature of events being described in the narrative, the overall degree of detail in which events are being described, and common knowledge about the usual temporal relationships among events. In (18), the elapsed time between the two reference times is naturally taken to be only a few seconds or minutes. But in the narrative in (19), the times elapsing between the first and second, and between the second and third will be taken to be a matter of days, weeks, or perhaps even longer.

(19) John moved to Boston in July. He took a job in a steel mill. His boss became a close friend of his.

The point is that in both cases the reference times "immediately" follow one another in the sense that each successive sentence presents the very next event that transpires that is important enough to merit the speaker's describing it to the hearer, given the purpose of the narration. In Kamp's terms (Kamp, 1979a), the successive events are "punctual" in the sense that no event of crucial importance to the narrative overlaps with the two successive events or intervenes temporally between them.

I should also add at this point that the TDIP will be compatible with the way past perfect sentences are interpreted when they are interspersed in a narrative in the simple past. A past perfect following a simple past superficially appears to be in violation of the TDIP, in that the event described in the past perfect is understood to have taken place before, not after, the event of the previous sentence. (20) illustrates this:

(20) John hurried to Mary's house after work. But Mary had already left for dinner.

But this situation will be in accord with the TDIP if we give the past perfect a semantics that places the event of its clause at a time i' before the reference time i. Thus if the reference time of the first sentence in (20) is i_1, the reference time for the second sentence will be a later time i_2; but the past perfect specifies that Mary's leaving takes place at a time i' earlier than i_2 (and therefore possibly earlier than i_1 as well).

(21) $\{\ \}\quad\quad\{\ \}\{\ \}\rightarrow$
$\quad\ \ i'\quad\quad\quad\ \ i_1\ \ i_2$

To be sure, nothing in the semantics of the past perfect or in the TDIP will exclude the possibility that i' here is simultaneous with i_1, but I believe this possibility is ruled out by Gricean principles: since the language has independent and unambiguous means for expressing simultaneity of events (for example *when*-clauses, or the locution *at the same time as*), the past perfect is conversationally implicated to exclude this possibility. This kind of semantics for the past perfect itself can be independently motivated on various grounds—for example, handling the semantics of sentences such as "Mary had left when John arrived"—but I will not take the time to discuss this motivation here.

In connection with the TDIP, note finally that this principle makes no mention of differences in aspectual class, and will therefore treat statives just the same as accomplishments and achievements in locating their reference times. But it is a central thesis of this paper that the inferences we draw in a narrative about which events or states overlap with others in the narrative is not really a consequence of the times sentences are *asserted* to be true, but rather also in part a consequence of the times at which we *assume* that states or events actually obtain or transpire in the real world, intervals of time which may in some cases be greater than the intervals of time for which they are simply asserted.

6   THE TDIP AND STATIVES

Before considering statives, let us look at accomplishments/achievements once more. The defining criterion (13c) for accomplishments/achievements states that if an accomplishment/achievement sentence is true at an interval I, then it is false at all subintervals of I. It also turns out that this criterion entails that if such a sentence is true at I, then it is false at all superintervals of I as well. To see this, let it be given that an accomplishment φ is true at I. Suppose that φ were also true of some superinterval of I, I'. But this would in turn violate the condition that if an accomplishment φ is true of any interval—in particular I'—then it must be false for all subintervals of I', and therefore false of I itself, which contradicts the assumption. Given this result, we can now see why the TDIP requires that if two accomplishment/achievement sentences occur successively in a discourse, they are *not* only asserted to be true at successive but non-overlapping intervals, there cannot even be overlapping intervals at which the two are true which are *not* explicitly asserted.[3]

The case of statives and activities is significantly different in this respect. If a stative sentence is asserted to be true at an interval *I*, then the criterion (13a) does nothing to exclude the possibility that it is actually true for larger intervals that properly include *I*. This is as it should be, for (22) is a perfectly normal assertion.

(22) Yes, John was asleep between 1:00 p.m. and 2:00 p.m. In fact, he fell asleep at noon and did not wake up until 3:00.

By contrast, (23) is anomalous, as *build a house* is an accomplishment.

(23) Yes, Mary built that house between July 1 and December 1: in fact, she began building it in June and did not finish it until January.

Indeed, I propose that for many stative predicates in many discourse contexts, when the stative is asserted to obtain at a certain point in a discourse, the *normal* assumption the hearer makes is that the stative began to obtain in advance of this point, perhaps well in advance of it. So in the discourse (24),

(24) Mary entered the president's office. There was a bound copy of the president's budget on his desk.

I argue that the TDIP actually tells us that the time of the budget's being on the president's desk was immediately after Mary entered the room, but that we are expected to assume in addition that this was not the first moment that it was there: it was no doubt there before Mary's entry. Similarly, if two or more stative sentences follow an accomplishment as in (25),

(25) Mary entered the president's office. A copy of the budget was on the president's desk. The president's financial advisor stood beside it. The president sat regarding both admiringly. The advisor spoke.

we not only assume that the second and third states began to obtain before Mary's entry, but that all three states continued beyond the asserted time and into the time of the accomplishment that ends the passage, *The advisor spoke*. Again, all these possibilities are consistent with the TDIP claim that the states are asserted to obtain in sequence.

Of course, we do not perceive that time "moves" in this narrative in the three middle sentences, but I do not find this disturbing. We have already seen in earlier examples like (19) and (20) that the duration which the hearer assigns to successive reference times in a discourse, and to the intervals between these reference times, depends on assumptions about the normal real-world duration and spacing of events of a given type. In the case

---

[3] This is not quite literally true. Since I have mentioned that there can in fact be a gap in time between the two "successive" reference time intervals in view of the TDIP, it is actually possible that the accomplishment mentioned by the second sentence was true another time at an interval lying partly in this gap which did not overlap with the reference time for the second sentence but which did overlap with that of the first sentence. The criterion for accomplishments/achievements, after all, does not exclude the possibility that a sentence of this class is true for two non-overlapping intervals. However, I believe we can ignore this possibility because this other, earlier occurrence of the accomplishment/achievement would be an event independent of the actually asserted event and also one that did not count among the events or states directly related to what the narrative describes.

of statives, the minimum duration can be arbitrarily small, so there would be no reason not to assign very brief and closely spaced reference times to stative sentences in a context like (25), given that we are assuming the actual times for which these states obtained were much longer than these reference times.

In fact, if there is any sense in which we assign a nontrivial duration to such stative reference times, I suggest that it is the following. In reading a narrative such as (25), we are invited to interpret such "scene-describing" statives as if they were the perceptual observations that a hypothetical human observer would make in the situation described by either the narrator or the protagonist from whose point of view the narrative is constructed. We as readers vicariously re-live these perceptual events. Thus we may take the duration of these stative reference times to be the time it would take a human observer to perceive these facts about the scene, and I believe the writer may even suggest that the order in which pragmatically overlapping statives are recorded in the discourse is the order in which the hypothetical observer notices them.

Now as I have mentioned earlier, there are also occurrences of statives in a discourse where the state is *not* interpreted to overlap with the previously described event; in this case, the stative sentence does "move" narrative time forward. Consider (26), a repetition of an earlier example.

(26) John went over the day's perplexing events once more in his mind.
Suddenly, he was fast asleep.

The thing to notice about the definition of statives in (13a) is that while this *allows* a state to begin earlier than its asserted reference time, it does not *require* it to be so. An adverb like *suddenly* will cancel the pragmatic inference that the state obtained earlier, for obvious reasons. This combination of the assertion of the state at the reference time with the inference that it did not obtain before this reference time constitutes a change of state, i.e. an inceptive interpretation for the stative. This inceptive interpretation is an event happening at a particular time, and thus we infer that narrative time "moves" here. But note that it is not at all necessary to regard the stative in this second sentence in (26) as lexically ambiguous between stative and inceptive interpretations. The inceptive reading arises purely from the ordinary stative reading of *be asleep* plus the semantics of *suddenly* and the resulting implicature that the state did not obtain earlier. (Certain stative predicates, such as *sit, stand*, and *lie*, admit the inceptive interpretation much more frequently and readily than other statives, and perhaps we should regard them as truly ambiguous between stative and inceptive readings. But this is not an issue which need be resolved here.)

An adverb like *suddenly* is not always necessary to produce the inceptive interpretation of a stative in a discourse. Sometimes the entailments of the stative sentence together with the entailments of the previous sentence lead us to conclude that the state has newly come about. So in (27), an example cited by Dry,

(27) Away in front, the engine whistled. Trees, hills and road, slid sideways and were gone. (from *A Wrinkle in Time*, by Madeleine L'Engle, cited by Dry 1978).

the state "were gone" in the last conjunct is inconsistent with the previous conjunct "trees, hills and road slid sideways", for in order for the narrator to perceive these objects sliding sideways, they must have been in view and therefore not yet "gone" in the intended sense of "out of view". Hence a kind of inceptive interpretation arises for the last conjunct. In (28) and (29), also examples cited by Dry from the same text, it is natural to infer a causal relation between the event in the first sentence and the coming about of the state mentioned in the second. Hence the state is a new one in the second sentence, and time accordingly "moves forward" in the second sentence:

(28) This time she was pushed out of the frightening fifth dimension with a sudden immediate jerk. There she was, herself again, standing with Calvin beside her. (cited by Dry)

(29) Then she was enfolded in the great wings of Mrs Whatsit, and she felt comfort and strength. (cited by Dry)

Now since I have attached a good deal of significance to the principle that statives are often assumed to obtain before and after their asserted reference time except when there are pragmatic reasons to infer the contrary, I think it is important to ask whether there is independent motivation for such a principle. Indeed, there is. In discussing the analysis of change of state predicates in artificial intelligence processing of discourse, Drew McDermott and others have pointed out that a processor must make this kind of assumption even for sentences widely separated in a discourse. Suppose a discourse, like that in (30), includes at an early stage the sentence *the book is on the table*.

(30) ... The book was on the table at t_0 ... Mary removed the book from the table at t_n.

The later sentence *Mary removed the book from the table* should be interpreted as having its presupposition satisfied, i.e. the presupposition of *remove* to the effect that the book must have been on the table at the time the act of removing it began. This will be the case no matter how many sentences intervene in the discourse represented by the second ellipsis, as long as no change in the location of the book has been mentioned. If on the other hand we alter the discourse to the form in (31),

(31) ?... The book was on the table at t_0 ... Mary put the book on the table at t_n.

still assuming that the position of the book is not mentioned in the intervening discourse, and interpreting the NP *the book* to refer to the same object in both cases, then the discourse is abnormal (and requires unusual assumptions about either the narrator of the discourse or forces which might affect the position of the book), because the presupposition of *put on the table* is that the object is not on the table at the beginning of the putting. It is apparently a conversational assumption in discourses that inanimate objects like books, which do not move under their own power, shall be assumed by the hearer to remain in the positions or other states ascribed to them, unless and until the narrator asserts otherwise. This kind of extremely common-sensical reasoning is one that seems trivial to us and hardly worth mentioning—until of course we attempt to program a computer to understand a discourse!

This principle of "inertia" in the interpretation of statives in discourse applies to many kinds of statives but of course not to all of them. For obvious reasons, a stative sentence like (32)

(32) The runner is at the finish line.

is not likely to generate any implicatures that the state extends earlier or later than the reference time in the context of a discourse, and in fact there must be a graded hierarchy of the likelihood that various statives will have this kind of implicature, depending on the nature of the state, the agent, and our knowledge of which states are long-lasting and which decay or reappear rapidly. Clearly, an enormous amount of real-world knowledge and expectation must be built into any system which mimics the understanding that humans bring to the temporal interpretations of statives in discourse, so no simple non-pragmatic theory of discourse interpretation is going to handle them very effectively.

7 THE TDIP AND ACTIVITIES

The definition for activities in (13b) is like that for statives in that it permits but does not require that an activity asserted to take place at interval I could perfectly well have begun before I or continued beyond I. So just as with statives, the question of overlap with surrounding sentences is determined by expectations as to which activities are likely to continue for a long time and which are not, as well as whether the surrounding discourse itself gives reason to believe that the asserted time of activity is the first or last interval for which it actually took place. At the one extreme are examples like (33), an example mentioned earlier, in which the clock's ticking is the kind of activity likely to have gone on before and after the asserted time and in which the discourse gives no indications to the contrary.

(33) John entered the president's office. The clock ticked loudly.

By contrast, the activity *look out the window* in (34), an example of Dry's, is understood to begin at its asserted reference time, hence not overlap with the previous sentence, because one infers a causal relation between the event of the previous sentence and the activity.

(34) John asked where the children were. Mary looked anxiously out the window. Their coats lay on the lawn, but they were not in sight. (Dry)

But even in this case, the activity of looking overlaps with the following sentence, because this last sentence reports states perceived by Mary as a consequence of the activity of looking and simultaneous with the looking.

8 THE TDIP AND PROGRESSIVES

Next I turn to the interpretation of progressive sentences in a discourse. I have already mentioned that progressives, like statives, allow the events they describe to overlap with those of the surrounding discourse, as for example in the middle sentence in (35).

(35) John entered the president's office. The president was writing a letter. The president's advisor signaled to John to take a chair.

But the explanation for this is somewhat different from the case of statives. The semantic clause (14) for the progressive tense asserts that the reference time of a progressive sentence falls within a larger interval over which the verb's action extends, and this larger interval may overlap with events described by the surrounding discourse, even though the reference time of the progressive sentence is disjoint from preceding and following ones. The normal interpretation of a case like (35), I would argue, is that diagrammed in (35'), where I_2 is the reference time

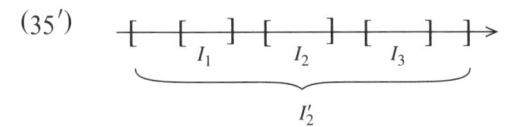

(35')

of the middle sentence but I'_2 is the interval over which the letter was written. Unlike the stative case, the larger, overlapping interval is here explicitly asserted, not just pragmatically inferred.

As I also pointed out earlier, progressives differ from statives in that the possibility of an inceptive interpretation is extremely remote with progressives, and thus the overlapping interpretation with surrounding discourse is highly consistent with progressives. To see an explanation for these facts, we must examine the interaction of the progressive with the TDIP in more detail. Note first that (14) does not really rule out the possibility that the reference time I might be an initial subinterval of the larger interval I' for which the atomic sentence is true. If this were allowed, an inceptive interpretation for a progressive ought to be possible. In fact, progressives are not normally used this way. Upon hearing (36), for example, one does not think of the possibility that 2 p.m. might be

(36) John was writing a letter at 2 p.m.

the first moment, or the last moment, of letter writing, but rather that it is somewhere in the middle of the event. We could if desired account for this fact directly by modifying the semantic clause for the progressive to stipulate that the reference time I is neither an initial nor a final subinterval of the atomic clause interval. But it is also possible that this added condition is simply a conversational implicature—one that arises for this reason: if the speaker knows that the reference time he would indicate with a progressive sentence is in fact the initial or final interval of the activity, there exist more explicit means in the language for indicating this, such as saying "John began to write a letter at 2 p.m." or "John finished writing a letter at 2 p.m.", etc. By the Maxim of Quantity, the speaker should use the more explicit expression in this case. We can try to test the status of this added condition in a familiar way: Suppose that I bet you $5 that John will be writing a letter at 2 p.m. At 1:59, he still has not started to write, but at precisely 2 p.m. he begins the letter. Have I won my bet? If so, this is an indication that the added condition is conversational. Now the status of this added condition may remain unclear, but it is not really necessary to resolve the issue here. Either way, there is clearly a preference for not using the progressive to indicate the initial subinterval of the verb's event.

But another possibility to worry about arises when we remember that the interpretation of "immediately after" in the TDIP might leave a gap between the reference time of the sentence preceding the progressive and the reference time of the progressive itself: Suppose S_2 is a progressive and I_2 its reference time:

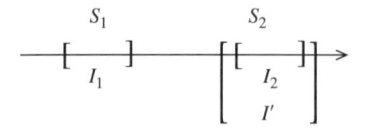

Even though this reference time is prohibited from being an initial subinterval of the time for the atomic clause of the progressive, I', I' might fail to overlap with the reference time of the preceding sentence, as in this diagram. The reason why this possibility might be excluded is a bit indirect, but would go something like this: As already mentioned, the intent of the phrase "immediately after" in the TDIP is that the reference time of the sentence S_i is to be the very next event or state (or narrator's perception of a state) of significance to the narrative. But the assumption that the time of the atomic sentence's truth, I', begins between I_1 and I_2 would violate the "immediately after" condition, since a potentially relevant event, the beginning of the activity or event denoted by the verb of the progressive sentence, would take place within this gap.

The possibility that this reasoning or something like it might be correct receives additional support, I believe, from the nature of the rare and exceptional examples in which this diagrammed temporal interpretation does arise. As far as I am aware, these exceptional examples are all similar to (37) and (38).

(37) In the darkness, John felt his way up the stairway of the dilapidated old house. Halfway up, there was a loud cracking noise under his feet, and suddenly he was falling through space.

(38) The president began the interview in a coldly official manner, much as Mary had expected. But the next thing she knew, the president was offering her the ambassador post.

These cases indicate a very particular psychological effect on the protagonist of the narrative: an event begins to happen, but it is only after it is already in progress that the protagonist realizes what is going on. This is made especially clear by the phrase *the next thing she knew* in (38), a phrase which seems to support this quasi-inceptive interpretation of the progressive better than any other. If as I suggested earlier the succession of reference times in a narrative can be exploited by the author to indicate the succession of perceptions of events and states by the person from whose point of view the narrative is constructed, then this quasi-inceptive interpretation of the progressive does not really violate the condition that the new reference time is the next significant event in the narrative. Rather, it indicates that the *perception* of this event already in progress is the next salient event in the consciousness of the protagonist.

By contrast, it seems very hard to get a felicitous inceptive reading of a progressive where this psychological effect cannot be inferred. Suppose we take the narrative in (39),

(39) John dropped the letter from the bridge and watched it hit the swiftly flowing water. The water carried the letter downstream and out of sight.

and change the second sentence to a progressive;

(40) ?John dropped the letter from the bridge and watched it hit the swiftly flowing water. (Suddenly/the next thing he knew), the water was carrying the letter downstream and out of sight.

Even with the insertion of *suddenly* or *the next thing he knew* into the second sentence, the narrative is rather strange. At best, we have to try to infer an unexplained momentary lapse of consciousness on John's part (or on the narrator's part); the "surprise effect" cannot be attributed to the letter since it is inanimate.

This section can be summarized as establishing that although progressives are like statives in certain respects according to this analysis (e.g. they both typically allow overlap with the previous sentence), it does seem to be consistent with this analysis that they are quite different in the way they allow an inceptive reading in the narrative.

9 SOME REMAINING MODIFICATIONS TO THE TDIP

Before concluding, I turn to some further modifications that need to be made in this method of handling temporal discourse interpretation and some further possible applications of it.

First, I have not discussed how sentences expressing iterative, or habitual, aspect are temporally ordered in a discourse. Dry (1983) has considered these, and has observed that iterative sentences behave like statives in that they are usually understood to overlap with the events of surrounding sentences in a discourse. Though I do not have at this point an explicit formal analysis of iterative aspect to propose (but cf. Vlach, ms.), it seems fairly obvious that any such analysis should give iteratives the subinterval property of statives, i.e. (13a). For example, if it is true at interval I that John smokes a pipe, in the iterative or habitual sense (i.e. John is a pipe smoker), then it surely should follow that "John smokes a pipe" is true in this same iterative sense at any subinterval of I (though of course he need not be actually smoking a pipe in the non-iterative, activity sense of "smoke a pipe" at any of these subintervals).

Secondly, the reader may have noticed that I have sometimes included examples of discourse ordering effects not just between independent main clauses of sentences, but also between conjuncts connected by *and*. Indeed, it seems that exactly the same sort of ordering principles apply whether we are dealing with successive main clauses or successive conjuncts with *and*, no matter what the syntactic category of these conjuncts, as long as they contain a verb. I am assuming that the semantics for natural language *and* is like that suggested by Cresswell (1977), approximately that in (41):

(41) [φ AND ψ] is true at I iff there are subintervals I' and I'' of I such that (a) φ is true at I', (b) ψ is true at I'' and (c) there is no subinterval of I that contains both I' and I''.

In other words, [φ AND ψ] is true of the smallest interval that contains times at which φ and ψ are true, but the semantics for AND itself does not specify what the relation is between these two times: φ and ψ might be true at the same time, at partially overlapping times, or at disjoint times. There seem to be two ways in which we could collapse the ordering of conjuncts with that of independent sentences. We could modify the definition of "reference time of a sentence" so that sentences with conjuncts connected by *and* have as many reference times as there are conjuncts. Or else we could leave the notion of "reference time of a sentence" as it is and try to generalize the TDIP so that it orders not only reference times proper but potentially any two times referred to in a sentence which are not explicitly ordered via time adverbials. One reason for preferring the latter is Hinrichs' (1981) observation that within passages of discourse entirely in the past perfect, the events mentioned are often ordered in accord with their aspectual classes in the same way that events in simple past clauses are. Since we want to be able to distinguish the true "reference time" of a past perfect from the time that its verb is true (or as Reichenbach would say, its "event time"), this is motivation for keeping the notion of "reference time" as it is. Under either method, many details remain to be worked out.

Thirdly, there are still a few exceptional examples of sentences with accomplishments/achievements which do not obey the TDIP as it stands. One of these, a case noted by Dry (1983) is where the second sentence in a discourse describes what is interpreted as the very same event as that described by the first sentence, but under a more detailed description, for example (42).

(42) John knelt at the edge of the stream and washed his face and hands. He washed slowly, feeling the welcome sensation of the icy water on his parched skin.

Since the event is the same, the reference time is also understood to be the same in the two sentences, even though both contain accomplishments.

Another, perhaps related exception arises when the discourse clearly implies that although events mentioned are distinct, they happen simultaneously. Consider the second and following sentences in (43).

(43) At the signal, everyone went to work at once. Mary searched the room for any of the items on the list that might be there. John went next door to do the same in Bill's apartment. Susan organized the rest of the players to canvass the block.

Kamp (ms.) has observed yet another kind of exceptional case: one in which a certain sentence is followed by a sequence of sentences each describing a "subevent" of the event mentioned in the first sentence, e.g. "Pedro dined at Madame Gilbert's. First there was an hors d'oeuvre. Then the fish. After that the butler brought a glazed chicken. The repast ended with a flaming dessert..."

It seems, therefore, that the TDIP must be modified to allow that if the discourse itself conveys some implication as to how events are to be specifically ordered, this should take priority over the third part of the rule that orders reference times successively. In other words, this third part is the "default case" to be followed when neither time adverbials nor entailments and implicatures of the discourse itself give clues to the ordering of events. (At this point, in fact, one is entitled to ask whether the TDIP is to be regarded as an independent principle of discourse interpretation per se, or merely as a description of the typical outcome of the interaction of various conversational principles and the speakers'/ hearers' knowledge of typical events and typical goals of narratives, any one clause of which may be overridden in various ways in exceptional cases. But this is not a question which can be profitably addressed here.)

A further application of this method of discourse interpretation is in adverbial subordinate clauses, such as those introduced by *when, while, before*, and *after*: Heinämäkki (1974), Smith (1978), Stump (1981) and especially Dry (1983) have called attention to the fact that the aspectual classes of verbs in these clauses, and also the aspectual classes of the verbs in the main clauses which these adverbials modify, have an effect on just what temporal relationship is conveyed by these connectives.

10 CONCLUSION

I believe that the main points of this paper are as follows. First, I have proposed that it is not really necessary for discourse construal rules of English to make reference to the aspectual class of lexical verbs directly nor to the progressive/non-progressive distinction. This is because semantic properties needed to explain these different effects on discourse are exactly those we would need to ascribe to the various aspectual classes independently in order to do lexical semantics and sentence-level compositional semantics. This "explanation" of discourse ordering of course has relied to a considerable degree upon pragmatics, but the pragmatic principles appealed to also seem to be those we would have to invoke anyway, such as the principle that a stative mentioned in a discourse should often be assumed to remain in effect long after it is explicitly mentioned and should likewise often be assumed to be in effect *before* it is explicitly mentioned.

A key thesis in this explanation therefore has been the assumption that we do not understand the perceived temporal ordering of discourse simply by virtue of the times that the discourse *asserts* events to occur or states to obtain, but rather also in terms of the additional larger intervals where we sometimes *assume* them to occur and obtain.

I conclude, therefore, that Kamp's conception of a discourse representation does not really seem to be motivated by the need to specify overlap versus non-overlap of successively described events in a discourse in English. Of course, there may be other sufficient motivation for the theory of discourse representations, such as pronominal reference, the conception of discourse representation as a psychological or computational representation of discourse meaning, or perhaps temporal discourse phenomena in French (though even here, I think one should first try to see whether the method I have proposed for English could be extended to French as well: the overlapping character of the French imparfait might fall out automatically, for example, if this tense were given a semantics akin to that of the progressive in English).

In fact, the considerations brought forth in this paper constitute obstacles for the theory of temporal discourse representations. If the aspectual class of sentences is determined by its compositional semantic interpretation and not its syntactic form,[4] then, given that aspectual class affects discourse ordering, discourse ordering must depend upon interpretation of individual sentences, not conversely. And since pragmatic inferences play a role in determining the ordering of events conveyed by a discourse, then, given that these inferences cannot be drawn without the hearer's having grasped the meanings of sentences to some extent, construction of implicature as well as literal semantic interpretation is needed for discourse ordering.

ACKNOWLEDGEMENT

This research was supported in part by a grant from the Alfred P. Sloan Foundation to the Ohio State University.

REFERENCES

Barwise, Jon and Perry, John (1983). *Situations and Attitudes.* Cambridge: Bradford Books.
Bennett, Michael and Partee, Barbara (1972). 'Toward the Logic of Tense and Aspect in English', distributed 1978 by the Indiana University Linguistics Club, Bloomington.
Cooper, Robin (1986). 'Tense and Discourse Location in Situation Semantics', *Linguistics and Philosophy* 9: 17–36.
Cresswell, M. J. (1977). 'Interval Semantics and Logical Words', in C. Rohrer (ed.), *On the Logical Analysis of Tense and Aspect.* Tübingen: TBL Verlag 7–29.
Dowty, David (1972). *Studies in the Logic of Tense and Aspect in English,* University of Texas dissertation.
——(1979). *Word Meaning and Montague Grammar.* Dordrecht: Reidel.
——(1982). 'Tenses, Time Adverbials and Compositional Semantic Theory', *Linguistics and Philosophy* **5**: 23–55.
——ms. 'Time Adverbials, Sequence of Tense, and the Temporal Interpretation of Discourse', Ohio State University, Athens.

---

[4] In connection with (1), Kamp has suggested (personal communication) that construction of discourse representation structures should not be strictly "top down" (in the sense that what is to be done with a sentence in constructing a representation depends not only on its top node but also on properties of various other syntactic nodes within it) and that semantics, likewise, should not be strictly compositional in the received sense. However, it seems to me that the issues raised in this paper pertain not to the question of compositionality per se, but rather whether only syntactic information, or also semantic information, is the input to discourse construction rules, no matter whether the information is derived compositionally (in either case) or not.

Dry, Helen (1978). 'Sentence Aspect and the Movement of Narrative Time', paper presented at the 1978 Annual Meeting of the Linguistic Society of America; published 1981 in *Text* 1 (3): 233–40.
——(1983). 'The Movement of Narrative Time', *Journal of Literary Semantics* **12**: 19–53.
Fillmore, Charles (1971). 'Lectures on Deixis', Indiana University Linguistics Club, Bloomington.
Heinämäkki, Orvokki (1974). *Semantics of English Temporal Connectives*. Bloomington: Indiana University Linguistics Club.
Hinrichs, Erhard (1981). 'Temporale Anaphora im Englischen', University of Tübingen *Staatsexamen thesis*.
Kamp, Hans (1979a). 'Events, Instants and Temporal Reference', in Egli and von Stechow (eds.), *Semantics from Different Points of View*. Berlin: Springer-Verlag, pp. 376–471.
——(1979b). 'On the Logic of Becoming', *Proceedings of the Stuttgart Conference on Quantifiers and Tenses*.
——(1980). 'A Theory of Truth and Semantic Representation', in Groenendijk et al. (eds.), *Formal Methods in the Study of Language*. Amsterdam: Mathematisch Centrum, 227–322.
—— ms., 'Discourse Representation and Temporal Reference'.
Nerbonne, John (1986). 'Reference Time and Time in Narration', *Linguistics and Philosophy* **9**: 83–95.
Partee, Barbara (1973). 'Some Structural Analogies between Tenses and Pronouns in English', *Journal of Philosophy* **70**: 601–9.
Reichenbach, H. (1947). *Elements of Symbolic Logic*. London: MacMillan.
Smith, Carlota (1978). 'The Syntax and Interpretation of Temporal Expressions in English', *Linguistics and Philosophy* **2**: 43–100.
——(1983). 'A Theory of Aspectual Choice', *Language* **59**: 479–501.
Stump, Gregory (1981). 'The Formal Semantics and Pragmatics of Free Adjuncts and Absolutes in English', Ohio State University dissertation, published 1985 in revised form as *The Semantic Variability of Absolutes*, Dordrecht: Reidel.
Taylor, Barry (1977). 'Tense and Continuity', *Linguistics and Philosophy* **1**: 199–220.
Vendler, Zeno (1967). *Linguistics in Philosophy*. Ithaca: Cornell University Press.
Verkuyl, Henk (1972). *On the Compositional Nature of the Aspects*. Dordrecht: Reidel.
Vlach, Frank ms. 'The Semantics of Tense and Aspect'.

16

Temporal Interpretation, Discourse Relations, and Commonsense Entailment*

ALEX LASCARIDES AND NICHOLAS ASHER

1 THE PROBLEM OF TEMPORAL RELATIONS

An essential part of text interpretation involves calculating the relations between the events described. But sentential syntax and compositional semantics alone don't provide the basis for doing this. The sentences in (1) and (2) have the same syntax, and so using compositional semantics one would predict that the events stand in similar temporal relations.

(1) Max stood up. John greeted him.
(2) Max fell. John pushed him.

But in (1) the order in which the events are described *matches* their temporal order, whereas in (2) descriptive order *mismatches* temporal order. At least, these are the natural interpretations of (1) and (2) unless the reader has information to the contrary. Similarly, the syntax of the sentences in texts (3) and (4) are similar, but the natural interpretations are different.

(3) Max opened the door. The room was pitch dark.
(4) Max switched off the light. The room was pitch dark.

The event and state in (3) temporally *overlap*, whereas in (4) they do not. An adequate account of temporal interpretation must capture these distinctions.

2 THE GOALS

Previous treatments of tense in Discourse Representation Theory (DRT) have investigated temporal relations in narrative texts like (1), (3) and (4) (Kamp and Rohrer 1983, Partee 1984, Hinrichs 1986). Dowty (1986) has explored the semantics of narrative text in an interval-based framework. These theories characterise tense as a tripartite relation

---

Alex Lascarides and Nicholas Asher, 'Temporal Interpretation, Discourse Relations, and Commonsense Entailment', *Linguistics and Philosophy* 16 (1993): 437–93. © 1993 Kluwer Academic Publishers.

* We would like to thank Mimo Caenepeel, Hans Kamp, Marc Moens, Michael Morreau, Jon Oberlander, Jeff Pelletier, and two anonymous reviewers for their helpful comments. The support of the Science and Engineering Research Council through project number GR/G22077 is gratefully acknowledged. HCRC is supported by the Economic and Social Research Council.

between event time, reference time and speech time. The reference time is anaphoric (cf. Reichenbach 1947): the forward movement of time in (1) is encoded in the logical form of the clauses through the forward movement of their reference times. In the case of DRT, statives don't invoke forward movement of reference times, and thus a distinction between (1) and (3) is achieved.

None of these theories attempts to account for the apparent backward movement of time in (2), and in texts like (5).

(5) The council built the bridge. The architect drew up the plans.

Moreover, they are unable to explain why the natural interpretations of (3) and (4) are different. We aim to extend these theories to solve the above problems. We will show that temporal relations must be calculated on the basis of semantic content, knowledge of causation, and knowledge of language use, as well as sentential syntax and compositional semantics. Consequently, temporal interpretation will *not* be determined by relations between reference times, where those relations are encoded in a logical form built from syntax alone. This is in sharp contrast to the traditional DRT interpretation of tense.

We'll argue that the basis for distinguishing (1) and (2) is a piece of defeasible causal knowledge relating falling and pushing, which is lacking for standing up and greeting: the knowledge is defeasible in the familiar sense that it is subject to exception. More generally, we'll suggest that defeasible reasoning underlies the interpretation of text: A defeasible logic is one where, informally, Γ defeasibly implies ϕ just in case from knowing only Γ one would infer ϕ. Thus conclusions following from a set of premises need not follow from a superset. We'll show that this type of logic provides a suitable system of inference for modelling the interactions between the Gricean pragmatic maxims and the world knowledge used to calculate temporal structure during interpretation.

Fixing NL interpretation in a defeasible reasoning system has been proposed before. In the realm of temporal interpretation, it has been defended by Hobbs (1979, 1985) and Dahlgren (1988). In certain respects, the approach developed in the current paper refines that outlined by Hobbs and Dahlgren. They encode world knowledge (WK) and linguistic knowledge (LK) in a declarative framework, and use this to determine the preferred interpretations of text. Our approach is similar in this respect. The main difference, in fact, lies in the utilisation of a constrained representation of defeasible knowledge, in which the underlying relation of logical consequence yields the interactions required.

In Hobbs' and Dahlgren's theories as they stand, it is not clear that the requisite notion of logical consequence could be defined, since the laws that need to interact in certain specific ways are not related in any obvious way. In particular, conflict can arise among the knowledge sources that they recruit during interpretation, and on occasion this conflict must be resolved. But since the resolution of conflict lacks logical justification, the interaction among the various knowledge sources appears arbitrary. We maintain that the only way of putting the reader's knowledge to work is to place it in the context of a logical language, for which a notion of logical consequence can be defined. Unlike Hobbs and Dahlgren, we will place the reader's knowledge in a logic where its implications can be precisely calculated.

Lascarides (1992) and Lascarides and Oberlander (1993*a*) calculate temporal structure by using WK and LK represented in terms of defeasible laws. But they dealt only with the temporal structure derived from two *consecutive* sentences in a text.

And Lascarides and Oberlander (1993a) didn't choose among the candidate logics which one should be used to calculate temporal structure. Here, we supply a logic that supports the inferences discussed in Lascarides and Oberlander (1993a). Indeed, the theory presented here can be viewed as an extension of that in Lascarides (1992) and Lascarides and Oberlander (1993a) in several ways. First, we suggest an analysis of the pluperfect that explains why (1) and (6) are different.

(6)   Max stood up. John had greeted him.

And secondly, we calculate the relation between sentences separated by intervening material, such as the relation between (7a) and (7e) in the text below:

(7) a. Guy experienced a lovely evening last night.
    b. He had a fantastic meal.
    c. He ate salmon.
    d. He devoured lots of cheese.
    e. He won a dancing competition.

In order to extend coverage to texts like (7) we assume, in line with Hobbs (1985), Grosz and Sidner (1986), Thompson and Mann (1987), and Scha and Polanyi (1988), that constraints must be imposed on which sentences in a text can be related to form text segments, and that these constraints are to be characterised in terms of *hierarchical discourse structure*. We therefore not only calculate the temporal structure of the events described in a text. We also investigate how WK and LK affect the interactions between discourse structure and temporal structure within very simple discourses. This is an important extension of the work in Lascarides (1992), where only event relations were calculated, making it impossible to analyse extended texts like (7).

The basic model of discourse structure we explore is one where units of a discourse are linked by discourse or rhetorical relations modelled after those proposed by Hobbs (1985). These discourse relations determine the hierarchical structure of the discourse, and hence the structural constraints on which sentences can attach together to form text segments. Because we're concerned only with temporal aspects of interpretation, we consider here only certain discourse relations that are central to temporal import. These are listed below, where the clause α appears in the text before β:

- *Explanation* (α, β): the event described in β explains why α's event happened (perhaps by causing it); e.g., text (2).
- *Elaboration* (α, β): β's event is part of α's (perhaps by being in the preparatory phase); e.g., text (5).[1]
- *Narration* (α, β): The event described in β is a consequence of (but not strictly speaking caused by) the event described in α; e.g., text (1).
- *Background* (α, β): The state described in β is the 'backdrop' or circumstances under which the event in α occurred (no causal connections but the event and state temporally overlap); e.g., text (3).
- *Result* (α, β): The event described in α caused the event or state described in β, e.g., text (4).

---

[1] We assume Moens and Steedman's (1988) tripartite structure of events, where an event consists of a preparatory phase, a culmination, and a consequent phase.

Explanation is in a sense the dual to *Result*; they both invoke causation, but the latter matches the textual and temporal orders of the events whereas the former doesn't. Both *Result* and *Narration* encode that textual order matches temporal order, but only the former relation induces a causal link between the events. We will provide an account of how these relations constrain the hierarchical structure of text, and we will supply logical mechanisms for inferring the relations from the reader's knowledge resources. It should be emphasised that this is not an exhaustive list of discourse relations: extensive classifications of discourse relations are offered in Hobbs (1985), Thompson and Mann (1987), Scha and Polanyi (1988), and Asher (1993). Here, since we are concerned with the temporal aspects of NL interpretation, we restrict our attention to the above relations.

The theory presented here lies at the intersection between formal semantics and computational linguistics. The relevance to formal semantics lies in our extension of existing DRT treatments of tense to solve the problems described. The extension will involve augmenting the DRT framework with the rhetorical relations mentioned above. We use this DRT-based theory of discourse structure so that direct comparisons with theories of tense in formal semantics can be made. But our account will be simpler than previous DRT treatments, in that we will not consider the role of temporal connectives in structuring discourse (but see Lascarides and Oberlander (1993b) for a proposed treatment in our framework). With regard to computational linguistics, we refine the proposal that defeasible reasoning underlies NL interpretation. We do this by examining in detail how a well-defined notion of nonmonotonic consequence can be used to calculate precisely the interactions between semantic content, causal knowledge, and pragmatic maxims. However, we offer no implementation, and we largely ignore communicative goals and intentions (cf. Grosz and Sidner 1986, Cohen, Morgan, and Pollack 1991).

3 THE BASIC STORY

A logic will be suitable for calculating temporal interpretation only if it supports all the patterns of inference we need to calculate temporal and rhetorical relations. These inferences are listed below; we motivate each one by a particular example. For simplicity, most of these examples will involve inferring temporal relations rather than discourse ones; the latter will be dealt with upon full formalisation.

Some formal notation is useful in order to clarify the logical structure of the inferences. We assume $A \mathrel{|\!\approx} B$ represents "B nonmonotonically follows from A" and $A \models B$ represents "B monotonically follows from A". $\phi > \psi$ is a gloss for the default rule "if ϕ, then normally ψ" and $\phi \to \psi$ is a gloss for "if ϕ, then (indefeasibly) ψ". We should stress that this formal notation is intended to be theory-neutral at this stage, for we simply wish to survey which patterns of inference we require from the logic. Thus for now, one can consider $\phi > \psi$ to be syntactic sugar for the way defaults are represented in default logic (i.e. $\phi, M\psi/\psi$, where M is the consistency operator), in autoepistemic logic (i.e. $L\phi \wedge \neg L \neg \psi \to \psi$, where L is the modal autoepistemic operator), in circumscription (i.e. $\phi \wedge \neg abnormal_n(\phi) \to \psi$, where $abnormal_n$ is an abnormality predicate), or in conditional logic (i.e. $\phi > \psi$, where $>$ is a modal connective). The two notions of entailment, i.e. $\mathrel{|\!\approx}$ and $\models$, can equally be regarded as syntactic sugar for the different notions of entailment supported in these various logics.

3.1 Defeasible Modus Ponens

Defeasible Modus Ponens is the following nonmonotonic inference:[2]

- **Defeasible Modus Ponens**
  $\phi > \psi, \phi \models \psi$
  E.g., Birds normally fly, Tweety is a bird $\models$ Tweety flies

We will show how it underlies the interpretation of text (1).

Intuitively, it's sometimes the case that the *only* information available to an interpreter regarding temporal structure is textual order. This is the case when no information about the temporal order of events is derivable from WK and LK, linguistic context, or syntactic clues like a change in tense, words like *because*, or adverbials. In such cases we claim the descriptive order of events typically matches temporal order. As explained in Lascarides (1992) and Lascarides and Oberlander (1993a), this claim is in line with Grice's (1975) Maxim of Manner, where it is suggested that text should be orderly. One way of interpreting this is that events should be described in the right order. Furthermore, Dowty (1986) claims that in some genres at least, the author typically describes events in the order of their discovery or perception, resulting in descriptive order matching temporal order. Our claim is that this LK plays a key role in interpreting (1). This is because in (1) it is indeed the case that the only information available for calculating temporal structure is textual order.

We represented this temporal information conveyed by textual order as a combination of two rules; one defeasible and one indefeasible.

- **Narration**
  If the clause β currently being processed is to be attached by a discourse relation to the clause α that's part of the text processed so far, then normally, *Narration*(α, β) holds.
- **Axiom on Narration**
  If *Narration*(α, β) holds, and α and β describe the eventualities e_1 and e_2 respectively, then e_1 occurs before e_2.

Narration exploits the dynamic processing of discourse familiar in DRT, where text structure is built by processing the successive sentences, and the information β portrayed in the current sentence must be added to some part α of the previous discourse. We define the constraints on which parts of the previous discourse are available for attachment below. Suffice for now to say that in a two-sentence text like (1), the only part of the previous discourse to which the second sentence can attach is the first sentence.

Since β is to be attached to α, α must have been in the text before β, and thus the textual order of α and β is coded in Narration's antecedent. Thus Narration and its Axiom together convey the information that textual order matches temporal order, unless there's information to the contrary. The idea that Gricean-style pragmatic maxims should be represented as defeasible rules has already been suggested in Joshi, Webber, and Weischedel (1984). Here, we've argued that the defeasible law Narration is a manifestation of Grice's Maxim of Manner. It is defeasible because there are exceptions, e.g., text (2).

---

[2] We ignore quantification and variables here, because the logic we ultimately use will be propositional.

Suppose that the logical forms of the sentences in (1) are respectively α and β; they describe the events e_1 of Max standing up and e_2 of John greeting him, but they do *not* impose any conditions on the relations between e_1 and e_2. Then Narration and its axiom can contribute to the interpretation of (1), providing the reader's knowledge base (KB) contains the following:

(a) α and β (so the reader believes the author is sincere);
(b) β is to be attached to α by a discourse relation (so the reader believes the text is coherent);
(c) the interpretation of the discourse so far (so interpretation is incremental, and the preceding discourse is taken as fixed);
(d) all defeasible WK, such as causal laws, and all defeasible LK, such as Narration;
(e) all indefeasible knowledge, like the Axiom on Narration and that causes precede effects;
(f) the laws of logic.

Defeasible Modus Ponens captures the preferred reading of (1) with respect to this KB:

(i) The premises of Narration are verified by the KB (assumption (b)).
(ii) The consequent of Narration is consistent with the KB.
(iii) (i) and (ii) form the premises of Defeasible Modus Ponens; *Narration*(α, β) is inferred.
(iv) Therefore, by the Axiom on Narration, Max standing up precedes John greeting him.

It must be stressed that this line of reasoning doesn't represent a psychologically plausible account of human text processing. Assumption (f) alone prevents us from making such claims. Nonetheless, the above reasoning predicts the correct analysis of (1) with respect to the reader's knowledge about the context, language use, and the world.

3.2 The Penguin Principle

The Penguin Principle is the following pattern of inference:

- **Penguin Principle**
  $\phi \to \psi, \phi > \neg\chi, \psi > \chi, \phi \models \neg\chi$
  E.g., Penguins are birds, penguins normally don't fly, birds normally fly, Tweety is a penguin $\models$ Tweety doesn't fly

The antecedents to two defeasible laws are verified, and the conclusions to both cannot hold in a consistent KB. In this sense, the rules conflict. The antecedent to one of the laws entails the antecedent to the other; in this sense, it is more specific. We want a defeasible logic to validate the inference in which the more specific rule is preferred. It will play a central role in resolving conflict among the reader's knowledge resources.

We now show how the Penguin Principle contributes to the interpretation of (2). First, we describe the relevant defeasible rules. By assumption (b) on the KB, an interpreter will infer a discourse connection between the sentences in a two-sentence text like (2). From the way we understand the discourse relations to which we limit ourselves in this paper, a discourse relation between two clauses entails one of the following relations between the *eventualities* (i.e. events and states) described: either one is a consequence of the other, one is part of (i.e. in the preparatory phase of) the other, they stand in causal relations, or they temporally overlap. For brevity, we state that if one of the above relations holds between two eventualities e_1 and e_2, then e_1 and e_2 are *e-connected*. Since the reader infers that the sentences in (1) and (2) are discourse-related, he infers that the events they describe are e-connected. In the case of (2), there is WK gained from perception and experience, that relates falling and pushing in a particular way:

- **Push Causal Law**
  If e_1 where x falls and e_2 where y pushes x are e-connected, then normally, e_2 causes e_1.

There is also indefeasible knowledge that causes precede effects:

- **Causes Precede Effects**
  If e_1 causes e_2, then (indefeasibly) e_2 does not precede e_1.

The Push Causal Law is a *defeasible* law. Unlike Dahlgren's (1988) probabilistic laws, it should *not* be read as pushings usually cause fallings. Indeed, we would claim that such a law would be far-fetched. For there will be plenty of pushings that don't cause fallings; and there may well be plenty of fallings that cause pushings. Rather, the Push Causal Law states that *if* a pushing and falling are e-connected, *then* although both causal directions may be permissible, one normally prefers one to the other.[3]

The Causal Law may seem very 'specific'. It could potentially be generalised, perhaps by re-stating e_1 as x moving and e_2 as y applying a force to x, and then having appropriate connections between pushings and applying force, and fallings and movement to interpret (2). A proposal for generalising causal knowledge in this way is discussed in Asher and Lascarides (1993). We're concerned here, however, with making the case for exploiting WK and LK in a logical framework to drive temporal interpretation, and this case can be made while glossing over generalisations like these. So we do so here.

There is no similar law for standing up and greeting; if one knows that a standing up and a greeting are e-connected but one knows nothing more, then it's not possible to conclude, even tentatively, exactly how the events are related. Our claim is that the Push Causal Law forms the basis for the distinction between (1) and (2).

In interpreting (2), there is conflict among the applicable knowledge resources, specifically between Narration and the Causal Law; given Narration's Axiom and Causes Precede Effects, the consequents of both laws can't hold in a consistent KB. Given that the natural interpretation of (2) in the 'null' context is one where the pushing caused the falling, this conflict must be resolved in that context in favour of the Causal Law.

In nonmonotonic logics, conflict between defeasible rules is resolvable if one is more specific than the other, cf. the Penguin Principle. We wish to provide a principled theory of how knowledge conflict is resolved during NL interpretation, and so we should ensure a Penguin Principle is formed in these cases. It's done like this: Given that constituents related by a discourse relation describe events that are e-connected, we can restate

---

[3] We are not concerned here with the metaphysics or meaning of causality. Suffice to say for now that our representation of causal relations is compatible with many of the current theories on causality. We also leave open the question of how these causal laws are acquired; suffice to say that they do not represent implausible knowledge.

the Push Causal Law as follows, making its antecedent entail that of Narration:

- **Push Causal Law**
  If β is to be attached to α, and α describes an event e_1 of x falling and β describes an event e_2 of y pushing x, then normally, e_2 causes e_1.

The new version of the Push Causal Law expresses a mixture of defeasible WK and LK, for it asserts that given the sentences are discourse-related somehow there is an e-connection between the events, and given the kinds of events they are, the second event described caused the first, if things are normal.

This new statement of the Causal Law ensures that together with Narration and the above contents of the reader's KB, the premises of a Penguin Principle are formed. α and β are now respectively the logical forms of the sentences in (2) rather than (1); the antecedents to the Causal Law and Narration are verified; these rules conflict and the more specific rule—the Causal Law—wins, resulting in an inference that the pushing caused the falling. This deals with the temporal structure of (2). We'll subsequently show that inferring the discourse structure of (2) also involves a Penguin Principle; in fact the inferences about temporal structure and discourse structure will be interleaved during interpretation.

To ensure that logic resolves the conflict in the right way when interpreting (2) with respect to the above context, we have essentially had to tailor the representation of causal knowledge to the particular task at hand, namely linguistic interpretation. For we have had to explicitly represent how the information is presented in the text in the 'causal' rule, in order to achieve the right logical interactions with other knowledge resources. Causal laws represented as "an event e_1 of type a normally causes an event e_2 of type b" would not bear the right logical relation to the available LK concerning textual order.

The result is a representation scheme that is nonmodular: WK and LK are mixed. Such a scheme has been viewed in computational linguistics to be undesirable. One reason for rejecting nonmodular approaches is that it makes it difficult to derive the laws from more fundamental knowledge resources in a systematic way. Asher and Lascarides (1993) address this problem, and show how lexical semantics can be used to generalise laws like the Push Causal Law, and suggest how they can be derived systematically. This is beyond the scope of this paper, however. We are not concerned with how the laws in the KB are acquired systematically. Rather, our purpose here is to investigate which logic provides the suitable inference regime for calculating temporal structure and discourse structure; and on this point we make the following claim. WK and LK can give conflicting messages about how to interpret discourse. This has two consequences. First, the logical consequence relation must be able to resolve conflict, and it can do this only if the conflicting laws are logically related. So second, this requires the causal knowledge to be represented in the nonmodular way we've suggested. Otherwise, conflicting defaults don't stand in the required relation of logical specificity.

The version of the Penguin Principle we've assumed here is one where the antecedents of the default rules are related by an indefeasible conditional. Intuitively, the same conclusion should follow when the indefeasible conditional is replaced by a defeasible one (cf. Asher and Morreau 1991). We haven't as yet found an example of discourse attachment that requires this version of the Penguin Principle however, and so we don't use a logic that supports it.

3.3 The Nixon Diamond

Conflict among defeasible rules is not resolvable when the antecedents of the rules aren't related. We refer to this (lack of) inference as the Nixon Diamond:

- **Nixon Diamond**
  $\phi > \chi, \psi > \neg\chi, \phi \not\models \chi$ (or $\neg\chi$)
  Quakers are normally pacifists, Republicans normally are non-pacifists, Nixon is a Quaker and a Republican $\not\models$ Nixon is a pacifist/Nixon is a non-pacifist.

We argue that the Nixon Diamond provides the key to textual incoherence, as in (8).

(8) ?Max won the race. He was home with the cup.

The appropriate KB when interpreting (8) verifies the antecedent of Narration. In addition, we claim that the following laws hold:

- **Win Law**
  If e_1 is Max winning, and e_2 is Max being at home, then normally, these eventualities don't overlap.
- **States Overlap**
  If the clause β is to be attached to the clause α, and β describes a state s, then normally s overlaps the eventuality e described by α.

The Win Law captures the WK that if Max wins the race and if Max is at home, then these events don't temporally overlap, if things are normal. In other words, it is unusual for the finish line of the race to be at the winner's house. Note that the Win Law doesn't require the antecedent to assert that the event and state are connected, nor in turn does it require the clauses that describe these eventualities to be discourse-related. For the intuition this law captures is that the event and state don't normally temporally overlap, *regardless* of whether they are connected or not.

States Overlap, on the other hand, is defeasible LK. This law can be seen as a manifestation of Grice's Maxim of Relevance, as suggested in Lascarides (1992). The argument goes as follows. An NL text describes a portion of the time-line, with events and states occurring on it. Let's call this a situation. To construct a full picture of the situation, the interpreter must infer the relative occurrences of the states and the culminations of events, including where states start and stop. Since culminations are punctual (holding at points of time), their relative order is inferred from rules like Narration, which models describing things in the order of perception as explained earlier. But states are extended, and the order of perception of states does not fully determine where the states start relative to the other eventualities. So order of perception is insufficient for determining where a state starts.

There are several linguistic mechanisms which can be used to indicate where a state starts. The author could explicitly refer in the text to what caused the state, and so from the law that causes precede effects, the interpreter will know the relative place where the state starts, cf. text (4). Alternatively, the author can use temporal adverbials to say where a state starts. But (3) shows that these two mechanisms are not enough: how do we determine where states start in text that do *not* feature adverbials or causes? States Overlap is then a vital mechanism for determining where a state starts relative to other eventualities described in text. It basically says that if there is no "explicit" indication of where the state starts—via the mention of causes or the use of temporal adverbials—then the start of the state is assumed to be *before* the situation that the text is concerned with occurs, resulting in overlap given the relation between textual order and order of perception. States Overlap asserts that (unless there's indication to the contrary) the point where a state starts is before the situation that the text describes, rather than part of it; and in that it's not part of the situation, it is irrelevant. Thus States Overlap models the following in accordance with Grice's Maxim of Relevance: the start of a state is relevant only if it is marked as such.

Assume that the reader's KB is as usual, save that α and β are now respectively the logical forms of the sentences in (8). Then the antecedents to States Overlap, the Win Law and Narration are all verified. By the general principle that the more specific default law overrides the less specific one when they conflict, the rule of Narration is deemed irrelevant here; States Overlap is more specific. States Overlap and the Win Law also conflict, but their antecedents aren't logically related. Hence as in the Nixon Diamond, we *fail* to infer any conclusion about the temporal relation between the eventualities described, leading to incoherence.

3.4 Closure on the Right

Closure on the Right is a *monotonic* inference of the following form:

- **Closure on the Right**
- $\phi > \psi, \psi \rightarrow \chi \models \phi > \chi$
  E.g., Lions normally walk, walkers (indefeasibly) have legs $\models$ lions normally have legs.

The theory of discourse attachment we propose requires this inference for several technical reasons, as will be clear in the appendix. It is also used, in conjunction with the Nixon Diamond, to account for discourse popping. Consider again text (7).

(7) a. Guy experienced a lovely evening last night.
  b. He had a fantastic meal.
  c. He ate salmon.
  d. He devoured lots of cheese.
  e. He won a dancing competition.

Intuitively, (7c,d) elaborate (7b), but (7e) does not. Thus (7e) should not attach to (7d) to form a text segment. Rather, (7e) should be related to (7b) by *Narration*. But (7d) and (7e) are consecutive sentences, and by our assumptions on the KB they will verify the antecedent to Narration. So something must block Narration's consequent. This is achieved as follows: In line with Scha and Polanyi (1988), we assume that if a text segment is narrative, it cannot also be an elaboration. Thus Rule 1 is part of the reader's KB:

- **Rule 1**
  If *Narration*(α, β) holds, then (indefeasibly) $\neg$ *Elaboration*(α, β) holds.

Rule 1 together with Narration and Closure on the Right produce Rule 2:

- **Rule 2**
  If β is to be attached to α with a discourse relation, then normally, $\neg$ *Elaboration*(α,β) holds.

The following defeasible law captures the intuition that if a clause γ is to attach with *Narration* to a clause β that elaborates α, then γ must also elaborate α:

- **Rule 3**
  If *Elaboration*(α, β) and $\neg$ *Elaboration*(α, γ) hold, then normally $\neg$ *Narration*(β, γ) holds.

Suppose that the logical forms of (7b), (7d), and (7e) are respectively α, β and γ. Suppose furthermore that in accordance with intuitions, the reader has inferred *Elaboration* (α, β). Then according to assumption (c) above, this is part of the contents of the KB. The task now is to attach γ to the preceding discourse. By Rule 2 with α and γ substituted in the schema, we infer $\neg$ *Elaboration*(α, γ). Thus from Rule 3 one would infer $\neg$ *Narration*(β, γ). But substituting β and γ in the schema Narration produces the conflicting conclusion *Narration*(β, γ). The antecedents of Rules 2 and 3 are not logically related to that of Narration, resulting in irresolvable conflict (cf. the Nixon Diamond). Thus no discourse relation between (7d) and (7e) is inferred, indicating that (7d,e) forms an incoherent text segment. Therefore, (7e) must attach to one of the remaining clauses in the preceding text. A full analysis of this example will be given upon formalisation. For now, suffice to say that Closure on the Right was required to block the attachment of (7e) to (7d).

3.5 Dudley Doorite

Dudley Doorite is also a monotonic inference:

- **Dudley Doorite**
  $\phi > \chi, \psi > \chi \models (\phi \vee \psi) > \chi$
  E.g., A Quaker is normally a pacifist, A Republican is normally a pacifist $\models$ A Quaker or Republican is normally a pacifist.

We use it to explain the ambiguity of text (9).

(9) The bimetallic strip changed shape. The temperature fell.

The appropriate KB contains the following laws:

- **Change = Bending or Straightening**
  A bimetallic strip changes shape if and only if it bends or straightens.
- **Bend Causal Law**
  If β is to be attached to α, and α describes the event e_1 of a bimetallic strip bending, and β describes an event e_2 of the temperature falling, then normally, e_1 causes e_2.
- **Straighten Causal Law**
  If β is to be attached to α, and α describes the event e_1 of a bimetallic strip straightening, and β describes an event e_2 of the temperature falling, then normally, e_2 causes e_1.

Neither of the above causal laws' antecedents are satisfied by the KB in the analysis of (9). However, Closure on the Right and Dudley Doorite can be used to infer the event structure for (9): Closure on the Right yields Law 1 and Law 2 respectively from the Bend Causal Law and the Straighten Causal Law:

- **Law 1**
  If β is to be attached to α, and α describes the event e_1 of a bimetallic strip bending, and β describes an event e_2 of the temperature falling, then normally, e_1 causes e_2 or e_2 causes e_1.
- **Law 2**
  If β is to be attached to α, and α describes the event e_1 of a bimetallic strip straightening, and β describes an event e_2 of the temperature falling, then normally, e_2 causes e_1 or e_1 causes e_2.

These then form the premises for Dudley Doorite which, together with Change = Bending or Straightening, produce the Change Causal Law:

- **Change Causal Law**
  If β is to be attached to α, and α describes the event e_1 of a bimetallic strip changing shape, and β describes an event e_2 of the temperature falling, then normally, e_2 causes e_1 or e_1 causes e_2.

The reader's KB verifies the antecedent to Change Causal Law when interpreting text (9). By Defeasible Modus Ponens, the reader infers that the two events are causally connected, but he fails to infer the *direction* of the causal connection, resulting in temporal ambiguity.

4 CHOOSING A NONMONOTONIC LOGIC

We will use all the above patterns of inference in text interpretation. So a logic is suitable for our purposes only if the logical consequence relation validates these inferences.

There are several different nonmonotonic logics which handle nonmonotonicity in various ways. For now, we simply survey which logics verify which of the above inferences. Reiter's (1980) default logic, auto-epistemic logic (Moore 1984) and the logic of All I Know (Levesque 1990) verify Defeasible Modus Ponens and the Nixon Diamond, but none of the others. Konolige's (1988) Hierarchical Autoepistemic logic (HAEL) verifies Defeasible Modus Ponens and the Penguin Principle, but the premises of a Nixon Diamond yield a contradiction rather than no conclusion. Furthermore, it fails to verify the monotonic patterns of inference. Veltman's (1990) Update Semantics verify all the nonmonotonic patterns of inference, but none of the monotonic ones. It would be difficult to extend these logics to support Closure on the Right (cf. Morreau 1993). Since we require Closure on the Right, these logics are not suitable for our purposes here.

Pearl (1988) shows how conditional probability theory can be used to model nonmonotonic reasoning. However, the system cannot represent or reason with embedded defaults; that is, default rules where one default condition is embedded in another. In Lascarides, Asher, and Oberlander (1992), we show that embedded defaults are needed to model how preceding discourse structure affects current discourse attachment. So Pearl's (1988) ε semantics is not suitable for our purposes either.

Circumscription (McCarthy 1980) represents defaults using abnormality predicates. For example, *birds fly* is represented as (10), which should be read as: for any x if x is a bird and is not abnormal in sense 1, then x flies.[4]

(10) $(\forall x)(bird(x) \land \neg ab_1(x) \to fly(x))$.

The language includes many abnormality predicates, to capture the many senses in which individuals can be abnormal. The default *Penguins don't fly*, for example, is represented in (11); it features a different abnormality predicate to (10) to reflect the intuition that being an abnormal penguin is different from being an abnormal bird.

(11) $(\forall x)(penguin(x) \land \neg ab_2(x) \to \neg fly(x))$

Defeasible entailment in circumscription is defined in terms of those admissible models where the abnormality predicates have as small an extension as is consistent with the premises: the so-called minimal models. ψ defeasibly follows from ϕ if for every minimal model in which ϕ holds, ψ holds. This definition of validity captures Defeasible Modus Ponens and the Nixon Diamond.

Prioritised Circumscription (Lifschitz 1984) captures the Penguin Principle by fixing a particular order to the abnormality predicates, preferring models which minimise over ab_2 to those that minimise over ab_1. Although this captures the intuitively compelling pattern of inference, it only does so in virtue of machinery that's extraneous to the semantics of defaults; namely the ordering of predicates in a hierarchy to guide inference. An alternative way of capturing the Penguin Principle, which does not require this extraneous machinery, is to assume the following law, which states that Penguins are abnormal birds (note we must use the abnormality predicate featured in (10) to express this).

(12) $(\forall x)(penguin(x) \to ab_1(x))$

The definition of validity in circumscription then captures the intuition that more specific defaults override less specific ones. But this is done at the sacrifice of a uniform translation of NL statements about defaults; for sometimes laws like (12) will have to be encoded in the translation of defaults into the object language.

The fact that NL statements about defaults do not translate uniformly into the formal representation is a general problem with Circumscription; it also raises difficulties when attempting to capture Closure on the Right. Consider the premises of this inference: that is $(\forall x)(A(x) \land \neg ab_1(x) \to B(x))$ and $(\forall x)(B(x) \to C(x))$. From this it follows that $(\forall x)(A(x) \land \neg ab_1(x) \to C(x))$. But given the multitude of abnormality predicates in Circumscription, we have no way of knowing whether ab_1 is the appropriate abnormality predicate for representing the default connection between A and C. The customary translation of default statements into Circumscription is to introduce a new abnormality predicate for each default statement. So suppose the abnormality predicate to be used when expressing the default connection between A and C is ab_n. Then we fail to support Closure on the Right: the above premises do not imply $(\forall x)(A(x) \land \neg ab_n(x) \to C(x))$. A similar tension arises between capturing Dudley Doorite and translations of NL default statements into Circumscription.

---

[4] We consider here the first-order language rather than the propositional version in order to clarify the discussion about abnormality predicates.

More recently, Delgrande (1988) has used conditional logic to model nonmonotonic reasoning. He defines a nonmonotonic consequence relation which is parasitic on his conditional connective >. The idea is that *can-fly(t)* follows from $(\forall x)(bird(x) > can\text{-}fly(x))$ and *bird(t)* just because $[\forall x(bird(x) > can\text{-}fly(x)) \wedge bird(t)]$ *can-fly(t)* is a theorem.

Delgrande notices a problem with the conditional logic approach to nonmonotonic reasoning: the conditionals seem to be too nonmonotonic for defeasible reasoning. Intuitively, if one adds *budgerigar(t)* to the above premises, then *can-fly(t)* should still follow. To ensure that the system supports this, Delgrande adds an external, syntactic mechanism for determining whether or not additional premises are irrelevant to the conclusions of arguments. Boutilier (1992) explains this problem, and our shared dissatisfaction with the solution: it invokes extra-logical machinery.

Commonsense Entailment (henceforward CE) (Asher and Morreau 1991, Morreau 1992) is a conditional logic for nonmonotonic reasoning that attempts to overcome the above problems in Circumscription and the above problems in Delgrande's logic. It is a different application of conditional logic to defeasible reasoning than Delgrande and Boutilier, in that it doesn't equate defeasible consequence with the conditional connective >. Morreau (1992) shows that consequently, one doesn't need the extra-logical machinery set up by Delgrande to solve the Irrelevance Problem.

It solves the above problems with Circumscription by restricting all representation of normality to the metalanguage. NL defaults are translated into the formalism in a uniform way. All defaults are represented using a nonmonotonic conditional operator >. Intuitively, $\phi > \psi$ is read as *If ϕ then normally ψ*, and *birds fly* is represented as $(\forall x)(bird(x) > fly(x))$. *All* default statements are translated in this way, regardless of their specificity. The need for a uniform translation of default statements is paramount when dealing with the complex commonsense knowledge required to reason about discourse.

CE captures all the patterns of inference we have mentioned. Its approach to Closure on the Right is more satisfactory than Circumscription's because multiple abnormality predicates are avoided. Furthermore, CE supports the Penguin Principle without resorting to machinery extraneous to the semantics of defaults, such as prioritising predicates as in Prioritised Circumscription, or forming hierarchies of defaults as in HAEL. We assume that whatever the semantics of default rules, that more specific defaults should override less specific ones when they conflict should be an inherent part of that semantics. We therefore favour the approach to the Penguin Principle taken in CE.

A further reason for using CE concerns the ability to carry out local inferences in a nonmonotonic framework. In general, it's not possible to divide nonmonotonic inference into a chain of deductions based on parts of the context. This is because adding premises to nonmonotonic deductions doesn't always preserve conclusions, making it necessary to look at the premises as a whole. In CE, however, it is possible to divide inferences into a chain of subtheories under special circumstances, as shown in the appendix. We will exploit this property upon formalisation, in order to interleave reasoning about temporal structure and discourse structure. We leave open the question of whether chains of local inferences would be possible in Prioritised Circumscription.

We now examine in detail how the ideas presented here can be formally pinned down. To do this, we augment the DRT framework with rhetorical relations, as proposed in Asher (1993); we show how to represent the appropriate LK and WK in CE; and we show how the appropriate temporal structures and discourse structures for NL texts are achieved.

5 DISCOURSE STRUCTURE IN DRT

The fragment of NL text considered here will be relatively simple, with no quantification, connectives, adverbials or future tense. We concentrate on characterising the pluperfect and simple past tenses alone. We employ an extension of DRT, so that we can compare directly our theory with previous, influential DRT theories of tense.

DRT represents discourse in terms of a discourse representation structure (DRS), which is a pair of sets identifying respectively the discourse entities and conditions on those entities. The individual sentences in this theory will be represented using DRSs. But the representation of text as a whole *extends* the framework of DRT. Text is represented in terms of a *discourse representation pair* (DRP). This consists of a set of DRSs which define the semantic content of the sentences of the text, and a set of conditions on those DRSs, which characterise the discourse relations between them. So in essence, DRPs are the logical forms of the individual sentences plus discourse relations between them.

This kind of representation is a natural extension of the DRT framework: A DRP is a simpler version of an SDRS (or segmented discourse representation structure) as introduced in Asher 1993. It is simpler in the sense that the discourse relations will relate only DRSs (corresponding to sentences) rather than SDRSs (corresponding to segments of text). Discourse relations between sentences rather than segments of text are adequate for the simple fragment considered here, but not adequate in general. For the sake of simplicity, we have chosen not to extend the DRT framework to SDRT here, although such an extension would be straightforward.

The formal definition of DRPs is as follows:

DEFINITION OF DRP and DRP CONDITIONS

- If $\alpha_1,\ldots,\alpha_n$ are DRSs, *Con* a set of DRP conditions on those DRSs, then $\{\{\alpha_1,\ldots,\alpha_n\}, Con\}$ is a DRP;
- If α_1 and α_2 are DRSs and R is a discourse Relation, then $R(\alpha_1, \alpha_2)$ is a DRP condition on α_1 and α_2.
- If α is a DRS, then the DRP $\{\{\alpha\}, \emptyset\}$ is equivalent to α and shall be referred to as such.

For our purposes, discourse relations are two-place predicates whose semantics are defined by the interpretation function in the model. Thus the semantics of DRPs are obtained from the semantics of DRT given in the appendix simply by extending the interpretation function in the appropriate way.

5.1 The logical form of sentences

We now turn to the question of representing sentences as DRSs. The logical form of sentences will introduce discourse entities denoting events and times to capture deictic reference (cf. Partee 1973). But since we are not concerned with NP reference, for simplicity we will assume NPs are represented by constants. We propose that the logical form of the sentence (13) is (13′).

(13) Max stood up.
(13′) $[e, t][t < now, hold(e, t), standup(max, e)]$

In words, (13′) introduces discourse entities e and t, and asserts that the event e is Max standing up and e holds at a point of time t earlier than *now*.

Contrary to traditional DRT, the semantics of (13′) is given in a modal framework (as CE is modal), with truth defined relative to possible worlds. Moreover, the movement of time through discourse will be determined by defeasible rules for discourse attachment rather than by syntactic-based rules for constructing DRSs.

The logical form of (14) is (14′):

(14) Max had stood up.
(14′) [s, t][s : [e][standup(m, e), s = cs(e)], hold(s, t), t < now]

In (14′), s is the consequent state of the event of Max standing up, and it holds at the time t which precedes *now*. So our semantics of the perfect is like that in Moens and Steedman (1988): a perfect transforms an event into a consequent state, and asserts that the consequent state holds. The pluperfect of a *state*, such as (15), therefore, is assumed to first undergo a transformation into an event.

(15) John had loved Mary.

The event is usually the inceptive reading of the state—in this case, *John started to love Mary*—although this can vary with the context. Then, the pluperfect asserts that the consequent state of this event holds—in this case, the consequent state is the state of John loving Mary itself.

We forego defining the function cs which takes events to consequent states here for reasons of space, but see Lascarides (1988) and Blackburn and Lascarides (1992) for a proposed semantics. We do, however, assume that the following relationship holds between an event and its consequent state:

- **Consequent States:**
  $\Box(\forall t)(hold(cs(e), t) \rightarrow (\exists t')(hold(e, t') \land t' < t))$
  $\Box(\forall t')(hold(e, t') \rightarrow (\exists t)(hold(cs(e), t) \land t' < t))$

So a consequent state holds if and only if the event holds at an earlier time. This relationship means that simple past and pluperfect tensed sentences are truth-conditionally equivalent, under the usual assumption that time is dense. They only differ in terms of which eventualities are available for future anaphoric reference.

This is unlike previous representations of the pluperfect, which invoke a tripartite relation between event time, reference time, and speech time (Kamp and Rohrer (1983), Partee (1984), Hinrichs (1986), Dowty (1986)). In these theories, the simple past and pluperfect tenses differ at the sentential level because the reference time is identified with the event time in the simple past and is after the event time in the pluperfect; thus the temporal structures are different.

But even though there is sentential equivalence, the pluperfect will play a distinct discourse role, as explained in Section 8. Because discourse structure doesn't arise solely from the logical form of sentences, the theory is rich enough to distinguish between the truth conditions of sentences and their discourse roles, thus allowing us to contrast the simple past and pluperfect in this way. Exploring this discourse level strategy for analysing the pluperfect is motivated by the fact that pluperfect sentences are understandable only in the context of preceding simple past tensed discourse.

This deals with sentences. Texts are represented as DRPs. The problem is to update the DRP: if τ is the DRP representing the first n sentences of the text, and β is the DRS representing the semantic content of the $n+1$th sentence, then τ must be updated with β

by adding β to τ's first set and adding discourse relations between β and DRSs in τ to τ's second set. Updating will consist of:

(1) Defining the constraints on the possible sites for attachment of the DRS β (these will be some subset of DRSs in the DRP τ); and
(2) Defining rules for attachment of β at an attachment site.

We now turn to the first task.

5.2 Constraints on possible sites for attachment

We mentioned in Section 2 the generally accepted view that only some components of a discourse structure are open in the sense that one may add new material to them as the discourse is processed. To update a DRP τ with the new information given by the sentence currently being processed, one has to relate the sentence's DRS by means of a discourse relation to an *open* DRS in τ, where openness is as defined below. From an intuitive point of view, the definition of openness captures the following: an open clause is either the previous clause (i.e. the last one added to the DRP), or a clause that it elaborates or explains. This is in line with the openness constraints described in Scha and Polanyi (1988) and Asher (1993).

DEFINITIONS OF DISCOURSE DOMINANCE

Suppose a DRP τ contains the DRSs α and β. Then:

- **Subordination**
  α is *subordinate* to β if:
  (i) *Explanation*(β, α) or *Elaboration*(β, α) holds; or
  (ii) γ is a DRS in τ such that *Explanation*(γ, α) or *Elaboration*(γ, α) holds, and γ is subordinate to β.

- **Openness**
  A DRS α is *open* in the DRP τ if and only if α is the DRS representing the previous clause in the text, or this DRS is subordinate to α.

One can represent DRPs as graphs, which are built in a depth-first left-to-right manner. The above definition of openness can then be represented pictorially as follows:

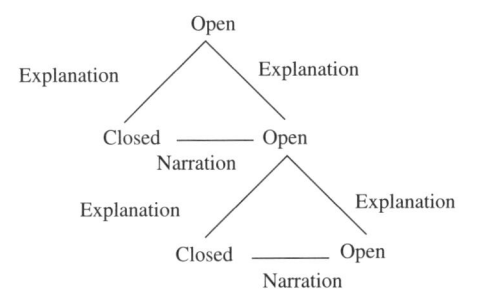

```
                        Open
                       /    \
            Explanation      Explanation
                       /    \
                 Closed ——— Open
                        Narration
                              /    \
                  Explanation      Explanation
                              /    \
                        Closed ——— Open
                              Narration
```

There are structural similarities between our notion of openness and Polanyi's (1985) and Webber's (1991); the open constituents are those on the right frontier of the discourse structure.

These constraints on the possible sites for attachment capture two intuitions noted in Scha and Polanyi (1988): first, the only clause to which the current clause can attach in narrative is the previous one; and second, an elaboration or explanation that occurs earlier than the previous clause cannot be resumed.[5]

The awkwardness of text (16) illustrates the first intuition: (16c) should intuitively be related to (16a); but (16a) isn't open since (16a,b) is narrative.

(16) a. Max stood up.
    b. John greeted him.
    c. ?Max got up slowly.

Text (17) illustrates the second intuition.

(17) a. John arrived late for work.
    b. He had taken the bus.
    c. He had totalled his car.
    d. His boss summoned him to his office.

Intuitively, (17b,c) explains (17a), but (17d) does not. Our definition of openness predicts that (17a–d,e) is awkward (because (17e) attempts to continue the 'closed' explanation (17b,c)), whereas (17a–d,f) is acceptable.

(17) e. ?John had taken his car to the garage.
    f. John realised that his chances of promotion looked bleak.

The definition of openness permits several possible attachment sites for the incoming material. Our theory of discourse attachment doesn't always choose which site among these possibilities is the preferred one. This is what one would want, because in some discourses there is no preference, leading to ambiguity (Asher 1993). However, our theory does predict that in some cases, the knowledge in the KB blocks attaching the incoming material to a particular open site. For example, we will formally pin down why even though (17c) is an open attachment site for (17d), (17d) doesn't attach there.

Having chosen a particular attachment site according to the above constraints, we have yet to formally pin down the reasoning that underlies choosing which discourse relation to use. For example, we must specify why (17f) is related to (17d) by *Narration*, and not by any of the other discourse relations. We must define the rules for attaching new information to a particular attachment site. We have argued that these rules must be defeasible, characterising causal laws and pragmatic maxims. We now turn to the problem of representing these defeasible rules within CE.

6   A BRIEF INTRODUCTION TO CE

CE supplies a modal semantics for defaults. On top of the truth conditional semantics there is a dynamic partial theory, which accounts for nonmonotonic inferences like those described above. Defeasible Modus Ponens intuitively goes as follows: first, one assumes the premises *birds fly* and *Tweety is a bird* and no more than this. Second, one assumes

---

[5] Definite noun phrases that refer to events previously described can occasionally allow one to refer back to segments of text which we claim are 'closed off'. It is debatable, however, whether we re-open closed attachment sites or whether we start a new structure in the discourse. For the sake of simplicity, we ignore these sorts of discourses here, but see Asher (1993).

that Tweety is as normal a bird as is consistent with these premises. Finally, from these two assumptions, one concludes that Tweety flies.

Let us first consider the semantics of defeasible statements. As already mentioned, "if ϕ then normally ψ" is represented as $\phi > \psi$. We augment the language to include DRPs, and strict conditionals of the form $\Box(A \to B)$ in order to represent *indefeasible* laws like the Axiom on Narration. But we also simplify the language in that we use a propositional version.

The semantics of defeasible statements are defined in terms of a function * from worlds and propositions to propositions. Intuitively, *(w, p) is the set of worlds where the proposition p holds together with everything else which, in world w, is normally the case when p holds. So * encodes assumptions about normality. The truth conditions of defeasible statements are defined as follows:

- $M, w \models \phi > \psi$ if and only if *(w, $[\![\phi]\!]$) $\subseteq [\![\psi]\!]$

In words, the above says that *If ϕ then normally ψ* is true with respect to the model M at the possible world w if the set of worlds that defines what is normally the case when ϕ is true in w all contain the information that ψ is also true. Thus CE is a conditional logic in the Acqvist (1972) tradition; it differs from previous conditional logics in the constraints it imposes on the function *. Three constraints are particularly relevant here: Facticity, Specificity, and Dudley Doorite, as defined in the appendix. Facticity captures the intuition that however few properties a normal bird has, one of them is that he is a bird. Specificity encodes the constraint that normal birds aren't penguins (because penguins don't have the flying property associated with normal birds). Dudley Doorite encodes the constraint that if Quakers are pacifists and Republicans are pacifists, then Quakers and Republicans are pacifists.

The truth definitions for the full language are given in the appendix, together with the monotonic axioms which make the monotonic part of CE sound and complete. We use a modified version of the logic of CE given in Asher and Morreau (1991): our axioms reflect 'modal closure' instead of just logical closure, where the background modal theory is S5. We show in the appendix that modal closure is necessary in order to build discourse structures.

Besides the monotonic axioms, CE develops a dynamic semantics of information states, which are sets of possible worlds, that verify defeasible inferences. This makes precise the notion of assuming no more than the premises of an argument (defined in terms of an update function + on information states), and assuming everything is as normal as is consistent with those premises (defined in terms of a normalisation function N). The functions *, + and N, which are defined in the appendix, characterize a further notion of (commonsense) validity, written $\approx$ (also described in the appendix). This supports (at least) Defeasible Modus Ponens, the Nixon Diamond, and the Penguin Principle. The monotonic validity $\models$ supports Closure on the Right, and Dudley Doorite (and since $\approx$ is supra-classical, these are also valid under $\approx$). Contrary to HAEL and Prioritised Circumscription, the Penguin Principle is verified without forming hierarchies of defaults. CE therefore captures in a satisfactory way all the patterns of inference we need. It may not do so in a minimal fashion, but it is the only candidate logic among those that we've discussed which does so at all. On the question of minimality, it should be noted that CE doesn't support case-based reasoning, which is what default logic and circumscription are designed to do. So CE is not a strictly more powerful logic than these ones. One of our claims here is that case-based reasoning isn't required to do discourse attachment, and so one doesn't need the full power of default logic.

7 THE DYNAMIC CONSTRUCTION OF DISCOURSE STRUCTURE

7.1 Narration and Defeasible Modus Ponens

The logical forms of the sentences in (1) are respectively α and β.

(1) Max stood up. John greeted him.
(α) $[e_1, t_1,][t_1 < now, \; hold \; (e_1, t_1), \; standup(max, e_1)]$
(β) $[e_2, t_2] \; [t_2 < now, \; hold(e_2, t_2), \; greet(max, john, e_2)]$

The DRP representing (1) is constructed by updating the DRP $\{\{\alpha\}, \emptyset\}$ with β. We now formalise this. Let $\langle \tau, \alpha, \beta \rangle$ be a function that updates the DRP τ with the DRS β via a discourse relation with α, where α is an open constituent of τ. Thus the output of this function is a new DRP τ', which is just like τ save that β is added to the first set and a discourse relation between α and β added to the second set. Let $me(\alpha')$ stand for the *main eventuality described in α'*. The formal definition of *me* is given in the appendix in a way that agrees with intuitions: for example, $me(\alpha)$ is the event e_1 of Max standing up. Then Narration and its Axiom, which were introduced in Section 3.1, are represented in CE as schemas:

- **Narration**
  $\langle \tau, \alpha, \beta \rangle > Narration(\alpha, \beta)$
- **Axiom for Narration**
  $\Box(Narration(\alpha, \beta) \rightarrow me \; (\alpha) < me(\beta))$

By the above assumptions (a) to (f) on the reader's KB, $Narration(\alpha, \beta)$ follows in CE from the KB by Defeasible Modus Ponens; and by modal closure in CE, the standing up precedes the greeting. So the DRP representing (1) is (1').

(1) Max stood up. John greeted him.
(1') $\{\{\alpha, \beta\}, \{Narration(\alpha, \beta)\}\}$

Discourse structure is related to topic structure, as defined in Asher (1993). Intuitively, the topic of a segment is the overarching description of what the segment is about. For example, the topic of (1) could be John's introduction to Max. In the case of *Narration*, the law below states that $Narration(\alpha, \beta)$ holds only if α and β have a distinct, common (and perhaps implicit) topic γ:

- **Topic of Narration**
  $\Box(Narration(\alpha, \beta) \rightarrow (\exists \gamma)(topic(\alpha) = \gamma \land topic(\beta) = \gamma \land \gamma \neq \alpha \land \gamma \neq \beta))$

This rule is used to explain the incoherence of (18): as long as WK about cars breaking down and the sun setting is represented as intuitions would dictate, one cannot find a common distinct topic, and so *Narration* between the clauses can't be inferred.

(18) ?My car broke down. The sun set.

But no other relation can be inferred given the defeasible LK and WK available. And hence no discourse structure for (18) is constructed. Note that we can improve the coherence of (18) by supplying a topic in a third clause, e.g. (19):

(19) Then I knew I was in trouble.

7.2 Knowledge Conflict and the Penguin Principle

The logical forms of the sentences in (2) are respectively α and β; they are constructed in the same way as those for the sentences in (1) because of the similar syntax:

(2) Max fell. John pushed him.
(α) $[e_1, t_1][t_1 < now, hold(e_1, t_1), fall(max, e_1)]$
(β) $[e_2, t_2][t_2 < now, hold(e_2, t_2), push(john, max, e_2)]$

We represent the Push Causal Law and the law that Causes Precede Effects in CE as:

- **Push Causal Law**
  $\langle \tau, \alpha, \beta \rangle \wedge fall(max, me(\alpha)) \wedge push(john, max, me(\beta)) > cause(me(\beta), me(\alpha))$
- **Causes Precede Effects**
  $\Box(cause(e_1, e_2) \to \neg\, e_2 < e_1)$

We also capture the LK that if β is to be attached to α, and moreover β's event caused α's then normally, β explains α:

- **Explanation**
  $\langle \tau, \alpha, \beta \rangle \wedge cause(me(\beta), me(\alpha)) > Explanation(\alpha, \beta)$

And finally, in accordance with Scha and Polanyi (1988), we assume that the same two clauses cannot be related by both *Explanation* and *Narration*:

- **Axiom on Explanation**
  $\Box(Explanation(\alpha, \beta) \to \neg Narration(\alpha, \beta))$

The KB contains α, β and $\langle \propto, \alpha, \beta \rangle$. So Narration and the Push Causal Law apply. This forms a complex Penguin Principle; it is complex because the consequents of the two defeasible laws are not χ and $\neg \chi$, but instead the laws conflict in virtue of the Axiom on Narration and Causes Precede Effects. CE supports the more complex Penguin Principle:

- **The Complex Penguin Principle**
  $\Box(\phi \to \psi), \psi > \chi, \phi > \zeta, \Box(\chi \to \theta), \Box(\zeta \to \neg\theta), \phi \mathrel{\!\mid\!\approx} \zeta$

Therefore, there is a defeasible inference that the pushing caused the falling, as required.

Given the results of the Complex Penguin Principle, the antecedent of Explanation is verified. Moreover, the antecedent to Explanation entails that of the conflicting law Narration. So there is another Complex Penguin Principle, from which *Explanation* (α, β) is inferred. So (2') is the representation of (2).

(2') $\{\{\alpha, \beta\}, \{Explanation(\alpha, \beta)\}\}$

The second application of the Penguin Principle in the above used the results of the first, but in nonmonotonic reasoning one must be wary of dividing theories into 'subtheories' in this way. We show in the appendix that the predicates involved in the above deduction are sufficiently independent that in CE one can indeed divide the above into two applications of the Penguin Principle to yield inferences from the theory as a whole. We call this double application of the Penguin Principle where the second application uses the results of the first the *Cascaded Penguin Principle*.

By the openness constraints on DRPs defined earlier, the only available sentence for attachment if one were to add a sentence to (1) is *John greeted him*, whereas in (2), both sentences are available. So although the sentences in (1) and (2) have similar syntax and logical forms, the texts have very different discourse structures. The events they describe also have different causal structures. The difference in the natural interpretations of (1) and (2) arose essentially from causal knowledge. But the difference is not that (1) is always a narrative and (2) is always an explanation. Rather, *in the absence of information to the contrary*, (1) is a narrative and (2) is an explanation. In Lascarides, Asher and Oberlander (1992), we demonstrate that this framework is sufficiently powerful to explain why the natural interpretation of (2) *in vacuo* is different from the interpretation of the same sentence pair in (20).

> (20) John and Max were at the edge of a cliff. Max felt a sharp blow to the back of his neck. *He fell. John pushed him.* Max rolled over the edge of the cliff.

In (20), the falling and pushing are related by *Narration* rather than *Explanation*.

The discourse structure for (5) is built in an exactly analogous way to (2), using the rules Elaboration and Axiom on Elaboration below, where $prep(me(\beta), me(\alpha))$ means β's eventuality is in the preparatory phase of α's.

> (5) The council built the bridge. The architect drew up the plans.

- **Elaboration**
  $\langle \tau, \alpha, \beta \rangle \land prep(me(\beta), me(\alpha)) > Elaboration(\alpha, \beta)$
- **Axiom on Elaboration**
  $\Box(Elaboration(\alpha, \beta) \rightarrow \neg Narration(\alpha, \beta))$

Now we fold states into the picture. States Overlap, which was introduced earlier, is formally represented as follows:

- **States Overlap**
  $\langle \tau, \alpha, \beta \rangle \land state(me(\beta)) > overlap(me(\alpha), me(\beta))$

There is also a version of States Overlap where $state(me(\beta))$ is replaced with $state(me(\alpha))$: this handles the cases where α is stative rather than an event sentence.

Background captures the intuition that if β is to be attached to α and the eventualities they describe overlap, then the discourse relation is *Background*, if things are normal, and the Axiom on Background prevents the text segment from being iconic:

- **Background**
  $\langle \tau, \alpha, \beta \rangle \land overlap(me(\alpha), me(\beta)) > Background(\alpha, \beta)$
- **Axiom on Background**
  $\Box(Background(\alpha, \beta) \rightarrow \neg me(\alpha) \prec me(\beta))$

The appropriate KB when interpreting (3) forms the premises of a Cascaded Penguin Principle: the pairs of conflicting laws are States Overlap and Narration and Background and Narration.

> (3) Max opened the door. The room was pitch dark.

Thus the event and state overlap and the clauses are related by *Background*. Now we turn to text (4).

> (4) Max switched off the light. The room was pitch dark.

We have the following causal law, which reflects the knowledge that the room being dark and switching off the light, if connected, are normally such that the event causes the state.[6]

- **Dark Causal Law**
  $\langle \tau, \alpha, \beta \rangle \wedge switchoff(max, light, me(\alpha)) \wedge dark(room, me(\beta)) > cause(me(\alpha)me(\beta))$

Suppose the reader's KB is as usual. Then this KB verifies the antecedents of Narration, Dark Causal Law and States Overlap. Narration conflicts with States Overlap, which in turn conflicts with the causal law. Moreover, the causal law is more specific than States Overlap (for we assume $dark(room, s_2)$ entails $state(s_2)$ by the stative classification of the predicate $dark$), and States Overlap is more specific than Narration. In CE the most specific rule wins, and so a causal relation between the event and state is inferred. Full details of the proof are given in the appendix.

A constraint on the use of the discourse relation Result is defined as follows:

- **Result**
  $\langle \tau, \alpha, \beta \rangle \wedge cause(me(\alpha), me(\beta)) > Result(\alpha, \beta)$

Given the above inference, the antecedents to Result and Narration are verified. Result and Narration don't conflict, so the consequents of both Narration and Result are inferred from the KB. Thus text (4) is a narrative, and moreover, the darkness is the *result* of switching off the light.

The Penguin Principle captures the following intuition concerning text processing: the reader never ignores information that is derivable from the text and relevant to calculating temporal structure and discourse structure. For example, in the case of (3) the Penguin Principle ensures the following information is not ignored: a stative expression was used instead of an event one.

There is an air of artificiality about the examples we've discussed in relation to the Penguin Principle, and there may be worries about the soundness of proceeding from our decontextualised cases to more realistic data. Texts containing more linguistic structure and information will in general mean that more information should be taken into account when attempting discourse attachment. Will this change the underlying inference patterns, and deem CE inappropriate? Any theory that makes precise the inferences that underlie language interpretation suffers from this problem of complexity, and our theory is no exception. Our conjecture, however, is that however complex the rules for discourse attachment, specificity will always govern the way in which knowledge conflict is resolved. Since CE supports resolution of conflict by specificity, it is hoped that it will be a suitable logic for handling more complex data. Some research on this is currently underway. In Asher and Lascarides (1993), we show how, through spreading the semantic processing load between the lexicon and rules for discourse attachment, generalisations on the rules for discourse attachment can be achieved, which enable a much wider coverage of data. But exploring the role of specificity when analysing real data from a corpus is an area of future research.

---

[6] For the sake of simplicity we ignore the problem of inferring that the light is in the room.

7.3 Discourse Popping and the Nixon Diamond

Consider text (7).

(7) a. Guy experienced a lovely evening last night.
    b. He had a fantastic meal.
    c. He ate salmon.
    d. He devoured lots of cheese.
    e. He won a dancing competition.

Let the logical forms of the respective clauses (7a-e) be α, β, γ, δ and ε. The discourse structure for (7a-d) involves Cascaded Penguin Principles and Defeasible Modus Ponens as before. Use is made of the defeasible knowledge connecting eating cheese and salmon with having a meal and experiencing a lovely evening.

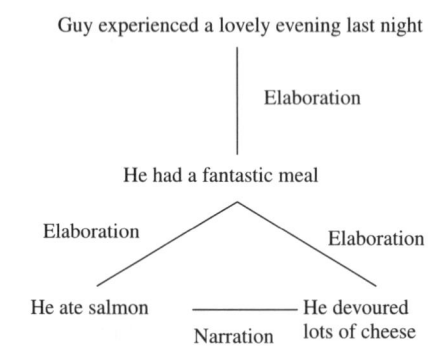

```
                Guy experienced a lovely evening last night
                                  |
                              Elaboration
                                  |
                        He had a fantastic meal
                          /              \
                   Elaboration         Elaboration
                      /                      \
             He ate salmon  ——————————  He devoured
                              Narration      lots of cheese
```

We study the attachment of ε to the preceding text in detail. The open clauses are δ, β and α. But intuitively ε is not related to δ at all, and so we must block the inference to Narration's consequent. $Elaboration(\beta, \delta)$ is in the KB because the interpretation of the text so far is taken to be fixed; $\langle \tau, \alpha, \varepsilon \rangle$, $\langle \tau, \delta, \varepsilon \rangle$ and $\langle \tau, \delta, \varepsilon \rangle$ are also in the KB. Rules 2 and 3 below are specifications of the rules introduced in Section 3.4; Rule 2 being obtained from Narration via Closure on the Right:

- **Rule 2**
  $\langle \tau, \beta, \varepsilon \rangle > \neg Elaboration(\beta, \varepsilon)$
- **Rule 3**
  $Elaboration(\beta, \delta) \wedge \neg Elaboration(\beta, \varepsilon) < \neg Narration(\delta, \varepsilon)$

The result is a 'Nixon Polygon'. There is *irresolvable conflict* between Narration on the one hand, and Rules 2 and 3 on the other because their antecedents are not logically related:

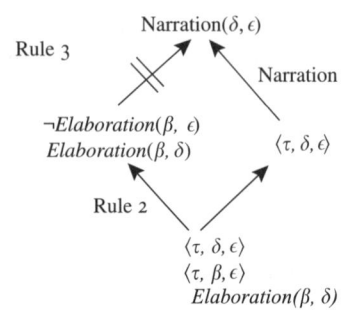

```
                         Narration(δ, ε)
               Rule 3    ↗          ↖
                       ✗              Narration
           ¬Elaboration(β, ε)
           Elaboration(β, δ)         ⟨τ, δ, ε⟩
                       ↑          ↗
                       Rule 2
                               ⟨τ, δ, ε⟩
                               ⟨τ, β, ε⟩
                               Elaboration(β, δ)
```

In CE, conflict is never resolved if the conflicting rules have unrelated antecedents (this is shown in the appendix). So neither *Narration*(δ, ε) nor ¬ *Narration*(δ, ε) are inferred from the above.

We assume that any KB that verifies $\langle \tau, \delta, \varepsilon \rangle$ but *fails* to verify any discourse relation between δ and ε is inconsistent. And because the linguistic processing is incremental, the interpretation of the preceding discourse is taken to be fixed. Consequently, the only assumption that can be dropped from the KB in order to ameliorate the inconsistency is $\langle \tau, \delta, \varepsilon \rangle$. So ε must be attached to α or β, but not δ. Using Cascaded Penguin Principles and Defeasible Modus Ponens, one infers *Elaboration*(α, ε) and *Narration*(β, ε), in agreement with intuitions.

The above shows that the Nixon Diamond provides the key to discourse popping: ε is attached to a constituent that dominates δ because a Nixon Diamond meant that ε couldn't be attached to δ itself.

7.4 Dudley Doorite and Text Ambiguity

We earlier indicated that interpreting text (9) requires Closure on the Right and Dudley Doorite.

(9) The bimetallic strip changed shape. The temperature fell.

We used these inferences to motivate the following causal law:

- **Change Causal Law**
  $\langle \tau, \alpha, \beta \rangle \land \textit{change}(\textit{strip}, \textit{me}(\alpha)) \land \textit{fall}(\textit{temperature}, \textit{me}(\beta)) > \textit{cause}(\textit{me}(\alpha), \textit{me}(\beta)) \lor \textit{cause}(\textit{me}(\beta), \textit{me}(\alpha))$

Now suppose we assume that the sentences in (9) are *not* dominated by a common topic. This conjecture is supported by standard heuristics for defining constraints on possible topics, which entail that sentences under a common topic should share actors and/or patients (cf. Grosz and Sidner 1986, Asher 1993). Then, by the contrapositive version of Common Topic for Narration, the relevant KB in analysing (9) verifies ¬ *Narration* (α, β). So although the antecedent to Narration is satisfied in analysing (9), *Narration* (α, β) cannot be inferred.

Closure on the Right and Dudley Doorite yield the following from Result and Explanation:

Closure on the Right on Result and Explanation

(i) $\langle \tau, \alpha, \beta \rangle \land \textit{cause}(\textit{me}(\alpha), \textit{m}(\beta)) > \textit{Result}(\alpha, \beta) \lor \textit{Explanation}(\alpha, \beta)$
(ii) $\langle \tau, \alpha, \beta \rangle \land \textit{cause}(\textit{me}(\beta), \textit{me}(\alpha)) > \textit{Result}(\alpha, \beta) \lor \textit{Explanation}(\alpha, \beta)$

Dudley Doorite on (i) and (ii)

(iii) $\langle \tau, \alpha, \beta \rangle \land (\textit{cause}(\textit{me}(\alpha), \textit{me}(\beta)) \lor \textit{cause}(\textit{me}(\beta), \textit{me}(\alpha))) > (\textit{Result}(\alpha, \beta) \lor \textit{Explanation}(\alpha, \beta))$

The antecedent of Change Causal Law is satisfied by the KB. So by Defeasible Modus Ponens (*cause*(*me*(α), *me*(β)) $\lor$ *cause*(*me*(β), *me*(α))) is inferred. By Defeasible Modus Ponens again on rule (iii), (21) is inferred.

(21) *Explanation* (α, β) $\lor$ *Result* (α, β)

Thus the discourse relation between the sentences in (9) is ambiguous.[7]

[7] Note that this is an informative ambiguity in that *Explanation*(α, β) $\lor$ *Result*(α, β) is not a tautology.

8 THE PLUPERFECT

We have so far examined how to infer discourse relations in simple past tensed texts. To explore what role the pluperfect plays in discourse, we first consider the following texts.

(22) ?Max poured a cup of coffee. He had entered the room.
(23) Max entered the room. He poured a cup of coffee.

Intuitively, the temporal order between entering the room and pouring a cup of coffee are the same in (22) and (23). So why is (22) awkward but (23) acceptable? Intuitively, we can find a connection between the events in (23) that is compatible with the tenses used; the connection is that Max entered the room so that he could pour himself a cup of coffee. On the other hand, this connection cannot be compatible with the tenses used in (22), since (22) is awkward. Theories that analyse the distinction between the simple past and pluperfect purely in terms of different relations between reference times and event times, rather than in terms of event-connections, fail to explain why (29) is acceptable but (22) is awkward.

Intuitively, a pluperfect clause β can be connected to a simple past tense clause α if β elaborates α (e.g. text (24)) or explains α (e.g. (25)).

(24) Max arrived late for work. He had taken the bus.
(25) The council built the bridge. The architect had drawn up the plans.

Indeed, it suffices for β to be *part of* an elaboration or explanation of α, for we can improve text (22) by adding to it a further clause that, together with the pluperfect clause, *explains* Max pouring the coffee (e.g. text (26), first cited in Caenepeel 1991):

(26) Max poured himself a cup of coffee. He had entered the room feeling depressed, but now felt much better.

Furthermore, pluperfect and simple past clauses can form a 'parallel' under a common topic, as in text (27) (cf. Asher 1993), and contrast each other, as in (28).

(27) Max was wrong. He had been wrong. He will always be wrong.
(28) Max got the answer wrong. But John had got the the answer right.

Both the contrast and parallels must be such that the event in the pluperfect happens before that in the simple past.

This seems to exhaust the possible connections between the simple past event and the pluperfect one. This is why (22) is awkward, for it is difficult to think of the circumstances under which the entering the room explains or elaborates pouring the coffee, and they clearly cannot form parallel or contrast. Of course, many more connections are allowed between two events described in the simple past. The task now is to formalise this intuition that the discourse role of the pluperfect is to restrict the kinds of discourse connections that can hold.

Let $C_{pp}(\alpha, \beta)$ mean that α and β are connected by the kind of discourse relation allowed between simple pasts and pluperfects: that is, β is (part of) an elaboration or explanation of α, or β and α form parallel or contrast, with the *event* described in β preceding that described in α. Then the discourse role of the pluperfect is captured as follows:

- **Connections When Changing Tense (CCT)**
  $\Box(\langle \tau, \alpha, \beta \rangle \wedge sp(\alpha) \wedge pp(\beta) \rightarrow C_{pp}(\alpha, \beta))$

It's important to stress that $C_{pp}(\alpha, \beta)$ *doesn't* necessarily follow if β is simple past rather than pluperfect. For simple past tensed texts, more connections are permissible, e.g., *Narration*(α, β).

Given the above rule one can explain the awkwardness of (22). If the WK is stated as intuitions would dictate, then the KB in analysing (22) would be one where the clauses described in (22) are not related by C_{pp}. So by the contrapositive version of CCT and the fact that information states incorporate modal closure, the sentences are not related by a discourse relation; for $\langle \tau, \alpha, \beta \rangle$ must be false. This makes (22) incoherent. Analysing (26) would involve relating whole discourse segments to a clause by a discourse relation; that is, the second and third clauses *together* must stand in the relation *Explanation* to the first. Providing such analysis is beyond our scope here since we have concentrated on relations between single sentences (but see Lascarides and Asher (1993) for a detailed discussion of such cases).

CCT captures the relevant distinction between the use of the simple past tense and the pluperfect as illustrated in (29) and (30).

(29) Max slipped. He had spilt a bucket of water.
(30) Max slipped. He spilt a bucket of water.

Intuitively, the discourse relation in (29) is *Explanation* and in (30) it is *Narration*. This difference must arise solely in virtue of the pluperfect. The analysis of (30) is exactly like that of (1): by Defeasible Modus Ponens on Narration, it's narrative. Now consider (29). The relevant KB satisfies the antecedents of Narration, States Overlap, and the indefeasible law CCT. CCT entails $C_{pp}(\alpha, \beta)$, where α and β are respectively the logical forms of the clauses. Now if spilling the water and slipping are connected so that either the spilling explains, elaborates, parallels, or contrasts the slipping, then normally the spilling explains the slipping. This intuition is reflected in the following law, where *Info*(α, β), is the gloss for "α describes Max slipping and β describes Max spilling a bucket of water".

- **Slipping Law**
  $\langle \tau, \alpha, \beta \rangle \wedge C_{pp}(\alpha, \beta) \wedge \mathit{Info}(\alpha, \beta) > \mathit{Explanation}(\beta, \alpha)$

Thus the KB satisfies the antecedents to the above law as well. Note that the Slipping Law is different from the causal laws considered so far, because $C_{pp}(\alpha, \beta)$ is in the antecedent. This added conjunct is crucial to the plausibility of the above law concerning spilling and slipping. For intuitively, there is *no* WK that normally the spilling caused the slipping if the choice of connection between these events encompasses the full range of possibilities, including that the slipping caused the spilling. It must be also stressed that this law plays no part in the analysis of (30); the relevant KB doesn't verify its antecedent, because $C_{pp}(\alpha, \beta)$ is not in the KB.

We must investigate what follows from Narration, States Overlap, and the Slipping Law in the interpretation of (29). The Slipping Law and States Overlap don't conflict, but they each conflict with Narration and are more specific than it. By the Penguin Principle, $\mathit{Explanation}(\alpha, \beta)$ and $\mathit{overlap}(me(\alpha), me(\beta))$ are inferred; thus the antecedent to Background is verified and $\mathit{Background}(\alpha, \beta)$ is inferred. So, spilling the water explains *why* Max slipped, and the consequences of spilling the water are still in force when Max slips.

These texts show that although simple past tensed sentences are equivalent to the corresponding pluperfects they play distinct roles in discourse. Our formalism reflects the intuition that the pluperfect acts as a syntactic discourse marker to indicate that only a restricted set of discourse relations is possible, thus yielding different inferences about discourse structure. We have used indefeasible and defeasible inference on LK to explain this and not formal devices like reference times.

We have investigated how the pluperfect sentences are related to simple past tensed ones. We now evaluate how pluperfect sentences are related to each other. Consider (31).

(31) a. Max arrived late for work.
b. He had taken the bus.
c. He had totalled his car.
d. His boss summoned him to his office.

The theory presented here is rich enough to reflect the intuition that each pluperfect sentence in (31) explains the previous pluperfect sentence. Let the logical forms of (31a) to (31d) be respectively α, β, γ and δ. The discourse relation between α and β is worked out in an analogous way to that in (29): *Background*(α, β) and *Explanation*(α, β) are inferred. α and β are both open clauses to γ. Again, by a similar inference to that for text (29), *Background*(α, γ) and *Explanation*(α, γ) are inferred.

In connecting β to γ, the KB satisfies the antecedents of States Overlap and Narration. There is also a causal law relating totalling the car and taking the bus. By the Penguin Principle, the consequents of States Overlap and the Causal Law are inferred, and subsequently, we infer *Background*(α, γ) and *Explanation*(β, γ).

The open clauses to δ are α, β and γ. A Nixon Polygon occurs when attempting to attach δ to γ and δ to β in a similar way to that which occurred in (7) described earlier. This time, we use a constraint on Narration defined in terms of *Explanation* rather than *Elaboration*:

- *Explanation*(β, γ) $\land$ $\neg$ *Explanation*(β, δ) $>$ $\neg$(*Narration*(γ, δ)

Thus δ must attach to α. By Defeasible Modus Ponens on Narration, *Narration*(α, δ) is inferred. Thus the DRP representing (31) is (31').

(31') {{α, β, γ, δ}, {*Explanation*(α, β), *Background*(α, β) *Explanation*(α, γ), *Background*(α,γ) *Explanation*(β, γ), *Background*(β, γ) *Narration*(α, δ)}}

```
Max arrived late for work  ————  His boss summoned
          |         /                him to his office
          |        /
      Explanation /
          |      / Explanation
          |     /
      He had taken the bus
          |    /
          |   / Explanation
          |  /
      He had totalled the car
```

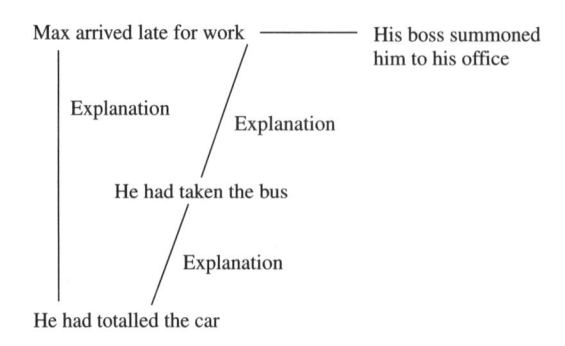

The pluperfect sentences in (31) each create further subordinations in the discourse structure. But pluperfects don't necessarily do this. Consider (32).

(32) a. Alexis was a really good girl by the time she went to bed yesterday.
b. She had done her homework.
c. She had helped her Mum with housework.

d. She had played piano.
e. We all felt good about it.

Suppose the logical forms of (32a) to (32e) are respectively α to ε. By a similar argument to the one above, common-sense inference yields *Explanation* (α, β), *Explanation* (α, γ), and *Explanation* (α, δ). World knowledge does not yield any preference as to the connections between the *event* in γ and the *event* in the open clause β. So β and γ satisfy the antecedents of States Overlap and Narration, and so a Cascaded Penguin Principle yields *Background*(β, γ). Similarly, we infer *Background*(γ, δ). And as in (31), a Nixon Diamond gives rise to discourse 'popping' for ε, and in fact we obtain *Background*(α, ε).

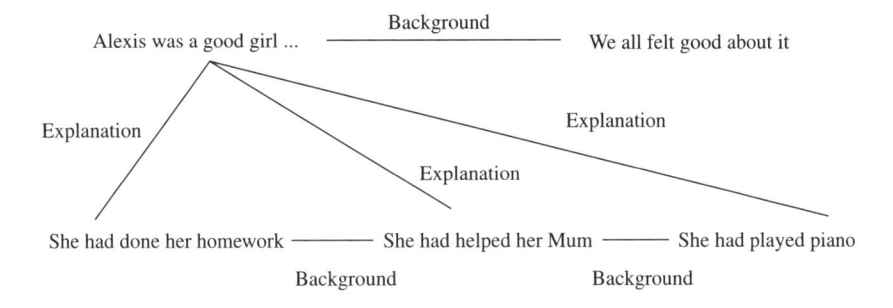

```
                          Background
    Alexis was a good girl ...  ─────────────  We all felt good about it
                 /│\                                   
     Explanation/ │ \                        Explanation
               /  │  \                      /
              /   │   Explanation          /
             /    │    \                  /
   She had done her homework ─── She had helped her Mum ─── She had played piano
                       Background                  Background
```

The fact that (32b–d) form background to each other entails nothing about how the events they describe are temporally ordered, for we cannot infer from *Background* where the consequent states start relative to each other, and the corresponding events are placed at the start of these consequent states. This is in agreement with the intuitive interpretation of (32), in contrast to the order of events inferred from Narration when analysing the corresponding simple past tensed text (33).

(33) Alexis did her homework. She helped her Mum with housework. She played piano.

The events described by a sequence of pluperfect clauses will occur in their textual order only if that order is inferrable from WK or other temporal information present in the text (cf. (34)).

(34) Max arrived at the summit at midday. He had got up at 5:30 a.m, had prepared his lunch, had chosen his route, and had passed base camp before 7 a.m.

This is in agreement with the claim made in Kamp (1991), that the temporal order of events described by a sequence of pluperfect clauses depends on the discourse type.

9 CONCLUSION

We have proposed a framework for calculating the structure of text, where the contributions made by syntax, semantic content, causal knowledge, and linguistic knowledge, are all explored within a single logic. The distinct discourse relations that are prevalent in texts with similar syntax arose from defeasible laws, by using intuitively compelling patterns of defeasible entailment.

We argued that a full account of the simple past and pluperfect tenses exemplify the inference patterns of Defeasible Modus Ponens, the Penguin Principle, the Nixon Diamond, Closure on the Right, and Dudley Doorite. Closure on the Right and Dudley Doorite provided the key to discourse structure ambiguity. The Nixon Diamond provided the key to 'popping' from subordinate discourse structure. And the Penguin Principle captured the intuition that the reader never ignores information relevant to calculating discourse structure.

We examined the effects of WK and LK on interpretation in a logical context. Consequently, the traditional DRT syntactic-based account for calculating relations between reference times in order to determine temporal structure was not needed. The distinct discourse roles of the simple past and the pluperfect were brought out through a mixture of defeasible and indefeasible reasoning, rather than by different relations between reference times determined in syntax.

APPENDIX

The language

The basic building blocks of DRPs are DRSs and discourse relations between them. In order to simplify the proofs in this appendix, we make some simplifying assumptions about the language for reasoning about discourse structure. In particular, the language in this appendix will not make full use of the truth definitions of DRSs. We are able to simplify things in this way because the only semantic information that's *part* of a DRS and relevant to constructing discourse structure—such as the information that the event described is Max falling—can be represented as a predicate which takes the DRS as an argument. In other words, for simplicity, we re-write *fall(max, me(α))* as *Max fall(α)*. The second simplification concerns the function *me* (standing for "main eventuality"). In the text, *me* is a partial function *me*: DRS. $\rightarrow U_{DRS}$, where U_α is the universe of the DRS α and *me(α)* is the main eventuality discourse referent as defined in Asher (1993). But we can for the sake of reasoning about DRP construction rephrase the function *me* and relations involving main events of DRSs as relations on the DRSs themselves. These two moves make the proof theory simpler. In particular our language will remain that of propositional logic. We call this propositional language for reasoning about DRP construction L_{DRP}.

We can essentially treat DRSs as atomic propositions in L_{DRP}. But this simplification comes with a cost. L_{DRP} is capable of expressing the fact that a DRS is true, but this assignment is independent of the assignment of truth values to DRSs given in the standard truth definition for DRSs below. If we wish, we may restrict our attention to those L_{DRP} models in which the assignment of truth values to DRSs and to predicates involving DRSs reflects the values assigned in the standard interpretation of DRSs. But we leave open the question of how the proofs in this appendix must be extended so as to apply to this class of models.

The standard truth definition for DRSs

We give here the semantics of atomic DRSs, which are the only kind used in this paper. A full truth definition for DRT can be found in Kamp and Reyle (in press).

- If ψ is an n-ary DRS predicate and $x_1, \ldots x_n$ are discourse references, then $\psi(x_1, \ldots, x_n)$ is an atomic condition.
- If x_1 and x_2 are discourse references (of any kind), then $x_1 = x_2$ is an atomic condition.
- A DRS is a pair $\langle U, Con \rangle$, where U is a set of discourse referents, and Con is a set of conditions.

The semantics of DRSs are defined with respect to a model $\langle W, T, D, E, [\![\ ]\!] \rangle$, where W is a non-empty set of possible worlds; T is a non-empty set of time points; D is a function from W into a family of non-empty sets ($D(w)$ is the domain of individuals in w); E is a function from W into a family of non-empty sets ($E(w)$ is the domain of eventualities in w); and $[\![\ ]\!]$ is an interpretation function that assigns to DRS predicates functions from W to $\wp(\cup_{n \in w}(D \cup E)^n \cup T)$.

A *proper embedding* of a DRS K in a model M is defined in terms of a function from discourse referents into objects O_M in M ($O_M = D_M \cup E_M \cup T_M$). Any such function from discourses references into O_M is an embedding function.

Define g to *extend* an embedding function f to an embedding of K in M at w (written $g \supseteq_K f$) just in case $Dom(g) = Dom(f) \cup U_K$.

Define an *external anchor* A for K in M to be a partial function from U_K into $\cup_{w \in W} D_w \cup T$, such that if *now* occurs in U_K then $A(now)$ is the utterance time of the discourse, and if i occurs in U_K, then $A(i)$ is the speaker of the discourse.

Now we define a *proper embedding* f of K in M at w (written $[f, K]^M w$) with respect to a possibly empty external anchor A for K in M and we define satisfaction of a condition in M relative to an embedding function f for the DRS in which the conditions occur at w (written $M \models_{w,f}$).

(i) If ψ is an atomic condition of the form $\phi(x_1, \ldots, x_n)n$ then $M \models_{w,f} \psi$ iff $\langle f, (x_1), \ldots, f(x_n) \rangle \in [\![\phi]\!](w)$.
(ii) If ψ is an atomic condition of the form $x_1 = x_2$, then, $M \models_{w,f} \psi$ iff $f(x_1) = f(x_2)$
(iii) If A is an external anchor for K in M, then $[f, K]^M_{w,g}$ iff (i) $f \supseteq_{kg}$; (ii) $A \subseteq f$;
   (iii) $\forall \theta \in Con_K$, $M \models_{w,f} \theta$.

DEFINITION OF MAIN EVENTUALITY: To define $me(\alpha)$, we assume the theory is expressed in DRT with the syntax analysed in GPSG. Under these circumstances, the definition is as follows: for a non-conjunctive clause α, $me(\alpha)$ is the eventuality discourse entity introduced by the verb phrase that heads the clause.

The language L_{DRP}

The language of L_{DRP} is built recursively in the usual way:

- DRS names α, β, γ are well-formed expressions of L_{DRP} and DRP names τ and τ' are well-formed expressions of L_{DRP}.
- If α is a DRS name or DRP name, then $\downarrow \alpha$ is a well-formed formula (WFF) of L_{DRP}.
- If $\alpha_1, \ldots, \alpha_n$ are DRS names, and p_n is an n-place predicate on DRS names, then $p_n(\alpha_1, \ldots, \alpha_n)$ is an atomic WFF.
- If φ and ψ are WFF, then $\varphi \wedge \psi, \varphi \vee \psi, \neg \varphi, \varphi \rightarrow \psi, \varphi > \psi$ and $\Box \varphi$ are WFF.
- If τ is a DRP name and α and β are DRS names, then $\langle \tau, \alpha, \beta \rangle$ is a WFF.
- If ϕ, ψ and χ are WFF, then $(\phi, \psi) > \chi$ is a WFF.

The truth definition for L_{DRP}

The well-formed expressions of the language are defined with respect to a model $\langle W, *, f \rangle$ for the language, where f assigns DRS and DRP names functions from W to propositions (which in turn are functions from W to $\{0, 1\}$), and assigns predicate constants functions from W to suitable sets of propositions.

(a) Where β is either a name constant or a predicate constant,
$[\![\beta]\!]^M(w) = f(\beta)(w)$. Where β is a DRS or DRP name, $[\![\downarrow \beta]\!]^M(w) = (f(\beta)(w))(w)$.

(b) Where β is an atomic WFF $p^n(d_1, \ldots, d_n)$,
$[\![\beta]\!]^M(w) = 1$ iff $\langle [\![d_1]\!]^M(w), \ldots, [\![d_n]\!]^M(w) \rangle$ belongs to $[\![p^n]\!]^M(w)$.

(c) $[\![\neg A]\!]^M(w) = 1$ iff $[\![A]\!]^M(w) = 0$.

(d) $[\![A \wedge B]\!]^M(w) = 1$ if $[\![A]\!]^M(w) = 1$ and $[\![\beta]\!]^M(w) = 1$.
$\rightarrow$ and $\vee$ are defined in terms of $\wedge$ and $\neg$ in the usual way.

(e) $[\![\phi > \psi]\!]^M(w) = 1$ iff $*(w, [\![\phi]\!]^M) \subseteq [\![\psi]\!]^M$.

(f) $[\![\Box \phi]\!]^M(w) = 1$ iff for all w', $[\![\phi]\!]^M(w') = 1$.

(g) $[\![(\phi, \psi) > \chi]\!]^M(w) = 1$ iff $*(w, [\![\phi]\!]) \cap *(w, [\![\psi]\!]) \subseteq [\![\chi]\!]$.

Constraints on the model

The function $*$ must satisfy the following constraints for the model to be admissible:

- **Facticity**
  $*(w, p) \subseteq p$
- **Specificity**
  If $p \subseteq q$, $*(w, p) \cap *(w, q) = \phi$, then $*(w, q) \cap p = \phi$
- **Dudley Doorite**
  $*(w, p \cup q) \subseteq *(w, p) \cup *(w, q)$

Facticity captures the intuition that whatever the properties of a normal bird, one is that he's a bird. Specificity captures the intuition that normal birds aren't penguins. Dudley Doorite captures the intuition that if Quakers are pacifists and Republicans are pacifists, then Quakers and Republicans are pacifists.[8] We will henceforth restrict ourselves to admissible models.

Monotonic proof in CE

The monotonic theory of CE in Asher and Morreau (1991) is to be strengthened by the following axiom schemata which reflect S5 'modal closure' instead of just logical closure.

(A1) ϕ where ϕ is a tautology.
(A2) $\phi > \phi$
(A3) $(\phi > \psi \wedge \zeta > \psi) \rightarrow ((\phi \vee \zeta) > \psi)$
(A4) $((\phi \psi) > \bot \wedge \Box (\phi \rightarrow \psi)) \rightarrow \psi > \neg \phi$
(A5) $(\phi > \psi) \rightarrow ((\phi, \psi) > \psi)$
(A6) $((\phi, \psi) > \chi) \leftrightarrow ((\psi, \phi) > \chi)$

---

[8] In fact, Specificity follows from Dudley Doorite.

(A7) $(\phi > \chi \wedge \psi > \chi) \rightarrow (\phi, \psi) > \chi$
(A8) $(\phi, \phi) > \psi \rightarrow \phi > \psi$
(A9) $\Box(\phi \leftrightarrow \psi) \rightarrow ((\phi > \zeta) \leftrightarrow (\psi > \zeta))$
(A10) $\Box(\phi \rightarrow \psi) \rightarrow ((\zeta > \phi) \rightarrow (\zeta > \psi))$
(A11) $\Box \phi \rightarrow \phi$
(A12) $\Box(\phi \rightarrow \psi) \rightarrow (\Box \phi \rightarrow \Box \psi)$
(A13) $\Diamond \phi \rightarrow \Box \Diamond \phi$.
(R) $((\phi \rightarrow \psi) \wedge \phi) \rightarrow \psi$
(R1) If $\vdash \phi$, then $\vdash \Box \phi$

Let the above axioms and rules be called T_0. We will write $\vdash_{T_0}$ for the derivability notion, and we define the L_{DRP} consequence to be the following:

- L_{DRP} **Consequence**
  $\Gamma \models_{L_{DRP}} \phi$ iff for every admissible L_{DRP} model M and for every world w in W_M if every element of Γ is true at w in M then ϕ is true at w in M.

Fact:

$$\Gamma \vdash_{T_0} \phi \Rightarrow \Gamma \models_{L_{DRP}} \phi$$

To prove completeness, we construct a canonical model in the usual fashion for propositional modal logic, except that we add a construction for *. Each world in the set of worlds ☺ in the canonical model is defined to be a maximal consistent set of sentences, and we may for each such set Γ and each formula ψ define:

$$\Gamma_\psi^+ = \{\phi : (\psi > \phi) \in \Gamma\}$$
$$\Gamma_\psi^- = \{\phi : \neg(\psi > \phi) \in \Gamma\}$$
$$*(\Gamma, \llbracket \psi \rrbracket) = \{\Gamma' \in W : \Gamma_\phi^+ \subseteq \Gamma'\}$$

This construction suffices to yield a canonical model such that one can then prove:

Fact:

$$\Gamma \models_{L_{DRP}} \phi \Rightarrow \Gamma \vdash_{T_0} \phi$$

We mention one other result about propositional CE, which one can prove using the filtration method (cf. Chellas 1980):

Fact: T_0 has the finite model property, and so is decidable.

The nonmonotonic part of CE

Just as in Asher and Morreau (1991), we define CE entailment, written $\approx$, in terms of the function * on information states, the update function +, and the normalisation function N. These three functions are defined as follows:

DEFINITION OF * ON INFORMATION STATES:

$*(s, p) = \cup_{w \in s} *(w, p)$.

DEFINITION OF $+$: $s + \Gamma = \{w \in S : W \models \Gamma\}$.

DEFINITION OF NORMALISATION:

$N *(s,p) = \{w \in s : w \notin p \setminus *(s,p)\}$ if $*(s, p) \cap S \neq \emptyset$
$= s$ otherwise

The definition of $\approx$ uses the notion of *normalisation chain* derived from N as follows:

DEFINITION OF $Ant(\Gamma)$: Where Γ is a set of sentences of L_{DRP} we define $Ant(\Gamma)$ to be $\{\phi: \phi > \psi$ occurs positively as a subset of a formula of $\Gamma\}$
$Cons(\Gamma)$—the set of consequents of conditionals in Γ—is defined analogously to $Ant(\Gamma)$.

DEFINITION OF Γ-NORMALISATION CHAIN. For $\Gamma \subseteq L_{DRP}$, the Γ-*normalisation chain* with respect to an enumeration μ of $Ant(\Gamma)$ is defined to be the following sequence:

$$N_\nu^0 = s$$
$$N_\nu^{\alpha+1} = N(N_\nu^\alpha(\phi_i)), \text{ where } \alpha = \lambda + n + 1, \text{ and } \nu(\phi_i) = n + 1$$
$$N_\nu^\lambda = \cap_{\mu \in \lambda} N_\nu^\mu.$$

DEFINITION OF $\approx$: $\Gamma \approx \phi$ iff for any Γ-normalisation chain C beginning from $\copyright + \Gamma$, $C * \approx$ where C^* is the fixpoint of C, where $\copyright$ is the set of worlds constructed in the canonical model.

When Γ is finite note that $Ant(\Gamma)$ is finite. And when $Ant(\Gamma)$ is finite and Γ has no embedded $>$-formulae within $>$-formulae, it is easy to see that all normalisation chains defined with respect to $Ant(\Gamma)$ reach a fixed point after finitely many normalisations. Together with the fact that T_0 has the finite model property, we can show the following:

Fact: $\approx$ is decidable.

We will be working in the canonical model $\copyright$. So in particular we will often define information states for various theories in terms of the operations of Asher and Morreau (1991)—e.g. the information state S corresponding to a theory T will be defined as $S = \copyright + T$. The following definitions will also be useful.

DEFINITION. Let T be a theory.
$Formula(T) = \{\phi: \phi \in Ant(T) \vee \phi \in Cons(T) \vee T \models \phi\}$.

DEFINITION. Let T be a theory. Then ϕ, ψ are T-independent iff any boolean combination of ϕ and ψ is consistent with T.

DEFINITION. Two sets of formulae X, Y are T-independent iff $\forall \phi \in X, \forall \psi \in Y, \phi, \psi$, are T-independent.

Fact: Let T be any theory, and let $T_1, \ldots, T_n$ be subtheories such that every $Formula(T_i)$ and $Formula(T_j), i \neq j$ are T-independent. Then $Formula(T_i) \cap Formula(T_j) = \emptyset$.

DEFINITION. A T survivor world w is a world that survives on every normalisation chain defined with respect to $Ant(T)$ and which verifies T in $\copyright$.

DEFINITION. A default theory is a set of $>$ conditionals.

DEFINITION. $* \upharpoonright (T, w)$ is the $*$ function restricted to $Ant(T)$ at w.

DEFINITION. $Th(w \upharpoonright L_T) = \{\phi \in L_{DRP} \cap L_T : w \models \phi\}$.

We will use the term *theory* here in a colloquial sense: we will not assume as is standard in logic that a theory is closed under some notion of logical consequence. Rather, our theories are collections of sentences that constitute the reader's knowledge, as described in the paper. We now prove the lemmas that enable us to divide these theories into subtheories in CE under special circumstances. These will be used to model the Cascaded Penguin Principle.

IRRELEVANCE LEMMA. Suppose T is a theory and $T_1, \ldots, T_n, T_i \subseteq T$ are default theories such that $\cup T_i = T$. If $Formula(T_i)$ and $Formula(T_j)$ for $i \neq j$ are T-independent, then for any T_i and T_i survivor world w_i, if each T_j for $j=1,\ldots n$ has a survivor world then there is a T survivor world w_1 such that $* \uparrow (T_i, w_1) = * \uparrow (T_i, w_i)$ and $Th(w_1 \uparrow Formula(T_i)) = Th(w_i \uparrow Formula(T_i))$.

Proof. Suppose $T_1, \ldots, T_n$ are as above and suppose all the individual T_j have survivor worlds. Let w_0 be a T_i survivor world. By assumption T_1 has a survivor world w_1. By independence, $\exists w'_1$ such that w'_1 is a survivor world for T_1 and $Th(w'_1, \uparrow Formula(T_i)) = Th(w_0, \uparrow Formula(T_i))$. Furthermore, by the assumption of independence, $Ant(T_1) \cap Ant(T_i) = \emptyset$. So we may choose w'_1 such that for each $p \in Ant(T_i)$, $*(w'_1, p) = *(w_0, p)$. Since by hypothesis each T_j is independent from T_i, we can repeat this for $T_2, \ldots, T_n$ and so construct a T survivor world.

STRENGTHENED IRRELEVANCE LEMMA. Suppose T is a theory and for $T_1 \ldots, T_n$, $T_i \subseteq T$ are default theories such that $\cup T_i = T$. If $Formula(T_i) - \Delta$ and $Formula(T_j) - \Delta$ for $i \neq j$ are T-independent for some $\Delta \subseteq L_{T_k} \cap \ldots \cap L_{T_m}$ and there are survivor worlds $w_k, \ldots, w_\mu$ for $T_k, \ldots, T_m$ respectively such that for each $\delta \in \Delta$ and each w, if $w' \in \{w_k, \ldots, w_\mu\}$ then $*(\llbracket \delta \rrbracket, w) = *(\llbracket \delta \rrbracket, w')$, then for any T_i survivor world w_0, there is a world w_1 such that w_1 is a T survivor, provided T has a survivor. And further $* \uparrow (T_i, w_1) = *(T_i, w_0)$, $Th(w_1 \uparrow Formula(T_i)) = Th(W_0 \uparrow Formula(T_j))$.

Proof. Suppose again w is a T_i survivor world and suppose that T_1 has a survivor world w_1. If every T_i formula is T-independent of every T_1 formula, then by the irrelevance lemma we have a survivor for T_i and T_1. Now suppose that T_i and T_1 share a common set of formulas Δ. By hypothesis the propositions p defined by the common formulas in $Ant(T_i)$ and $Ant(T_1)$ are such that any T_i survivor world w_i, $*(w_i, p) = *(w_1, p)$. Again by using the irrelevance lemma on the independent formulae in $Formula(T_j) - \Delta$, we can show that there is a survivor w_2 such that $Th(w_2 \uparrow Formula(T_i)) = Th(w \uparrow Formula(T_1))$. Again by extending the argument to all the subtheories, we get the desired result. □

It seems that we may strengthen the irrelevance still further in the case where for each of the common formulae in Δ among the theories $T_k, \ldots, T_m$ there are survivor worlds $w_k, \ldots, w_m$ that can be ordered in such a way that $*\llbracket \delta \rrbracket, w_j) \subseteq *\llbracket \delta \rrbracket, w_i)$ for $i \leq j$ then a T survivor world may be constructed from any T_i survivor by following the procedure already outlined and then taking for the common predicates the strongest or smallest set of normal worlds. That a world w is a T_i survivor depends solely on the structural relationship between the survivor world and the set of normal worlds it assigns to $\llbracket \phi \rrbracket$ for $\phi \in Ant(T_i)$. By the hypothesis and the construction procedure suggested, this relationship is preserved. We formalise this observation in the following lemma, but first some definitions:

DEFINITION. Suppose $T_1, \ldots, T_n$ are sets of $>$-sentences, such that $T = T_1 \cup \ldots \cup T_n$ and either:

(a) $Formula(T_1), \ldots, Formula(T_n)$ are T-independent (if distinct), or
(b) $T_j \ldots T_m$ have a common set of formulae Δ such that
$Formula(T_1), \ldots, Formula(T_{j-1})$,
$Formula(T_j) - \Delta, \ldots, Formula(T_m) - \Delta$,
$Formula(T_{m+1}), \ldots, Formula(T_n)$
are T-independent (if distinct), and there are survivor worlds $w_j, \ldots, w_m$ of $T_j, \ldots, T_m$ that can be ordered such that for each $\delta \in \Delta$ $*(w_i, \delta) \subseteq *(w_j, \delta)$ for $i < j$.

Then we say $T_1, \ldots, T_n$ has the *chain survivor property*.

DEFINITION. Suppose $T_1,\ldots,T_m$ are theories such that $T_1 \approx \phi_1$ and $\phi_1 \in T_2$, $T_2 \approx \phi_2$ and $\phi_2 \in T_3,\ldots,T_{m-1} \approx \phi_{m-1}$ and $\phi_{m-1} \in T_m$ and that $\cup\, T_i \backslash \{\phi_1,\ldots,\phi_m\} = T$. Then we say that $T_1,\ldots,T_m$ are *default expanded subtheories of T.*

STARKLY STRENGTHENED IRRELEVANCE LEMMA (SSI). Suppose T is a theory and $T_1,\ldots,T_n$ are default expanded subtheories of T. If $Formula(T_i) - \Delta$, $Formula(T_j) - \Delta$, are T-independent for $i \neq j$ for some set $\Delta \subseteq L_{T_k} \cap \cdots \cap L_{T_m}$ and there are survivor worlds $w_k,\ldots,w_m$ for $T_k,\ldots,T_m$ respectively such that for each $\delta \in \Delta$ such that $T_k,\ldots,T_m$ have the chain survivor property with respect to δ, then for any T_i survivor world w_0 there is a world w_1 such that w_1 is a T survivor and $*(w_1, \psi) = *(w_0, \psi)$ for all independent formulae in $Formula(T_i)$ and for any common formula $\delta \in \Delta$, $*(w_1, [\![\delta]\!]) \subseteq *(w_0, [\![\delta]\!])$ and if $w_0 \in S_i \cap *(w, [\![\delta]\!])$ then $w_1 \in S_i \cap *(w, [\![\delta]\!])$.

COROLLARY. Given a theory T and subtheories $T_1,\ldots T_n$ such that $Formula(T_i) - \Delta$ and $Formula(T_j) - \Delta$ are T-independent for $i \neq j$ for some set $\Delta \subseteq T_k \cap \cdots \cap T_m$ and these subtheories have the chain survivor property with respect to any $\delta \in \Delta$, then if $T_i \approx \phi$, then $T \approx \phi$.

The proof of this follows from the fact that for any T_i subtheory the nonmonotonic consequences are verified by the construction of a survivor world (see Propositions 1–6 in Asher and Morreau 1991). By the starkly strengthened irrelevance lemma (SSI) we can construct a survivor world that also survives through all of the normalisation chains defined by $Ant(T)$.

We now turn to the patterns that are commonly used in this paper to explain the examples. There are three: the Cascaded Penguin Principle, the Nixon Polygon, and the Double Penguin Principle. We give a short analysis of each one within this framework.

We will make use of the following fact: If A is an admissible model of L_{DRP} in which there is a T-survivor world w then the theory of w is an element of ☺. We will plan to construct small models to verify the defeasible inference patterns that we use.

The cascaded Penguin Principle

Consider text (2).

(2) Max fell. John pushed him.

The theory T relevant to this example consists of the following:
The Basic Axioms

$\langle \tau, \alpha, \beta \rangle > Narration(\alpha, \beta)$
$\langle \tau, \alpha, \beta \rangle \wedge Cause(\beta, \alpha) > Explanation(\alpha, \beta)$
$\langle \tau, \alpha, \beta \rangle \wedge Info(\alpha, \beta) > Cause(\beta, \alpha)$

The Axioms of Temporality

$\Box(Cause(\beta, \alpha) \rightarrow \neg Narration(\alpha, \beta))$
$\Box(Narration(\alpha, \beta) \rightarrow \neg Explanation(\alpha, \beta))$

The information state S_0 that is to be normalised contains all this information. In addition it verifies: $\langle \tau, \alpha, \beta \rangle$ and $Info(\alpha, \beta)$. And by axiom (A4) we also have:

$\langle \tau, \alpha, \beta \rangle > \neg Cause(\beta, \alpha)$
$\langle \tau, \alpha, \beta \rangle > \neg Info(\beta, \alpha)$

We will isolate the following default expanded subtheories of T that allow us to use the SSI.

T_1:

$\langle \tau, \alpha, \beta \rangle \wedge \mathit{Info}(\alpha, \beta)$
$\langle \tau, \alpha, \beta \rangle > \mathit{Narration}(\alpha, \beta)$
$\langle \tau, \alpha, \beta \rangle \wedge \mathit{Info}(\alpha, \beta) > \mathit{Cause}(\beta, \alpha)$
$\langle \tau, \alpha, \beta \rangle \wedge \mathit{Info}(\alpha, \beta) > \langle \tau, \alpha, \beta \rangle$
$\langle \tau, \alpha, \beta \rangle \wedge \mathit{Info}(\alpha, \beta) > \neg \mathit{Narration}(\alpha, \beta)$
$\Box(\mathit{Cause}(\beta, \alpha) \to \neg \mathit{Narration}(\alpha, \beta))$
$\Box(\mathit{Narration}(\alpha, \beta) \to \neg \mathit{Explanation}(\alpha, \beta))$

T_2:

$\langle \tau, \alpha, \beta \rangle \wedge \mathit{Cause}(\beta, \alpha)$
$\langle \tau, \alpha, \beta \rangle > \mathit{Narration}(\alpha, \beta)$
$\langle \tau, \alpha, \beta \rangle \wedge \mathit{Cause}(\beta, \alpha) > \mathit{Explanation}(\alpha, \beta)$
$\langle \tau, \alpha, \beta \rangle \wedge \mathit{Cause}(\beta, \alpha) > \langle \tau, \alpha, \beta \rangle$
$\Box(\mathit{Narration}(\alpha, \beta) \to \neg \mathit{Explanation}(\alpha, \beta))$

T_1 and T_2 have common formulas except for $\mathit{Info}(\alpha, \beta)$, which is independent of all the others. We want to check that T_1 and T_2 have the chain survivor property with respect to their common vocabulary. Of course, all this can only be checked given the construction of an appropriate T_1 and T_2 survivor world and checking the properties. First, we turn to a T_1 survivor world. w_0 below is an appropriate T_1 survivor world.

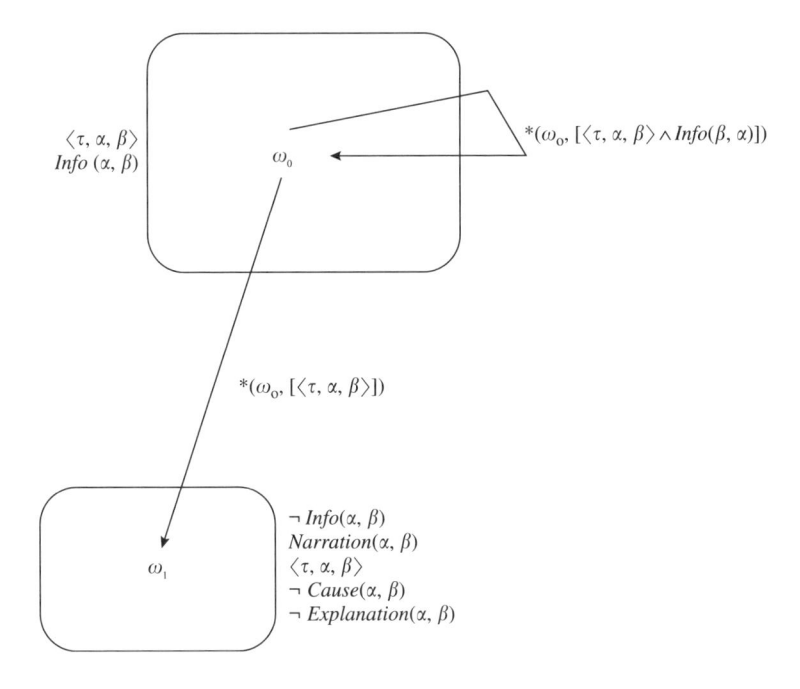

The normal worlds above (drawn as the quadrangles) verify the formulae to their sides. It can be checked that the model above is an admissible L_{DRP} model subject to the following proviso: for any proposition $p \neq [\![\langle \tau, \alpha, \beta \rangle \wedge \mathit{Info}(\alpha, \beta)]\!]$ and $p \neq [\![\langle \tau, \alpha, \beta \rangle]\!]$, $*(w_1, p) = *(w_0, p) = p$.

We now show that w_0 is a survivor world for T_1. Typically in CE we do so by induction on the length of normalisation chains. Given that $Ant(T_0)$ is finite, however, the chains are finite; in fact there are just two sorts of normalisations one with $[\![\langle \tau, \alpha, \beta \rangle]\!]$ and one with $[\![\langle \tau, \alpha, \beta \rangle \wedge Info(\alpha, \beta)]\!]$ The information state S_0 verifies the axioms and the information $\langle \tau, \alpha, \beta \rangle$ and $Info(\alpha, \beta)$. So clearly, $w_0 \in S_0$.

LEMMA 1. If $w_0 \in S$, then $w_0 \in N^*(S, p)$, where $p \in \{[\![\langle \tau, \alpha, \beta \rangle]\!], [\![\langle \tau, \alpha, \beta \rangle \wedge Info(\alpha, \beta)]\!]\}$.

Proof. Suppose $w_0 \in S_0$ and $\phi = [\![\langle \tau, \alpha, \beta \rangle \wedge Info(\alpha, \beta)]\!]$. $w_0 \in *(w_0, [\![\langle \tau, \alpha, \beta \rangle \wedge Info(\alpha, \beta)]\!])$ and so $w_0 \in *(S, [\![\langle \tau, \alpha, \beta \rangle \wedge Info(\alpha, \beta)]\!])$ and so

$N^*(S, [\![\langle \tau, \alpha, \beta \rangle \wedge Info(\alpha, \beta)]\!])$
$= \{w \in S : w \notin [\![\langle \tau, \alpha, \beta \rangle \wedge Info(\alpha, \beta)]\!] \setminus$
$*(w_0, [\![\langle \tau, \alpha, \beta \rangle \wedge Info(\alpha, \beta)]\!])\}$

Now suppose $\phi = [\![\langle \tau, \alpha, \beta \rangle]\!]$. Then $w_0 \notin *(w_0, [\![\langle \tau, \alpha, \beta \rangle]\!])$. But $*(S, [\![\langle \tau, \alpha, \beta \rangle]\!]) \models \neg Info(\alpha, \beta)$ and $S \models Info(\alpha, \beta)$. So $S \cap *(S, [\![\langle \tau, \alpha, \beta \rangle]\!]) = \emptyset$. So $N^*(S, [\![\langle \tau, \alpha, \beta \rangle]\!]) = S$ and so $w_0 \in N^*(S, [\![\langle \tau, \alpha, \beta \rangle]\!])$. □

Given that w_0 is a T_1 survivor world, we now show that the fixpoint of every normalisation chain leading from S_0 verifies $\neg Narration(\alpha, \beta) \wedge Cause(\beta, \alpha)$.

Fact 2.

$T_1 \approx \neg Narration(\alpha, \beta) \wedge Cause(\beta, \alpha)$

Proof. Suppose that there is a chain C such that the fixpoint C_λ contains a world ν such that $\nu \models \neg(\neg Narration(\alpha, \beta) \wedge Cause(\beta, \alpha))$. So $\nu \models Narration(\alpha, \beta) \vee \neg Cause(\beta, \alpha)$. $N^*(C_\lambda, [\![\langle \tau, \alpha, \beta \rangle \wedge Info(\alpha, \beta)]\!]) = C_\lambda$. But then $\nu \in *(C_\lambda, [\![\langle \tau, \alpha, \beta \rangle \wedge Info(\alpha, \beta)]\!])$. So then $\nu \models \neg Narration(\alpha, \beta) \wedge Cause(\beta, \alpha)$, which contradicts our hypothesis.

Now we turn to the appropriate T_2 survivor world W_2. Given T_1, T_2 is a default expanded subtheory of T. Here now is the normal worlds set-up for T_2.

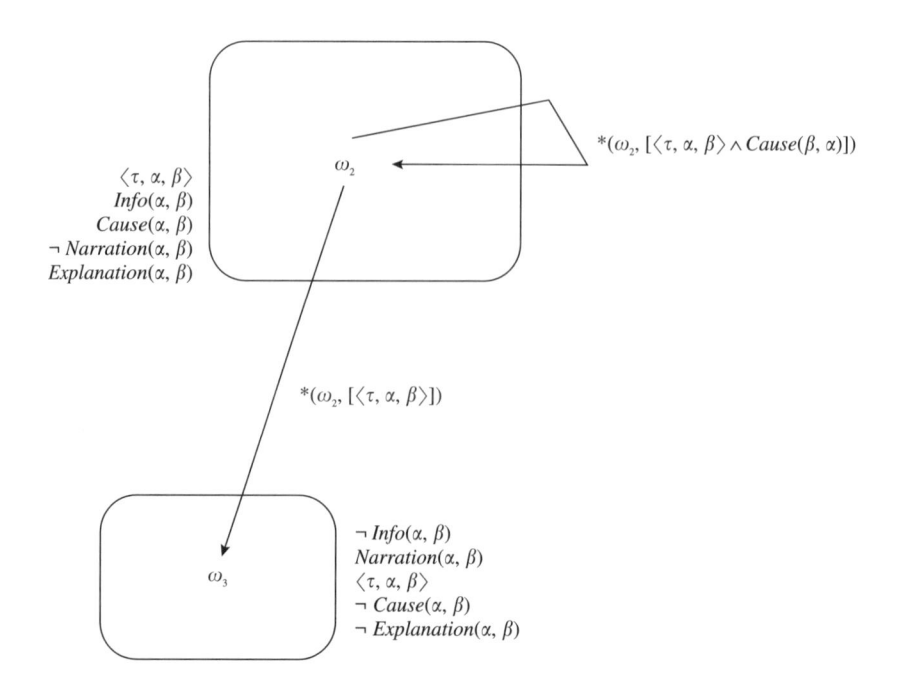

$\langle \tau, \alpha, \beta \rangle$
$Info(\alpha, \beta)$
$Cause(\alpha, \beta)$
$\neg Narration(\alpha, \beta)$
$Explanation(\alpha, \beta)$

ω_2

$*(\omega_2, [\langle \tau, \alpha, \beta \rangle \wedge Cause(\beta, \alpha)])$

$*(\omega_2, [\langle \tau, \alpha, \beta \rangle])$

ω_3

$\neg Info(\alpha, \beta)$
$Narration(\alpha, \beta)$
$\langle \tau, \alpha, \beta \rangle$
$\neg Cause(\alpha, \beta)$
$\neg Explanation(\alpha, \beta)$

The normal worlds for the other propositions can be filled in; only the above are relevant to making our point. This is also a DRP admissable model subject to the following proviso: for any proposition $p \neq [\![\langle \tau, \alpha, \beta \rangle \wedge Cause(\beta, \alpha)]\!]$, $p \neq [\![\langle \tau, \alpha, \beta \rangle]\!]$, $*(w_2, p) = *(w_3, p) = p$.

Suppose $S_1 \models T_2$. The proof that w_2 is a T_2 survivor world and that the fixpoints of every normalisation chain defined on S_1 goes exactly as before. But note that by the construction the common predicates for T_1 and T_2 have the chain survivor property with respect to these formulas. By SSI, there is a common survivor world for T and the fixpoint of every normalisation chain defined with respect to T verifies the conjunction of all formulas verified by each local fixpoint: i.e. $\neg Narration(\alpha, \beta)$, $Explanation(\alpha, \beta)$ and $Cause(\beta, \alpha)$.

This verifies the desired conclusions of the Cascaded Penguin.

The Nixon Polygon

Consider text (7).

(7) a. Guy experienced a lovely evening last night.
  b. He had a great meal.
  c. He ate salmon.
  d. He devoured lots of cheese.
  e. He won a dancing competition.

Let us assume a constituent α about a dinner is elaborated by constituents β_1 and β_2—about various courses. We now consider how to attach a constituent β_3 about winning a dance competition to this text structure. Both β_2 and α are open for β_3 and we have to look at both possibilities.

We suppose a basic information state verifying the following subtheories:

T_1:

$Elaboration\,(\alpha, \beta_2) \wedge \langle \tau, \alpha, \beta_3 \rangle \wedge \langle \tau, \beta_2, \beta_3 \rangle$
$\langle \tau, \alpha, \beta_3 \rangle > \neg Elaboration(\beta_3, \alpha)$
$\Box(Narration(\alpha, \beta_3) \to \neg Elaboration(\alpha, \beta_3))$

T_2:

$\langle \tau, \alpha, \beta_3 \rangle \wedge \neg Elaboration(\alpha, \beta_3) \wedge \langle \tau, \beta_2, \beta_3 \rangle \wedge$
$Elaboration\,(\alpha, \beta_2)$
$\langle \tau, \beta_2, \beta_3 \rangle > (Narration(\beta_2, \beta_3)$
$Elaboration(\alpha, \beta_2) \wedge \neg Elaboration(\alpha, \beta_3) > \neg Narration(\beta_2, \beta_3)$
$\Box(Narration(\alpha, \beta_3) \to \neg Elaboration(\alpha, \beta_3))$

A survivor world for T_1 is not difficult to construct. But a survivor world for T_2 is more involved. Let w_0 verify $Narration(\beta_2, \beta_3)$, $\langle \tau, \beta_2, \beta_3 \rangle$ and $\langle \tau, \alpha, \beta_3 \rangle$. And let w_1 verify $\neg Narration(\beta_2, \beta_3)$, $\neg(Elaboration(\alpha, \beta_3)$, $Elaboration\,(\alpha, \beta_2)$ and $\langle \tau, \alpha, \beta_3 \rangle$. Then we show:

LEMMA 5. w_0 survives to the fixpoint of any T_2 normalisation chain in which no normalisation of the form $N * (S_n, [\![\neg Elaboration(\alpha, \beta_3)]\!])$ occurs in C prior to a normalisation of the form $N * (S_m, [\![\langle \tau, \beta_2, \beta_3 \rangle]\!])$ And w_1 survives to the fixpoint of any T_2 normalisation chain in which no normalisation of the form $N * (S_m, [\![\langle \tau, \beta_2, \beta_3 \rangle]\!])$ occurs before a normalisation of the form $N * (S_n, [\![\neg Elaboration\,(\alpha, \beta_3)]\!])$.

The proof of the two cases is completely symmetric. So let us illustrate by taking the case of w_0 first. Suppose no normalisation of the form $N * (S_n, [\![\neg Elaboration\,(\alpha, \beta_3)]\!])$

occurs in C prior to a normalisation of the form $N * (S_m, [\![\langle \beta_2, \beta_3 \rangle]\!])$. There are only three sorts of links in a T_2 normalisation chain: $N * (S_m, [\![\langle \tau, \beta_2, \beta_3 \rangle]\!])$, $N * (S_n, [\![\neg \text{Elaboration}(\alpha, \beta_3)]\!])$ and $N * (S_n, [\![\text{Elaboration}(\alpha, \beta_2) \wedge \neg \text{Elaboration}(\alpha, \beta_3)]\!])$. By the specification of w_0 above $w_0 \models T_2$. If $S = \odot + T_2$, then $w_0 \in S$. $w_0 \in *(w_0, [\![\langle \tau, \beta_2, \beta_3 \rangle]\!])$, so $*(S, [\![\langle \tau, \beta_2, \beta_3 \rangle]\!]) \cap S \neq \emptyset$ and so

$$N * (S, [\![\langle \tau, \beta_2, \beta_3 \rangle]\!]) = \{w \in S : w \notin [\![\langle \tau, \beta_2, \beta_3 \rangle]\!] \setminus *(S, \langle \tau, \beta_2, \beta_3 \rangle)\}$$

and

$$w_0 \in N * (S_m, [\![\langle \tau, \beta_2, \beta_3 \rangle]\!]).$$

Let $N *(S_m, [\![\langle \tau, \beta_2, \beta_3 \rangle]\!]) = S'$. Suppose now that $N * (S', [\![\neg \text{Elaboration}(\alpha, \beta_3)]\!])$ is the next normalisation in the chain prior to the fixpoint of $N (S'', [\![\text{Elaboration}(\alpha, \beta_2) \wedge \neg \text{Elaboration}(\alpha, \beta_3)]\!])$. Since

$S'' \models \text{Narration}(\beta_2, \beta_3)$ but
$S'' \models \text{Elaboration}(\alpha, \beta_2) \wedge \neg \text{Elaboration}(\alpha, \beta_3)$
$\quad > \neg \text{Narration}(\beta_2, \beta_3)$
$S'' \cap *(S'', [\![\text{Elaboration}(\alpha, \beta_2) \wedge \neg \text{Elaboration}(\alpha, \beta_3)]\!]) = \emptyset$.
So $N *(S'', [\![\text{Elaboration}(\alpha, \beta_2) \wedge \neg \text{Elaboration}(\alpha, \beta_3)]\!]) = S''$.

But then $w_0 \in N *(S'', [\![\text{Elaboration}(\alpha, \beta_2) \wedge \neg \text{Elaboration}(\alpha, \beta_3)]\!])$. A similar argument shows that w_0 survives if the normalisation chain with respect to:

$$[\![\text{Elaboration}(\alpha, \beta_2) \wedge \neg \text{Elaboration}(\alpha, \beta_3)]\!]$$

comes prior to the normalisation chain with respect to $[\![\neg \text{Elaboration}(\alpha, \beta_3)]\!]$. Since this exhausts all the types of T_2 normalisation chains in which no normalisation of the form $N * (S_n, [\![\neg \text{Elaboration}(\alpha, \beta_3)]\!])$ occurs in C prior to a normalisation of the form $N * (S_m, [\![\langle \tau, \beta_2, \beta_3 \rangle]\!])$, we have the desired result: w_0 survives in every T_2 normalisation chain in which no normalisation of the form $N * (S_n, [\![\neg \text{Elaboration}(\alpha, \beta_3)]\!])$ occurs in C prior to a normalisation of the form $N * (S_m, [\![\langle (\beta_2, \beta_3) \rangle]\!])$. □

By Lemma 5, we see that in some fixpoints w_0 survives: in others w_1. By an argument parallel to that in Fact 2, we conclude then that at those fixpoints C_λ in which w_0 survives $C_\lambda \models \text{Narration}(\beta_2, \beta_3)$ and at those fixpoints C'_λ in which w_1 survives $C'_\lambda \models \neg \text{Narration}(\beta_2, \beta_3)$. So we conclude:

Fact 6

$$T_2 \not\models \text{Narration}(\beta_2, \beta_3)$$

But further, since no other axiom of T_2 allows us to conclude any other discourse relation between β_2 and β_3 we have that $S = \odot + T_2$ is such that $S \models \langle \beta_2, \beta_3 \rangle$ and $S \not\models R(\beta_2, \beta_3)$ for any discourse relation R. We assume such a state S to be incoherent.

Because we must avoid whenever possible incoherent information states, we seek another attachment. We thus look at the information state S''' that is the update of $\odot$ with T_3:

T_3:

$\quad \langle \tau, \alpha, \beta_3 \rangle$
$\quad \langle \tau, \alpha, \beta_3 \rangle > \text{Narration}(\alpha, \beta_3)$

An easy survivor argument shows that:

$$T_3 \not\models \text{Narration}(\alpha, \beta_3)$$

Double Penguin Principle

The relevant example for the Double Penguin is text (4).

(4) Max switched off the light. The room was dark.

The axioms for this example involve two resolvable conflicts—one between States Overlap and Narration and one between States Overlap and Result.

T:

$\langle \tau, \alpha, \beta \rangle > Narration(\alpha, \beta)$
$\langle \tau, \alpha, \beta \rangle \wedge Info(\alpha, \beta)$
$\langle \tau, \alpha, \beta \rangle \wedge State(\beta) > Overlap(\alpha, \beta)$
$\langle \tau, \alpha, \beta \rangle \wedge State(\beta) > \langle \tau, \alpha, \beta \rangle$
$\langle \tau, \alpha, \beta \rangle \wedge Info(\alpha, \beta) > \langle \tau, \alpha, \beta \rangle$
$\langle \tau, \alpha, \beta \rangle \wedge Info(\alpha, \beta) > Cause(\alpha, \beta)$
$\langle \tau, \alpha, \beta \rangle \wedge Cause(\alpha, \beta) > Results(\alpha, \beta)$
□ $(Overlap(\alpha, \beta) \rightarrow \neg Narration(\alpha, \beta))$
□ $(Overlap(\alpha, \beta) \rightarrow \neg Result(\alpha, \beta))$
□ $(Info(\alpha, \beta) \rightarrow state(\beta))$

Because of the connections between the various formulas in $Ant(T)$—e.g. between $\langle \tau, \alpha, \beta \rangle$, $\langle \tau, \alpha, \beta \rangle \wedge Info(\alpha, \beta)$ and $\langle \tau, \alpha, \beta \rangle \wedge State(\beta)$, subtheories that each do one of the Penguin inferences will not have the required chain survivor property with respect to their common vocabulary. So we require one large survivor proof. This proof depends on the following T survivor:

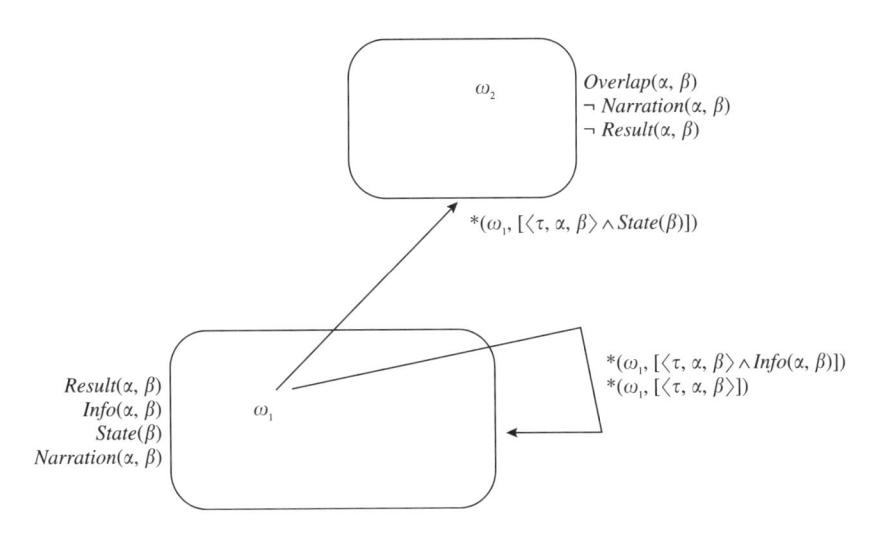

Again, analogous proofs to those in Lemmas 2–5, we may show:
LEMMA 8. w_1 is a T survivor and from this follows:

Fact
$T \mathrel{\vert\approx} Result(\alpha, \beta) \wedge Narration(\alpha, \beta) \wedge \neg Overlap(\alpha, \beta)$.

REFERENCES

Aqvist, L. (1972). 'Logic of Conditionals', *Journal of Philosophical Logic*, 1.

Asher, N. (1993). *Reference to Abstract Objects in English: A Philosophical Semantics for Natural Language Metaphysics*. Dordrecht: Kluwer Academic Publishers.

—— and Lascarides, A. (1993). 'Lexical Disambiguation in a Discourse Context', in *Proceedings of the International Workshop on Universals in the Lexicon*, Dagstuhl, Germany.

—— and Morreau, M. (1991). 'Common Sense Entailment: A Modal Theory of Nonmonotonic Reasoning', in *Proceedings to the 12th International Joint Conference on Artificial Intelligence*, Sydney, Australia, August 1991, 1–30.

Blackburn, P. and Lascarides, A. (1992). 'Sorts and Operators for Temporal Semantics', in *Proceedings of the Fourth International Symposium on Logic and Language*, Budapest, August 1992.

Boutilier, C. (1992). 'Conditional Logics for Default Reasoning and Belief Revision', Ph.D. Thesis, University of British Columbia, Technical Report 92-1.

Caenepeel, M. (1991). 'Event Structure vs. Discourse Structure', in *Proceedings of the DANDI Workshop on Discourse Coherence*, Edinburgh, April 1991.

Chellas, B. F. (1980). *Modal Logic*. Cambridge: Cambridge University Press.

Cohen, P. R., Morgan, J. and Pollack, M. E. (eds.) (1991). *Intentions in Communication*. Cambridge, MA: MIT Press.

Dahlgren, K. (1988). *Naive Semantics for Natural Language Understanding*. Dordrecht: Kluwer Academic Publishers.

Delgrande, J. P. (1988). 'An Approach to Default Reasoning based on a First-Order Conditional Logic: Revised Report', *Artificial Intelligence* **36**(1): 63–90.

Dowty, D. (1986). 'The Effects of Aspectual Class on the Temporal Structure of Discourse: Semantics or Pragmatics?' *Linguistics and Philosophy* **9**: 37–61.

Grice, H. P. (1975). 'Logic and Conversation', in P. Cole and J. L. Morgan (eds.), *Syntax and Semantics, Volume 3: Speech Acts*. New York: Academic Press, 1–58.

Grosz, B. J. and Sidner, C. L. (1986). 'Attention, Intentions, and the Structure of Discourse', *Computational Linguistics* **12**: 175–204.

Hinrichs, E. (1986). 'Temporal Anaphora in Discourses of English', *Linguistics and Philosophy* **9**: 63–82.

Hobbs, J. R. (1979). 'Coherence and Coreference', *Cognitive Science* **3**: 67–90.

—— (1985). 'On the Coherence and Structure of Discourse', Report No. CSLI-85-7, Center for the Study of Language and Information, October, 1985.

Joshi, A., Webber, B., and Weischedel, R. (1984). 'Default reasoning in interaction', in *Proceedings of the Non-Monotonic Reasoning Workshop*, AAAI, New York, October, 1984, 144–50.

Kamp, H. (1991). 'The Perfect and Other Tenses in French and English', in H. Kamp (ed.), *Tense and Aspect in English and French*, DYANA deliverable 2.3B, available from the Centre for Cognitive Science, University of Edinburgh, 41–64.

—— and Reyle, U. (in press). *From Discourse to Logic; Introduction to Modeltheoretic Semantics of Natural Language, Formal Logic and Discourse Representation Theory*. Dordrecht: Kluwer Academic Publishers.

—— and Rohrer, C. (1983). 'Tense in Texts', in R. Bauerle, C. Schwarze, and A. von Stechow (eds.), *Meaning, Use and Interpretation of Language*. Berlin: de Gruyter, 250–69.

Konolige, K. (1988). 'Hierarchic Autoepistemic Theories for Nonmonotonic Reasoning: Preliminary Report', Technical Note No. 446, SRI International, Menlo Park, August 1988.

Lascarides, A. (1988). 'The Semantics of Aspectual Classes Using Reference to Intervals', Research Report, EUCCS/RP-22, Centre for Cognitive Science, University of Edinburgh.

—— (1992). 'Knowledge, Causality and Temporal Representation', *Linguistics* **30**(5): 941–73.

—— and Asher, N. (1993). 'A Semantics and Pragmatics for the Pluperfect', in *Proceedings of the Sixth European Chapter of the Association of Computational Linguistics*, Utrecht, 250–9.

——and Oberlander, J. (1992). 'Inferring Discourse Relations in Context', in *Proceedings of the 30th Annual Meeting of the Association for Computational Linguistics*, Delaware, June 1992, 1–8.
——and Oberlander, J. (1993a). 'Temporal Coherence and Defeasible Knowledge', *Theoretical Linguistics* **19**(1): 1–37.
—— ——(1993b). 'Temporal Connectives in a Discourse Context', in *Proceedings of the Sixth European Chapter of the Association of Computational Linguistics*, Utrecht, 260–8.
Levesque, H. (1990). 'All I Know: A Study in Autoepistemic Logic', *Artificial Intelligence* **42**: 263–309.
Lifschitz, V. (1984). 'Some Results on Circumscription', in *Proceedings of the Non-Monotonic Reasoning Workshop*, AAAI, New York, October 1988, 151–64.
McCarthy, J. (1980). 'Circumscription: A Form of Nonmonotonic Reasoning', *Artificial Intelligence* **13**: 27–39.
Moens, M. and Steedman, M. J. (1988). 'Temporal Ontology and Temporal Reference', *Computational Linguistics* **14**: 15–28.
Moore, R. C. (1984). 'A Formal Theory of Knowledge and Action', Technical Note, SRI International Number 320, February 1984.
Morreau, M. (1992). 'Conditionals in Philosophy and Artificial Intelligence', Ph.D. thesis, IMS Universität Stuttgart, Report number 26-1992.
——(1993). 'Norms or Inference Tickets? A Frontal Collision Between Intuitions', in E. J. Briscoe, A. Copestake, and V. de Paiva (eds.), *Default Inheritance in Unification-based Approaches to the Lexicon*. Cambridge: Cambridge University Press.
Partee, B. (1973). 'Some Structural Analogies between Tenses and Pronouns in English', *Journal of Philosophy* **70**(18): 601–9.
——(1984). 'Nominal and Temporal Anaphora', *Linguistics and Philosophy* **7**, 243–86.
Pearl, J. (1988). *Probabilistic Reasoning in Intelligent Systems: Networks of Plausible Inference*. San Mateo, CA: Morgan Kaufmann.
Polanyi, L. (1985). 'A Theory of Discourse Structure and Discourse Coherence', in W. H. Eilfort, P. D. Kroeber and K. L. Peterson (eds.), *Papers from the General Session at the Twenty-First Regional Meeting of the Chicago Linguistics Society*, Chicago, April 25–27, 1985.
Reichenbach, H. (1947). *Elements of Symbolic Logic*. London: Macmillan.
Reiter, R. (1980). 'A Logic for Default Reasoning', *Artificial Intelligence* **13**: 81–132.
Scha, R. and Polanyi, L. (1988). 'An Augmented Context Free Grammar for Discourse', in *Proceedings of the 12th International Conference on Computational Linguistics and the 24th Annual Meeting of the Association for Computational Linguistics*, Budapest, Hungary, 22–27 August 1988, 573–7.
Thompson, S. and Mann, W. (1987). 'Rhetorical Structure Theory: A Framework for the Analysis of Texts', *IPRA Papers in Pragmatics* **1**: 79–105.
Veltman, F. (1990). *Defaults in Update Semantics*, DYANA deliverable 2.5a, available from Centre for Cognitive Science, University of Edinburgh.
Webber, B. (1991). 'Structure and Ostension in the Interpretation of Discourse Deixis', *Language and Cognitive Processes* **6**(2): 107–35.

17

News Stories as Narratives

ALLAN BELL

Journalists do not write articles. They write stories. A story has structure, direction, point, viewpoint. An article may lack these. Stories come in many kinds and are known in all cultures of the world. They include fairy tales, fables, parables, gospels, legends, epics and sagas. Stories are embedded in all sorts of language use, from face-to-face conversation to public addresses. The role of the storyteller is a significant one both in language behaviour and in society at large. Much of humanity's most important experience has been embodied in stories.

Journalists are professional storytellers of our age. The fairy tale starts: 'Once upon a time.' The news story begins: 'Fifteen people were injured today when a bus plunged ...' The journalist's work is focused on the getting and writing of stories. This is reflected in the snatches of phrases in which newsroom business is conducted. A good journalist 'gets good stories' or 'knows a good story'. A critical news editor asks: 'Is this really a story?' 'Where's the story in this?'

[...]

NEWS STORIES AND PERSONAL NARRATIVES

As a first approach to the nature of the news story, I will compare news with another kind of story which has been researched in recent decades: narratives of personal experience told in face-to-face conversation. The similarities and differences between these two kinds of stories will illuminate what news has in common with other storytelling, and where it differs. Labov and Waletzky (1967) and Labov (1999) have analysed the structure of such narratives into six elements:

1. The abstract summarizes the central action and main point of the narrative. A storyteller uses it at the outset to pre-empt the questions, what is this about, why is this story being told?
2. The orientation sets the scene; the who, when, where, and initial situation or activity of the story.
3. The complicating action is the central part of the story proper answering the question, what happened (then)?

Allan Bell, 'News Stories as Narratives', in A. Jaworski and N. Coupland (eds.), *The Discourse Reader* (London and New York: Routledge, 1999), 236–51. Reprinted from Allan Bell, *The Language of News Media* (Oxford: Blackwell Publishers, 1991), excerpts from Chapter 8, 'Telling Stories', 147–74. © 1991 Blackwell Publishers.

4 The evaluation addresses the question, so what? A directionless sequence of clauses is not a narrative. Narrative has point, and it is narrators' prime intention to justify the value of the story they are telling, to demonstrate why these events are reportable.
5 The resolution is what finally happened to conclude the sequence of events.
6 Finally, many narratives end with a coda—'and that was that.' This wraps up the action, and returns the conversation from the time of the narrative to the present.

These six elements occur in the above order, although evaluation can be dispersed throughout the other elements. Only the complicating action, and some degree of evaluation, are obligatory components of the personal narrative. To what extent do news stories follow this pattern, and where do they depart from it? [...]

The examples I use in this chapter are from the press. Because press stories are generally longer and carry much more detail than broadcast news, the structure of press stories is more complex. A framework which handles press news is likely to be adequate for the text of broadcast stories. Even long broadcast stories such as those carried by Britain's *Channel Four News* or *World at One*, with their multiple inputs, are shorter and less complex than many press stories. The use of the newsmaker's actual voice in broadcast news is in principle no different from direct quotation in printed news. For television news one would require additional apparatus to relate voiceover commentary to the visuals. This is less of a problem than it seems. The Glasgow University Media Group's analysis (see, for instance, 1976: 125) indicates that despite television news-workers' efforts and beliefs to the contrary, the written text remains paramount and the visual subsidiary. In practice, news pictures are often tangential to the spoken text of a story, because it is impossible for cameras to be regularly in the right place at the right time. There are differences between printed and broadcast news styles, which we will touch on below, but the differences are less than the similarities.

Figure 1 displays a hard news story typical of those which appear daily on the international pages of any newspaper. The international news agencies are the chief suppliers of hard news and custodians of its style (as, for example, in Cappon's *Associated Press Guide to Good News Writing* (1982)). We can expect such stories to embody the core components of news discourse. Our example story contains some but not all of the elements of the personal narrative, and their order and importance are different.

Abstract

The importance of the lead or first paragraph in establishing the main point of a news story is clear. The lead has precisely the same function in news as the abstract in personal narrative. It summarizes the central action and establishes the point of the story. For major news stories, the lead paragraph is often set off from the remainder of the story in larger type or across several columns of the body copy.

In Figure 1, the first paragraph presents two main actions—the wounding of the US soldiers, and the consequent alert for US troops in Honduras. The story has a double abstract, a feature which can also occur in personal narratives. The consequence is treated as the prior point, with the violent incident second. The lead as summary or abstract is obligatory in hard news, where in personal narrative it remains optional. The lead is the device by which copy editor or audience can get the main point of a story from reading a single opening sentence, and on that basis decide whether to continue.

Press news has headlines as well as lead paragraphs. The headline is an abstract of the abstract. The lead pares the story back to its essential point, and the headline abstracts

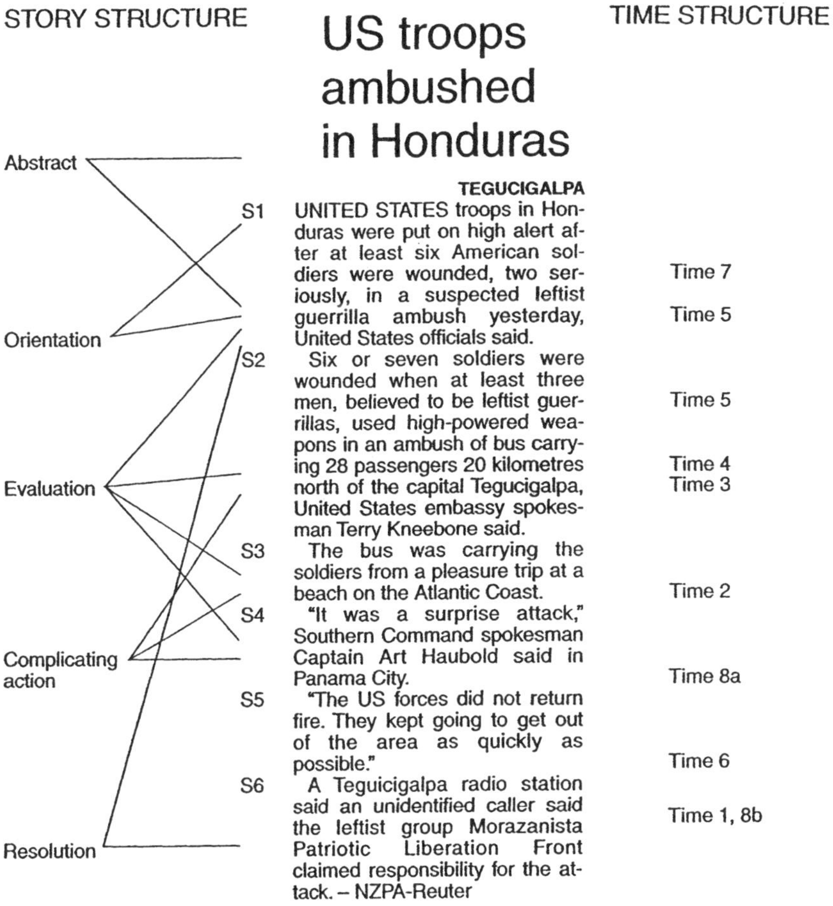

STORY STRUCTURE		TIME STRUCTURE
	US troops ambushed in Honduras	
Abstract		
	TEGUCIGALPA	
S1	UNITED STATES troops in Honduras were put on high alert after at least six American soldiers were wounded, two seriously, in a suspected leftist guerrilla ambush yesterday, United States officials said.	Time 7 Time 5
Orientation		
S2	Six or seven soldiers were wounded when at least three men, believed to be leftist guerrillas, used high-powered weapons in an ambush of bus carrying 28 passengers 20 kilometres north of the capital Tegucigalpa, United States embassy spokesman Terry Kneebone said.	Time 5 Time 4 Time 3
Evaluation		
S3	The bus was carrying the soldiers from a pleasure trip at a beach on the Atlantic Coast.	Time 2
S4	"It was a surprise attack," Southern Command spokesman Captain Art Haubold said in Panama City.	Time 8a
Complicating action		
S5	"The US forces did not return fire. They kept going to get out of the area as quickly as possible."	Time 6
S6	A Teguicigalpa radio station said an unidentified caller said the leftist group Morazanista Patriotic Liberation Front claimed responsibility for the attack. – NZPA-Reuter	Time 1, 8b
Resolution		

FIG. 1 Narrative structure and time structure of international spot news story.
Source: *The Dominion*, Wellington, 2 April 1990.

the lead itself. In Figure 1 the headline highlights the ambush, even though the lead begins with the consequent military alert. The lead paragraph is the journalist's primary abstract of a story. While to the reader the headline appears as first abstract in the printed story, in fact headlines are absent from broadcast news and even in press news are a last-minute addition. Broadcast news has no headlines, except in so far as stories are summarized at the beginning and/or end of a news bulletin. There are no headlines in news agency copy, from which most published news derives. Nor do journalists put headlines on their own stories: that is the work of subeditors. For journalists and news agencies, stories are identified by the ultimate in abstracts—a one-word catchline or slugline, unique to the story.

Orientation

In personal narrative, orientation sets the scene: who are the actors, where and when did the events take place, what is the initial situation? In news stories, such orientation is obligatory. For journalists *who, what, when* and *where* are the basic facts which concentrate at the beginning of a story, but may be expanded further down. The lead in Figure 1 crams in no less than five sets of people: United States troops in Honduras, the six wounded soldiers, the two seriously wounded, leftist guerrillas and US officials.

International agency stories as received off the wire are 'datelined' at the top for time and place origin, with the deictics *here* and *today* used in the lead paragraph.[1] In this story the time of the ambush is given as *yesterday*. The time of the alert is unspecified (but in fact was also *yesterday* because this was published in the morning paper, and Honduras is some 18 hours behind New Zealand time). The dateline specifies the location from which the journalist 'filed' the story to the news agency. Here as in many newspapers, the dateline is carried below the headline and above the lead. The lead paragraph names Honduras, the second sentence (S2) specifies the exact site of the ambush and identifies the capital city, a necessary detail for news about a country whose geography will not be well known to the readers. Further detail of place is given in S3. In S4 there is a change of country with a regional command spokesperson outside Honduras quoted. This may indicate that the story has been combined by agency copy editors from separate despatches from both Tegucigalpa and Panama City.

Evaluation

Evaluation is the means by which the significance of a story is established. In personal narrative, evaluation is what distinguishes a directionless sequence of sentences from a story with point and meaning. In the case of the fight stories studied by Labov (1999), the point is often the self-aggrandizement of the narrator. Evaluation pre-empts the question, so what? It gives the reason why the narrator is claiming the floor and the audience's attention.

News stories also require evaluation, and in their case its function is identical to that in personal narrative: to establish the significance of what is being told, to focus the events, and to justify claiming the audience's attention. The story in Figure 1 stresses repeatedly the importance of what has happened. *High alert, at least six wounded, two seriously* in the lead paragraph all stake claims on the reader to take these events, quite literally, seriously. The claims continue in the remaining paragraphs, but with diminishing frequency and force: *at least three men, high-powered weapons* (S2), *surprise attack* (S4), *as quickly as possible* (S5).

The lead paragraph is a nucleus of evaluation, because the function of the lead is not merely to summarize the main action. The lead focuses the story in a particular direction. It forms the lens through which the remainder of the story is viewed. This function is even more obvious for the headline, especially when it appears to pick up on a minor point of the story. Focusing a story is a prime preoccupation of the journalist. Until a journalist finds what to lead a story with, the story remains unfocused. It is an article but not a story, and may be rejected or rewritten by editors on those grounds. On the other hand, once the journalist decides what the lead is, the rest of the story often falls into place below it. If no good lead can be found, the material may be rejected altogether as a non-story.

---

[1] In the days of wire despatches both the place and date were carried on the dateline. Most of the elements surrounding news copy are named after the line above the body copy of which they traditionally occurred—headline, catchline, dateline, byline. 'Datelined Moscow' means the story was 'filed'—written and supplied to the news agency—from Moscow. The slugline is named for the 'slugs' of hard metal type used in the original letterpress technology before the advent of offset printing and computer typesetting.

In personal narrative, evaluative devices may occur throughout the narrative but are typically concentrated near the end, just before the resolution of the events. In the news story, evaluation focuses in the lead. Its function is to make the contents of the story sound *as X as possible*, where *X* is big, recent, important, unusual, new; in a word—newsworthy. The events and news actors will be given the maximum status for the sake of the story. In the same fashion, narrators of fight stories are at pains to enhance the scale of their adversary—'the baddest girl in the neighborhood'—and hence the magnitude of their own eventual victory (Labov 1999).

Action

At the heart of a personal narrative is the sequence of events which occurred. In Labov's analysis (1999), a defining characteristic of narrative as a form is the temporal sequence of its sentences. That is, the action is invariably told in the order in which it happened. News stories, by contrast, are seldom if ever told in chronological order. Even within the lead paragraph of Figure 1, result (the military alert) precedes cause (the ambush). Down in the story proper, the time sequence is also reversed. The sequence of events as one of the participants might have told it is:

About 30 of us went by bus for a day at the beach.
On the way back we got to 20 kilometres north of Tegucigalpa.
There some guerrillas ambushed us and shot up the bus with high powered rifles.
They wounded six or seven of the soldiers.

Figure 1 shows the time structure of events in the story. S2 and S3 of the news story run these events in precisely the reverse order to which they happened. The result is placed before the action which caused it. This is a common principle of news writing, that it is not the action or the process which takes priority but the outcome. Indeed, it is this principle which enables news stories to be updated day after day or hour by hour. If there is a new outcome to lead with, the previous action can drop down in the story. Our example shows traces of just such an origin in the dual abstract of its lead paragraph, which reads like an updating story from the international wires. A previous story probably carried news of the ambush, and Figure 1 is a follow-up which leads with the more recent information of the military alert.

The time structure of the story is very complex. In S1 the latest occurring event is presented first, followed by its antecedent. S2 and S3 pick up the action at that antecedent point in time and trace it backwards as described above. S4 shifts the story into another setting and timeframe for commentary on what happened, and S5 describes the final action of the main incident, namely the bus's escape from the ambush. The last paragraph moves into a third setting and presents what is in fact temporally the beginning of the events, the group (possibly) responsible for the ambush.

Where chronological order defines the structure of personal narrative, a completely different force is driving the presentation of the news story. Perceived news value overturns temporal sequence and imposes an order completely at odds with the linear narrative point. It moves backwards and forwards in time, picking out different actions on each cycle. In one case, at the start of S2, it even repeats an action—*six or seven soldiers were wounded*—from the previous sentence. This wilful violation of our expectations that narratives usually proceed in temporal succession is distinctive of news stories. It may also have repercussions for how well audiences understand news stories.

Resolution

The personal narrative moves to a resolution: the fight is won, the accident survived. News stories often do not present such clearcut results. When they do, as noted above, the result will be in the lead rather than at the end of the story. In Figure 1, the nearest thing to a resolution is the general military alert. But this, of course, is only the latest step in a continuing saga. The news is more like a serial than a short story. The criminal was arrested, but the trial is in the future. The accident occurred, but the victims are still in hospital. One kind of news does follow the chronology of the personal narrative more closely: sports reporting. Sport makes good news just because there is always a result. A sports story will lead in standard news fashion with the result of the game and a few notable incidents, but then settle down to chronological reporting of the course of the game.

News stories are not rounded off. They finish in mid-air. The news story consists of instalments of information of perceived decreasing importance. It is not temporally structured, or turned in a finished fashion. One very good reason for this is that the journalist does not know how much of her story will be retained by copy editors for publication. Stories are regularly cut from the bottom up, which is a great incentive to get what you believe to be the main points in early.

Coda

Nor is there a coda to the news story. The reason lies in the function which the coda performs in personal narrative. It serves as an optional conclusion to the story, to mark its finish, to return the floor to other conversational partners, and to return the tense from narrative time to the present. None of these functions is necessary in the newspaper, where the floor is not open, and where the next contribution is another story. But the coda does have some parallel in broadcast news. The end of a news bulletin or programme—but not of individual news stories—will usually be explicitly signalled by 'that is the end of the news' or a similar formula. Between broadcast stories there is no discourse marker to mark one off from the other, although intonation or (on television) visual means will be used to flag the change of topic.

Our first approach to the structure of news stories indicates interesting similarities and differences to personal narrative. In news, the abstract is obligatory not optional. Orientating and evaluative material occurs in a similar fashion to personal narrative, but tends to concentrate in the first sentence. The central action of the news story is told in non-chronological order, with result presented first followed by a complex recycling through various time zones down through the story. One characteristic which news and personal narrative share is a penchant for direct quotation. The flavour of the eyewitness and colour of direct involvement is important to both forms.

The Honduras example story also points up four features which are typical of news stories but alien to the face-to-face narrative. First, the personal narrative is just that—*personal*. It relates the narrator's own experience, while the news story reports on others' experiences. The reporter has usually not witnessed these, and first person presentation is conventionally excluded from standard news reporting. Second, and consequently, where the personal narrative is told from one viewpoint—the narrator's—in news a range of sources is often cited. In Figure 1 at least four separate sources are named in the space of six paragraphs. Third, the news revels in giving numbers with a precision which is foreign to conversational stories. In the Honduras story, six sets of figures counting the guerrillas, passengers, casualties, distance to the location occur in the first two paragraphs. Fourth, the syntax of personal narratives is simple, with mostly main clauses and little subordination. The syntax of news stories can be complex, as S1 and S2 show (although these are unusually long sentences for hard news). [...]

[Bell goes on to review previous studies of the discourse structure of news reports, including Teun van Dijk's 1988 analysis of topic-based 'macropropositions' and his 1985 analysis of 'news schemata'.]

Analysing a political news story's structure

In Figure 1 we looked at a spot news story from the international news agencies. Figure 2 displays a typical example of the other predominant product of the same agencies, diplomatic and political news. The possible component categories of the story's structure are annotated alongside the copy. In Figure 3, that linear structure is redisplayed as a tree diagram, which reunites the components of different events from where they are scattered throughout the story. The structure as diagrammed in Figure 3 looks complex, and so it is, but in fact I have here telescoped levels and omitted nodes in order to simplify the presentation as much as possible. The complexity is a true reflection of the structure of such international diplomatic/political stories.

The news text consists of abstract, attribution and the story proper (Figure 3). The attribution is outside the body copy of the story, and indicates place at the top (*Moscow*, Figure 2) and source at the bottom (*NZPA—Reuter*). In many papers all three constituents of the attribution would conventionally be presented at the start of the lead paragraph: *Moscow, 31 March, NZPA-Reuter*. Here the time is not stated in attribution, headline or lead, but is explicit within the story—*yesterday* (S2, S12). The NZPA-Reuter attribution means that the story originates from one of the principal international agencies, channelled through London, New York, or Paris, and finally Sydney and Wellington. Although most of the action takes place in Lithuania, the story is datelined Moscow. This may indicate a reporter working from Lithuania through a Moscow office. More likely the reporting is in fact being done from Moscow itself. Such off-the-spot reporting is completely standard in international news. Within the story other media are named as sources of specific information—Vilnius radio (S15) and Tass (S19) for Events 5 and 2 respectively. Unusually, and in contrast to the Honduras story, no non-media sources of information are credited.

The abstract breaks down into headline and lead. The headline covers only Event 1, the occupation—the subeditor gratefully picking out the only hard action from a generally verbal story. The lead covers the occupation plus Event 2, the Byelorussian

Troops take over Lithuanian office

HEADLINE
Event 1

ATTRIBUTION
Place

LEAD
Evaluation S1 — STEPPING up the pressure on rebel Lithuania, Soviet troops seized a government office in the capital – and neighbouring Byelorussia threatened to claim a slice of the republic if it secedes from the Soviet Union.

Event 1
Event 2

EVENT 3 S2 — The parliament in Lithuania's sister Baltic republic of Estonia, meanwhile announced yesterday it wanted to break with Moscow too, declaring the beginning of a transitional period that would end in full independence.

Previous episodes S3 — Moscow has refused to recognise Lithuania's March 11 declaration of independence.

EVENT 1 S4 — Instead it has waged what Lithuanians call a war of nerves, with soldiers occupying public buildings and arresting Lithuanian military deserters.

EVENT 4 S5 — United States President George Bush sent Soviet President Mikhail Gorbachev a note urging peaceful settlement of the dispute.

Action S6 — A few hours later, Interior Ministry troops moved into the public prosecutor's office in the Lithuanian capital Vilnius.

EVENT 1
Context S7 — It was the first Lithuanian building to be occupied by Soviet troops since Wednesday, when the Communist Party headquarters was seized.

Previous episodes S8 — It was also the first to be taken over from the government as opposed to the party.

Context
Reaction S9 — Lithuanian President Vytautas Landsbergis went on television yesterday to denounce the move, saying it would bring shame on Moscow.

S10 — "We have endured all these years . . . we will this time as well," he said.

S11 — "What the USSR is doing now will bring only shame in the eyes of all the world."

S12 Action — Earlier yesterday, deputy Soviet prosecutor Alexei Vasilyev told staff at the prosecutor's office that Moscow had relieved their boss, Alturas Paulauskas, from his post.

S13 Action — In his place Mr Vasilyev announced Moscow had appointed Antanas Petrauskas, who quickly told journalists he did not recognise Lithuanian independence.

S14 Evaluation — Control of the prosecutor's office is considered crucial for Moscow to enforce Soviet law which it says still holds sway in Lithuania, including penalties for army desertion.

Attribution
S15 EVENT 5 — Vilnius Radio said, Interior Ministry troops had also taken over the history institute of the Lithuanian Communist Party.

S16 EVENT 6 — Chief military prosecutor Alexander Katusev said yesterday a defence ministry amnesty announced on Friday for any Lithuanian deserters who returned to their units was invalid.

S17 — They would be considered on a case-by-case basis, he said.

S18 EVENT 2 — Lithuanian was also set upon by its neighbour Byelorussia, where the parliamentary leadership said it would lay claim to Vilnius and six other districts if Lithuania seceded.

S19 — "We shall be obliged to insist on the return of Byelorussian land to the Byelorussian Soviet Socialist Republic," the presidium of the republic's Supreme Soviet, or parliament said, according to the official news agency Tass. – NZPA-Reuter.

Attribution

ATTRIBUTION

FIG. 2 Components of an international news agency story (capitals represent major categories, lower-case labels are subordinate categories).

Source: *Dominion Sunday Times*, Wellington, 1 April 1990.

threat, as well as evaluating their effect on the situation. The evaluative clause *stepping up the pressure on rebel Lithuania* generalizes on the significance of the two separate events reported in the lead. This kind of explicit evaluation is a common device for drawing together the often disparate threads of such a story. There is no expansion or justification of the evaluation within the body of the story.

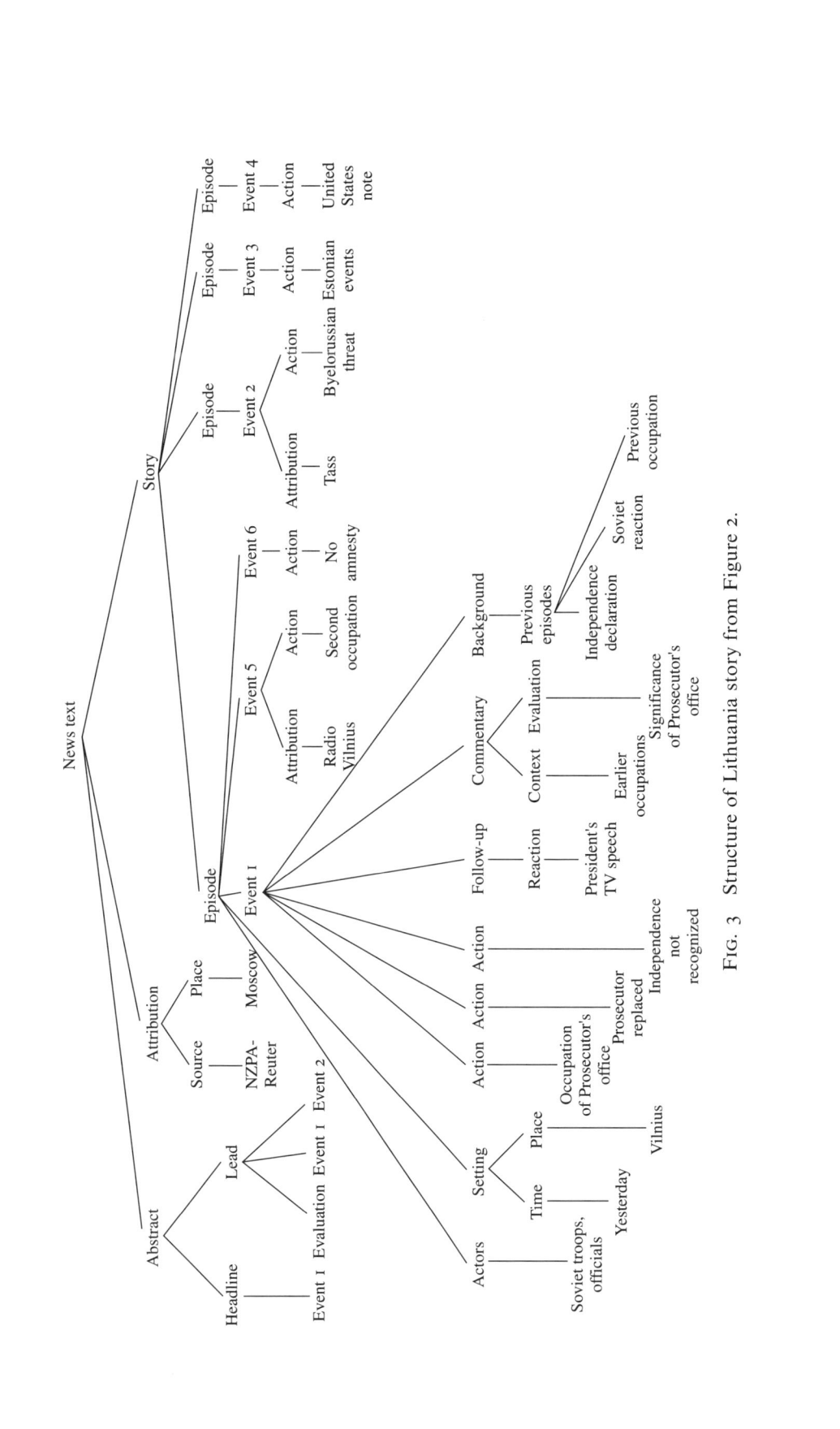

FIG. 3   Structure of Lithuania story from Figure 2.

406   *The Language of Time: A Reader*

The story itself covers no fewer than six events:

1 Occupation of the prosecutor's office (S1, S3–4, S6–14);
2 Byelorussian threat to claim territory (S1, S18–19);
3 Estonia's announcement of desired independence (S2);
4 Bush's note to Gorbachev (S5);
5 Occupation of the Communist Party history institute (S15);
6 Withdrawal of deserter amnesty (S16–17).

In Figure 3 I subsume events 1, 5, and 6 under a single episode. They share a common setting of place (Vilnius) as well as principal actors (Soviet troops and officials). However, it is not clear from the story how related these happenings are, and further information might lead us to treat them as separate episodes. Events 2 and 4 are related to the main episode only through the general theme of the Lithuanian independence issue. Event 3 is even more remote, drawing parallels between happenings in Estonia and Lithuania. The story as published bears all the hallmarks of a shotgun marriage by the news agency of up to four originally separate stories covering the occupation, the Byelorussian threat, Bush's note, and the Estonian situation.

Events 3–6 are picked up and dropped within a paragraph or so each (Figure 2). In the diagram I have not specified all the categories required in the analysis. For example, each event implies actors and setting as well as action. Although Events 1 and 2 are treated at greater length, they are delivered by instalments in a manner characteristic of news narrative. A number of devices are used to bring cohesion out of these diverse components. The inclusion of Event 3 is justified (S2) by describing Estonia as *Lithuania's sister Baltic republic*, together with the use of *meanwhile*—a sure signal that a journalist is about to draw a tenuous connection between disparate events (cf. Glasgow University Media Group 1976: 118). Event 4, Bush's note, is said to deal with *the dispute* (S5), the label under which everything is here subsumed. (In fact, the Bush note was covered in an adjacent story in the newspaper.) A time relationship is specified (S6), linking Bush's note with the occupation which occurred *a few hours later*. The juxtaposition seems to imply not just a temporal but a causal or at least concessive relationship. The occupation is interpreted as taking place in disregard of Bush's plea for a peaceful settlement. *Also* is used both to tie Event 5 in to the main occupation (S15), and when Event 2—mentioned in the lead then dropped—reappears in S18.

The actors, time and place structure are as complicated as the action. News narrative, as Manoff (1987) notes, is a means of knitting diverse events together. The story ranges across several locations. Each event belongs to a different place, principally the Lithuanian capital Vilnius (several sites), Byelorussia, Estonia, Washington, and Moscow. As well as the complex interleaving of other events between the two main events, the time structure of the main events themselves is presented nonchronologically. Event 2 is included in the lead by the rather clumsy punctuation device of the dash, and surfaces again only at the end of the story. Event 1 consists of three actions (Figure 3), plus follow-up, commentary and background. The event moves from the occupation itself (S1), back in time to previous episodes which form the broad background to it (S3–4). It then presents detail about the occupation (S6) plus background about previous occupation events (S7–8), moves forward in time to Lithuanian verbal reaction to the occupation (S9–11), and returns to the occupation again (S12–13) plus evaluative background on its significance (S14). Such a to-and-fro time structure is completely standard for this kind of story—which does not make it any easier for the reader to keep track of. As van Dijk (1988: 65) says, getting coherence out of the discontinuous nature of news can be a demanding comprehension task. The analysis of a standard fire story from the *Baltimore Sun* undertaken by Pollard-Gott et al. (1979) shows how the same kind of non-chronological presentation, cycling through different actions, consequences and causes, occurs in a local spot news item.

[...]

THE STRUCTURE OF NEWS STORIES

We are now in a position to draw some general conclusions about the categories and structure of news discourse. Most of the categories which van Dijk has identified in news discourse—and others in other story types—are needed, with a few relabellings and additions. A news text will normally consist of an abstract, attribution and the story proper (Figure 4). Attribution of where the story came from is not always explicit. It can include agency credit and/or journalist's byline, optionally plus place and time. The abstract consists of the lead and, for press news, a headline. The lead will include the main event, and possibly a second event. This necessarily entails giving some information on actors and setting involved in the event. The lead may also incorporate attribution (as in the Honduras story), and supplementary categories such as evaluation (see the Lithuania story).

A story consists of one or more episodes, which in turn consist of one or more events. Events must contain actors and action, usually express setting, and may have explicit attribution. The categories of attribution, actors and setting (time and place) need to be recognized as part of the structure of news stories. They perform the orientation which Labov (1999) found in narratives, as well as embedding all or part of a story as information given by a particular source. These are also part of the journalist's mental analysis of what goes in a story: who, when, where, who said?

As well as those elements which present the central action, we recognize three additional categories that can contribute to an event: *follow-up, commentary and background* (Figure 4). The Lithuanian story contained all three of these, and all but three of the lower categories of which they can be composed: consequences, expectations, and history.

Follow-up covers any action subsequent to the main action of an event. It can include verbal reaction, as in the Lithuania story, or non-verbal consequences—for example, if the upshot of the occupation had been demonstrations in Vilnius instead of a presidential speech. Because it covers action occurring after what a story has treated as the main action, follow-up is a prime source of subsequent updating stories—themselves called 'follow-ups'. We can easily imagine a subsequent story where the lead reads *Lithuanian President Vytautas Landsbergis has gone on television to condemn Soviet occupation of....* If the follow-up action had in fact been a demonstration, that would certainly have claimed the lead on a later agency story.

Commentary provides the journalist's or news actors' observations on the action. It may be represented by context, such as the S7–8 information comparing this occupation with previous ones. It may be by explicit evaluation, as in the S14 presentation of the significance of occupying the prosecutor's office. Third, and not exemplified in the Lithuania story, it may express expectations held by the journalist or a news actor on how the situation could develop next.

The category of background covers any events prior to the current action. These are classed as 'previous episodes' if they are comparatively recent. They probably figured as

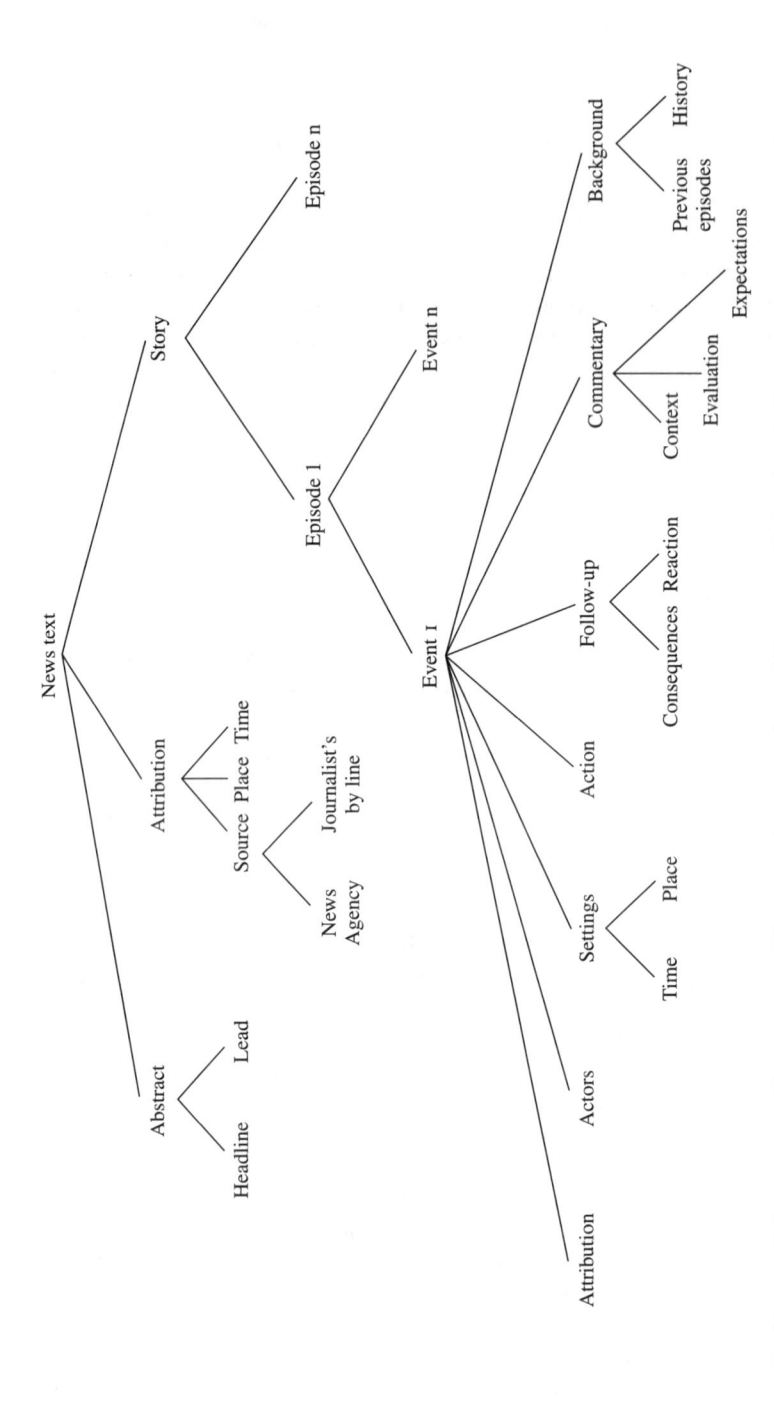

FIG. 4 Outline model structure of news texts. There can be a number of Events or Episodes. Follow-up and Background Categories can have Episodes embedded into them. Headline and Lead pick-up components from the Story itself. Categories such as Attribution or Setting can be components of either an Event or an Episode.

news stories in their own right at an earlier stage of the situation. If the background goes beyond the near past, it is classed as 'history'. Information on the relationship of Lithuania to the Soviet Union during the Second World War was included in stories on other events around this time.

Follow-up and background can have the character of episodes in their own right. That is, episode is a recursive category and can be embedded under consequences, reaction, history, or background. If the previous episodes outlined in S3–4 of the Lithuanian story had been more fully expanded, they could easily have incorporated the apparatus of a full episode within them, including categories such as context or evaluation. Similarly, follow-up reaction or consequences can be complex. These are by nature categories which were full stories in their own right at a previous time, or may become so tomorrow.

[...]

REFERENCES

Cappon, R. J. (1982). *The Word: An Associated Press Guide to Good News Writing*. New York: Associated Press.

Glasgow University Media Group (1976). *Bad News*. London: Routledge & Kegan Paul.

Labov, W. L. (1999). 'The Transformation of Experience in Narrative', in A. Jaworski and N. Coupland (eds.), *The Discourse Reader*. London and New York: Routledge, 221–35.

—— and Waletzky, J. (1967). 'Narrative analysis: oral versions of personal experience', in J. Helm (ed.), *Essays on the Verbal and Visual Arts* (*Proceedings of the 1966 Annual Spring Meeting of the American Ethnological Society*). Seattle: University of Washington Press, 12–44.

Manoff, R. (1987). 'Writing the news (by telling the "story")', in R. K. Manoff and M. Schudson (eds.), *Reading the News*. New York: Pantheon, 197–229.

Pollard-Gott, L., McCloskey, M., and Todres, A. K. (1979). 'Subjective story structure', *Discourse Processes* 2(4): 251–81.

Van Dijk, T. A. (1985). 'Structures of news in the press', in T. A. Van Dijk (ed.), *Discourse and Communication: New Approaches to the Analysis of Mass Media Discourse and Communication*. Berlin: de Gruyter, 69–93.

—— (1988). *News as Discourse*. Hillsdale, NJ: Lawrence Erlbaum.

18

Tense as Discourse Anaphor

BONNIE LYNN WEBBER

1 INTRODUCTION

In this paper, I consider a range of English expressions and show that their context-dependency can be characterized in terms of two properties:

1. They specify entities in an evolving model of the discourse that the listener is constructing;
2. the particular entity specified depends on another entity in that part of the evolving "discourse model" that the listener is currently attending to.

Two types of expressions have previously been described in these terms: definite pronouns and certain definite noun phrases (NPs). Researchers in computational linguistics and in artificial intelligence have called these expressions **anaphors** (cf., Woods 1978, Sidner 1983, Bobrow 1986, Hirst 1981, Webber 1983).

Linguists, however, have used this term somewhat differently. Many have restricted its use to expressions (usually pronouns) that can be treated analogously to variables in a logical language (Chomsky 1980). A view in linguistics that comes somewhat closer to the AI model can be found in a paper by Sag and Hankamer (1984), who distinguish what they call **deep** (or **model-interpretive**) anaphora from what they call **surface** anaphora (or **ellipsis**). Under the former, they include personal pronouns, sentential "it," and null-complement anaphora, and under the latter, verb phrase (VP) ellipsis, sluicing, gapping, and stripping. The two types are distinguished by whether they make reference to the interpretation of an antecedent—i.e., some object in a model of the world constructed by the interpreter of the sentence of discourse (deep anaphora)—or whether they are interpreted with respect to a previous logical form (surface anaphora). While their deep anaphors include pronouns, Hankamer and Sag do not consider other expressions like NPs in discourse that might also be described in similar model-interpretive terms, nor do they describe in any detail how model interpretation works for the expressions they consider.

To avoid confusion then, I will use the term **discourse anaphors** for expressions that have these two properties.[1] My main point will be that tensed clauses share these properties as well, and hence should also be considered discourse anaphors. This will

---

Bonnie Lynn Webber, 'Tense as Discourse Anaphor', *Computational Linguistics* 14 (2) (1988), 61–73. © 1988 Association for Computational Linguistics.

[1] Computationally, these properties imply particular things about processing. For example, in interpreting an NP, one may always have to consider the possibility—probably in parallel with other possibilities—that it is a discourse anaphor. For this alternative, the processor will need to (a) keep track of entities whose specification the NP may depend on and (b) make appropriate inferences with respect to these entities. Other forms of context dependencies will have other implications for processing. In this paper, I will touch on processing issues for discourse anaphora, but not other context-dependent phenomena.

capture in a simple way the oft-stated, but difficult-to-prove intuition that *tense is anaphoric*.

To begin with, in Section 2, I characterize the dependency of an anaphoric expression X_b on a discourse entity E_a in terms of an anaphoric function $\alpha(X_b, E_a)$, that itself depends on (1) the **ontology** of the specified entity E_a, and (2) **discourse structure** and its **focusing** effect on which E_a entities the listener is attending to. With respect to definite pronouns and NPs, this will essentially be a review of previous research. However, I will argue that some indefinite NPs should also be considered discourse anaphors in just this same way. In Section 3, I will move on to tensed clauses and the notion of *tense as anaphor*, a notion that goes back to at least Leech in his monograph *Meaning and the English Verb* (1987). I will review previous attempts to make the notion precise, attempts that require special-purpose machinery to get them to work. Then I will show, in contrast, that the notion can more simply be made precise in terms of a set of similar anaphoric functions that again depend on ontology and discourse structure. Making clear these dependencies contributes to our knowledge of what is needed for understanding narrative text.

2 BACKGROUND

2.1 Discourse models and specification

The notion **specify** that I am using in my definition of discourse anaphora is based on the notion of a **Discourse Model**, earlier described in Webber (1983). My basic premise is that in processing a narrative text, a listener is developing a model of at least two things: (1) the entities under discussion, along with their properties and relationships to one another, and (2) the events and situations under discussion, along with their relationships to one another (e.g., consequential relations, simple ordering relations, elaboration relations, etc.). The representation as a whole I call the listener's **Discourse Model**.[2]

In this section, I will focus on NPs. (In Section 3, I will turn attention to tensed clauses.) NPs may **evoke** entities into the listener's Discourse Model corresponding to individuals (Example 1), sets (Example 2), abstract individuals (Example 3), classes (Example 4), etc.[3]

1. a. Wendy gave Eliot *a T-shirt* for Christmas.
   b. Unfortunately, (*it, the T-shirt*) had the logo "You ate it, Ralph".
2. a. Wendy gave each boy *a T-shirt*.
   b. (*They, the T-shirts*) each had a different logo on the front.
3. a. *The vice president* must be over 35 years old.
   b. *He or she* must also be able to count.
4. a. *The dachshund* down the block bit me yesterday.
   b. *They're* really vicious beasts.

---

[2] In earlier work, it was only the former that I discussed under the concept of Discourse Model. The notion is not all that different from Kamp's "Discourse Representation Structures" (Kamp 1984) or Heim's "File Cards" (Heim 1982).

[3] This does not mean that all NPs evoke entities in the listener's Discourse Model: for example, I would not want to say that a predicate nominal (as in "John is a neuro-surgeon.") evokes a separate entity. On the other hand, I do assume that NPs in a quantified context evoke discourse entities that are accessible as long as that context holds. For example, "Whenever a philosopher debates a computer scientist, *the philosopher* turns out to have a naive idea of what *the computer scientist* is doing. Of course, *the computer scientist* always does her best to explain." (I thank Rich Thomason for the example.) Keith Stenning has also discussed examples such as this one.

An NP which **evokes** a discourse entity also **specifies** it.[4] One way an NP would be considered anaphoric by the above definition would be if it specified an entity E_a in the model that had already been evoked by some other NP. (In that case, one would say that the two NPs **co-specified** the same entity.) This basic arrangement is illustrated in Examples 1–3 above and is shown in Figure 1a.[5] Formally, one could say that there is an anaphoric function α, whose value, given the anaphoric noun phrase NP_b and the discourse entity E_a, is E_a—that is, $\alpha(NP_b, E_a) = E_a$. This can also be read as *NP_b specifies E_a by virtue of E_a*. Definite pronouns are most often anaphoric in just this way.

The other way an NP would be considered a discourse anaphor would be if it used some existing discourse entity E_a to evoke and specify a new discourse entity E_b, as in

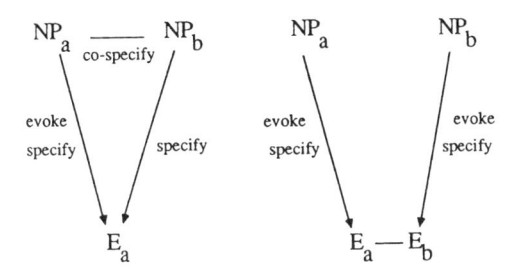

FIG. 1   Evoke, specify, and co-specify.

5. a. A bus came round the corner.
   b. I signaled to *the driver* to stop.

where NP_b—*the driver*—makes use of the entity associated with the bus mentioned in 5a to specify a new entity—*the driver of that bus*.

Here the anaphoric function is of the form $\alpha(NP_b, E_a) = E_b$. In cooperative discourse, there have to be constraints on the value of $\alpha(NP_b, E_a)$, since only NP_b is given explicitly. In short, a cooperative speaker must be able to assume that the listener is able to both infer a possible α and single out E_a in his/her evolving Discourse Model.[6] (This is illustrated in Figure 1b.) I will consider each of these two types of constraints in turn.

Speakers assume listeners will have no problem with α when $\alpha(NP_b, E_a) = E_a$. Inferring α in other cases follows in large part from the **ontology** of the entities specified by NPs—i.e., the ontology of our concepts of individuals, sets, mass terms, generics, etc. We view these as having parts (e.g., car: the engine, the wheels), having functional relations (e.g., car: the driver), having roles (e.g., wedding: the bride), etc. These needn't be necessary parts, relations, roles, etc. Our ontology includes possible parts, relations, etc., and these too make it possible for the listener to infer an α such that $\alpha(NP_b, E_a) = E_b$ (e.g., room: the chandelier; car: the chauffeur; wedding: the flower girl). Such inferences are discussed at length in the literature, including Clark and Marshall 1981, and Hobbs 1987.[7]

---

[4] In this use of "specify", I am following Sidner, who used it to mean, essentially, *refer in a model*, as opposed to *refer in the outside world* (cf. Sidner 1983).

[5] Note that a discourse entity may or may not stand for some real-world individual or set. Whether it does or doesn't, however, is irrelevant to these model-based notions of evoke, specify, and co-specify.

[6] As with any aspect of discourse that relies on the speaker making assumptions about the listener's knowledge, those assumptions may in some cases be wrong. Listeners, for their part, try to do their best in making sense anyhow—for example, hoping that the further discourse will provide enough information to work things out.

[7] The inferrability of α in other cases follows from the ontology of entities specified clausally. This I will touch upon in Section 3. Often a speaker can assume that α relates an individual to the generic class it belongs

Before closing this section, there are two more things to say about NPs. First, the above definition of discourse anaphor does not apply to all definite NPs: a definite NP can be used to refer to something unique in the speaker and listener's shared spatio-temporal context (e.g., the telephone—i.e., the one that they both hear ringing) or their shared culture (e.g., the government), to the unique representative of a class (e.g., the duck-billed platypus), to an entire class or set (e.g., the stars), or to a functionally defined entity (e.g., the largest tomato in Scotland). None of these would be considered discourse anaphoric by the above definition.

Secondly, though the definition implies that one must consider some indefinite NPs to be discourse anaphors, since they are essentially parasitic on a corresponding anaphoric definite NP, as in the following example:

6. a. The driver stopped the bus when *a passenger* began to sing, "Aida".
   b. The driver stopped the bus when *the passengers* began to sing "Aida".

The indefinite NP *a passenger* in (6a) can be paraphrased as *some one of the passengers*, and thus is parasitic on the anaphoric definite NP *the passengers* mentioned explicitly in (6b). This does not imply that all indefinite NPs are discourse anaphors. In *Mary met a boy with green hair* or *Fred built an oak desk*, the indefinite NPs do not need to be interpreted with respect to another discourse entity and some inferrable relationship with that entity, in order to characterize the discourse entity they specify.

In the next section, I will discuss the second kind of constraint on the function $\alpha(NP_b, E_a)$ necessary for cooperative use of an anaphor—constraints on identifiable E_as. These involve notions of **discourse structure** and **discourse focus.** Before I close, though, I want to point to where I'm going vis-à-vis the anaphoric character of tense and tensed clauses. In contrast with previous accounts of tense as pronoun or tense as loosely context-dependent, I am going to claim that, like an anaphoric definite NP,

- a tensed clause C_b may either **specify** an existing event or situation E_b in the listener's Discourse Model, or it may both **evoke** and **specify** a new entity.
- As with anaphoric NPs, there are constraints on possible anaphoric functions and on the E_as that can participate in them at any one time.
- These functions are sensitive to that part of a tensed clause C_b called by Reichenbach (1947) **point of reference** (here abbreviated RT), as well as its relationship to Reichenbach's **point of the event** (ET).
- These functions can be defined in part in terms of an independently justifiable ontology of events proposed (independently) by Moens and Steedman (chapter 6, this volume) and Passonneau (Chapter 8, this volume).
- The constraints on E_a are tied in with a temporal analogue of discourse focus that I have called **temporal focus** (TF), and through TF, with discourse structure as well.

2.2 Discourse focus and discourse structure

The ideas presented in this section have been formulated and developed by Barbara Grosz and Candy Sidner, originally independently and later in joint research. It is not a

---

to, as in Example 4, or the intension of a definite description to its extension—or vice versa—as in "The President is elected by the Electoral College. In the 1964 election, he got all but two of the votes." I am not claiming that all inferrable α's follow from ontology—only that ontology sanctifies a great many.

summary of their work:[8] it is limited to those of their ideas that are necessary to the concept of anaphor that I am advancing here and the concept of tense as anaphor, in particular.

Sidner's thesis (1979, 1983) presents an account of understanding definite pronouns and anaphoric definite NPs that reflects the ease with which people identify the intended specificand of definite pronouns (except in highly ambiguous cases), as well as the intended specificand of anaphoric definite NPs.

With respect to noun phrases (but not clauses), Sidner makes the same assumption about evoking, specifying, and co-specifying in a Discourse Model that I have made here. To understand anaphoric expressions, Sidner postulates three mechanisms:

1. a current discourse focus (DF)
2. an ordered list of potential foci (PFL) for the next utterance
3. a stack for saving the current DF and resuming it later.

The DF corresponds to that entity the listener is most attending to. Pronouns can most easily specify the current DF, slightly less easily a member of the PFL, and with slightly more difficulty, a stacked focus. Specifying an entity pronominally can shift the listener's attention to it, thereby promoting it to be the next DF. Anything else specified in the clause ends up on the PFL, ordered by its original syntactic position. (Sidner introduced a separate "agent focus" to allow two entities to be specified pronominally in the same clause, but it was not a critical feature of her approach.) As for anaphoric definite NPs, they can specify anything previously introduced (whether on the PFL, a stacked focus, or anything else) or anything related in a mutually inferrable way with the current DF or a member of the PFL. In terms of the constraints I mentioned above, it is only those discourse entities that are either the DF or on the PFL that can serve as E_a for an anaphoric definite NP.[9]

In Sidner (1983) DFs always are stacked for possible resumption later. In Grosz and Sidner (1986) it is an entire **focus space** (FS) (Grosz 1977) that gets stacked (i.e., the collection of entities L is attending to by virtue of the current **discourse segment** (DS)) but only when the **purpose** of the current DS is taken to **dominate** that of the one upcoming. **Dominance** relations are also specified further according to the type of discourse. In Grosz and Sidner, they are defined for task-related dialogues and arguments. For example, in arguments, one DS purpose (DSP) dominates another if the second provides evidence for a point made in the first. When the dominated DSP is satisfied, its corresponding FS is popped. This stack mechanism models the listener's **attentional state**. The relations between DSPs constitute the **intentional structure** of the text. Getting a listener to resume a DS via the stack mechanism is taken to require less effort on a speaker's part than returning to elaborate an argument or subtask description later on.

The significance of Sidner (1983) and Grosz and Sidner (1986) for the current enterprise is that:

- Sidner essentially shows how DF can move gradually among the discourse entities that make up a focus space, as the listener is processing its associated discourse segment;

---

[8] Nor does it indicate wholesale acceptance of their theory of discourse as has so far emerged. I believe that they would be the first to admit that it's a "theory in progress".

[9] Grosz, Joshi, and Weinstein (1983) have reinterpreted part of Sidner's work in terms of their theory of **centering**. Her DF becomes their "backward-looking center" C_b and her PFL becomes their ordered list of "forward-looking centers" C_f. They have proposed heuristics for which entities (C_b and/or C_fs) will be specified pronominally (when specified at all) and for the consequences for such specification on subsequent C_b and C_fs.

- Grosz and Sidner show how DF can make a radical jump to a different (possibly newly evoked) discourse entity as the listener moves to process the next discourse segment.[10]

I reinterpret this in the current framework in terms of the anaphoric function $\alpha(NP_b, E_a)$. Within a discourse segment, the entity that is the DF is the most likely E_a. Over the discourse segment, other discourse entities in the segment's focus space may in turn become DF. With a change in discourse segment, however, the DF can change radically to an entity in the focus space associated with the new segment.

To hint again at what is to come: in Section 3.2, I will propose a temporal analogue of DF, which I have called **temporal focus** (TF). In Section 3.3, I will show how gradual movements of the TF are tied in with the ontology of what a tensed clause specifies—i.e., an ontology of events and situations—while more radical movements reflect the effect of discourse structure on TF.

3 TENSE AS ANAPHOR

Tense may not seem *prima facie* anaphoric: an isolated sentence like *John went to bed* or *I met a man who looked like a basset hound* appears to make sense in a way that a stand-alone *He went to bed* or *The man went to bed* does not. On the other hand, if some time or event is established by the context (i.e., either by an event or situation described in the previous discourse or by a temporal adverbial in the current sentence—cf. Passonneau, and Moens and Steedman, Chapters 8 and 6, this volume), tense will invariably be interpreted with respect to it, as in:

7. a. After he finished his chores, John went to bed.
   b. John partied until 3 am. He came home and went to bed.

In each case, the interpretation of John's going to bed is linked to an explicitly mentioned time or event. This is what underlies all discussion of the anaphoric quality of tense.

3.1 Background

The assumption that tense is anaphoric (i.e., that its interpretation is linked to some time or event derived from context) goes back many years, although it is not a universally held belief (cf. Comrie 1985). Leech seems to express this view in his *Meaning and the English Verb:*

63 INDEFINITE TIME Whereas the Present Perfect, in its indefinite past sense, does not name a specific point of time, a definite POINT OF ORIENTATION in the past is normally required for the appropriate use of the Simple Past Tense. The point of orientation may be specified in one of three ways: (a) by an adverbial express of time-when; (b) by a preceding use of a Past or Perfect Tense; and (c) by implicit definition; i.e., by assumption of a particular time from context.

73 The Past Perfect Tense has the meaning of past-in-the-past, or more accurately, 'a time further in the past, seen from the viewpoint of a definite point of time already in the past'. That is, like the

---

[10] This jump is not necessary: the DF can stay the same over discourse segments—for example, discussing the same entity from different points of view.

Simple Past Tense, the Past Perfect demands an already established past point of reference. (Leech 1987: 47)

Leech did not elaborate further on how reference points are used in the interpretation of simple past tense and past perfect tense, or on what has become the main problem in the semantics and pragmatics of tense: reconciling the (usual) forward movement of events in narratives with a belief in the anaphoric (or context-dependent) character of tense.

The first explicit reference I have to tense being anaphoric like a definite pronoun is in an article by McCawley (1971:110), who said:

However the tense morpheme does not just express the time relationship between the clause it is in and the next higher clause—it also refers to the time of the clause that it is in, and indeed, refers to it in a way that is rather like the way in which personal pronouns refer to what they stand for.

McCawley also tried to fit in his view of tense as pronoun with the interpretation of tense in simple narratives. Here he proposed that the event described in one clause serves as the antecedent of the event described in the next, but that it may be related to that event by being either at the same time or "shortly after" it. He did not elaborate on when one relation would be assumed and when the other.

Partee (1973) also noted the similarities between tense and definite pronouns. However, she subsequently recognized that taking simple past tense as directly analogous with pronouns was incompatible with the usual forward movement of time in the interpretation in a sequence of sentences denoting events (Partee 1984). Her response was a modification of the claim that tense is anaphoric, saying:

I still believe it is reasonable to characterize tense as anaphoric, or more broadly as context-dependent, but I would no longer suggest that this requires them to be viewed as 'referring' to times as pronouns 'refer' to entities, or to treat times as arguments of predicates (256).

The particular context-dependent process she proposes for interpreting tensed clauses follows that of Hinrichs 1986, briefly described below.

The examples presented above to illustrate the anaphoric quality of tense were all simple past. However, as Leech notes (see above), the past perfect also makes demands on having some reference point already established in the context. Thus it cannot be in terms of the event described in a tensed clause that tense is anaphoric. Instead, several people (Steedman 1982, Hinrichs 1986, Bauerle 1979) have argued that it is that part of tense called by Reichenbach (1947) the **point of reference** (here abbreviated RT) that is anaphoric. This can be seen by considering the following example:

8. a. John went to the hospital.
   b. He had twisted his ankle on a patch of ice.

It is not the **point of the event** (here abbreviated ET) of John's twisting his ankle that is interpreted anaphorically with respect to his going to the hospital. Rather, it is the RT of the second clause: its ET is interpreted as prior to that because the clause is in the past perfect (see above).

I will now review briefly Hinrichs's proposal as to how tensed clauses are interpreted in context, in order to contrast it with the current proposal.

In Hinrichs 1986, Hinrichs makes the simplifying assumption that in a sequence of simple past sentences, the temporal order of events described cannot contradict the order of the sentences. This allows him to focus on the problem of characterizing those circumstances in which the event described by one sentence *follows* that described by the previous one (Example 9—Hinrichs's Example 15) and when it overlaps it (Example 10—Hinrichs's Example 21):

9. The elderly gentleman wrote out the check, tore it from the book, and handed it to Costain.
10. Mr. Darby slapped his forehead, then collected himself and opened the door again. The brush man was smiling at him hesitantly.

Hinrichs bases his account on the *Aktionsart* of a tensed clause (i.e., its Vendlerian classification as an accomplishment, achievement, activity, or state—including progressives). Assuming an initial reference point in a discourse, the event described by a tensed clause interpreted as an accomplishment or achievement will be included in that reference point and will also introduce a new reference point ordered after the old one. Events associated with the other *Aktionsarten* include the current reference point in the event time. This means that given a sequence of two clauses interpreted as accomplishments or achievements, their corresponding events will follow one another (cf. Example 9). On the other hand, given a sequence with at least one tensed clause interpreted as an activity or state (including progressive), their corresponding events will be interpreted as overlapping each other (cf. Example 10).

Hinrichs relates his reference point to that of Reichenbach. (Thus, the anaphoric character of tense is based on RT and not on the events directly.) However, Hinrichs's notion and Reichenbach's differ with respect to the time of the event described in the tensed clause. While Reichenbach talks about ET and RT being the same for nonprogressive past-tense clauses, in Hinrichs's account the reference point can fall after the event if a nonprogressive past is interpreted as an accomplishment or an achievement. This is necessary to achieve the forward movement of narrative that Hinrichs assumes is always the case (his simplifying assumption) but it is not the same as Reichenbach's RT. It also leads to problems in cases where this simplifying assumption is just wrong—where in a sequence of simple past tenses, there is what appears to be a "backward" movement of time, as in

11. a. For an encore, John played the "Moonlight Sonata".
    b. The opening movement he took rather tentatively, but then...

where the second clause should be understood as describing the beginning of the playing event in more detail, not as describing a subsequent event.

In the account given below, both forward and backward movement of time fall out of the anaphoric character of tensed clauses, and the dependency of discourse anaphora on discourse structure.[11]

3.2 Tense as discourse anaphor: in what sense "specify"?

With that background, I will now show how tensed clauses share the two properties I set out in Section 1 (repeated here) and hence are further examples of discourse anaphora:

---

[11] Dowty 1986 gives an account similar to Hinrichs's in its *a priori* assumption of the non-backward-movement of time in simple narratives and its focus on how different *Aktionsarten* lead to interpretation of co-temporal versus subsequent events. The two accounts differ in how the latter is achieved. Dowty's account avoids some problems that Hinrichs's cannot, but still cannot deal with the fact that time sometimes "moves backwards" even in sequences of simple past tense.

1. Anaphors specify entities in an evolving model of the discourse that the listener is constructing;
2. the particular entity specified depends on another entity in that part of the evolving Discourse Model that the listener is currently attending to.

To do this, I need to explain the sense in which tensed clauses specify and the way in which that specification can depend on another element in the current context.

Recall that I presume that a listener's developing discourse model represents both the entities being discussed, along with their properties and relations, and the events and situations being discussed, along with their relationships with another. For the rest of this paper, I want to ignore the former and focus on the latter. This I will call **event/situation structure**, or **E/S structure**. It represents the listener's best effort at interpreting the speaker's ordering of those events and situations in time and space. One problem in text understanding, then, is that of establishing where in the evolving E/S structure to integrate the event or situation description in the next clause.

In this framework, a tensed clause C_b provides two pieces of semantic information: (a) a description of an event or situation, and (b) a particular configuration of ET, RT, and **point of speech** (abbreviated ST). (Here I may be departing from Reichenbach in treating ET, RT, and ST explicitly as elements of linguistic semantics, quite distinct from entities of type "event" in the Discourse Model.) C_b then specifies an entity E_b in the Discourse Model whose temporal relationship to other events in the model follows (in part) from C_b's particular configuration of ET, RT, and ST. Both the characteristics of E_b (i.e., its ontology) and the configuration of ET, RT, and ST are critical to my account of tense as discourse anaphor.

The event ontology I assume follows that of Moens and Steedman (chapter 6, this volume) and of Passonneau (chapter 8, this volume). Both propose that people interpret events as having a tripartite structure (a "nucleus" in Moens and Steedman's terminology) consisting of a preparatory phase (**prep**), a culmination (**cul**), and a consequent phase (**conseq**)—as in Figure 2. This tripartite structure permits a uniform account to be given of aspectual types in English and of how the interpretation of temporal adverbials interacts with the interpretation of tense and aspect. For example, the coercion of clauses from one interpretation to another is defined in terms of which parts of a nucleus they select and how those parts are described.[12]

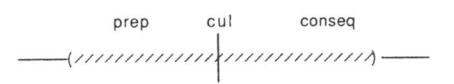

FIG. 2 Tripartite ontology of events.

The ET/RT/ST configuration is significant in that, like Steedman 1982, Dowty 1986, Hinrichs 1986, and Partee 1984, I take RT as the basis for anaphora. To indicate this, I single it out as an independent argument to anaphoric functions, here labelled β. In particular, the following schema holds of a clause C_b linked anaphorically to an event E_a through its RT:

$$\beta(C_b, E_a, RT_b) = E_b$$

---

[12] The ontology of an event/situation also includes its role structure. This latter appears to play a part in possible anaphoric relations between an NP and an event entity, but not between a tensed clause and an event entity.

420   The Language of Time: A Reader

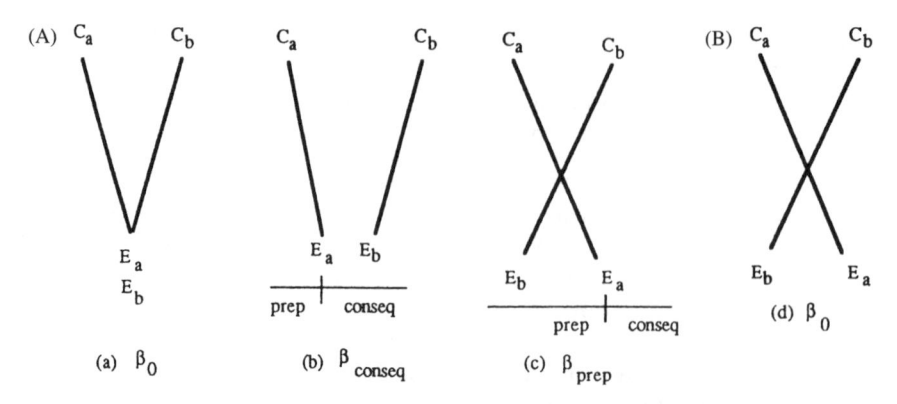

FIG. 3 Anaphoric relations for tensed clauses where (A) ET = RT, (B) ET < RT.

The relationship between E_b and E_a then falls out as a **consequence** of (1) the particular ET/RT/ST configuration of C_b; and (2) the particular function β involved.

One possibility is that β links RT_b directly to E_a—i.e.:

$$\beta_0(C_b, E_a, RT_b) = E_b$$

In this case, the relationship between E_b and E_a then depends on the configuration of RT_b and ET_b. If $ET_b = RT_b$, then (minimally) E_b is taken to coincide in some way with E_a. This is shown in Figure 3a. If $ET_b < RT_b$ (as in the perfect tenses), E_b is taken to precede E_a. This is shown in Figure 3d.

Alternatively, β may embody part of the tripartite ontology of events mentioned earlier: β_{prep} links RT_b to the preparatory phase of E_a (as shown in Figure 3b)—i.e.:

$$\beta_{prep}(C_b, E_a, RT_b) = E_b$$

while β_{conseq} links RT_b to the consequent phase of E_a (as shown in Figure 3c)—i.e.:

$$\beta_{conseq}(C_b, E_a, RT_b) = E_b$$

(There is a third possibility—that RT_b links to the culmination of E_a—but it is not clear to me that it could be distinguished from the simpler β_0 function given above, which links RT_b to E_a itself. Also, while β_{prep} and β_{conseq} relations for RT_b might theoretically be possible for a perfect, it is not clear to me that these cases could be distinguished from the simpler β_0. In the case of perfects therefore, the relation between E_b and E_a is correspondingly indirect.[13]

The following example illustrates the case where $\beta = \beta_0$ and $ET_b = RT_b$.

12. a. John played the piano.
    b. Mary played the kazoo.

Sentence 12a. evokes a new event entity E_a describable as the event of John playing the piano. Since the tense of (12b) is simple past, $ET_b = RT_b$. Given $\beta_0(C_b, E_a, RT_b) = E_b$,

---

[13] I have not considered other aspectual types in English (such as progressive) vis-à-vis possible anaphoric relations. Integrating the current account with work on aspect and *Aktionsarten* (cf. Moens & Steedman (chapter 6), Passonneau (chapter 8), Hinrichs (1988), Nakhimovsky (1988)) is left to future work.

then E_b is interpreted as coextensive with E_a. (Whether this is further interpreted as two simultaneous events or a single event of their playing a duet depends on context and, perhaps, world knowledge as well.) This is illustrated in Figure 4. Example 8 (repeated here) illustrates the case β_0 where $ET_b < RT_b$.

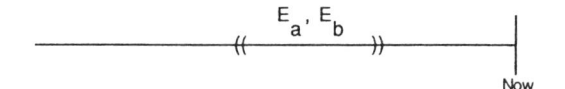

FIG. 4   Co-extensive events.

8. a. John went to the hospital.
   b. He had twisted his ankle on a patch of ice.

Clause 8a evokes an entity E_a describable as John's going to the hospital. Since 8b is past perfect, $ET_b < RT_b$. Thus if $\beta_0 (C_b, E_a, RT_b) = E_b$, the event E_b described by 8b is taken to be prior to E_a. As Moens and Steedman (Chapter 6, this volume) point out, the *consequences* of an event described with a perfect tense are still assumed to hold. Hence the overlap shown in Figure 5:

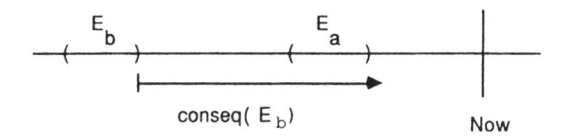

FIG. 5   Ordered events.

The next example illustrates β_{conseq}:

13. a. John went into the florist shop.
    b. He picked out three red roses, two white ones and one pale pink.

Clause 13a evokes an entity E_a describable as John's going into a flower shop. Since Clause 13b is simple past, $ET_b = RT_b$. Thus given $\beta_{conseq}(C_b, E_a, RT_b) = E_b$, event E_b is taken as being part of the consequent phase of E_a. That is, John's picking out the roses is taken as happening after his going into the florist shop. This is shown in Figure 6.

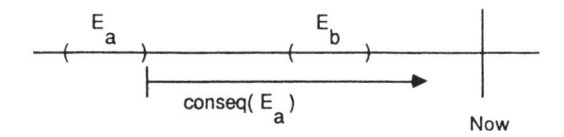

FIG. 6   Consequent-phase relation.

The next example illustrates the case of β_{prep}:

14. a. John bought Mary some flowers.
    b. He picked out three red roses, two white ones and one pale pink.

Since 14b is simple past, $ET_b = RT_b$. Thus given $\beta_{prep}(C_b, E_a, RT_b) = E_b$, event E_b—the event of picking out some roses—is taken as being part of the preparatory phase of the event E_a, which when completed, can be described as having bought some flowers. This is shown in Figure 7.

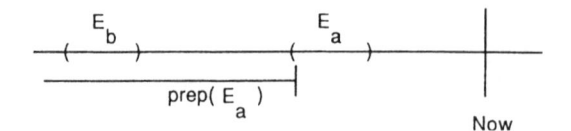

FIG. 7 Preparatory-phase relation.

To summarize, I have claimed that: (1) the notion of **specification** makes sense with respect to tensed clauses; (2) one can describe the anaphoric relation in terms of the RT of a tensed clause C_b, its ET/RT configuration, and an existing event or situation entity E_a—that is, $\beta(C_b, E_a, RT_b) = E_b$; and (3) there are (at least) three β functions—one, β_0, linking RT_b to E_a itself, the other two (β_{prep} and β_{conseq}) embodying parts of a tripartite ontology of events. In the next section, I will discuss constraints on the second argument to $\beta(C_b, E_a, RT_b)$—that is, constraints on which entities in the evolving E/S structure the specification of a tensed clause can depend on.

3.3   Temporal focus

Recall from Section 2.2 that Sidner introduced the notion of a dynamically changing **discourse focus** (DF) to capture the intuition that at any point in the discourse, there is one discourse entity that is the prime focus of attention and that is the most likely (although not the only possible) specificand of a definite pronoun. In parallel, I propose a dynamically changing **temporal focus** (TF), to capture a similar intuition that at any point in the discourse, there is one entity in E/S structure that is most attended to and hence most likely to stand in an anaphoric relation with the RT of the next clause. That is, $\beta(C_b, TF, RT_b) = E_b$. If C_b is interpreted as part of the current discourse segment, after its interpretation there are three possibilities:

1. With β_0, the TF will stay where it is, independent of whether $ET = RT$ or $ET < RT$.
2. With β_{conseq}, RT_b's link to the consequent phase of the TF locates event E_b there, shifting the TF forward (to E_b). This is the "natural" forward progression of narrative.
3. With β_{prep}, RT_b's link to the preparatory phase of the TF locates E_b there, shifting the TF backward to (E_b). This is used to elaborate an event or situation in more detail.

These relationships, which I will call **maintenance** and **local movement** of the TF, correspond to Sidner's DF moving gradually among the discourse entities in a discourse segment. (They cover the same phenomena as the **micromoves** that Nakhimovsky describes in his paper (Nakhimovsky, 1988).) More radical movements of TF correspond to changes in discourse structure. (These cover similar phenomena to the **macromoves** described in Nakhimovsky, 1988.) In cases involving movements into and out of an embedded discourse segment, either 1. The TF will shift to a different entity in E/S structure—either an existing entity or one created in recognition of an embedded narrative; or 2. It will return to the entity previously labeled TF, after completing an embedded narrative. Such movements are described in Section 3.3.2. Other movements, signaled by temporal adverbials and *when* clauses, are not discussed in this paper.[14]

---

[14] I should also note that Rohrer 1985 suggests that there may exist a set of possible temporal referents, possibly ordered by saliency, among which the tense in a sentence may find its reference time, but doesn't elaborate how. That is the only thing I have seen that comes close to the current proposal.

3.3.1 Temporal focus: maintenance and local movement

The following pair of examples illustrate maintenance and local movement of TF within a discourse segment and its link with E/S structure construction. The first I discussed in the previous section to illustrate β_{conseq}. The second is a variation on that example:

13. a. John went into the florist shop.
    b. He picked out three red roses, two white ones and one pale pink.

15. a. John went into the florist shop.
    b. He had promised Mary some flowers.
    c. He picked out three red roses, two white ones, and one pale pink.

First consider Example 13. The first clause (13a) evokes an event entity E_a describable as *John's going into the florist shop*. Since its tense is simple past, E_a is interpreted as prior to ST. Since it begins the discourse, its status is special vis-à-vis both definite NPs and tensed clauses. That is, since no previous TF will have been established yet, the listener takes that entity E_a to serve as TF.[15] This is shown in Figure 8:

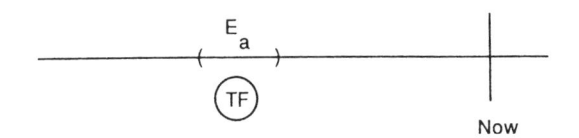

FIGURE 8   E/S structure after processing Clause 13a.

If Clause 13b is interpreted as being part of the same discourse segment as (13a) it must be the case that $\beta(C_{13b}, TF, RT_{13b})$. Assume the listener takes β to be β_{conseq} on the basis of world knowledge—that is, $\beta_{conseq}(C_{13b}, TF, RT_{13b})$. Since the tense of (13b) is simple past, its RT and ET coincide. Thus (13b) specifies a new entity E_b, located within the consequent phase of the TF—that is, E_a—and hence after it. I assume that, following the computation of the anaphoric function, TF becomes associated with the event entity located at RT_b. In this case, it is E_b, and TF thereby moves forward (cf. Figure 9). As noted, this is the gradual forward movement of simple narratives that Hinrichs, Partee, and Dowty were out to achieve. Here it falls out simply from the discourse notion of a TF and from the particular anaphoric function β_{conseq}.[16]

Now consider Example 15 (repeated here) whose first clause is the same as Example 13a and hence would be processed in the same way.

15. a. John went into the florist shop.
    b. He had promised Mary some flowers.
    c. He picked out three red roses, two white ones, and one pale pink.

The tense of the next clause (15b) is past perfect. As I noted above, the only anaphoric function on RT_{15b} and an event entity that makes sense for perfect tenses is β_0—that is,

$$\beta_0(C_{15b}, TF, RT_{15b}) = E_{15b}$$

---

[15] This is similar to the listener's response to the definite NP *the florist shop*, which in the middle of a discourse would have to be taken anaphorically. At the beginning of a discourse, the listener will just create a new discourse entity.

[16] In parallel with this, given β_{prep}, TF will move incrementally back into the preparatory phase of the event that was the previous TF. Given β_0, RT_b is at the TF and TF does not move.

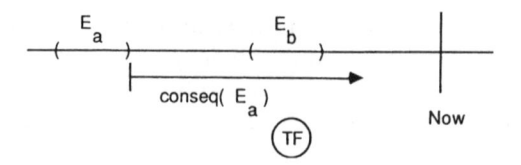

FIG. 9 E/S structure after processing Clause 13b.

Given that perfect tenses imply $ET < RT$, the event E_b specified by (15b) will be interpreted as being prior to E_a. Moreover, since (15b) is past perfect, the consequent phase of E_b is assumed to still hold with respect to RT_{15b}. Hence the consequent phase of E_b overlaps E_a. Finally, since TF is associated with the event entity at RT_b, it remains at E_a. E/S structure at this point resembles Figure 10:

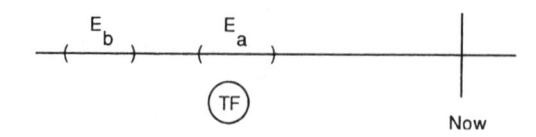

FIG. 10 E/S structure after processing Clause 15b.

Now Clause 15c is the same as (13b), and TF is the same as it was at the point of interpreting (13b). Thus not surprisingly, 15c produces the same change in E/S structure and in the TF as (13b), resulting in the diagram shown in Figure 11.

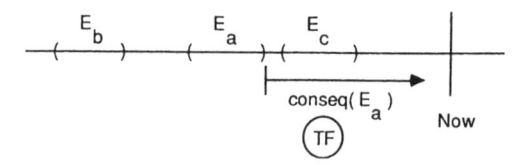

FIG. 11 E/S structure after processing Clause 15c.

3.3.2 Temporal focus: discourse-structure movements

To illustrate the effect of discourse structure on TF, consider the following variation on Example 15, which had the same structure vis-à-vis sequence of tenses.

16. a. John went into the florist shop.
    b. He had promised Mary some flowers.
    c. She said she wouldn't forgive him if he forgot.

The first two clauses (a) and (b) are the same as in Example 15 and lead to the same configuration of event entities in E/S structure (as shown in Figure 10). But the most plausible interpretation of (16c) is where the "saying" event is interpreted anaphorically with respect to the "promising" event—that is, where (16b–c) are taken together as (the start of) an embedded discourse, describing an event prior to John's going to the florist's.

To handle this, I assume, following Grosz and Sidner 1986, that when the listener recognizes an embedded discourse segment, s/he stores the current TF for possible resumption later.[17] However, I also assume the listener recognizes the embedding *not*

---

[17] While Sidner and thereafter Grosz and Sidner assume a stack of focus spaces with their associated DFs, each of which is resumable, I do not have evidence that the listener can keep track of more than one other node of E/S structure in addition to the TF. Resuming any other node seems to require more effort—such as using a *when* clause. Hence I assume a single item cache for the previous value of TF.

when s/he first encounters a perfect-tensed clause C_b, since it needn't signal an embedded discourse, but *later*, when an immediately following simple past tense clause C_c is most sensibly interpreted with respect to the event entity E_b that C_b evoked.[18] At this point, the listener moves TF from its current position to E_b, caching the previous value for possible resumption later. Following this gross movement, $\beta(C_c, TF, RT_c)$ will be computed. If β is then interpreted as β_{conseq} or β_{prep}, there will be a second movement of TF.[19]

Coming back to Example 16, if Clause 16c is taken as being part of a single discourse segment with (16a–b), *she saying something* would have to be interpreted with respect to the current $TF(E_a)$—John's going to the florist. This is implausible under all possible interpretations of β.[20] However, under the assumption that E_b is part of an embedded narrative, the listener can *a posteriori* shift TF to E_b and consider the anaphoric relation

$$\beta(C_{16c}, TF, RT_{16c}) = E_{16c}$$

with E_b as TF. At this point, the listener can plausibly take β to be β_{conseq} based on world knowledge. Since (16c) is simple past, $ET_c = RT_c$, the "saying" event E_c is viewed as part of the consequent phase of (and hence following) the "promising" event E_b. As in the first case, TF moves to the event located at RT_c—i.e., to E_c. This is shown roughly in Figure 12. Notice that this involved *two* movements of TF—once in response to a perceived embedded segment and a second time, in response to interpreting β as β_{conseq}.

Now consider the following extension to (16):

17. a. John went into the florist shop.
    b. He had promised Mary some flowers.
    c. She said she wouldn't forgive him if he forgot.
    d. So he picked out three red roses, two white ones, and one pale pink.

As before, Clauses 17b–c form an embedded narrative, but here the main narrative of John's visit to the florist shop, started at (17a), is continued at (17d). To handle this, I again assume that TF behaves much like Sidner's DF in response to the listener's recognition of the **end** of an embedded narrative: that is, the cached TF is resumed and processing continues.[21]

---

[18] One could say, in parallel with Sidner 1983, that this E_b was a potential focus (PF). However, I do not postulate a Potential Focus List as in Sidner, because I do not think there is ever more than one PF that one can shift to without using a temporal adverbial.

[19] This is clearly an **inertial** strategy: it assumes that the listener will prefer to interpret clauses as being in the same discourse segment, unless forced to do otherwise, say by a continuation such as (16c) or a lexical item that signals a possible embedded narrative. This I will discuss later on. In spoken text, the speaker might give an intonation to (16b) that conveys that it and the following clauses should be understood as an embedded discourse segment. This would be what breaks the inertia and causes the listener to shift the TF.

[20] It is rarely the case that one cannot come up with a story linking two events and/or situations. Thus it would be impossible to reject a hypothesis on grounds of inconsistency. All one can say is that one of such stories might be more plausible than the others by requiring, in some sense not explored here, fewer inferences. Crain and Steedman 1985 make a similar argument about prepositional phrase (PP) attachment. For example, it is not impossible for a cat to own a telescope—e.g., by inheritance from its former owner. Thus *a cat with a telescope* is not an inconsistent description. However, it must compete with other plausible interpretations like *seeing with a telescope* in *I saw a cat with a telescope*. Thus I assume that interpretations are computed in parallel, with the most plausible prediction being the one that ends up updating both E/S structure and the TF.

[21] Recall my prediction that if any but the most recently cached TF is to be resumed, a cooperative speaker will explicitly indicate this with a temporal adverbial or a *when* clause.

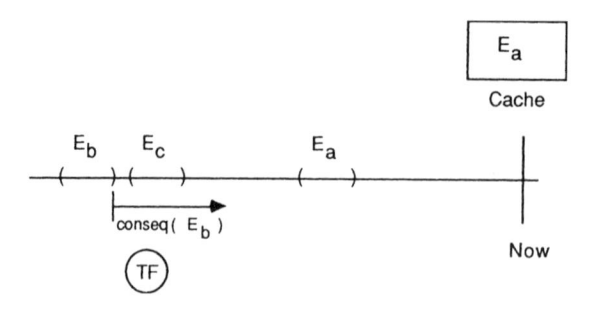

FIG. 12 E/S structure after processing Clause 16c.

Under this assumption, Clauses 17a–c are interpreted as in the previous example (cf. Figure 12). Recognizing Clause 17d as resuming the embedding segment,[22] the previously cached TF (E_a—the *going into the florist shop* event) is resumed. Again assume that the listener takes the anaphoric function to be $\beta_{conseq}(C_d, TF, RT_d) = E_d$ on the basis of world knowledge. Since Clause 17d is simple past (ET = RT), the *picking out roses* event E_d is viewed as part of the consequent phase and hence following the *going into the florist shop* event. This is shown roughly in Figure 13:

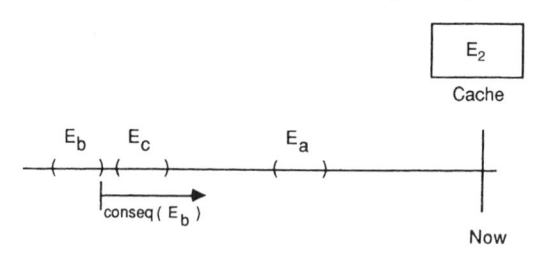

FIG. 13 E/S structure after processing Clause 17d.

Now getting the listener to interpret a text as an embedded narrative requires providing him/her with another event or situation that TF can move to. One way in English is via a perfect-tensed clause, which explicitly evokes another event, temporally earlier than the one currently in focus. Another way is by lexical indications of an embedded narrative, such as verbs of telling and NPs that themselves denote events or situations (e.g., ones headed by de-verbal nouns).

This is illustrated in Example 18. Even though all its clauses are simple past (ET = RT), Clauses 18c–d are most plausibly interpreted as *indirect speech* describing an event that has occurred prior to the "telling" event. I assume that in response to recognizing this kind of embedded narrative, the listener creates a new node of E/S structure and shifts TF there, caching the previous value of TF for possible resumption later. The temporal location of this new node vis-à-vis the previous TF will depend on information in the tensed clause and on the listener's world knowledge.

18. a. I was at Mary's house yesterday.
    b. We talked about her sister Jane.
    c. She spent five weeks in Alaska with two friends.
    d. Together, they climbed Mt. McKinley.
    e. Mary asked whether I would want to go to Alaska some time.

---

[22] *So* is one cue. In spoken discourse, intonation would be another.

Notice that, as with embedded narratives cued by the use of a perfect tense, caching the previous TF for resumption later enables the correct interpretation of Clause 18e, which is most plausibly interpreted as following the *telling about her sister* event.

An NP denoting an event or situation (such as one headed by a noun like *trip* or by a de-verbal noun like *installation*) can also signal the upcoming possibility of an embedded narrative that will elaborate that event or situation (past, upcoming, or hypothetical) in more detail, as in Example 19. In this case, the original NP and the subsequent clause(s) will be taken as co-specifying the same thing. The question here is how and when TF moves.

19. a. I was talking with Mary yesterday.
    b. She told me about her trip to Alaska.
    c. She spent five weeks above the Arctic Circle with two friends.
    d. The three of them climbed Mt. McKinley.

After interpreting Clause 19b, the TF is at the "telling" event. I claim that the NP *her trip to Alaska*, while evoking a discourse entity, does not affect the TF. If Clause 19c is interpreted as the start of an embedded narrative (as it is here), TF moves to the event entity E_c it evokes (caching the previous value E_b). At this point, using additional reasoning, the listener may recognize an anaphoric relation between Clause 19c and the discourse entity evoked by *her trip to Alaska*. Support for this, rather than assuming that an event-denoting NP sets up a potential focus, just as I claim a perfect-tensed clause does, comes from the reasoning required to understand the following parallel example, where I would claim TF does not move.

20. a. I was talking with Mary yesterday.
    b. She told me about her trip to Alaska.
    c. She had spent five weeks above the Arctic Circle with two friends.
    d. The three of them had climbed Mt. McKinley.
    e. She said that next year they would go for Aconcagua.

The event described in Clause 20c is the same as that described in Clause 19c, and should be interpreted anaphorically with respect to the entity *her trip to Alaska* in the same way. If this is the case, however, then the anaphoric link does not follow from the movement of TF.

3.3.3 Temporal focus: miscellany

Example 20 above illustrates one case of an anaphoric function on an NP and a tensed clause, specifically $\beta\,(C_b, E_a, RT_b)$ where the entity E_a has been evoked by an NP rather than a clause. Another possibility is that $\beta\,(NP_b, E_a) = E_b$, where NP_b is definite by virtue of an entity evoked by a clause rather than an NP—that is, E_b is associated with either the preparatory/culmination/consequent structure of E_a, as in

21. a. Mary climbed Mt. McKinley.
    b. *The preparations* took her longer than *the ascent*.

or its associated role structure, as in

22. a. John bought a television.
    b. Although he had intended to buy a 13" b/w set, *the salesman* convinced him to buy a 25" color, back-projection job.

where *the salesman* fills a particular role in the buying event.

Next, notice that ambiguities arise when there is more than one way to plausibly segment the discourse, as in the following example:

23. a. I told Frank about my meeting with Ira.
    b. We talked about ordering a Butterfly.

Here it is plausible to take Clause 23b as the beginning of an embedded narrative, whereby the "talking about" event is interpreted against a new node of E/S structure, situated prior to the "telling Frank" event. (In this case, *we* is Ira and me.) It is also plausible to take (23b) as continuing the current narrative, whereby the "talking about" event is interpreted with respect to the "telling Frank" event. (In contrast here, *we* is Frank and me.)

Finally, consider things from the point of view of generation. If some event E_b is part of the preparatory phase of some event E_a, and a description of E_a has just been generated using the simple past tense, then E_b could be described using either the simple past, as in Example 24 or past perfect, as in Example 25.

24. a. John went to the hospital.
    b. He took a taxi, because his car was in the shop.
25. a. John went to the hospital.
    b. He had taken a taxi, because his car was in the shop.

In the case of Example 24, the listener/reader recognizes that E_b is part of the preparatory phase of E_a and that E_b therefore precedes E_a. In the case of Example 25, the listener would first recognize that E_b precedes E_a because of the past perfect, but then recognize E_b as part of the preparatory phase of E_a.

On the other hand, if E_b simply precedes E_a, but a description of E_a has been generated first, then E_b must be described with a past perfect (Example 26): simple past would not be sufficient (Example 27).

26. a. John went to the hospital.
    b. He had broken his ankle, walking on a patch of ice.
27. a. John went to the hospital.
    b. *He broke his ankle, walking on a patch of ice.

4 CONCLUSION

In this paper, I have presented a uniform characterization of discourse anaphora in a way that includes definite pronouns, definite NPs, and tensed clauses. In doing so, I have argued that the successful use of discourse anaphors depends on two different things: (1) speakers' and listeners' (mutual) beliefs about the ontology of the things and events being discussed, and (2) speakers' and listeners' (mutual) focus of attention. The former implicates semantics in the explanation of discourse anaphora, the latter, discourse itself. It is important that we as researchers recognize these as two separate systems, as the properties of discourse as an explanatory device are very different from those of semantics.

ACKNOWLEDGEMENTS

This work was partially supported by ARO grant DAA29-884-9-0027, NSF grant MCS-8219116-CER, and DARPA grant N00014-85-K-0018 to the University of

Pennsylvania, by DARPA grant N00014-85-C-0012 to UNISYS Paoli Research Center, and an Alvey grant to the Centre for Speech Technology Research, University of Edinburgh.

My thanks to Becky Passonneau, Debby Dahl, Mark Steedman, Ethel Schuster, Candy Sidner, Barbara Grosz, Ellen Bard, Anne Anderson, Tony Sanford, Simon Garrod, and Rich Thomason for their helpful comments on the many earlier versions of this paper.

REFERENCES

Bauerle, R. (1979). *Temporal Deixis, temporale Frage*. Tübingen: Gunter Narr Verlag.
Bobrow, D. and the PARC Understander Group (1986). 'GUS, A Frame-Driven Dialog System', *Artificial Intelligence* 8: 155–73.
Chomsky, N. (1980). *Rules and Representations*. New York, NY: Columbia University Press.
Clark, H. and Marshall, C. (1981). 'Definite Reference and Mutual Knowledge,' in A. Joshi, B. Webber, and I. Sag (eds), *Elements of Discourse Understanding*. Cambridge: Cambridge University Press, 10–63.
Comrie, B. (1985). *Tense*. Cambridge: Cambridge University Press.
Crain, S. and Steedman, M. (1985). 'On not being Led up the Garden Path: the Use of Context by the Psychological Syntax Processor', in [*Natural Language Parsing*] D. Dowty, L. Karttunen, and A. Zwicky, (eds.). Cambridge: Cambridge University Press, 320–58.
Dowty, D. (1986). 'The Effects of Aspectual Class on the Temporal Structure of Discourse: Semantics or Pragmatics', *Linguistics and Philosophy* 9(1): 37–62.
Grosz, B. (1977). 'The Representation and Use of Focus in Dialogue Understanding'. Ph.D. dissertation. University of California, Berkeley, CA.
——, Joshi, A., and Weinstein, S. (1983). 'Providing a Unified Account of Definite Noun Phrases in Discourse', in *Proceedings of the 22nd Annual Meeting of the Association for Computational Linguistics*. MIT, Cambridge, MA, 44–50.
—— and Sidner, C. (1986). 'Attention, Intention, and the Structure of Discourse', *Computational Linguistics* 12(3): 175–604.
Heim, I. (1982). 'The Semantics of Definite and Indefinite Noun Phrases'. Ph.D. dissertation. Department of Linguistics, University of Massachusetts, Amherst, MA.
Hinrichs, E. (1986). 'Temporal Anaphora in Discourses of English', *Linguistics and Philosophy* 9(1): 63–82.
——(1988). 'Tense, Quantifiers, and contexts', *Computational Linguistics* 14 (2): 3–14.
Hirst, G. (1981). *Anaphora in Natural Language Understanding: A Survey*. Berlin: Springer-Verlag.
Hobbs, J. (1987). 'Implicature and Definite Reference'. CSLI-87-99. Center for the Study of Language and Information, Stanford University, Stanford, CA.
Kamp, H. (1984). 'A Theory of Truth and Semantic Representation', in [*Truth, Interpretation, and Information.*] J. Groenendijk, T. M. V. Janssen, and M. Stokhof, (eds.). Dordrecht: Foris.
Leech, G. (1987). *Meaning and the English Verb* (2nd edn.). London: Longman.
McCawley, J. (1971). 'Tense and Time Reference in English', in C. Fillmore and D.J. Langendoen (eds.), *Studies in Linguistic Semantics*. New York, NY: Holt, Rinehart and Winston, 97–114.
Moens, M. and Steedman, M. (1987). Temporal Ontology in Natural Language. *Proceedings of the 25th Annual Meeting of the Association for Computational Linguistics*. Stanford, CA: Stanford University, 1–7.
Nakhimovsky, A. (1988). 'Aspect, Aspectual class, and the Temporal structure of Narrative', *Computational Linguistics* 14 (2): 29–43.
Partee, B. (1973). 'Some Structural Analogies between Tenses and Pronouns in English', *Journal of Philosophy* 70: 601–9.

Partee, B. (1984). 'Nominal and Temporal Anaphora', *Linguistics and Philosophy* 7(3): 287–324.
Passonneau, R. (1987). 'Situations and Intervals', in *Proceedings of the 25th Annual Meeting of the Association for Computational Linguistics*. Stanford, CA: Stanford University, 16–24.
Reichenbach, H. (1947). *The Elements of Symbolic Logic*. New York, NY: The Free Press.
Rohrer, C. (1985). 'Indirect Discourse and "Consecutio Temporum"', in [*Temporal Structure in Sentence and Discourse*]. V. LoCascio and C. Vet (eds.). Dordrecht: Foris Publications, 79–98.
Sag, I. and Hankamer, J. (1984). 'Toward a Theory of Anaphoric Processing', *Linguistics and Philosophy* 7(3): 325–45.
Sidner, C. (1979). 'Towards a Computational Theory of Definite Anaphora Comprehension in English Discourse'. Ph. D. dissertation. Dept. of Electrical Engineering and Computer Science, MIT, Cambridge, MA.
—— (1983). 'Focusing in the Comprehension of Definite Anaphora', in [*Computational Models of Discourse.*] M. Brady and R. Berwick (eds.). Cambridge, MA: MIT press, 267–330.
Steedman, M. (1982). 'Reference to Past Time', in [*Speech, Place, and Action*] R. Jarvella and W. Klein (eds.). New York, NY: Wiley, 125–57.
Webber, B. (1983). 'So can we Talk about Now?' in M. Brady and R. Berwick (eds.), *Computational Models of Discourse*. Cambridge, MA; MIT Press, 331–71.
—— (1987). 'The Interpretation of Tense in Discourse'. *Proceedings of the 25th Annual Meeting of the Association for Computational Linguistics*. Stanford University, Stanford, CA 147–54.
Woods, W.A. (1978). 'Semantics and Quantification in Natural-Language Question Answering'. in M. Yovits (ed.), *Advances in Computing* 17. New York, NY: Academic Press, 2–64.

19

Tense Interpretation in the Context of Narrative

FEI SONG AND ROBIN COHEN

1 INTRODUCTION

Tense interpretation plays an important role in determining the temporal ordering between the states and events mentioned in a narrative. Following Mourelatos (1978), we generally call states and events "situations." Determining temporal ordering is useful for many research problems of artificial intelligence. In story understanding, for example, knowing the temporal ordering allows us to answer questions like "what happened after a particular event occurred?"

Both tense and aspect are important expressions that contribute to the determination of temporal ordering (Passonneau, 1987; Dowty, 1986; Comrie, 1985)[1]. This paper focuses on tense interpretation and adopts a simplified treatment of aspect as proposed in Passonneau (1987). A more detailed treatment of aspect can be found in Song (1990).

Although tense has long been studied by linguists (Reichenbach, 1947; Dowty, 1986; Comrie, 1985), it is fairly recently that people have started to construct computational models to interpret it (Hinrichs, 1987; Passonneau, 1987; Webber, 1987; Moens and Steedman, 1987). Among these researchers, Webber (1987) is the first to extend tense interpretation from individual utterances to a whole discourse. Webber's main contributions include: recognizing the similarities between tense and other referential expressions such as pronoun and definite noun phrases, introducing the concept of temporal focus to maintain a dynamically changing entity, and presenting a set of heuristics on the possible movements of the temporal focus to interpret the tense of a new utterance. However, Webber allows all the heuristics to be applied in parallel and does not elaborate further on how the most plausible interpretation can be decided. Also, Webber did not consider the effects of aspect on the determination of the temporal ordering between situations.

In this paper, we extend Webber's work in several respects. First, we propose more detailed heuristics for determining the temporal ordering between situations. Second, we suggest constraints for capturing coherent tense sequences; only coherent sequences are further processed. Last, we arrange the heuristics and constraints in a fixed order to get a

---

Fei Song and Robin Cohen, 'Tense Interpretation in the Context of Narrative', *Proceedings of the Ninth National Conference on Artificial Intelligence (AAAI-91)*. (Menlo Park, CA: AAAI Press, 1991), 131–6. ©1991 American Association for Artificial Intelligence.

[1] Of course, other indicators such as temporal adverbials and connectives, discourse clues, and in general, real world knowledge of events also contribute to the analysis.

processing algorithm. The algorithm works for a restricted set of narratives which we call "simple narratives," but it can be made more general when more knowledge from discourse processing is added.

2 REPRESENTATION ISSUES

We can use Vilain and Kautz's point algebra (Vilain and Kautz, 1986) to represent the temporal ordering between situations. We can also use the same algebra to describe the underlying structure of an English tense. Similar to Reichenbach's account (Reichenbach, 1947), we still use the three points: S (the speech time), R (the reference time, a theoretical entity used to describe some complex tenses and distinguish between certain tenses), and E (the event time). However, in addition to assuming "precedes" and "coincides", we also allow "follows", the inverse relation of "precedes", to be used to describe a tense structure. As a result, we can have the following list of SRE triples for describing English tenses[2]:

Simple Present   [S = R = E]
    e.g., John runs.
Simple Past   [S > R = E]
    e.g., John ran.
Simple Future   [S < R = E]
    John will run.
Present Perfect   [S = R > E]
    John has run.
Past Perfect   [S > R > E]
    John had run.
Future Perfect   [S < R > E]
    John will have run.
Present Prospective   [S = R < E]
    John is going to run.
Past Prospective   [S > R < E]
    John was going to run.
Future Prospective   [S < R < E]
    John will be going to run.

The above list covers the same number of tenses as Reichenbach's account does, but it is both unambiguous and precise. For example, a Future Perfect would be described by three structures in Reichenbach's account, while by only one SRE triple in our description above. A situation, as argued in Allen (1983), typically holds or occurs over a time interval, which we denote as ET. It is not clear in Reichenbach's account how the E point is related to the ET interval. Our description is precise in that the relationships between E and ET are clearly specified according to the aspect of a situation.

In this paper, we follow Passonneau (1987) and treat aspect as the type of a situation. According to Passonneau (1987), situations can be classified into four types: states, temporally unbounded processes, temporally unspecified processes, and transition events,

---

[2] Here, <, =, and > stand for "precedes", "coincides" and "follows" respectively.

based on the verb type and whether the tense is progressive. Then, the relationships between E and ET can be specified as follows:

state: $\quad$ Start $< E <$ End
ub-process: $\quad$ Start $< E <$ End
us-process: $\quad$ Start $\leq E \leq$ End
event: $\quad$ Start $< E =$ End

where Start and End denote the start and end points of the interval ET. Given "John is reading a book", for example, we can decide an ub-process, since "read" is an event-verb and its grammatical aspect is "progressive." As in Passonneau (1987), we can also decide that E should be marked as an interior point of the ET interval.

3 TENSE INTERPRETATION FOR NARRATIVES

3.1 Temporal Focus Structure

Tense is widely regarded as anaphoric: its interpretation is usually linked to some time or situation derived from context. Webber (1987), following (Bauerle, 1979; Steedman, 1982; Hinrichs, 1986), argues that it is the R point in a Reichenbach's tense description that is anaphoric. Webber suggests that one needs to maintain a dynamically changing entity as the temporal focus, denoted as TF, which is usually the E point of a previous utterance and is most likely to be used as the referent of the R point of the next utterance.

However, as the following example implies, treating only R as anaphoric is not enough, especially when the same tense is used to describe several situations.

a. John went to a hospital.
   ($Sa > Ra = Ea$)
b. He had fallen on a patch of ice
   ($Sb > Rb > Eb$)
c. and had twisted his ankle.
   ($Sc > Rc > Ec$)

Intuitively, we should be able to decide that $Ea > Eb$, $Ea > Ec$, and $Eb < Ec$. Following Webber's approach, we can decide $Ea > Eb$ after the interpretation of utterance (b). Now, for the current TF, we can either maintain Ea as the TF or establish Eb as a new TF. If we take Ea as the referent for Rc, then we can only decide $Ea > Ec$, without knowing the relation between Eb and Ec. Alternatively, if we take Eb as the referent for Rc, then we can conclude $Eb > Ec$, a contradiction to $Eb < Ec$ above. To get the right interpretation, we need to take Rb as the referent for Rc and a point after Eb as the referent for Ec. In other words, both R and E in a Reichenbach description should be treated as anaphoric.

After taking both R and E as anaphoric, we must consider how to decide the referents for them. Webber's one-point focus is not enough since R and E may not coincide for some tenses, and therefore, cannot refer to the same point. To get around this problem, we introduce the concept of temporal focus structure, denoted as TFS, to help interpret the R and E of a new situation. A TFS is also in the form of a SRE triple. It is different from a tense structure in that it is a variable—the values referred to by R and E can be changed from time to time[3]. In fact, TFS is an extension of Webber's one point TF: it not only contains the focus point for interpreting R, but also the point for interpreting E in a new utterance. A tense structure can be interpreted if it shares the same ordering relations between S, R, and E with a TFS. This is done by taking the values of R and E of the TFS (at a specific time, of course) as the referents for the R and E of the given tense structure.

As the above example indicates, tense can maintain an existing TFS, as is the case from (b) to (c) (similar to using a pronoun to maintain a noun in focus). Further, tense can create a new TFS based on an existing TFS, as is the case from (a) to (b) (similar to using a definite noun phrase to create a new focus). However, unlike the static objects referred to by pronoun or definite noun phrases, the time referred to by tense is a dynamic entity, which typically shifts forward, as is the case from (b) to (c).

3.2 Detailed Heuristics for Tense Interpretation

In order to describe the heuristics for tense interpretation, we organize all nine SRE triples into the tense hierarchy in Figure 1. Here, a thin link from a father to its son

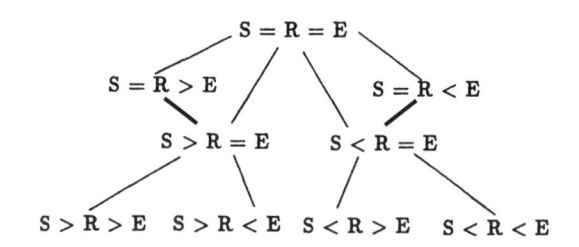

$$S = R = E$$
$$S = R > E \quad S = R < E$$
$$S > R = E \quad S < R = E$$
$$S > R > E \quad S > R < E \quad S < R > E \quad S < R < E$$

FIG. 1   Tense hierarchy in English.

denotes a creation case, where the father is taken as the current TFS and the son as the tense structure of a new utterance, and a thick link or the repetition of the same structure suggests a maintenance case.

In the following, we assume that from prior processing, we have (1) set the current TFS, and (2) determined ST(n) and TS(n), the situation type and the tense structure of the current utterance. Also, we use S(n), R(n), and E(n) to denote all the points in TS(n), and S(f), R(f), and E(f) all the points in the current TFS.

There are two rules for the maintenance case: (1) progression rule, applicable when the same tense is used to described several situations; (2) elaboration rule, applicable when the tense sequence is from a Present Perfect to a Simple Past or from a Present Prospective to a Simple Future, marked by the two thick links in our tense hierarchy.

```
procedure maintain(TS(n), TFS)
begin
    if TS(n) = TFS then /* progression rule */
        if ST(n) is a state or ub-process
            then record E(n) = E(f)
            else record E(n) > E(f);
        if R(n) ≠ E(n) then set R(n) = R(f);
```

---
[3] The reason for including S in a TFS is that the speech time will shift forward for the on-line description of events, as illustrated in "John is making a phone call. Now, he has finished." In this paper, however, we assume that the difference between the S's is negligible, since in a simple narrative most of the events occur either in the past or future.

```
        if there exists m such that m ≠ n and
           (E(f) < E(m) or E(f) ≤ E(m)) then
           if E(f) ≠ E(m) then
              replace E(f) < E(m) with
                 E(n) < E(m)
           else replace E(f) ≤ E(m) with
                 E(n) ≤ E(m);
        else /* elaboration rule */
           record E(f) ≥ E(n)
end
```

The progression rule captures the forward shifts of time from situation to situation, depending on the type of a situation, as time typically shifts for events and bounded processes, but stays the same for states and unbounded processes (Dowty, 1986; Hinrichs, 1986). Also in the progression rule, we check for a prior situation E(m) such that E(f) occurs earlier than E(m), and if such a situation exists, we replace the ordering relation with E(n) located earlier than E(m). This step is intended to update the global representation of the ordering relations in the narrative, by collapsing certain binary relations. In contrast, the elaboration rule shifts time backwards in order to add details to a previously introduced situation. For example, it is often the case that a speaker uses a Present Perfect to introduce an event in the past and then uses several Simple Pasts to elaborate the event in detail.

There are also two rules for the creation case: R-creation and E-creation. The former can be applied to the sequence from a Simple Present to a Simple Past or a Simple Future, and the latter to the other thin links in our tense hierarchy, i.e., sequences from a Simple tense to a Perfect tense or a Prospective tense.

```
procedure create(TS(n), TFS)
begin
     if R(n) = E(n) then/* R-creation rule */
        if S(n) < R(n) then record E(f) < E(n)
        else record E(f) > E(n)
     else /* E-creation rule */
        set R(n) = E(f)
        if R(n) < E(n) then record E(f) < E(n)
        else record E(f) > E(n)
end
```

3.3 Constraints on Coherent Tense Sequences

In the previous subsection, we assumed that the current TFS was given for interpreting the tense structure of a new utterance. Now, we need to consider how to set and maintain the current TFS, in particular, what to use as the initial TFS and how to save the old TFS for later resumption every time a new TFS is created.

Since from the current TFS, we can either maintain the TFS or create a new TFS based on the TFS, it is natural to take the tense structure [S = R = E] at the root of our tense hierarchy as the initial TFS. Another reason is that all points in this structure refer to the speech time which is obvious to both the speaker and the hearer. In Comrie (1985), the speech time is also called the deictic center, since the speaker can always use clue words like "now", "at present", to direct the hearer's attention to this time. Then, starting from this initial TFS, we can either maintain the TFS or create one of the four new structures: [S = R > E], [S > R = E], [S = R < E], and [S < R = E].

However, there are cases where a narrative starts with a Past Perfect. Such a Past Perfect is often used to set up the background in the past and from then on, more past situations can be given to make up the narrative. That is, the deictic center is actually moved to a time in the past and we can take [S > R = E], the structure of a Simple Past, as the initial TFS.

Once setting up the initial TFS, we can then maintain or create a new TFS based on the TFS. However, at some point of the narrative, the speaker may need to return back to a previously introduced TFS. Following (Grosz and Sidner, 1986; Webber, 1988), we can use a focusing stack to store all the existing TFSs, with the top element always being the current TFS. When a new TFS is created, it will be pushed on top of the stack so that it becomes the current TFS. When a previous TFS is resumed, all the elements above it will be eliminated so that the previous TFS becomes the current TFS again.

Referring to our tense hierarchy, maintenance and creation correspond to the repetition of the same node or the links from a father to its son, while resumption corresponds to the links from a son to its father. In other words, the links in the hierarchy can be seen as bidirectional. However, our heuristics for tense interpretation only apply to the links that go from a father to its son. For example, a switch from a Simple Past to a Simple Present requires us to first resume a previous Present TFS in the focusing stack and then apply the heuristic for the maintenance case to interpret the Present tense.

Using a stack to manage the change of TFS is similar to the management of some other kinds of focuses in discourse processing (Grosz, 1977; Sidner, 1983; McKeown, 1985). The reason that we prefer the most recent TFS is that a speaker can only create a new TFS based on an existing TFS. Once a TFS is created, the speaker tends to make full use of it before returning to a previous TFS, otherwise the TFS has to be reintroduced into the focusing stack.

The above rules of setting up the initial TFS and managing the existing TFSs form the constraints on coherent tense sequences. Tense sequences that do not satisfy these constraints are said to be incoherent, i.e., where there are no possible links between some tense structure and the existing TFSs. Consider the following example,

a. John is staying at home.
   ($S_a = R_a = E_a$)
b. He had finished his homework.
   ($S_b > R_b > E_b$)

After interpreting utterance (a), the current TFS will have the structure [$S_a = R_a = E_a$]. Now, given utterance (b), we cannot maintain the current TFS since it does not match the tense structure of utterance (b), nor can we create a new TFS to interpret utterance (b) as a Past Perfect is not a son structure of a Simple Present. Therefore, we decide that the given tense sequence is incoherent.

3.4 An Algorithm for Tense Interpretation

Based on the detailed heuristics for tense interpretation and the constraints on coherent tense sequences, we can now present a context-based algorithm for tense interpretation. It will terminate since all the rules are arranged in a fixed order and it stops only when all the utterances in a narrative are processed or the tense sequence of the narrative is incoherent.

Tense Interpretation and Narrative 437

input a list of (n, ST(n), TS(n)), where n is the order, and ST(n) and TS(n) are the situation type and tense structure of a new situation;
output a network of E points and the ordering relations between them;
begin
   if TS(n) = [S(1) > R(1) > E(1)] then
     push [S(0) > R(0) = E(0)] to the focusing stack
   else
     push [S(0) = R(0) = E(0)] to the focusing stack;
   while Input is not empty do
     begin
       get the next TS(n) from Input;
       search through from top of the focusing
         stack for a TFS such that TS(n) = TFS
         or TS(n) = a son of TFS;
       if no such TFS exists then
         report incoherent discourse and stop;
       eliminate all the elements above TFS in
         the stack;
       if TS(n) = TFS or (S(f) = R(f) and
         R(f) ≠ E(f)) then
         call maintain(TF(n), TFS);
         update TFS with TS(n);
       else
         call create(TS(n), TFS);
         push TS(n) onto the focusing stack;
     end
end

In order to save space, we choose a small example to illustrate the above algorithm.

(1) John is boiling the fettucini noodles.
(2) He has already made the marinara sauce.
(3) He is going to put them together to get a pasta dish.

The corresponding input list can be given as follows:

    [(1, [S(1) = R(1) = E(1)], ub-process),
    (2, [S(2) = R(2) > E(2)], event),
    (3, [S(3) = R(3) < E(3)], event)]

At the beginning, we initialize the current TFS to be [S(0) = R(0) = E(0)] since the first utterance is not described in a Past Perfect. Taking the first utterance, we find that its tense structure [S(1) = R(1) = E(1)] matches the current TFS. Following the "maintain" procedure, we record E(1) = E(0) since the given utterance describes a temporally unbounded process. After this interpretation, we update the current TFS with [S(1) = R(1) = E(1)]. Taking the second utterance, we find that its tense structure [S(2) = R(2) > E(2)] is a son structure of the current TFS in our tense hierarchy. So we call the "create" procedure to record E(2) < E(1) and push [S(2) = R(2) > E(2)] on top of the focusing stack to get a new TFS. Here, the creation is a case of E-creation. Taking the last utterance, we find that its tense structure [S(3) = R(3) < E(3)] does not match the current TFS; nor can the structure be created from the current TFS, as there is no creation link between them in our tense hierarchy. However, this tense structure can be created from a previous TFS, the one that is obtained from the first utterance. So we eliminate the current TFS in the stack and resume [S(1) = R(1) = E(1)] below it to be the current TFS. Then, we call the "create" procedure to record E(3) > E(1) and push [S(3) = R(3) < E(3)] on top of the stack. Since all of the utterances have been interpreted, our algorithm will now terminate and give us the temporal structure shown in Figure 2. Note that E(0) is used as a dummy situation, which is only useful for setting up the initial TFS and is not shown in the figure.

$$ \text{———} E(2) \xrightarrow{<} E(1) \xrightarrow{<} E(3) \text{———>} $$

FIG. 2   Temporal structure of example 1.

4   EXPERIMENTS WITH NATURAL EXAMPLES

Our rules for tense interpretation are intended to capture the most likely cases. Exceptions to these cases do arise in contexts where other temporal indicators, such as temporal adverbials and connectives, and discourse cue phrases (see Grosz and Sidner, 1986) are provided.

To further test our algorithm, we chose a total of twenty examples from the book *Real Stories* (Katz et al., 1975). Our experiments may go through two possible rounds. First, we test whether our algorithm can produce the expected temporal ordering that would be decided by a human reader.

Our algorithm uses heuristics to prefer certain interpretations, in the absence of other temporal indicators. For example, in the case when the same tense is repeated in a subsequent sentence, our rule would prefer progression over elaboration as a speaker tends to describe situations at the same level of detail and when the speaker wants to add details to some situation, he usually uses cue phrases such as "first" and "for example" to clearly indicate such a shift[4].

For examples with interpretations that are inconsistent with the results of round one, we run a second round, allowing a user to provide information suggested by other temporal indicators. If there are such linguistic expressions available, the user provides the focus movement suggested; otherwise, our algorithm simply assumes the heuristics used at the first round analysis. Depending on how many focus movements are explicitly provided by a user, we compute the number of utterances that are correctly interpreted by our tense algorithm.

The number of utterances that are interpreted correctly is shown in the table below. An example that shows the natural flavor of our experiments can be found in Appendix A.

#Stories	#Utterances		
	Average	Tense&Aspect	With User
20	16.15	14.15	16.0

---

[4] Similar heuristics are also used in Cohen (1983), Litman (1985), and Carberry (1986). The general rule seems to be that we prefer continuation over resumption and prefer resumption over creation.

As our results suggest, further work should extend our current algorithm to interact with a module which has additional discourse information.

5 SUMMARY AND FUTURE DIRECTIONS

We have presented an algorithm that uses tense interpretation in the analysis of simple narratives. Our work can be seen as an extension to Webber's. More specifically, we proposed detailed heuristics for interpreting tense, suggested constraints for capturing coherent tense sequences, and organized these rules into an algorithm for determining the temporal ordering between the situations mentioned in a narrative.

One of our future directions is to provide a detailed treatment of aspect. Readers are referred to Song (1990) for more discussion. In addition, temporal adverbials (e.g., yesterday, at three o'clock, in a week) and temporal connectives (e.g., when, before, after, while) are also effective ways of describing ordering relations. The problem with these expressions is that they are not always available and are widely diversified. They may also require a mechanism for combining quantitative temporal information (often incomplete) with qualitative temporal information (usually uncertain) (see Allen, 1983).

In short, we believe that our work provides the basis for building more complex algorithms to implement these possible extensions.

REFERENCES

Allen, James F. (1983). 'Maintaining knowledge about temporal intervals', *Communications of the ACM* 26(11): 832–43.

Bauerle, R. (1979). *Temporal Deixis, Temporale Frage*. Tübingen: Gunter Narr Verlag.

Carberry, Sandra (1986). *Pragmatic Modeling in Information System Interfaces*. Ph.D. dissertation, University of Delaware.

Cohen, Robin (1983). *A Computational Model for the Analysis of Arguments*. Ph.D. dissertation, University of Toronto.

Comrie, Bernard (1985). *Tense*. Cambridge: Cambridge University Press.

Dowty, David (1986). 'The effects of aspectual class on the temporal structure of discourse: semantics or pragmatics', *Linguistics and Philosophy* 9(1): 37–62.

Grosz, Barbara. J. (1977). 'The representation and use of focus in a system for understanding dialogs', in *Proceedings of the International Joint Conference on Artificial Intelligence*, 67–76.

——and Sidner, Candace L. (1986). 'Attention, intentions, and the structure of discourse', *Computational Linguistics* 12(3): 175–204.

Hinrichs, Erhard W. (1986). 'Temporal anaphora in discourses of English', *Linguistics and Philosophy* 9: 63–82.

——(1987). 'A compositional semantics of temporal expressions in English', in *Proceedings of the 25th ACL Conference*, 8–15.

Katz, Milton, Chakeres, Michael, and Bromberg, Murray (1975). *Real Stories*. Book 1, 2nd edn. New York: Globe Book Company.

Litman, Diane (1985). *Plan Recognition and Discourse Analysis: An Integrated Approach for Understanding Dialogues*. Ph.D. dissertation, University of Rochester.

McKeown, Kathleen R. (1985). *Text Generation: Using Discourse Strategies and Focus Constraints to Generate Natural Language Text*. Cambridge: Cambridge University Press.

Moens, Marc and Steedman, Mark (1987). 'Temporal ontology in natural language', in *Proceedings of the 25th ACL Conference*, 1–7.

Mourelatos, Alexander P. D. (1978). 'Events, processes, and states', *Linguistics and Philosophy* 2: 415–34.
Passonneau, Rebecca J. (1987). 'Situations and intervals', in *Proceedings of the 25th ACL Conference*, 16–24.
Reichenbach, Hans (1947). *The Elements of Symbolic Logic*. New York, NY: The Free Press.
Sidner, Candace L. (1983). 'Focusing in the comprehension of definite anaphora', in M. Brady and R.C. Berwick (eds.), *Computational Models of Discourse*. Cambridge, MA: MIT Press, 267–330.
Song, Fei (1990). 'A Processing Model for Temporal Analysis and its Application to Plan Recognition'. Ph.D. dissertation, University of Waterloo.
Steedman, Mark (1982). 'Reference to past time', in R. Jarvella and W. Klein (eds.), *Speech, Place, and Action*. Chichester Wiley, 125–57.
Vilain, M. and Kautz, H. (1986). 'Constraint propagation algorithms for temporal reasoning', in *Proceedings of the Fifth National Conference on Artificial Intelligence*, 377–82.
Webber, Bonnie L. (1987). 'The interpretation of tense in discourse', in *Proceedings of the 25th ACL Conference*, 147–54.
Webber, Bonnie L. (1988). 'Tense as discourse anaphor', *Computational Linguistics* 14(2): 61–73.

A. ONE REAL EXAMPLE

The examples used in our experiments are all adopted from *Real Stories* [Katz et al., 1975]. Many of these examples may need to be transcribed so that certain linguistic constructions (such as indirect speech and non-actual situations) are stripped off or restated for the purpose of tense interpretation. One transcribed example is shown as follows:

(1) King is a watchdog at an Air Force base in Tennessee.
(state, simple present)
(2) At one point, King was about to be destroyed.
(state, simple past)
(3) He was too mean to train.
(state, simple past)
(4) He was vicious.
(state, simple past)
(5) He hated everybody, everything that moves and everything touching him.
(state, simple past)

(6) King had been raised by a Spanish-speaking family
(event, past perfect)
(7) before he was sold to the Air Force.
(event, simple past)
(8) All that King wanted was someone to give him his orders in Spanish.
(state, simple past)
(9) Spanish was the only language he knew.
(state, simple past)

(10) King was given a new trainer who speaks Spanish.
(event, simple past)
(11) Now King is happy and
(state, simple present)
(12) the Air Force is happy with him.
(state, simple present)

Here, each utterance is associated with a description indicating the type and the tense of the situation described. Also, an empty line between utterances is used to separate different paragraphs.

Our tense interpretation algorithm can interpret correctly 10 out of the 12 utterances. The two exceptions are utterance (7), where a progression case is indicated by the connective "before", and utterance (10), where a resumption case is suggested by the start of a new paragraph, which can be seen as a clue to discourse structures.

An Empirical Approach to Temporal Reference Resolution

JANYCE WIEBE, TOM O'HARA, KENNETH MCKEEVER, THORSTEN ÖHRSTRÖM-SANDGREN

1 INTRODUCTION

Temporal information is often a significant part of the meaning communicated in dialogs and texts, but is often left implicit, to be recovered by the listener or reader from the surrounding context. Determining all of the temporal information that is being conveyed can be important for many interpretation tasks. For instance, in machine translation, knowing the temporal context is important in translating sentences with missing information. This is particularly useful when dealing with noisy data, as with spoken input (Levin et al. 1995). In the following example, the third utterance could be interpreted in three different ways.

    s1: (Ahora son las once y diez)
        Now it is eleven ten
    s1: (Qué tal a las doce)
        How about twelve
    s1: (Doce a dos)
        Twelve to two
    or The twelfth to the second
    or The twelfth at two

By maintaining the temporal context (i.e., the 5th of March 1993 at 12:00), the system will know that "12:00 to 2:00" is a more probable interpretation than "the 12th at 2:00".

In addition, maintaining the temporal context would be useful for information extraction tasks dealing with natural language texts such as memos or meeting notes. For instance, it can be used to resolve relative time expressions, so that absolute dates can be entered in a database with a uniform representation.

This paper presents the results of an empirical investigation of temporal reference resolution in scheduling dialogs (i.e., dialogs in which participants schedule a meeting with one another). This work thus describes how to identify temporal information that is missing due to ellipsis or anaphora, and it shows how to determine the times evoked by deictic expressions. In developing the algorithm, our approach was to start with a straightforward, recency-based approach and add complexity as needed to address problems encountered in the data. The algorithm does not include a mechanism for handling global focus (Grosz and Sidner 1986), for centering within a discourse segment (Sidner 1979; Grosz et al. 1995), or for performing tense and aspect interpretation. Instead, the algorithm processes anaphoric references with respect to an Attentional State (Grosz and Sidner 1986) structured as a linear list of all times mentioned so far in the current dialog. The list is ordered by recency, no entries are ever deleted from the list, and there is no restriction on access. The algorithm decides among candidate antecedents based on a combined score reflecting recency, a priori preferences for the type of anaphoric relation(s) established, and plausibility of the resulting temporal reference. In determining the candidates from which to choose the antecedent, for each type of anaphoric relation the algorithm considers only the most recent antecedent for which that relationship can be established.

The algorithm was primarily developed on a corpus of Spanish dialogs collected under the JANUS project (Shum et al. 1994) (referred to hereafter as the "CMU dialogs") and has also been applied to a corpus of Spanish dialogs collected under the Artwork project (Wiebe et al. 1996) (hereafter referred to as the "NMSU dialogs"). In both cases, subjects were told that they were to set up a meeting based on schedules given to them detailing their commitments. The CMU protocol is akin to a phone conversation between people who do not know each other. Such strongly task-oriented dialogs would arise in many useful applications, such as automated information providers and automated phone operators. The NMSU data are face-to-face dialogs between people who know each other well. These dialogs are also strongly task-oriented, but only in these, not in the CMU dialogs, do the participants stray significantly from the scheduling task. In addition, the data sets are challenging in that they both include negotiation, both contain many disfluencies, and both show a great deal of variation in how dates and times are discussed.

To support the computational work, the temporal references in the corpus were manually annotated according to explicit coding instructions. In addition, we annotated the seen training dialogs for anaphoric chains, to support analysis of the data.

A fully automatic system has been developed that takes as input the ambiguous output of a semantic parser (Lavie and Tomita 1993, Levin et al. 1995). The system performance on unseen, held-out test data is good, especially on the CMU data, showing the usefulness of our straightforward approach. The performance on the NMSU data is worse but surprisingly comparable, given the greater complexity of the data and the fact that the system was primarily developed on the simpler data.

Rosé et al. (1995), Alexandersson et al. (1997), and Busemann et al. (1997) describe other recent NLP systems that resolve temporal expressions in scheduling dialogs as part of their overall processing, but they do not give results of system performance on any temporal interpretation tasks. Kamp and Reyle (1993) address many representational and processing issues in the interpretation of temporal expressions, but they do not attempt coverage of a data set or present results of a working system. To our knowledge, there are no other published results on unseen test data of systems performing the same temporal resolution tasks.

The specific contributions of this paper are the following. The results of an intercoder reliability study involving naive subjects are presented (in Section 2) as well as an abstract presentation of a model of temporal reference resolution (in Section 3). In addition, the high-level algorithm is given (in Section 4); the fully refined algorithm, which distinguishes many more subcases than can be presented here, is available online at < http://crl.nmsu.edu/Research/Projects/artwork >. Detailed results of an implemented system are also presented (in Section 5), showing the success of the algorithm. In the final part of the paper, we abstract away from matters of implementation and analyze the challenges presented by the dialogs to an algorithm that does not include a model of global focus (in Section 6). We found surprisingly few such challenges.

2 THE CORPUS AND INTERCODER RELIABILITY STUDY

Consider this passage from the corpus (translated into English):

Preceding time: Thursday 19 August
s1 1 On Thursday I can only meet after two pm
    2 From two to four
    3 Or two thirty to four thirty
    4 Or three to five
s2 5 Then how does from two thirty to
       four thirty seem to you
    6 On Thursday
s1 7 Thursday the thirtieth of September

An example of temporal reference resolution is that (2) refers to 2–4pm Thursday 19 August. Although related, this problem is distinct from tense and aspect interpretation in discourse (as addressed in, e.g., Webber 1988, Song and Cohen 1991, Hwang and Schubert 1992, Lascarides et al. 1992, and Kameyama et al. 1993).

Because the dialogs are centrally concerned with negotiating an interval of time in which to hold a meeting, our representations are geared toward such intervals. Our basic representational unit is given in Figure 1. To avoid confusion, we refer to this basic unit throughout as a *Temporal Unit (TU)*.

The time referred to in, for example, "From 2 to 4, on Wednesday the 19th of August" is represented as:

((August, 19th, Wednesday, 2, pm)
 (August, 19th, Wednesday, 4, pm))

Thus, the information from multiple noun phrases is often merged into a single representation of the underlying interval evoked by the utterance.

An utterance such as "The meeting starts at 2" is represented as an interval rather than as a point in time, reflecting the orientation of the coding scheme toward intervals. Another issue this kind of utterance raises is whether or not a speculated ending time of the interval should be filled in, using knowledge of how long meetings usually last. In the CMU data, the meetings all last two hours. However, so that the instructions will be applicable to a wider class of dialogs, we decided to be conservative with respect to filling in an ending time, given the starting time (or vice versa), leaving it open unless something in the dialog explicitly suggests otherwise.

| ((start-month, | start-date, | start-day-of-week, | start-hour&minute, | start-time-of-day) |
| (end-month, | end-date, | end-day-of-week, | end-hour&minute, | end-time-of-day)) |

FIG. 1   Temporal units.

There are cases in which times are considered as points (e.g., "It is now 3pm"). These are represented as Temporal Units with the same starting and ending times (as in Allen (1984)). If just one ending point is represented, all the fields of the other are null. And, of course, all fields are null for utterances that do not contain temporal information. In the case of an utterance that refers to multiple, distinct intervals, the representation is a list of Temporal Units.

A Temporal Unit is also the representation used in the evaluation of the system. That is, the system's answers are mapped from its more complex internal representation (an *ILT*, see Section 4.1) into this simpler vector representation before evaluation is performed.

As in much recent empirical work in discourse processing (e.g., Arhenberg et al. 1995; Isard and Carletta 1995; Litman and Passonneau 1995; Moser and Moore 1995; Hirschberg and Nakatani 1996), we performed an intercoder reliability study investigating agreement in annotating the times. The goal in developing the annotation instructions is that they can be used reliably by non-experts after a reasonable amount of training (cf. Passonneau and Litman 1993, Condon and Cech 1995, and Hirschberg and Nakatani 1996), where reliability is measured in terms of the amount of agreement among annotators. High reliability indicates that the encoding scheme is reproducible given multiple labelers. In addition, the instructions serve to document the annotations.

The subjects were three people with no previous involvement in the project. They were given the original Spanish and the English translations. However, as they have limited knowledge of Spanish, in essence they annotated the English translations.

The subjects annotated two training dialogs according to the instructions. After receiving feedback, they annotated four unseen test dialogs. Intercoder reliability was assessed using Cohen's Kappa statistic (κ) (Siegel and Castellan 1988, Carletta 1996).

κ is calculated as follows, where the numerator is the average percentage agreement among the annotators (Pa) less a term for chance agreement (Pe), and the denominator is 100% agreement less the same term for chance agreement (Pe):

$$\kappa = \frac{Pa - Pe}{1 - Pe}$$

(For details on calculating Pa and Pe see Siegel and Castellan 1988). As discussed in (Hays 1988), κ will be 0.0 when the agreement is what one would expect under independence, and it will be 1.0 when the agreement is exact. A κ value of 0.8 or greater indicates a high level of reliability among raters, with values between 0.67 and 0.8 indicating only moderate agreement (Hirschberg and Nakatani 1996; Carletta 1996).

In addition to measuring intercoder reliability, we compared each coder's annotations to the evaluation Temporal Units used to assess the system's performance. These evaluation Temporal Units were assigned by an expert working on the project.

The agreement among coders (κ) is shown in table 1. In addition, this table shows the average pairwise agreement of the coders and the expert (κ_{avg}), which was assessed by averaging the individual κ scores (not shown). There is a moderate or high level of agreement among annotators in all cases except the ending time of day, a weakness we are investigating. Similarly, there are reasonable levels of agreement between our evaluation Temporal Units and the answers the naive coders provided.

Busemann et al. (1997) also annotate temporal information in a corpus of scheduling dialogs. However, their annotations are at the level of individual expressions rather than

TABLE I Agreement among Coders (kappa coefficients by field)

Field	Pa	Pe	κ	κ_avg
start				
Month	.96	.51	.93	.94
Date	.95	.50	.91	.93
WeekDay	.96	.52	.91	.92
HourMin	.98	.82	.89	.92
TimeDay	.97	.74	.87	.74
end				
Month	.97	.51	.93	.94
Date	.96	.50	.92	.94
WeekDay	.96	.52	.92	.92
HourMin	.99	.89	.90	.88
TimeDay	.95	.85	.65	.52

at the level of Temporal Units, and they do not present the results of an intercoder reliability study.

3 MODEL

This section presents our model of temporal reference in scheduling dialogs. The treatment of anaphora in this paper is as a relationship between a Temporal Unit representing a time evoked in the current utterance, and one representing a time evoked in a previous utterance. The resolution of the anaphor is a new Temporal Unit that represents the interpretation of the contributing words of the current utterance.

Fields of Temporal Units are partially ordered as in Figure 2, from least to most specific.

In all cases below, after the resolvent has been formed, it is subjected to highly accurate, trivial inference to produce the final interpretation (e.g., filling in the day of the week given the month and the date).

The cases of non-anaphoric reference:
1. A deictic expression is resolved into a time interpreted with respect to the dialog date (e.g., "Tomorrow", "last week"). (See rule NA1 in Section 4.2.)
2. A forward time is calculated by using the dialog date as a frame of reference. Let F be the most specific field in $TU_{current}$ above the level of *time-of-day*. Resolvent: The next F after the dialog date, augmented with the fillers of the fields in $TU_{current}$ at or below the level of *time-of-day*. (See rule NA2.)

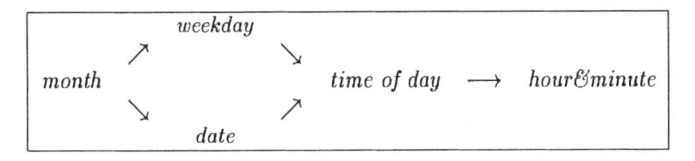

FIG. 2 Specificity ordering.

For both this and anaphoric relation (3), there are subcases for whether the starting and/or ending times are involved. Note that tense can influence the choice of whether to calculate a forward or a backward time from a frame of reference (Kamp & Reyle 1993), but we do not account for this in our model due to the lack of tense variation in the corpora.

> Ex: Dialog date is Mon, 19th, Aug
> "How about Wednesday at 2?"
> interpreted as 2 pm, Wed 21 Aug

The cases of anaphora considered:
1. The utterances evoke the same time, or the second is more specific than the first. Resolvent: the union of the information in the two Temporal Units. (See rule A1.)

    > Ex: "How is Tuesday, January 30th?"
    > "How about 2?"

    (See also (1)–(2) of the corpus example.)

2. The current utterance evokes a time that includes the time evoked by a previous time, and the current time is less specific. (See rule A2.)
    Let F be the most specific field in $TU_{current}$. Resolvent: All of the information in $TU_{previous}$ from F on up.

    > Ex: "How about Monday at 2?"
    > resolved to 2pm, Mon 19 Aug
    > "Ok, well, Monday sounds good."

    (See also (5)–(6) in the corpus example.)

3. This is the same as non-anaphoric case (2) above, but the new time is calculated with respect to $TU_{previous}$ instead of the dialog date. (See rule A3.)

    > Ex: "How about the 3rd week in August?"
    > "Let's see, Monday sounds good."
    > interpreted as Mon, 3rd week in Aug

    > Ex: "Would you like to meet Wed, Aug 2nd?"
    > "No, how about Friday at 2."
    > interpreted as Fri, Aug 4 at 2pm

4. The current time is a modification of the previous time; the times are consistent down to some level of specificity X and differ in the filler of X. Resolvent: The information in $TU_{previous}$ above level X together with the information in $TU_{current}$ at and below level X. (See rule A4.)

    > Ex: "Monday looks good."
    > resolved to Mon 19 Aug
    > "How about 2?"
    > resolved to 2pm Mon 19 Aug
    > "Hmm, how about 4?"
    > resolved to 4pm Mon 19 Aug

    (See also (3)–(5) in the example from the corpus.)

Although we found domain knowledge and task-specific linguistic conventions most useful, we observed in the NMSU data some instances of potentially exploitable syntactic information to pursue in future work (Grosz et al. 1995, Sidner 1979). For example, "until" in the following suggests that the first utterance specifies an ending time.

"... could it be until around twelve?"
"12:30 there"

A preference for parallel syntactic roles might be used to recognize that the second utterance specifies an ending time too.

4 THE ALGORITHM

This section presents our algorithm for temporal reference resolution. After a brief overview, the rule-application architecture is described and then the rules composing the algorithm are given. As mentioned earlier, this is a high-level algorithm. Description of the complete algorithm, including a specification of the normalized input representation (see Section 4.1), can be obtained from a report available at the project web page (http://crl.nmsu.edu/Research/Projects/artwork).

There is a rule for each of the relations presented in Section 3. Those for the anaphoric relations involve various applicability conditions on the current utterance and a potential antecedent. For the current not-yet-resolved Temporal Unit, each rule is applied. For the anaphoric rules, the antecedent considered is the most recent one meeting the conditions. All consistent maximal mergings of the results are formed, and the one with the highest score is the chosen interpretation.

4.1 Architecture

Following (Qu et al. 1996) and (Shum et al. 1994), the representation of a single utterance is called an *ILT* (for InterLingual Text). An ILT, once it has been augmented by our system with temporal (and speech-act) information, is called an *augmented ILT* (an *AILT*). The input to our system, produced by a semantic parser (Shum et al. 1994; Lavie and Tomita 1993), consists of multiple alternative ILT representations of utterances. To produce one ILT, the parser maps the main event and its participants into one of a small set of case frames (for example, a *meet* frame or an *is busy* frame) and produces a surface representation of any temporal information, which is faithful to the input utterance. Although the events and states discussed in the NMSU data are often outside the coverage of this parser, the temporal information generally is not. Thus, the parser provides us with a sufficient input representation for our purposes on both sets of data. This parser is proprietary, but it would not be difficult to produce just the portion of the temporal information that our system requires.

Because the input consists of alternative sequences of ILTs, the system resolves the ambiguity in batches. In particular, for each input sequence of ILTs, it produces a sequence of AILTs and then chooses the best sequence for the corresponding utterances. In this way, the input ambiguity is resolved as a function of finding the best temporal interpretations of the utterance sequences in context (as suggested in Qu et al. 1996).

A focus list keeps track of what has been discussed so far in the dialog. After a final AILT has been created for the current utterance, the AILT and the utterance are placed together on the focus list (where they are now referred to as a *discourse entity*, or *DE*). In the case of utterances that evoke more than one Temporal Unit, a separate entity is added for each to the focus list in order of mention.

Otherwise, the system architecture is similar to a standard production system, with one major exception: rather than choosing the results of just one of the rules that fires (i.e., conflict resolution), multiple results can be merged. This is a flexible architecture that accommodates sets of rules targeting different aspects of interpretation, allowing the system to take advantage of constraints that exist between them (for example, temporal and speech act rules).

Step 1. The input ILT is *normalized*. In the input ILT, different pieces of information about the same time might be represented separately in order to capture relationships among clauses. Our system needs to know which pieces of information are about the same time (but does not need to know about the additional relationships). Thus, we map from the input representation into a normalized form that shields the reasoning component from the idiosyncracies of the input representation. After the normalization process, highly accurate, obvious inferences are made and added to the representation.

Step 2. All rules are applied to the normalized input. The result of a rule application is a *partial AILT (PAILT)*—information this rule would contribute to the interpretation of the utterance. This information includes a certainty factor representing an a priori preference for the type of anaphoric or non-anaphoric relation being established. In the case of anaphoric relations, this factor gets adjusted by a term representing how far back on the focus list the antecedent is (in rules A1-A4 in Section 4.2, the adjustment is represented by *distance factor* in the calculation of the certainty factor *CF*). The result of this step is the set of PAILTs produced by the rules that fired (i.e., those that succeeded).

Step 3. All maximal mergings of the PAILTs are created. Consider a graph in which the PAILTs are the vertices, and there is an edge between two PAILTs iff the two PAILTs are compatible. Then, the maximal cliques of the graph (i.e., the maximal complete subgraphs) correspond to the maximal mergings. Each maximal merging is then merged with the normalized input ILT, resulting in a set of AILTs.

Step 4. The AILT chosen is the one with the highest certainty factor. The certainty factor of an AILT is calculated as follows. First, the certainty factors of the constituent PAILTs are summed. Then, critics are applied to the resulting AILT, lowering the certainty factor if the information is judged to be incompatible with the dialog state.

The merging process might have yielded additional opportunity for making obvious inferences, so that process is performed again, to produce the final AILT.

4.2 Temporal resolution rules

The rules described in this section (see Figure 3) apply to individual temporal units and return either a more fully specified TU or an empty structure to indicate failure.

Many of the rules calculate temporal information with respect to a frame of reference, using a separate calendar utility. The following describe these and other functions assumed by the rules below, as well as some conventions used.

Rules for non-anaphoric relations

Rule NA1: All cases of non-anaphoric relation 1.
if there is a deictic term, *DT*, in *TU* then
    return {[when, resolve_deictic(*DT, Todays Date*)], [certainty, 0.9]}

Rule NA2: The starting-time cases of non-anaphoric relation 2.
if (most_specific(starting_fields(*TU*)) < **time_of_day**) then
    Let *f* be the most specific field in starting_fields(*TU*)
    return {[when, next(*TU*→*f, Todays Date*)], [certainty, 0.4]}

Rules for anaphoric relations

Rule A1: All cases of anaphoric relation 1.
for each non-empty temporal unit TU_{fl} from *FocusList* (starting with most recent)
    if specificity (TU_{fl}) ≤ specificity (*TU*) and not empty merge(TU_{fl}, *TU*) then
        CF = 0.8 − distance_factor(TU_{fl}, *FocusList*)
        return {[when, merge(TU_{fl}, *TU*)], [certainty, *CF*]}

Rule A2: All cases of anaphoric relation 2.
for each non-empty temporal unit TU_{fl} from *Focus List* (starting with most recent)
    if specificity (TU_{fl}) > specificity (*TU*) and not empty merge_upper(TU_{fl}, *TU*) then
        CF = 0.5 − distance_factor(TU_{fl}, *FocusList*)
        return {[when, merge_upper(TU_{fl}, *TU*)], [certainty, *CF*]}

Rule A3: Starting-time case of anaphoric relation 3.
if (most_specific(starting_fields(*TU*)) < **time_of_day**) then
    for each non-empty temporal unit TU_{fl} from *FocusList* (starting with most recent)
        if specificity (*TU*) ≥ specificity (TU_{fl}) then
            Let *f* be the most specific field in starting_fields(*TU*)
            CF = 0.6 − distance_factor (TU_{fl}, *FocusList*)
            return {[when, next(*TU*→*f*, TU_{fl}→start_date)], [certainty, *CF*]}

Rule A4: All cases of anaphoric relation 4.
for each non-empty temporal unit TU_{fl} from *FocusList* (starting with most recent)
    if specificity (*TU*) ≥ specificity (TU_{fl}) then
        $TU_{temp} = TU_{fl}$
        for each {*f* | *f* ≥ most specific field in *TU*}
            TU_{temp}→*f* = null
        if not empty merge(TU_{temp}, *TU*) then
            CF = 0.5 − distance_factor(TU_{fl}, *FocusList*)
            return {[when, merge(TU_{temp}, *TU*)], [certainty, *CF*]}

FIG. 3 Main Temporal Resolution Rules.

next (*TimeValue, RF*): returns the next *timeValue* that follows reference frame *RF*.
    next(Monday, [... Friday, 19th, ...]) = Monday, 22nd.

resolve_deictic(*DT, RF*): resolves the deictic term *DT* with respect to the reference frame *RF*.

merge(*TU1*, *TU2*): if temporal units *TU1* and *TU2* contain no conflicting field fillers, returns a temporal unit containing all of the information in the two; otherwise returns {}.

merge_upper(*TU1*, *TU2*): like the previous function, except includes only those field fillers from *TU1* that are of the same or less specificity as the most specific field filler in *TU2*.

specificity(*TU*): returns the specificity of the most specific field in *TU*.

starting_fields(*TU*): returns a list of starting field names for those in *TU* having non-null values.

structure → component: returns the named component of the structure.

conventions: Values are in **bold face** and variables are in *italics*. *TU* is the current temporal unit being resolved. *TodaysDate* is a representation of the dialog date. *FocusList* is the list of discourse entities from all previous utterances.

The algorithm does not cover a number of subcases of relations concerning the ending times. For instance, rule NA2 covers only the starting-time case of non-anaphoric relation 2. An example of an ending-time case that is not handled is the utterance "Let's meet until Thursday," under the meaning that they should meet from today through Thursday. This is an area for future work.

5 RESULTS

As mentioned in Section 2, the main results are based on comparisons against human annotation of the held out test data. The results are based on straight field-by-field comparisons of the Temporal Unit representations introduced in Section 2. Thus, to be considered as correct, information must not only be right, but it has to be in the right place. Thus, for example, "Monday" correctly resolved to Monday, 19th of August, but incorrectly treated as a starting rather than an ending time, contributes 3 errors of omission and 3 errors of commission (and no credit is given for recognizing the date).

Detailed results for the test sets are presented next, starting with results for the CMU data (see Table 2). Accuracy measures the degree to which the system produces the correct answers, while precision measures the degree to which the system's answers are correct (see the formulas in the tables). For each component of the extracted temporal structure, counts were maintained for the number of correct and incorrect cases of the system versus the tagged file. Since null values occur quite often, these two counts exclude cases when one or both of the values are null. Instead, additional counts were used for those possibilities. Note that each test set contains three complete dialogs with an average of 72 utterances per dialog.

These results show that the system is performing with 81% accuracy overall, which is significantly better than the lower bound (defined below) of 43%. In addition, the results show a high precision of 92%. In some of the individual cases, however, the results could be higher due to several factors. For example, our system development was inevitably focussed more on some types of slots than others. An obvious area for improvement is the time-of-day handling. Also, note that the values in the Missing column are higher than those in the Extra column. This reflects the conservative coding convention, mentioned in Section 2, for filling in unspecified end points. A system that produces extraneous values is more problematic than one that leaves entries unspecified.

TABLE 2 Evaluation of System on CMU Test Data

Label	Cor	Inc	Mis	Ext	Nul	AccLB	Acc	Prec
start								
Month	49	3	7	3	0	0.338	0.831	0.891
Date	48	4	7	3	0	0.403	0.814	0.873
WeekDay	46	6	7	3	0	0.242	0.780	0.836
HourMin	18	0	7	0	37	0.859	0.887	1.000
TimeDay	9	0	18	0	35	0.615	0.710	1.000
end								
Month	48	3	7	1	3	0.077	0.836	0.927
Date	47	5	6	3	1	0.048	0.814	0.857
WeekDay	45	7	6	3	1	0.077	0.780	0.821
HourMin	9	0	9	0	44	0.862	0.855	1.000
TimeDay	4	0	13	1	44	0.738	0.787	0.980
overall	323	28	87	17	165	0.428	0.809	0.916

Legend
Cor(rect):   System and key agree on non-null value
Inc(orrect):   System and key differ on non-null value
Mis(sing):   System has null value for non-null key
Ext(ra):   System has non-null value for null key
Nul(l):   Both System and key give null answer

Acc(uracy)LB: accuracy lower bound
Acc(uracy):   percentage of key values matched correctly
                (Correct + Null)/(Correct + Incorrect + Missing + Null)
Prec(ision):   percentage of System answers matching the key
                (Correct + Null)/(Correct + Incorrect + Extra + Null)

TABLE 3 Evaluation of System on NMSU Test Data

Label	Cor	Inc	Mis	Ext	Nul	AccLB	Acc	Prec
start								
Month	55	0	23	5	3	0.060	0.716	0.921
Date	49	6	23	5	3	0.060	0.642	0.825
WeekDay	52	3	23	5	3	0.085	0.679	0.873
HourMin	34	3	7	6	36	0.852	0.875	0.886
TimeDay	18	8	31	2	27	0.354	0.536	0.818
end								
Month	55	0	23	5	3	0.060	0.716	0.921
Date	49	6	23	5	3	0.060	0.642	0.825
WeekDay	52	3	23	5	3	0.060	0.679	0.873
HourMin	28	2	13	1	42	0.795	0.824	0.959
TimeDay	9	2	32	5	38	0.482	0.580	0.870
overall	401	33	221	44	161	0.286	0.689	0.879

Table 3 contains the results for the system on the NMSU data. This shows that the system performs respectably, with 69% accuracy and 88% precision, on this less constrained set of data. The precision is still comparable, but the accuracy is lower since more of the entries were left unspecified. Furthermore, the lower bound for accuracy (29%) is almost 15% lower than the one for the CMU data (43%), supporting the claim that this data set is more challenging.

More details on the lower bounds for the test data sets are shown next (see Table 4). These values were derived by disabling all the rules and just evaluating the input as is (after performing normalization, so the evaluation software could be applied). Since 'null' is the most frequent value for all the fields, this is equivalent to using a naive algorithm that selects the most frequent value for a given field. The rightmost column shows that there is a small amount of error in the input representation. This figure is 1 minus the precision of the input representation (after normalization). Note, however, that this is a close but not entirely direct measure of the error in the input, because there are a few cases of the normalization process committing errors and a few of it correcting them. Recall that the input is ambiguous; the figures in Table 4 are based on the system selecting the first ILT in each case. Since the parser orders the ILTs based on a measure of acceptability, this choice is likely to have the relevant temporal information.

Since the above results are for the system taking ambiguous semantic representations as input, the evaluation does not isolate focus-related errors. Therefore, two tasks were performed to aid in developing the analysis presented in Section 6. First, anaphoric chains and competing discourse entities were manually annotated in all of the seen data. Second, to aid in isolating errors due to focus issues, the system was evaluated on unambiguous, partially corrected input for all the seen data (the test sets were retained as unseen test data).

The overall results are shown in Table 5. This includes the results described earlier to facilitate comparisons. Among the first, more constrained data, there are twelve dialogs in the training data and three dialogs in a held out test set. The average length of each

TABLE 4 Lower Bounds for both Test Sets

Set	Cor	Inc	Mis	Ext	Nul	Acc	Input Error
cmu	84	6	360	10	190	0.428	0.055
nmsu	65	3	587	4	171	0.286	0.029

TABLE 5 Results on Corrected Input (to isolate focus issues)

seen/unseen	cmu/nmsu	Ambiguous/unambiguous	#dialogs	#utterances	Accuracy	Precision
seen	cmu	ambiguous	12	659	0.883	0.918
seen	cmu	unambiguous	12	659	0.914	0.957
unseen	cmu	ambiguous	3	193	0.809	0.916
seen	nmsu	ambiguous	4	358	0.679	0.746
seen	nmsu	unambiguous	4	358	0.779	0.850
unseen	nmsu	ambiguous	3	236	0.689	0.879

dialog is approximately 65 utterances. Among the second, less constrained data, there are four training dialogs and three test dialogs.

As described in the next section, our approach handles focus effectively. In both data sets, there are noticeable gains in performance on the seen data going from ambiguous to unambiguous input, especially for the NMSU data. Therefore, the ambiguity in the dialogs contributes much to the errors.

The better performance on the unseen, ambiguous NMSU data over the seen, ambiguous, NMSU data is due to several reasons. For instance, there is vast ambiguity in the seen data. Also, numbers are mistaken by the input parser for dates (e.g., phone numbers are treated as dates). In addition, a tense filter, to be discussed below in Section 6, was implemented to heuristically detect subdialogs, improving the performance of the seen NMSU ambiguous dialogs. This filter did not, however, significantly improve the performance for any of the other data, suggesting that the targeted kinds of subdialogs do not occur in the unseen data.

The errors remaining in the seen, unambiguous NMSU data are overwhelmingly due to parser error, errors in applying the rules, errors in mistaking anaphoric references for deictic references (and vice versa), and errors in choosing the wrong anaphoric relation. As will be shown in the next section, very few errors can be attributed to the wrong entities being in focus due to not handling subdialogs or "multiple threads" (Rosé et al. 1995).

6 GLOBAL FOCUS

The algorithm is conspicuously lacking in any mechanism for recognizing the global structure of the discourse, such as in Grosz and Sidner (1986), Mann and Thompson (1988), Allen and Perrault (1980), and their descendants. Recently in the literature, Walker (1996) has argued for a more linear-recency based model of Attentional State (though not that discourse structure need not be recognized), while Rosé et al. (1995) argue for a more complex model of Attentional State than is represented in most current computational theories of discourse.

Many theories that address how Attentional State should be modeled have the goal of performing intention recognition as well. We investigate performing temporal reference resolution directly, without also attempting to recognize discourse structure or intentions. We assess the challenges the data present to our model when only this task is attempted.

We identified how far back on the focus list one must go to find an antecedent that is appropriate according to the model. Such an antecedent need not be unique. (We also allow antecedents for which the anaphoric relation would be a trivial extension of one of the relations in the model.)

The results are striking. Between the two sets of data, out of 215 anaphoric references, there are fewer than 5% for which the immediately preceding time is not an appropriate antecedent. Going back an additional time covers the remaining cases.

The model is geared toward allowing the most recent Temporal Unit to be an appropriate antecedent. For example, in the example for anaphoric relation 4, the second utterance (as well as the first) is a possible antecedent of the third. A corresponding speech act analysis might be that the speaker is suggesting a modification of a previous suggestion. Considering the most recent antecedent as often as possible supports robustness, in the sense that more of the dialog is considered.

There are subdialogs in the NMSU data (but none in the CMU data) for which our recency algorithm fails because it lacks a mechanism for recognizing subdialogs. There are five temporal references within subdialogs that recency either incorrectly interprets to be anaphoric to a time mentioned before the subdialog or incorrectly interprets to be the antecedent of a time mentioned after the subdialog. Fewer than 25 cumulative errors result from these primary errors. In the case of one of the primary errors, recency commits a "self-correcting" error; without this luck, the remainder of the dialog would have represented additional cumulative error.

In a departure from the algorithm, the system uses a simple heuristic for ignoring subdialogs: a time is ignored if the utterance evoking it is in the simple past or past perfect. This prevents a number of the above errors and suggests that changes in tense, aspect, and modality are promising clues to explore for recognizing subdialogs in this kind of data (cf., e.g., Grosz and Sidner 1986; Nakhimovsky 1988). The CMU data has very little variation in tense and aspect, the reason a mechanism for interpreting them was not incorporated into the algorithm.

Rosé et al. (1995) report that "multiple threads", when the participants are negotiating separate times, pose challenges to a stack-based discourse model on both the intentional and attentional levels. They posit a more complex representation of Attentional State to meet these challenges. They report improved results on speech-act resolution in a corpus of scheduling dialogs.

Here, we focus on just the attentional level. The structure relevant for the task addressed in this paper is the following, corresponding to their figure 2. There are four Temporal Units mentioned in the order TU_1, TU_2, TU_3, TU_4 (other times could be mentioned in between). The (attentional) multiple thread case is when TU_1 is required to be an antecedent of TU_3, but TU_2 is also needed to interpret TU_4. Thus, TU_2 cannot be simply thrown away or ignored once we are done interpreting TU_3. This structure would definitely pose a difficult problem for our algorithm, but there are no realizations, in terms of our model, of this structure in the data we analyzed.

The different findings might be due to the fact that different problems are being addressed. Having no intentional state, our model does not distinguish times being negotiated from other times. It is possible that another structure is relevant for the intentional level: Rosé et al. (1995) do not specify whether or not this is so. The different findings may also be due to differences in the data: although their scheduling dialogs were collected under similar protocols, their protocol is like a radio conversation in which a button must be pressed in order to transmit, resulting in less dynamic interaction and longer turns (Villa 1994).

An important discourse feature of the dialogs is the degree of redundancy of the times mentioned (Walker 1996). This limits the ambiguity of the times specified, and it also leads to a higher level of robustness, since additional DE's with the same time are placed on the focus list. These "backup" DE's might be available in case the rule applications fail on the most recent DE. Table 6 presents measures of redundancy. For illustration,

TABLE 6 Redundancy in the Training Dialogs

Dialog Set	Temporal Utterances	Redundant	Reiteration	%
cmu	210	36	20	26.7
nmsu	122	11	13	19.7

the redundancy is broken down into the case where redundant plus additional information is provided ("redundant") versus the case where the temporal information is just repeated ("reiteration"). This shows that roughly 25% of the CMU utterances with temporal information contain redundant temporal references, while 20% of the NMSU ones do.

7 CONCLUSIONS

This paper presented an intercoder reliability study showing strong reliability in coding the temporal information targeted in this work. A model of temporal reference resolution in scheduling dialogs was presented which supports linear recency and has very good coverage; and, an algorithm based on the model was described. The analysis of the detailed results showed that the implemented system performs quite well (for instance, 81% accuracy vs. a lower bound of 43% on the unseen CMU test data).

We also assessed the challenges presented by the data to a method that does not recognize discourse structure, based on an extensively annotated corpus and our experience developing a fully automatic system. In an overwhelming number of cases, the last mentioned time is an appropriate antecedent with respect to our model, in both the more and the less constrained data. In the less constrained data, some error occurs due to subdialogs, so an extension to the approach is needed to handle them. But in none of these cases would subsequent errors result if, upon exiting the subdialog, the offending information were popped off a discourse stack or otherwise made inaccessible. Changes in tense, aspect, and modality are promising clues for recognizing subdialogs in this data, which we plan to explore in future work.

8 ACKNOWLEDGEMENTS

This research was supported in part by the Department of Defense under grant number 0-94-10. A number of people contributed to this work. We want to especially thank David Farwell, Daniel Villa, Carol Van Ess-Dykema, Karen Payne, Robert Sinclair, Rocio Guillén, David Zarazua, Rebecca Bruce, Gezina Stein, Tom Herndon, and CMU's Enthusiast project members, whose cooperation greatly aided our project.

REFERENCES

Alexandersson, Jan, Reithinger, Norbert, and Maier, Elisabeth (1997). 'Insights into the dialogue processing of VERBMOBIL', in *Proceedings of the 5th Conference on Applied Natural Language Processing*, Washington DC, 33–40.

Allen, J.F. (1984). 'Toward a general theory of action and time', *Artificial Intelligence* 23: 123–54.

—— and Perrault, C.R. (1980). 'Analyzing intention in utterances', *Artificial Intelligence* 15: 143–78.

Arhenberg, L., Dahlbäck, N., and Jönsson, A. (1995). 'Coding schemes for natural language dialogues' in *Working Notes of AAAI Spring Symposium: Empirical Methods in Discourse Interpretation and Generation*, 8–13.

Busemann, Stephan, Declerck, Thierry, Diagne, Abdel Kader, Dini, Luca, Klein, Judith, and Schmeier, Sven (1997). 'Natural language dialogue service for appointment scheduling agents', in *Proceedings of the 5th Conference on Applied Natural Language Processing*, Washington DC, 25–32.

Carletta, J. (1996). 'Assessing agreement on classification tasks: the kappa statistic', *Computational Linguistics* 22(2): 249–54.

Condon S. and Cech C. (1995). 'Problems for reliable discourse coding schemes', in *Proceedings of the AAAI Spring Symposium on Empirical Methods in Discourse Interpretation and Generation*, 27–33.

Grosz, B., Joshi, A., and Weinstein, S. (1995). 'Centering: A Framework for Modeling the Local Coherence of Discourse', *Computational Linguistics* 21(2): 203–25.

Grosz, B. and Sidner, C. (1986). 'Attention, intention, and the structure of discourse', *Computational Linguistics* 12(3): 175–204.

Hays, W.L. (1988). *Statistics*. Fourth Edition. New York: Holt, Rinehart, and Winston.

Hirschberg, J. and Nakatani, C. (1996). 'A prosodic analysis of discourse segments in direction-giving monologues', in *Proceedings of the 34th Annual Meeting of the Association for Computational Linguistics*, Santa Cruz, CA., 286–93.

Hwang, C.H. and Schubert, L. (1992). 'Tense trees as the "fine structure" of discourse', in *Proceedings of the 30th Annual Meeting of the Association for Computational Linguistics*, Newark, DE., 232–40.

Isard, A. and Carletta, J. (1995). 'Replicability of transaction and action coding in the map task corpus', in *Working Notes of AAAI Spring Symposium: Empirical Methods in Discourse Interpretation and Generation*, 60–6.

Kameyama, M., Passonneau, R., and Poesio, M. (1993). 'Temporal centering', in *Proceedings of the 31st Annual Meeting of the Association for Computational Linguistics*, Columbus, Ohio, 70–7.

Kamp, Hans, and Reyle, Uwe (1993). *From Discourse to Logic*, Studies in Linguistics and Philosophy, Volume 42, part 2. Dordrecht, Kluwer Academic Publishers.

Lascarides, A., Asher, N., and Oberlander, J. (1992) 'Inferring discourse relations in context', in *Proceedings of the 30th Annual Meeting of the Association for Computational Linguistics*, Newark, DE., 1–8.

Lavie, A. and Tomita, M. (1993). 'GLR*—An efficient noise skipping parsing algorithm for context free grammars', in *Proceedings of the 3rd International Workshop on Parsing Technologies*. Tilburg, The Netherlands, 123–34.

Levin, L., Glickman, O., Qu, Y., Gates, D., Lavie, A, Rosé, C.P., Van Ess-Dykema, C., and Waibel, A. (1995). 'Using context in the machine translation of Spoken Language', in *Proceedings of the Theoretical and Methodological Issues in Machine Translation*, (TMI-95).

Litman, D. and Passonneau, R. (1995). 'Combining multiple knowledge sources for discourse segmentation', in *Proceedings of the 33rd Annual Meeting of the Association for Computational Linguistics*, MIT, 130–43.

Mann, W. and Thompson, S. (1988). 'Rhetorical Structure Theory; Toward a functional theory of text organization', *Text* 8(3): 243–81.

Moser, M. and Moore, J. (1995). 'Investigating cue selection and placement in tutorial discourses,' in *Proceedings of the 33rd Annual Meeting of the Association for Computational Linguistics*, MIT, 130–43.

Nakhimovsky, A. (1988). 'Aspect, aspectual class, and the temporal structure of narrative', *Computational Linguistics* 14(2): 29–43.

Passonneau, R.J. and Litman, D.J. (1993). 'Intention based segmentation: human reliability and correlation with linguistic cues', in *Proceedings of the 31st Annual Meeting of the Association for Computational Linguistics*, 148–55.

Qu, Y., Di Eugenio, B., Lavie, A., Levin, L., and Rosé, C.P. (1996). 'Minimizing cumulative error in discourse context', in *ECAI Workshop Proceedings on Dialogue Proceeding in Spoken Language Systems*.

Rosé, C.P., Di Eugenio, B., Levin, L., and Van Ess-Dykema, C. (1995). 'Discourse processing of dialogues with multiple threads', in *Proceedings of the 33rd Annual Meeting of the Association for Computational Linguistics*, 31–8.

Shum, B., Levin, L., Coccaro, N., Carbonell, J., Horiguchi, K., Isotani, H., Lavie, A., Mayfield, L., Rosé, C.P., Van Ess-Dykema, C., & Waibel, A. (1994). 'Speech-language integration in a multilingual speech translation system', in *Proceedings of the AAAI Workshop on Integration of Natural Language and Speech Processing*, 73–9.

Sidner, C. (1979). 'Towards a Computational Theory of Definite Anaphora Comprehension in English Discourse.' Doctoral dissertation, Artificial Intelligence Laboratory, MIT, Cambridge, MA. Technical Report 537.

Siegel, S., and Castellan, Jr. N.J. (1988). *Nonparametric Statistics for the Behavioral Sciences*. Second edition. New York: McGraw-Hill.

Song, F. and Cohen, R. (1991). 'Tense interpretation in the context of narrative', in *Proceedings of the 9th National Conference on Artificial Intelligence (AAAI-91)*, 131–6.

Villa, D. (1994). 'Effects of protocol on discourse internal and external illocutionary markers in Spanish dialogs'. Presented at Linguistic Association of the Southwest Conference XXIII, Houston, TX, October 21–23, 1994.

Walker, L. (1996). 'Limited attention and discourse structure', *Computational Linguistics* 22(2): 255–64.

Webber, B.L. (1988). 'Tense as discourse anaphor', *Computational Linguistics* 14(2): 61–73.

Wiebe, J., Farwell, D., Villa, D., Chen, J.-L., Sinclair, R., Sandgren, T., Stein, G., Zarazua, D., and O'Hara, T. (1996). 'ARTWORK: Discourse processing in machine translation of dialog'. Technical report MCCS-96-294, Computing Research Laboratory, New Mexico State University.

21

Tense Trees as the 'Fine Structure' of Discourse

CHUNG HEE HWANG* AND LENHART K. SCHUBERT*

1 INTRODUCTION

Work on discourse structure (e.g., Reichman, 1985; Grosz and Sidner, 1986; Allen, 1987) has so far taken a rather coarse, high-level view of discourse, mostly treating sentences or sentence-like entities ("utterance units," "contributions," etc.) as the lowest-level discourse elements. To the extent that sentences are analyzed at all, they are simply viewed as carriers of certain features relevant to supra-sentential discourse structure: cue words, tense, time adverbials, aspectual class, intonational cues, and others. These features are presumed to be extractable in some straightforward fashion and provide the inputs to a higher-level discourse segment analyzer.

However, sentences (or their logical forms) are not in general "flat," with a single level of structure and features, but may contain multiple levels of clausal and adverbial embedding. This substructure can give rise to arbitrarily complex relations among the contributions made by the parts, such as temporal and discourse relations among subordinate clausal constituents and events or states of affairs they evoke. It is therefore essential, in a comprehensive analysis of discourse structure, that these intra-sentential relations be systematically brought to light and integrated with larger-scale discourse structures.

Our particular interest is in tense, aspect and other indicators of temporal structure. We are developing a uniform, compositional approach to interpretation in which a parse tree leads directly (in rule-to-rule fashion) to a preliminary, *indexical* logical form, and this LF is *deindexed* by processing it in the current *context* (a well-defined structure). Deindexing simultaneously transforms the LF and the context: context-dependent constituents of the LF, such as operators *past, pres* and *perf* and adverbs like *today* or *earlier*, are replaced by explicit relations among quantified *episodes*; (anaphora are also deindexed, but this is not discussed here); and new structural components and episode tokens (and other information) are added to the context. This dual transformation is accomplished by simple recursive equivalences and equalities. The relevant context structures are called *tense trees*; these are what we propose as the "fine structure" of discourse, or at least as a key component of that fine structure.

Chung Hee Hwang and Lenhart K. Schubert, 'Tense Trees as the "Fine Structure" of Discourse', *Proceedings of the Thirtieth Annual Meeting of the Association for Computational Linguistics* (1992), 232–40. © 1992 Association for Computational Linguistics.

*Department of Computer Science, University of Rochester, Rochester, New York 14627, U.S.A. {hwang, schubert}@cs.rochester.edu.

In this paper, we first review Reichenbach's influential work on tense and aspect. Then we describe temporal deindexing using tense trees, and extensions of the mechanism to handle discourse involving shifts in temporal perspective.

2 FAREWELL TO REICHENBACH

Researchers concerned with higher-level discourse structure, e.g., Webber (1987; 1988), Passonneau (1988) and Song and Cohen (1991), have almost invariably relied on some Reichenbach (1947)-like conception of tense. The syntactic part of this conception is that there are nine tenses in English, namely *simple* past, present and future tense, past, present and future *perfect* tense, and *posterior* past, present and future tense[1] (plus progressive variants). The semantic part of the conception is that each tense specifies temporal relations among exactly three times particular to a tensed clause, namely the event time (E), the reference time (R) and the speech time (S). On this conception, information in discourse is a matter of "extracting" one of the nine Reichenbachian tenses from each sentence, asserting the appropriate relations among E, R and S, and appropriately relating these times to previously introduced times, taking account of discourse structure cues implicit in tense shifts.

It is easy to understand the appeal of this approach when one's concern is with higher-level structure. By viewing sentences as essentially flat, carrying tense as a top-level feature with nine possible values and evoking a triplet of related times, one can get on with the higher-level processing with minimum fuss. But while there is much that is right and insightful about Reichenbach's conception, it seems to us unsatisfactory from a modern perspective. One basic problem concerns embedded clauses. Consider, for instance, the following passage.

(1) John will find this note when he gets home.
(2) He *will think*(a) Mary *has left*(b).

Reichenbach's analysis of (2) gives us $E_b < S$, $R_b < R_a$, E_a, where $t_1 < t_2$ means t_1 is before t_2, as below.

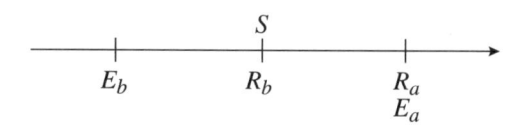

$$\underset{E_b \qquad\qquad R_b \qquad\qquad \underset{E_a}{R_a}}{\xrightarrow{\qquad\qquad\quad \overset{S}{|} \qquad\qquad\qquad}}$$

That is, John will think that Mary's leaving took place some time before the speaker uttered sentence (2). This is incorrect; it is not even likely that John would know about the utterance of (2). In actuality, (2) only implies that John will think Mary's leaving took place some time before the time of his thinking, i.e., $S < R_a$, E_a and $E_b < R_b$, R_a, as shown below.

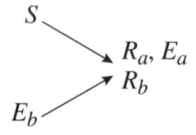

$$S \searrow \atop E_b \nearrow \quad {R_a, E_a \atop R_b}$$

---

[1] Examples of expressions in posterior tense are *would*, *was going to* (posterior past), *is going to* (posterior present), and *will be going to* (posterior future).

Thus, Reichenbach's system fails to take into account the local context created by syntactic embedding.

Attempts have been made to refine Reichenbach's theory (e.g., Hornstein, 1977; Smith, 1978; Nerbonne, 1986), but we think the lumping together of tense and aspect, and the assignment of *E, R, S* triples to all clauses, are out of step with modern syntax and semantics, providing a poor basis for a systematic, compositional account of temporal relations within clauses and between clauses. In particular, we contend that English past, present, future and perfect are separate morphemes making separate contributions to syntactic structure and meaning. Note that perfect *have*, like most verbs, can occur untensed ("She is likely to have left by now"). Therefore, if the meaning of other tensed verbs such as *walks* or *became* is regarded as composite, with the tense morpheme supplying a "present" or "past" component of the meaning, the same ought to be said about tensed forms of *have*. The modals *will* and *would* do not have untensed forms. Nevertheless, considerations of syntactic and semantic uniformity suggest that they too have composite meanings, present or past tense being one part and "future modality" the other. This unifies the analyses of the modals in sentences like "He knows he *will* see her again" and "He knew he *would* see her again," and makes them entirely parallel to paraphrases in terms of *going to*, viz., "He knows he is going to see her again" and "He knew he was going to see her again." We take these latter "posterior tense" forms to be patently hierarchical (e.g., *is going to see her* has 4 levels of VP structure, counting to as an auxiliary verb) and hence semantically composite on any compositional account. Moreover, *going to* can both subordinate, and be subordinated by, perfect *have*, as in "He is going to have left by then." This leads to additional "complex tenses" missing from Reichenbach's list.

We therefore offer a compositional account in which operators corresponding to past (*past*), present (*pres*), future (*futr*) and perfect (*perf*) contribute separately and uniformly to the meanings of their operands, i.e., formulas at the level of LF. Thus, for instance, the temporal relations implicit in "John will have left" are obtained not by extracting a "future perfect" and asserting relations among *E, R* and *S*, but rather by successively taking account of the meanings of the nested *pres, futr* and *perf* operators in the LF of the sentence. As it happens, each of those operators implicitly introduces exactly one *episode*, yielding a Reichenbach-like result in this case. (But note: a simple present sentence like "John is tired" would introduce only *one* episode concurrent with the speech time, not two, as in Reichenbach's analysis.) Even more importantly for present purposes, each of *pres, past, futr* and *perf* is treated uniformly in deindexing and context change. More specifically, they drive the generation and traversal of *tense trees* in deindexing.

3 TENSE TREES

Tense trees provide that part of a discourse context structure[2] which is needed to interpret (and deindex) temporal operators and modifiers within the logical form of English sentences. They differ from simple lists of Reichenbachian indices in that they organize episode tokens (for described episodes and the utterances themselves) in a way that *echoes the hierarchy of temporal and modal operators* of the sentences and clauses

---

[2] In general, the context structure would also contain speaker and hearer parameters, temporal and spatial frames, and tokens for salient referents other than episodes, among other components—see Allen, 1987.

from which the tokens arose. In this respect, they are analogous to larger-scale representations of discourse structure which encode the hierarchic segment structure of discourse. (As will be seen, the analogy goes further.) Tense trees for successive sentences are "overlaid" in such a way that related episode tokens typically end up as adjacent elements of lists at tree nodes. The traversal of trees and the addition of new tokens is simply and fully determined by the logical forms of the sentences being interpreted.

The major advantage of tense trees is that they allow simple, systematic interpretation (by deindexing) of tense, aspect, and time adverbials in texts consisting of arbitrarily complex sentences, and involving implicit temporal reference across clause and sentence boundaries. This includes certain relations implicit in the ordering of clauses and sentences. As has been frequently observed, for a sequence of sentences within the same discourse segment, the temporal reference of a sentence is almost invariably connected to that of the previous sentence in some fashion. Typically, the relation is one of temporal precedence or concurrency, depending on the *aspectual class* or *Aktionsart* involved (cf., "John closed his suitcase; He walked to the door" *versus* "John opened the door; Mary was sleeping"). However, in "Mary got in her Ferrari. She bought it with her own money," the usual temporal precedence is reversed (based on world knowledge). Also, other discourse relations could be implied, such as *cause-of, explains, elaborates,* etc. (more on this later). Whatever the relation may be, finding the right pair of episodes involved in such relations is of crucial importance for discourse understanding. Echoing Leech (1987: 41), we use the predicate constant *orients*, which subsumes all such relations. Note that the *orients* predications can later be used to make probabilistic or default inferences about the temporal or causal relations between the two episodes, based on their aspectual class and other information. In this way they supplement the information provided by larger-scale discourse segment structures. We now describe tense trees more precisely.

Tense Tree Structure
The form of a tense tree is illustrated in Figure 1. As an aid to intuition, the nodes in Figure 1 are annotated with simple sentences whose indexical LFs would lead to those nodes in the course of deindexing. A tense tree node may have up to three branches—a leftward *past* branch, a downward *perfect* branch, and a rightward *future* branch. Each node contains a stack-like list of recently introduced episode tokens (which we will often refer to simply as episodes).

In addition to the three branches, the tree may have (horizontal) *embedding links* to the roots of embedded tense trees. There are two kinds of these embedding links, both illustrated in Figure 1. One kind, indicated by dashed lines, is created by subordinating constructions such as VPs with *that*-complement clauses. The other kind, indicated by dotted lines, is derived from the surface speech act (e.g., telling, asking or requesting) implicit in the mood of a sentence. On our view, the utterances of a speaker (or sentences of a text, etc.) are ultimately to be represented in terms of modal predications expressing these surface speech acts, such as [Speaker tell Hearer (That Φ)] or [Speaker ask Hearer (Whether Φ)]. Although these speech acts are not explicitly part of what the *speaker* uttered, they are part of what the *hearer* gathers from an utterance. Speaker and Hearer are indexical constants to be replaced by the speaker(s) and the hearer(s) of the utterance context. The two kinds of embedding links require slightly different tree traversal techniques as will be seen later.

A set of trees connected by embedding links is called a *tense tree structure* (though we often refer loosely to tense tree structures as tense trees). This is in effect a tree of tense

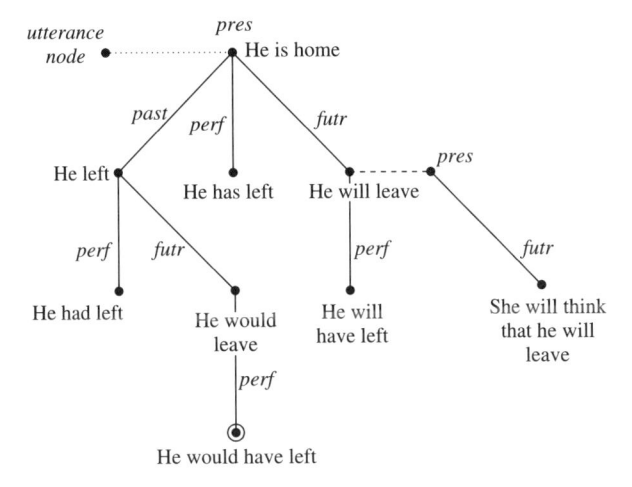

FIG. 1 A Tense Tree.

trees, since a tense tree can be embedded by only one other tree. At any time, exactly one node of the tense tree structure for a discourse is in focus, and the focal node is indicated by ⊙. Note that the "tense tree" in Figure 1 is in fact a tense tree structure, with the lowest node in focus.

By default, an episode added to the right end of a list at a node is "oriented" by the episode which was previously rightmost. For episodes stored at different nodes, we can read off their temporal relations from the tree roughly as follows. At any given moment, for a pair of episodes e and e' that are rightmost at nodes n and n', respectively, where n' is a daughter of n, if the branch connecting the two nodes is a past branch, [e' before e][3]; if it is a perfect branch, [e' impinges-on e] (as we explain later, this yields entailments [e' before e] if e' is nonstative and [e' until e] if e' is stative, respectively illustrated by "John has left" and "John has been working"); if it is a future branch, [e' after e]; and if it is an embedding link, [e' at-about e]. These orienting relations and temporal relations are not extracted *post hoc*, but rather are automatically asserted in the course of deindexing using the rules shown later.

As a preliminary example, consider the following passage and a tense tree annotated with episodes derived from it by our deindexing rules:

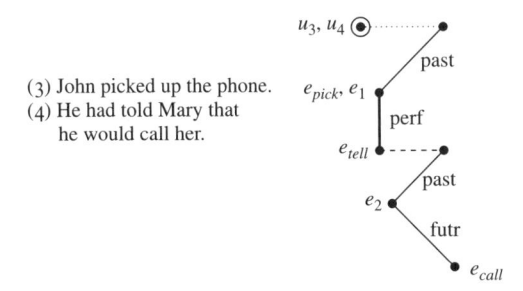

(3) John picked up the phone.
(4) He had told Mary that he would call her.

u_3 and u_4 are utterance episodes for sentences (3) and (4) respectively.

---

[3] Or, sometimes, *same-time* (cf., "John noticed that Mary *looked* pale" *vs.* "Mary realized that someone *broke* her vase"). This is not decided in an *ad hoc* manner, but as a result of systematically interpreting the context-charged relation bef_T. More on this later.

Intuitively, the temporal content of sentence (4) is that the event of John's *telling*, e_{tell}, took place *before* some time e_1, which is at the same time as the event of John's *picking up the phone*, e_{pick}; and the event of John's *calling*, e_{call}, is located *after* some time e_2, which is the at the same time as the event of John's *telling*, e_{tell}. For the most part, this information can be read off directly from the tree: [e_{pick} orients e_1], [e_{tell} before e_1] and [e_{call} after e_2]. In addition, the deindexing rules yield [e_2 same-time e_{tell}]. From this, one may infer [e_{tell} before e_{pick}] and [e_{call} after e_{tell}], assuming that the *orients* relation defaults to *same-time* here.

How does [e_{pick} orients e_1] default to [e_{pick} same-time e_1]? In the tense tree, e_1 is an episode evoked by the past tense operator which is part of the meaning of *had* in (4). It is a *stative* episode, since this past operator logically operates on a sentence of form (perf Φ), and such a sentence describes a *state* in which Φ has occurred—in this instance, a state in which John has told Mary that he will call her. It is this stativity of e_1 which (by default) leads to a *same-time* interpretation of *orients*.[4] Thus, on our account, the tendency of past perfect "reference time" to align itself with a previously introduced past event is just an instance of a general tendency of stative episodes to align themselves with their orienting episode. This is the same tendency noted previously for "John opened the door. Mary was sleeping." We leave further comments about particularizing the *orients* relation to a later subsection.

We remarked that the relation [e_2 same-time e_{tell}] is obtained directly from the deindexing rules. We leave it to the reader to verify this in detail (see Past and Futr rules stated below). We note only that e_2 is evoked by the past tense component of *would* in (4), and denotes a (possible) *state* in which John will call Mary. Its stativity, and the fact that the subordinate clause in (4) is "past-dominated,"[5] causes [e_2 bef$_T$ e_{tell}] to be deindexed to [e_2 same-time e_{tell}].

We now show how tense trees are modified as discourse is processed, in particular, how episode tokens are stored at appropriate nodes of the tense tree, and how deindexed LFs, with *orients* and temporal ordering relations incorporated into them, are obtained.

Processing of Utterances
The processing of the (indexical) LF of a new utterance always begins with the root node of the current tense tree (structure) in focus. The processing of the top-level operator immediately pushes a token for the surface speech act onto the episode list of the root node. Here is a typical indexical LF:

(*decl* (*past* [John know (*That* (*past* (¬ (*perf* [Mary leave])))))]))
"John knew that Mary had not left."

(*decl* stands for *declarative*; its deindexing rule introduces the surface speech act of type "tell"). As mentioned earlier, our deindexing mechanism is a compositional one in which operators *past, futr, perf,* ¬, *That, decl,* etc., contribute separately to the meaning of their operands. As the LF is recursively transformed, the tense and aspect operators encountered, *past, perf* and *futr*, in particular, cause the focus to shift "downward" along existing branches (or new ones if necessary). That is, processing a *past* operator shifts the current focus down to the left, creating a new branch if necessary. The resulting tense

---

[4] More accurately, the default interpretation is [(end-of e_{pick}) same-time e_1], in view of examples involving a longer preceding event, such as "John painted a picture. He was pleased with the result."
[5] A node is *past-dominated* if there is a *past* branch in its ancestry (where embedding links also count as ancestry links).

tree is symbolized as ∕ T. Similarly *perf* shifts straight down, and *futr* shifts down to the right, with respective results ↓ T and ∖ T. *pres* maintains the current focus. Certain operators embed new trees at the current node, written ↦ T (e.g., *That*), or shift focus to an existing embedded tree, written ↪ T (e.g., *decl*). Focus shifts to a parent or embedding node are symbolized as ↑T and ←T respectively. As a final tree operation, ○T denotes storage of episode token e_T (a new episode symbol not yet used in T) at the current focus, as rightmost element of its episode list. As each node comes into focus, its episode list and the lists at certain nodes on the same tree path provide explicit reference episodes in terms of which *past, pres, futr, perf*, time adverbials, and implicit "orienting" relations are rewritten nonindexically. Eventually the focus returns to the root, and at this point, we have a nonindexical LF, as well as a modified tense tree.

Deindexing Rules
Before we proceed with an example, we show some of the basic deindexing rules here.[6] In the following, "**" is an episodic operator that connects a formula with the situation it characterizes. Predicates are infixed and quantifiers have restrictions (following a colon).[7]

Decl: (decl Φ)$_T$
 ↔ (∃e_T:[[e_T same-time Now$_T$] ∧
  [Last$_T$ immediately-precedes e_T]]
  [[Speaker tell Hearer (That Φ$_↪$ ○$_T$)]
  ** e_T])
 Tree transform : (decl Φ) · T = ← (Φ · (↪ ○T))

Pres: (pres Φ)$_T$
 ↔ (∃e_T:[[e_T at-about Emb$_T$] ∧ [Last$_T$ orients e_T]]
  [Φ$_{○T}$ ** e_T])
 Tree transform : (pres Φ) · T = (Φ · (○T))

Past: (past Φ)$_T$
 ↔ (∃e_T:[[e_T bef$_T$ Emb$_T$] ∧ [Last$_{∕T}$ orients e_T]]
  [Φ$_{○∕T}$ ** e_T])
 Tree transform : (past Φ) · T = ↑ (Φ · (○∕T))

Futr: (futr Φ)$_T$
 ↔ (∃e_T:[[e_T after Emb$_T$] ∧ [Last$_{∖T}$ orients e_T]]
  [Φ$_{○∖T}$ ** e_T])
 Tree transform : (futr Φ) · T = ↑ (Φ · (○∖T))

Perf: (perf Φ)$_T$
 ↔ (∃e_T:[[e_T impinges-on Last$_T$] ∧
  [Last$_{↓T}$ orients e_T]]
  [Φ$_{○↓T}$ ** e_T])
 Tree transform : (perf Φ) · T = ↑(Φ · (○↓T))

That: (That Φ)$_T$ ↔ (That Φ$_{↦T}$)
 Tree transform : (That Φ) · T = ←(Φ · (↦T))

---

[6] See (Hwang, 1992) for the rest of our deindexing rules. Some of the omitted ones are: **Fpres** ("futural present," as in "John has a meeting tomorrow"), **Prog** (progressive aspect), **Pred** (predication), K, Ka and Ke ("kinds"), those for deindexing various operators (especially, negation and adverbials), etc.

[7] For details of *Episodic Logic*, our semantic representation, see (Schubert and Hwang, 1989; Hwang and Schubert, 1991).

As mentioned earlier, Speaker and Hearer in the Decl-rule are to be replaced by the speaker(s) and the hearer(s) of the utterance. Note that each equivalence pushes the dependence on context one level deeper into the LF, thus deindexing the top-level operator. The symbols Now_T, $Last_T$, and Emb_T refer respectively to the speech time for the most recent utterance in T, the last- stored episode at the current focal node, and the last-stored episode at the current embedding node. bef_T in the Past-rule will be replaced by either *before* or *same-time*, depending on the aspectual class of its first argument and on whether the focal node of T is past-dominated. In the Perf-rule, $Last_T$ is analogous to the Reichenbachian reference time for the perfect. The *impinges-on* relation confines its first argument e_T (the situation or event described by the sentential operand of *perf*) to the temporal region preceding the second argument. As in the case of *orients*, its more specific import depends on the aspectual types of its arguments. If e_T is a stative episode, *impinges-on* entails that the state or process involved persists to the reference time (episode), i.e., [e_T until $Last_T$]. If e_T is an event (e.g., an accomplishment), *impinges-on* entails that it occurred sometime before the reference time, i.e., [e_T before $Last_T$], and (by default) its main effects persist to the reference time.[8]

An Example
To see the deindexing mechanism at work, consider now sentences (5a) and (6a).

(5) a. John went to the hospital.
   b. $(decl_{\uparrow a} (past_{\uparrow b} [\text{John goto Hospital}]))_{\uparrow c}$
   c. ($\exists$ e1:[e1 same-time*Now1*]
       [[*Speaker* tell *Hearer* (That
           ($\exists$ e2:[e2 before e1]
               [[John goto Hospital] ** e2]))]
       ** e1])

(6) a. The doctor told John he had broken his ankle.
   b. $(decl_{\uparrow d} (past_{\uparrow e} [\text{Doctor tell John (That}_{\uparrow f}$
       $(past_{\uparrow g} (perf_{\uparrow h} [\text{John break Ankle}])))]))_{\uparrow i}$
   c. ($\exists$ e3: [[e3 same-time *Now2*] $\wedge$
           [e1 immediately-precedes e3]]
       [[*Speaker* tell *Hearer* (That
           ($\exists$ e4: [[e4 before e3] $\wedge$ [e2 *orients* e4]]
               [[Doctor tell John (That
                   ($\exists$ e5: [e5 same-time e4]
                       [($\exists$ e6: [e6 before e5]
                           [[John break Ankle] ** e6])
                       ** e5]))]
               ** e4]))]
       ** e3])

The LFs before deindexing are shown in (5,6b) (where the labelled arrows mark points we will refer to); the final, context-independent LFs are in (5,6c). The transformation from (b)s to (c)s and the corresponding tense tree transformations are done with the deindexing rules shown earlier. Anaphoric processing is presupposed here.

---

[8] We have formulated tentative meaning postulates to this effect but cannot dwell on the issue here. Also, we are setting aside certain well-known problems involving temporal adverbials in perfect sentences, such as the inadmissibility of *"John has left yesterday." For a possible approach, see (Schubert and Hwang, 1990).

The snapshots of the tense tree while processing (5b) and (6b), at points $\uparrow_a$–$\uparrow_i$, are as follows (with a null initial context).

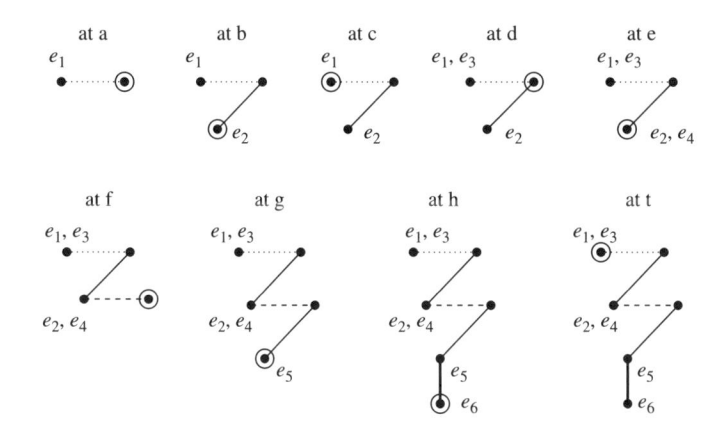

```
at a          at b          at c          at d          at e
e₁            e₁            e₁            e₁, e₃        e₁, e₃
●······⊙      ●······●      ●······●      ●······●      ●······●
                   ⊙         ╲             ╲             ╲
                    e₂         ● e₂          ● e₂         ⊙ e₂, e₄

at f          at g          at h          at t
e₁, e₃        e₁, e₃        e₁, e₃        e₁, e₃
●······●      ●······●      ●······●      ⊙······●
 ╲             ╲             ╲             ╲
 ●----⊙       ●----●        ●----●        ●----●
  e₂, e₄        e₂, e₄        e₂, e₄        e₂, e₄
                 ⊙             │             │
                  e₅            e₅            e₅
                                ⊙ e₆          ● e₆
```

The resultant tree happens to be unary, but additional branches would be added by further text, e.g., a future branch by "It will take several weeks to heal."

What is important here is, first, that Reichenbach-like relations are introduced compositionally; e.g., [e6 before e5], i.e., the breaking of the ankle, e6, is *before* the state John is in at the time of the doctor's talking to him, e4. In addition, the recursive rules take correct account of embedding. For instance, the embedded present perfect in a sentence such as "John will think that Mary has left" will be correctly interpreted as relativized to John's (future) thinking time, rather than the speech time, as in a Reichenbachian analysis.

But beyond that, episodes evoked by successive sentences, or by embedded clauses within the same sentence, are correctly connected to each other. In particular, note that the orienting relation between John's going to the hospital, e2, and the doctor's diagnosis, e4, is automatically incorporated into the deindexed formula (6c). We can plausibly *particularize* this orienting relation to [e4 after e2], based on the aspectual class of "goto" and "tell" (see below). Thus we have established inter-clausal connections automatically, which in other approaches require heuristic discourse processing. This was a primary motivation for tense trees. Our scheme is easy to implement, and has been successfully used in the TRAINS interactive planning advisor at Rochester (Allen and Schubert, 1991).

More on Particularizing the ORIENTS Relation
The *orients* relation is essentially an indicator that there could be a more specific discourse relation between the argument episodes. As mentioned, it can usually be particularized to one or more temporal, causal, or other "standard" discourse relation. Existing proposals for getting these discourse relations right appear to be of two kinds. The first uses the aspectual classes of the predicates involved to decide on discourse relations, especially temporal ones (e.g., Partee, 1984, Dowty, 1986, and Hinrichs, 1986). The second approach emphasizes inference based on world knowledge, (e.g., Hobbs, 1985, Lascarides and Asher, 1991, and Lascarides and Oberlander, 1992). The work by Lascarides et al. is particularly interesting in that it makes use of a default logic and is capable of retracting previously inferred discourse relations.

Our approach fully combines the use of aspectual class information and world knowledge. For example, in "Mary got in her Ferrari. She bought it with her own money," the successively reported "achievements" are by default in chronological order. Here, however, this default interpretation of *orients* is reversed by world knowledge: one owns things *after* buying them, rather than before. But sometimes world knowledge is mute on the connection. For instance, in "John raised his arm. A great gust of wind shook the trees," there seems to be no world knowledge supporting temporal adjacency or a causal connection. Yet we tend to infer both, perhaps attributing magical powers to John (precisely because of the lack of support for a causal connection by world knowledge). So in this case default conclusions based on *orients* seem decisive. In particular, we would assume that if e and e' are nonstative episodes,[9] where e is the performance of a volitional action and e' is not, then [e orients e'] suggests [e right-before e'] and (less firmly) [e cause-of e'].[10]

4 BEYOND SENTENCE PAIRS

The tense tree mechanism, and particularly the way in which it automatically supplies orienting relations, is well suited for longer narratives, including ones with tense shifts. Consider, for example, the following (slightly simplified) text from Allen (1987: 400):

(7) a. Jack and Sue went$_{\{e_1\}}$ to a hardware store
  b. as someone had$_{\{e_2\}}$ stolen$_{\{e_3\}}$ their lawnmower.
  c. Sue had$_{\{e_4\}}$ seen$_{\{e_5\}}$ a man take it
  d. and had$_{\{e_6\}}$ chased$_{\{e_7\}}$ him down the street,
  e. but he had$_{\{e_8\}}$ driven$_{\{e_9\}}$ away in a truck.
  f. After looking$_{\{e_{10}\}}$ in the store, they realized$_{\{e_{11}\}}$ that they couldn't afford$_{\{e_{12}\}}$ a new one.

Even though {b–e} would normally be considered a subsegment of the main discourse {a, f}, both the temporal relations *within* each segment and the relations *between* segments (i.e., that the substory temporally precedes the main one) are automatically captured by our rules. For instance, e_1 and e_{11} are recognized as successive episodes, both preceded at some time in the past by e_3, e_5, e_7, and e_9, in that order.

This is not to say that our tense tree mechanism obviates the need for larger-scale discourse structures. As has been pointed out by Webber [1987; 1988] and others, many subnarratives introduced by a past perfect sentence may continue in simple past. The following is one of Webber's examples:

(8) a. I was$_{\{e_1\}}$ at Mary's house yesterday.
  b. We talked$_{\{e_2\}}$ about her sister Jane.
  c. She had$_{\{e_3\}}$ spent$_{\{e_4\}}$ five weeks in Alaska with two friends.
  d. Together, they climbed$_{\{e_5\}}$ Mt. McKinley.
  e. Mary asked$_{\{e_6\}}$ whether I would want to go to Alaska some time.

---

[9] Non-statives could be achievements, accomplishments, culminations, etc. Our aspectual class system is not entirely settled yet, but we expect to have one similar to that of Moens and Steedman, 1988.

[10] Our approach to plausible inference in episodic logic in general, and to such default inferences in particular, is probabilistic (see Schubert and Hwang, 1989; Hwang, 1992). The hope is that we will be able to "weigh the evidence" for or against alternative discourse relations (as particularizations of *orients*).

Note the shift to simple past in *d*, though as Webber points out, past perfect *could* have been used. The abandonment of the past perfect in favor of simple past signals the temporary abandonment of a perspective anchored in the main narrative–thus bringing readers "closer" to the scene (a *zoom-in* effect). In such cases, the tense tree mechanism, unaided by a notion of higher-level discourse segment structure, would derive incorrect temporal relations such as [e_5 orients e_6] or [e_6 right-after e_5].

We now show possible deindexing rules for perspective shifts, assuming for now that such shifts are independently identifiable, so that they can be incorporated into the indexical LFs. *new-pers* is a sentence *operator* initiating a perspective shift for its operand, and *prevpers* is a *sentence* (with otherwise no content) which gets back to the previous perspective. Recent$_T$ is the episode most recently stored in the subtree immediately embedded by the focal node of T.

New-pers: (new-pers Φ)$_T$
　　　　　↔ [Φ$_{\hookrightarrow T}$ ∧ [Recent$_T$ orients Recent$_{T'}$]]
　　　　　where Tree T' = Φ · (↦T)
　　　　　Tree transform :
　　　　　(new-pers Φ) · T = Φ · (↦T)
Prev-pers: prev-pers$_T$ → ⊤ (True)
　　　　　Tree transform : prev-pers · T = ↞ T

When *new-pers* is encountered, a new tree is created and embedded at the focal node, the focus is moved to the root node of the new tree, and the next sentence is processed in that context. In contrast with other operators, *new-pers* causes an overall focus shift to the new tree, rather than returning the focus to the original root. Note that the predication [Recent$_T$ orients Recent$_{T'}$] connects an episode of the new sentence with an episode of the previous sentence. *prev-pers* produces a trivial *True*, but it returns the focus to the embedding tree, simultaneously blocking the link between the embedding and the embedded tree (as emphasized by use of ↞ instead of ←).

We now illustrate how tense trees get modified over perspective changes, using (8) as example. We repeat (8d,e) below, augmenting them with perspective changes, and show snapshots of the tense trees at the points marked. In the trees, $u_1, \ldots, u_5$ are utterance episodes for sentences a, ..., e, respectively.

(8) d. ↑T1 (*new-pers* Together, they climbed$_{\{e_5\}}$ Mt. McKinley.)↑T2
　　　prev-pers↑T3
　　e. Mary asked$_{\{e_6\}}$ whether I would want to go to Alaska some time.↑T4

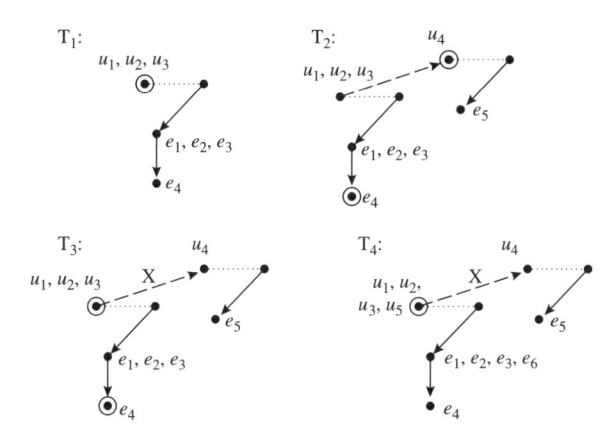

Notice the blocked links to the embedded tree in T3 and T4. Also, note that Recent$_{T1}$ = e4 and Recent$_{T2}$ = e5. So, by New-pers, we get [e4 orients e5], which can be later particularized to [e5 during e4]. It is fairly obvious that the placement of *new-pers* and *prev-pers* operators is fully determined by discourse segment boundaries (though not in general coinciding with them). So, as long as the higher-level discourse segment structure is known, our perspective rules are easily applied. In that sense, the higher-level structure supplements the "fine structure" in a crucial way.

However, this leaves us with a serious problem: deindexing and the context change it induces is supposed to be *independent* of "plausible inferencing"; in fact, it is intended to *set the stage* for the latter. Yet the determination of higher-level discourse structure—and hence of perspective shifts—is unquestionably a matter of plausible inference. For example, if *past perfect* is followed by *past*, this could signal either a new perspective within the current segment (see 8c,d), or the closing of the current subsegment with no perspective shift (see 7e,f). If *past* is followed by *past*, we may have either a continuation of the current perspective and segment (see 9a,b below), or a perspective shift with opening of a new segment (see 9b,c), or closing of the current segment, with resumption of the previous perspective (see 9c,d).

(9) a. Mary found that her favorite vase was broken.
    b. She was upset.
    c. She bought it at a special antique auction,
    d. and she was afraid she wouldn't be able to find anything that beautiful again.

Only plausible inference can resolve these ambiguities. This inference process will interact with resolution of anaphora and introduction of new individuals, identification of spatial and temporal frames, the presence of modal/cognition/ perception verbs, and most of all will depend on world knowledge. In (9), for instance, one may have to rely on the knowledge that one normally would not buy broken things, or that one does not buy things one already owns.

As approaches to this general difficulty, we are thinking of the following two strategies: (A) Make a best initial guess about presence or absence of *new-pers/prev-pers*, based on *surface* (syntactic) cues and then use failure-driven backtracking if the resulting interpretation is incoherent. A serious disadvantage would be lack of integration with other forms of disambiguation. (B) Change the interpretation of Last$_T$, in effect providing multiple alternative referents for the first argument of *orients*. In particular, we might use

Last$_T$ = {e_i | e_i is the last-stored episode at the focus of T, or was stored in the subtree rooted at the focus of T *after* the last-stored episode at the focus of T}.

Subsequent processing would resemble anaphora disambiguation. In the course of further interpreting the deindexed LF, plausible inference would particularize the schematic orienting relation to a temporal (or causal, etc.) relation involving just two episodes. The result would then be used to make certain structural changes to the tense tree (*after* LF deindexing).

For instance, suppose such a schematic orienting relation is computed for a simple past sentence following a past perfect sentence (like 8c,d). Suppose further that the most coherent interpretation of the second sentence (i.e., 8d) is one that disambiguates the orienting relation as a simple temporal inclusion relation between the successively reported events. One might then move the event token for the second event (reported in simple past) from its position at the past node to the rightmost position at the past perfect node, just as if the second event had been reported in the past perfect. (One might in addition record a perspective shift, if this is still considered useful.) In other words, we would "repair" the distortion of the tense tree brought about by the speaker's "lazy" use of simple past in place of past perfect. Then we would continue as before.

In both strategies we have assumed a general coherence-seeking plausible inference process. While it is clear that the attainment of coherence entails delineation of discourse segment structure and of all relevant temporal relations, it remains unclear in which direction the information flows. Are there independent principles of discourse and temporal structure operating *above* the level of syntax and LF, *guiding* the achievement of full understanding, or are higher-level discourse and temporal relations a mere byproduct of full understanding? Webber (1987) has proposed independent temporal focusing principles similar to those in (Grosz and Sidner, 1986) for discourse. These are not deterministic, and Song and Cohen (1991) sought to add heuristic constraints as a step toward determinism. For instance, one constraint is based on the presumed incoherence of simple present followed by past perfect or posterior past. But there are counterexamples; e.g., "Mary is angry about the accident. The other driver had been drinking." Thus, we take the question about independent structural principles above the level of syntax and LF to be still open.

5 CONCLUSION

We have shown that tense and aspect can be analyzed compositionally in a way that accounts not only for their more obvious effects on sentence meaning but also, via tense trees, for their cumulative effect on context and the temporal relations implicit in such contexts. As such, the analysis seems to fit well with higher-level analyses of discourse segment structure, though questions remain about the flow of information between levels.

ACKNOWLEDGEMENTS

We gratefully acknowledge helpful comments by James Allen and Philip Harrison on an earlier draft and much useful feedback from the members of Trains group at the University of Rochester. This work was supported in part by NSERC Operating Grant A8818 and ONR/DARPA research contract no. N00014-82-K-0193, and the Boeing Co. under Purchase Contract W-288104.

A preliminary version of this paper was presented at the AAAI Fall Symposium on Discourse Structure in Natural Language Understanding and Generation, Pacific Grove, CA, November 1991.

REFERENCES

Allen, J. (1987). *Natural Language Understanding*, Chapter 14. Reading, MA: Benjamin/Cummings Publ. Co.

—— and Schubert, L. K. (1991). 'The TRAINS project', TR 382, Dept. of Comp. Sci., University of Rochester, Rochester, NY.

Dowty, D. (1986). 'The effect of aspectual classes on the temporal structure of discourse: semantics or pragmatics?' *Linguistics and Philosophy*, 9(1): 37–61.

Grosz, B. J. and Sidner, C. L. (1986). 'Attention, intentions, and the structure of discourse', *Computational Linguistics* 12: 175–204.

Hinrichs, E. (1986). 'Temporal anaphora in discourses of English', *Linguistics and Philosophy*, 9(1): 63–82.

Hobbs, J. R. (1985). 'On the coherence and structure of discourse', Technical Report CSLI-85-37, Stanford, CA.

Hornstein, N. (1977). 'Towards a theory of tense', *Linguistic Inquiry* 3: 521–57.

Hwang, C. H. (1992). 'A logical Framework for Narrative Understanding', Ph.D. thesis, University of Alberta, Edmonton, Canada.

——and Schubert, L. K. (1991). 'Episodic Logic: A situational logic for natural language processing', in *3rd Conference on Situation Theory and its Applications (STA-3)*, Oiso, Kanagawa, Japan, November 18–21, 1991.

Lascarides, A. and Asher, N. (1991). 'Discourse relations and defeasible knowledge', in *Proceedings of the 29th Annual Meeting of the ACL*, Berkeley, CA, June 18–21, 1991, 55–62.

——and Oberlander, J. (1992). 'Temporal coherence and defeasible knowledge', *Theoretical Linguistics* 8: 1–37.

Leech, G. (1987). *Meaning and the English Verb (2nd edn.)*, London: Longman.

Moens, M. and Steedman, M. (1988). 'Temporal ontology and temporal reference', *Computational Linguistics* 14(2): 15–28.

Nerbonne, J. (1986). 'Reference time and time in narration', *Linguistics and Philosophy* 9(1): 83–95.

Partee, B. (1984). 'Nominal and Temporal Anaphora', *Linguistics and Philosophy* 7: 243–86.

Passonneau, R. J. (1988). 'A Computational model of the semantics of tense and aspect', *Computational Linguistics* 14(2): 44–60.

Reichenbach, H. (1947). *Elements of Symbolic Logic*. New York, NY: Macmillan.

Reichman, R. (1985). *Getting Computers to Talk Like You and Me*. Cambridge, MA: MIT Press.

Schubert, L. K. and Hwang, C. H. (1989). 'An Episodic knowledge representation for Narrative Texts', in *Proceedings of the 1st International Conference on Principles of Knowledge Representation and Reasoning (KR '89)*, Toronto, Canada, May 15–18, 1989, 444–58. Revised, extended version available as TR 345, Dept. of Comp. Sci., U. of Rochester, Rochester, NY, May 1990.

—— —— (1990). 'Picking reference events from tense trees: A formal, implementable theory of English tense-aspect semantics', in *Proceedings of the Speech and Natural Language, DARPA Workshop*, Hidden Valley, PA, June 24–27, 1990, 34–41.

Smith, C. (1978). 'The syntax and interpretations of temporal expressions in English', *Linguistics and Philosophy* 2: 43–99.

Song, F. and Cohen, R. (1991). 'Tense interpretation in the context of narrative', in *Proceedings of the AAAI-91*, Anaheim, CA, July 14–19, 1991, 131–6.

Webber, B. L. (1987). 'The Interpretation of tense in discourse', in *Proceedings of the 25th Annual Meeting of the ACL*, Stanford, CA, July 6–9, 1987, 147–54.

Webber, B. L. (1988). 'Tense as discourse anaphor', *Computational Linguistics* 14(2): 61–73.

22

Algorithms for Analysing the Temporal Structure of Discourse*[†]

JANET HITZEMAN, MARC MOENS, AND CLAIRE GROVER

1 INTRODUCTION

In this paper we describe a method for analysing the temporal structure of a discourse. This component was implemented as part of a discourse grammar for English. The goals of the temporal component were to yield a detailed representation of the temporal structure of the discourse, taking into account the effect of tense, aspect, and temporal expressions while at the same time minimising unnecessary ambiguity in the temporal structure. The method combines a constraint-based approach with an approach based on preferences: we exploit the HPSG type hierarchy and unification to arrive at a temporal structure using constraints placed on that structure by tense, aspect, rhetorical structure and temporal expressions, and we use the *temporal centering* preferences described by (Kameyama et al., 1993; Poesio, 1994) to rate the possibilities for temporal structure and choose the best among them.

The starting point for this work was Scha and Polanyi's discourse grammar (Scha and Polanyi 1988; Prüst et al. 1994). For the implementation we extended the HPSG grammar (Pollard and Sag, 1994) which Gerald Penn and Bob Carpenter first encoded in ALE (Carpenter, 1993). This paper will focus on our temporal processing algorithm, and in particular on our analysis of narrative progression, rhetorical structure, perfects, and temporal expressions.

2 CONSTRAINTS ON NARRATIVE CONTINUATIONS

Probably the best known algorithm for tracking narrative progression is that developed by Kamp (1979), Hinrichs (1981), and Partee (1984), which formalises the observation that an event will occur *just after* a preceding event, while a state will *overlap* with a preceding event. This algorithm gives the correct results in examples such as the following:

(1) John entered the room. Mary stood up.
(2) John entered the room. Mary was seated behind the desk.

Janet Hitzeman, Marc Moens, and Claire Grover, 'Algorithms for Analysing the Temporal structure of Discourse', *Proceedings of the Annual Meeting of the European Chapter of the Association for Computational Linguistics*, Dublin, Ireland, 1995, 253–60. © 1995 Association for Computational Linguistics.

* We would like to thank Alex Lascarides and Massimo Poesio for comments on an earlier draft.
[†] This work was supported in part by the European Commission's programme on *Linguistic Research and Engineering* through project LRE-61-062, "Towards a declarative theory of discourse."

In (1) the event of Mary's standing is understood to occur just after John enters the room, while in (2) the state in which Mary is seated is understood to overlap with the event of John's entering the room.

However, if there is a rhetorical relationship between two eventualities such as causation, elaboration, or enablement, the temporal defaults can be overridden, as in the following examples:

(3) a. John fell. Mary pushed him.
    b. Local builders constructed the Ford St. Bridge. They used 3 tons of bricks.

In (3a) there is a causal relationship between Mary's pushing John and his falling, and the second event is understood to precede the first. In (3b), the second sentence is an elaboration of the first, and they therefore refer to aspects of the same event rather than to two sequential events.

It has been suggested that only world knowledge allows one to detect that the default is being overridden here. For example, Lascarides and Asher (1991) suggest that general knowledge postulates (in the case of (3a): that a pushing can cause a falling) can be invoked to generate the backward movement reading.

The problem for practical systems is twofold: we could assume that in the case of narrative the Kamp/Hinrichs/Partee algorithm is the default, but each time the default is applied we would need to check all our available world knowledge to see whether there isn't a world knowledge postulate which might be overriding this assumption. Clearly this would make the processing of text a very expensive operation.

An alternative is to assume that the temporal ordering between events in two consecutive sentences can be any of the four possibilities (*just_after*, *precede*, *same-event* and *overlap*). But then the resulting temporal structures will be highly ambiguous even in small discourses. And sometimes this ambiguity is unwarranted. Consider:

(4)   Mary stared at John. He gave her back her slice of pizza.

Here, it would appear, only one reading is possible, i.e. the one where John gave Mary her slice of pizza *just after* she stared or started to stare at him. It would be undesirable for the temporal processing mechanism to postulate an ambiguity in this case.

Of course, sometimes it is possible to take advantage of certain cue words which either indicate or constrain the rhetorical relation. For example, in (5) the order of the events is understood to be the reverse of that in (1) due to the cue word *because* which signals a causal relationship between the events:

(5)   John entered the room because Mary stood up.

As Kehler (1994) points out, if forward movement of time is considered a default with consecutive event sentences, then the use of "because" in (5) should cause a temporal clash—whereas it is perfectly felicitous. Temporal expressions such as *at noon* and *the previous Thursday* can have a similar effect: they too can override the default temporal relations and place constraints on tense. In (6), for example, the default interpretation would be that John's being in Detroit overlaps with his being in Boston, but the phrase *the previous Thursday* overrides this, giving the interpretation that John's being in Detroit precedes his being in Boston:

(6)   John was in Boston. The previous Thursday he was in Detroit.

This suggests that the temporal information given by tense acts as a weaker constraint on temporal structure than the information given by temporal adverbials.

The possibilities for rhetorical relations (e.g., whether something is narration, or elaboration, or a causal relation) can be further constrained by aspect. For example, a state can elaborate another state or an event:

(7) a. Mary was tired. She was exhausted.
    b. Mary built a dog house. It was a labour of love.

But an event can only elaborate another event, as in (8):

(8) a. Mary built a dog house. She used two tons of bricks.
    b. Mary was tired/working hard. ?She built a dog house.

For the eventive second sentence of (8b) to be an elaboration of the first sentence, it must occur in a stative form—for example as a progressive (i.e., *She was building a dog house*).

Because of considerations like these, our aim in the implementation work was to treat tense, aspect, cue words, and rhetorical relations as mutually constraining, with more specific information such as explicit cue words having higher priority than less specific information such as tense. The main advantage of this approach is that it reduces temporal structure ambiguity without having to rely on detailed world knowledge postulates.

Table 1 lists the possible temporal relations between the eventualities described by two consecutive sentences without temporal expressions or cue words, where the first sentence (S_1) may have any tense and aspect and the second sentence (S_2) expresses a simple past event. We constrain S_2 in this way because of lack of space; additional constraints are given in (Hitzeman et al., 1994). For example, if a simple past eventive sentence follows a simple past eventive sentence the second event can be understood to occur just after the first, to precede the first or to refer to the same event as the first (an elaboration relation), but the two events cannot overlap; these constraints are weaker, however, than explicit clues such as cue words to rhetorical relations and temporal expressions. When S_1 expresses a state, it is possible for the temporal relation to hold between the event described by S_2 and the event or activity most closely preceding S_1, i.e., the temporal focus of S_1, here referred to as TF_1.[1]

However, we haven't solved the problem completely at this point: although tense can provide a further constraint on the temporal structure of such discourses, it can also add a further ambiguity. Consider (9):

(9)   Sam rang the bell. He had lost the key.

Clearly, the event described by the past perfect sentence must precede the event described by the first, simple past sentence. However, if a third sentence is added, an ambiguity results. Consider the following possible continuations of (9):

(10) a. ...Hannah opened the door.
     b. ...It fell through a hole in his pocket.

The temporal relation between these continuations and the portion of earlier text they attach to is constrained along the lines sketched before. The problem here is determining which thread in (9) they continue; (10a) continues the thread in which Sam rings the bell, but (10b) continues the thread in which Sam loses the key.

---

[1] In this chart it appears that whether the tense is simple past or past perfect makes no difference, and that only aspect affects the possible temporal relations between S_1 and S_2. However, it is important not to ignore tense because other combinations of tense and aspect do show that tense affects which relations are possible, e.g., a simple past stative S_2 cannot have a *precede* relation with any S_1, while a past perfect stative S_2 can.

TABLE 1 Possible relations when S2 expresses a simple past event

S_1	Relation	Example
past event	just-after S_1	Mary pushed John. He fell.
	precede S_1	John fell. Mary pushed him.
	overlap S_1	NO
	same-event S_1	I assembled the desk myself. The drawers only took me ten minutes.
past activity	just-after S_1	Mary stared at John. He gave her back her slice of pizza.
	precede S_1	NO
	overlap S_1	NO
	same-event S_1	NO
past state	just-after S_1	NO
	just-after TF_1	Sam arrived at eight. He was tired. He rang the bell.
	precede S_1	NO
	precede TF_1	?John fell. He was in pain. Mary pushed him.
	overlap S_1	Mary was angry. She pushed John.
	overlap TF_1	NO
	same-event S_1	NO
	same-event TF_1	I assembled the desk myself. It was beautiful. The drawers only took me ten minutes.
past perf event	just-after S_1	Sam had arrived at the house. He rang the bell.
	precede S_1	Sam arrived at the house. He had lost the key. He rang the bell.
	overlap S_1	NO
	same-event S_1	I had assembled the desk myself. The drawers only took me ten minutes.
past perf activity	just-after S_1	Mary had stared at John. He gave her back her slice of pizza.
	precede S_1	NO
	overlap S_1	NO
	same-event S_1	NO
past perf state	just-after S_1	NO
	just-after TF_1	Martha discovered the broken lock. Someone had been in the garage. They rearranged the tools.
	precede S_1	NO
	precede TF_1	NO
	overlap S_1	Martha discovered the broken lock. Someone had been in the garage. They rearranged the tools.
	overlap TF_1	NO
	same-event S_1	NO
	same-event TF_1	Mary built the desk herself. She had been happy taking it on. The drawers only took her ten minutes.

A further ambiguity is that when the third sentence is past perfect, it may be a continuation of a preceding thread or the start of a new thread itself. Consider:

(11) a. Sam rang the bell. He had lost the key. It had fallen through a hole in his pocket.
b. John got to work late. He had left the house at 8. He had eaten a big breakfast.

In (a) the third sentence continues the thread about losing the key; in (b) the third starts a new thread.[2]

For the problem with multi-sentence discourses, and the "threads" that sentences continue, we use an implementation of temporal centering (Kameyama et al., 1993; Poesio, 1994). This is a technique similar to the type of centering used for nominal anaphora (Sidner, 1983; Grosz et al., 1983). Centering assumes that discourse understanding requires some notion of "aboutness." While nominal centering assumes there is one object that the current discourse is "about," temporal centering assumes that there is one thread that the discourse is currently following, and that, in addition to tense and aspect constraints, there is a preference for a new utterance to continue a thread which has a parallel tense or which is semantically related to it and a preference to continue the current thread rather than switching to another thread. Kameyama et al. (1993) confirmed these preferences when testing their ideas on the Brown corpus.

As an example of how the temporal centering preference techniques can reduce ambiguity, recall example (9) and the possible continuations shown in (10). The difficulty in these examples is determining whether the third sentence continues the thread begun by the first or second sentence. For example, in (10a) the preference technique which allows us to choose the first thread over the second is one which assigns a higher rating to a thread whose tense is parallel to that of the new sentence; in this case both *Sam rang the bell* and *Hannah opened the door* are in the simple past tense. In example (10b) the fact that the key is mentioned only in the second sentence of (9) links (10b) with the second thread. To handle an example like (12), we employ a preference for relating a sentence to a thread that has content words that are rated as semantically "close" to that of the sentence:

(12) Sam rang the bell. He had lost the key. His keyring broke.

We store semantic patterns between words as a cheap and quick form of world knowledge; these patterns are easier to provide than are the detailed world knowledge postulates required in some other approaches, and result in similar and sometimes more precise temporal structures with less processing overhead. Using the semantic patterns we know that *key* and *keyring* are semantically close, and through that semantic link between the second and third sentences we prefer to connect the third sentence to the thread begun by the second.[3] The approach to representing semantic relationships we take is one used by Morris and Hirst (1991) wherein the words in the lexicon are associated with each other in a thesaurus-like fashion and given a rating according to how semantically "close" they are. We thus avoid relying on high-level inferences and very specific world knowledge postulates, our goal being to determine the temporal structure as much as possible prior to the application of higher-level inferences.

3 AN HPSG IMPLEMENTATION OF A DISCOURSE GRAMMAR

Following Scha and Polanyi (1988) and Prüst et al. (1994), our model of discourse consists of units called Discourse Constituent Units (DCUs) which are related by various

---

[2] We will not discuss the additional problem that if the final sentence in (11b) is the end of the text, the text is probably ill-formed. This is because a well-formed text should not leave threads "dangling" or unfinished. This is probably also the reason for the awkwardness of the well-known example *Max poured a cup of coffee. He had entered the room.*

[3] Semantic closeness ratings won't help in examples (9)–(10) because there is as strong a relationship between *door* and *bell* as there is between *door* and *key*.

temporal and rhetorical relations. A basic DCU represents a sentence (or clause), and complex DCUs are built up from basic and complex DCUs.

In our ALE implementation, a DCU contains the following slots for temporal information:

CUE_WORD: Cues to rhetorical structure, e.g., "because."
V_AND_NP_LIST: Contains content words found in this DCU, and is used to compare the content words of the current DCU with those in previous threads, in order to rate the semantic "closeness" of the DCU to each thread.
SEM_ASPECT: Contains the semantic aspect (*event, state, activity*). We have extended the Penn and Carpenter implementation of the HPSG grammar so that semantic aspect is calculated compositionally (and stored here).
RHET_RELN: The relation between this DCU and a previous one. Lexical items and phrases such as cue words (stored in CUE_WORD) affect the value of this slot.
TEMP_CENTER: Used for temporal centering; Keeps track of the thread currently being followed (since there is a preference for continuing the current thread) and all the threads that have been constructed so far in the discourse.
FWD_CENTER: Existing threads
BKWD_CENTER: The thread currently being followed
CLOSED_THREADS: Threads no longer available for continuation
TEMP_EXPR_RELNS: Stores the semantic interpretation of temporal expressions associated with this DCU.
TEMP_RELNS: Stores the temporal relations between the eventualities in the discourse.
TEMPFOC: The most recent event in the current thread which a subsequent eventuality may elaborate upon (*same-event*), *overlap*, come *just_after* or *precede*.
TENASP: Keeps track of the tense and syntactic aspect of the DCU (if the DCU is simple).
TENSE: past, pres, fut
ASPECT: simple, perf, prog, perf_prog

To allow the above-mentioned types of information to mutually constrain each other, we employ a hierarchy of rhetorical and temporal relations (illustrated in Figure 1), using the ALE system in such a way that clues such as tense and cue words work together to reduce the number of possible temporal structures. This approach improves upon earlier work on discourse structure such as (Lascarides and Asher, 1991) and (Kehler, 1994) in reducing the number of possible ambiguities; it is also more precise than the Kamp/Hinrichs/Partee approach in that it takes into account ways in which the apparent defaults can be overridden and differentiates between events and activities, which behave differently in narrative progression.

Tense, aspect, rhetorical relations, and temporal expressions affect the value of the RHET_RELN type that expresses the relationship between two DCUs: cue words are

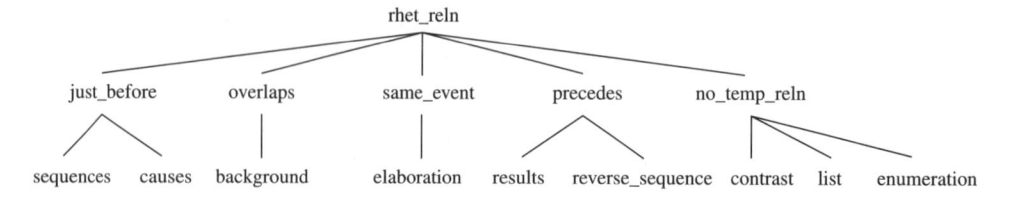

FIG. 1 The type hierarchy used for constraints.

lexically marked according to what rhetorical relation they specify, and this relation is passed on to the DCU. Explicit relation markers such as cue words and temporal relations must be consistent and take priority over indicators such as tense and aspect. For example, sentence (13) will be ruled out because the cue phrase *as a result* conflicts with the temporal expression *ten minutes earlier:*

(13) #Mary pushed John and as a result ten minutes earlier he fell.

On the other hand, if temporal expressions indicate an overlap relation and cue words indicate a background relation as in (14), these contributions are consistent and the RHET_RELN type will contain a *background* value (the more specific value of the two):

(14) Superman stopped the train just in time. Meanwhile, Jimmy Olsen was in trouble.

4 THE ALGORITHM

For reasons of space it is difficult to give examples of the sign-based output of the grammar, or of the ALE rules, so we will restrict ourselves here to a summary of the algorithm and to a very limited rendition of the system output. The algorithm used for calculating the temporal structure of a discourse can be summarised as follows. It consists of two parts, the constraint-based portion and the preference-based portion:

1. The possible temporal/rhetorical relations are constrained.
   (a) If there is a temporal expression, it determines the temporal relationship of the new DCU to the previous ones, and defaults are ignored.
   (b) Lexical items such as cue words influence the value of the RHET_RELN type. (See Figure 1.)
   (c) If steps (a) and (b) attempt to place conflicting values in the RHET_RELN slot, the parse will fail.
   (d) If there is no temporal expression or cue phrase, tense and semantic aspect also influence the value of the RHET_RELN type (see Table 1), so that rhetorical relations, tense, and aspect constrain each other.

2. If more than one possibility exists, semantic preferences are used to choose between the possibilities.
   (a) A "semantic distance" rating between the new DCU and each previous thread is determined. (If there are no existing threads a new thread is started.)
   (b) Other preferences, such as a preference for relating the new DCU to a thread with parallel tense, are employed (see (Kameyama et al., 1993; Poesio, 1994) for details), and the resulting ratings are factored into the rating for each thread.
   (c) If the thread currently being followed is among the highest rated threads, this thread is continued. (This corresponds to temporal centering's preference to continue the current thread.)
   (d) If not, the DCU may continue any of the highest rated threads, and each of these solutions is generated.

Charts such as Table 1 provide the observations we use to fill in the value of RHET_RELN. Those observations are summarised below. In what follows, the event variable associated with DCU$_i$ is e$_i$ and the TEMPFOC of e$_1$ is the most recent event/activity processed, possibly e$_1$ itself:

- e$_2$ can overlap with e$_1$ if
  - DCU$_2$ describes a state, or
  - DCU$_1$ describes a state and DCU$_2$ describes an activity.

- e$_2$ can occur just-after the TEMPFOC of e$_1$ if
  - DCU$_2$ describes a simple tense event, or
  - DCU$_1$ describes a complex tense clause and DCU$_2$ describes a complex tense event, or
  - DCU$_1$ describes an event and DCU$_2$ describes an atelic or a simple tense state, or
  - DCU$_1$ describes a state and DCU$_2$ describes a simple tense activity.

- e$_2$ can precede e$_1$ if
  - DCU$_2$ describes an event, or
  - DCU$_1$ doesn't describe an activity and DCU$_2$ describes a past perfect stative.

- e$_2$ can elaborate on e$_1$ if
  - DCU$_1$ describes an event, or
  - DCU$_1$ describes an activity and DCU$_2$ describes an atelic, or
  - DCU$_1$ and DCU$_2$ describe states and either DCU$_2$ describes a simple tense state or DCU$_1$ describes a complex tense state.

Using this algorithm, we can precisely identify the rhetorical and temporal relations when cue words to rhetorical structure are present, as in (15):

(15) John fell (e$_1$) because Mary pushed him (e$_2$).
TEMP_RELNS: e$_2$ precedes e$_1$

We can also narrow the possibilities when no cue word is present by using constraints based on observations of tense and aspect interactions such as those shown in Table 1. For example, if DCU$_1$ represents a simple past eventive sentence and DCU$_2$ a past perfect eventive sentence, then in spite of the lack of rhetorical cues we know that e$_2$ precedes e$_1$, as in (16):

(16) Sam rang the doorbell (e$_1$). He had lost the key (e$_2$).
TEMP_RELNS: e$_2$ precedes e$_1$

Also, when several structures are possible we can narrow the possibilities by using preferences, as in the examples below:

(17) Sam arrived at the house at eight (e$_1$).
He had lost the key (e$_2$).
  a. ...He rang the bell (e$_3$).
  TEMP_RELNS: e$_2$ precedes e$_1$,
  e$_3$ just-after e$_1$
  b. ...It fell through a hole in his pocket (e$_{3'}$).
  TEMP_RELNS: e$_2$ precedes e$_1$,
  e$_{3'}$ just_after e$_2$

If we allow any of the four possible temporal relations between events, both continuations of sentence (17) would have 17 readings (4 × 4 + 1 reading in which the third sentence begins a new thread). Using constraints, we reduce the number of readings to 4. Using preferences, we reduce that to 2 readings for each continuation. The correct temporal relations are shown in (17).[4]

5 AN UNDERSPECIFIED REPRESENTATION

By using constraints and preferences, we can considerably reduce the amount of ambiguity in the temporal/rhetorical structure of a discourse. However, explicit cues to rhetorical and temporal relations are not always available, and these cases result in more ambiguity than is desirable when processing large discourses.

Consider, however, that instead of generating all the possible temporal/rhetorical structures, we could use the information available to fill in the most restrictive type possible in the type hierarchy of temporal/rhetorical relations shown in Figure 1. We can then avoid generating the structures until higher-level information can be applied to complete the disambiguation process.

6 CONCLUSION

We presented a brief description of an algorithm for determining the temporal structure of discourse. The algorithm is part of an HPSG-style discourse grammar implemented in Carpenter's ALE formalism. Its novel features are that it treats tense, aspect, temporal adverbials, and rhetorical relations as mutually constraining; it postulates less ambiguity than current temporal structuring algorithms do; and it uses semantic closeness and other preference techniques rather than full-fledged world knowledge postulates to determine preferences over remaining ambiguities. We also recommended using an underspecified representation of temporal/rhetorical structure to avoid generating all solutions until higher-level knowledge can aid in reducing ambiguity.

REFERENCES

Carpenter, Bob (1993). *ALE: The Attribute Logic Engine User's Guide*. Laboratory for Computational Linguistics, Philosophy Department, Carnegie Mellon University, version β, May.

Grosz, Barbara J., Joshi, Aravind, and Weinstein, Scott (1983). 'Providing a unified account of definite noun phrases in discourse', in *Proceedings of the 21st Annual Meeting of the Association for Computational Linguistics*, 44–50.

Hinrichs, Erhard W. (1981). 'Temporale anaphora in englischen'. StaatsExamen thesis, Universität Tübingen.

Hitzeman, Janet, Grover, Claire, and Moens, Marc (1994). 'The implementation of the temporal portion of the discourse grammar'. Deliverable D.2. Temporal, LRE 61-062, University of Edinburgh, December.

Kameyama, Megumi, Passonneau, Rebecca, and Poesio, Massimo (1993). 'Temporal centering' in *Proceedings of the 31st Annual Meeting of the Association for Computational Linguistics*, Columbus, OH, 70–7.

---

[4] The other reading, in which the third sentence is an elaboration of one of the preceding events, must not be ruled out because there are cases such as *Sam arrived at the house at eight. He rang the bell. He let it ring for two minutes*, in which such elaboration is possible.

Kamp, Hans (1979). 'Events, instants and temporal reference', in R. Bauerle, U. Egli, and A. von Stechow (eds.), *Semantics from Different Points of View*. Berlin, Springer-Verlag, 376–417.

Kehler, Andrew (1994). 'Temporal relations: Reference or discourse coherence?' in *Proceedings of the 32nd Annual Meeting of the Association for Computational Linguistics*, June, 319–21.

Lascarides, Alex and Asher, Nicholas (1991). 'Discourse relations and defeasible knowledge', in *Proceedings of the 29th Annual Meeting of the Association for Computational Linguistics*. University of California at Berkeley, 55–63.

Morris, J. and Hirst, Graeme (1991). 'Lexical cohesion computed by thesaural relations as an indicator of the structure of text', *Computational Linguistics* 17(1): 21–48.

Partee, Barbara Hall (1984). 'Nominal and temporal anaphora', *Linguistics and Philosophy* 7: 243–86.

Poesio, Massimo (1994). 'Discourse Interpretation and the Scope of Operators'. Ph.D. dissertation, University of Rochester, Department of Computer Science, Rochester, NY.

Pollard, Carl and Sag, Ivan A. (1994). *Head-Driven Phrase Structure Grammar*. Chicago: University of Chicago Press and CSLI Publications.

Prüst, Hub, Scha, Remko, and van den Berg, Martin (1994). 'Discourse grammar and verb phrase anaphora', *Linguistics and Philosophy* 17: 261–327.

Scha, Remko and Polanyi, Livia (1988). 'An augmented context-free grammar for discourse', in *Proceedings of the 12th Conference on Computational Linguistics*, Prague, August, 573–7.

Sidner, Candace L. (1983). 'Focusing in the comprehension of definite anaphora', in M. Brady and R. Berwick (eds.), *Computational Models of Discourse*. Cambridge, MA: MIT Press.

PART IV
Temporal Annotation

Introduction to Part IV

1 INTRODUCTION

The work presented in earlier sections of this book has, by and large, followed the methods of analytical linguistics, philosophy, and symbolic AI. That is, aspects of how temporal information is conveyed in language have been analyzed and modeled in formal (in varying degrees) or computational systems. The emphasis, however, has been on the analytical approach or model, and not on the data being analyzed. Native speaker intuitions both about acceptability and about the nature of the phenomena to be studied are taken as sufficient to ground the work in 'real' language. This methodology tends not to be explicitly defended; the presumption is that while theories or models remain unable to account for obvious usage, there is no need to go hunting in data for new challenges.

In the last decade, however, there has been a growing movement in both computational and noncomputational linguistics to place more emphasis on the study of real language as evidenced in collections of texts or **corpora**. Linguistic judgments about these texts are then recorded in the form of **annotations** associated with the texts, sometimes called **metadata**, which serve to label or flag phenomena of interest in the texts. The reasons for this shift in emphasis in the field are complex, and this is not the place either to defend this shift (see, for example McEnery and Wilson (1996) for strong advocacy for this move in linguistics) or to engage in speculation as to why it has come about. However, we can cite some of the clear benefits it brings:

- Corpus-guided research reveals both the variety of forms of expression in real samples of language and the distribution of these forms of expression. The former is important as it may direct attention to forms that the intuitions of armchair linguists have either overlooked or ruled out. The latter is important to help focus efforts of algorithm builders on the most frequently occurring cases, to aid in the construction of probabilistic models, and to guide psycholinguistic or cognitive psychological research.
- Annotation schemes, together with corpora annotated according to them, provide an objective data resource that can be shared, argued over, and refined by the (computational) linguistic community. Comparisons between human annotators annotating the same data according to the same scheme can be used to decide how well-defined and comprehensive the scheme is.
- Annotated corpora are resources that can be exploited by machine-learning algorithms to acquire annotation capability without the necessity of implementing an underlying analytical model.
- Annotated corpora provide an objective basis to evaluate competing algorithms.

This general movement towards corpus-based research has not been without effect on the study of temporal phenomena in text, and the papers in this part reflect this work. Unlike work in the previous sections, some of which dates back over fifty years, work on the annotation of temporal phenomena is quite recent, all of it less than ten years old, much of it more recent than that. As a consequence, no consensus about how temporal information in text should be annotated can yet be said to have emerged, though the collaboration of several research groups to produce the TimeML annotation scheme, described by PUSTEJOVSKY et al. (Chapter 27) is an ambitious attempt to provide a comprehensive approach which subsumes earlier efforts.

As an introduction to the papers in this part, the following provides a background to the issues these papers address. These issues include what to annotate and the status of automatic annotators, the process of and tools to support manual annotation, and the existing resources which are outcomes from annotation work.

The programme of defining appropriate standards for temporal annotation and then building algorithms that can carry out this annotation automatically is an exciting one and one which is only partially complete. The coming years will see to what extent it can be realized and what the impact of temporal annotation capability will be on applications of language technology.

2 ANNOTATING TEMPORAL REFERRING EXPRESSIONS

The most obvious temporal feature to annotate in texts, and the one which historically was addressed first, is **temporal referring expressions** (as found in temporal adverbials, for example); that is, expressions which refer to **times** (*July 1, 1867*), **durations** (*three months*), or **frequencies** (*weekly*). Being able to identify and distinguish these types of expression is crucial to being able to situate the events described in text either absolutely in terms of some conventional calendrical time frame or relatively with respect to other events.

The examples just given perhaps understate the complexity of the phenomena to be addressed. When devising an annotation scheme to capture temporal referring expressions one must deal with a variety of complications:

(1) *indexicals*: expressions like *now, yesterday*—and other contextually dependent expressions such as partially specified calendrical times (e.g. *Wednesday*—which Wednesday?) or relatives such as *next week, three weeks ago*, all of which depend for their interpretation on knowledge of a deictic centre;

(2) *relational expressions*: expressions which explicitly specify times in relation to other times (*two weeks after Christmas*) or to events (*5 seconds after the first explosion*); and

(3) *vagueness*: expressions referring to times whose boundaries are inherently vague (*spring, evening*) or which contain modifiers which blur the time reference (*several days ago, sometime after 7 p.m.*).

Work to devise annotation schemes for temporal referring expressions appears to have begun as part of the Named Entity (NE) tagging subtask within the DARPA Message Understanding Conference (MUC) series of evaluations, specifically in MUC-6 (MUC 1995). In this task participants' systems were to tag (by inserting SGML tags into running text) expressions which named persons, organizations, locations, dates, times, monetary amounts, and percentages. A key part of this exercise was that a set of texts was manually tagged by human annotators to provide a 'gold standard' measure of correctness. Metrics, principally the **recall** and **precision** metrics adapted from information retrieval research, were used to compare system-supplied annotations (or **responses**) against human-supplied annotations (or **answer keys**). Recall, the proportion of the answer keys for which a correct response is supplied, is a measure of coverage or completeness of a system; precision, the proportion of responses which are correct, i.e. match the answer key, is a measure of correctness or soundness of a system.

In MUC-6 date and time (of day) expressions were labeled using a TIMEX tag. Only **absolute** time expressions were to be annotated, i.e. expressions which indicated a specific minute, hour, day, month, season, year, etc. **Relative** time expressions (e.g. *last July*) were excluded, though subexpressions within them (e.g. *July* in this example) were to be tagged. A set of thirty manually annotated newswire texts were used for a blind evaluation. The top scoring automated system scored .97 recall and .96 precision on the TIMEX tagging task.

In MUC-7 (MUC 1998) the principal change was to capture relative as well as absolute date and time expressions, though the two did not need to be distinguished in the tagging. Thus indexicals, such as *yesterday, last July*, were to be marked, as were so-called 'time-relative-to-event' phrases such as *the morning after the July 17 disaster*. For the final blind evaluation a set of 100 tagged texts was used and the highest scoring system scored .89/.99 recall/precision on the date tagging task and .81/.97 recall/precision on the time tagging task.

One of the principal limitations of the date and time NE task in both MUC-6 and MUC-7 is that while identifying temporal referring expressions in text is useful, what is really needed is the ability to interpret or evaluate or dereference these expressions to obtain the time they denote. Thus, according to the MUC-7 TIMEX tagging guidelines, an expression such as *yesterday* in an article datelined *June 12, 1998* would be tagged as a TIMEX of type DATE. However, what applications really need is the knowledge that in this context *yesterday* refers to *June 11, 1998*. This requirement is addressed by the TIMEX2 tagging guidelines, reviewed by WILSON et al. (Chapter 23). Interpretation is handled by adding the full calendrical time value for every temporal referring expression as an attribute of the tagged element, using an ISO standard time format as the attribute's value. Wilson et al. also describe an implemented tagger which annotates newswire text (in English and Spanish) with TIMEX2 tags with impressively high scores, achieving 96.2 f-measure (a combined measure of recall and precision) for tagging surface expressions and 83.2 f-measure in interpreting them.

The ability to evaluate a relational or indexical time expression, returning a calendrical time value, is clearly needed as part of the temporal interpretation process. However, there is utility in separating the evaluation process into two stages, first mapping the time expression into a semantic representation in the form of a functional expression, and second evaluating the functional expression. So, for example *last Thursday* might in the first stage be mapped into the expression thursday (predecessor (week DCT)), where DCT is the document-creation time of the article and in the second stage an absolute calendrical time is computed from this latter representation given the DCT. This separation of semantic interpretation from full evaluation has a number of advantages. It fosters discussion of the correct semantic interpretation of complex temporal referring expressions, it permits separate evaluation of the two stages (an algorithm could be good at working out the semantics of *last* expressions, but bad at finding their anchors), it allows unevaluated semantic representations to be made available to other interpretation components which may require them rather than their values, and it permits taggers to defer the evaluation of temporal functions until their values are actually required. Pustejovsky et al. propose an extension of the TIMEX2 standard to include temporal functional representations, and call the extended standard TIMEX3 (TIMEX3 includes a number of other refinements to the TIMEX2 standard, but this is the most significant).

Most of the work described above has been driven by the English-speaking research community, though as noted TIMEX2 has been applied to English and Spanish, and recently to Korean, French, Chinese, and Hindi. However, SCHILDER AND HABEL (Chapter 26) independently propose an approach for annotating German newswire texts which aims to capture the same sort of temporal referring expressions as the TIMEX2 and 3 standards. Their tagger outputs a semantic representation of relative time expressions which are evaluated in a subsequent stage, making its handling of these expressions similar to that proposed in TIMEX3.

3 ANNOTATING EVENTS AND STATES

To interpret a text temporally means not just identifying the times, durations, and frequencies mentioned in a text; it means positioning the events and states described in the text with respect to these times and to each other. However, before it is possible to discuss how to annotate relations between events, states, and times, agreement must be reached on how to annotate events and states themselves. To do this in turn requires making decisions about (a) what we are trying to annotate—just events? events and states? and what do we take the difference to be? (b) how events/states are realized in text; (c) what textual representative of the event/state will be annotated; (d) what attributes should be associated with annotated events/states.

3.1 What semantic types to annotate

To answer the first of these questions requires taking some position with respect to questions of event ontology raised in several places in the Introduction to Part I in this volume. At the most general level, temporal annotation can be taken as the task of correctly annotating the temporal position of all temporal entities in a text, i.e. of all *things that happen or are situated in time*. If, for purposes of the following discussion, we assume a top-level ontological class of eventualities or situations which is divided into events and states (cf. Introduction to Part I, 3.1.2), this would mean annotating all events and states.

Such a task is daunting, and since practical applications are primarily concerned with events, it might appear reasonable to start out with the more modest aim of annotating events, but excluding states. However, drawing a firm *conceptual* distinction between events and states is not straightforward, as the discussion in Part I has shown. One common distinguishing test is the so-called subinterval property (Dowty, Chapter 15): for any state p that holds over an interval t, p must hold for every subinterval of t. However, this is not a particularly easy test to apply and not one to expect annotators of texts to be able to carry out efficiently or effectively.

A second way to distinguish events and states, also discussed at greater length in Part I, is via *linguistic* tests. States tend to be expressed via constructions with the copula, or via certain verbs such as *have, know, believe*. This is perhaps a more practical approach in the context of producing realistic guidelines for annotation. If the point of making the distinction is to capture genuine semantic differences between events and states, however, then this approach depends on determining an accurate and complete set of linguistic correlates for states.

Most approaches to event annotation reported in this part, however, do not attempt to make a distinction between events and states. In general, the approach is to treat all verbs as expressing temporal entities suitable for tagging. This lumping together assumes that the distinction is not important, or is too difficult, for purposes of annotation. While dismissing the problem in the short term, this ignores the fact that there are genuine semantic differences between events and states, and that these have consequences in terms of the inferences that can be drawn and the likely questions that can be asked concerning each. For example, states typically invite questions about when they began, ended, and how long they lasted; events invite questions about when they happened, but not so typically about their duration. Furthermore, the process of positioning states in time may differ from that of positioning events, so that an algorithm that attempts to do this positioning automatically would need to know which it was dealing with.

The only work in this part which does propose to distinguish events and states and to annotate both is that of Pustejovsky et al. Note, however, that they treat states as a subtype of events—effectively identifying events with what we have here termed eventualities. In fact they go further than simply distinguishing events and states, and propose distinguishing seven types of events in their annotation scheme, two of which are stative and all of which are held to have distinctive temporal significance. Their distinguishing criteria, as presented, are primarily linguistic, though concerning states they do appeal to something like the subinterval property cited above. Further, they do not propose to annotate all states: they propose to annotate only those states which 'are directly related to a temporal expression... including those states that identifiably change over the course of a document'.

3.2 The linguistic realization of events and states

To date then, the work on temporal annotation of 'events' in text has not worried overly about the semantic distinction between events and states and has assumed that the 'things which are situated in time' which need to be annotated can be identified via a set of syntactic or lexical linguistic criteria.

KATZ AND AROSIO (Chapter 24), for example, define their task in a (deliberately) restrictive way: 'The temporal interpretation of a sentence, for our purposes, can simply be taken to be the set of temporal relations that a speaker naturally takes to hold among the states and events described by the *verbs* of the sentence' (italics added). Thus, for example, event nominals such *destruction, election, war* are excluded, as are, presumably, stative adjectives such as *sunken*. However, their investigation is exclusively concerned with sentence-internal temporal relations and they are not aiming to position every event or state reference in time, or in relation to another event or state.

FILATOVA AND HOVY (Chapter 25) take the locus of events to be syntactic clauses which contain a subject (one or more noun phrases) and predicate (verb phrase with one or more verbs), as output by a specific parser. Their concern is to time-stamp these clauses, that is, to associate a calendrical time reference with each clause. They, too, ignore event nominals and stative adjectives. However, again, they are not aiming at complete temporal interpretation, but at a more limited task.

Schilder and Habel have a broader target. They identify two types of event-denoting expressions: sentences and event-denoting nouns, especially nominalizations. The most inclusive treatment is that of Pustejovsky et al., who consider events expressed by tensed or untensed verbs, nominals, adjectives, predicative clauses, or prepositional clauses.

3.3 Textual representatives to annotate

Once a set of linguistic signals for events has been decided there is still the issue of deciding precisely what text spans will be annotated, i.e. what will count as the textual representative of the event. For the most part this follows straightforwardly from decisions made about the linguistic realizations of events and states. However, those decisions do not entirely specify the annotation.

Concerning events conveyed by clauses containing verbs, one could decide that the entire clause is the appropriate span to be annotated. This is the position taken by Filatova and Hovy. Or, one could decide to annotate just verb groups or just the heads of verb groups. This latter approach has been adopted by the other authors in this part, perhaps because it simplifies matters when dealing with embedded clauses or clauses with multiple verbs (Filatova and Hovy acknowledge problems with their approach for cases of co-ordinated verb phrases where the verbs have different tenses).

3.4 Attributes of events and states

As well as tagging a text span as event representative, some approaches choose to associate attributes with the event. In Schilder and Habel's approach, for example, each event has a sem attribute that holds a predicate-argument representation of the event. It also has a temp attribute whose value is triple consisting of a binary temporal relation, the time id of the event itself, and the id of a time related to the event time by the temporal relation. This attribute gets its value computed as part of the interpretation process.

These event attributes are effectively part of Schilder and Habel's implementation of a computational mechanism to assign times to events. Another sort of information that can be associated with events is descriptive linguistic information which may be of use during the interpretation process. So, for example, Filatova and Hovy make use of tense information associated with event clauses by their parser. Pustejovsky et al. associate tense, aspect, and subtype information with events. The event subtypes they propose are: occurrence (*crash, merge*), state (*on board, love*), reporting (*say, report*), i-action (*attempt, offer*), i-state (*believe, want*), aspectual (*begin, stop*), and perception (*see, hear*). These classes are distinguished because of the distinctive sorts of temporal inferences that may be drawn for events within them.

3.5 Automated event tagging

In the foregoing we have discussed *what* is to be annotated when annotating events or states. Now we briefly discuss the state of play with implemented systems that do event tagging. Of the papers in this part only three describe implemented systems that do event tagging: Filatova and Hovy, Schilder and Habel and Li et al. However, for none of these researchers is event tagging itself a goal—rather they are aiming to anchor events in time and possibly also to relate events to each other temporally (Li et al.). Only Filatova and Hovy provide separate evaluation results for their system's ability to recognize events—in their case the ability to recognize clauses, since for them clauses are the textual representatives of events. They report figures of around 61 per cent recall and 56 per cent precision, errors being due in part to the parser they use and in part to their shallow algorithm for extracting clauses from the parse tree. As noted the others do not evaluate event recognition separately from temporal relation annotation.

4 ANNOTATING TEMPORAL RELATIONS

Given an approach to annotating temporal referring expressions and event/state denoting expressions, the next challenge for a programme of temporal annotation is to establish conventions for annotating the **relations** between times and events or between events and events (from now on we will use the term 'event' loosely to refer to events and possibly to states as well, making clear if necessary where remarks may only pertain to states or to nonstative eventualities).

4.1 Annotating relations between times and events

Time–event relational information may be conveyed in a variety of ways. The most explicit route is via a prepositional phrase in which a preposition signals a relation between a temporal referring expression (the complement of the phrase) and an event denoting expression (typically a verb or an event nominal modified by the phrase); for example, *John flew to Boston on Friday*. Sometimes the explicit prepositional marker is omitted and temporal referring expressions are used in adverbial (*Friday John flew to Boston*), nominal modifier (*John's Friday flight to Boston*) or elliptical/reduced relative clause (*John's flight, Friday at 5, will be crowded*) contexts. We refer to these cases as instances of **syntactically implicit** time–event relations.

However, in many cases the relational information may be implicit in a much less direct way, to be derived by the reader using world or lexical semantic knowledge, or narrative convention and discourse interpretation. In many of these cases relations between times and events are established indirectly by first establishing relations between events and then inferring relations between times and events. For example, consider the mini-narrative in (1):

(1) John arrived home at 9 p.m. He opened the door, dropped his briefcase, and poured himself a stiff whisky. Sipping his drink, he moved into the living room and collapsed in front of the TV.

The only explicit temporal relation here—between the event of arriving home and 9 p.m.—is asserted in the first sentence. The most likely interpretation of the ordering and absolute positioning of subsequent events is that they happened in the order they are recounted and within minutes of John's arrival home. This interpretation is made by assuming this narrative follows the general convention of recounting events in the order they occurred, and by drawing on script-like (Schank and Abelson 1977) world knowledge that tells us that on arrival home people don't drop their briefcases or pour themselves drinks before they open the door. Furthermore, since carrying around briefcases is cumbersome and at odds with what appears to be John's mood of exhaustion/release from toil, suggested by what appears to be a late arrival home from work and by his need for relaxation, we assume John dropped the briefcase immediately after entering the house, and that the other events also occurred very soon thereafter. This interpretation is also boosted by the presumption, again based on narrative convention, that had other events intervened (e.g. half an hour spent walking the dog) we would have been told. We refer to time–event relations such as those in this example (excluding the time–event relation in the first sentence) as **semantically implicit** time–event relations.

The question that arises here for a temporal annotation scheme is whether or not times ought to be associated with events when the relation is implicit, in either of the two senses just identified. Different positions are possible here and some of these are found in the work of authors in this part, reflecting fundamentally different conceptions of the ultimate goal of temporal annotation.

One position to take is that relations between time and events should be marked only in cases where explicitly signaled by prepositions or where they are syntactically implicit. This position is adopted by Schilder and Habel, who assume a default semantic relation of inclusion for all syntactically implicit relations. Time–event relations for events which do not occur in such syntactic contexts are simply not supplied.

Another possible position is to assign a calendrical time point or interval to *all* events in a text—so-called **time-stamping** of events. Filatova and Hovy pursue this line, developing a heuristic algorithm for news texts which assigns to each event (for them a verb-bearing clause, as discussed in 3.2 above) a calendrical date, date range, or open-ended date interval (i.e. the interval before or after a given date). They use one set of rules which apply to cases of explicit time reference (e.g. temporal PPs), and another set that apply when no implicit information is available.

A further position to take is that time–event relations should only be marked in cases where they are explicitly signaled or are syntactically implicit (as with Schilder and Habel), but that event–event temporal relations (to be discussed later) should also be marked, so that calendrical time-points for some events can be recovered by inference from combinations of time–event and event–event relations (so, for example, if e_1 occurs at t and e_2 occurs after e_1 then we know e_2 occurs after t). The approaches of both Li et al. and Pustejovsky et al. admit event–event relations to be tagged as well as time–event relations and hence support this sort of indirect positioning of events in time.

4.2 Time-stamping events

Before discussing the annotation of event–event relations in detail, it is worth considering the time-stamping project in more detail. Time-stamping—by which we mean the assignment of a calendrical time reference (point or interval) to *every* event in running text—is an appealing aim. Motivating it is the intuition or wish, which is especially strong as concerns narrative texts such as newswires, that all events should be placeable on a **time-line**. This goal suggests that the target representation for a temporal annotator should be a mapping or anchoring of all events in a text on a calendrical time-line.

Despite its intuitive appeal, time-stamping all events has serious drawbacks which stem ultimately from the fact that natural language narratives underspecify event positions in time in a way that makes a time-line representation problematic. Put another way, narratives may only specify a partial ordering between events; a time-line representation commits one to assigning a total ordering, information which simply may not be present in the text. This position is elaborated by Setzer and Gaizauskas (2002) who prefer a **time–event graph**, in which the nodes are times or events and the arcs are temporal relations, to a time-line as a target representation for temporal relation annotation. They present two arguments for this position which we repeat here in slightly modified form.

First, in many cases texts position events in time explicitly by relation to other events and any attempt to coerce these events onto a time-line must either lose information, invent information, or rely on a notion of an underspecified time-point constrained by temporal relations (i.e. introduce a representation of temporal relations by the back door). Consider this example:

(2) After the plane crashed, a search was begun. Later the coastguard reported finding debris.

and assume that an earlier sentence explicitly specifies the calendrical time of the plane crash. Attempting to map the information presented in this example onto a time-line we are faced with the situation depicted in Figure 1. While the crash event can be placed on the time-line the other two events cannot. Either time-points must be guessed, or an interval must be assigned. The first option is clearly not satisfactory. But if an interval is assigned the only possible interval, for both the searching and finding events, is the interval from the crash till the date of the article. However, if this is assigned to both events then the information about their ordering with respect to each other is lost.

A simpler representation, which does not attempt to be as specific but actually carries more information, is shown in Figure 2. This representation preserves the information that the searching event precedes the finding event, without forcing any early commitment to points on a time-line.

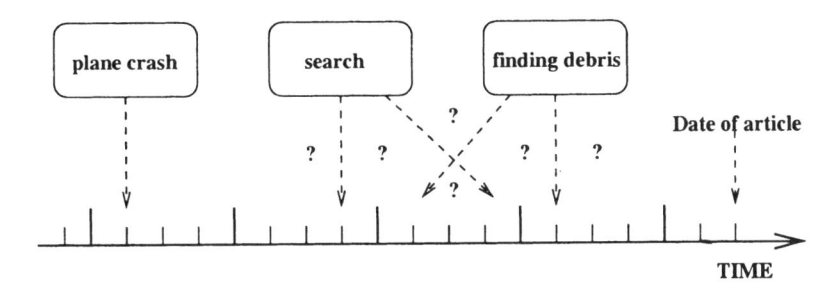

FIG. 1   A Time-line Representation.

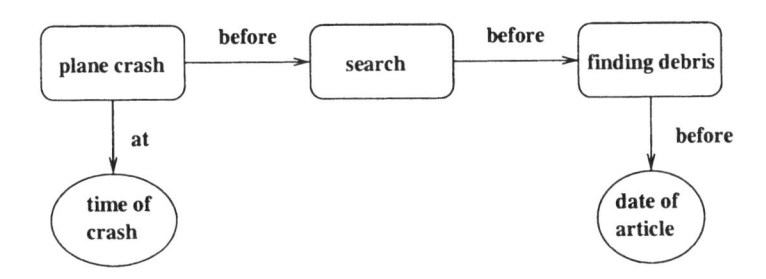

FIG. 2   A Time-Event Graph Representation.

The second argument for preferring a time-event graph representation that captures event–event temporal relations as well as time–event relations is that to position events on a time-line accurately requires the extraction of event–event relational information. In the example, the placing of the searching and finding events in the interval between the plane crash and the date of the article requires the recognition that these events occurred after the crash as signaled by the words 'after' and 'later'. Without identifying the relations conveyed by these words the searching and finding events could only be positioned before the time of the article, and not following the plane crash. Thus, even if a time-stamp representation is viewed as the best target representation, achieving it requires the extraction of temporal relational information. In this case adopting a time–event graph as an intermediate representation is still a good idea, which begs the question of why it should not simply be taken as the final target representation.

4.3 Annotating relations between events and events

As with time–event relations, event–event temporal relations may be conveyed explicitly or implicitly. The primary mechanism for explicit relation is the temporal conjunction, typically used to relate the event expressed in a subordinated clause to one in a main clause; for example: *While chopping vegetables, John cut his finger* or *After the game John called Bob*. As with time–event relations, event–event temporal relations are frequently expressed implicitly, relying on world or lexical semantic knowledge, or narrative convention and discourse interpretation. Arguably all of the time–event relations in the mini-narrative (1) in Section 4.1 above (excluding the one in the first sentence) are established indirectly by first establishing event–event relations and then using plausible reasoning to position approximately the ordered events on a time-line. The event–event ordering is implicit in the narrative and established as described above.

Three of the papers in this part address the identification or annotation of event–event relation, though their concerns are different. Katz and Arosio are interested in the temporal relations between events, as signaled by verbs, within single sentences. Their primary concern is the study of how temporal information is conveyed within sentences such as *John kissed the girl he met at the party* where there are no explicit temporal relational markers. Is, for example, our knowledge that the kissing took place after the meeting dependent on lexical semantic knowledge of these two verbs? or on the recognition of the syntactic structure of matrix and subordinate clauses both with past tense verbs? To answer this question they propose adding to a large corpus of syntactically annotated sentences further annotations which capture temporal relational information. This resource could then be used for the induction of the sort of knowledge needed to resolve questions of temporal ordering in implicit contexts.

In their annotation scheme a human annotator adds labeled, directed edges between nodes in a graph which are the verbs in a syntactically annotated sentence. In addition to verb nodes, each sentence also has associated with it a node corresponding to its speech time (cf. Reichenbach, part I). The edges represent temporal relations and the edge labels and direction specify the relation (their set of relations contains just the two relations of precedence and inclusion, though their duals are also available by reversing the directionality of an edge). As noted above in the discussion of event annotation (Section 3.2), they do not consider event nominals.

While Katz and Arosio are concerned only with intrasentential temporal relations between verbs, the TimeML scheme proposed by Pustejovsky et al. aims to capture event–event temporal relations as completely as possible and in a way that will facilitate the development of time, event, and temporal relational tagging systems for use in applications such as question answering and summarization. To that end they propose an approach to relational tagging that allows event–event relations to be marked between any two event-denoting expressions (recall from Section 3.2 that for them events can be denoted by verbs, nominals, adjectives, predicative clauses, and even prepositional phrases). The approach relies on implementing a relational graph by using XML elements which consume no text but link, via pointers, XML elements surrounding event representatives and associate a relation type with the link. The set of relation types they employ are the thirteen proposed by Allen (Chapter 12). Note that these links, called TLINKS, can be asserted between any two event-denoting expressions (or between event and temporal referring expressions), regardless of whether or not they occur in the same sentence. This permits temporal relations that hold between events in different sentences to be recorded as in, for example, *John ate dinner. Later he phoned Bob*. However, it raises the question of whether temporal relations between *all* event–event pairs should be annotated in an extended text (an overwhelming task for a human annotator) or if not, which subset of them. This question is further addressed in Sections 5 and 6.2 below.

Li et al. are concerned to build a working temporal information extraction system for Chinese newswire texts. They distinguish single event, multiple event, and declared event statements which are statements reporting one event, two or more events, and events as asserted by a person or organization, respectively. In their model, single event statements are related to times (i.e. placed in a temporal relation to a calendrical time-point), while in multiple event statements the events are related to each other, using one of Allen's thirteen temporal relations. Thus, like Katz and Arosio, event–event relations are only marked within sentences. However, presumably event–event temporal relational information for events in separate sentences is available indirectly via the temporal relation of these single events to times on a time-line.

4.4 Subordinating and aspectual relations

If one considers verbs as event signals and examines sentences with multiple verbal elements with a view to labeling their temporal relations, several problem cases soon emerge. Consider, for example, *John might have kissed the girl he met at the party* or *John hoped to kiss the girl he met at the party (and did/did not)*. In neither case can we mark a temporal relation between *kiss* and *met*, because we do not know whether or not it occurred. These cases reveal that in contexts where verbs are modally subordinated, or occur as arguments in intensional constructions, they cannot straightforwardly be taken as denoting real events. However, there are some such contexts where the events the subordinated verbs denote are guaranteed to have occurred, such as *John forgot that he had already paid the bill* or *John knew Bill had gone*.

A further class of problem cases are those involving aspectual verbs, such as *start*, *keep*, which may signal the beginning, culmination, termination, or continuation of an activity, as in *John started chopping vegetables* or *Sue kept talking*. These verbs do not signal events distinct from the ones denoted by their verbal arguments, but rather draw attention to an *aspect* of these events. Attempting to assert a temporal relation between them, therefore, is problematic.

These cases demonstrate that proposing to annotate *temporal* relations between *all* verbs within a sentence is not sensible. There are two other possibilities. One is to ignore them; the other is to annotate these verb–verb relations in some other way. Ignoring these contexts might have no impact on certain uses of temporal annotation, for example on Katz and Arosio's project of building an annotated corpus from which to induce the temporal profile of lexical items. For other applications, such as question answering or summarization, however, the ability to distinguish these contexts is certainly needed. Either to learn to ignore them, or to handle them appropriately, an annotation scheme for these contexts is desirable. This has been proposed in the TimeML specification, via the addition of two further sorts of relational links. Subordination links (SLINKS) are introduced to deal with cases of subordinate relations, and aspectual links (ALINKS) are introduced to deal with the cases of relations introduced by aspectual verbs.

4.5 Automated temporal relation tagging

The preceding discussion has focused on elucidating the targets of temporal relation tagging, rather than the implementation and performance of systems that actually attempt to do this automatically. As with automated event tagging discussed in Section 3.5 above we note that only three of the papers in this part describe implemented systems that actually do relation tagging: Filatova and Hovy, Schilder and Habel, and Li et al. As noted above, Filatova and Hovy are concerned with time-stamping all events (clauses). Their implementation does this using a rule-based system with two classes of rules: those for clauses with explicit date information and those for clauses without explicit date information. In the latter case tense information from the clause together with information about the most recently assigned time or the date of the article are used to assign a time-stamp to the clause. They report evaluation figures of 82 per cent correctly assigned time-stamps to clauses correctly identified. Schilder and Habel describe an implementation which extracts temporal relation information only from sentences containing time expressions and event expressions. They report figures of 84.49 per cent recall and precision for the system in extracting temporal relational information from these sentences. Finally, Li et al. describe an implemented system which extracts both time–event and event–event relational information from Chinese sentences. Their system relies on a complex set of rules which map from surface temporal indicators to temporal relations between times and events and events and events. They report figures of close to 93 per cent correct extraction of these relations. Given the differences in tasks and test corpora, these figures are not directly comparable.

5 COMPARING ANNOTATIONS: SEMANTIC APPROACHES TO EVALUATION

One of the clear lessons to have emerged from the corpus annotation programme is the necessity, for any given annotation scheme, of some means to compare quantitatively two annotations of the same text created by separate annotators (human or machine). As noted above in Section 1, precise quantitative comparison permits validation of the annotation scheme (if two humans cannot agree then the scheme must be unclear), evaluation of competing algorithms, and hill-climbing approaches to machine learning of automated annotators.

Typically one wants to ensure that an annotator has annotated all the things it ought to and none that it ought not. These intuitions are captured in the metrics of precision and recall, mentioned above in Section 2. Defining these metrics concretely can only be done with reference to a specific annotation scheme. For annotation schemes which specify a single correct annotation for any piece of text (i.e. are deterministic) this is relatively simple. For example, for texts annotated according to an annotation scheme for temporal referring expressions, there is typically a single way to tag the text correctly, tagging certain character sequences as times and perhaps associating additional attribute information, such as normalized time values, with these sequences. It may be desirable to decouple the evaluation of the accuracy with which text **extents** have been correctly tagged from the accuracy with which **types** or other attributes have been assigned to them. For example, one can separately assess the accuracy of a temporal referring expression tagger at marking the beginnings and endings of character sequences referring to times or dates, from its ability to distinguish which are times and which are dates, and this again from its ability to assign the correct normalized time. All this is quite straightforward, given the presumption of a single correct tagging.

What are much more problematic are annotation schemes which permit alternative equivalent taggings, particularly when it is not independent strings that are being tagged, but *relations* between multiple strings. However, this is precisely the situation which is likely to arise with annotating temporal relations *since the same information can be captured by distinct annotations*. Consider the abstract case, where two events A and B are said to occur at the same time and a third event C occurs later. If one annotator marks A and B as simultaneous and C after A and a second annotator also marks A and B as simultaneous, but instead marks C after B, then they do not differ in terms of their views on what happened when. Nor indeed would they differ from a third annotator who marked A and B as simultaneous and marked C after A *and* C after B.

This example is used by SETZER et al. (Chapter 29) to motivate their proposal for a semantic basis for comparing temporal annotations. They define the **temporal closure** of an annotation (of a specific text) to be the deductive closure, i.e. the set of all temporal consequences that may be drawn from the annotation using a set of inference rules which capture essential properties of the temporal relations used in the annotation scheme. Two annotations are then said to be equivalent if their temporal closures are equivalent. So, for example, suppose the set of inference rules contains the plausible rule that says that for all times or events x, y, and z, if x and y are simultaneous and z is later than x then z is later than y. Using this rule, the temporal closures of each of the three annotations of the temporal relations between events A, B, and C introduced above are the same. Thus, we have means of abstracting away from the surface form an annotation to the temporal information it conveys, and based on this a way of comparing temporal annotations semantically. Setzer et al. go on to define measures of precision and recall in terms of the notion of temporal closure. In essence recall is the proportion of temporal closure of the key annotation which is found in the temporal closure of the response and precision is the proportion of the response annotation which is found in the key. They note that the problem of defining semantically based metrics for comparing temporal relation annotations is related to the problem of comparing coreference chain annotations, originally addressed in MUC-6, to which similar semantically based solutions have been proposed. A key difference is that whereas coreference is an equivalence relation which induces equivalence classes over sets of linked entities in the text, temporal relations are not, in general, equivalence relations. Thus, solutions based on the number of links which need to be added to transform the response (key) equivalence class into the key (response) equivalence class are not sufficient. Rather, the full implicational consequences of the annotations, i.e. the temporal closures, need to be compared instead.

Katz and Arosio propose a similar semantically based solution to the problem of comparing annotations, though with a more overtly model-theoretic character. They define the **model of an annotation** to be the assignment of pairs of entities in the domain of the annotation (the verbs, i.e. event realizations, in the annotation) to the two binary temporal relations in their annotation scheme—precedence and inclusion—that satisfy a set of axioms (for example, transitivity of precedence). An annotation is **satisfied** by a model if and only if all temporal relations in the annotation are satisfied by, i.e. are found in, the model. A distance measure may then be defined between annotations in terms of the numbers of models they share. More precisely, the distance is the sum of the number of models satisfying one annotation but not satisfying the other normalized by the number of models satisfying both.

Taken together, the measures already in use for evaluating temporal referring expressions (e.g. for TIMEX and TIMEX2) and the proposals discussed here for evaluating temporal relation annotations form the basis of a comprehensive framework for evaluating temporal annotations. This framework itself is part of an emerging publicly available set of resources for temporal annotation, to which we now turn.

6 ANNOTATION RESOURCES: STANDARDS, TOOLS, CORPORA

The preceding sections have discussed issues in the annotation of times, events, and temporal relations, and in the evaluation of these annotations. While a consensus in all these matters has not yet been achieved, sufficient progress has been made that various groups have made, or are in process of making, available annotation standards, tools to assist in the process of annotation and annotated corpora to promote research and reduce duplicated effort in this area. This section details some of these resources.

6.1 Annotation standards

Experience in creating annotated resources has shown that the creation and publication of an **annotation guidelines** or **specification** document is a key step towards creating an open standard. This document has as its ideal that two randomly selected individuals should, by following the annotation instructions in the document, produce identical annotations over any set of appropriate texts. Clearly this is an ideal, but it is a key aspect of an objective, scientific methodology (repeatability by independent observers) in this area. It also has the salutary effect of forcing would-be implementers of automated taggers to separate the 'what' from the 'how' in their work.

For some of the work reported in papers in this part it is not clear whether full temporal annotation specifications exist. The only temporal annotation proposals for which we are certain that annotation guidelines or specifications are publicly available are: TIMEX (MUC 1995, 1998), TIMEX2 (Ferro et al. 2001), TIMEX3 (available as part of the TimeML specification), and TimeML <http://www.timeml.org>. This is not to condemn work carried out without independent annotation specifications. In many cases the broad shape of what is proposed as a target annotation is clear from papers concerned with reporting algorithms as well as target representation. Furthermore, creating an annotation guidelines document suitable for creating large-scale annotated resources and for carrying out interannotator reliability experiments is a lot of work that is not feasible and arguably not necessary for initial exploratory research, which characterizes much of the work reported here. It is to be hoped, however, that agreement can be reached on multilingual standards for temporal annotation, since this will benefit everyone engaged in this research area.

Apropos annotation standards, another topic of relevance is the language in which the annotations are to be expressed. A consensus appears to be emerging in the corpus linguistic community that linguistic annotations should be represented in some form of XML. Some annotated corpora, however, such as the TIMEX-annotated MUC corpora, were annotated prior to the advent of XML and are available with naive SGML-based annotation only (naive in the sense that no DTD is supplied, making the corpora unprocessable by an SGML parser). TimeML, including TIMEX3, has been specified in XML and an XML schema is available. Annotated corpora that are TimeML compliant should be possible to validate with an XML parser. The broader question of whether temporal annotations can or should become compliant with overarching schemes which have been proposed for linguistic annotation, such as the Text Encoding Initiative <http://www.tei-c.org> or the Corpus Encoding Standard <http://www.cs.vassar.edu/CES>, remains to be addressed.

6.2 Annotation tools and the process of annotation

As noted in the discussion of the TimeML approach to event–event annotation in Section 4.3 above, since any two events in a text may potentially be temporally related by an annotator, the issue arises as to whether an annotator should be directed to annotate *all* event pairs (probably infeasible) or only a subset, in which case it must be decided which subset. One solution that has been proposed to this problem (Setzer et al.) is to exploit further the notion of temporal closure to assist manual annotation. They propose a three-stage process for the manual annotation of all times, events, and temporal relations in a text. First, all times and events are marked, possibly with automated assistance as a preprocessing step (for example a tagger for temporal referring expressions could be run and its output corrected by a human). In the second stage a subset of the temporal relations is marked. These could be those which are explicitly expressed via temporal prepositions or conjunctions (if TimeML is adopted these signals are required to be annotated) and perhaps others which are particularly obvious (e.g. what were called syntactically implicit time–event relations in Section 4.1 above) or salient to the annotator. The key point here is that this set need not be defined precisely. In the final stage, the annotator takes part in an interactive process in which the temporal closure of the relations previously entered is computed and an as yet unrelated time–event or event–event pair from the set of all possible time–event/event–event pairs (as defined by the first stage) is selected and the annotator is promoted to supply the relation between them (possibly undefined). This process is repeated until a relation has been supplied or inferred for every time–event/event–event pair in the text. The advantage of the above procedure is that it significantly reduces the burden on the annotator. A pilot experiment reported by Setzer et al. revealed that almost 80 per cent of the relational pairs in the temporal closures of a small set of texts were supplied automatically by inference, with approximately 4 per cent being initially annotated and 16 per cent annotated under interactive prompting.

Regardless of whether an interactive annotation tool built on top of a closure procedure is available, the task of annotating text according to a scheme as rich as TimeML is clearly demanding and requires sophisticated support. To this end a temporal annotation tool (TANGO) is under development; see <http://www.timeml.org>. TANGO allows a user to see the text being annotated in one window, a time–event graph within a second window, and the underlying XML annotation in a third. Temporal, subordination, or aspectual links may be added or removed and a temporal closure algorithm run to add links by inference.

6.3 Temporally annotated corpora

As with annotation standards, the publication of annotated resources is a boon to the research community, enabling researchers to build on and contribute to prior work. Existing publicly available, though not necessarily free, temporally annotated corpora are the MUC-6 and MUC-7 TIMEX annotated corpora, which can be obtained from the Linguistic Data Consortium: <http://www.ldc.org>. The TIMEX2-tagged Enthusiast corpus and Korean corpus, as described in Wilson et al., are freely available to those who have licensed access to the underlying text (details at <http://timex2.mitre.org>). As part of the TERQAS workshop which stimulated the creation of the TimeML standard and the TANGO annotation tool a corpus of 300 newswire texts, called TimeBank (Pustejovsky et al. 2003), has been annotated with a subset of the full TimeML annotations. Further refinement of this corpus is still on-going, but it will in due course become available from the LDC.

7 CONCLUSION: ISSUES AND CHALLENGES

In the foregoing we have attempted to give an overview of the issues involved in the temporal annotation of text, as well as a snapshot of the current state of affairs concerning automated annotators and the resources that are publicly available to support research and development in this area. There remain many issues to be addressed and challenges to be overcome before either the scientific project of understanding how temporal information is conveyed in text or the engineering project of building reliable temporal annotators that can be embedded in language technology applications can be said to be complete. In concluding we raise some of these outstanding issues and challenges.

7.1 Multilinguality

Most of the work done to date on temporal annotation is for English, though Schilder and Habel's work for German and Li et al.'s work for Chinese are exceptions. Wilson et al. report that they have applied their TIMEX2 annotation standard to documents in Spanish, Korean, French, Hindi, and Chinese as well as to English. Katz and Arosio claim they have applied their temporal relation tagging scheme to sentences 'from a variety of languages', but give no indication of just which languages or how many. Clearly this work just scratches the surface of the world's languages. Applying ambitious annotation schemes such as TimeML to multiple languages will bring many benefits: the adequacy of annotation schemes will be further tested, rich insights will be gained into the range and distribution of mechanisms employed across the world's languages to convey temporal information, more researchers will be drawn into work in

Introduction to Part IV 503

this area, and many of the resulting resources, tools, and applications will be sharable across languages.

7.2 Annotation tools and resources

The foregoing should have made clear the need for, and the utility of, annotated resources. To date there is still a serious shortage of these, particularly for more complex relational annotations, such as those found in TimeML. The creation of such resources is difficult and time-consuming, hence expensive. Further development of specialized annotation tools, such as TANGO, should help, as will the integration into such tools of robust preprocessing components that will relieve some of the annotator's burden. More studies need to be made of the levels of agreement obtainable by annotators, with a view to improving annotation specifications, or recognizing fundamental limitations in the process.

7.3 Building temporal relation taggers

While automated taggers for annotating temporal referring expressions have achieved good levels of accuracy, even for the difficult task of evaluating indexicals and contextually sensitive expressions, the programme of constructing taggers to tag temporal relational information is still in its infancy. Some progress has been made, as reported by some authors in this part, but there are as yet no automated taggers that can begin to approximate the rich annotation proposed in TimeML. Building such taggers is an exciting challenge. However, achieving this capability may be a long-term project, and researchers may be well advised to target simpler, intermediate goals. So, for example, while in Section 4.2, we presented arguments against time-stamping as a suitable target representation for capturing *all* temporal relational information in text, this does not mean that taggers that accurately time-stamp a subset of events in text would be of no utility. In the short term, the creation of taggers that focus solely on relating times and events where these are explicitly signaled or straightforwardly associated may be a sensible goal. Of course defining this goal sufficiently precisely as to allow quantitative evaluation is itself no small task.

7.4 Applications

As automated temporal annotation taggers with increasing functionality become available, applications will be able to take advantage of this. Obvious examples, cited repeatedly by authors in this part, are question answering, information extraction, and summarization. Questions may explicitly request temporal information (*When did the French Revolution begin?*) or be time-sensitive in less direct ways (*Who was president of Enron in 2000/when its share price was highest?*). Information extraction is concerned with extracting attributes of entities (e.g. titles of persons) or relations between entities (e.g. the `employee_of` relation). However, for most real applications attributes and relations will hold of entities in temporally bounded ways, and knowing these temporal bounds is critical for the extracted information to be of value. Summarization of multiple documents which overlap in their description of events and need to be reduced to a single nonredundant chronological narrative is a requirement in numerous areas, ranging from assembling background information from news reports to condensing clinical records and courtroom proceedings. As with many areas of language technology, the challenge will be to deploy imperfect technology in settings where it can be of genuine value and where the lessons learned in its deployment can be fed back to fuel a positive development cycle.

REFERENCES

Ferro, L., Mani, I., Sundheim, B., and Wilson, G. (2001). 'TIDES temporal annotation guidelines, version 1.0.2'. Technical Report MTR 01W0000041, MITRE Corporation.

McEnery, T. and Wilson, A. (1996). *Corpus Linguistics*. Edinburgh: Edinburgh University Press.

MUC (1995). *Proceedings of the Sixth Message Understanding Conference (MUC-6)*. California: Morgan Kaufmann.

MUC (1998). *Proceedings of the Seventh Message Understanding Conference (MUC-7)*. California: Morgan Kaufmann. Available at <http://www.itl.nist.gov/iaui/894.02/related_projects/muc/>.

Pustejovsky, J., Hanks, P., Saurí, R., See, A., Gaizauskas, R., Setzer, A., Radev, D., Sundheim, B., Day, D., Ferro, L., and Lazo, M. (2003). 'The TIMEBANK corpus', in D. Archer, P. Rayson, A. Wilson, and T. McEnery (eds.), *Proceedings of the Corpus Linguistics 2003 Conference*, Lancaster, March 2003, 647–56.

Schank, R. and Abelson, R. (1977). *Scripts, Plans, Goals, and Understanding*. Hillsdale, NJ: Lawrence Erlbourm Associates.

Setzer, A. and Gaizauskas, R. (2002). 'On the importance of annotating temporal event–event relations in text', in *Proceedings of the Third International Conference on Language Resources and Evaluation (LREC2002) Workshop on Annotation Standards for Temporal Information in Natural Language*, Las Palmas de Gran Canaria. European Language Resources Association, 52–60.

A Multilingual Approach to Annotating and Extracting Temporal Information*

GEORGE WILSON, INDERJEET MANI,
BETH SUNDHEIM, LISA FERRO

1 INTRODUCTION

The processing of temporal information poses numerous challenges for NLP. Progress on these challenges may be accelerated through the use of corpus-based methods. This paper introduces a set of guidelines for annotating time expressions with a canonicalized representation of the times they refer to, and describes methods for extracting such time expressions from multiple languages. Applications that can benefit include information extraction (e.g., normalizing temporal references for database entry), question answering (answering "when" questions), summarization (temporally ordering information), machine translation (translating and normalizing temporal references), and information visualization (viewing event chronologies).

Our annotation scheme, described in detail in (Ferro et al. 2000), has several novel features. It goes well beyond the one used in the Message Understanding Conference (MUC7 1998), not only in terms of the range of expressions that are flagged, but also, more importantly, in terms of representing and normalizing the time *values* that are communicated by the expressions. In addition to handling fully specified time expressions (e.g., *September 3rd, 1997*), it also handles *context-dependent* expressions. This is significant because of the ubiquity of context-dependent time expressions; a recent corpus study (Mani and Wilson 2000) revealed that more than two-thirds of time expressions in print and broadcast news were context-dependent ones. The context can be local (within the same sentence), e.g., *In 1995, the months of June and July were devilishly hot*, or global (outside the sentence), e.g., *The hostages were beheaded that afternoon*. A subclass of these context-dependent expressions are 'indexical' expressions, which require knowing when the speaker is speaking to determine the intended time value, e.g., *now, today, yesterday, tomorrow, next Tuesday, two weeks ago*, etc.

The annotation scheme has been designed to meet the following criteria:

- *Simplicity with precision*: We have tried to keep the scheme simple enough to be executed confidently by humans, and yet precise enough for use in various natural language processing tasks.

George Wilson, Inderjeet Mani, Beth Sundheim, and Lisa Ferro, 'A Multilingual Approach to Annotating and Extracting Temporal Information', *Proceedings of the ACL 2001 Workshop on Temporal and Spatial Information Processing*, 39th Annual meeting of the ACL (ACL'2001), Toulouse (2001), 81–7. © 2001 Association for Computational Linguistics.

*This work has been funded by DARPA's Translingual Information Detection, Extraction, and Summarization (TIDES) research program, under contract number DAA-B07-99-C-C201 and ARPA Order H049.

- *Naturalness*: We assume that the annotation scheme should reflect those distinctions that a human could be expected to reliably annotate, rather than reflecting an artificially defined smaller set of distinctions that automated systems might be expected to make. This means that some aspects of the annotation will be well beyond the reach of current systems.
- *Expressiveness:* The guidelines require that one specify time values as fully as possible, within the bounds of what can be confidently inferred by annotators. The use of 'parameters' and the representation of 'granularity' (described below) are tools to help ensure this.
- *Reproducibility:* In addition to leveraging the ISO-8601 (1997) format for representing time values, we have tried to ensure consistency among annotators by providing an example-based approach, with each guideline closely tied to specific examples. While the representation accommodates both points and intervals, the guidelines are aimed at using the point representation to the extent possible, further helping enforce consistency.

The annotation process is decomposed into two steps: flagging a temporal expression in a document (based on the presence of specific *lexical trigger* words), and identifying the time value that the expression designates, or that the speaker intends for it to designate. The flagging of temporal expressions is restricted to those temporal expressions which contain a reserved time word used in a temporal sense, called a 'lexical trigger', which include words like *day, week, weekend, now, Monday, current, future*, etc.

2 INTERLINGUAL REPRESENTATION

2.1 Introduction

Although the guidelines were developed with detailed examples drawn from English (along with English-specific tokenization rules and guidelines for determining tag extent), the semantic representation we use is intended for use across languages. This will permit the development of temporal taggers for different languages trained using a common annotation scheme.

It will also allow for new methods for evaluating machine translation of temporal expressions at the level of interpretation as well as at the surface level. As discussed in Hirschman et al. (2000), time expressions generally fall into the class of so-called *named entities*, which includes proper names and various kinds of numerical expressions. The translation of named entities is less variable stylistically than the translation of general text, and once predictable variations due to differences in transliteration, etc. are accounted for, the alignment of the machine-translated expressions with a reference translation produced by a human can readily be accomplished. A variant of the word-error metric used to evaluate the output of automatic speech transcription can then be applied to produce an accuracy score. In the case of our current work on temporal expressions, it will also be possible to use the normalized time values to participate in the alignment and scoring.

2.2 Semantic distinctions

Three different kinds of time values are represented: points in time (answering the question "when?"), durations (answering "how long?"), and frequencies (answering "how often?").

- *Points in time* are calendar dates and times-of-day, or a combination of both, e.g., *Monday 3 p.m., Monday next week, a Friday, early Tuesday morning, the weekend*. These are all represented with values (the tag attribute VAL) in the ISO format, which allows for representation of date of the month, month of the year, day of the week, week of the year, and time of day, e.g., <TIMEX2 VAL="2000-11-29-T16:30">*4:30 p.m. yesterday afternoon*</TIMEX2>.
- *Durations* also use the ISO format to represent a period of time. When only the period of time is known, the value is represented as a duration, e.g., <TIMEX2 VAL="P3D">*a three-day*</TIMEX2> *visit*.
- *Frequencies* reference *sets* of time points rather than particular points. SET and GRANULARITY attributes are used for such expressions, with the PERIODICITY attribute being used for regularly recurring times, e.g., <TIMEX2 VAL="XXXX-WX-2" SET="YES" PERIODICITY="F1W" GRANULARITY="G1D">*every Tuesday*</TIMEX2>. Here "F1W" means frequency of once a week, and the granularity "G1D" means the set members are counted in day-sized units.

The annotation scheme also addresses several semantic problems characteristic of temporal expressions:

- *Fuzzy boundaries*. Expressions like *Saturday morning* and *Fall* are fuzzy in their intended value with respect to when the time period starts and ends; *the early 60s* is fuzzy as to which part of the 1960s is included. Our format for representing time values includes parameters such as FA (for *Fall*), EARLY (for *early*, etc.), PRESENT_REF (for *today, current*, etc.), among others. For example, we have <TIMEX2 VAL="1990-SU">*Summer of 1990*</TIMEX2>. Fuzziness in modifiers is also represented, e.g., <TIMEX2 VAL="1990" MOD="BEFORE">*more than a decade ago*</TIMEX2>. The intent here is that a given application may choose to assign specific values to these parameters if desired; the guidelines themselves don't dictate the specific values.
- *Non-specificity*. Our scheme directs the annotator to represent the values, where possible, of temporal expressions that do not indicate a specific time. These non-specific expressions include generics, which state a generalization or regularity of some kind, e.g., <TIMEX2 VAL="XXXX-04" NON_SPECIFIC="YES">*April*</TIMEX> *is usually wet*, and non-specific indefinites, like <TIMEX2 VAL="1999-06-XX" NON_SPECIFIC="YES" GRANULARITY="G1D">*a sunny day in*<TIMEX2 VAL="1999-06">*June*</TIMEX2></TIMEX2>.

3 REFERENCE CORPUS

Based on the guidelines, we have arranged for six subjects to annotate an English reference corpus, consisting of 32,000 words of a telephone dialog corpus—English translations of the 'Enthusiast' corpus of Spanish meeting scheduling dialogs used at CMU and by Wiebe et al. (1998), 35,000 words of New York Times newspaper text, and 120,000 words of broadcast news (TDT2 1999).

4 TIME TAGGER SYSTEM

4.1 Architecture

The tagging program takes in a document which has been tokenized into words and sentences and tagged for part-of-speech. The program passes each sentence first to a module that flags time expressions, and then to another module (SC) that resolves self-contained (i.e., '*absolute*') time expressions. Absolute expressions are typically processed through a lookup table that translates them into a point or period that can be described by the ISO standard.

The program then takes the entire document and passes it to a discourse processing module (DP) which resolves context-dependent (i.e., '*relative*') time expressions (indexicals as well as other expressions). The DP module tracks transitions in temporal focus, using syntactic clues and various other knowledge sources.

The module uses a notion of *Reference Time* to help resolve context-dependent expressions. Here, the *Reference Time* is the time a context-dependent expression is relative to. The reference time (italicized here) must either be described (as in "a week from *Wednesday*") or implied (as in "three days ago [from *today*]"). In our work, the reference time is assigned the value of either the *Temporal Focus* or the document (creation) date. The *Temporal Focus* is the time currently being talked about in the narrative. The initial reference time is the document date.

4.2 Assignment of time values

We now discuss the assigning of values to identified time expressions. Times which are fully specified are tagged with their value, e.g, "June 1999" as 1999-06 by the SC module. The DP module uses an ordered sequence of rules to handle the context-dependent expressions. These cover the following cases:

- *Explicit offsets from reference time*: indexicals like "yesterday", "today", "tomorrow", "this afternoon", etc., are ambiguous between a specific and a non-specific reading. The specific use (distinguished from the generic one by machine-learned rules discussed in Mani and Wilson (2000)) gets assigned a value based on an offset from the reference time, but the generic use does not.
- *Positional offsets from reference time:* Expressions like "next month", "last year" and "this coming Thursday" use *lexical markers* (underlined) to describe the direction and magnitude of the offset from the reference time.
- *Implicit offsets based on verb tense*: Expressions like "Thursday" in "the action taken Thursday", or bare month names like "February" are passed to rules that try to determine the direction of the offset from the reference time, and the magnitude of the offset. The tense of a neighboring verb is used to decide what direction to look to resolve the expression.
- *Further use of lexical markers*: Other expressions lacking a value are examined for the nearby presence of a few additional markers, such as "since" and "until", that suggest the direction of the offset.
- *Nearby dates*: If a direction from the reference time has not been determined, some dates, like "Feb. 14", and other expressions that indicate a particular date, like "Valentine's Day", may still be untagged because the year has not been determined.

TABLE I Performance of Time Tagger (English)

Type	Human Found Correct	System Found	System Correct	F-measure
TIMEX2	728	719	696	96.2
VAL	728	719	602 (234)	83.2 (32.3)

If the year can be chosen in a way that makes the date in question less than a month from the reference date, that year is chosen. Dates more than a month away are not assigned values by this rule.

4.3 Time tagging performance

The system performance on a test set of 221 articles from the print and broadcast news section of the reference corpus (the test set had a total of 78,171 words) is shown in Table 1.[1] Note that if the human said the tag had no value, and the system decided it had a value, this is treated as an error. A baseline of just tagging values of absolute, fully specified expressions (e.g., "January 31st, 1999") is shown for comparison in parentheses.

5 MULTILINGUAL TAGGING

The development of a tagging program for other languages closely parallels the process for English and reuses some of the code. Each language has its own set of lexical trigger words that signal a temporal expression. Many of these, e.g. day, week, etc., are simply translations of English words.

Often, there will be some additional triggers with no corresponding word in English. For example, some languages contain a single lexical item that would translate in English as "the day after tomorrow". For each language, the triggers and lexical markers must be identified.

As in the case of English, the SC module for a new language handles the case of absolute expressions, with the DP module handling the relative ones. It appears that in most languages, in the absence of other context, relative expressions with an implied reference time are relative to the present. Thus, tools built for one language that compute offsets from a base reference time will carry over to other languages.

As an example, we will briefly describe the changes that were needed to develop a Spanish module, given our English one. Most of the work involved pairing the Spanish surface forms with the already existing computations, e.g. we already computed "yesterday" as meaning "one day back from the reference point". This had to be attached to the new surface form "ayer". Because not all computers generate the required character encodings, we allowed expressions both with and without diacritical marks, e.g., mañana and manana.

Besides the surface forms, there are a few differences in conventions that had to be accounted for. Times are mostly stated using a 24-hour clock. Dates are usually written in the form day/month/year rather than the idiosyncratic US-English convention of month/day/year.

---

[1] The evaluated version of the system does not adjust the Reference Time for subsequent sentences.

A difficulty arises because of the use of multiple calendric systems. While the Gregorian calendar is widely used for business across the world, holidays and other social events are often represented in terms of other calendars. For example, the month of Ramadan is a regularly recurring event in the Islamic calendar, but shifts around in the Gregorian.[2]

Here are some examples of tagging of parallel text from Spanish and English with a common representation.

<TIMEX2 VAL="2001-04-01">hoy</TIMEX2>
<TIMEX2 VAL="2001-04-01">today</TIMEX2>
<TIMEX2 VAL="1999-03-13">el trece de marzo de 1999</TIMEX2>
<TIMEX2 VAL="1999-03-13">the thirteenth of March, 1999</TIMEX2>
<TIMEX2 VAL="2001-W12">la semana pasada</TIMEX2>
<TIMEX2 VAL="2001-W12">last week</TIMEX2>

6 RELATED WORK

Our scheme differs from the recent scheme of Setzer and Gaizauskas (2000) in terms of our in-depth focus on representations for the values of specific classes of time expressions, and in the application of our scheme to a variety of different genres, including print news, broadcast news, and meeting scheduling dialogs. Others have used temporal annotation schemes for the much more constrained domain of meeting scheduling, e.g., Wiebe et al. (1998), Alexandersson et al. (1997), and Busemann et al. (1997). Our scheme has been applied to such domains as well, our annotation of the Enthusiast corpus being an example.

7 CONCLUSION

In the future, we hope to extend our English annotation guidelines into a set of *multilingual* annotation guidelines, which would include *language-specific* supplements specifying examples, tokenization rules, and rules for determining tag extents. To support development of such guidelines, we expect to develop large keyword-in-context concordances, and would like to use the time-tagger system as a tool in that effort. Our approach would be (1) to run the tagger over the desired text corpora; (2) to run the concordance creation utility over the annotated version of the same corpora, using not only TIMEX2 tags but also lexical trigger words as input criteria; and (3) to partition the output of the creation utility into entries that are tagged as temporal expressions and entries that are not so tagged. We can then review the untagged entries to discover classes of cases that are not yet covered by the tagger (and hence, possibly not yet covered by the guidelines), and we can review the tagged entries to discover any spuriously tagged cases that may correspond to guidelines that need to be tightened up.

We also expect to create and distribute multilingual corpora annotated according to these guidelines. Initial feedback from machine translation system grammar writers (Levin 2000) indicates that the guidelines were found to be useful in extending an existing interlingua for machine translation. For the existing English annotations, we are currently carrying out interannotator agreement studies of the work of the six annotators.

---

[2] Our annotation guidelines state that a holiday name is markable but should receive a value only when that value can be inferred from the context of the text, rather than from cultural and world knowledge.

8 UPDATE

Since 2001, several new developments have occurred, including:

- *Interannotator Agreement:* Interannotator reliability across five annotators (graduate students) on 193 TDT2 English documents was .79F for TIMEX2 extent and .86F for time values. In addition, detailed error analyses have been carried out to determine the main classes of disagreements among annotators. The time tagger TempEx described above scored .76F (extent) and .82F (value) on these documents. The reason the value F-measures are higher than the extent F-measures is because of a new and improved version of the scorer (version 3). This version of the scorer flags occurrences of tags in a candidate annotation that occur in almost but not exactly the same position in the reference annotation as errors of extent. It nevertheless compares the values of such overlapping tags, scoring the values correct if the candidate and reference values are equivalent.
- *Multilingual Corpora:* In addition to the English annotated corpora created above, additional corpora in different languages have been annotated. These include 95 Spanish dialogs from the Enthusiast corpus, Spanish portions of the UN Parallel Corpus, 200 Korean news articles, as well as miscellaneous collections of documents in French, Hindi, and Chinese. Some of these corpora are available at <http://timex2.mitre.org>.
- *Multilingual Taggers*: Automatic taggers have been developed for the above languages based on machine-learning from annotated corpora.
- *Adoption*: The annotation scheme has been adopted by the DARPA TIDES program, the ACE (Automatic Content Extraction) Program (ACE 2003), and the TimeML annotation scheme (Pustejovski et al, Chapter 27 in this volume). In the course of doing so, the basic annotation scheme has remained relatively stable, though several improvements have been made, most notably to the SET-valued tags, where interannotator agreement had been lower.

All in all, the annotation framework described here appears robust and likely to serve the needs of temporal information processing in the future.

REFERENCES

Alexandersson, J., Reithinger, N., and Maier, E. (1997). 'Insights into the Dialogue Processing of VERBMOBIL', in *Proceedings of the Fifth Conference on Applied Natural Language Processing*, Washington, DC, 33–40.

Busemann, S., Declerck, T., Diagne, A. K., Dini, L., Klein, J., and Schmeier, S. (1997). 'Natural Language Dialogue Service for Appointment Scheduling Agents', in *Proceedings of the Fifth Conference on Applied Natural Language Processing*, Washington, DC, 25–32.

Ferro, L., Mani, I., Sundheim, B., and Wilson, G. (2000). 'TIDES Temporal Annotation Guidelines. Draft Version 1.0'. MITRE Technical Report, MTR 00W0000094, October 2000.

Hirschman, L., Reeder, F., Burger, J., and Miller, K. (2000). 'Name Translation as a Machine Translation Evaluation Task', in *Proceedings of the Workshop on the Evaluation of Machine Translation*, Second International Conference On Language Resources And Evaluation (LREC'2000), Athens, 31 May–2 June 2000.

ISO-8601 (1997). ftp://ftp.qsl.net/pub/g1smd/8601v03.pdf.

Levin, L. (2000). Personal Communication.

Mani I., and Wilson, G. (2000). 'Robust Temporal Processing of News', *Proceedings of the ACL'2000 Conference*, 3–6 October 2000, Hong Kong, 69–76.

MUC-7 (1998). *Proceedings of the Seventh Message Understanding Conference*, DARPA. 1998. <http://www.itl.nist.gov/iad/894.02/related_projects/muc/>.

Setzer, A. and Gaizauskas, R. 'Annotating Events and Temporal Information in Newswire Texts', in *Proceedings of the Second International Conference on Language Resources and Evaluation* (LREC-2000), Athens, Greece, 31 May–2 June 2000, 1287–94.

TDT2 (1999). <http://morph.ldc.upenn.edu/Catalog/LDC99T37.html>.

Wiebe, J. M., O'Hara, T. P., Öhrström-Sandgren, T., and McKeever, K. J. (1998). 'An Empirical Approach to Temporal Reference Resolution', *Journal of Artificial Intelligence Research* 9: 247–93.

APPENDIX 1   ANNOTATED CORPUS: ENTHUSIAST DIALOG
EXAMPLE (ONE UTTERANCE)

Transcript of Spanish source:
EL LUNES DIECISIETE IMAGINO QUE QUIERE DECIR EL DIECISIETE TENGO UN SEMINARIO DESDE LAS DIEZ HASTA LAS CINCO
Annotated English translation:
<TIMEX2 VAL="2000-05-17">MONDAY THE SEVENTEENTH</TIMEX2> I IMAGINE YOU MEAN <TIMEX2 VAL="2000-05-17">THE SEVENTEENTH </TIMEX2> I HAVE A SEMINAR FROM <TIMEX2 VAL="2000-05-17T10"> TEN </TIMEX2> UNTIL <TIMEX2 VAL="2000-05-17T17">FIVE </TIMEX2>
Note: Elements of range expressions are tagged separately. The VAL includes date as well as time because of the larger context. The annotator has confidently inferred that the seminar is during the daytime, and has coded the time portion of the VAL accordingly.

APPENDIX 2   ANNOTATED CORPUS: NEW YORK
TIMES ARTICLE (EXCERPT)

Dominique Strauss-Kahn, France's finance minister, said: "<TIMEX2 VAL= "1999-01-01"> Today</TIMEX2> is clearly <TIMEX2 NON_SPECIFIC="YES"> a historic day for the European enterprise</TIMEX2>. Europe will be strong, stronger than in <TIMEX2 VAL="PAST_REF">the past</TIMEX2>, because it will speak with a single monetary voice."

But even on <TIMEX2 VAL="1998-12-31"> Thursday </TIMEX2>, there were signs of potential battles ahead.

One hint came from Duisenberg, a former Dutch central banker who was named president of the European Central Bank only after a bitter political fight <TIMEX2 VAL="1998-05">last May</TIMEX2> between France and Germany. Duisenberg, a conservative on monetary policy, was favored by Helmut Kohl, who was <TIMEX2 VAL="1998-05">then</TIMEX2> chancellor of Germany. But President Jacques Chirac of France insisted on the head of the Bank of France, Jean-Claude Trichet.

Germany and France eventually cut a deal under which Duisenberg would become president of the new European bank, but "voluntarily" agree to step down well ahead of <TIMEX2 VAL="P8Y" MOD="END"> the end of his eight-year term</TIMEX2>.

24

The Annotation of Temporal Information in Natural Language Sentences

GRAHAM KATZ AND FABRIZIO AROSIO

1 INTRODUCTION

In interpreting narratives the most essential information to be extracted is who did what where, when, and why, the classic journalistic imperatives. The 'who' and 'what' information is usually expressed overtly, and this has made it possible to apply stochastic techniques to problems in this domain (such as word-sense classification and argument structure mapping). The 'when' and 'where' information is, however, often left implicit, or, at least, only partially specified. The 'why' information is rarely explicit.

Formal semantic theories of temporal interpretation (e.g. Kamp and Reyle 1993, Ogihara 1996, Abusch 1997) have been quite successful at specifying the contribution that such overt markers as tenses and temporal adverbials make to the meaning of a sentence or discourse. Investigations into the interpretation of narrative discourse (Lascarides and Asher 1993, Reyle and Rossdeutscher 2000) have, however, shown that very specific lexical information plays an important role in determining temporal interpretation. As of yet it is not clear how this kind of lexical information could be automatically acquired. The most promising avenue for acquiring lexical information appears to be automatic induction from very large annotated corpora (Rooth et al. 1998). Our task here is to provide a system whereby the temporal information can be made explicit so as to make the application of these empirical methods possible, i.e., a system of temporal annotation.

The systems for temporal annotation we are familiar with have been concerned either with absolute temporal information (Wiebe et al. 1998, Androutsopoulos, Ritchie, and Thanisch 1998), or with the annotation of overt markers (Setzer and Gaizauskas 2000). Much temporal information, however, is not absolute but relative and not overtly marked but implicit. We are frequently only interested (and only have information about) the order events occurred in. And while there are sometimes overt markers for these temporal relations, the conjunctions *before, after*, and *when* being the most obvious, usually this kind of relational information is implicit. The examples in (1) illustrate the phenomenon.

(1) a. John kissed the girl he met at the party.
    b. Leaving the party, John walked home.
    c. He remembered talking to her and asking her for her name.

Although there are no obvious markers for the temporal ordering of the events described in these sentences, native speakers have clear intuitions about what happened when: we know that the kissing took place after the meeting and that the asking was part of the talking. But how do we know this, and—more importantly—how could this information be automatically extracted from these sentences? We don't know the answers to these questions.

We believe, however, that the development of a large-scale treebank annotated with relational temporal information as well as standard morphological and syntactic information is an appropriate way to begin this line of research. "Large scale" for the obvious reason that the application of stochastic methods requires this. "Syntactically annotated" because we cannot know beforehand to what degree the cues used by speakers are lexical and to what degree they are grammatical. We don't know, for example, in (1a) whether it is the lexical relationship between *kiss* and *meet* that is crucial to determining the temporal interpretation, or whether the grammatical relation—the fact that *meet* is in a subordinate clause—also plays a role. To answer these kinds of questions it is necessary to encode the temporal information conveyed by a sentence in a way which makes answering such questions possible.

What we describe below is a practical system for encoding relational temporal information that is suited to large-scale hand annotation of texts. This system has a number of applications beyond this, both in the domain of cross-linguistic investigation and in empirical NLP.

2 TEMPORAL ANNOTATION

The idea of developing a treebank enriched with semantic information is not new. In particular such semantically annotated corpora have been used in research on word sense disambiguation (*WordNet, Eagles, Simple*) and semantics role interpretation (*Eagles*). The public availability of large syntactically annotated treebanks (*Penn, Verbmobil, Negra*) makes such work attractive, particularly in light of the success that empirical methods have had (Kilgarriff and Rosenzweig 2000). Traditional semantic representational formalisms such as DRT make this much more difficult. Additionally, since these formalisms are developed in the service of theories of natural language interpretation, they are—rightly—both highly articulated and highly constrained. In short, they are too complex for the purposes at hand (as the experience of Poesio et al. (1999) makes clear). Our proposal here is to adopt a radically simplified semantic formalism which, by virtue of its simplicity, is suited to the tagging application.

The temporal interpretation of a sentence, for our purposes, can simply be taken to be the set of temporal relations that a speaker naturally takes to hold among the states and events described by the verbs of the sentence. To put it more formally, we associate with each verb a temporal interval, and concern ourselves with relations among these intervals. Of the interval relations discussed by Allen (1984), we will be concerned with only two: precedence and inclusion. The basic idea is that the sentences in the treebank be marked with a semantic representation that accords with a native speaker's natural interpretation of the sentence. Taking t_{talk} to be the time of talking, t_{ask} to be the time of asking, and $t_{remember}$ to be the time of remembering, the temporal interpretation of (1c), for example, can be given by the following table:

	t_{talk}	t_{ask}	$t_{remember}$
t_{talk}			$<$
t_{ask}	$\subseteq$		$<$
$t_{remember}$			

Such a table, in effect, stores the native speaker's judgment about the most natural temporal interpretation of the sentence.

Since our goal was to annotate a large number of sentences with their temporal interpretations and to examine the interaction between the lexical and syntactic structure, it was imperative that the interpretation be closely tied to its syntactic context. We needed to keep track of both the semantic relations among times and the syntactic relations among the words in the sentences that refer to these times, but not much more. By adopting existing technology for syntactic annotation, we were able do this quite directly, by essentially building the information in this table into the syntax.

2.1 The annotation system

To carry out our temporal annotation, we made use of the *Annotate* tool for syntactic annotation developed in Saarbrücken by Brants and Plaehn (2000). We exploited an aspect of the system originally designed for the annotation of anaphoric relations: the ability to link two arbitrary nodes in a syntactic structure by means of labeled "secondary edges." This allowed us to add a layer of semantic annotation directly to that of syntactic annotation.

A sentence was temporally annotated by linking the verbs in the sentence via secondary edges labeled with the appropriate temporal relation. As we were initially only concerned with the relations of precedence and inclusion, we only had four labels: "$<$", "$\subseteq$", and their duals.

Sentence (1a), then, is annotated as in (2).

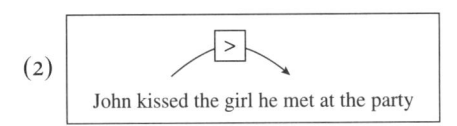

(2) John kissed the girl he met at the party [>]

The natural ordering relation between the kissing and the meeting is indicated by the labeled edge. Note that the edge goes from the verb associated with the event that fills the first argument of the relation to the verb associated with the event that fills the second argument of the relation.

The annotation of (1c), which was somewhat more complex, indicates the two relations that hold among the events described by the sentence.

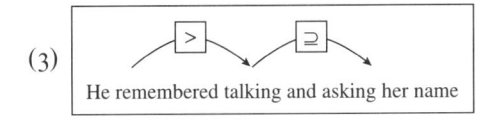

(3) He remembered talking and asking her name [>] [⊇]

In addition to encoding the relations among the events described in a sentence, we anticipated that it would be useful to also encode the relationship between these events and the time at which the sentence is produced. This is, after all, what tenses usually convey. To encode this temporal indexical information, we introduce into the annotation an explicit representation of the speech time. This is indicated by the "°" symbol, which is automatically prefaced to all sentences prior to annotation.

The complete annotation for sentence (1a), then, is (4).

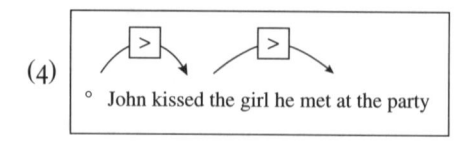

(4)   ° John kissed the girl he met at the party

As we see in (5), this coding scheme enables us to represent the different interpretations that past tensed and present tensed clauses have.

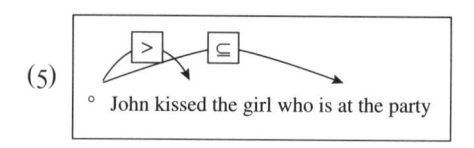

(5)   ° John kissed the girl who is at the party

Notice that we do not annotate the tenses themselves directly. It should be clear that we are not concerned with giving a semantics for temporal markers, but rather with providing a language within which we can describe the temporal information conveyed by natural language sentences. With the addition of temporal indexical annotation, our annotation system gains enough expressive power to account for most of the relational information conveyed by natural language sentences.

2.2 Annotation procedure

The annotation procedure is quite straightforward. We begin with a syntactically annotated treebank. Then the speech-time marker is added to the sentences and the temporal relations among verbs and the speech time are annotated. This is accomplished in accordance with the following conventions:

(i) temporal relations are encoded with directed "secondary edges";
(ii) the edge goes from the element that fills the first argument of the relation to the element that fills the second;
(iii) edge labels indicate the temporal relation that holds;
(iv) edge labels can be " $>$ ", " $<$ ", " $\subseteq$ " and " $\supseteq$ ".

Annotators are instructed to annotate the sentences as they naturally understand it. When the treebank is made up of a sequence of connected text, the annotators are encouraged to make use of contextual information.

The annotation scheme is simple, explicit, and theory neutral. The annotator needs only to exercise his native competence in his language and he doesn't need any special training in temporal semantics or in any specific formal language; in pilot studies we have assembled small temporal annotated databases in a few hours.

2.3 Comparing annotations

It is well known that hand-annotated corpora are prone to inconsistency (Marcus, Santorini, and Marcinkiewicz, 1993) and to that end it is desirable that the corpus be multiply annotated by different annotators and that these annotations be compared. The kind of semantic annotation we are proposing here introduces an additional complexity to inter-annotation comparison, in that the consistency of an annotation is best defined not in formal terms but in semantic terms. Two annotations should be taken to be equivalent, for example, if they express the same meanings, even if they use different sets of labeled edges.

To make explicit what semantic identity is, we provide our annotations with a model-theoretic interpretation. The annotations are interpreted with respect to a structure $\langle D, <, \subseteq \rangle$, where D is the domain (here the set of verb tokens in the corpus) and $<$ and $\subseteq$ are binary relations on D. Models for this structure are assignments of pairs of entities in D to $<$ and $\subseteq$ satisfying the following axioms:

- $\forall x, y.\ x < y \rightarrow \neg y < x$
- $\forall x, y, z.\ x < y\ \&\ y < z \rightarrow x < z$
- $\forall x.\ x \subseteq x$
- $\forall x, y, z.\ x \subseteq y\ \&\ y \subseteq z \rightarrow x \subseteq z$
- $\forall x, y.\ x < y \vee y < z \vee x \subseteq y \vee y \subseteq x$
- $\forall w, x, y, z.\ x < y\ \&\ z \subseteq x\ \&\ w \subseteq y \rightarrow z < w$
- $\forall w, x, y, z.\ x < y\ \&\ y < z\ \&\ x \subseteq w\ \&\ z \subseteq w \rightarrow y \subseteq w$

Thus all entities in the domain are related by $<$ or $\subseteq$, and $<$ and $\subseteq$ have the properties one would expect for the precedence and inclusion relation. An annotation

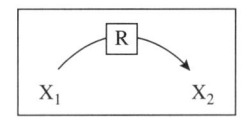

is satisfied in a model iff the model assigns $\langle X_1, X_2 \rangle$ to R if R is $<$ or $\subseteq$, or $\langle X_2, X_1 \rangle$ to R if R is $>$ or $\supseteq$.

There are four semantic relations that can hold between two annotations. These can be defined in model-theoretic terms:

- Annotation A and B are **equivalent** if all models satisfying A satisfy B and all models satisfying B satisfy A.
- Annotation A **subsumes** annotation B iff all models satisfying B satisfy A.
- Annotations A and B are **consistent** iff there are models satisfying both A and B.
- Annotations A and B are **inconsistent** if there are no models satisfying both A and B.

We can also define a minimal model satisfying an annotation in the usual way. We can then compute a distance measure between two annotations by comparing sets of models satisfying the annotations. Let M_A be the models satisfying A and M_B be those satisfying B and M_{AB} be those satisfying both (simply shorthand for the intersection of M_A and M_B). Then the distance between A and B can be defined as:

$$d(A, B) = (|M_A - M_{AB}| + |M_B - M_{AB}|)/|M_{AB}|$$

Since models are individuated by the extensions of their relations, this value is determined by the number of relation pairs that two annotations have in common. We can use this metric to quantify the "goodness" of both annotations and annotators.

Consider again (1c). We gave one annotation for this in (3). In (6) and (7) there are two alternative annotations.

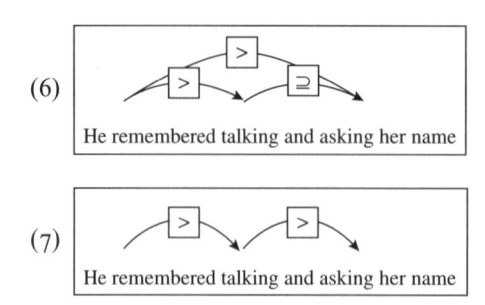

(6) [diagram: He remembered talking and asking her name]

(7) [diagram: He remembered talking and asking her name]

As we can compute on the basis of the semantics for the annotations, (6) is equivalent with (3)—they are no distance apart, while (7) is inconsistent with (3)—they are infinitely far apart. The annotation (8) is compatible with (7) and is a distance of 3 away from it.

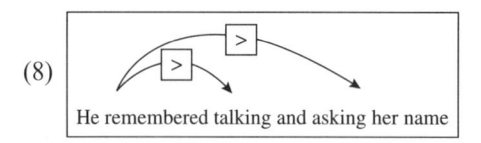

(8) [diagram: He remembered talking and asking her name]

As in the case of structural annotation, there are a number of ways of resolving interannotator variation. We can choose the most informative annotation as the correct one, or the most general. Or we can combine annotations. The intersection of two compatible annotations gives an equally compatible annotation which contains more information than either of the two alone. We do not, as of yet, have enough data collected to determine which of these strategies is most effective.

3 APPLICATIONS OF TEMPORAL ANNOTATION

There are any number of applications for a temporally annotated corpus such as that we have been outlining. Lexicon induction is the most interesting, but, as we indicated at the outset, this is a long-term project, as it requires a significant investment in hand annotation. We hope to get around this problem. But even still, there are a number of other applications which require less extensive corpora, but which are of significant interest. One of these has formed the initial focus of our research, and this is the development of a searchable multilingual database.

3.1 Multilingual database

Our annotation method has been applied to sentences from a variety of languages, creating a searchable multi-language treebank. This database allows us to search for sentences that express a given temporal relation in a language. We have already developed

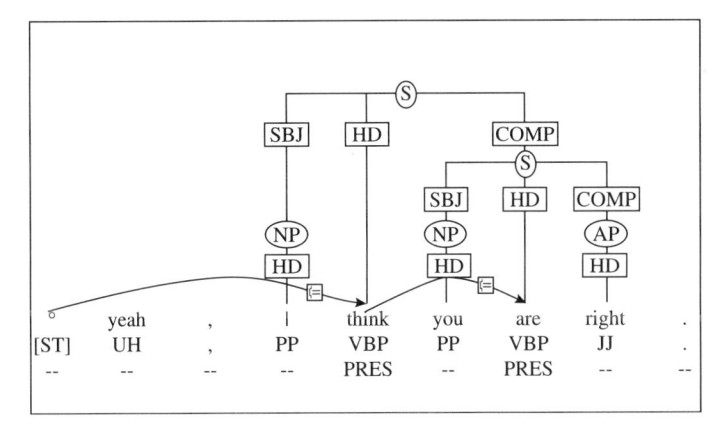

FIG. 1 A temporally annotated sentence from the *Verbmobil* English treebank as displayed by *Annotate*.

a pilot multilingual database with *Verbmobil* sentences (see the example in Figure 1) and we have developed a query procedure in order to extract relevant information. As can be seen, the temporal annotation is entirely independent of the syntactic annotation.

In the context of the *Annotate* environment a number of tools have been developed (and are under development) for the querying of structural relations. Since each sentence is stored in the relational database with both syntactic and temporal semantic annotations, it is possible to make use of these querying tools to query on structures, on meanings, and on structures and meanings together. For example a query such as: "Find the sentences containing a relative clause which is interpreted as temporally overlapping the main clause" can be processed. This query is encoded as a partially specified tree, as indicated below:

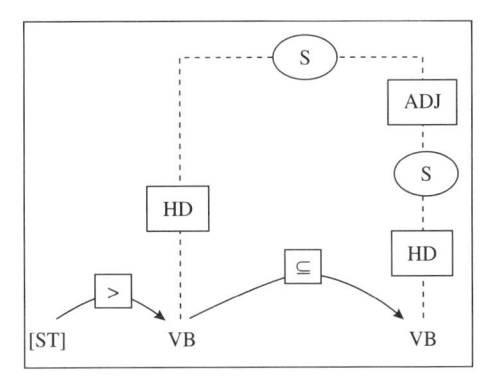

In this structure, both the syntactic configuration of the relative clause and the temporal relations between the matrix verb and the speech time and between the matrix verb and the verb occurring in the relative clause are represented. Querying our temporally annotated treebank with this request yields the result in Figure 2. The application to cross-linguistic research should be clear. It is now possible to use the annotated treebank as an informant by storing the linguistically relevant aspects of the temporal system of a language in a compact searchable database.

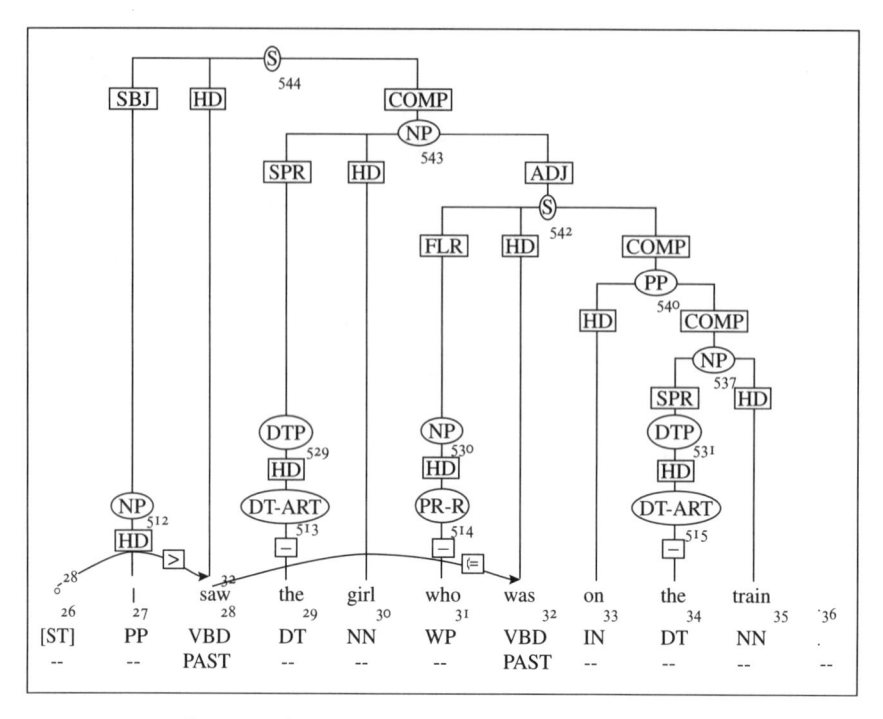

FIG. 2 Query result from the English treebank.

3.2 Aid for translation technology

Another potential application of the annotation system is as an aid to automatic translation systems. That the behaviour of tenses differs from language to language makes the translation of tenses difficult. In particular, the application of example-based techniques faces serious difficulties (Arnold, et al. 1994). Adding the intended temporal relation to the database of source sentences makes it possible to moderate this problem.

For example in Japanese (9a) is properly translated as (10a) on one reading, where the embedded past tense is translated as a present tense, but as (10b) on the other, where the verb is translated as a past tense.

(9) a. Bernard said that Junko was sick.
(10) a. Bernard-wa Junko ga byookida to it-ta lit: Bernard said Junko is sick.
  b. Bernard-wa Junko-ga byookidata to it-ta. lit: Bernard said Junko was sick.

Only the intended reading can distinguish these two translations. If this is encoded as part of the input, we can hope to achieve much more reasonable output.

3.3 Extracting cues for temporal interpretation

While we see this sort of cross-linguistic investigation as of intrinsic interest, our real goal is the investigation of the lexical and grammatical cues for temporal interpretation. As already mentioned, the biggest problem is one of scale. Generating a temporally annotated treebank of the size needed is a serious undertaking.

It would, of course, be of great help to be able to partially automate this task. To that end we are currently engaged in research attempting to use overt cues such as perfect marking and temporal conjunctions such as *before* and *after* to bootstrap our way towards a temporally annotated corpus. Briefly, the idea is to use these overt markers to tag a corpus directly and to use this to generate a table of lexical preferences. So, for example, the sentence (11) can be tagged automatically, because of the presence of the perfect marking.

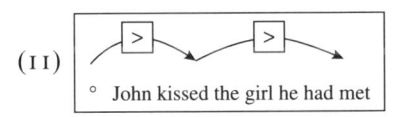

(11) ○ John kissed the girl he had met

This automatic tagging will allow us to assemble an initial data set of lexical preferences, such as would appear to hold between *kiss* and *meet*. If this initial data is confirmed by comparison with hand-tagged data, we can use this information to automatically annotate a much larger corpus based on these lexical preferences. It may then be possible to begin to carry out the investigation of cues to temporal interpretation before we have constructed a large hand-coded temporally annotated treebank.

4 CONCLUSIONS

We have described a simple and general technique for the annotation of temporal information. The annotations are provided with a model-theoretic semantics and have a number of fascinating applications. Of particular interest is the promise such annotated databases bring to the automatic extraction of lexical information about stereotypical ordering relations among events.

ACKNOWLEDGMENTS

An earlier version of this paper appeared in the *Proceedings of the ACL 2001 Workshop on Spatial and Temporal Information Processing*. Thanks to Rob Gaizauskas and Mark Hepple for pointing out errors in section 2.3 of that paper and for useful general discussion.

REFERENCES

Abusch, Dorit. (1997). 'Sequence of Tense and Temporal De Re', *Linguistics and Philosophy* 20: 1–50.
Allen, James F. (1984). 'A General Model of Action and Time', *Artificial Intelligence 23 (2)*: 123–54.
Androutsopoulos, Ion, Ritchie, Graeme D., and Thanisch, Peter (1998). 'Time, Tense and Aspect in Natural Language Database Interfaces', *Natural Language Engineering 4 (3)*. Cambridge: Cambridge University Press, 229–76.
Arnold, Doug, Balkan, Lorna, Humphreys, R. Lee, Meijer, Siety, and Sadler, Louisa (1994). *Machine Translation: an Introductory Guide*. London: Blackwells/NCC.
Brants, Thorsten and Plaehn, Oliver (2000). 'Interactive Corpus Annotation', in *Second International Conference on Language Resources and Evaluation (LREC-2000)*, Athens, Greece.

Kamp, Hans and Reyle, Uwe (1993). *From Discourse to Logic*. Dordrecht: Kluwer Academic Publishers.

Kilgarriff, Adam and Rosenzweig, Joseph (2000). 'Framework and Results for English SENSEVAL'. *Special Issue on SENSEVAL: Computers and the Humanities*, 34 (1–2): 15–48.

Lascarides, Alex and Asher, Nicholas (1993). 'A Semantics and Pragmatics for the Pluperfect', in *Proceedings of the Sixth European Chapter of the Association of Computational Linguistics*, Utrecht, 250–9.

Marcus, Mitchell P., Santorini, Beatrice, and Marcinkiewicz, Mary Ann (1993). 'Building a large annotated corpus of English: the Penn Treebank', *Computational Linguistics* 19: 313–30.

Ogihara, Toshiyuki. (1996). *Tense, Scope and Attitude Ascription*. Dordrecht: Kluwer Academic Publishers.

Poesio, Massimo, Henschel, Renate, Hitzeman, Janet, Kibble, Rodger, Montague, Shane, and van Deemter, Kees (1999). 'Towards an Annotation Scheme for Noun Phrase Generation', *Proceedings of the EACL Workshop on Linguistically Interpreted Corpora*. Bergen.

Reyle, Uwe and Rossdeutscher, Antje (2000). 'Understanding very short stories', ms. Institut für Maschinelle Sprachverarbeitung, Universität Stuttgart.

Rooth, Mats, Riezler, Stefan, Prescher, Detlef, Schulte im Walde, Sabine, Carroll, Glenn, and Beil, Franz (1998). *Inducing Lexicons with the EM Algorithm*. AIMS Report *4(3)*. Institut für Maschinelle Sprachverarbeitung, Universität Stuttgart.

Setzer, Andrea and Gaizauskas, Robert (2000). 'Annotating Events and Temporal Information in Newswire Texts', in *Second International Conference on Language Resources and Evaluation (LREC-2000)*, Athens, Greece, 1287–94.

Vazov, Nikolay and Lapalme, Guy (2000). 'Identification of Temporal Structure in French'. *Proceedings of the Workshop of the 7th International Conference on Principles of Knowledge Representation and Reasoning*, Breckenridge, Colorado, 79–86.

Wiebe, Janyce, O'Hara, Tom, McKeever, Kenneth, and Öhrström-Sandgren, Thorsten (1998). 'An Empirical Approach to Temporal Reference Resolution', *Journal of Artificial Intelligence Research* 9: 247–93.

25

Assigning Time-Stamps to Event-Clauses

ELENA FILATOVA AND EDUARD HOVY

1 INTRODUCTION

Linguists who have analyzed news stories (Schokkenbroek, 1999; Bell, 1997; Ohtsuka and Brewer, 1992, etc.) noticed that "narratives[1] are about more than one event and these events are temporally ordered. Though it seems most logical to recapitulate events in the order in which they happened, i.e. in chronological order, the events are often presented in a different sequence"(Schokkenbroek, 1999). The same paper states that "it is important to reconstruct the underlying event order[2] for narrative analysis to assign meaning to the sequence in which the events are narrated at the level of discourse structure.... If the underlying event structure cannot be reconstructed, it may well be impossible to understand the narrative at all, let alone assign meaning to its structure".

Several psycholinguistic experiments show the influence of event arrangement in news stories on the ease of comprehension by readers. Duszak (1991) had readers reconstruct a news story from the randomized sentences. According to his experiments, readers follow a default strategy by which—in the absence of cues to the contrary—they re-impose chronological order on events in the discourse.

The problem of reconstructing the chronological order of events becomes more complicated when we deal with separate news stories, written at different times and describing the development of some situation, as is the case in multidocument summarization.

By judicious definition, one can make this problem easy or hard. Selecting only specific items to assign time-points to, and then measuring correctness on them alone, may give high performance but leave much of the text unassigned. We address the problem of assigning a time-point to *every* clause in the text.

Our approach is to break the news stories into their clause-sized constituent events and to assign time-stamps—either time-points or time-intervals—to these events. When assigning time-stamps we analyze both implicit time references (mainly through the tense system) and explicit ones (temporal adverbials) such as "on Monday", "in 1998", etc. The result of the work is a prototype program which takes as input a set of news stories broken into separate sentences and produces as output a text that combines all the events from all the articles, organized in chronological order.

Elena Filatova and Eduard Hovy, 'Assigning Time-Stamps to Event-Clauses', *Proceedings of the ACL-2001 Workshop on Temporal and Spatial Information Processing*, 39th Annual Meeting of the ACL (ACL' 2001) Toulouse, 2001, 104–11. © 2001 Association for Computational linguistics.

[1] Schokkenbroek (1999) uses the term *narrative* for news stories that relate more than one event.
[2] i.e., chronological order.

2 DATA

As data we used a set of news stories about an earthquake in Afghanistan that occurred at the end of May in 1998. These news stories were taken from the CNN, ABC, and APW websites for the Document Understanding Conference Workshop (DUC-2000). The stories were all written within one week. Some of the texts were written on the same day. In addition to a description of the May earthquake, these texts contain references to another earthquake that occurred in the same region in February 1998.

3 IDENTIFYING EVENTS

To divide sentences into event-clauses we use CONTEX (Hermjakob and Mooney, 1997), a parser that produces a syntactic parse tree augmented with semantic labels. CONTEX applies machine-learning techniques to induce a grammar from a given treebank.

To divide a sentence into event-clauses the parse tree output by CONTEX is analyzed from left to right (root to leaf). The *::CAT* field for each node provides the necessary information about whether the node under consideration forms a part of its upper level event or whether it introduces a new event. *::CAT* features that indicate new events are: S-CLAUSE, S-SNT, S-SUB-CLAUSE, S-PART-CLAUSE, S-REL-CLAUSE. These features mark clauses that contain both subject (one or several NPs) and predicate (VP containing one or several verbs).

The above procedure classifies a clause containing more than one verb as a simple clause. Such clauses are treated as one event and only one time-point will be assigned to them. This is fine when the second verb is used in the same tense as the first, but may be wrong in some cases, as in *He **lives** in this house now and **will stay** here for one more year*. There are no such clauses in the analyzed data, so we ignore this complication for the present.

The parse tree also gives information about the tense of verbs, used later for time assignment.

In order to facilitate subsequent processing, we wish to rephrase relative clauses as full independent sentences. We therefore have to replace pronouns by their antecedents, where possible. Very often the parser gives information about the referential antecedents (in the example below, *Russia*). Therefore we introduce the rule: if it is possible to identify a referent, insert it into the event-clause:

> *Original sentence: Russia, which has loaned helicopters in the previous disasters, said, it would consider sending aid.*
> *Event clauses:*
> 1. *Russia <2.> said;*
> 2. ***which** <Russia> has loaned helicopters in previous disasters,*
> 3. ***it** <Russia> would consider sending aid.*

But sometimes the antecedent is identified incorrectly:

> *Qulle charged that the United Nations and non-governmental organizations involved in the relief were poorly coordinated, **which** was costing lives.*

Here the antecedent for *which* is identified as *the relief*, giving *which <the relief> was costing lives* instead of *which <poor coordination> was costing lives*. Fortunately, in most cases our rule works correctly.

TABLE 1 Recall and precision scores for event identifier

Text number	# of clauses by human	# of clauses by system	# correct	Recall	Precision
Text 1	7	6	5	5/7 = 71.42%	5/6 = 83.33%
Text 2	27	31	15	15/27 = 55.55%	15/31 = 48.38%
Text 3	5	8	3	3/5 = 60%	3/8 = 37.5%
Text 4	28	28	18	18/28 = 64.28%	18/28 = 64.28%
Text 5	33	36	19	19/33 = 57.57%	19/36 = 52.77%
Text 6	58	63	36	36/58 = 62.07%	36/63 = 57.14%
Total	**158**	**172**	**96**	**96/158 = 60.76%**	**96/172 = 55.81%**

Recall = (# of event-clauses correctly identified by system)/(# of event-clauses identified manually), *Precision* = (# of event-clauses correctly identified by system)/(# of event-clauses identified by system)

Although the event identifier works reasonably well, breaking text into event-clauses needs further investigation. Table 1 shows the performance of the system. Two kinds of mistakes are made by the event identifier: those caused by CONTEX (it does not identify clauses with omitted predicate, etc.) and those caused by the fact that our clause identifier does too shallow an analysis of the parse tree.

4 THE TIME-STAMPER

According to (Bell, 1997) "time is expressed at different levels—in the morphology and syntax of the verb phrase, in time adverbials whether lexical or phrasal, and in the discourse structure of the stories above the sentence".

4.1 Representation of Time-points and -intervals

For the present work we adopt a slight modification of the time representation suggested in (Allen, 1991), using the following formats:

- **{YYYY:DDD:W}**[3] Used when it is possible to point out the particular day the event occurred.
- **{YYYY1:DDD1:W1},{YYYY2:DDD2:W2}**... Used when it is possible to point out several concrete days when the events occurred.
- **{YYYY1:DDD1:W1}---{YYYY2:DDD2:W2}** Used when it is possible to point out a range of days when the event occurred.
- **≪{YYYY:DDD:W}** Used when it is possible to say the event occurred {YYYY:DDD:W} or earlier.
- **≫{YYYY:DDD:W}** Used when it is possible to say the event occurred {YYYY:DDD:W} or later.

---

[3] YYYY—year number, DDD—absolute number of the day within the year (1–366), W—number of the day in a week (1–Monday, ... 7–Sunday). If it is impossible to identify the day of the week then W is assigned 0.

4.2 Time-points used for the Time-stamper

We use two anchoring time-points:

1. *Time of the article*

We require that the first sentence for each article contain time information. For example:

T1 (05/30/1998:Saturday 18:35:42.49) PAKISTAN MAY BE PREPARING FOR ANOTHER TEST.

The date information is in bold. We denote by **Ti** the reference time-point for article *i*. The symbol *Ti* is used as a comparative time-point if the time the article was written is unknown. The information in brackets gives the *exact date* the article was written, which is the main anchor point for the time-stamper. The information about hours, minutes, and seconds is ignored for the present.

2. *Last time point assigned in the same sentence*

While analyzing different event-clauses within the same sentence we keep track of what time-point was most recently assigned within this sentence. If needed, we can refer to this time-point. In case the most recent time information assigned is not a date but an interval we record information about both time boundaries. When the program proceeds to the next sentence, the variable for the most recently assigned date becomes undefined. In most cases this assumption works correctly (examples 5.2–5.3):

> 5.2.1 *In the village of Kol, hundreds of people swarmed a United Nations helicopter*
> 5.2.2 *that ⟨a United Nations helicopter⟩ touched down three days after Saturday's earthquake*
> 5.2.3 *⟨after Saturday's earthquake⟩ struck a remote mountainous area rocked three months earlier by another massive quake*
> 5.2.4 *that ⟨another massive quake⟩ claimed some 2,300 victims.*
> 5.3.1 *On Monday and Tuesday, U.N. helicopters evacuated 50 of the most seriously injured to emergency medical centers.*

The last time interval assigned for sentence 5.2 is {1998:53:0}---{1998:71:0}, which gives an approximate range of days when the previous earthquake happened (nominally, three months earlier). But the information in sentence 5.3 is about the recent earthquake and not about the previous one of three months earlier, so it would be a mistake to place Monday and Tuesday within that range. Similarly, Mani and Wilson (2000) point out that "over half of the errors [made by their time-stamper] were due to propagation of spreading of an incorrect event time to neighboring events". The rule of dropping the most recently assigned date as an anchor point when proceeding to the next sentence very often helps us to avoid this problem.

There are however cases where dropping the most recent time as an anchor when proceeding to the next sentence causes errors:

> 4.8.1 *But in February a devastating earthquake in the same region killed 2,300 people and left thousands of people homeless.*
> 4.9.1 *At the time international aid workers suffered through a logistical nightmare to reach the snow-bound region with assistance.*

It is clear that sentence 4.9 is the continuation of sentence 4.8 and refers to the same time point (February earthquake). In this case our rule assigns the wrong time to 4.9.1. Still, since we don't interpret phrases like "at the time", we retain this rule because it is more frequently correct than incorrect.

4.3 Preprocessing

First, the text divided into event-clauses is run through a program that extracts all explicit date-stamps (made available by Kevin Knight, ISI). In most cases this program does not miss any date-stamps and extracts only the correct ones. The only cases in which it did not work properly for the texts were:

1.H1 PAKISTAN MAY BE PREPARING FOR ANOTHER TEST.

Here the modal verb *MAY* was assumed to be the month, given that it started with a capital letter.

6.24 Tuberculosis is already common in the area where people live in close **quarters** *and have poor hygiene*

Here the noun *quarters*, which in this case is used in the sense *immediate contact or close range* (Merriam-Webster dictionary), was interpreted in the sense *the fourth part of a measure of time* (Merriam-Webster dictionary).

After extracting all the date-phrases we proceed to time assignment.

4.4 Rules of time assignment

When assigning a time to an event, we select the time to be either the most recently updated value or, if it is undefined, the date of the article. We use a set of rules to perform this selection. These rules can be divided into two main categories: those that work for sentences containing explicit date information, and those that work for sentences that do not.

4.4.1 Assigning Time-Stamps to clauses with explicit date information
Day of the Week
If the day-of-the-week used in the event-clause is the same as that of the article (or the most recently assigned date, if it is defined), and no words before it could signal that the described event happened earlier or will happen later, then the time-point of the article (or the most recently assigned date, if it is defined) is assigned to this event. If before or after a day-of-the-week there is a word/words signaling that the event happened earlier or will happen later then the time-point is assigned in accordance with this signal-word and the most recently assigned date, if it is defined.

If the day-of-the-week used in the event-clause is not the same as that of the article (or the most recently assigned date, if it is defined), then if there are words pointing out that the event happened before the article was written or the tense used in the clause is past, then the time for the event-clause is assigned in accordance with this word (such words we call signal words), or the most recent day corresponding to the current day-of-the-week is chosen. If the signal word points out that the event will happen after the article was written or the tense used in the clause is future, then the time for the event-clause is assigned in accordance with the signal word or the closest subsequent day corresponding to the current day-of-the-week. For example,

5.3.1 **On Monday and Tuesday**, *U.N. helicopters evacuated 50 of the most seriously injured to emergency medical centers.*

Since the time for article 5 is *(06/06/1998:Tuesday 15:17:00)*, the time assigned to event-clause 5.3.1 is *{1998:151:1}, {1998:152:2}*.

Name of the Month

The rules are the same as for a day-of-the- week, but in this case a time-range is assigned to the event-clause. The left boundary of the range is the first day of the month, the right boundary is the last day of the month, and though it is possible to figure out the days of weeks for these boundaries, this aspect is ignored for the present.

> 4.8.1 But in **February** a devastating earthquake in the same region killed 2,300 people and left thousands of people homeless.

Since the time for article 4 is *(05/30/1998:Saturday 14:41:00)*, the time assigned to this event-clause is {*1998:32:0*}- - -{*1998:60:0*}.

In the analyzed corpus there is a case where the presence of a name of month leads to a wrong time-stamping:

> 6.3.1 *Estimates say*
> 6.3.2 *up to 5,000 people died from the May 30 quake,*
> 6.3.3 *more than twice as many fatalities as in the* **February** *disaster.*

Because of *February*, a wrong time-interval is assigned to clause 6.3.3, namely {*1998:32:0*}- - -{*1998:60:0*}. As this event-clause compares latest news to earlier figures it should have the time-point of the article. Such cases present a good possibility for the use of machine-learning techniques to disambiguate between the cases where we should take into account date-phrase information and where not.

Weeks, Days, Months, Years

We might have date-stamps where the words *weeks, days, months, years* are used with modifiers. For example

> 5.2.1 *In the village of Kol, hundreds of people swarmed a United Nations helicopter*
> 5.2.2 *that <a United Nations helicopter> touched down three days after Saturday's earthquake*
> 5.2.3 *after Saturday's earthquake struck a remote mountainous area rocked* **three months earlier** *by another massive quake*
> 5.2.4 *that <another massive quake> claimed some 2,300 victims.*

In event-clause 5.2.3 the expression *three months earlier* is used. It is clear that to obtain the time for this event it is not enough to subtract three months from the time of the article because the above expression gives an approximate range within which this event could happen and not a particular date. For such cases we invented the following rule:

Time = multiplier*length[4]; (in this case, 3 * 30);
Day = DDD-Time; for *years* Year = YYYY-Time;
Left boundary of the range =
        Day–round (10%*Day)
    (for *years* = Year – round(10%*Year));
Right boundary of the range =
    Day + round (10%*Day);
(for *years* = Year + round (10%*Year)).

Thus for event 5.2.3 the time range will be {*1998:53:0*}- - -{*1998:71:0*} (the exact date of the article is {1998:152:2}).

---

[4] For *days*, length is equal to 1, *weeks*–7, *months*–30.

If the modifier used with *weeks, days, months* or *years* is *several*, then the multiplier used equals 2.

When, Since, After, Before, etc.
If an event-clause does not contain any date- phrase but contains one of the words *when, since, after, before,* etc., it might mean that this clause refers to an event, the time of which can be used as a reference point for the event under analysis. In this case we ask the user to insert the time for this reference event manually.

This rule can cause problems in cases where *after* or *before* are used not as temporal connectors but as spatial ones, though in the analyzed texts we did not face this problem.

4.4.2 Assigning Time-Stamps to Clauses without Explicit Date Information
Present/Past Perfect
If the current event-clause refers to a time-point in Present/Past Perfect tense, then an open-ended time-interval is assigned to this event. The starting point is unknown; the end-point is either the most recently assigned date or (if that is undefined) the time-point of the article.

Future Tense
If the current event-clause contains a verb in future tense (one of the verbs *shall, will, should, would, might* is present in the clause) then the open-ended time-interval assigned to this event-clause has the starting point at either the most recently assigned date or (if that is undefined) the date of the article.

Other Tenses
Other tenses that can be identified with the help of CONTEX are *Present* and *Past Indefinite*. In the analyzed data all the verbs in Present Indefinite are given the most recently assigned date (or the date of the article). The situation with Past Indefinite is much more complicated and requires further investigation of more data. News stories usually describe the events that already took place at some time in the past, which is why even if the day when the event happened is not over, past tense is very often used for the description (this is especially noticeable for US news of European, Asian, African and Australian events). This means that very often an event-clause containing a verb in Past Indefinite Tense can be assigned the most recently assigned date (or, if that is undefined, the date of the article). It might prove useful to use machine-learned rules for such cases.

No verb in the event-clause
If there is no verb in the event-clause then the most recently assigned date (or the date of the article) is assigned to the event-clause.

4.5 Sources of Errors for Time-stamper

We ran the time-stamper program on two types of data: a list of event-clauses extracted by the event identifier and a list of event-clauses created manually. Tables 2 and 3 show the results.[5] In the former case we analyzed only the correctly identified clauses. One can see that even on manually created data the performance of the time-stamper is not 100%. Why?

---
[5] If an event happened at some time-point but according to the information in the sentence we can assign only a time-interval to this event (for example, *February earthquake*) then we say that the time-interval is assigned correctly if the necessary time-point is within this interval.

TABLE 2 Time-stamper performance on automatically claused texts (only correctly identified clauses are analyzed)

Text number	Number of event-clauses identified correctly	Number of time-points correctly assigned to correctly identified clauses	Percentage correct assignment
text 1	5	4	80.00
text 2	15	15	100
text 3	3	2	66.67
text 4	18	17	94.44
text 5	19	17	89.47
text 6	36	24	66.66
Total	96	79	82.29

TABLE 3 Time-stamper performance on manually (correct) claused texts

Text number	Number of manually created event-clauses	Number of time-points correctly assigned to manually created clauses	Percentage correct assignment
target 1	7	6	85.71
target 2	27	20	74.07
target 3	5	4	80.00
target 4	28	26	92.85
target 5	33	30	90.91
target 6	58	37	63.79
Total	158	123	77.85

Some errors are caused by assigning the time based on the date-phrase present in the event-clause, when this date-phrase is not an adverbial time modifier but an attribute. For example,

1. *Estimates say*
2. *up to 5,000 people died from the May 30 earthquake,*
3. *more than twice as many fatalities as in the February disaster.*

As described in Section 4.4.1, the third event describes the May 30 earthquake but the time interval given by our rules for this event is {1998:32:0}---{1998:60:0} (i.e., the event happened in February). It might be possible to use machine-learned rules to correct such cases.

Another significant source of errors is writing style:

1. *"When I left early this morning,*
2. *everything was fine.*
3. *After the earthquake, I came back,*
4. *and the house had collapsed.*
5. ***I looked for two days** and gave up.*
6. *Everybody gave up...*

When the reader sees *early this morning* he or she tends to assign to this clause the time of the article, but later on seeing *looked for two days* realizes that the time of the clause containing *early this morning* is two days earlier than the time of the article. Such verbatim quotes introduce distinct temporal environments that have to be handled separately. It seems that errors caused by such writing style can hardly be avoided.

The approx. 5% discrepancy between averages in Tables 2 and 3 is interesting. We surmise that the system performs worse on manually delimited (and hence correct) clauses because some of them are simply more difficult to handle. The same reasons that make them hard to delimit—they are brief and syntactically hidden—also make it harder to find time-stamping clues.

5 TIME-LINE FOR SEVERAL NEWS STORIES AND ITS APPLICATIONS

After stamping all the news stories from the analyzed set, we arrange the event-clauses from all the articles into a chronological order. We obtain a new set of event-clauses which can easily be divided into two subsets: the first containing all references to the February earthquake, the second containing event-clauses describing what happened in May, in chronological order. Such rewriting of the text into chronological order may be helpful when creating updates in multidocument summaries, where it is important to include into the final summary not only the most important information but also the most recent events.

6 RELATED WORK

Allen presents a detailed logic-based apparatus for time representation and temporal reasoning. Unfortunately, the problem of what part of text is an event and should be assigned a time-stamp is not discussed, which makes the application of this theoretical framework difficult.

A few computational applications have focused on temporal expressions in scheduling dialogs (Busemann et al., 1997; Alexandresson et al., 1997). Since such dialogs contain many explicit temporal references, these systems deliver quite high performance, but the specificity of the application makes it hard to transfer the systems to the general case.

Several other studies describe parts of the time-stamping problem, but interpret temporal information just where it occurs in the text and ignore clauses without any explicit time marking. Of course, the accuracy scores in these studies are much higher than those we obtain here. For example, systems participating in the Message Understanding Conferences (MUC, 1997) also extracted time information from given documents. However, MUC systems were restricted to a predefined template and thus extracted time phrases only for specific events in the template's focus, not for each clause. In fact, they usually extracted only a single phrase per text for a given template.

More recently, interest has been growing in creating a corpus manually annotated with time-stamps (Setzer and Gaizauskas, 2000). In this corpus time phrases are given values according to the time phrase type, and verbs are marked as events and assigned the corresponding time-stamps.

The prior work most relevant to ours is (Mani and Wilson, 2000), who implemented their system on news stories, introduced rules spreading time-stamps obtained with the help of explicit temporal expressions throughout the whole article, and invented machine-learning rules for disambiguating between specific and generic use of temporal expressions (for example, whether *Christmas* is used to denote the 25th of December or to denote some period of time around the 25th of December). They also mention the problem of disambiguating between temporal expressions and proper names, as in the newspaper name *USA Today*.

7 CONCLUSION

We agree with Bell (1997) that "more research is needed on the effects of time structure on news comprehension. The hypothesis that the non-canonical news format does adversely affect understanding is a reasonable one on the basis of comprehension research into other narrative genres, but the degree to which familiarity with news models may mitigate these problems is unclear". Research of this topic may greatly improve the performance of the time-stamper and might lead to a list of machine-learning rules for time detection.

In this paper we make an attempt to not just analyze and decode temporal expressions where they occur explicitly, but to apply this analysis throughout the whole text and assign time-stamps to each clause, which may later be used to form new sentences in such applications as multidocument summarization.

REFERENCES

Alexandresson, J., Reithinger, N., and Maier, E. (1997). 'Insights into the Dialogue Processing of VERBMOBIL', in *Proceedings of the Fifth Conference on Applied Natural Language Processing*, 33–40.

Allen, J. (1991). 'Time and Time Again: The Many Ways to Represent Time', *International Journal of Intelligent Systems* 4, 341–56.

—— and Ferguson, G. (1994). 'Actions and Events in Interval Temporal Logic'. Technical Report 521, University of Rochester.

Bell, A. (1997). 'The Discourse Structure of News Structure', in A. Bell (ed.), *Approaches to Media Discourse*. Oxford: Blackwell, 64–104.

Busemann, S., Declerck, T., Diagne, A. K., Dini, L., Klein, J., and Schmeier, S. (1997). 'Natural Language Dialogue Service for Appointment Scheduling Agents', *Proceedings of the Fifth Conference on Applied Natural Language Processing*, 25–32.

Document Understanding Conference (DUC) (2000). <http://www_nlpir.nist.gov/projects/duc/guidelines/2000.html>.

Duszak, A. (1991). 'Schematic and Topical Categories in News Story Reconstruction', *Text 11(4)*: 503–22.

Hermjakob, U., and Mooney, R. (1997). 'Learning Parse and Translation Decisions from Examples with Rich Context', in *Proceedings of the 35th Annual Meeting of the Association for Computational Linguistics, 481–89*.

Mani, I. and Wilson, G. (2000). 'Robust Temporal Processing of News'. *Proceedings of the ACL-2000 Conference*, 3–6 October 2000, Hong kong, 69–76.

Message Understanding Conference (MUC). (1997). *Proceedings of the Seventh Message Understanding Conference*.

Ohtsuka, K. and Brewer, W. F. 1992. Discourse organization in the comprehension of temporal order in narrative texts. *Discourse Processes*, 15, 317–36.

Schokkenbroek, S. (1999). 'News Stories: Structure, Time and Evaluation', *Time and Society* 8(1): 59–98.

Setzer, A. and Gaizauskas, R. (2000). 'Annotating Events and Temporal Information in Newswire Texts', in *Proceedings of the Second International Conference on Language Resources and Evaluation*(LREC-2000), Athens, Greece, 31 May–2 June 2000, 1287–94.

From Temporal Expressions to Temporal Information: Semantic Tagging of News Messages

FRANK SCHILDER AND CHRISTOPHER HABEL

1 INTRODUCTION

This paper describes a semantic tagging system that extracts temporal information from news messages. Temporal expressions are defined for this system as chunks of text that express some sort of direct or inferred temporal information. The set of these expressions investigated in the present paper includes dates (e.g. 08.04.2001), prepositional phrases (PPs) containing some time expression (e.g. *on Friday*), and verbs referring to a situation (e.g. *opened*). Related work by Mani and Wilson (2000) focuses only on the core temporal expressions neglecting the temporal information conveyed by prepositions (e.g. *Friday* vs. **by** *Friday*).

The main part of the system is a temporal expression tagger that employs finite state transducers based on hand-written rules. The tagger was trained on economic news articles obtained from two German newspapers and an online news agency (*Financial Times Deutschland, die tageszeitung*, and <http://www.comdirect.de>).

Based on the syntactic classification of temporal expressions a semantic representation of the extracted chunks is proposed. A clear-cut distinction between the syntactic tagging process and the semantic interpretation is maintained. The advantage of this approach is that a second level is created that represents the *meaning* of the extracted chunks. Having defined the semantic representation of the temporal expressions, further inferences, in particular on temporal relations, can be drawn. Establishing the temporal relations between all events mentioned by a news article is the ultimate goal of this enterprise. However, at the current stage of this work the semantic analysis is still in progress. For the time being, we focus on the anchoring of the temporal expressions in the absolute time-line and present an already substantial subset of a full semantics that will eventually cover the entire set of temporal expressions extracted.

Finally, the evaluation of the temporal expression tagger provides precision and recall rates for tagging temporal expressions and drawing temporal inferences.

Frank Schilder and Christopher Habel, 'From Temporal Expressions to Temporal Information: Semantic Tagging of News Messages', *Proceedings of the ACL-2001 Workshop on Temporal and Spatial Information Processing*. 39th Annual Meeting of the ACL (ACL-2001). Toulouse, 2001. 88–95. © 2001 Association for Computational Linguistics.

2 REPRESENTING TIME IN NEWS ARTICLES

Since we focus on a particular text domain (i.e. news articles), the classification of temporal expressions can be kept to a manageable set of classes.

2.1 Classification of temporal expressions

The main distinction we make is between time-denoting and event-denoting expressions. The first group comprises chunks expressing temporal information that can be stated with reference to a calendar or clock system. Syntactically speaking, these expressions are mainly expressed by prepositional, adverbial or noun phrases (e.g. *on Friday* or *today* or *the fourth quarter*).

The second group, event-denoting expressions, refers to events. These expressions have an implicit temporal dimension, since all situations possess a temporal component. For these expressions, however, there is no direct or indirect link to the calendar or clock system. These expressions are verb or noun phrases (e.g. *increased* or *the election*).

2.1.1 Time-denoting expressions

Temporal reference can be expressed in three different ways:

Explicit reference. Date expressions such as *08.04.2001* refer explicitly to entries of a calendar system. Also time expressions such as *3 p.m.* or *Midnight* denote a precise moment in our temporal representation system.

Indexical reference. All temporal expressions that can only be evaluated via a given index time are called indexical. Expressions such as *today, by last week*, or *next Saturday* need to be evaluated with respect to the article's time-stamp.

Vague reference. Some temporal expressions express only vague temporal information and it is rather difficult to precisely place the information expressed on a time-line. Expressions such as *in several weeks, in the evening*, or *by Saturday the latest* cannot be represented by points or exact intervals in time.

For the given domain of a news article, the extraction of a time-stamp for the given article is very important. This time-stamp represents the production time of the news information and is used by the other temporal expressions as an index time to compute the correct temporal meaning of the expression. Note that an explicit date expression such as *24.12* can only be evaluated with respect to the year that the article was written. This means that even an explicit temporal expression can contain some degree of indexicality.

2.1.2 Event-denoting expressions

Two types of event-denoting expressions have to be distinguished, on the one hand, sentences, and, on the other, specific noun phrases. In the former case, the verb is the lexical bearer of information about the event in question, in the latter case, specific nouns, especially those created by nominalization, refer to an event.

Since temporal information is the topic of the system described in this paper, only a subset of event-denoting nouns have to be considered. These expressions—as *election* in the phrase *after the election*—which serve as temporal reference pointers in building the temporal structure of a news event, can be marked by a specific attribute in their lexical entry. Furthermore, in the text classes we have investigated, there is a small number of *event nouns*, which are used as domain dependent pointers to elements of temporal structures. For the domain of business and stock market news, phrases such as *opening of the stock exchange, opening bell*, or *the close* are examples of domain specific event expressions.

2.2 Representation of temporal information: the time domain

The primary purpose of the present paper is to anchor the temporal information obtained from natural language expressions in news messages in *absolute time*, i.e. in a linearly ordered set of abstract time-entities, which we call *time-set* in the following. One of the major tasks in this anchoring process is to augment the temporal information in case of indexical and vague temporal descriptions (see Section 4.3 for more details). Since these expressions do not specify an individual time-entity of the time-set, it is necessary to add temporal information until the temporal entity build-up from natural language is fully specified, i.e. can be anchored in the time-set.

2.2.1 The granular system of temporal entities

The temporal information obtained from news messages is organized in a granular system of temporal entities including such granularity levels as GL-day, GL-week, GL-month, and GL-year.[1] Individual days are anchored by a date, e.g. date (2001, 3, 23), on the *time-line*, i.e. the time-set. Further information, for example, the *day of the week*, can also be included by an additional slot of the time entity: time = ['Fri', date (2001, 3, 23)]. Time entities of coarser granularity levels, e.g. weeks, are represented on the basis of intervals, which can be determined by a start, that is an entity of GL-day, and a specific duration: time = ['Mon', date (2001, 4, 2), '7 days'].[2]

The concept of temporal granularity is reflected linguistically, for example, in the use of demonstratives as determiners of time expressions in German: *dieser Freitag* ('this Friday') refers to that Friday which is located in the current week (i.e. the time entity of the next coarser level of temporal granularity). The same phenomenon holds with *dieser Monatserste* ('this first day of the month').

In the following we will apply the granularity structure of temporal expressions only with respect to the *finer than—coarser than* relation between levels of granularity, which is different from the *is part of* relation between temporal entities. For example, whereas between days and weeks there is a unique functional relationship, namely that there is exactly one week (as standard calendar unit) that an individual day is a part of, a week can temporally *overlap* with one or two months (Technically, *overlap* can be realized by temporal relations of Allen-style; see Allen (1983)). Nevertheless, GL-week *finer than* GL-month holds in the granularity system.[3]

---

[1] In the present paper we focus on the conception of *granularity level* in semantic and pragmatic inferences. Therefore, we do not discuss the formal notions of granular systems for temporal entities here. Compare, e.g. Bettini et al. (2000), for a framework of temporal granularity, which could be used for the purposes we discuss here.

[2] Whether the GL-week information remains implicit, i.e. is inferable from duration, or is made explicit, i.e. coded by a GL-week-stamp, depends on some design decisions dependent on the conceptual richness of domain modeling. For example, in a standardized world of ISO-weeks, which start on Monday only, it is not necessary to use GL-week-stamps. On the other hand, if ISO-weeks, and business weeks—of five-day length—are conceptual alternatives, then it is appropriate to use explicit granularity-level stamps.

[3] The phenomena of overlapping temporal entities of different granularity systems, for example the *system of calendar time-entities* vs. the *system of business time-entities*, or the *astronomical system of seasons of the year* vs. the *meteorological seasons of the year* are especially relevant for processing vague and ambiguous temporal expressions. Due to the temporal and spatial limitations of this paper, we cannot go into the details here.

TABLE 1 The temporal relations used

before	$\{b, m\}$
after	$\{bi, mi\}$
incl	$\{d, s, f, eq\}$
at	$\{di, si, fi, eq\}$
starts	$\{s\}$
finishes	$\{f\}$
excl	$\{b, bi, m, mi\}$

2.2.2 Definition of temporal relations

Temporal relations are explicitly marked by temporal prepositions (e.g. *before*, *on*, or *by*). We use the following seven temporal relations: before, after, incl, at, starts, finishes, excl. The preposition *on* as in *on Friday*, for instance, denotes the inclusion relation incl, whereas the preposition *by* as in *by Friday* is represented as finishes.

Note that the seven temporal relations employed by the current version are equivalent to sets of Allen's interval relations (Allen, 1983).[4]

3 EXTRACTION OF TEMPORAL INFORMATION

Similar to other approaches to information extraction or tagging, a cascade of Finite State Transducers (FST) was employed. The following sections provide a brief introduction to this technique before the overall system architecture is described in more detail.[5]

3.1 Preliminaries

The temporal expression chunks are extracted via an FST. FSTs are basically automata that have transitions labeled with a translation instruction. A label of the form *a:b*

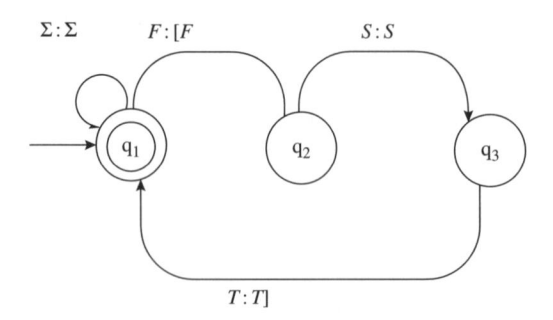

FIG. 1 A simple FST

---

[4] Allen (1983) proposes a temporal reasoning system that contains all thirteen conceivable relations between intervals: b(efore), m(eets), o(verlaps), s(tarts), d(uring), f(inishes), eq(ual), and the six reverse relations bi, mi, oi, si, di, and fi.
[5] The semantic tagging system is written in SWI-PROLOG 4.0.2.

indicates such a translation from *a* to *b*. Take as an example the simple FST in Figure 1. If the input contains the sequence of the three subsequent characters *F, S*, and *T*, the same output is produced with the sequence of these three characters put into brackets. The input stream "*FSTs are basically automata*" is, for instance, translated, into "*[FST]s are basically automata*".

3.2 Classes of temporal information

The FSTs defined are fed by the output of a Part of Speech (POS) tagger.[6] The POS tagger specifies the syntactic categories and a lemma for every word of the input text. The syntactic information is then stored in an XML file.[7] Given the derived syntactic categories and the lemma information for every word of the text, several FSTs specialized into different classes of temporal expressions are run.

Temporal Expressions. One FST, consisting of 15 states and 61 arcs, tags all occurrences of time-denoting temporal expressions. The POS information stored in an XML file as well as a predefined class of temporal lemmas are used by this FST. The class of temporal lemmas used includes days of the week (e.g. *Friday*), months (e.g. *April*), as well as general temporal descriptions such as *midday, week*, or *year*. Since German is a very productive language regarding compound nouns, a simple morphological analysing tool was integrated into this FST as well. This tool captures expressions such as *Rekordjahr* ('record year') or *Osterferien* ('Easter holiday').

The extracted temporal expression chunks are marked by the CHUNK tag and an attribute type=time. See the first row of Table 2 for an example. Note that the attributes sem and time carry semantic information. The meanings of these values are explained in Section 4 in detail.

Document time-stamp. The document time-stamp for a given article is crucial for the computation of almost all temporal expressions (e.g. *now*).[8] In particular, this index time is indispensable for the computation of all temporal expressions that express an indexical reference (see the second row of Table 2).[9]

Verbal descriptions. Another FST that contains 4 states and 27 arcs marks all verbs as previously tagged by the POS tagger. As already pointed out these temporal expressions denote an event. The tag for such expressions is <CHUNK type=event> </CHUNK> (see Table 2; third row).

Nominal descriptions. So far there is only an experimental FST that extracts also nominal descriptions of events such as *the election*. More tests have to be carried out to determine a subset of nouns for the given domain. These nouns should then also be used to denote events mentioned in the text which can be combined with time-denoting expressions, as in *after the election in May*.

---

[6] A decision-tree-based POS tagger developed by Schmid (1994) was integrated into the system.
[7] Some of the XML and HTML handling predicates the system uses stem from the PiLLoW package developed by Manuel Hermenegildo and Daniel Cabeza (URL <http://www.clip.dia.fi.upm.es/miscdocs/pillow/pillow.html>).
[8] See Wiebe et al. (1998) for an empirical approach to temporal reference resolution in dialogue.
[9] This FST consists of 7 states and 15 arcs. It also extracts the name of the newspaper or agency as indicated by the attribute ag. So far only the newspaper names and agencies mentioned by the article of the training set can be extracted. A future version of the temporal expressions tagger should also be capable of tagging previously unknown names. However, note that this is rather a named entity recognition task and therefore goes beyond the scope of this paper.

TABLE 2 Examples of tagged temporal expressions

on Monday (*time-denoting expression*)	\<CHUNK id=t43 type=time sem=[incl, [E, t42]] time=['Mon', date (2001, 4, 2), time (_,_,_), gl (_, day, _)]> on Monday \</CHUNK>
ftd.de, Fr, 16.3.2001, 11:00 (*document time-stamp*)	\<CHUNK id=t1 type=time ag='FTD' sem=now time=['Fri', date (2001, 3, 16), time (11,00,_), gl (_, second, now)]> ftd.de, Fr, 16.3.2001, 11:00 \</CHUNK>
closed (*event-denoting expression*)	\<CHUNK id=e23 type=event sem=close (e23) temp=[_, [t (e23) ,_]] closed \</CHUNK>

3.3 System output

After all expressions have been tagged, an HTML file is produced highlighting the respective expressions. See the snapshot in Figure 2.[10] While reading the output stream from the FSTs temporal inferences are drawn by the system. In particular, expressions bearing indexical references are resolved and the event descriptions are matched with the time-denoting temporal expressions.

Note that the values for CHUNK attributes sem, time, and temp as indicated by the three examples in Table 2 are PROLOG expressions. While translating the tagged text a PROLOG predicate triggers other predicates that compute the correct temporal information. An additional HTML file is also generated that contains the derived temporal information in standard ISO format, provided an explicit reference was given or was resolved. In the case of vague reference (e.g. *afternoon*) the semantic description is kept (e.g. 20:01:04:03:afternoon).[11] In addition, the temporal relations holding between the events and times expressed by the text are stored as well.

---

[10] Time-denoting expressions are indicated by a dark (or magenta) background, while event-denoting expressions are indicated by a lighter (or yellow) background. The document time-stamp is tagged by a very dark (or green) background.

[11] Future research will focus on the temporal inferences that can be drawn with these vague descriptions taking into account the different granularity levels.

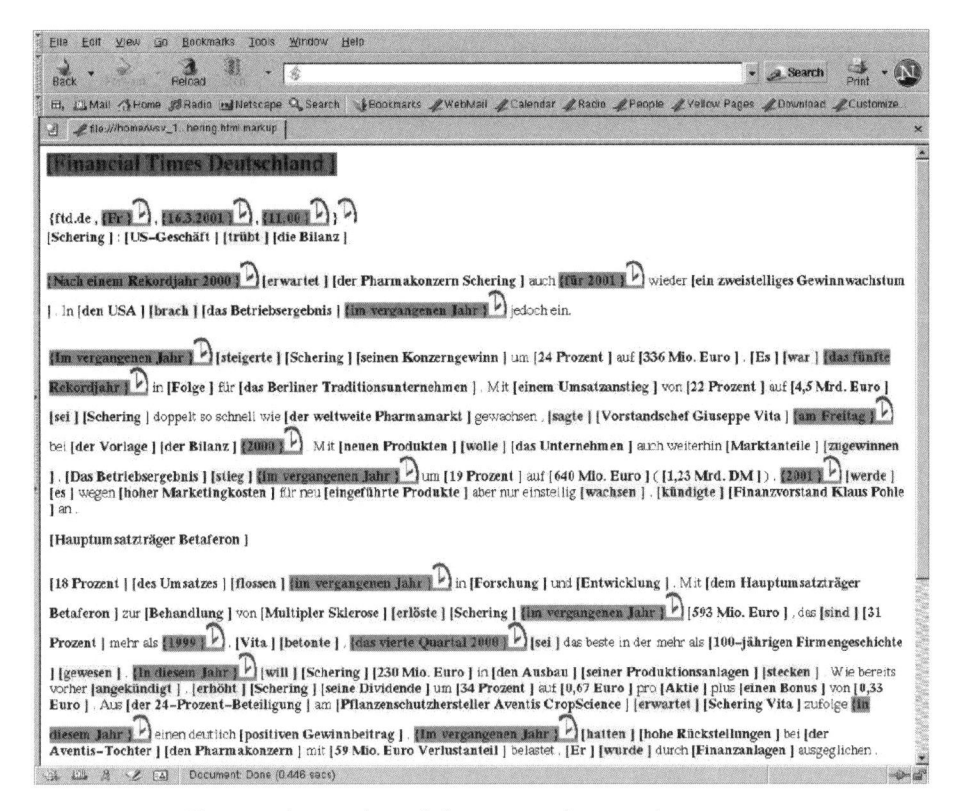

FIG. 2   A snapshot of the temporal expressions tagger.

4   SEMANTIC DESCRIPTIONS AND TEMPORAL INFERENCES

4.1   Semantics for temporal expressions

With respect to processing temporal information, the crucial distinction between time-denoting and event-denoting expressions is that event-denoting expressions lack the direct link to temporal entities. An event-denoting expression (e.g. a verb) refers to an event of a certain type. The verb *to meet*, for instance, can be formalized as `meet(e1)`. In order to add the temporal information to the event, a function `temp` is defined that gives back the time when the event occurred (i.e. run-time of the event). A time-denoting expression such as *on Monday* that is combined with the event description carries some temporal information that can further specify the run-time `temp(e1)` of the event `e1`.

4.2   Semantics for temporal prepositions

PPs are the carrier of temporal relations. The semantics for a preposition is, therefore, as follows: `rel(t,e)`. For each preposition a temporal relation `rel` was defined. The preposition *by* expresses, for instance, the finishes relation, as in *by Friday*. Temporal expressions that do not contain a preposition are assumed to express an inclusion relation, as in *Die Pflegeversicherung war 1995 [...] in Kraft getreten* ('the statutory health insurance coverage of nursing care for the infirm took effect in 1995').

4.3 Derivation of meaning

The temporal information expressed by a sentence as in example sequence (1) is derived via unification of the semantic attributes derived for the temporal expression chunks.

(1) Die   US-Technologiebörse   Nasdaq
    The   US-technology stock market   Nasdaq
    hatte   {am   Montag}   mit   einem   Minus
    had   on   Monday   with   a   minus
    von   3,11   Prozent   bei   1782   Punkten
    of   3.11   per cent at   1782   points
    [geschlossen].
    closed.

'The Nasdaq closed with a minus of 3.11 per cent at 1782 points on Monday.'

Two temporal expressions are marked by the tagger: *am Montag* ('on Monday') and *geschlossen* ('closed'). The former expression is a time-denoting expression that consists of a preposition and a time-denoting expression that is stored by the FST. The derivation of the semantics for this expression is done during the tagging process for the temporal expressions.

First, the preposition *am* ('on') denoting an inclusion relation between an event and a time is processed. The expressed temporal relation is represented by a PROLOG list (i.e. [incl, [E, T]]). After having processed the following noun referring to a time (i.e. *Monday*), the following semantic representation is obtained via unification: sem = [incl, [E, t1]], where t1 refers to the following time-stamp time = ['Mon', date (_,_,_), time (_,_,_), gl ([_, '1 day',_])].[12]

In the next step, the verbal expression tagger combines the temporal information derived for *am Montag* with the event representation for *geschlossen*. The following semantic representation is assigned to the verb *geschlossen* during the tagging of the verbal expressions: sem = close (e23) temp = [_, [t (e23),_]]. This means that event e23 is of type closing and the run-time t (e23) of this event stands in some to-be-specified relation with another expression. Next, the temporal information extracted by the FST specialized in time-denoting expressions is unified with the value of the temp-attribute. The result is [incl, [t (e23), t1]].

So far, only the temporal relation that the event of closing happened within a time frame of one day has been determined. Since *Montag* contains an indexical reference, this reference has to be resolved. The document time-stamp is needed here. All references regarding this index time are resolved during the generation of the HTML output file. Accordingly, the following time-stamp is generated for *am Montag*: time = ['Mon', date (2001, 4, 2), time (_,_,_), gl([_, '1 day',_])]. The time information is left open because the current granularity level is GL-day.

However, this information could be further specified by modifiers such as *nächstes Jahr* ('next year'). The third slot in gl is reserved for these modifiers. The first slot can be filled by temporal modifiers that refer to a subpart of the expressed temporal entity, as in *Beginn des Jahres* ('beginning of the year'). The resulting representation of an expression such as *Beginn letzten Jahres* ('beginning of last year') is gl ([begin, year, last]).

---

[12] Note that the underscore "_" refers to an anonymous variable in PROLOG.

4.4 Pragmatic inferences for anchoring indexicals: the case of 'last'

Temporal expressions of the type *last Friday* are similar to the phenomena discussed in the section above. German has three lexemes, namely *letzt, vergangen* and *vorig* that express this idea. The differences in meaning are—in referring to a specific day—more of the type of individual preferences than of real alternatives in meaning. Which day is referred to by using *vorigen Montag*? This depends on the time of utterance. In general, there seems to be a tendency to interpret this expression as synonymous to *Monday of the previous week*, i.e. to make use of the *previous*-operation on the coarser level GL-week, instead of using this operation on the level GL-day. But, if uttered on Friday, our informants would give the Monday of the same week a preference in their interpretation.

Thus the *granularity-level up strategy* is not always successful. As an alternative strategy we propose the *strategy of the gliding time window*. Similar to the first proposal a granularity of week-size is relevant, but the relevant time entity in question is centered around the focused day of the week. In other words, looking forward and backward in time from the perspective of a Friday, the next Monday is nearer—or more activated—than the last Monday, although it is in the same calendar week. Thus, this Monday, i.e. the last Monday, has to be marked explicitly by *vorige*, and therefore, the Monday before this has to be specified as *Montag der vorigen Woche* ('Monday of last week').

5 EVALUATION

We evaluated the temporal expression tagger with respect to a small corpus consisting of 10 news articles taken from Financial Times Deutschland. We can report precision and recall rates regarding the recognition of simple temporal expressions (i.e. NPs or AdvPs) and complex temporal expression phrases (i.e. PPs). Based on the extracted temporal expression chunks the temporal information was derived and evaluated.

5.1 Tagging results

First, the class of simple temporal expressions was tagged and analysed. Mani and Wilson (2000) call this class TIMEX expression (of type TIME or DATE). We computed the precision and recall values for our data regarding this type of expression in order to obtain a better comparability with the results obtained by this earlier study. However, as pointed out earlier, we consider PPs carrying information regarding temporal relations as quite crucial for the derivation of temporal information. This class of complex temporal expressions provides more detailed information about the temporal information expressed by a text.

Table 3 contains the results of the evaluation with respect to the two classes of temporal expressions. There was a total of 186 simple and 182 complex temporal expressions previously annotated.

An error analysis showed that the main source of missed temporal expressions was the occurrence of a combined temporal expression, as in *2000/01*. There were 6 cases when the tagger did not correctly analyze this type of expression.

Another error source for *complex* temporal expressions was the preposition *für* ('for'). We wrongly assumed that *für* expresses the inclusion relation incl, as in *für Montag*

TABLE 3 Performance of the temporal expressions tagger

	Simple temp. Expr.	Complex temp. Expr.
Precision	92.11	87.30
Recall	94.09	90.66

TABLE 4 Performance of the temporal inference derivation

	Reference expressed		
	explicit	implicit	vague
Total	49	109	7
Wrong	0	25	0
Precision		84.49	

('for Monday'). However, we found quite a few occurrences of constructions such as in *der Bericht für 2001* ('the report for 2001'), where a prediction for an interval in the future is made at the time of the document time-stamp.

5.2 Temporal information

The analysis of the temporal expressions included an evaluation of the temporal relations derived. Since all temporal prepositions and the class of temporal expressions that can be recognized by the FSTs come with a predefined semantics, precision and recall rates are the same. The overall performance showed a precision and recall rate of 84.49. As indicated by Table 4, errors were only made for expressions that express an indexical reference. These errors were in most cases due to a missing semantics assigned to the respective expression. Since this part of the system is still work in progress, we have not yet defined a complete semantics for all temporal expressions. Hence the performance of the system regarding temporal inference is likely to improve in the future.

6 CONCLUSION AND OUTLOOK

We presented a semantic tagging system that automatically tags the occurrence of temporal expressions such as *3. June, on Monday*, and *last month* for German news messages. In addition, a semantics for most of the temporal expressions was defined so that temporal inferences were drawn regarding dates and events described. A more complex set of temporal expressions as extracted by recent systems (e.g. (Mani and Wilson, 2000)) was tagged. Our definition of temporal expressions also includes PPs capturing temporal relations. The system achieved an overall precision rate of 84.49 which is likely to go up as soon as the semantic definition of all temporal expressions is completed.

Our system also covers indexical and vague temporal expressions. Temporal reasoning and pragmatic inferences drawn on the basis of these expressions is the focus of on-going and future work.

The system we described in the present paper is intended to become a part of an experimental multi-document summarization system currently under development. Our studies focus on financial news messages obtained from on-line information services in Germany. The task the system has to solve is the production of summaries of the most recent—and especially, most referred to—topics. Our experience in this domain shows that there is one topic which leads to five to twenty news messages almost every day. These news messages are mostly unrelated, and they often only focus on the last one or two hours. Thus a bare collection of such messages is nearly useless for a reader who wants to be informed at the end of the day. For a user of an on-line information service summarizations of several articles on the same *hot topics* would have an enormous advantage compared to unsummarized collections of news messages.

The processing of temporal expressions plays a major role in building up these summaries, because temporal information is ubiquitous in this class of news. In addition, developing stories are reported via a stream of in-coming news messages. Producing coherent news depends heavily on the correct extraction of temporal information expressed by these messages.[13]

7 SUBSEQUENT RESEARCH

The temporal tagger presented in this paper has been improved in recent years. One focus of our current work is the temporal anchoring of described events. For this purpose a tagger for event descriptions had to be implemented, since, as already pointed out in the current paper, events are not expressed solely by verbal phrases. Events can be encoded in German as tensed or untensed verbs (e.g. *hatte geschlossen* 'had closed' or *zu öffnen* 'to open'), adjectives derived from participles (e.g. *der von den Arbeitgebern abgelehnte Vorschlag* 'the proposal that was rejected by the employers') or noun phrases (e.g. *Tariferhöhung* 'pay rise').

An event tagger based on morphological cues and a set of event nouns typical for the business news domain is presented in Schilder and Habel (2003). The use of the event tagger improves the 'time-stamping' algorithm in comparison with the naive algorithm that maps the meaning of the temporal expression to the event description of the main verb phrase in the same clause.

However, there is also still room for improvement in the temporal tagger. Sundheim (2002) discusses difficult time-stamping tasks that involve more context than normally considered for the derivation of the meaning of temporal expressions. Some suggestions on how to deal with these challenges are made in Schilder (2003).

After successfully time-stamping the event description, the next important step is the derivation of temporal relations between all events described in the text (cf. Filatova and Hovy (2001); Mani et al. (2003)). The next phase of our research addresses this problem. First results regarding a more elaborate semantics for temporal PPs can be found in Schilder (2004).

---

[13] Cf. Radev and McKeown (1998); Barzilay et al. (1999)

REFERENCES

Allen, James F. (1983). 'Maintaining Knowledge about Temporal Intervals', *Communications of the ACM*, 26(1): 832–43.

Barzilay, Regina, McKeown, Kathleen, and Elhadad, Michael (1999). 'Information fusion in the context of multi-document summarization', in *Proceedings of the 37th Annual Meeting of the ACL*, Maryland, MD, 550–7.

Bettini, Claudio, Jajodia, Sushil, and Wang, Sean X. (2000). *Time Granularities in Databases, Data Mining, and Temporal Reasoning*. Berlin: Springer-Verlag.

Filatova, Elena and Hovy, Eduard (2001). 'Assigning time-stamps to event-clauses', in *Proceedings of ACL'01 Workshop on Temporal and Spatial Information Processing*, Toulouse, France, 88–95.

Mani, Inderjeet and Wilson, George (2000). 'Robust temporal processing of news', in *Proceedings of the 38th Annual Meeting of the ACL*, Hong Kong, 69–76.

——Schiffman, Barry, and Zhang, Jianping (2003). 'Inferring temporal ordering of events in news', in *Proceedings of Human Language Technology Conference and the Conference of the North American Chapter of the Association for Computational Linguistics (HLT-NAACL 2003)*, Edmonton, Canada, 55–7.

Radev, Dragomir R. and McKeown, Kathleen R. (1998). 'Generating natural language summaries from multiple on-line sources', *Computational Linguistics* 24(3): 469–500.

Schilder, Frank (2003). 'Deriving meaning from temporal expressions', in Raffaella Bernardi and Michael Moortgat (ed.), *Proceedings of the Linguistic Corpora and Logic-Based Grammar Formalisms workshop*, Utrecht, The Netherlands, 86–93.

——(2004). 'Extracting meaning from temporal nouns and temporal prepositions', *ACM Transactions on Asian Language Information Processing (TALIP)*. Special issue on Spatial and Temporal Information Processing, to appear.

——and Habel, Christopher (2003). 'Temporal information extraction for temporal question answering', in *Working Notes of the AAAI Spring Symposium on New Directions in Question Answering*, Palo Alto, USA, 35–44.

Schmid, Helmut (1994). 'Probabilistic part-of-speech tagging using decision trees', in *Proceedings of International Conference on New Methods in Language Processing*, 44–9.

Sundheim, Beth (2002). 'Association of absolute times with events: Current status and future challenges'. Technical report, TERQAS report. Available at <http://timem/.org>.

Wiebe, Janyce, O'Hara, Thomas P., Öhrström-Sandgren, Thorsten, and McKeever, Kenneth J. (1998). 'An empirical approach to temporal reference resolution', *Journal of Artificial Intelligence Research*, 9: 247–93.

27

The Specification Language TimeML

JAMES PUSTEJOVSKY, ROBERT INGRIA,
ROSER SAURÍ, JOSÉ CASTAÑO,
JESSICA LITTMAN, ROB GAIZAUSKAS,
ANDREA SETZER, GRAHAM KATZ, AND
INDERJEET MANI

I INTRODUCTION

The automatic recognition of temporal and event expressions in natural language text has recently become an active area of research in computational linguistics and semantics. In this paper, we report on TimeML, a specification language for events and temporal expressions, which was developed in the context of a six-month workshop, TERQAS (<http://www.timeml.org>), funded under the auspices of the AQUAINT program. The ARDA-funded program AQUAINT is a multiproject effort to improve the performance of question answering systems over free text, such as that encountered on the Web. An important component to this effort is the access of information from text through content rather than keywords. Named entity recognition (Chinchor et al., 1999) has moved the fields of information retrieval and information exploitation closer to access by content, by allowing some identification of names, locations, and products in texts. Beyond these metadata tags (ontological types), however, there is only a limited ability at marking up text for real content. One of the major problems that has not been solved is the recognition of events and their temporal anchorings. In this paper, we report on an AQUAINT project to create a specification language for event and temporal expressions in text.

Events in articles are naturally anchored in time within the narrative of a text. For this reason, temporally grounded events are the very foundation from which we reason about how the world changes. Without a robust ability to identify and extract events and their temporal anchoring from a text, the real "aboutness" of the article can be missed. Moreover, since entities and their properties change over time, a database of assertions about entities will be incomplete or incorrect if it does not capture how these properties are temporally updated. To this end, event recognition drives basic inferences from text.

For example, currently questions such as those shown below are not supported by question answering systems.

1. a. Is Gates currently CEO of Microsoft?
   b. When did Iraq finally pull out of Kuwait during the war in the 1990s?
   c. Did the Enron merger with Dynegy take place?

What characterizes these questions as beyond the scope of current systems is the following: they refer, respectively, to the temporal aspects of the properties of the entities being questioned, the relative ordering of events in the world, and events that are mentioned in news articles, but which have never occurred.

There has recently been a renewed interest in temporal and event-based reasoning in language and text, particularly as applied to information extraction and reasoning tasks (cf. Mani and Wilson, 2000, *ACL Workshop on Spatial and Temporal Reasoning*, 2001, *Annotation Standards for Temporal Information in Natural Language*, LREC 2002). Several papers from the workshop point to promising directions for time representation and identification (cf. Filatova and Hovy, 2001, Schilder and Habel, 2001, Setzer, 2001). Many issues relating to temporal and event identification remain unresolved, however, and it is these issues that TimeML was designed to address. Specifically, four basic problems in event-temporal identification are addressed:

(a) Time-stamping of events (identifying an event and anchoring it in time);
(b) Ordering events with respect to one another (lexical versus discourse properties of ordering);
(c) Reasoning with contextually underspecified temporal expressions (temporal functions such as *last week* and *two weeks before*);
(d) Reasoning about the persistence of events (how long does an event or the outcome of an event last).

The specification language, TimeML, is designed to address these issues, in addition to handling basic tense and aspect features.

2 INTRODUCTION TO TimeML

Unlike most previous attempts at event and temporal specification, TimeML separates the representation of event and temporal expressions from the anchoring or ordering dependencies that may exist in a given text. There are four major data structures that are specified in TimeML (Ingria and Pustejovsky, 2002, Pustejovsky et al., 2002): EVENT, TIMEX3, SIGNAL, and LINK. These are described in some detail below. The features distinguishing TimeML from most previous attempts at event and time annotation are summarized below:

1. It extends the TIMEX2 annotation attributes.
2. It introduces **Temporal Functions** to allow intensionally specified expressions: *three years ago, last month*.
3. It identifies signals determining interpretation of temporal expressions:
   (a) Temporal Prepositions: *for, during, on, at*.
   (b) Temporal Connectives: *before, after, while*.
4. It identifies all classes of event expressions:
   (a) Tensed verbs: *has left, was captured, will resign*.
   (b) Stative adjectives and other modifiers: *sunken, stalled, on board*.
   (c) Event nominals: *merger, Military Operation, Gulf War*.
5. It creates dependencies between events and times:
   (a) Anchoring: *John left on Monday*.
   (b) Orderings: *The party happened after midnight*.
   (c) Embedding: *John said Mary left*.

In the design of TimeML, we began with the core of the TIDES TIMEX2 annotation effort (Ferro et al., 2001)[1] and the temporal annotation language presented in Andrea Setzer's thesis (Setzer, 2001). Consideration of the details of this representation, however, in conjunction with problems raised in trying to apply it to actual texts, resulted in several changes and extensions to Setzer's original framework. The most significant extension is the logical separation of event descriptions and the relations they enter into, defined relative to temporal expressions or other events. This resulted in a natural reification of these relations as LINK tags. Details on motivations for introducing the class of LINK tags can be found in Ingria and Pustejovsky (2002). Briefly, Setzer (2001) defines events as having the following attribute structure:

```
attributes ::=
   eid class [argEvent] [tense] [aspect]
   [([signalID] relatedToEvent eventRelType)
   | ([signalID] relatedToTime timeRelType)] ...
```

That is, an EVENT has as attributes a unique id, a class (see below), optionally another event which is its argument, a tense and an aspect, and then, importantly, but also optionally, either another event to which it is temporally related or a time to which it is temporally related, perhaps in each case, by a signal. One thing that is striking in looking at this specification is that for both the case where the event is related to another event and the case where it is related to a time, we are dealing not with three unrelated attributes (eid relatedtoEvent eventRelType), but with three attributes that only make sense as a unit. The same triad also appears in the attribute structure of Setzer's definition of complex time expressions, time-denoting expressions which inherently involve reference to an event, such as *five seconds after the explosion*: her specification for such complex TIMEX's includes the attributes tid relatedtoEvent relType. Moreover, as the specification of the values for the eventRelType and timeRelType attributes of EVENT and the relType attribute of TIMEX indicates, we are really dealing with one property, whose values are specified three times. This is forced in the case of eventRelType and timeRelType for EVENT by virtue of the fact that only the name of the attribute can link it to relatedToEvent or relatedToTime, respectively. And, of course, since relType is defined on TIMEX, not EVENT, it must repeat the specification of permissible values.

All these considerations suggest that these triplets of attributes should be factored out into the form of a new abstract tag (i.e. one which consumes no input text). This would formally express the fact that these attributes are linked, allow eventRelType, timeRelType and relType to be collapsed into a single attribute, and allow the specification of the possible values of this single attribute to be stated only once.

TimeML considers "events" (and the corresponding tag <EVENT>) a cover term for situations that *happen* or *occur*. Events can be punctual or last for a period of time. We also consider as events those predicates describing *states* or *circumstances* in which something obtains or holds true. Not all stative predicates are marked up, however. Only those states that are directly related to a temporal expression are annotated, including those states that identifiably change over the course of a document. Events are generally expressed by means of tensed or untensed verbs, nominalizations, adjectives,

---

[1] TIMEX2 introduces a value attribute whose value is an ISO time representation in the ISO 8601 standard.

predicative clauses, or prepositional phrases. The specification of EVENT is shown below:

```
attributes ::= eid class
eid ::= EventID
%EventID ::= e<integer>
class ::= 'OCCURRENCE'|'PERCEPTION'|'REPORTING'|'ASPECTUAL'
         |'STATE'|'I_STATE'|'I_ACTION'
```

Examples of each of these event types are given below:

1. **Occurrence**: *die, crash, build, merge, sell*
2. **State**: *on board, kidnapped, love*
3. **Reporting**: *say, report, announce*
4. **I-Action**: *attempt, try, promise, offer*
5. **I-State**: *believe, intend, want*
6. **Aspectual**: *begin, finish, stop, continue*
7. **Perception**: *see, hear, watch, feel.*

MAKEINSTANCE is a realization tag that is used to annotate information about a given event. One can create as many instances as are motivated by the text, for example in dealing with quantified event references such as *John taught three times*. All relations indicated by links (Section 3) are stated over these instances. Because of this, every EVENT introduces at least one corresponding MAKEINSTANCE. The specification of MAKEINSTANCE is shown below:

```
attributes ::= eiid eventID tense aspect [polarity] [modality]
[signalID] [cardinality]
%eiid ::= ID
eiid ::= EventInstanceID
{%EventInstanceID ::= ei<integer>}
eventID ::= IDREF
%{eventID ::= EventID}
tense ::= 'PAST' | 'PRESENT' | 'FUTURE' | 'NONE'
aspect ::= 'PROGRESSIVE' | 'PERFECTIVE'
| 'PERFECTIVE_PROGRESSIVE'| 'NONE'
polarity ::= 'NEG' | 'POS'
modality ::= CDATA
signalID ::= IDREF
%{signalID ::= SignalID}
cardinality ::= CDATA
```

The TIMEX3 tag is used to mark up explicit temporal expressions, such as times, dates, durations, etc. It is modeled on both Setzer's (2001) TIMEX tag, as well as the TIDES (Ferro, et al. (2001)) TIMEX2 tag. There are four major types of TIMEX3 expressions: (a) Fully Specified Temporal Expressions, *June 11, 1989, Summer, 2002*; (b) Underspecified Temporal Expressions, *Monday, Next month, Last year, Two days ago*; (c) Durations, *Three months, Two years*; (d) Sets, *Twice a month, Daily*.

```
attributes ::= tid type [functionInDocument] [beginPoint]
               [endPoint] [quant]
               [freq] [temporalFunction]
               (value | valueFromFunction)
               [mod] [anchorTimeID]
tid ::= TimeID
%TimeID ::= t<integer>
type ::= 'DATE' | 'TIME' | 'DURATION' | 'SET'
functionInDocument ::= 'CREATION_TIME' | 'EXPIRATION_TIME' |
                      'MODIFICATION_TIME' |
                      'PUBLICATION_TIME' | 'RELEASE_TIME' |
                      'RECEPTION_TIME' | 'NONE'
temporalFunction ::= 'true' | 'false'
%{temporalFunction ::= boolean}
beginPoint ::= IDREF
%{beginPoint ::= TimeID}
endPoint ::= IDREF
%{endPoint ::= TimeID}
quant ::= CDATA
freq ::= CDATA
%value ::= CDATA
value ::= duration | dateTime | time | date | gYearMonth |
          gYear | gMonthDay | gDay | gMonth
valueFromFunction ::= IDREF
%{valueFromFunction ::= TemporalFunctionID
%TemporalFunctionID ::= tf<integer>}
mod ::= 'BEFORE' | 'AFTER' | 'ON_OR_BEFORE' | 'ON_OR_AFTER' |
        'LESS_THAN' | 'MORE_THAN' | 'EQUAL_OR_LESS' |
        'EQUAL_OR_MORE' | 'START' | 'MID' | 'END' | 'APPROX'
anchorTimeID ::= TimeID
```

The optional attribute, functionInDocument, indicates the function of the TIMEX3 in providing a temporal anchor for other temporal expressions in the document. If this attribute is not explicitly supplied, the default value is "NONE". The non-empty values take their names from the temporal metadata tags in the Prism draft standard (available at <http://www.prismstandard.org/>).

The treatment of temporal functions in TimeML allows any time-value dependent algorithms to delay the computation of the actual (ISO) value of the expression. The following informal paraphrase of some examples illustrates this point, where DCT is the Document Creation Time of the article.

1. *last week* = (predecessor (week DCT)): That is, we start with a temporal anchor, in this case, the DCT, coerce it to a week, then find the week preceding it.
2. *last Thursday* = (thursday (predecessor (week DCT))): Similar to the preceding expression, except that we pick out the day named 'thursday' in the predecessor week.
3. *the week before last* = (predecessor (predecessor (week DCT))): Also similar to the first expression, except that we go back two weeks.
4. *next week* = (successor (week DCT)): The dual of the first expression: we start with the same coercion, but go forward instead of back.

SIGNAL is used to annotate sections of text, typically function words, that indicate how temporal objects are to be related to each other. The material marked by SIGNAL constitutes several types of linguistic elements: indicators of temporal relations such as temporal prepositions (e.g. *on*, *during*) and other temporal connectives (e.g. *when*) and subordinators (e.g. *if*). The basic functionality of the SIGNAL tag was introduced by Setzer (2001). In TimeML it has been expanded to also mark indicators of temporal quantification such as *twice*, *three times*, and so forth. The specification for SIGNAL is given below:

```
attributes ::= sid
%sid ::= ID
sid ::= SignalID
%SignalID ::= s<integer>}
```

To illustrate the application of these tags, consider the example annotation shown below.

John left 2 days before the attack.

```
John
<EVENT eid="e1" class="OCCURRENCE">
left
</EVENT>
<MAKEINSTANCE eiid="ei1"
eventID="e1" tense="PAST" aspect="PERFECTIVE"/>
<TIMEX3 tid="t1" type="DURATION" value="P2D"
temporalFunction="false">
2 days
</TIMEX3>
<SIGNAL sid="s1">
before
<SIGNAL>
the
<EVENT
eid="e2" class="OCCURRENCE">
attack
</EVENT>
<MAKEINSTANCE eiid="ei2" eventID="e2"
tense="NONE" aspect="NONE"/>.
```

3   LINKS

One of the major innovations introduced in TimeML is the LINK tag. As mentioned above, the set of LINK tags encode the various relations that exist between the temporal elements of a document, as well as establishing ordering between events directly. There are three types of link tags:

1. **TLINK:** a Temporal Link representing the temporal relationship holding between events or between an event and a time;
2. **SLINK:** a Subordination Link used for contexts introducing relations between two events, or an event and a signal;
3. **ALINK:** an Aspectual Link representing the relationship between an aspectual event and its argument event.

3.1 TLINK

TLINK represents the temporal relationship holding between events or between an event and a time, and establishes a link between the involved entities, making explicit if they are:[2]

1. Simultaneous;
2. Identical (referring to the same event);
   John drove to Boston. During his drive he ate a donut.
3. One before the other;
   John left before Mary arrived.
4. One after the other (cf. 3);
5. One immediately before the other;
   All passengers died when the plane crashed into the mountain.[3]
6. One immediately after the other (cf. 5);
7. One including the other;
   John arrived in Boston last Thursday.
8. One being included in the other (cf. 7);
9. One holding during the duration of the other;
   John was on vacation for two months.
10. One being the beginning of the other;
    John has lived in Boston since 1998.
11. One being begun by the other (cf. 10);
12. One being the ending of the other;
    John stayed in Boston till 1999.
13. One being ended by the other (cf. 12).

The specification for TLINK is given below.

```
attributes ::= [lid] [origin] (eventInstanceID | timeID)
               [signalID]
               (relatedtoEventInstance | relatedtoTime) relType
%lid ::= ID
lid ::= LinkID
%LinkID ::= l<integer>}
origin ::= CDATA
eventInstanceID ::= IDREF
timeID ::= IDREF
signalID ::= IDREF
relatedToEventInstance ::= IDREF
relatedToTime ::= IDREF
relType ::= 'BEFORE' | 'AFTER' | 'INCLUDES' | 'IS_INCLUDED'
            | "DURING" | 'SIMULTANEOUS' | 'IAFTER' | 'IBEFORE' |
            'IDENTITY' | 'BEGINS' | 'ENDS' | 'BEGUN_BY' | 'ENDED_BY'
```

---

[2] See Allen (1984), Allen and Kautz (1985) for motivation.
[3] In terms of causal reasoning, these two events must be ordered rather than simultaneous.

To illustrate the function of this link, let us return to the sentence above, now adding the annotation of the TLINK, which orders the two events mentioned in the sentence.

John left 2 days before the attack.

```
<TLINK eventInstanceID = "ei1" signalID = "s1"
relatedToEventInstance = "ei2" relType = "BEFORE"/>
```

3.2 SLINK

SLINK or Subordination Link is used for contexts introducing relations between two events, or an event and a signal, of the following sort.

1. MODAL: Events that introduce a reference to a possible world; these are mainly I_STATEs.
   a. *Mary wanted John to buy some wine.*
2. FACTIVE: Certain verbs introduce an entailment (or presupposition) of the argument's veracity. They include *forget* in the tensed complement, *regret, manage*.
   a. *John forgot that he was in Boston last year.*
   b. *Mary regrets that she didn't marry John.*
   c. *John managed to leave the party.*
3. COUNTERFACTIVE: The event introduces a presupposition about the non-veracity of its argument: *forget* (to), *unable* to (in past tense), *prevent, cancel, avoid, decline,* etc.
   a. *John forgot to buy some wine.*
   b. *Mary was unable to marry John.*
   c. *John prevented the divorce.*
4. EVIDENTIAL: Evidential relations are introduced by REPORTING or PERCEPTION.
   a. *John said he bought some wine.*
   b. *Mary saw John carrying only beer.*
5. NEGATIVE EVIDENTIAL: Introduced by REPORTING and some PERCEPTION events conveying negative polarity.
   a. *John denied he bought only beer.*

The specification for the SLINK relation is given below:

```
attributes ::= [lid] [origin] [eventInstanceID]
               subordinatedEventInstance [signalID]
               relType
%lid ::= ID
lid ::= LinkID
%LinkID ::= l<integer>}
origin ::= CDATA
eventInstanceID ::= IDREF
subordinatedEventInstance ::= IDREF
signalID ::= IDREF
relType ::= 'MODAL'|'EVIDENTIAL'|'NEG_EVIDENTIAL' |
            'FACTIVE'|'COUNTER_FACTIVE'
```

A modally subordinating predicate such as *want* is typed as introducing a SLINK, as shown below.

    Bill wants to teach on Monday.

```
Bill
<EVENT eid="e1" class="I_STATE">
wants
</EVENT>
<MAKEINSTANCE eiid="ei1"
eventID="e1" tense="PRESENT" aspect="NONE"/>
<SIGNAL sid="s1">
to
</SIGNAL>
<EVENT eid="e2"
class="OCCURRENCE">
teach
</EVENT>
<MAKEINSTANCE eiid="ei2" eventID="e2" tense="NONE"
aspect="NONE"/>
<SIGNAL sid="s2">
on
</SIGNAL>
<TIMEX3 tid="t1" type="DATE"
temporalFunction="true"
value="XXXX-WXX-1">
Monday
</TIMEX3>
<TLINK
eventInstanceID="ei2" relatedToTime="t1"
relType="IS_INCLUDED"/>
<SLINK
eventInstanceID="ei1" signalID="s1"
subordinatedEventInstance="ei2"
relType="MODAL"/>
```

3.3 ALINK

The ALINK or Aspectual Link represents the relationship between an aspectual event and its argument event. Examples of the possible aspectual relations that are encoded are shown below.

1. Initiation:
   John started to read.
2. Culmination:
   John finished assembling the table.
3. Termination:
   John stopped talking.

4. Continuation:
   John kept talking.

```
attributes ::= [lid] [origin] eventInstanceID [signalID]
    relatedToEventInstance relType
%lid ::= ID
lid ::= LinkID
%LinkID ::= l<integer>}
origin ::= CDATA
eventInstanceID ::= IDREF
signalID ::= IDREF
relatedToEventInstance ::= IDREF
relType ::= 'INITIATES' | 'CULMINATES' | 'TERMINATES' | CONTINUES'
```

To illustrate the behavior of ALINKs, notice how the aspectual predicate *begin* is treated as a separate event, independent of the logically modified event; the "phase" is introduced as the relation within the ALINK.

   The boat began to sink.

```
The boat
<EVENT eid="e1" class="ASPECTUAL">
began
</EVENT>
<MAKEINSTANCE eiid="ei1" eventID="e1" tense="PAST"
aspect="NONE"/>
<SIGNAL sid="s1">
to
</SIGNAL>
<EVENT eid="e2" class="OCCURRENCE">
sink
</EVENT>
<MAKEINSTANCE eiid="ei2" eventID="e2" "tense="NONE"
aspect="NONE"/>
<ALINK eventInstanceID="ei1" signalID="s1"
relatedToEventInstance="ei2" relType="INITIATES"/>
```

4 EVENTS AND CAUSATION IN TimeML

Event causation involves more than proximate (or related) temporal precedence of events. However, for a significant number of cases in text, the axioms associated with temporal ordering together with information linked to specific lexical items is sufficient for deriving causal-like inferences between events.

Causative predicates raise issues as to whether the event signaled by the causative is genuinely distinct from the event which may be the causative's logical subject. For example, in

   The rains caused the flooding.

is the *cause* event distinct from the *rain* event for annotation purposes? We have identified three distinct cases of event causal relations that must be identified in texts:

1. EVENT cause EVENT
    The [**rains**] [**caused**] *the* [**flooding**].
2. ENTITY cause EVENT
    John [**caused**] *the* [**fire**].
3. EVENT Discourse marker EVENT
    He [**kicked**] *the ball, and it* [**rose**] *into the air.*

In the current specification, we adopt the following treatment for explicit causative predicates in TimeML. For Case (1) above, we treat the causal predicate as denoting a separate event, which is identified as identical to the initial event in the logical subject position. A second TLINK establishes the precedence relation between this event and the "caused" event in object position. This is illustrated below.

The rains caused the flooding.

```
The
<EVENT eid="e1" class="OCCURRENCE">
rains
</EVENT>
<MAKEINSTANCE eiid="ei1"
eventID="e1" tense="NONE" aspect="NONE"/>
<EVENT eid="e2" class="OCCURRENCE">
caused
</EVENT>
<MAKEINSTANCE
eiid="ei2" eventID="e2" tense="PAST" aspect="NONE"/>
the
<EVENT eid="e3" class="OCCURRENCE">
flooding
</EVENT>
<MAKEINSTANCE eiid="ei3" eventID="e3"
tense="NONE" aspect="NONE"/>
<TLINK eventInstanceID="ei1" relatedToEventInstance="ei2"
relType="IDENTITY"/>
<TLINK eventInstanceID="ei2"
relatedToEventInstance="ei3" relType="BEFORE"/>
```

For Case (2) above, there is no explicit event in subject position, hence the causal predicate alone will be temporally ordered relative to the object event, thereby obviating an "event metonymy" interpretation of the sentence (Pustejovsky, 1993).

Kissinger secured the peace at great cost.

```
Kissinger
<EVENT eid="e1" class="OCCURRENCE">
secured
</EVENT>
```

```
<MAKEINSTANCE
eiid="ei1" eventID="e1" tense="PAST" aspect="NONE"/>
the
<EVENT eid="e2"
class="OCCURRENCE">
peace
</EVENT>
<MAKEINSTANCE eiid="ei2" eventID="e2"
tense="NONE" aspect="NONE"/>
at great cost.
<TLINK eventInstanceID="ei1"
relatedToEventInstance="ei2"
relType="BEFORE"/>
```

Both solutions are adopted for verbs such as the following, in their causative senses: *cause, stem from, lead to, breed, engender, hatch, induce, occasion, produce, bring about, secure*.

For Case (3) above, the annotation can optionally identify the discourse marker *and* as a signal for a TLINK introducing the `relType` BEFORE (and hence the reading of causation).

5 CONCLUSION AND FUTURE DEVELOPMENTS

In this paper, we have reported on work done towards establishing a broad and open standard metadata mark-up language for natural language texts, examining events and temporal expressions. What is novel in this language, TimeML, we believe, is the integration of three efforts in the semantic annotation of text: TimeML systematically anchors event predicates to a broad range of temporally denoting expressions; it provides a language for ordering event expressions in text relative to one another, both intrasententially and in discourse; and it provides a semantics for underspecified temporal expressions, thereby allowing for a delayed interpretation. Most of the details of this last component of TimeML have, unfortunately, not been discussed in this paper.

Significant efforts have been launched to annotate the temporal information in large textual corpora, according to the specification of TimeML described above. The result is a gold standard corpus of 300 articles, known as TIMEBANK, which has been completed and will be released early in 2004 for general use. We are also working towards integrating TimeML with the DAML-Time language (Hobbs, 2002), for providing an explicit interpretation of the mark-up described in this paper. It is hoped that this effort will provide a platform on which to build a multilingual, multidomain standard for the representation of events and temporal expressions. We are currently working on a semantics for TimeML expressions and their compositional properties as seen in the LINK relations. This will be reported in Pustejovsky and Gaizauskas (2004). Further information may be found at <http://www.timeml.org>.

ACKNOWLEDGEMENTS

The authors would like to thank the other members of the TERQAS and TANGO Working Groups on TimeML for their contribution to the specification language presented here: Antonio Sanfilippo, Jerry Hobbs, Beth Sundheim, and Andy Latto, as well as Andrew See, Patrick Hanks, and Bob Knippen. This work was performed in support of the Northeast Regional Research Center (NRRC), which is sponsored by the Advanced Research and Development Activity in Information Technology (ARDA), a U.S. Government entity which sponsors and promotes research of import to the Intelligence Community, which includes but is not limited to the CIA, DIA, NSA, NIMA, and NRO. It was also funded in part by the Defense Advanced Research Projects Agency as part of the DAML program under Air Force Research Laboratory contract F30602-00-C-0168.

REFERENCES

Allen, J. F. (1984). 'Towards a general theory of action and time', *Artificial Intelligence* 23: 123–54.
—— and Ferguson, G. (1997). 'Actions and events in interval temporal logic', in Oliveiro Stock (ed.), *Spatial and Temporal Reasoning*. Dordrecht: Kluwer Academic Publishers, 205–45.
—— and Hayes, P. J. (1989). 'Moments and points in an interval-based temporal logic', *Computational Intelligence* 5: 225–38.
—— and Kautz, Henry A. (1985). 'A Model of Naive Temporal Reasoning', in Jerry R. Hobbs and Robert C. Moore (eds.), *Formal Theories of the Commonsense World*. Norwood, NJ: Ablex Publishing Corp., 251–68.
Chinchor, Nancy, Brown, Erica, Ferro, Lisa, and Robinson, Patty (1999). 'Named Entity Recognition Task Definition, version 1.4'. MITRE Technical Report.
Ferro, Lisa, Mani, Inderjeet, Sundheim, Beth, and Wilson, George (2001). 'TIDES Temporal Annotation Guidelines. Version 1.0.2'. MITRE Technical Report, MTR 01W0000041.
Filatova, Elena and Hovy, Eduard (2001). 'Assigning Time-Stamps To Event-Clauses', in *Proceedings of the ACL-2001 Workshop on Temporal and Spatial Information Processing*, ACL-2001. Toulouse, France, 6–11 July, 88–95.
Gaizauskas, Robert and Setzer, Andrea (eds.) (2002). *Annotation Standards for Temporal Information in Natural Language*, LREC 2002.
Hobbs, Jerry (2002). 'An Ontology of Time', available at DAML Website, <http://www.cs.rochester.edu/~ferguson/daml/>.
Ingria, Robert and Pustejovsky, James (2002). 'TimeML Specification 1.0', available at <http://time2002.org>.
McDermott, Drew, Borden, Jonathan, Burstein, Mark, Smith, Doug, and Waldinger, Richard (2001). 'A Proposal for Encoding Logic in RDF/DAML', available at <http://www.cs.yale.edu/homes/dvm/daml/>.
Mani, Inderjeet and Wilson, George (2000). 'Robust Temporal Processing of News', *Proceedings of the ACL'2000 Conference*, 3–6 October 2000, Hong Kong, 69–76.
Pustejovsky, J. (1993). 'Type Coercion and Lexical Selection', in J. Pustejovsky (ed.), *Semantics and the Lexicon*. Dordrecht: Kluwer Academic Publishers.
Pustejovsky, James, Gaizauskas, Robert, Sauri, Roser, Setzer, Andrea, and Ingria, Robert (2002). 'Annotation Guideline to TimeML 1.0', available at <http://timeml.org>.
Pustejovsky, James and Gaizauskas, Robert (2004). *Time and Event Recognition in Natural Language*. Amsterdam: John Benjamins Publishers.
Schilder, Frank and Habel, Christopher (2001). 'From Temporal Expressions To Temporal Information: Semantic Tagging Of News Messages' in *Proceedings of the ACL-2001 Workshop on Temporal and Spatial Information Processing*, ACL-2001. Toulouse, France, 6–11 July, 65–72.
Setzer, Andrea (2001). 'Temporal Information in Newswire Articles: an Annotation Scheme and Corpus Study', Ph.D. dissertation, University of Sheffield.

A Model for Processing Temporal References in Chinese

WENJIE LI, KAM-FAI WONG, AND CHUNFA YUAN

1 INTRODUCTION

Information Extraction (IE) is an upcoming challenging research area to cope with the increasing volume of unwieldy, distributed information resources, such as information over WWW. Among them, temporal information is important in domains where the task of extracting and tracking information over time occurs frequently, such as planning, scheduling, and question-answering. It may be as simple as an explicit or direct expression in a written language, such as "the company closed down in May, 1997"; or it may be left implicit, to be recovered by readers from the surrounding texts. For example, one may know the fact that "the company closed down before an earthquake", yet without knowing the exact time of the bankruptcy. Relative temporal knowledge such as this, where the precise time is unavailable, is typically determined by a human. An information system which does not account for this properly is thus rather restrictive.

It is hard to separate temporal information discovery (in particular this refers to temporal relations in this paper) from natural language processing. In English, tenses and aspects reflected by different verb forms are important elements in a sentence for expressing temporal reference (Steedman, 1997) and for transforming situations into temporal logic operators (Bruce, 1972). The pioneering work of Reichenbach (Reichenbach, 1947) on tenses forms the basis of many subsequent research efforts in temporal natural language processing, e.g. the work of Prior in tense logic (Prior, 1967), and of Hwang et al. in tense-tree (Hwang, 1992) and temporal adverbial analysis (Hwang, 1994), etc. Reichenbach argued that the tense system provided predication over three underlying times, namely S (speech time), R (reference time), and E (event time). Later, a multiple temporal references model was introduced by Bruce (Bruce, 1972). He defined the set $(S_1, S_2, \ldots, S_n)$, which is an element of a tense. S_1 corresponds to the time of speech. Each S_i ($i=2, \ldots, n-1$) is a time of reference, and S_n, the time of an event. To facilitate logic manipulation, Bruce proposed seven first-order logic relations based on time intervals and a method to map nine English tenses into temporal first-order logic expressions[1]. His work laid down the foundation of temporal logic in

---

Wenjie Li, Kam-Fai Wong, and Chunfa Yuan, 'A Model for Processing Temporal References in Chinese', *Proceedings of the ACL-2001 Workshop on Temporal and Spatial Information Processing*, 39² Annual Meeting of the ACL (ACL '2001), Toulouse, 2001, 33–40. © 2001 Association for Computational Linguistics.

[1] The seven relations are symbolized as $R(A, B)$ for relation R and time intervals A and B, where R includes *before, after, during, contains, same-time, overlaps,* or *overlapped-by*.

natural language. These relations were then gradually expanded to nine in (Allen, 1981) and further to thirteen in (Allen, 1983)[2].

In contrast, Chinese verbs appear in only one form. The lack of regular morphological tense markers renders Chinese temporal expressions complicated. For quite a long time, linguists argued whether tenses existed in Chinese; and if they did how are they expressed. We believe that Chinese does have tenses. But they are determined with the assistance of temporal adverbs and aspect auxiliary words. For example, 在...呢 (*being*), 已经...了 (*was/been*) and 要...(*will be*) express an ongoing action, a situation started or finished in the past, and a situation which will occur in the future, respectively. Therefore, the conventional theory to determine temporal information based on verb affixation is inapplicable. Over the past years, there has been considerable progress in the areas of information extraction and temporal logic in English (Galton, 1987; Bruce, 1972; MUC-6, 1997). Nevertheless, only a few researchers have investigated these areas in Chinese.

The objective of our research is to design and develop a temporal information extraction system. For practical and cultural reasons, the application target is on-line financial news in Chinese. The final system, referred to as *TICS* (Temporal Information-extraction from Chinese Sources), will accept a series of Chinese financial texts as input, analyze each sentence one by one to extract the desired temporal information, represent each piece of information in a concept frame, link all frames together in chronological order based on inter- or intra-event relations, and finally apply this linked knowledge to fulfill users' queries.

In this paper, we introduce a fundamental model of *TICS*, which is designed to mine and organize temporal relations embedded in Chinese sentences. Three kinds of event expressions are accounted for, i.e. single event, multiple events, and declared event(s). This work involved four major parts, (1) build temporal model; (2) construct rules sets; (3) develop the algorithm; and (4) set up the experiments and perform the evaluation.

2   A MODEL FOR TEMPORAL RELATION DISCOVERY

2.1   Temporal Concept Frame

In IE, it is impossible as well as impractical to extract all the information from an incoming document. For this reason, all IE systems are geared for specific application domains. The domain is determined by a pre-specified concept dictionary. Then a certain concept is triggered by several lexical items and activated in the specific linguistic contexts. Each concept definition contains a set of slots for the extracted information. In addition, it contains a set of enabling conditions which are constraints that must be satisfied in order for the concept to be activated. Due to its versatility, a frame structure is generally used to represent concepts (as shown in Figure 1).

Slots in a temporal concept frame are divided into two types: activity-related and time-related. Activity-related slots provide the descriptions of objects and actions concerning the concept. For example, *company predator*, *company target*, and *purchase value* are the attributes of the concept (收购, *TAKEOVER*). Meanwhile, time-related slots provide information related to when a concept begins or finishes, how long it lasts, and how it relates to another concept, etc.

---

[2] *meet, met-by, starts, started-by, finishes* and *finished-by* are added into temporal relations.

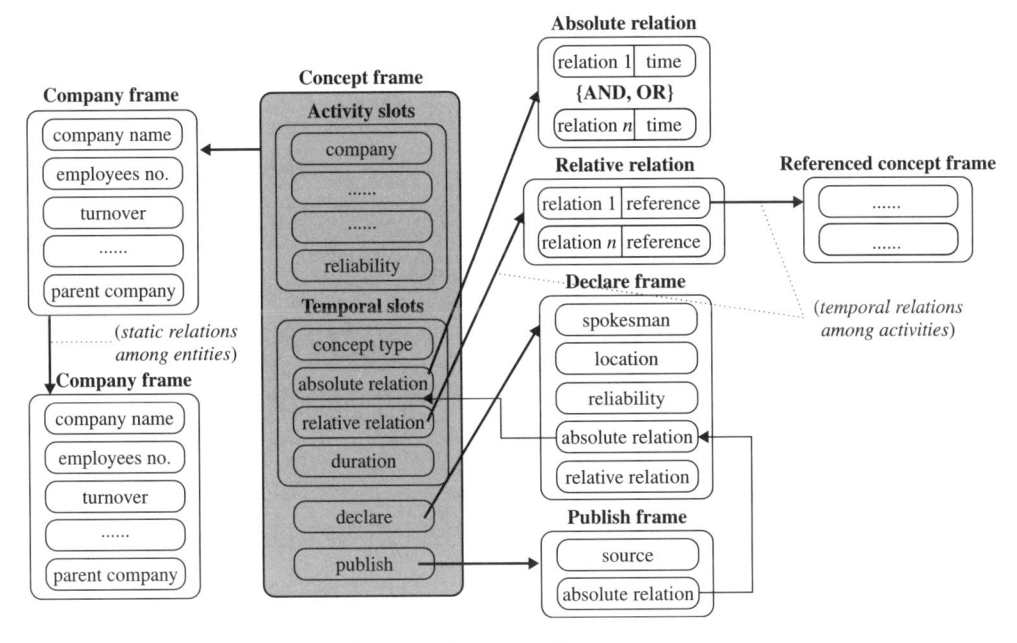

FIG. 1 Temporal concept frame construction.

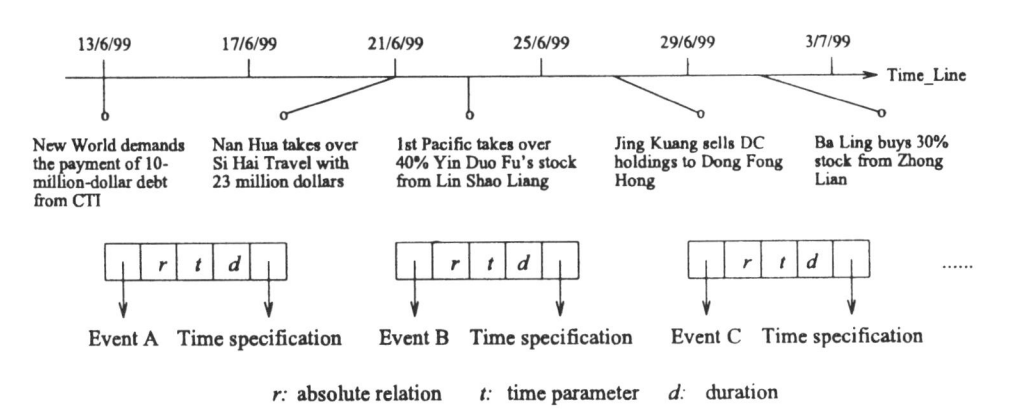

FIG. 2 The *Time_Line* organization for absolute relations in *TICS*.

2.2 Temporal Relations

The system is designed with two sets of temporal relations, namely *absolute* and *relative* relations. The role of absolute temporal relations is to position situation occurrences on a time axis. These relations depict the beginning and/or ending time bounds of an occurrence or its relevance to reference times, see $TR(T)$ in Section 2.3. Absolute relations are organized by *Time_Line* in the system; see Figure 2.

In many cases, the time when an event takes place may not be known. But its relevance to another occurrence time is given. Relative temporal knowledge such as this is manifested by relative relations. Allen has proposed thirteen relations. The same

562   *The Language of Time: A Reader*

FIG. 3   The *Relational_Chain* organization for relative relations in *TICS*.

is adopted in our system, see $TR(E_i, E_j)$ in Section 2.3. The relative relations are derived either directly from a sentence describing two situations, or indirectly from the absolute relations of two individual situations. They are organized by *Relational_Chains*, as shown in Figure 3.

2.3   Temporal Model

This section describes our temporal model for discovering relations from Chinese sentences. Suppose *TR* indicates a temporal relation, *E* indicates an event, and *T* indicates time. The absolute and relative relations are symbolized as: $OCCUR(E_i, TR(T))$[3] and $TR(E_i, E_j)$, respectively. The sets of *TR* are:

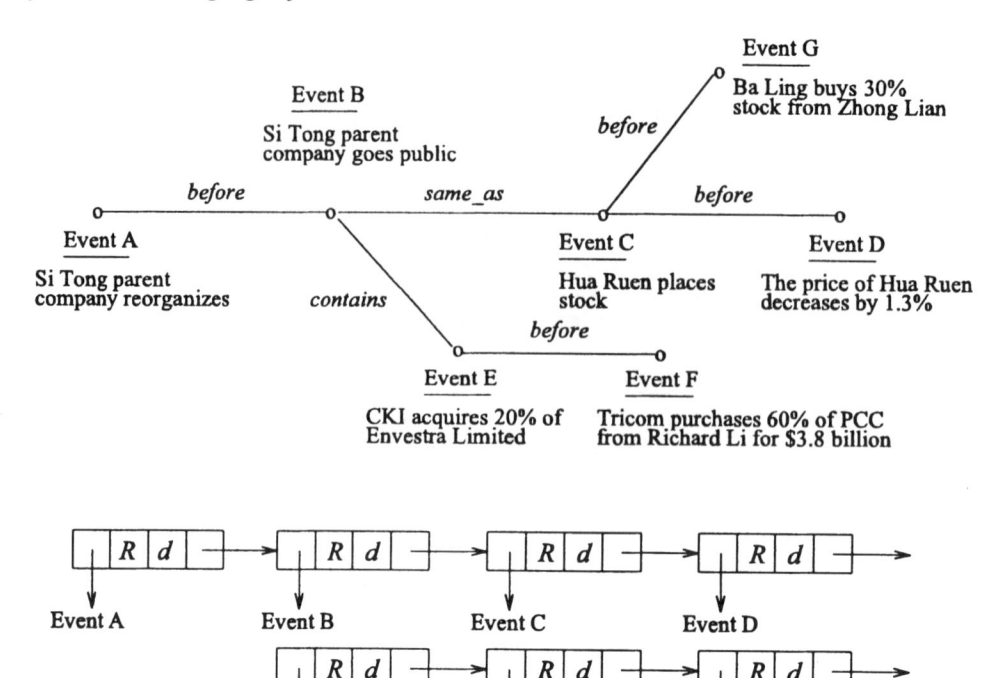

$TR(T) = \{ON, BEGIN, END, PAST, FUTURE, ONGOING, CONTINUED\}$

$TR(E_i, E_j) = \{BEFORE, AFTER, MEETS, METBY, OVERLAPS, OVERLAPPED,$
    $DURING, CONTAINS, STARTEDBY, STARTS, FINISHES, FINISHEDBY,$
    $SAME\_AS\}$

---
[3] *OCCUR* is a predicate for the happening of a single event. Under situations where there is no ambiguity, E_i can be omitted. $OCCUR(E_i, TR(T))$, is simplified as $TR(T)$.

A Model for Processing Temporal References in Chinese   563

For an absolute relation of a single event, T is an indispensable parameter, which includes event time t_e, reference time t_r[4] and speech time t_s:

$$T = \{t_e, t_r, t_s\}$$

Some Chinese words can function as temporal indicators. These include time words (TW), time position words (F), temporal adverbs (ADV), auxiliary words (AUX), preposition words (P), auxiliary verbs (VA), trend verbs (VC), and some special verbs (VV). They are all regarded as the elements of the set of temporal indicators TI:

$$TI = \{TW, F, ADV, AUX, VA, VC, VV, P\}$$

Each type of indicator, e.g. TW, contains a set of words, such as $TW = twlist = \{tw_1, tw_2, \ldots tw_n\}$, with each word having a temporal attribute, indicated by ATT.

The core of the model is thus a rule set R which maps the combined effects of all the indicators, TI, in a sentence to its corresponding temporal relation, TR,

$$R: TI \rightarrow \begin{cases} TR(T) \\ TR(E_i, E_j) \end{cases}$$

Regarding temporal relations, the language has three basic forms in representation:

- Single event statement: in which only one single event is stated.
- Multiple events statement: in which two or more events are stated.
- Declaration statement: in which the event(s) are declared by a person or an organization.

3 RULE CONSTRUCTION

3.1 General Rules for Temporal References (GR)

Some general temporal characteristics, approximations and assumptions are examined to understand and uncover the hidden reference times, or to refine the identified solutions in order to make them more natural. For example, $PAST$ (报道日期, *reporting date*) is probably better than ON (日前 *a few days ago*). Or, when no explicit reference time is given, the default value of T, i.e. the "reporting date" (thereafter referred to as RD), would be assumed. It must be noted that the rules given below are not for the immediate use of extracting TR. But they are necessary to design the $TICS$ program.

1. **$TR(T)$ (single event) supports the following rules**:

   (1) Approximation:
   $ON(t_e) \oplus (ATT(T) = \text{"present"}) \Rightarrow ON(\text{RD})$
   $ON(t_e) \oplus (ATT(T) = \text{"past"}) \Rightarrow PAST(\text{RD})$
   $ON(t_e) \oplus (ATT(T) = \text{"future"}) \Rightarrow FUTURE(\text{RD})$
   $PAST(t_r) \oplus (ATT(T) = \text{"past"}) \Rightarrow PAST(\text{RD})$
   $FUTURE(t_r) \oplus (ATT(T) = \text{"future"}) \Rightarrow FUTURE(\text{RD})$
   $TR(t_r) \oplus (ATT(T) = \text{"present"}) \Rightarrow TR(\text{RD})$
   $TR(?) \Rightarrow TR(\text{RD})$

---

[4] There maybe exist more than one reference time in a statement.

(2) Negation:
$\neg END(t_r) \Rightarrow CONTINUED(t_r)$
$\neg BEGIN(t_r) \Rightarrow FUTURE(t_r)$
$\neg PAST(t_r) \Rightarrow FUTURE(t_r)$
$\neg FUTURE(t_r) \Rightarrow FUTURE(t_r)$

2. $TR(E_i, E_j)$ (**multiple events**) **supports the following rules**:

(3) Symmetry:
$BEFORE(E_i, E_j) \equiv AFTER(E_j, E_i)$
$CONTAINS(E_i, E_j) \equiv DURING(E_j, E_i)$
$OVERLAPS(E_i, E_j) \equiv OVERLAPPED(E_j, E_i)$
$STARTS(E_i, E_j) \equiv STARTEDBY(E_j, E_i)$
$FINISHES(E_i, E_j) \equiv FINISHEDBY(E_j, E_i)$
$SAME\_AS(E_i, E_j) \equiv SAME\_AS(E_j, E_i)$

3. $TR_s(T)$ and $TR_e(T)$ (**declared event**) **supports the following rules**:

(4) $TR_s(t_s) \oplus TR_e(t_r) \Rightarrow TR_e(t_s)$:
$ON(t_s) \oplus TR(?) \Rightarrow TR(t_s)$
$ON(t_s) \oplus ?(?) \Rightarrow ON(t_s)$

(5) $TR_s(t_r) \oplus TR_e(t_r) \Rightarrow TR_e(t_r)$:
$PAST(?) \oplus PAST(?) \Rightarrow PAST(RD)$
$?(?) \oplus TR(?) \Rightarrow TR(RD)$
$?(?) \oplus ?(?) \Rightarrow PAST(RD)$

3.2 Impact Coefficients of Temporal Indicators (Ro)

The combined effect of all the temporal indicators in a sentence determines its temporal relation. However, in different situations, a certain indicator may have different effects. Compare (a) 他看了今天的报纸 (*He read today's newspaper*) and (b) 昨天我读了两本书 (*I read two books yesterday*). The two sentences are alike as they both embody an indicator 了, which implies *PAST* in principle. The sole difference is that a definite time is present in (b). (a) means the reading is finished at the speech time and the person must have known some news or information from his reading. Thus $TR = PAST(t_s)$ for (a). However, (b) means the event took place yesterday but not before yesterday. Consequently, for (b), $TR = ON$ (昨天, *yesterday*) is appropriate. In the database, the impact coefficients are defined for the temporal indicators when T does or does not present in the sentence.

Remark:
It is likely for a sentence to contain two or more indicators. For example, the adverb 已经 and the aspectual auxiliary word 了 together express a past tense and they both share the same reference time t_r. The same kind of instances include 将...要 (*will*) and 正...着 (*being*), etc. Another example, such as 国庆 前 已经 (*before the National Day, one has already*), however includes two reference times. Here, 国庆 (*National Day*) is t_r, location word 前 (*before*) indicates *PAST* between t_r and t'_r (i.e. $t'_r < t_r$), and adverb 已经 indicates the same relativity but between t_e and t'_r (i.e. $t_e < t'_r$).

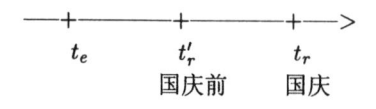

```
—+————+————+—>
 $t_e$    $t'_r$    $t_r$
         国庆前    国庆
```

TABLE 1 Rule set R1 for single event statements

$PAST(t_s) \oplus BEGIN(t_r) \Rightarrow CONTINUED(t_s)$
$PAST(t_s) \oplus END(t_r) \Rightarrow PAST(t_s)$
$PAST(t_s) \oplus FUTURE(t_r) \Rightarrow FUTURE(t_s)$
$PAST(t_s) \oplus ONGOING(t_r) \Rightarrow CONTINUED(t_s)$
$PAST(t_s) \oplus CONTINUED(t_r) \Rightarrow CONTINUED(t_s)$
$FUTURE(t_s) \oplus BEGIN(t_r) \Rightarrow FUTURE(t_s)$
$FUTURE(t_s) \oplus END(t_r) \Rightarrow CONTINUED(t_s)$
$FUTURE(t_s) \oplus PAST(t_r) \Rightarrow FUTURE(t_s)$
$FUTURE(t_s) \oplus ONGOING(t_r) \Rightarrow FUTURE(t_s)$
$FUTURE(t_s) \oplus CONTINUED(t_r) \Rightarrow CONTINUED(t_s)$

The current proposed algorithm is unable to mine the implicit reference time (i.e. t'_r). But this does not affect the work at all. It does not matter even if we cannot discover a relation like $PAST(t'_r)$. As we know $t'_r < t_r$ and $t_e < t'_r$, we can deduce a conclusion such as $t_e < t_r$ by rule $PAST(t'_r) \oplus PAST(t_r) \Rightarrow PAST(t_r)$ (for t_e). Thus, for this example, a relation of $PAST$ (国庆, National Day) is enough to provide sufficient information to the users. To cater for these cases, we define a general rule: if all the indicators in a sentence indicate the same relation, then it is identified as TR (hereafter this rule together with impact coefficients is referred to as R0).

3.3 Rules for resolving conflicts (R1)

In many situations, the indicators in a sentence may introduce more than one relation. For example, adverbs 已经 (*have already*) and 在 (*being*) indicate $PAST$ and $ONGOING$, respectively. But they could be collocated to represent some event which began in the past and continued to the reference time. For example 他 已经 在 看报 (*He has been reading newspaper*). Such a problem is regarded as conflict. In the following, five cases are illustrated with examples. To resolve this conflict, a set of rules are defined in Table 1 (R1).

Case I: t_e to t_r and t_r to t_s (t_r is unknown)
深信 证券 市场 (adv仍) (va会) (v是) 香港 经济 发展 的 主要 动力。
(*believe stock market still can be HK economy development of major motivation.*)
(*They believed that the stock market will still be the major motivation for the development of the HK economy.*)

$TR = CONTINUED$ (二千年), $T = t_s$

```
                    t_e
                  ─────
      ────+────────+────>
         t_s      t_r
```

(仍) → $CONTINUED$ (t_e is continued in t_r)
(会) → $FUTURE$ (t_r is future for t_s)
$FUTURE(t_s) \oplus CONTINUED(t_r)$
$\Rightarrow CONTINUED(t_s)$[5]

---
[5] See the last rule in Table 1

TABLE 2 Rule set R2 for two event statements

$(ATT(F) = "ON") \oplus (TR(E_2) = "PAST") \Rightarrow (TR(E_1, E_2) = "BEFORE")$
$(ATT(F) = "ON") \oplus (TR(E_2) = "CONTINUED") \Rightarrow (TR(E_1, E_2) = "CONTAINS")$
$(ATT(F) = "ON") \oplus (TR(E_2) = "FUTURE") \Rightarrow (TR(E_1, E_2) = "DURING")$
$(ATT(F) = "ON") \oplus (TR(E_2) = "ONGOING") \Rightarrow (TR(E_1, E_2) = "CONTAINS")$
$(ATT(F) = "ON") \oplus (TR(E_2) = "BEGIN") \Rightarrow (TR(E_1, E_2) = "STARTED\ BY")$
$(ATT(F) = "FUTURE") \oplus (TR(E_2) = "PAST") \Rightarrow (TR(E_1, E_2) = "AFTER")$
$(ATT(F) = "FUTURE") \oplus (TR(E_2) = "FUTURE") \Rightarrow (TR(E_1, E_2) = "AFTER")$
$(ATT(F) = "FUTURE") \oplus (TR(E_2) = "ONGOING") \Rightarrow (TR(E_1, E_2) = "AFTER")$
$(ATT(F) = "FUTURE") \oplus (TR(E_2) = "BEGIN") \Rightarrow (TR(E_1, E_2) = "AFTER")$
$(ATT(F) = "FUTURE") \oplus (TR(E_2) = "CONTINUED") \Rightarrow$
  $(TR(E_1, E_2) = "CONTAINS")$
$(ATT(F) = "PAST") \oplus (TR(E_2) = "PAST") \Rightarrow (TR(E_1, E_2) = "BEFORE")$
$(ATT(F) = "PAST") \oplus (TR(E_2) = "FUTURE") \Rightarrow (TR(E_1, E_2) = "BEFORE")$
$(ATT(F) = "PAST") \oplus (TR(E_2) = "CONTINUED") \Rightarrow (TR(E_1, E_2) = "BEFORE")$

TABLE 3 Templates in rule set R3

Templates	Relations
V1 + 了 + V2	AFTER
一 + V1 + 就 + V2	AFTER
V1 + (的)同时 + V2	SAME_AS
V1 + 着 + V2	SAME_AS
(一)边 + V1 + (一)边 + V2	SAME_AS

A Special Situation of Case I: t_e to t_r and t'_r to t_r (t_r is given)
基本上 (p在) (t二千年) (f后), 香港 在 国际 金融界 (adv仍) (va会) (v占)一席位$_r$,
(*Basically in 2000 after HK in international financial sector still can occupy a seat,*)
(*Basically, HK will continue to be important in the world global financial sector after 2000,*)
$TR = CONTINUED(二千年), T = t_r$

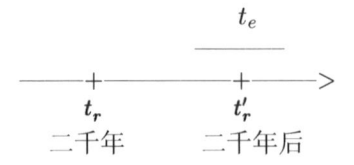

```
                    t_e
                ─────────
    ───────+───────────+──────>
           t_r          t'_r
          二千年       二千年后
```

(仍) → $CONTINUED$ (t_e is continued in t'_r)
(后) ... (会) → $FUTURE$ (t'_r is future for t_r)
$FUTURE(t_r) \oplus CONTINUED(t'_r)$
$\Rightarrow CONTINUED(t_r)^6$

Case II: t_e to t_r and t_s (t_r is given)
(t八七年) (f以后) 市场 (adv已) (v打下) 良好 基础
(*1987 after market have lay good foundation,*)
(*It has laid a good foundation for the market after 1987,*)

---

[6] See the last rule in Table 1. To fit for this case, t_s is replaced with t_r and t_r is replaced with t'_r in the rule.

TR = *FUTURE* (八七年) and *PAST*(报道日期)

```
——+————+————+——>
   $t_r$     $t_e$     $t_s$
  八七年  八七年以后  报道日期
```

(以后) → *FUTURE* (t_e is future for t_r)
(已) → *PAST*   (t_e is past for t_s)
$FUTURE(t_r) \oplus PAST(t_s) \Rightarrow FUTURE(t_r)$[7]

Case III: Composition of Cases I and II

t_e to t_r and t_s, t_r to t_s (t_r is unknown)
但 他 (vs估计)， (p在) (d两个月) (f内) (adv已) (va可) (v落实),
(*But he estimate, in two months within have can secure,*)
(*But he estimated that it would be secured within two months,*)

TR = *FUTURE*(报导日期) and PAST(报导日期+两个月), t_s = 报导日期

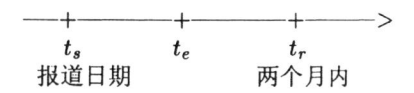

```
——+————+————+——>
   $t_s$    $t_e$    $t_r$
 报道日期          两个月内
```

(在) (两个月) (内) → *FUTURE*   (t_r is future for t_s)
(已) → *PAST*   (t_e is past for t_r)
(可) → *FUTURE*   (t_e is future for t_s)
$FUTURE(t_s) \oplus PAST(t_r) \Rightarrow FUTURE(t_s)$

Case IV: t_e to t_s and t'_r, t'_r to t_r (t_r is given)

但 他 (vs估计)， (t十二月) (f前) (adv已) (va可) (v落实),
(*But he estimate, December before have can secure,*)
(*But he estimated that it would be secured before December,*)

TR = *PAST*(十二月) and *FUTURE*(报道日期), t_s = 报导日期

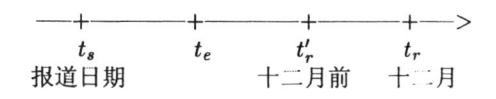

```
——+————+————+————+——>
   $t_s$    $t_e$   $t'_r$   $t_r$
 报道日期         十二月前  十二月
```

(前); → *FUTURE*   (t'_r is past for t_r)
(已) → *PAST*   (t_e is past for t'_r)
(可) → *FUTURE*   (t_e is future for t_s)
$PAST(t_r) \oplus PAST(t'_r) \Rightarrow PAST(t_r)$ (see Ro)

Case V: Multiple implicit reference times

保险业，尤其 是 一般 保险业务，(adv已经) (va要) (vv开始) (v受到) 亚洲 金融 风暴 的 影响。
(*insurance business, especially is general insurance, have will begin be Asian financial crisis of influence.*)
(*The insurance business, especially general insurance, has been affected by the Asian financial crisis.*)

---

[7] See the eighth rule in Table 1. For those rules in Table 1, the parameters t_r and t_s are changeable.

$TR = FUTURE(十二月)$

```
                  t_e
                  +———
——+—————————+———————+——>
  t_r        t'_r   t_s
                    报道日期
```

(已经) → $PAST$ (t_r is past for t_s)
(要) → $FUTURE$ (t'_r is future for t_r)
(开始) → $BEGIN$ (t_e is begin for t'_r)
$PAST(t_s) \oplus FUTURE(t_r) \Rightarrow FUTURE(t_s)$
$FUTURE(t_s) \oplus BEGIN(t'_r) \Rightarrow FUTURE(t_s)$

3.4 Rules for discovering the relevance of two events (R2 & R3)

To express two relevant events is straightforward. In general, one of them is treated as the reference event, say E_1, which is expressed by the subordinate clause. Another one, say E_2, i.e. the event concerned, is expressed by the main clause. The position words (F), such as 前 (*before*) and 后 (*after*), and some special nouns, such as 时候 (*when*) and 期间 (*during*) between the two event expressions play an important role in determining their relevance in time. Also, it is noticed that the impact of $TR(E_2)$ cannot be ignored. Practically, $TR(E_2)$ relates E_2 to t_s or E_1. Especially for the latter, the influence of $TR(E_2)$ is indispensable. The rules for this are defined in the rule set R2. In addition, some special templates are also necessary for relating two events, which are defined in the rule set R3, when F is absent.

4 ALGORITHM DESCRIPTION

BEGIN:
input temporal statements;
(1) for a single event statement:
   IF t_e is found in a temporal statement, let $T = t_e$; ELSE let $T = t_s =$ "报道日期" (reporting date, i.e. the default value);
   ENDIF;
   DETERMINE(TR):
   IF $\cap_{ATT(TI_i) \neq \phi} ATT(TI_i) = \psi \neq \phi$, return $TR = \psi$;
   ELSEIF $\cup ATT(TI_i) = \phi$,
     IF $T = t_e$, return $TR =$ "ON";
     ELSE return $TR =$ "PAST" (default value);
     ENDIF;
   ELSE check rule set R1;
     IF TR is found, return TR;
     ELSE return $TR = \phi$;
     ENDIF;
   ENDIF;
   go to END.

(2) for a declaration statement:
   IF t_e is found for v, let $T=t_e$;
   ELSE let $T=t_r$;
   ENDIF;
   IF t_s is found for s, let $t_r=t_s$;
   ELSE let $t_r=t_s=$ "报道日期"(reporting date, i.e. the default value);
   ENDIF;
   do DETERMINE(TR) (for the declared event).
(3) for a multiple event statement or a declared multiple event statement:
   IF f is found in a temporal statement, find $ATT(F)$ and $TR^{(E2)}$, then check rule set $R2$;
      IF TR is found, return TR;
      ELSE return $TR=\phi$;
      ENDIF;
   ELSE check $R3$;
      IF TR is found, return TR;
      ELSE return $TR=$ "BEFORE" (default value);
      ENDIF;
   ENDIF;
   IF one of the events contains time definition (i.e. t), do (1);
   ELSE go to END;
   ENDIF.
END.

5 EXPERIMENT SETUP AND ERROR ANALYSIS

943K bytes of test data are collected from one month of financial pages of 《大公报》 (*Ta Kung Bao*). In total, 7,429 temporal relations are discovered from the data. The distribution of temporal relations in test data is shown in Table 4. Considering the ultimate objective of this research is to find the temporal relations embedded in sentences, the focus of the evaluation is therefore to figure out the number of the temporal relations of single event (i.e. $TR(E)$) and of multiple events (i.e. $TR(E_i, E_j)$),

TABLE 4 Temporal expressions in the test data

	Straight	
	Single event	Multiple events
Number	5,235	603
Percentage	70.47%	8.12%

	Declared	
	Single event	Multiple events
Number	1,507	84
Percentage	20.29%	1.13%

570   *The Language of Time: A Reader*

TABLE 5   Experimental results of temporal relation discovery

TR	No.	Corr. Mark	Accu.
$TR(T)$	6,742	6,249	92.69%
$TR(E_i, E_j)$	687	643	93.60%
Overall	7,429	6,892	92.77%

TABLE 6   *TR* classified by the program in descending order

	Pattern	Number	Percentage
1	ON	2,087	28.09%
2	FUTURE	1,728	23.26%
3	PAST	1,441	19.40%
4	CONTINUED	975	13.12%
5	AFTER	387	5.21%
6	ONGOING	299	4.02%
7	BEGIN	139	1.87%
8	DURING	128	1.73%
9	BEFORE	69	0.93%
10	BEGIN&END	66	0.89%
11	SAME_AS	59	0.79%
12	CONTAINS	41	0.55%
13	END	7	0.09%
14	STARTEDBY	3	0.04%

which are correctly marked by the program. Table 5 shows the results. Table 6 gives the order of *TR* classified by the program.

After analyzing the outputs, it was discovered that most errors were due to:

(1) *t* as a noun modifier
Since the proposed method does not integrate the mechanism of parsing, the association between a modifier and the element modified is not clear. A time expression (indicated by *t*) could either modify a verb as an adverb, or modify a noun as a restricted modifier. Only the adverb *t* determines the temporal reference of the event described by the verb. Thus, the mistake is unavoidable when a noun modifier *t* appears in the text.

(2) Ambiguous rules
All the rules are defined on the basis of indicators' attributes. In case multiple attributes of an indicator assign different temporal relations, the final relation chosen is the one assigned by the attribute used more frequently in the text. However, some special words may lead to exceptional results. These special words are possible sources of errors. Following is the example of a typical ambiguous rule.

$FUTURE(t_s) \oplus CONTINUED(t_r)$
$\Rightarrow CONTINUED(t_s)$ or

$\Rightarrow (FUTURE(t_s))$

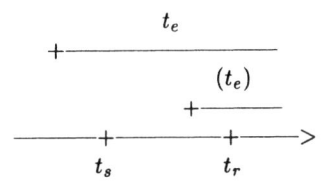

```
                t_e
        +───────────────
                    (t_e)
                    +───────
    ────────+───────+───────>
            t_s     t_r
```

(a) 集团 (将) (adv继续) 专注 (v发展) 电脑 显示器 及 有关 产品，扩阔 产品 系列。
(*group will continue concentrate on develop computer monitors and related product, widen product series.*)
(*The group will continue concentrating on the development of computer monitors, and related items in order to widen the product.*)

$TR = CONTINUED$(报导日期)

(b) (vs估计) 欧洲元 在 长线 的 走势 (va会) 在 经济 因素 支持 下 (adv逐步) (v向好)，
(*estimate Euro in long-term trend can under economic factor support gradually become better.*)
(*It is estimated that supported by economic factors, in the long run, the Euro will gradually become better.*)

$TR = CONTINUED$(报导日期)
correct: $TR = FUTURE$(报导日期)
reason: The word 逐步 has the essence of CONTINUED, but it is independent to any reference time.

(3) Noisy Annotation
Some errors result from noisy annotations. For example,

- noun or verb?
  切实 (v拉动) (aux了) 国民 经济 的 (v增长) (?)
  (*do push were national economy of growth*)
  (*did push the growth of national economy*)

- vs or v?
  (t本周) 半岛豪庭新盘，(va会) (vs公布) (?) (v订价)，
  (*this week new island houses, will announce price*)
  (*the price of the new island houses will be announced this week*)

- vv or v?
  (t下周一) 两 所 会 就 合并 建议 (vv进行) (?) (v表决)，
  (*next Monday two department will for merger do suggestion vote*)
  (*the two departments will vote for the suggestion of the merger on next Monday*)

(4) Co-reference
The program searches for a solution within a sentence bounded by a full stop. As the connections between two sentences are ignored, it is incapable of resolving the coreference problem. As such, the following two sentences are all identified as $TR = PAST$, which is acceptable for the first and correct for the second. Nevertheless, since 同时 links the current event to the event described in the last sentence (indicated by ?), a solution of $SAME\_AS$(?, 接受) would be more accurate. Similarly, $BEFORE$(此?,发出) is more

proper in the second sentence with 此 referring to the event stated before. The problem of coreference will be studied in our future work.

(a) 另 方面，同时 (v接受) 内购 登记 的 粉岭叠茵庭，
(*the other side, meanwhile accept internal registration of Fenling Dieyinting...*)
(*On the other side, the Fenling Dieyinting accepts internal registration...*)

(b) 此 (f前) 中国 信息 产业 部 (adv曾) (v发出) 通知，
(*it before China Information Industry Department once send out a notice,*)
(*Before this, China Information Industry Department sent out a notice,*)

6 CONCLUSIONS AND FUTURE WORK

The issues of mapping linguistic patterns to temporal relations are addressed in the paper. These mappings are preconditioned by temporal indicators and achieved via a set of predefined rules. The mapping mechanism was validated. On 7429 sentences describing temporal relevance, we achieved 92.77% accuracy on average.

These relations will be useful for information extraction, information retrieval, and question-answering applications, once the corresponding frames have been instantiated and their slots filled after temporal natural language processing. The related temporal concepts will be linked together according to their chronological orders, to be applied as the knowledge to fulfill users' queries.

We have identified two interesting questions as our future work.

(1) Reference Time Shift
In the current work, we considered sentences as independent units. The evaluation is also performed on this basis. However, some sentences in an article may be temporally related. They may share the same reference time which is indicated in an preceding sentence, or the event time in one sentence serves as a reference point for the next. How to identify whether a reference time is continued from the preceding sentence or is the same as an omitted speech time, and how the reference times shift should be a good topic in the future work.

(2) The Focus of Negation
The negation form of a verb may have two focuses. One emphasizes the event, which is expected to become the fact but, still has not yet happened. It implies that the event will take place in the future. Another emphasizes a status where the event didn't happen throughout a specified duration. Is it possible to find out the focus of the negation?

REFERENCES

Allen, J. F. (1981). 'An Interval-based Represent Action of Temporal Knowledge', in *Proceedings of 7th International Joint Conference on Artificial Intelligence*, 221–6.
Allen, J. F. et al. (1983). 'Planning Using a Temporal World Model', in *Proceedings of 8th International Joint Conference On Artificial Intelligence*, (1998). 741–7.
Androutsopoulos, I., Ritchie, G., and Thanisch, P. (1998). 'Time, Tense and Aspect in Natural Language Database Interfaces', cmp-lg/9803002, 22 March, 1998.
Bruce, B. C. (1972). 'A Model for Temporal References and its Application in Question-answering Program', *Artificial Intelligence*, 3: 1–25.

Galton, A. (1987). *Temporal Logics and their Applications*. Department of Computer Science, University of Exeter, Academic Press.

Glasgow, B., Mandell, A., Binney, D., and Fisher, F. (1997). 'An Information Extraction Approach to Analysis of Free Form Text in Life Insurance application', in *Proceedings of the 9th Conference on Innovative Applications of Artificial Intelligence*. Menlo Park, CAS, 992–9.

Hwang, C. H., and Schubert, L. K. (1992). 'Tense Trees as the Fine Structure of Discourse', in *Proceedings of 30th Annual Meeting of the Association for Computational Linguistics*, 232–40.

——(1994). 'Interpreting Tense, Aspect and Time Adverbials: A Compositional, Unified Approach', in *Proceedings of 1st International Conference in Temporal Logic*, Bonn, Germany, July 1994, 238–64.

Kaufmann, M. (1995). 'Advanced Research Project Agency', in *Proceedings of the Sixth Message Understanding Conference* (MUC-6), USA.

Lehnert, W. et al. (1993) 'UMass/Hughes: Description of the CIRCUS System Used for MUC-5', in *Proceedings of the Fifth Message Understanding Conference* (MUC-5), San Francisco, CA, 277–91.

Prior, A. N. (1967). *Past, Present and Future*. Oxford: Clarendon Press.

Reichenbach, H. (1947). *Elements of Symbolic Logic*. Berkeley CA: University of California Press.

Soderland, S., Aronow, D., Fisher, D., Aseltine, J., and Lehnert, W. (1995). 'Machine Learning of Text Analysis Rules for Clinical Records', Technical Report, TE39, Department of Computer Science, University of Massachusetts.

Steedman, M. (1997). 'Temporality' in J. van Benthem and A. ter Meulen, (eds.), *Handbook of Logic and Language*. Amsterdam: Elsevier North Holland, 895–935.

Wong, K.F., Li, W.J., Yuan, C.F., and Zhu, X.D. 'Temporal Representation and Classification in Chinese', submitted to *International Journal of Computer Processing of Oriental Languages*, 2000.

李临定，《现代汉语动词》，中国社会科学出版社, (1990). (Li Linding (1990), *Modern Chinese Verbs*, Chinese Social Science Press; in Chinese.)

Using Semantic Inferences for Temporal Annotation Comparison

ANDREA SETZER, ROBERT GAIZAUSKAS, AND MARK HEPPLE

1 INTRODUCTION

The automatic recognition and annotation of temporal expressions as well as event expressions have become active areas of research in computational linguistics, as evidenced by workshops such as the ACL2001 workshop on Temporal and Spatial Information Processing (Harper et al. 2001), the LREC 2002 workshop on Annotation Standards for Temporal Information in Natural Language (Setzer 2002), and the TERQAS[1] workshop on Time and Event Recognition for Question-Answering Systems (Pustejovsky.et al. 2003). Temporal information is important to many application areas, including Question Answering, Information Extraction (IE), and Topic Detection and Tracking.

To enable the development and evaluation of systems that recognize and annotate temporal information, annotated corpora must be created—and often the goal is to do this automatically. Before this is possible, the annotation scheme must be validated, which is often done by hand-annotating a trial corpus and analysing the results. To overcome the potential inconsistencies to which hand-annotated corpora are prone and to ensure the quality of the description of the scheme used by the annotators during annotation, it is necessary to be able to compare annotations and to assess their quality. This is frequently done by manually creating a 'gold-standard' annotation against which other manual annotations are compared. These comparisons are used to calculate interannotator agreement figures, which are one way of judging how well the scheme is defined and with how much agreement.

In this paper we will present a way of comparing temporal annotations and an approach to support the creation of a gold-standard annotation. We introduce the notion of the temporal closure that can be computed over an annotation as well as methods for computing precision and recall figures for different annotations.

A. Setzer, R. Gaizauskas, and M. Hepple,'Using Semantic Inferences for Temporal Annotation Comparison', *Proceedings of the Fourth International Workshop on Inference in Computational Semantics* (ICOS-4), INRIA Lorraine, Nancy, France, September 25–26, 2003, 185–96. © 2003 A. Setzer, R. Gaizauskas, and Mark Hepple.

[1] <http:// www.timeml.org>.

2 AN APPROACH FOR COMPARING TEMPORAL ANNOTATIONS

2.1 Temporal annotation schemes

Annotation schemes for temporal information usually include entities such as events, times, and the temporal relations holding between them, and they annotate expressions in text conveying these entities. The set of temporal relations used varies between annotation schemes. For this paper, we consider only a small set of uncontroversial relations, namely: BEFORE, INCLUDES and SIMULTANEOUS.[2] We assume further that events and times are annotated (putting aside the finer details of how they would be defined and annotated), and that events and times are assigned unique identifiers.

2.2 The equivalence of temporal annotations

Temporal annotations, like for example co-reference chain annotations (see Section 3), are of a semantic nature and should be compared in semantic terms. Two annotations are equivalent if they convey the same 'temporal information', even if different ways of annotating this information are chosen. For example, consider the first diagram in Figure 1, which shows two simultaneous events A and B, which both precede a third event C. The two further diagrams in the figure, representing possible partial annotations, differ from the first but are nonetheless equivalent to it, as the omitted relations are implied by simple inference rules. For Version 1, for example, we can infer the omitted fact that *B is before C* from *A is simultaneous to B* and *A is before C*. Any comparison of annotations should take into account this observation that annotations can be distinct but equivalent.

2.3 Calculating the temporal closure

The above discussion suggests an approach in which the temporal relations made explicit in a particular annotation of a text might be expanded, using an appropriate set of inference rules, to provide a complete (i.e. maximal) representation of the temporal consequences of that annotation. Such a representation will be termed the *temporal closure* of the annotation. Two annotations of a text can then be compared in terms of the equivalence or overlap of their temporal closures. To formalize this idea, let us allow that identifiers for annotated event and time expressions form two sets, E and T, respectively. Our temporal relations are all binary relations between event and time expressions, and so the denotation of each is a subset of $(E \cup T) \times (E \cup T)$. A set of inference rules for our temporal relations are given in Figure 2, using S, B, and I to denote the extension of the relations SIMULTANEOUS, BEFORE, and INCLUDES, respectively. Some of the inference rules concern only one of the relations, and follow logically from the formal properties of the relation, e.g. that SIMULTANEOUS is an equivalence relation, whilst BEFORE and INCLUDES are transitive, asymmetric, and irreflexive. Other inference rules capture interactions between relations that follow naturally from their intuitive meaning, e.g. if x and y are simultaneous, and x is before z, then y also is before z.

---

[2] In (Setzer 2001), a larger set is used, which includes also the relations AFTER and IS-INCLUDED. These additional relations are the inverses of BEFORE and INCLUDES, and so their omission does not reduce expressiveness, whilst allowing a simpler presentation of the approach.

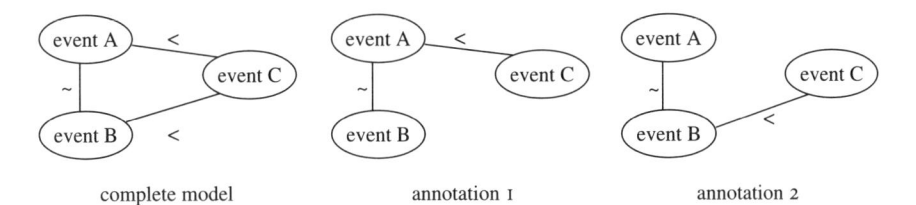

FIG. 1 Comparing annotations.

$\forall x, y, z \in (E \cup T):$

(1) $\quad (x,y) \in S \Rightarrow (y,x) \in S$

(2) $\quad (x,y) \in B \wedge (y,z) \in B \Rightarrow (x,z) \in B$

(3) $\quad (x,y) \in I \wedge (y,z) \in I \Rightarrow (x,z) \in I$

(4) $\quad (x,y) \in B \wedge (y,z) \in I \Rightarrow (x,z) \in B$

(5) $\quad (x,y) \in I \wedge (x,z) \in B \Rightarrow (y,z) \in B$

(6) $\quad (x,y) \in S \wedge (y,z) \in S \Rightarrow (x,z) \in S$

(7) $\quad (x,y) \in B \wedge (y,z) \in S \Rightarrow (x,z) \in B$

(8) $\quad (x,y) \in I \wedge (y,z) \in S \Rightarrow (x,z) \in I$

(9) $\quad (x,y) \in S \wedge (y,z) \in I \Rightarrow (x,z) \in I$

(10) $\quad (x,y) \in B \wedge (x,z) \in S \Rightarrow (z,y) \in B$

(11) $\quad (x,y) \in S \wedge (x,z) \in I \Rightarrow (y,z) \in I$

FIG. 2 Inference rules.

Let S_t denote the simultaneity pairs explicitly specified by a temporally annotated text t, and likewise for B_t and I_t. These components combine to give the overall temporal model of the text $\mathcal{M}_t = \langle S_t, B_t, I_t \rangle$. The inference rules can be applied to this model to generate its deductive closure $\mathcal{M}_t^\vDash$. Let $S_t^\vDash$ denote the SIMULTANEOUS relation that results in $\mathcal{M}_t^\vDash$, and likewise for $B_t^\vDash$ and $I_t^\vDash$. For this approach, we can say that two alternative annotations t and t' of a text are equivalent just in case the deductive closures of their models are equivalent, i.e. $\mathcal{M}_t^\vDash = \mathcal{M}_{t'}^\vDash$. Furthermore, we can say that a model $\mathcal{M}_t$ is a *minimal* model if it has no proper subset which has an equivalent temporal closure. Minimal models need not be unique, as the example in Figure 1 shows.

2.4 Recall and precision

This approach allows comparison between alternative annotations of a text in terms of the degree of overlap between their temporal closures. In particular, a given annotation of a text can be compared to a 'gold-standard' annotation of the same text by computing figures of precision and recall between their temporal closures. Let k and r denote key and response annotations of the same text. The precision and recall for the SIMULTANEOUS relation S_r as compared to S_k is given by:

$$ R = \frac{|S_k^\vDash \cap S_r^\vDash|}{|S_k^\vDash|} \qquad P = \frac{|S_k^\vDash \cap S_r^\vDash|}{|S_r^\vDash|} $$

Parallel definitions can be provided for the other temporal relations. Precision and recall measures for the overall temporal model $\mathcal{M}_t$ can be defined as:[3]

$$R = \frac{|S_k^\models \cap S_r^\models| + |B_k^\models \cap B_r^\models| + |I_k^\models \cap I_r^\models|}{|S_k^\models| + |B_k^\models| + |I_k^\models|} \qquad P = \frac{|S_k^\models \cap S_r^\models| + |B_k^\models \cap B_r^\models| + |I_k^\models \cap I_r^\models|}{|S_r^\models| + |B_r^\models| + |I_r^\models|}$$

2.5 Related work

In the next section we discuss at some length the relation between our approach to comparing temporal annotations and approaches to comparing co-reference annotations. Here, we mention briefly the only other work of which we are aware that addresses the specific issue of comparing temporal annotations, viz., Katz and Arosio's work (2001) on annotating sentence-internal temporal relations. Their overall project is somewhat different from ours in that they are interested only in annotating temporal relations between multiple event signals (verbs) within single sentences, whilst we are interested in annotating all temporal relations between times and events, or events and events, across an entire discourse. However, they have confronted the same problem of how to compare different annotations expressing the same temporal relational content and have arrived at a somewhat different solution, though one which is closely related to ours. Put abstractly, their approach has a model-theoretic flavour while ours is more proof-theoretic. To compare annotations they compare the sets of models—models here in the sense of model-theoretic semantics—that satisfy each of the annotations. Models are mappings over a structure consisting of a domain and a set of binary relations which assign verbs (event signals) to elements of the domain and verb pairs to the relations in such a fashion as to satisfy several axioms (e.g. transitivity of *before*). A model is then said to satisfy an annotation iff it assigns the appropriate relation to the verbs in a sentence. Given this framework, annotations may be compared based on whether the set of models satisfying one is the same as the other (such annotations are said to be *equivalent*), includes the other (*subsumes*), has a nonempty intersection with the other (*consistent*), or has an empty intersection with the other (*inconsistent*). Katz and Arosio go on to define a notion of distance between two annotations which is defined as the number of models satisfying one but not both annotations, normalized by the number satisfying both.

The obvious differences between Katz and Arosio's approach and our own are that (1) the approaches use different sets of axioms, and (2) they define a distance measure for annotations while we define notions of precision and recall. However, these differences are relatively minor as we could easily adopt the same axioms and move to a common set of measures, i.e. we could define a distance measure between deductive closures and they could define recall and precision measures in terms of sets of satisfying models, nominating one annotation to be the key and the other the response. However even with such harmonizations, it is not clear that the two approaches become equivalent. In particular the measures the two approaches compute might exhibit somewhat different behaviour given that our approach relies upon comparing the deductive closures of annotations whilst Katz and Arosio's relies upon comparing sets of models of annotations. This matter merits further investigation. The only further consideration in comparing the two approaches is the ease with which they lend themselves to implementation. Katz and

---

[3] This method can be compared to Crowe's way (1997) of evaluating clause-event grids.

Arosio have not as yet implemented their approach (personal communication). Our approach lends itself straightforwardly to implementation as a forward-chaining inference procedure. It has been implemented and used in the annotation procedure discussed below in Section 4.

3 COMPARISON TO CO-REFERENCE SCORING APPROACHES

Temporal annotation is not the only case that should be compared in semantic terms. As mentioned earlier, a similar situation arises for comparing differently annotated co-reference chains. We will briefly introduce two co-reference annotation scoring methods, and then compare them to our approach.

3.1 The MUC co-reference scoring scheme

Co-reference is a form of equivalence relation, and co-reference annotations generate equivalence classes. Alternative annotations can generate identical equivalence classes, i.e. we see a situation similar to that discussed for temporal annotation, where distinct annotations can produce equivalent results. For example, the co-reference linkages <A-B, B-C> and <A-B, A-C> both generate the equivalence class {A, B, C}.

The co-reference scoring approach used for MUC6 (1995) was developed to avoid this problem of equivalent annotations being semantically distinct. The approach exploits the fact that co-reference is an equivalence relation, and provides precision and recall metrics that are computed relative to the minimal size of linkage required to generate the given equivalence classes. The minimal size of linkage required to generate an equivalence class containing n elements is always $n-1$.

We will introduce the MUC6 precision and recall metrics using a simple example, taken from the MUC 6 *Proceedings*. (Please refer to this source for a more detailed explanation of the approach.) Assume that elements {A, B, C, D} are present, of which {B, C, D} co-refer, as captured by a key annotation <B-C, C-D>. The response annotation is <B-C,A-D>.

Recall: Intuitively, recall for the example should be 0.5 since the minimal number of links needed to link the three elements in the key class is two and the response provides only one correct link. If c is the minimal number of correct links needed and m is the number of links missing in the response then recall is:

$$Recall = \frac{c - m}{c} \quad (e.g.\ Recall = \frac{2 - 1}{2} = 0.5)$$

Precision: Precision for the example should intuitively be 0.5 since only one of the two given links is correct. To calculate precision the above approach is reversed: the number of links which must be added to the key to yield the equivalence class of the response is counted. If c' is the minimal number of links to generate the response equivalence class and m' the number of links missing in the key to generate that class, then the formula for precision is:

$$Precision = \frac{c' - m'}{c'} \quad (e.g.\ Precision = \frac{2 - 1}{2} = 0.5)$$

3.2 The B-CUBED scoring algorithm

Bagga and Baldwin (1998) make the following three criticisms of the MUC6 co-reference scoring approach:

(i) Separating out singletons, i.e. entities that occur only in chains of which they are the only member, from other chains is not given credit by the MUC6 scoring algorithm.
(ii) All errors are considered equal, i.e. precision is penalized equally for any type of error, though some are more damaging than others, e.g. it is more damaging to incorrectly link together two long chains than to link a long chain with a short one, i.e. as more entities are incorrectly made co-referent. This distinction is not reflected in the MUC6 algorithm.
(iii) The MUC6 approach gives equal weight to all instances of co-reference. Bagga and Baldwin argue that this is appropriate for IE (where the MUC6 metric has been used), but that alternative weighting schemes are more suitable in other contexts, such as Information Retrieval.

Bagga and Baldwin propose an alternative scoring method for co-reference, the *B-CUBED algorithm*, which looks at the absence/presence of entities relative to each of the other entities in the equivalence classes produced, rather than concentrating on the links produced. Precision and recall for each entity are defined as follows:

$$Precision_i = \frac{\text{number of correct elements in the output chain containing entity}_i}{\text{number of elements in the output chain containing entity}_i}$$

$$Recall_i = \frac{\text{number of correct elements in the output chain containing entity}_i}{\text{number of elements in the key (true) chain containing entity}_i}$$

Final recall and precision are computed by the following formulae:

$$FinalRecall = \sum_{i=1}^{N} w_i * Recall_i \qquad FinalPrecision = \sum_{i=1}^{N} w_i * Precision_i$$

In these formulae, N is the number of entities in the document and w_i the weight assigned to entity i in the document. In a case where all entities are equally important, the value $1/N$ could be assigned for all w_i, so that the *Final* scores are just the mean of the scores for each entity. However, the possibility of varying these weights allows the third criticism above to be addressed. The method also addresses the other criticisms, i.e. it gives merit for correctly identified singletons, and it will more severely punish a linkage that incorrectly co-refers more elements than one co-referring less.

3.3 Comparing the co-reference and temporal annotation scoring methods

The two co-reference scoring methods both avoid the problem of distinct annotations being semantically equivalent by looking beyond the specific linkages to the equivalence classes they induce. This is possible of course only because co-reference is an equivalence relation which induces such classes. For temporal annotation, such an approach is not possible, because although the SIMULTANEOUS relation is an equivalence relation, the BEFORE and INCLUDES are not (being asymmetric and irreflexive), and so we cannot put aside the unimportant differences between distinct but equivalent annotations by 'flattening' them down to a representation based purely on equivalence classes. Instead our approach overcomes irrelevant differences by expanding each annotation's model to its temporal closure, allowing comparisons to be made between annotations in terms of their full informational consequences. The question of whether a scoring scheme could be developed for temporal annotations which is based on some more complicated notion of a minimal model is nontrivial and one that deserves research attention in its own right.

Despite this important difference between our approach and the co-reference scoring methods, we would observe that our approach exhibits some similar characteristics to that of Bagga and Baldwin (1998) in regard to their point that some errors are more damaging than others, for which we noted the specific case that an incorrect linking of two long chains should be more damaging to precision than an incorrect linking of a long and a short chain. We can construct a similar example for temporal annotation rather than co-reference in terms of 'chains' of entities deemed *simultaneous*. Imagine a key forming three such 'simultaneity chains' such as the following (where $\sim$ denotes simultaneity):

$$\text{KEY}: e_1 \sim e_2 \sim e_3 \sim e_4 \sim e_5 \quad e_6 \sim e_7 \sim e_8 \sim e_9 \sim e_{10} \quad e_{11} \sim e_{12}$$

A response A might incorrectly link the two larger chains, whilst a response B might incorrectly link a large chain to a small one:

$$\text{Resp-A}: e_1 \sim e_2 \sim e_3 \sim e_4 \sim e_5 \sim e_6 \sim e_7 \sim e_8 \sim e_9 \sim e_{10} \quad e_{11} \sim e_{12}$$
$$\text{Resp-B}: e_1 \sim e_2 \sim e_3 \sim e_4 \sim e_5 \sim e_{11} \sim e_{12} \quad e_6 \sim e_7 \sim e_8 \sim e_9 \sim e_{10}$$

Our temporal closure-based precision metric does treat the mistake in A as worse than that in B, assigning a precision score of 0.45 for A and 0.67 for B. This is because connecting the two long chains results in a greater number of false inferences linking entities from the two chains during deductive closure. (The recall for both responses is 1, because all the relations that are in the key are also in the response.) Using the MUC scoring method, the precision is 0.9 for both responses, as only one additional link is introduced in each case. For more information about this example refer to Setzer 2001.

4 USING TEMPORAL INFERENCE TO FACILITATE ANNOTATION

We now turn to the process of creating gold-standard annotations manually, and consider how this process might be facilitated using insights from the approach described above. A gold-standard annotation of temporal information should be such as to determine correctly all the temporal relations holding between all entities (events and times) within the text, insofar as the text does support this information. Note that there is a separation between an annotation that supports this information and one that makes it explicit, i.e. because an annotation that does not explicitly state all the relations may yet imply them under deductive closure, and, with our approach to temporal evaluation, a lesser annotation that supports the full information is functionally equivalent to one that makes it all explicit.

The central question here is how the manual annotation process should be formulated so as to enable annotators to produce gold-standard annotations that are of high quality, with the least effort. Assume that annotators will firstly identify and mark temporal entities, i.e. times and events. Then, for temporal relations, we might ask annotators simply to mark those relations that are salient to them from the text. Such an approach, however, runs the risk that many relation instances that are supported by the text but which are not immediately salient will be missed, so that incomplete annotations are produced. An alternative strategy would be to ask annotators to consider *every* possible pairing amongst the identified entities, and consider which if any of the temporal relations might hold between the paired elements. Such an approach seems much more likely to elicit an annotation capturing the full temporal content of the text, perhaps even one that makes all relations explicit. However, even if the annotation software were to provide support for the enumeration of pairings to be addressed (which could easily be done), such an approach threatens to impose too high a burden upon the annotator, e.g. a text containing only 20 events and times (which would be quite a small text), would give rise to around 200 entity pairs for consideration (assuming we treat $a+b$ and $b+a$ as the same pair), whilst a text with 50 entities would yield over 1,000 pairs.

We propose an alternative annotation strategy which combines the above two approaches and additionally uses temporal inference to facilitate the process and reduce the amount of work required of the annotator. In this approach, the annotator initially marks up some portion of the temporal relations within a text, presumably the most salient ones. In a second, interactive stage, the annotator is questioned regarding the temporal relationship between pairs of entities for which this information is unknown. (Note that a valid response at this point is that the relation is not determined by the text.) Crucially, throughout this second phase, temporal inference is used to compute the deductive closure of the annotation done so far. Such inference will resolve the relational status of many entity pairs which are not explicitly linked by the annotation, so that the annotator need only be questioned about those pairs whose relationship is unknown. Each additional annotation that results from questioning may itself have consequences under inference, further reducing the number of unresolved pairs. The process terminates when the relational status of all pairs of entities has been resolved.

The effectiveness of this approach in reducing the work required to produce complete annotations is supported by the results of the following experiment, which is discussed in greater detail in Setzer (2001). Six texts were used, of average length 312 words and containing on average 31 temporal entities. The texts were annotated by 2 or 3 subjects each, producing 16 annotations in total. In the initial phase, 200 temporal relations were marked up across all 16 annotated texts. In the second phase, annotators were prompted with a total of 865 questions until the phase reached completion, giving an average of 54 prompts per annotated text. The temporal closure of these annotations contained in total 5,288 relational pairs, of which 3.8 percent (i.e. the 200) were manually annotated in the initial phase, 16.3 percent were generated under prompting, and the remaining 79.9 percent were automatically inferred. While an average of 54 prompts to the annotator is not ideal, it shows a significant improvement over the alternative without temporal inference, which would have required 318 prompts per document on average during the second phase.

In the above experiment, the selection of the next unresolved entity pair to question the annotator about was made randomly. This approach could be improved by using a more intelligent method for selecting these pairs, with a view to minimizing the number of prompts that must be made. To illustrate this possibility, consider an example where the only relation is BEFORE (denoted $<$), and where the current annotation of a text produces an ordering of entities of $a<b<c$ and $d<e<f$. The selection of different pairs from amongst $a-f$ will determine the relation of more or less unresolved pairs, depending on the answer given. Prompting for (b, e), for example, will resolve four

relation pairs whether the answer is $b<e$ or $e<b$ (we ignore here the possibility of a 'not related' response), whilst prompting for (a, d) will resolve three pairs, again with either answer. This suggests that (b, e) is a better prompt pair than (a, d). A prompt for (c, d) will resolve nine relation pairs if the answer is $c<d$, but only one if the answer is $d<c$, so the preference between (c, d) and (b, e) is less obvious. If we assume that answers are equally likely, then (c, d) is better, resolving five pairs *on average*, but we might instead go for the best guaranteed result, which favours (b, e). A further possibility is that we might find cues to suggest that one answer is more likely than another for a given pair (e.g. perhaps from the position of temporal entities within the text), and use this to determine the likely outcome for each pair as a basis for choosing. This topic merits further investigation.

Two annotation tools have been developed which incorporate the above approach (using random selection of pairs for prompting). The first, described in Setzer (2001), prompts the user textually for missing relations, while at the same time highlighting the entities involved (the text itself being shown in a separate window). The annotation tool developed during the TERQAS workshop[4] is based on the same method, but uses a more sophisticated visual method of aiding the user in asserting missing temporal relations.

5 PROBLEMATIC CASES

The few temporal relations used in this paper are only a small subset of those possible. Allen (1984), for example, uses 13 different temporal relations.[5] These relations all have very clear-cut definitions. In analysing real text, however, we find many cases where the relations encountered are not as clear cut as one might hope. For the SIMULTANEOUS relation, for example, we observe cases where the information given is only enough to establish that events occurred 'at roughly the same time', as in the following real example:

> All 75 people on board the Aeroflot Airbus died when it ploughed into a Siberian mountain in March 1994.

Here, the exact temporal relation between died and ploughed is not clear, and yet it is important to capture the relation that holds between them.

To handle such cases, Setzer (2001) proposes that the SIMULTANEOUS relation be allowed a more 'fuzzy' definition which admits the 'at roughly the same time' reading. This change, however, has significant ramifications in relation to inference, requiring either that some inference rules must be withdrawn, or an acceptance that some consequences of inference are such as would appear invalid under a strict view of validity. The following sentence, for example, suggests the fuzzy simultaneity of the radioed and crashed events, and of the crashed and died events, but the simultaneity of the radioed and died events which is thereby implied contradicts the natural intuition that the former preceded the latter. See Setzer (2001) for more detailed discussion of these issues.

> The pilot radioed for help as the plane crashed into the mountain, killing all on board.

---

[4] <http://www.time2002.org>.
[5] The same relations were used in the annotation scheme developed during the TERQAS workshop (Pustejovsky et al. 2003).

6 CONCLUSION AND FUTURE WORK

Comparing and evaluating temporal annotations is an important part of developing annotation schemes and, using these schemes, annotated corpora. In this paper, we have described a method to do this; a method based on computing the temporal closure over different temporal annotations, using inference rules. The algorithm used works in semantic rather than formal terms—a requirement for temporal annotations. We have also described how our approach can be used to support the creation of gold-standard annotation and we have illustrated the effectiveness of this approach.

As we have mentioned in the section above, the way annotators are prompted for missing temporal relations needs improvement before this method can be used for annotating large corpora.

The temporal relations used in this paper to demonstrate the approach are only a small set. More temporal relations, and potentially relations that have different properties, will require a reworking of the set of inference rules used.

Another area of future work are relations that are not temporal as such but that have temporal consequences on the events involved. Examples are hypothetical events, relations of cause and effect, and subevents.

REFERENCES

Allen, J. (1984). 'Towards a General Theory of Action and Time', *Artificial Intelligence* **23**: 123–54.

Bagga, A. and Baldwin, B. (1998). 'Algorithms for Scoring Coreference Chains', in *Proceedings of the Linguistic Co-reference Workshop at The First International Conference on Language Resources and Evaluation (LREC '98)*, 563–6.

Crowe, J. (1997). 'Constraint Based Event Recognition for Information Extraction', Ph.D. thesis, University of Edinburgh.

Harper, L., Mani, I., and Sundheim, B., (eds.), (2001). *Proceedings of the ACL-EACL 2001, Workshop for Temporal and Spatial Information Processing*, Toulouse, France, 2001.

Katz, G. and Arosio, F. (2001). 'The Annotation of Temporal Information in Natural Language Sentences', in *Proceedings of the ACL-EACL 2001 Workshop for Temporal and Spatial Information Processing*, Toulouse, France, 2001, 104–11.

MUC-6 (1995). *Proceedings of the Sixth Message Understanding Conference*. California: Morgan Kaufman.

Pustejovsky, P., Castao, J., Ingria, R., Saur, R., Gaizauskas, R., Setzer, A., and Katz, G. (2003). 'TimeML: Robust Specification of Event and Temporal Expressions in Text', in *Proceedings of the IWCS-5 Fifth International Workshop on Computational Semantics*, 1–16.

Setzer, A. (2001). 'Temporal Information in Newswire Articles: An Annotation Scheme and Corpus Study', Ph.D. thesis, University of Sheffield.

Setzer, A. (ed.), (2002). *Proceedings of LREC 2002, Workshop on Annotation Standards for Temporal Information in Natural Language*, Las Palmas, Gran Canaria, 2002.

Index

The letter f indicates figure, n a textual note and t a table.

abstracts: news stories 401, 402–3
accomplishments: verbs 5, 6, 7, 26, 31, 34, 35, 36, 94n, 117, 119, 120, 121, 335, 340–1
achievements: verbs 5, 6, 7, 26, 31, 34, 35, 36, 117, 120, 122, 335, 340–1
actions: artificial intelligence 251–71; event ontology 199–209; news stories 397, 401–2
active intervals 134
activities: verbs 6, 7, 25, 26, 31, 117, 119, 335, 345
actual time *see* PUNDIT text-processing system
adverbials 35, 36, 95, 101–4, 112, 134, 153, 335; durative 35–6, 53–4; modification of 49–53
Aktionsarten *see* lexical aspect
ALINK tags 303, 305–6, 550, 553–4 *see also* LINK tags
anaphoric binding 47–8
anaphoric reference *see* temporal anaphora
anaphors *see* discourse anaphors
annotations: comparison of 598–9; events and states 496–9; resources 500–2; schemes 505–6
AQUAINT program: and free text 301, 302, 545
argument structure 53–6
artificial intelligence 161–2 *see also* temporal interval algebra
Artwork project *see* NMSU dialogs
aspect 10–13; in discourse representation theory (DRT) 321
aspectual composition 7
aspectual markers: Mandarin Chinese 4
aspectual relations: and subordinating 497–8
aspectual verbs 139–40
Attentional State 455

belief: artificial intelligence 266–7
Bend Causal Law 363, 364
bounded processes 34, 35
'Brouwersche' system 88
Burmese: realis/irrealis distinctions in 4

calculus *see* event calculus; situation calculus
Carnap, R. 91
CASREPS 129, 155
causal laws *see* Bend Causal Law; Change Causal Law; Dark Causal Law; Push Causal Law; Straighten Causal Law
causal verbs 4
causality: problem solving 185–93
causation *see* event causation
Change Causal Law 364, 377
Chinese: temporal references in 4, 8, 559–71
chronicles: states 177–9, 180
chronsets: data structures 210–14
clausal subordination 328–9
clauses *see* event-clauses; *when* clauses
Closure on the Right: monotonic inferences 362–3
CMU dialogs 444, 445, 453t, 454, 456, 457

codas: news stories 402–3
common-sense knowledge 325
commonsense entailment (CE): nonmonotonic reasoning 366, 370, 385–9
complex sentences 155
computing aspect 14–17
conditionals 25
CONTEX: parsing 524–5
continuous change *see* fluents: continuous change
continuous tenses 22–32
culminated process 95, 98

DAML program: temporal concepts 301
DAML-Time *see* OWL-Time: temporal relations
Dark Causal Law 375
databases 228; multilingual 518–20; temporal 111, 112
date information *see* time assignment
datelines: news stories 400
DCT *see* document creation time
DCUs *see* Discourse Constituent Units (DCUs)
decomposition 137, 141 *see also* lexical semantics
defeasible modus ponens: textual interpretation 357–8, 372
defeasible reasoning 324
definite noun phrases *see* discourse anaphors: tense
definite pronouns *see* discourse anaphors: tense
definiteness *see* past tense: English
discourse: temporal structure analysis 475–83; ORIENTS relation 469–70
discourse anaphors: tense 411–28
Discourse Constituent Units (DCUs) 479–82
discourse focus: and discourse structure 414–16
discourse history 319
discourse popping: and Nixon Diamond 376–7
discourse representation theory (DRT) 320–1, 325, 334–6, 353–93
discreteness: time 162
document creation time 489
document time-stamps 537
Dudley Dooright: monotonic inferences 363–4, 365; and text ambiguity 377
durative adverbials 35–6, 153–4

English: discourses 334–6; tenses 4, 8, 10–11, 71–3, 74–8
evaluations: news stories 398, 400–1
event calculus 166–7; Temporal Granularity and Indeterminacy event Calculus (TGIC) 241–50
event causation 554–6
event-clauses 523
event composition 44–9
EVENT data structure 547–8, 555–6
event-denoting expressions 534–5
event descriptions, incomplete 229–35
event ontologies 3, 15–16, 419–22; actions 199–209

Index

event ordering 329
event structures 3, 8–10, 34–57
event time 104, 134, 149, 432–3
events 61–9, 95, 292–3, 302–3; annotating 490–3; identifying 524–5; partially-ordered 245–7 *see also* causality: problem solving; times and events
eventualities: lexical aspect 5–6
expressions: time-denoting 534 *see also* discourse anaphors
extended tenses 73–8

felicity conditions: present perfect 13
fluents: continuous change 193–9
frame problems: temporal reasoning 170, 188
French: adverbials 102; tenses 8, 73, 74, 76n, 77n, 78, 334, 350
future tense: 4, 107–11

German: adverbials 102; extended tenses 73, 74, 76, 78n
Germanic languages: future tense 4
grammatical aspects 3, 7–8
granular system: temporal entities 535–6 *see also* Temporal Granularity and Indeterminacy event Calculus (TGIC)
Greek: extended tenses 74

headlines: news stories 398–9
Hinrichs, E. 334–6
Horn clauses *see* logic: and notion of time

imperfective aspects 7, 8; inertia worlds 13
imperfective paradox 36
inertia worlds 13
inflected verbs: temporal analysis 141–3
information retrieval *see* AQUAINT program: and free text
intentional action 266–71
interlingual representation 506–7
interval temporal logic (ITL) 165
intervals *see* active intervals
irrealis distinctions *see* realis/irrealis distinctions
isa links *see* event ontologies

JANUS project *see* CMU dialogs
Japanese: translation technology 520
Jesperson, J. 72n

Kamp, H. 334–6, 341, 349, 350
kinesis: temporal structure 132
knowledge conflict: and Penguin Principle 373–5

Latin: extended tenses 74, 77, 78n
lexical aspect 3, 5–7, 115–25, 132, 139, 141
lexical conceptual structures 117–25
lexical semantics 37–9
Link, G. 9, 62, n, 63, 64, 65–6, 68
LINK tags 303–5, 547 *see also* ALINK tags
logic: and notion of time 217

machine translations 124–5, 444, 520
MAKEINSTANCE realization tag 548
Mandarin Chinese: expression of tense in 4, 8 *see also* Chinese: temporal references in

markup languages *see* TimeML markup language
maximal validity intervals (MVIs) 242–5
Message Understanding Conference (MUC) evaluations: temporal referring expressions 488–9, 579–80
minimal tense logic 163
modifiers 97
monotonic inferences *see* Closure on the Right; Dudley Dooright: monotonic inferences
Moore, R. 175
multilinguality: temporal annotation 502–4, 509–10, 518–20
MVIs *see* maximal validity intervals (MVIs)

narrative discourse *see* Kamp, H.
narratives: news stories 397–409; tense interpretation 431–9 *see also* time stamps: assigning event-clauses to
natural language sentences: temporal information in 513–21
Nixon Diamond 361–2, 365, 376
NLITDB 17
NMSU dialogs 444, 453t, 454, 455, 456, 457
nominal descriptions: temporal information 537
nominal system 62–4
non-monotonic logics: text interpretation 188–90, 364–7
noun phrases *see* discourse anaphors
nucleus: temporal ontology 111

ontologies *see* event ontologies; temporal ontology
orientations: news stories 398, 399–400
ORIENTS relation: discourse 469–70
OWL-Time: temporal relations 301, 305–14

parsing *see* CONTEX: parsing
part-of links 3
partially ordered events 245–7
Past, Present and Future 87
past tense: English 4 *see also* perfect tenses; tense trees: discourse
Penguin Principle: textual interpretation 358–9, 365, 366, 373–5, 388–93
perfect tenses 152
perfective aspect 7, 8, 13, 99–101
personal narratives *see* news stories
plans: artificial intelligence 267–8
pluperfect: discourse relations 378–81
plurals: nominal system 62–4
point adverbials 35
point expressions 95
point of speech: tense 71, 72, 419
points of reference: tense 71, 72
pragmatics: and default reasoning 324–5
predicates 33, 36, 39, 47–9, 225–39, 248
predications *see* PUNDIT text-processing system
present tense: English 4
processes 293–4; and plans: temporal logic 173–214; verbs 5, 34, 36, 40, 62, 64–5, 95, 134, 145–7
progressive sentences: analysis 294–6
progressive state 98–9
progressives: imperfective aspect 12–13; and Temporal Discourse Interpretation Principal (TDIP) 345–7

Index

PROLOG programs 222, 225–8, 239, 538
property negations 278–9, 281–2
propositions 94, 97
psychological predicates 47–9
PUNDIT text-processing system 129, 131–3, 137, 138, 140–1, 144, 148, 151–2
Push Causal Law 359–60

qualia structures 38–9

realis events 16
realis/irrealis distinctions 4
realization tags *see* MAKEINSTANCE realization tag
recency: present perfect 13
reference point: narrative 322
reference time 10, 104, 149–50, 322, 339, 508 *see also* temporal reference
resolutions: news stories 402
resultative constructions 46
Russian: tenses 8

scalar adverbials 36
semantic structure 118–20
semantic tagging: news messages 533–43
semantics: aspectual classes 336–9
semelfactives 6–7
sentences: aspectual class 335–6; complex 155; logical form: discourse representaion structure 367–9 *see also* temporal annotation; tense trees: discourse
SIGNAL text annotation 550
situation calculus 165–6
situations: temporal structure 132–8 *see also* eventualities: lexical aspect
SLINK tags 303, 304, 550, 552–3
Slipping Law 379
Spanish: imperfective 7; machine translations 124–5
speech point: English 4
speech time 151–2
states: tense 25, 26, 35–6, 40, 62, 95–6, 117, 119, 120, 122, 133–4, 144–5, 176; annotating 490–3
states of motion 285–6, 289–91
states of position 285–6, 288–9
States Overlap 361, 362, 375
stative predications 133–4
statives 5–7; and Temporal Discourse Interpretation Principal (TDIP) 341–5
stories *see* narratives: news stories
Straighten Causal Law 363–4
subordinating: and aspectual relations 497–8
subordinating clauses *see* clausal subordination
systems *see* temporal awareness: systems

tags *see* ALINK tags; LINK tags; MAKEINSTANCE realization tag; TIMEX tags: temporal expressions; TLINK tags
Taylor, B. 336–9
TDIP *see* Temporal Discourse Interpretation Principal (TDIP)
temporal adverbials 44, 52–3, 152–3
temporal anaphora 326–8, 448

temporal annotation 514–1, 575–84 *see also* TimeML markup language
temporal aspect 34
temporal awareness: systems ix
temporal centering 329
temporal closure: annotation of 499; calculation of 576–7
temporal databases 111, 112
Temporal Discourse Interpretation Principal (TDIP) 339–49
temporal expressions: classification 534–5, 537–8; semantics for 539 *see also* TIMEX tags: temporal expressions
temporal focus 422–8, 433–8
Temporal Granularity and Indeterminacy event Calculus (TGIC) 241–50
temporal information 130; extraction 536; machine translation 444; in natural language sentences 513–21; representation of 535–7
temporal interval algebra 168–70, 277–98
temporal locations *see* PUNDIT text-processing system
temporal logic 163–4, 173–214, 253, 254–7
temporal narratives: empirical structure of 325–6
temporal ontology 93–111 *see also* temporal interval algebra
temporal ordering 330, 431
temporal prepositions: semantics for 539
temporal reasoning 162–3, 170–1, 188, 330–1 *see also* reason: ancestors' ability to
temporal references 131–2, 488–90; time values 508–9 *see also* reference time; Chinese 560–72
temporal relations 322, 353, 561–2; annotating 497–502; OWL-Time 301, 305–14; and pragmatics 323–4
temporal structures *see* discourse: temporal structure analysis; PUNDIT text-processing system
tense interpretation: narrative 431–9
tense logics 79–91, 163, 164–5
tense trees: discourse 461–2, 463–73
tenses 3, 4, 10–13, 21, 71–8, 104–11, 149–52, 462–3; as discourse anaphors 416–22; in Discourse Representation Theory (DRT) 321, 353–6 *see also* CONTEX: parsing; pluperfect: discourse relations; states: tenses
text ambiguity *see* Dudley Dooright: and text ambiguity
text-processing systems *see* PUNDIT text-processing system
textual interpretation *see* Penguin Principle: textual interpretation
TGIC *see* Temporal Granularity and Indeterminacy event Calculus (TGIC)
third-order verbs 140
TICS (Temporal Information-extraction from Chinese Sources) 560, 561f, 562f
time assignment 527–9
time-denoting expressions 534
time instants 227, 282–4
time stamps: assigning event-clauses to 523, 525–32; documents 537
time values: temporal references 508–9
times and events 301–14; annotating relations between 493–4; mechanisms for expressing 4; notion of 21

TimeML markup language 301, 302–5, 545–56; interpretation in OWL-Time 312–14
TIMEX tags: temporal expressions 489, 490, 500, 501, 502, 548–50
TLINK tags 303–4, 550, 551–2 *see also* ALINK tags
transition events 40, 45–6, 135–6, 147–8
translations: machine 124–5, 520
treebanks *see* temporal annotation
Turkish: extended tenses 73

verbal descriptions: temporal information 537
verbs 4; causal 136; Chinese 560; temporal properties, 5; tenses 3, 21, 71–8 *see also* accomplishments: verbs; activities: verbs; CONTEX: parsing; event structures; lexical aspect; temporal information

when clauses 105–7, 112
Win Law 361